S.A.L. Butler

Mesopotamian Conceptions of
Dreams and Dream Rituals

Alter Orient und Altes Testament

Veröffentlichungen zur Kultur und Geschichte des Alten Orients
und des Alten Testaments

Band 258

Herausgeber

Manfried Dietrich • Oswald Loretz

1998
Ugarit-Verlag
Münster

Mesopotamian Conceptions of

Dreams and Dream Rituals

S.A.L. Butler

1998
Ugarit-Verlag
Münster

Die Deutsche Bibliothek - CIP-Einheitsaufnahme

Butler, Sally A. L.:
Mesopotamian conceptions of dreams and dream rituals / S. A. L. Butler. - Münster : Ugarit-Verl., 1998
(Alter Orient und Altes Testament ; Bd. 258)
ISBN 3-927120-65-0

Herstellung: Weihert-Druck GmbH, Darmstadt

Printed in Germany

ISBN 3-927120-65-0

Printed on acid-free paper

CONTENTS

ABBREVIATIONS AND REFERENCES

ABBREVIATIONS

A. Tablet signature of Mari letters in the Louvre Museum, Paris.

AbB *Altbabylonische Briefe in Umschrift und Übersetzung;* E. J. Brill.

Volume 5: F. R. Kraus (1972): *Briefe aus dem Istanbuler Museum.*

Volume 9: M. Stol (1981): *Letters from Yale.*

Volume 10: F. R. Kraus (1985): *Briefe aus kleineren Westeuropäischen Sammlungen.*

Volume 11: M. Stol (1986): *Letters from Collections in Philadelphia, Chicago, and Berkeley.*

ABL *Assyrian and Babylonian Letters Belonging to the Kouyunjik Collection of the British Museum Volumes 1-14,* R. F. Harper (1892-1914). University of Chicago Press.

ABRT *Assyrian and Babylonian Religious Texts . . . Volumes 1-2,* J. A. Craig (1895 and 1897). J. C. Hinrichs.

ABZ *Assyrisch-babylonische Zeichenliste. 3. Auflage,* R. Borger (1986). *AOAT* 33/33A.

ADD *Assyrian Deeds and Documents Recording the Transfer of Property . . . Volumes 1-4,* C. H. W. Johns (1898-1923). Deighton Bell and Co.

ADRC *Ashur Dream Ritual Compendium.* Edited here.

AEM 1/1 *Archives épistolaires de Mari 1/1,* J.-M. Durand (1988) (= *ARMT* 26). Editions recherche sur les Civilisations, A. D. P. F.

AfO *Archiv für Orientforschung.*

AGS *Assyrische Gebete an den Sonnengotte für Staat und konigliches Haus aus der Zeit Asarhaddons und Asurbanipals Volumes 1-2,* J. A. Knudtzon (1893). Eduard Pfeiffer.

AHw *Akkadisches Handwörterbuch Volumes 1-3,* W. von Soden (1965-1981). Otto Harrassowitz.

AJSL *American Journal of Semitic Languages and Literatures.*

Akk. Akkadian

AMT *Assyrian Medical Texts from the Originals in the British Museum,* R. Campbell Thompson (1923). Oxford University Press.

ANET[3] *Ancient Near Eastern Texts Relating to the Old Testament* (third edition with supplement), edited by J. B. Pritchard (1969). Princeton University Press.

AnSt *Anatolian Studies.*

AOAT *Alter Orient und Altes Testament Veröffentlichungen zur Kultur und Geschichte des Alten Orients und des Alten Testaments;* Butzon und Bercker, Kevelaer - Neukirchener Verlag, Neukirchen-Vluyn.

ARM 10 *Archives royales de Mari* (Texts) Volume 10: G. Dossin (1967): *La correspondance féminine* (= *TCL* 31). Libraire Orientaliste, Paul Geuthner, S. A.

ARMT *Archives royales de Mari* (Transliteration and translation); Libraire Orientaliste Paul Geuthner, S. A.

Volume 13: G. Dossin, J. Bottéro, M. Bírot, M. Lurton Burke, J. Kupper, and A. Finet (1964): *Textes divers.*

Volume 21: J.-M. Durand (1983): *Textes administratifs des salles 134 et 160 du palais de Mari.*

Volume 26: J.-M. Durand (1988) (= *AEM* 1/1).

ARRIMP *Annual Review of the Royal Inscriptions of Mesopotamia Project.*

ASKT *Akkadische und sumerische Keilschrifttexte nach den Originalen im Britischen Museum . . . ,* P. Haupt (1881-1882). Assyriologische Bibliothek 1, J. C. Hinrichs.

BA *Beiträge zur Assyriologie und semitischen Sprachwissenschaft.*

BAM *Die babylonisch-assyrische Medizin in Texten und Untersuchungen Volumes 1-6,* F. Köcher (1963-1980). Walter de Gruyter and Co.

Volume 1 = Numbers 1-113.

Volume 2 = Numbers 114-198.

Volume 3 = Numbers 199-319.

Volume 4 = Numbers 320-420.

Volume 5 = Numbers 421-509.

Volume 6 = Numbers 510-584.

BBR *Beiträge zur Kenntnis der babylonischen Religion Volumes 1-2,* H. Zimmern (1896 and 1901). J. C. Hinrichs.

BHT *Babylonian Historical Texts Relating to the Capture and Downfall of Babylon,* S. Smith (1924). Methuen and Co. Ltd.

BIN 6 *Babylonian Inscriptions in the Collection of James B. Nies* Volume 6: F. J. Stephens (1944): *Old Assyrian Letters And Business Documents.* Yale University Press - Oxford University Press.

BiOr *Bibliotheca Orientalis.*

BM British Museum; tablet signature of the British Museum, London.

BMS *Babylonian Magic and Sorcery Being 'the Prayers of the Lifting of the Hands'*, L. W. King (1896). Luzac and Co.

Bu. Budge; tablet signature of the British Museum, London.

BWL *Babylonian Wisdom Literature,* W. G. Lambert (1960). The Clarendon Press.

CAD *The Assyrian Dictionary of the Oriental Institute of the University of Chicago,* (1956 on). The Oriental Institute - J. J. Augustin.

Cap. Namburbi Texts in the British Museum, R. I. Caplice.

Part 1: *OrNS* 34 (1965), pages 105-131 (Numbers 1-11).
Part 2: *OrNS* 36 (1967), pages 1-38 (Numbers 12-24).
Part 3: *OrNS* 36 (1967), pages 273-298 (Numbers 25-33).
Part 4: *OrNS* 39 (1970), pages 111-151 (Numbers 34-43).
Part 5: *OrNS* 40 (1971), pages 133-183 (Numbers 44-III).

CBS Catalogue of the Babylonian Section; tablet signature of the University of Pennsylvania Museum, Philadelphia.

2 Chron. *The Second Book of the Chronicles.*

CLAM *The Canonical Lamentations of Ancient Mesopotamia Volumes 1-2,* M. E. Cohen (1988). Capital Decisions Ltd.

CRRA Compte rendu, Rencontre assyriologique internationale.

CT *Cuneiform Texts from Babylonian Tablets in the British Museum;* British Museum Publications, London.

R. Campbell Thompson: Volumes 11 (1900), 15 (1902), 16 (1903), 17 (1903), 18 (1904), 20 (1904), 22 (1906), and 23 (1906).
L. W. King: Volumes 13 (1901), 24 (1908), 29 (1910), and 34 (1914).
P. S. P. Handcock: Volumes 28 (1910), and 31 (1911).
C. J. Gadd: Volumes 39 (1926), 40 (1927), and 41 (1931).
S. Smith: Volume 37 (1923).
H. W. Figulla: Volume 43 (1963).
W. G. Lambert and A. R. Millard: Volume 46 (1965).
C. B. F. Walker: Volume 51 (1972).

CT 23, pls. 15-22 +
CT 23, pls. 15-22 + K. 2431 + *AMT* 29/1 + 89/3 + K. 10454 + *KMI* 74c + *AMT* 38/6 + K. 14738.

DAB *A Dictionary of Assyrian Botany,* R. Campbell Thompson (1949). The British Academy.

DACG	*A Dictionary of Assyrian Chemistry and Geology,* R. Campbell Thompson (1936). The Clarendon Press.
DB	*The Interpretation of Dreams in the Ancient Near East with a Translation of an Assyrian Dream-Book,* A. L. Oppenheim (1956). Transactions of the American Philosophical Society NS 46/3.
D.T.	Daily Telegraph; tablet signature of the British Museum, London.
Gen.	*Genesis.*
IM	Iraq Museum, Baghdad; tablet signature.
JAOS	*Journal of the American Oriental Society.*
JCS	*Journal of Cuneiform Studies.*
Jer.	*Jeremiah.*
JNES	*Journal of Near Eastern Studies.*
K.	Kuyunjik; tablet signature of the British Museum, London.
KAR	*Keilschrifttexte aus Assur Religiösen Inhalts Volumes 1-2,* E. Ebeling (1919 and 1923). Wissenschaftliche Veröffentlichungen der Deutschen Orient-Gesellschaft 28 and 34.
KAV	*Keilschrifttexte aus Assur verschiedenen Inhalts,* O. Schroeder (1920). Ausgrabungen der Deutschen Orientgesellschaft in Assur 3, J. C. Hinrichs.
KMI	*Keilschrifttexte medicinischen Inhalts Volumes 1-2,* E. Ebeling (1922-1923). Published by the author in Berlin.
Kraus No.	F. R. Kraus (1939), *Texte zur babylonische physiognomatik, AfO* Beiheft 3.
KUB	*Keilschrifttexte aus Boghazköi.* Gebr. Mann. Volume 7: H. Otten (1954): *Texte der Grabung* 1952. Volume 9: H. Otten (1957): *Vorwiegend Texte der Grabungen 1955 und 1956.*
LKA	*Literarische Keilschrifttexte aus Assur,* E. Ebeling (1953). Akademie.
LM	*ŠU-ILA-Gebete: Supplement zu L. W. King, Babylonian Magic and Sorcery,* O. Loretz and W. R. Mayer (1978). *AOAT* 34.
MAOG	*Mitteilungen der altorientalischen Gesellschaft.*
MSL	*Materialen zum sumerischen Lexikon;* Pontificium Institutum Biblicum. Volume 12: M. Civil, R. D. Biggs, H. G. Güterbock, H. J. Nissen, and E. Reiner (1969). Volume 13: M. Civil, H. G. Güterbock, W. W. Hallo, H. A. Hoffner, and E. Reiner (1971). Volume 14: M. Civil, M. W. Green, and W. G. Lambert (1979).

Volume 17: A. Cavigneaux, H. G. Güterbock, and M. T. Roth (1985).

MVAG *Mitteilungen der Vorderasiatisch-Ägyptischen Gesellschaft.*

Nabonidus No.

These follow the order of H. Tadmor in *Assyrological Studies* 16 [1965], p. 351, n. 2.

1: 5 *R.* 64; R. J. Lau and J. Dyneley Prince (1905).

4*: *CT* 34, pls. 26-37 (and duplicates).

8: *MVAG* 1 (1896), pages 73-83.

24: *AnSt* 8 (1958), pls. 4-8.

NADR *Nusku Apotropaic Dream Ritual.* Edited here.

ND Nimrud Documents; tablet signature of collections at Baghdad and London.

Ni. Nippur; tablet signature of the Museum of the Ancient Orient, Istanbul.

NROD *Nusku Ritual to Obtain a Pleasant Dream.* Edited here.

NRGD *Neo-Assyrian Royal Grants and Decrees,* J. N. Postgate (1969). Studia Pohl: Series Maior, Dissertationes Scientificae de Rebus Antiqui 1; Pontificial Biblical Institute.

OECT 6 Oxford Editions of Cuneiform Texts Volume 6: S. Langdon (1927): *Babylonian Penitential Psalms . . .* Libraire Orientaliste Paul Geuthner.

OrNS *Orientalia Nova Series.*

PBS *The Publications of the Babylonian Section of the Museum of the University of Pennsylvania.*

Volume 1/1: D. W. Myhrmann (1911): *Babylonian Hymns and Prayers.*

Volume 1/2: H. F. Lutz (1919): *Selected Sumerian and Babylonian Texts.*

Volume 5: A. Poebel (1914): *Historical and Grammatical Texts.*

Volume 7: A. Ungnad (1915): *Babylonian Letters of the Hammurapi Period.*

Volume 12/1: S. Langdon (1917): *Sumerian Grammatical Texts.*

Volume 13: L. Legrain (1922): *Historical Fragments.*

PRT *Politisch-religiöse Texte aus der Sargonidenzeit,* E. G. Klauber (1913). Eduard Pfeiffer.

n. *R.* n. *The Cuneiform Inscriptions of Western Asia . . . . Volumes 1-5;* London.

Volume 3: E. Norris (1866).

Volume 4^2: Second edition, T. G. Pinches (1891).

Volume 5: T. G. Pinches (1909).

RA — *Revue d'assyriologie et d'archéologie orientale.*

RLA — *Reallexikon der Assyriologie Vols. 1 on* (1932 on); Walter de Gruyter and. Co.

Rm. — Rassam; tablet signature of the British Museum, London.

ROP — *Rituals to Obtain a Purussû.* Edited here.

SAA — *State Archives of Assyria;* Helsinki University Press.

Volume 3: A. Livingstone (1989): *Court Poetry and Literary Miscellanea.*

Volume 4: I. Starr (1990): *Queries to the Sun God: Divination and Politics in Sargonid Assyria.*

Volume 7: F. M. Fales and J. N. Postgate (1992): *Imperial Administrative Records, Part 1: Palace and Temple Administration.*

Volume 10: S. Parpola (1993): *Letters from Assyrian and Babylonian Scholars.*

Volume 12: L. Kataja and R. Whiting (1995): *Grants, Decrees and Gifts of the Neo-Assyrian Period.*

SDR — *Shamash-shum-ukin Dream Ritual.* Edited here.

Si — Sippar; tablet signature of collections at Istanbul and London.

SLTN — *Sumerian Literary Texts from Nippur in the Museum of the Ancient Orient at Istanbul,* S. N. Kramer (1944). The Annual of the American Schools of Oriental Research 23.

Sm. — Smith; tablet signature of the British Museum, London.

SOED — *The Shorter Oxford English Dictionary on Historical Principals Volumes 1-2* (third edition, reprinted), revised by G. W. S. Friedrichsen (1987). The Clarendon Press.

SpTU — *Spätbabylonische Text aus Uruk Volumes 1-3;* Ausgrabungen der Deutschen Forschungsgemeinschaft in Uruk-Warka 9-10 and 12; Gebr. Mann. Volume 1: H. Hunger (1976); Volume 2: E. von Weiher (1983); Volume 3: E. von Weiher (1988).

Volume 4: E. von Weiher (1993). Deutsches Archäologisches Institut Ableitung - Phillip von Zabern.

STT — *The Sultantepe Tablets Volumes 1-2;* Occasional Publications 3 and 7, the British Institute of Archaeology at Ankara.

Volume 1: O. R. Gurney and J. J. Finkelstein (1957) (Numbers 1-111).

Volume 2: O. R. Gurney and P. Hulin (1964) (Numbers 112-407).

S.U.	Sultantepe-Urfa; tablet signature.
Sum.	Sumerian
ŠRT	*The Shamash Religious Texts Classified in the British Museum Catalogue as Hymns, Prayers and Incantations,* C. D. Gray (1901). University Of Chicago Press.
TCL	*Textes cunéiformes, Musée du Louvre Départment des Antiquités Orientales;* Libraire Orientaliste Paul Geuthner S.A. Volume 1: F. Thureau-Dangin (1910): *Lettres et contrats de l'epoque de la première dynastie babylonienne.* Volume 8: F. Thureau-Dangin (1925): *Les cylindres de Goudéa découverts par Ernest de Sarzec à Tello.* Volume 18: G. Dossin (1934): *Lettres de la première dynastie babylonienne 2.* Volume 31: G. Dossin (1967): *La correspondance féminine* (= *ARM* 10).
TDP	*Traité akkadien de diagnostics et pronostics médicaux Volumes 1-2,* R. Labat (1951). Collection de travaux de l'Académie Internationale d'Histoire des Sciences 7; E. J. Brill.
TUAT 2/2	*Texte aus der Umwelt des Alten Testaments Band 2 Lieferung 2: Rituale und Beschwörungen 1;* Gütersloher Verlagshaus Gerd Mohn. (1987).
U.	Ur; artifacts excavated at Ur.
UET 7	*Ur Excavation Texts* Volume 7: O. R. Gurney (1974): *Middle Babylonian Legal Documents and Other Texts.* British Museum Publications, London.
UFGB	*Untersuchungen zur Formensprache der babylonischen 'Gebetsbeschwörungen',* W. Mayer (1976). Studia Pohl, Series Maior 5; Biblical Institute Press.
UHF	*Forerunners to UDUG-HUL: Sumerian Exorcistic Incantations,* M. J. Geller (1985). Freiburger Altorientalische Studien 12; Franz Steiner - GMBH.
VAT	Vorderasiatische Abteilung T(h)on Tafeln; tablet signature of the Staatliche Museen, Berlin.
VS 7	*Vorderasiatische Schriftdenkmäler der Königlichen Museen du Berlin* Volume 7: A. Ungnad (1909). J. C. Hinrichs, Leipzig.
W	Warka; tablet signature of collections at Baghdad and Berlin.
YBC	Yale Babylonian Collection; tablet signature of Yale University.
YOS	*Yale Oriental Series, Babylonian Texts;* Yale University Press.

Volume 1: A. T. Clay (1915): *Miscellaneous Inscriptions in the Yale Babylonian Collection.*

Volume 10: A. Goetze (1966): *Old Babylonian Omen Texts* (second edition).

Volume 11: J. van Dijk, A. Goetze, M. I. Hussey (1985): *Early Mesopotamian Incantations and Rituals.*

ZA *Zeitschrift für Assyriologie und vorderasiatische Archäologie.*

ZI *Zaqiqu Incantation.* Edited here.

(Tablets given a registration date only (e.g., 79-7-8, 77) are in the British Museum, London.)

REFERENCES

ABUSCH, (I.) T.

[1989] The Demonic Image of the Witch in Standard Babylonian Literature: The Reworking of Popular Conceptions by Learned Exorcists. Pages 27-58 in *Religion, Science, and Magic in Concert and in Conflict,* ed. J. Neusner, E. S. Frerichs, and P. V. McCracken Flesher. Oxford University Press.

[1990] An Early Form of the Witchcraft Ritual Maqlû and the Origin of a Babylonian Magical Ceremony. Pages 1-57 in *Lingering Over Words: Studies in Ancient Near Eastern Literature in Honor of William L. Moran,* ed. T. Abusch, J. Huehnergard, and P. Steinkeller. Scholars Press.

AL-RAWI, F. N. H.

[1990] Tablets from the Sippar Library 1. The "Weidner Chronicle": A Supposititious Royal Letter Concerning a Vision. *Iraq* 52, pages 1-13.

AUSTIN, M. M.

[1981] *The Hellenistic World from Alexander to the Roman Conquest: A Selection of Ancient Sources in Translation.* Cambridge University Press.

BAYLISS, M.

[1973] The Cult of the Dead Kin in Assyria and Babylonia. *Iraq* 35, pages 115-125.

BEHRENS, E.

[1906] *Assyrisch-babylonische Briefe kultischen Inhalts aus der Sargonidenzeit.* Leipziger semitistische Studien 2/1. J. C. Hinrichs.

BENITO, C. A.

[1969] *"Enki and Ninmah" and "Enki and the World Order".* Ph.D. thesis for the University of Pennsylvania. University Microfilms Inc.

BERLIN, A.

[1979] *Enmerkar and Ensuhkeshdanna: A Sumerian Narrative Poem.* Occasional Publications of the Babylonian Fund 2. The University Museum, Phildadelphia.

BIGGS, R. D.

[*OIP* 99] *Inscriptions from Tell Abū Ṣalābīkh.* (1974). The University of Chicago Oriental Institute Publications 99. University of Chicago Press.

[*ŠZG*] *ŠÀ.ZI.GA: Ancient Mesopotamian Potency Incantations.* (1967). Texts from Cuneiform Sources 2. J. J. Augustin.

BÖLLENRÜCHER, J.

[1904] *Gebete und Hymnen an Nergal.* Leipziger semitistische Studien 1/6. J. C. Hinrichs.

BORGER, R.

[*BAL*] *Babylonisch-assyrische Lesestücke Volumes 1-3.* (1963). Pontificium Institutum Biblicum.

[*HKL*] *Handbuch der Keilschriftliteratur Volumes 1-2.* (1967 and 1975). Walter de Gruyter and Co.

[1956] *Die Inschriften Asarhaddons, Königs von Assyrien. AfO* Beiheft 9.

[1957-1958] Review of A. L. Oppenheim [*DB*] *AfO* 18, pages 415-418.

[1961] Review of *CAD* E. *BiOr* 18, pages 151-154.

[1969] Die erste Teiltafel der ZI-PÀ-Beschwörungen (ASKT 11). Pages 1-22 in *AOAT* 1 = *lišān mithurti. Festschrift W. F. von Soden,* ed. M. Dietrich and W. Röllig.

[1974] Die Beschwörungsserie bīt mēseri und die Himmelfahrt henochs. *JNES* 33, pages 183-196.

BOTTÉRO, J.

[1985] *Mythes et rites de Babylone.* (1985). Bibliothèque de l'Ecole des Hautes Etudes IVe Section, Sciences historiques et philologiques 328. Libraire Honoré Champion.

[1985a] Les exorcismes complémentaires des oracles: Comment on se gardait du mal prédit par les oracles. Pages 29-64 in J. Bottéro [1985]. (Written 1973-1974).

[1985b] Le manuel de l'exorciste et son calendrier. Pages 65-112 in J. Bottéro [1985]. (Written 1974-1975).

BRINKMAN, J. A.

[*PHPKB*] *A Political History of Post-Kassite Babylonia 1158-722 B.C.* (1968). Analecta Orientalia Commentationes Scientificae de Rebus Orientis Antiqui 43. Pontificium Institutum Biblicum.

BUREN, E. DOUGLAS VAN

[1930] *Clay Figurines of Babylonia and Assyria.* Yale Oriental Series, Researches 16. Yale University Press.

[1936-1937] Mesopotamian Fauna in the Light of the Monuments: Archaeological Remarks upon Landsberger's *Fauna des alten Mesopotamien. AfO* 11, pages 1-37.

CAPLICE, R. I.

[1965] Namburbi Texts in the British Museum. I. *OrNS* 34, pages 105-131

[1974] *The Akkadian Namburbi Texts: An Introduction.* Sources from the Ancient Near East 1/1. Undena Publications.

COMBE, E.

[1908] *Histoire du cult de Sin en Babylonie et en Assyrie.* Paul Geuthner.

COUPRIE, P. C.

[1960] Review of A. L. Oppenheim [*DB*]. *BiOr* 17, pages 184-187.

CRAIG, J. A.

[1894-1895] An Assyrian Incantation to the God Sin (cir. 650 B.C.). *Hebraica* 11, pages 101-109.

CURTIS, J.

[1982] Balawat. Pages 113-119 in *Fifty Years of Mesopotamian Discovery: The Work of the British School of Archaeology in Iraq 1932-1982,* ed. J. Curtis. British School of Archaeology in Iraq.

DALLEY, S.

[1991] *Myths from Mesopotamia: Creation, the Flood, Gilgamesh, and Others.* The World's Classics, Oxford University Press.

DEIMAL, A.

[*Fara* 2] *Die Inschriften von Fara 2.* (1969, reprinted). Otto Zeller.

DeMARTINO, M. F. (ed.)

[1959] *Dreams and Personality Dynamics.* Charles C. Thomas.

DEVEREUX, G.

[1966] Pathogenic Dreams in Non-Western Societies. Pages 213-228 in *The Dream and Human Societies,* ed. G. E. von Grunebaum and R. Caillois. University of California Press.

DIJK, J. J. A. VAN

[*SSA*] *La sagesse suméro-accadienne: Recherches sur les genres littéraires des textes sapientiaux avec choix de textes.* (1953). Commentationes Orientales 1. Nederlandsch Instituut voor het Nabije Oosten. E. J. Brill.

DONNER, H.

[1957-1958] Zur Inschrift von Südschen Aa 9. *AfO* 18, pages 390-392.

DURAND, J.-M.

[*AEM* 1/1] *Archives épistolaires de Mari 1/1.* (1988). *ARMT* 26. Editions Recherche sur les Civilisations, A. D. P. F.

[1982] In Vino Veritas. *RA* 76, pages 43-50.

EBELING, E.

[*AGH*] *Die akkadische Gebetsserie „Handerhebung" von neuen Gesammelt und Herausgegeben.* (1955). Deutsche Akademie der Wissenschaften zu Berlin Institut für Orientforschung Publication 20. Akademie.

[1918] Quellen zur Kenntnis der babylonischen Religion 1. *MVAG* 23, pages 1-8.

[1954] Beiträge zur Kenntnis der Beschwörungsserie Namburbi. *RA* 48, pages 1-15, 76-83, 130-141, and 180-191.

[1955] Beiträge zur Kenntnis der Beschwörungsserie Namburbi. *RA* 49, pages 32-41, 138-149, and 178-193.

ELLMAN, S. J., and J. S. ANTROBUS (ed.)

[1991] *The Mind in Sleep: Psychology and Pscytiophysiology* (Second edition). John Wiley and Sons, Inc.

FALKENSTEIN, A.

[1966] ≪Wahrsagung≫ in der sumerischen Überlieferung. Pages 45-68 in *La divination en Mésopotamie ancienne et dans les régions voisines* = 14th. CRAA. (Strasbourg, 1965). Presses Universitaires de France.

FALKENSTEIN, A., and W. VON SODEN

[*SAHG*] *Sumerische und akkadische Hymnen und Gebete.* (1953). Die Bibliothek der Alten Welt, Artemis.

FARBER, W.

[*SKS*] *Schlaf, Kindchen, Schlaf!: Mesopotamische Baby-Beschwörungen und -Rituale.* (1989). Mesopotamian Civilizations 2. Eisenbrauns.

[1973] ina KUŠ.DÙ.DÙ(.BI) = *ina maški tašappi.* *ZA* 63, pages 59-68.

FINET, A.

[1982] Un cas de clédomancie a\ Mari. Pages 48-53 in *Zikir Šumim: Assyriological Studies Presented to F. R. Kraus on the Occasion of his Seventieth Birthday,* ed. G. van Driel, T. J. H. Krispijn, M. Stol, and K. R. Veenhof. Nederlands Instituut voor het Nabije Oosten Studia Francisci Scholten Memoriae Dicata 5. E. J. Brill.

FINKEL, I. L.

[1983] The Dream of Kurigalzu and the Tablet of Sins. *AnSt* 33, pages 75-80.

[1983-1984] A New Piece of Libanomancy. *AfO* 29-30, pages 50-55.

FISHER, C., J. BYRNE, A. EDWARDS, and E. KAHN

[1970] A Psychophysiological Study of Nightmares. *Journal of the American Psychoanalytic Association* 18, pages 747-782.

FOSTER, B. R.

[*BM* 2] *Before the Muses: An Anthology of Akkadian Literature Volume 2.* (1993). CDL Press.

FRAZER, J. G.

[1900] *The Golden Bough: A Study in Magic and Religion Volume 1* (Second edition, revised and enlarged). Macmillan and Co., Ltd.

GADD, C. J.

[1948] *Ideas of Divine Rule in the Ancient Near East.* The Schweich Lectures of the British Academy, 1945. Oxford University Press.

GEORGE, A. R., and F. N. H. AL-RAWI

[1996] Tablets from the Sippar Library VI: Atra-hasis. *Iraq* 58, pages 147-190.

GOETZE, A.

[1939] Cuneiform Inscriptions from Tarsus. *JAOS* 59, pages 1-16.

GORDON, C. H.

[1952] *Smith College Tablets: 110 Cuneiform Texts Selected from the College Collection.* Smith College Studies in History 38. Department of History of Smith College.

GORDON, E. I.

[1960] A New Look at the Wisdom of Sumer and Akkad. *BiOr* 17, pages 122-152.

GRAY, C. D.

[*ŠRT*] *The Shamash Religious Texts Classified in the British Museum Catalogue as Hymns, Prayers, and Incantations.* (1901). University of Chicago Press.

GRAYSON, A. K.

[*ABC*] *Assyrian and Babylonian Chronicles.* (1975). Texts from Cuneiform Sources 5. J. J. Augustin.

[*ARI* 2] *Assyrian Royal Inscriptions Part 2: From Tiglath-pileser I to Ashur-nasir-apli II.* (1976). Records of the Ancient Near East 2. Otto Harrassowitz.

[1991] *Assyrian Rulers of the Early First Millennium BC 1 (1114-859 BC).* University of Toronto Press.

[1991a] A Text of Shalmaneser III on an Amulet-Shaped Stone. *ARRIMP* 9, pages 19-22.

[1996] *Assyrian Rulers of the Early First Millennium BC 2 (858-745 BC).* University of Toronto Press.

GREENGUS, S.

[1979] *Old Babylonian Tablets from Ischali and Vicinity.* Nederlands Historisch-Archaeologisch Instituut Te Istanbul 23.

GURNEY, O. R.

[1954] Two Fragments of the Epic of Gilgamesh. *JCS* 8, pages 87-95.

[1981-1982] The Sultantepe Tablets: Addenda and Further Corrigenda. *AfO* 28, pages 92-112.

HADFIELD, J. A.

[1954] *Dreams and Nightmares* (Reprint). Penguin Books Ltd.

HALLO, W. W.

[1983] Lugalbanda Excavated. *JAOS* 103, pages 165-180.

HAMILTON, M.

[1906] *Incubation or the Cure of Disease in Pagan Temples and Christian Churches.* W. C. Henderson and Son - Simpkin, Marshall, Hamilton, Kent, and Co.

HARPER, R. F.

[1898-1899] Assyriological Notes V. *AJSL* 15, pages 129-144.

HEIMPEL, W.

[1986] The Sun at Night and the Doors of Heaven in Babylonian Texts. *JCS* 38, pages 127-151.

HELD, M.

[1961]: A Faithful Lover in an Old Babylonian Dialogue. *JCS* 15, pages 1-26.

HIRSCH, H.

[1968-1969] Den Toten zu beleben. *AfO* 22, pages 39-58.

HOROWITZ, W.

[1989] The Akkadian Name for Ursa Minor: ^{mul}mar.gíd.da.an.na = eriqqi šamê/šamāmi. *ZA* 79, pages 242-244.

HOWARD, M.

[1955] Technical Description of the Ivory Writing-Boards from Nimrud. *Iraq* 17, pages 14-20.

HUNGER, H.

[*BAK*] *Babylonische und assyrische Kolophone.* (1968). *AOAT* 2.

IDEL, M.

[1988] *Kabbalah: New Perspectives.* Yale University Press.

JACOBSEN, T.

[1939] *The Sumerian King List.* The Oriental Institute of the University of

Chicago, Assyriological Studies 11. University of Chicago Press.

[1970] *Towards the Image of Tammuz and Other Essays on Mesopotamian History and Culture.* Edited by W. L. Moran. Harvard Semitic Series 21. Harvard University Press.

[1976] *The Treasures of Darkness: A History of Mesopotamian Religion.* Yale University Press.

[1989] The lil_2 of ^{d}En-lil_2. Pages 267-276 in *DUMU-E_2-DUB-BA-A: Studies in Honor of Åke W. Sjöberg,* ed. H. Behrens, D. Loding, and M. T. Roth. Occasional Publications of the Samuel Noah Kramer Fund 11. The University Museum, University of Pennsylvania.

JACOBSON, H.

[1976] An.zaqar: A Conjecture. *OrNS* 45, page 269.

JASTROW, M.

[1905] *Das Religion babyloniens und assyriens Volume 1.* J. Richer.

JASTROW, M., and A. T. CLAY

[1920] *An Old Babylonian Version of the Gilgamesh Epic on the Basis of Recently Discovered Texts.* Yale Oriental Series Researches 4/3. Yale University Press.

KAMMENHUBER, A.

[1976] *Orakelpraxis, Träume, und Vorzeichenschau bei den Hethiten.* Carl Winter.

KILBORNE, B.

[1987] On Classifying Dreams. Pages 171-193 in *Dreaming: Anthropological and Psychological Interpretations,* ed. B. Tedlock. School of American Research Advanced Seminar Series. Cambridge University Press.

KING, L. W.

[*AKA* 1] *Annals of the Kings of Assyria . . . . Volume 1.* (1902). The British Museum

[*BMS*] *Babylonian Magic and Sorcery Being 'the Prayers of the Lifting of the Hand'.* (1896). Luzac and Co.

KLAUBER, E. G.

[*PRT*] *Politisch-religiöse Texte aus der Sargonidenzeit.* (1913). Eduard Pfeiffer.

KLEIN, J.

[1970-1971] Sum. GA-RAŠ = Akk. *purussû.* *JCS* 23, pages 118-122.

KÖCHER, F.

[*KADP*] *Keilschrifttexte zur assyrisch-babylonischen Drogen- und Pflanzen-*

kunde: Texte der Serien uru.an.na : maltakal, HAR.ra : hubullu und Ú GAR-šú. (1955). Akademie.

[1963] Ein verkannter neubabylonsicher Texte aus Sippar. *AfO* 20, pages 156-158.

KÖCHER, F., and A. L. OPPENHEIM

[1957-1958] The Old-Babylonian Omen Text VAT 7525. *AfO* 18, pages 62-77.

KRACKE, W.

[1987] Myths in Dreams, Thought in Images: An Amazonian Contribution to the Psychoanalytic Theory of Primary Process. Pages 31-54 in *Dreaming: Anthropological and Psychological Interpretations,* ed. B. Tedlock. School of American Research Advanced Seminar Series. Cambridge University Press.

KRAMER, S. N.

[1960] *Two Elegies on a Pushkin Museum Tablet: A New Sumerian Literary Genre.* Oriental Literature Publishing House.

KRAUS, F. R.

[1936] Ein Sittenkanon in Omenform. *ZA* 43, pages 77-113.

[1970] Akkadisch Wörter und Ausdrücke I-III. *RA* 64, pages 53-61.

[1985] Mittelbabylonische Opferschauprotokolle. *JCS* 37, pages 127-218.

KRECHER, J.

[1978] Das sumerische Phonem |ĝ|. Pages 7-73 in *Festschrift Lubor Matouš Volume 2,* ed. B. Hruška and G. Komoróczy. Assyriologia 5. Eötvös Loránd Tudományegyetem Ókon Történeti.

KUNSTMANN, W. G.

[1932] *Die babylonische Gebetsbeschwörung.* Leipziger semitistische Studien NF 2. J. C. Hinrichs.

LABAT, R.

[*TDP*] *Traité akkadien de diagnostics et pronostics médicaux Volumes 1-2.* (1951). Collection de Travaux de l'Académie Internationale d'Histoire des Sciences. E. J. Brill.

[1970] *Les religions du Proche-Orient Asiatique: Texts babyloniens, ougaritiques, hittites.* With A. Caquot, M. Sznycer, and M. Vieyra. A. Fayard/ Denoël.

LACKENBACHER, S.

[1971] Note sur l'*ardat-lilî.* *RA* 65, pages 119-154.

LAESSØE, J.

[1955] *Studies in the Assyrian Ritual and Series bît rimki.* Ejnar Munksgaard.

LAMBERT, W. G.

[*BWL*] *Babylonian Wisdom Literature.* (1960). The Clarendon Press.

[1959] The Sultantepe Tablets: A Review Article. *RA* 53, pages 119-138.

[1960] New Light on the Babylonian Flood Story. *Journal of Semitic Studies* 5, pages 113-123.

[1974] DINGIR.ŠÀ.DIB.BA Incantations. *JNES* 33, pages 267-322.

[1974-1977] Review of W. R. Mayer [*UFBG*]. *AfO* 25, pages 197-199.

[1976] A Late Assyrian Catalogue of Literary and Scholarly Texts. Pages 313-318 in *AOAT* 25 = *Cuneiform Studies in Honour of Samuel Noah Kramer,* ed. B. L. Eiehler.

[1980] The Theology of Death. Pages 53-66 in *Death in Mesopotamia,* ed. B. Alster. Copenhagen Studies in Assyriology, Mesopotamia 8 = 26th. CRAA (Copenhagen, 1979). Akademisk.

LAMBERT, W. G., and A. R. MILLARD

[1969] *Atra-hasīs: The Babylonian Story of the Flood.* The Clarendon Press.

LANDSBERGER, B.

[1967] *The Date Palm and its By-Products According to the Cuneiform Sources. AfO* Beiheft 17.

[1968] Zur vierten und siebenten Tafel des Gilgamesch-Epos. *RA* 62, pages 97-135.

LANGDON, S.

[*NBK*] *Die neubabylonsichen Königsinschriften.* (1912). Translated into German by R. Zehnpfund. J. C. Hinrichs.

[*TI*] *Tammuz and Ishtar: A Monograph upon Babylonian Religion and Theology* . . . . (1914). The Clarendon Press.

[1915-1916] New Inscriptions of Nabuna'id. *AJSL* 32, pages 102-117.

[1918] A Hymn to the Moon-God, Adapted for the Use of Shamash-shum-ukin, Viceroy of Babylon. *Proceedings of the Society of Biblical Archaeology* 40, pages 104-110.

LAWSON, J. N.

[1994] *The Concept of Fate in Ancient Mesopotamia of the First Millennium: Towards an Understanding of šīmtu.* Orientalia Biblica et Christiana 7. Harrassowitz.

LEBRUN, R.

[1980] *Hymnes et prières hittites.* Centre d'Historie des Religions.

LEICHTY, E.

[*ŠI*] *The Omen Series šumma izbu.* (1970). Texts from Cuneiform Sources 4. J. J. Augustin.

[1990] A Tamītu from Nippur. Pages 301-304 in *Lingering Over Words: Studies in Ancient Near Eastern Literature in Honor of William L. Moran,* ed. T. Abusch, J. Huehnergard, and P. Steinkeller. Scholars Press.

LIVINGSTONE, A.

[1986] *Mystical and Mythological Explanatory Works of Assyrian and Babylonian Scholars.* The Clarendon Press.

LLOYD, S.

[1980] *Foundations in the Dust: The Story of Mesopotamian Exploration* (Revised and enlarged edition). Thames and Hudson Ltd.

LUCKENBILL, D. D.

[*ARAB* 1] *Ancient Records of Assyria and Babylonia Volume 1: Historical Records of Assyria from the Earliest Times to Sargon.* (1926). University of Chicago Press.

MALLOWAN, M. E. L.

[1954] The Excavations at Nimrud (Kalhu), 1953. *Iraq* 16, pages 59-163.

[1956] *Twenty-five Years of Mesopotamian Discovery (1932-1956).* The British School of Archaeology in Iraq.

MALUL, M.

[1986] 'Sissiktu' and 'Sikku' - Their Meaning and Function. *BiOr* 43, pages 18-36.

[1988] *Studies in Mesopotamian Legal Symbolism. AOAT* 221.

MARGALIT, B.

[1989] *The Ugaritic Poem of Aqht.* Walter de Gruyter.

MAUL, S. M.

[1988] *Herzberuhigungsklagen: Die sumerisch-akkadischen Eršahunga-Gebete.* Otto Harassowitz.

[1994] *Zukunftsbewältigung: Eine Untersuchung altorientalischen Denkens anhand der babylonisch-assyrischen Löserituale (Namburbi).* Baghdader Forschungen 18. Philipp von Zabern.

MAUSS, M.

[1972] *A General Theory of Magic.* Translated by R. Brain. Routledge and Kegan Paul Ltd. (Written 1950).

MAVROMATIS, A.

[1987] *Hypnagogia: The Unique State of Consciousness between Wakefulness and Sleep.* Routledge and Kegan Paul.

MAYER, W.

[*UFBG*] Untersuchungen zur Formensprache der babylonischen 'Gebetsbeschwörungen'. (1976). Studia Pohl, Series Maior 5. Biblical Institute Press.

[1980] Corrigenda zu O. Loretz - W. R. Mayer, ŠU-ILA-Gebet (AOAT 34; 1978). *Ugarit-Forschungen* 12, pages 422-424.

MEISSNER, B.

[*BuA* 2] *Babylonien und Assyrien Volume 2.* (1925). Carl Winters Universitätsbuchhandlung.

MOOREY, P. R. S.

[1994] *Ancient Mesopotamian Materials and Industries: The Archaeological Evidence.* The Clarendon Press.

NOUGAYROL, J.

[1941] Textes hépatoscopiques d'epoque ancienne conservés au Musée du Louvre. *RA* 38, pages 67-88.

OATES, D.

[1974] Balawat (Imgur Enlil): The Site and its Buildings. *Iraq* 36, pages 173-178.

OLMSTEAD, A. T.

[1923] *History of Assyria.* Charles and Scribner's Sons.

OPPENHEIM, A. L.

[*DB*] *The Interpretation of Dreams in the Ancient Near East with a Translation of an Assyrian Dream-Book.* (1956). Transactions of the American Philosophical Society NS 46/3.

[1941] Idiomatic Akkadian. *JAOS* 61, pages 251-271

[1954-1956] Sumerian: INIM.GAR, Akkadian: *egirrû* = Greek: kledon. *AfO* 17, pages 49-55.

[1969] New Fragments of the Assyrian Dream-Book. *Iraq* 31, pages 153-165.

[1970] *Glass and Glassmaking in Ancient Mesopotamia.* With R. H. Brill, D. Barag, and A. von Saldern. Monographs 3. The Corning Museum of Glass.

PARKER, B.

[1963] Economic Tablets from the Temple of Mamu at Balawat. *Iraq* 25, pages 86-103.

PARPOLA, S.

[*LAS*] *Letters from Assyrian Scholars to the Kings Esarhaddon and Assurbanipal Volumes 1-2.* Volume 1: Texts, *AOAT* 5/1 (1970); Volume 2: Commentary and Appendices, *AOAT* 5/2 (1983).

[*SAA* 10] *Letters from Assyrian and Babylonian Scholars.* (1993). State Archives of Assyria 10. Helsinki University Press.

[1983] Assyrian Library Records. *JNES* 42, pages 1-29.

[1993] The Assyrian Tree of Life: Tracing the Origins of Jewish Monotheism and Greek Philosphy. *JNES* 52, pages 161-208.

PEDERSÉN, O.

[1986] *Archives and Libraries in the City of Assur: A Survey of the Material from German Excavations Part 2.* Acta Universitatis Upsaliensis, Studia Semitica Upsaliensia 8.

PERRY, E. G.

[1907] *Hymnen und Gebete an Sin.* Leipziger semitistische Studien 2/4. J. C. Hinrichs.

PFEIFFER, R. H.

[*SLA*] *State Letters of Assyria: A Transliteration and Translation of 355 Official Assyrian Letters Dating from the Sargonid Period (722-625 B.C.).* (1935). American Oriental Series 6. American Oriental Society.

POSTGATE, J. N.

[*NRGD*] *Neo-Assyrian Royal Grants and Decrees.* (1969). Studia Pohl, Series Maior 1. Pontificium Institutum Biblicum.

[1987] A Dedication Text on an 'Amulet'. *State Archives of Assyria Bulletin* 1, pages 57-61.

PRINCE, J. DYNELEY

[1912-1913] The God-Name ZAQ-QAR. *AJSL* 29, pages 284-287.

QUIRKE, S.

[1992] *Ancient Egyptian Religion.* British Museum Press.

REINER, E.

[1956] Lipšur Litanies. *JNES* 15, pages 129-149.

[1959-1960] ME.UGU = *mēlu. AfO* 19, pages 150-151.

[1960] Plague Amulets and House Blessings. *JNES* 19, pages 148-155.

[1960a] Fortune-Telling in Mesopotamia. *JNES* 19, pages 23-35.

[1965] Dead of Night. *Assyriological Studies* 16, pages 247-251.

[1967] Another Volume of Sultantepe Tablets. *JNES* 26, pages 177-200.

[1995] *Astral Magic in Babylonia.* Transactions of the American Philosophical Society 85/4.

RITTER, E. K.

[1965] Magical-expert (= āšipu) and Physician (= asû): Notes on Two Complementary Professions in Babylonian Medicine. *Assyriological Studies* 16, pages 299-321.

RITTER, E. K., and J. V. KINNIER WILSON

[1980] Prescription for an Anxiety State: A Study of BAM 234. *AnSt* 30, pages 23-30.

RITTIG, D.

[1977] *Assyrisch-babylonische Kleinplastik magischer Bedeutung vom 13.-6. Jh. v. Chr.* Münchener Universitäts-Schriften Phil. Fachbereich 12, Münchener Vorderasiatische Studien 1. Uni-Druck.

ROCHBERG-HALTON, F.

[1982] Fate and Divination in Mesopotamia. Pages 363-371 in *AfO* Beiheft 19 = 28th. CRAA (Vienna, 1981).

RÖMER, W. H. P.

[1971] *Frauenbriefe über Religion, Politik und Privatleben in Mari: Untersuchungen zu G. Dossin, Archives Royales de Mari X (Paris 1967). AOAT* 12.

ROUX, G.

[1980] *Ancient Iraq* (Third Edition). Penguin Books Ltd.

ROWTON, M. B.

[1967] The Woodlands of Ancient Western Asia. *JNES* 26, pages 261-277.

SAGGS, H. W. F.

[1978] *The Encounter with the Divine in Mesopotamia and Israel.* Jordan Lectures 1976. The Athlone Press.

SASSON, J. M.

[1983] Mari Dreams. *JAOS* 103, pages 283-293.

SAX, M., D. COLLON, and M. N. LEESE

[1993] The Availability of Raw Materials for Near Eastern Cylinder Seals during the Akkadian, Post Akkadian and Ur III Periods. *Iraq* 55, pages 77-90.

SCHEIL, (M.) V.

[SFS] *Une saison de fouilles à Sippar.* (1902). Memoires publiés par les membres de l'Institut Français d'Archéologie Orientale du Cairo 1/1.

[1913] Tablette des présages. *Mémoires de la Mission Archéologique de Perse* 14, pages 48-57.

[1925] Un catalogue de présages. *RA* 22, pages 141-143.

SCHMIDT, E. F.

[1957] *Persepolis Volume 2: Contents of the Treasury and Other Discoveries.* The University Of Chicago Oriental Institute Publications 69. University of Chicago Press.

SCHRAMM, W.

[1970] Die Annalen des assyrischen Königs Tukulti-Ninurta II (890-884 B.C.). *BiOr* 27, pages 147-160.

SCURLOCK. J. A.

[1988] *Magical Means of Dealing with Ghosts in Ancient Mesopotamia.* Unpublished Ph.D. thesis for the University of Chicago (courtesy of M. J. Geller).

SEUX, M.-J.

[1976] *Hymnes et prieres aux dieux de Babylonie et d'Assyrie.* Littératures ancienne du Proche-Orient. Les Editions du Cerf.

SHAFFER, A.

[1963] *Sumerian Sources of Tablet XII of the Epic of Gilgamesh.* Ph.D. thesis for the University of Pennsylvania. University Microfilms Inc.

SMITH, G.

[1871] *History of Assurbanipal Translated from the Cuneiform Inscriptions.* British Museum.

SODEN, W. VON

[1967] *Das akkadische Syllabar 2., völlig neubearbeitete Auflage.* W. Röllig. Analecta Orientalia Commentationes Scientificae de Rebus Orientis Antiqui 42. Pontificium Institutum Biblicum.

SOLLBERGER, E.

[1987] A Bead for Sennacherib. Pages 379-381 in *Language, Literature, and History: Philological and Historical Studies Presented to E. Reiner,* ed. F. Rochberg-Halton. American Oriental Series 67. American Oriental Society.

SPELEERS, L.

[1925] *Recueil des inscriptions de l'Asie Antérieure des Musées Royaux du Cinquantenaire à Bruxelles . . .* Vanderpoorten et Co.

SPERL, S.

[1994] The Literary Form of Prayer: Qu'ran sūra One, the Lord's Prayer, and a Babylonian Prayer to the Moon God. *Bulletin of the School of Oriental and African Studies* 57, pages 213-227.

STARR, I.

[1977] Extispicy Reports from the Old Babylonian and Sargonid Periods. Pages 200-208 in *Essays on the Ancient Near East in Memory of Jacob Joel Finkelstein,* ed. M. de Jong Ellis. Memoirs of the Connecticut Academy of Arts and Sciences 19. Archon Books.

STOL, M.

[1993] *Epilepsy in Babylonia.* Cuneiform Monographs 2. Styx Publications.

STRASSMAIER, J. V.

[*AV*] *Alphabetisches Verzeichniss der assyrischen und akkadischen Wörter der Cuneiform Inscriptions of Western Asia Vol. II sowie anderer meist unveröffentlichter Inschriften.* (1886). J. C. Hinrichs.

STRECK, M.

[*VAB* 7] *Assurbanipal und die letzten assyrischen Könige bis zum Untergange Niniveh's Parts 1-3.* (1916). Vorderasiatische Bibliothek 7. J. C. Hinrichs.

TALLQVIST, K. L.

[*AGE*] *Akkadische Götterepitheta, mit einem Götterverzeichnis und einer Liste der prädikativen Elemente der sumerischen Götternamen.* (1938). Studia Orientalia 7.

TEDLOCK, B.

[1987] Dreaming and Dream Research. Pages 1-30 in *Dreaming: Anthropological and Psychological Interpretations,* ed. B. Tedlock. School of American Research Advanced Seminar Series. Cambridge University Press.

TSUKIMOTO, A.

[1985] *Untersuchungen zur Totenpflege (kispum) im alten Mesopotamien. AOAT* 216.

TUCKER, D. J.

[1994] Representations of Imgur-Enlil on the Balawat Gates. *Iraq* 56, pages 107-116.

VOGELZANG, M.

[*BŠD*] *Bin Šar Dadmē: Edition and Analysis of the Akkadian Anzu Poem.* (1988), Styx Publications.

VORLÄNDER, H.

[1975] *Mein Gott: Die Vorstellungen vom persönlichen Gott im Alten Orient und in Alten Testament. AOAT* 23.

WALTERS, S. D.

[1970] *Water for Larsa: An Old Babylonian Archive Dealing with Irrigation.* Yale University Press.

WASSERMAN, N.

[1994] A Neo-Babylonian Imposture of an Old-Babylonian Amulet? *RA* 88, pages 49-57.

WATERMAN, L.

[*RCAE*] *Royal Correspondence of the Assyrian Empire Volumes 1-4.* (1930-6). University of Michigan Studies, Humanistic Series 17-20. University of Michigan Press.

WEBSTER, H.

[1948] *Magic: A Sociological Study.* Stanford University Press.

WEIDNER, E. F.

[1921-1923] Studien zu babylonischen Himmelskunde, III: Astrologie im Traume. *Rivista degli Studi Orientali* 9, pages 287-300 (especially pages 297-299).

[1924-1925] Altbabylonische Götterlisten. *AfO* 2, pages 1-18, and 71-82.

LIST OF TABLES

LIST OF PLATES

The author is grateful to the Trustees of the British Museum for permission to publish the BM and Kuyunjik tablets, and for supplying the photographs; similarly to Professor Maul of the Seminar für Sprachen und Kulturen des Vorderen Orients, Ruprecht-Karls-Universität, Heidelberg for the Geers Copies of Si 884 and Si 904.

CHAPTER ONE: INTRODUCTION

It is now over forty years since A. L. Oppenheim's pioneering work on ancient Near Eastern dreams (*DB*, published in 1956), and the publication of numerous texts in the interim calls for a re-examination of Mesopotamian oneirology. The writer has concentrated on how the Mesopotamians regarded dreams and on the rituals associated with dreams, and intends to write a companion volume on the Akkadian dream omens and reports. This study developed from a doctoral thesis presented to the Oriental Board of the University of London in 1992, and has benefited from the comments of the writer's supervisor, M. J. Geller, and examiners, A. R. George and J. V. Kinnier Wilson.

DREAMS

Modern research in sleep laboratories is revealing details of the sleeping and dreaming processes (chapter 2). All humans dream each night, with various factors affecting the amount of dream recall in the morning.

The *SOED* defines a dream as:

i). A train of thoughts, images, or fancies passing through the mind during sleep; a vision during sleep; the state in which this occurs.

ii). A vision of the fancy indulged in when awake (especially as being unreal or idle); a reverie; castle-in-the-air; cf. day-dream.

Therefore, a dream is a type of mental activity which differs in its sleeping or waking forms. The vast majority of the Akkadian citations will be seen to concern nocturnal dreams (henceforth dreams). However, it is possible that the Mesopotamians used the word *munattu* to denote waking dreams (pages 34-35; also see the reference to day-time dreams on *BMS* 12 (with *LM* 40) + K. 20155, rev. 113; page 95).

The definitions above do not mention the extremely intimate nature of a dream, namely, that the dreamer cannot share his experience with anyone else at the time it happens. This contrasts with the waking world where events may be experienced in common by those present, although often with varying degrees of emotion or comprehension. Yet, there are two Mesopotamian accounts of large groups apparently seeing the same nocturnal dream:

i). Ashurbanipal *Annals*, col. V lines 97-99 (M. Streck [*VAB* 7], p. 48):

97). ^{d}XV *a-ši-bat* ^{URU}*Ar-ba-ilu ina šat mu-ši*

98). *a-na* ÉRIN.HI.A-*ia* MÁŠ.GE$_6$ *ú-šab-ri-ma*

99). *ki-a-am iq-bi-šu-nu-ti*

[97-98] Ishtar, who resides at Arbela, caused my army to see a dream during the night. [99] She spoke to them thus (in the dream):

ii). Nabonidus 4*, col. I lines 67-70:

67). *i-na šu-ut-ti šá a-mu-ru ù* UN.MEŠ *i-tam-ma-ru-ni*

68). *a-na* UGU *te-me-en-na É-babbar-ra la-bi-ri šu-a-tú*

69). *É-babbar-ra a-na áš-ri-šú tur-ru šu-bat ṭu-ub lìb-bi-šú*

70). *ú-ma-'i-⌜ir⌝-an-ni*

[67] In a dream which I saw, and the people also saw, [68-70] he (Shamash) sent me to return Ebabbar to its place (i.e., former glory) on top of the foundation platform of that ancient Ebabbar, the dwelling of his heart's delight.

Such a uniform sharing of a dream is very unlikely. On the rare occasions when dreams are shared, dreamer A dreams about dreamer B, and vice versa, rather than both seeing exactly the same dream.

For centuries Man has been convinced that his dreams (however weird) contain a message, which often requires interpretation; hence the existence of Dream-Books (see pages 99-101 on the Mesopotamian examples) and, in recent times, psychoanalysts. People are reluctant to accept that anything so personal and vivid as a dream might be insignificant. Ancient and 'primitive' peoples believed that dreams were divine communications, while psychoanalysts claim that our sub-conscious is trying to express itself while the conscious censor is dormant. Even if one derides the idea that dreams are applicable to reality, these subjective experiences affect one's mood, and nightmares are impossible to ignore.

FATE AND DIVINATION IN MESOPOTAMIA

The Mesopotamian universe was an orderly one, with everyone and everything having its fortune and function pre-ordained (see J. N. Lawson's [1994] discussion of *šīmtu*). Something in the primordial world may have determined the individual fates of the deities (*Enūma eliš*, Tab. 1, lines 7-8), namely their own role within the cosmos. Each person's lot was allocated by the major gods; several of whom were given the epithet *mušīm šimāti*, "the one who decrees (something's) destiny" (see K. L. Tallqvist [*AGE*], pp. 222-223 for examples).

The deities were not remote figures but were actively concerned with human affairs, both of the individual and of the state. Divine intentions or warnings about the future were transmitted to mankind via:

i). Direct communication, namely prognostic dreams, and the inspired speech of ecstatics.

ii). The more usual method of "ominous signs, omens", *ittu*(GISKIM).

An omen indicated, to a skilled interpreter, possible alterations in a person's circumstances, within divinely established limits. No element of chance was involved, but neither was a prediction inevitable. If event A occurred, then result B could be expected, from previous observation, unless a namburbi ritual was performed to dissolve the evil portended by an unfavourable omen. H. W. F. Saggs [1978, p. 126]:

> "The logical contradiction inherent in the idea of taking steps to frustrate destiny does not appear to have been faced in the ancient Near East."

For instance, divination is only meaningful if it is believed that the future is predetermined.

The only free will a mortal appeared to have had was to lead a pious life, either hoping the gods would heed one's prayers and relent (but the problem of the Righteous Sufferer arose); or to seek indications as to the future by divination, and then perform the appropriate ritual to avert any evil predicted. The recipient of a divine warning could ignore it, albeit at his peril. The prime example is the *Cuthaean Legend of Naram-Sin* (*AnSt* 5 [1955], pp. 97-109), which describes how this king of Agade scornfully disregarded the omens, and went out to fight the enemy, with disastrous results.

J. N. Lawson [1994], p. 71:

> "In the final analysis, we can only take the position that to the ancient Mesopotamian, life's events were understood to be fixed, determined - but they were not inevitable!"

Yet some things could not be avoided: e.g., the extispicy omen *CT* 31, pl. 36, rev. 9:

> 9). *a-di* u_4*-um a-dan-ni* TI-*uṭ* EGIR *a-dan-ni-šú* ÚŠ
>
> He will live until the predetermined time; he will die after his allotted period (is over).

Man was created to toil for the gods (*Enūma eliš,* Tab. 6, lines 33-34), and his ultimate destiny was death; the Old Babylonian Version of the *Epic of Gilgamesh,* (*MVAG* 7/1 [1902], pp. 1-14, with photographs on pls. 1-2) Tab. 10, col. III lines 3-5:

> 3). *i-nu-ma* DINGIR.MEŠ *ib-nu-ú a-wi-lu-tam*
>
> 4). *mu-tam iš-ku-nu a-na a-wi-lu-tim*

5). *ba-la-ṭam i-na qá-ti-šu-nu iṣ-ṣa-ab-tu*

[3] When the gods created mankind [4] they assigned death to mankind [5] (while eternal) life they reserved for themselves (lit., they seized in their hands).

There were different categories of Mesopotamian omens:

i). Those deduced from the (un)natural behaviour of creatures, such as the malformed births recorded in *Šumma izbu,* or from occurrences in every-day life, in *Šumma ālu.* Dream omens come into this group.

ii). Regularly occurring astronomical and meteorological phenomena: e.g. *Enūma Anu Enlil.*

iii). Those sought by elaborate ceremonies involving ritual experts: e.g., extispicy, and the non-literary examples of incubation (chapter 19).

Extispicies were performed in most periods of Mesopotamian history. The earliest reference comes from c. 2,500 B.C., in the expression maš/máš šu mu.gíd, "He placed (his) hand in the sheep". (One of the logograms for the haruspex was MÁŠ.ŠU.GÍD.GÍD.) This occurs in two difficult and duplicating texts: R. D. Biggs [*OIP* 99], No. 114, col. V line 13; and A. Deimal [*Fara* 2], No. 37, col. III line 10, col. IV line 4, etc. Haruspical texts emerge in the Old Babylonian period, and from then on extispicy is attested throughout the centuries, rising to a very prominent position in the Neo-Assyrian era.

The other methods used to obtain omens varied with time: for example, libanomancy (omens deduced from smoke patterns) is known only from four Old Babylonian texts, which partially duplicate each other (see I. L. Finkel [1983-1984]). (*DB,* p. 22 mentioned *YOS* 10, Nos. 57-58, but these are lecanomantic omens; i.e., omens deduced from the colours and patterns of oil dropped onto water.)

It seems that divinatory techniques became associated with social stratification. For instance, extispicy was performed in the Old Babylonian period for 'ordinary' people (e.g., YBC 16148; I. Starr [1977], p. 207) but, by the Neo-Assyrian period, it was applied only to public matters (namely, the destinies of the state, the royal family, or of important officials), as was astrology-astronomy. This social division may explain why the many 'minor' or 'private' methods of divination are poorly attested, probably these were practised mainly outside the official and royal circles in which the writers of our sources seem to have moved. Even these minor techniques would have required scholarly interpretation by a ritual expert, although a few omens could be explained, on a popular level, by their recipient or by another untrained person: e.g., some oracular utterances (page 152); and see pages 7 and 114-115 on dreams.

MESOPOTAMIAN ONEIROLOGY

There are references to dreams and dream experts in nearly all the Mesopotamian textual genres, from the Sumerian (largely ignored in this study) to the Seleucid epochs: administrative texts; charm lists; incantations, with or without rituals; letters; lexical works; literature; medical texts; omen series; rituals prefaced with long catalogues of woes; and royal inscriptions. This extraneous material has been used here to supplement the technical dream literature.

TABLE 1: SUMMARY OF DREAM ASPECTS

	Significant/True			**Irrational/False**
Causes	various deities			demons, ill health, Marduk's wrath, sorcery (pages 50-58)
Types	message (pages 15-18)	symbolic-message (pages 18-19)	dream omen (pages 19-20)	symptomatic, night-mares (pages 23-24 and 59-65)
Approaches	objective-passive			objective-passive
Field	direct divine communication	indirect		
	theological divination		scientific divination	folklore, morals, religion
Ritual Method	incubation (chapter 19)	interpretation		aversion or turning to good luck (chapters 12-17)
Modern Terms	paranormal - causes unknown			caused by problems in the self, requiring psychoanalysis
Connections	prophecies		omens	demonology, medicine, sorcery

Table 1 on page 5 shows a fundamental separation between the significant/true dreams originating from the gods, presenting a message concerning the future (prognostic dreams); and the irrational/false dreams, either nightmares sent by hostile deities or evil powers, or merely pleasant dreams, neither having any mantic import (symptomatic dreams). It is very difficult to determine how any culture decides on what constitutes an omen. Since unpleasant symptomatic dreams are usually one item in a list of disasters befalling an individual due to divine wrath, the Mesopotamians may have used 'context' to separate the 'irrationality' of such dreams from the complicated content of 'everyday' dreams; i.e., dream omens. (Clairvoyant dreams, examples of the objective-active approach, and Death Dreams have been omitted from Table 1, but are discussed on pages 20-23.)

This separation appears in the Akkadian sources, with dream omens and reports referring to prognostic dreams, while dream rituals (excluding incubation) and references outside the technical literature apply to symptomatic dreams.

The bulk of this study is concerned with symptomatic dreams rather than with prognostic dreams so it is not the place to analyse in detail A. L. Oppenheim's conviction that oneiromancy (divination by dreams) in Mesopotamia was a very minor and socially dubious technique [*DB,* pp. 212, 221-223, 238, and 242]. However, the following points should be noted:

i). While there are less sources and references to oneiromancy than for extispicy, the body of evidence (from all ages) is considerably larger than for many of the 'private' methods: e.g., there is only one text on casting special dice (*LKA* 137).

ii). Tablets of dream omens (and ceremonies) were included in Ashurbanipal's Library at Nineveh, even if only for curiosity value, whereas examples of some other techniques have yet to surface: e.g., smoke omens.

iii). There are royal dream reports, and a possible royal *Dream-Book* (see page 100).

iv). Contrary to *DB,* p. 200, the letters of the ritual experts to Esarhaddon and Ashurbanipal do include dream reports: *ABL* 1347 (pages 237-238, although no details were recounted), *ABL* 1021 (page 17), and the very fragmentary *ABL* 1336 (= *SAA* 10, No. 365).

The practice of oneiromancy was limited by nature because an individual would have seen far more symptomatic than prognostic dreams in his life.

We know little about the relevance of any divinatory method to the 'ordinary', non-official Mesopotamians (nor about their access to the ritual experts). Dreams are mentioned infrequently in private letters: e.g.:

i). Old Babylonian - *AbB* 5, No. 10; S. Greengus [1979], No. 23 (page 156); *TCL* 18, No. 100 (page 35); *TCL* 1, No. 53 (page 21); and *PBS* 7, No. 17 (page 53; the last reference is to symptomatic dreams).

ii). Old Assyrian - *BIN* 6, No. 179 (page 29).

iii). Middle Babylonian - *JCS* 6 [1952], p. 143; L. Speleers [1925], p. 28, No. 260 (= *AbB* 10, No. 158); and *PBS* 1/2, No. 60 (see *DB*, p. 196 on the last text, but the object was stolen from Ninlil).

There are no accounts of Dream-Book consultation apart from the mention in a non-dream omen on a tablet in a private collection (page 20). A letter reveals that sometimes people felt competent 'to interpret' their acquaintances' dreams, if not their own: S. D. Walters [1970], No. 69 (= *AbB* 9, No. 263), obv. 1 to rev. 13:

1). *a-na Ba-a-nu-u*[*m*]
2). *qí-bí-ma*
3). *um-ma Nu-ú*[*r*]-^{d}ZUEN-*ma*
4). *im-me-r*[*a*]-*am*
5). *iš-te-en*
6). *ša-am-ma i-na* [X X] X *mi/im*
7). *ša* ^{d}IŠKUR *i-qí-i*
8). *aš-šum ki-i-a-am*
9). *šu-ut-ta-a-am*
10). *ta-mu-ur*
11). *ù pi-ta-a-am*
12). *i-ta-at* AŠA$_5$-*li-im*
13). *pe-et a-pu-tum*

[1-2] Speak to Banum [3] thus (from) Nur-Sin:
[4-7] Buy one ram, and sacrifice (it) in the [. .] . . of Adad
[8 to rev. 10] because this is why you saw a dream.
[11-13] Also, please open the dike outlet adjacent to the field!

On the other hand, many prognostic dream reports by individuals are attested from Sumerian times onwards. These are predominantly message dreams or symbolic-message dreams; explanations being attached to the latter only in the literary examples. It is interesting that reputed message dreams were used to support a variety of causes in waking life (see pages 40-41 for examples).

It is surprising that there are so many specific rites to counteract unpleasant symptomatic dreams (chapters 12-17), instead of this evil being covered by the *Universal Namburbi* rituals (pages 111-112). Obviously unpleasant symptomatic dreams were regarded as an important source of malefic influence and, thus, a major manifestation of divine anger.

CHAPTER TWO: RESULTS FROM SLEEP LABORATORIES

Research in sleep laboratories has increased our knowledge of the mechanisms of sleeping and dreaming states. The following summary derives mainly from chapters in S. J. Ellman and J. S. Antrobus [1991] and those by W. Dement and his co-authors in M. F. DeMartino [1959].

A Sumerian proverb (*JCS* 12 [1958], p. 54, 5.76) mentions a dog dreaming:

ur.gi$_{15}$ máš.ge$_{6}$ bi.e.àm

The dog mutters in its dream(s).

Apparently all mammals experience two types of sleep, with distinctive physiological characteristics, during a normal night's rest: rapid eye movement (REM) sleep and non-REM sleep. (REMs also occur in the waking state.)

REM SLEEP

In 1953 E. Aserinsky and N. Kleitman published their discovery of what became known as REM sleep (*Science* 118, pp. 273-274). The features of human REM sleep include:

i). Binocular synchronised rapid, jerky movements of the eye-balls in all directions, as opposed to the slow, rolling movements noticed at sleep onset, measured by an electro-oculogram (EOG). These jerky eye movements occur in irregular bursts throughout a REM period, interspersed with intervals of quiescence. The end of a REM period is frequently indicated by a quiescent state lasting more than five minutes.

ii). Brain waves of low voltage and mixed frequency, recorded on an electroencephalograph (EEG).

iii). Inhibition of the muscles of the face and neck, indicated by an electromyogram (EMG). (Major body movements also are rare.)

iv). Accelerated and irregular heart and respiratory rates.

The researchers' different views as to what constituted 'a dream' and their reluctance to accept non-REM mentation as 'dreaming' led to 'results' of high recall rates of vivid and complex dreams from REM periods and hardly anything from non-REM periods in the early experimental awakenings. The theory that REM sleep was the time of dreaming seemed to be 'proven' by the discovery in 1957 by W. C. Dement and E. Wolpert that there was a correspondence between the direction of the REMs and the actions in a dream: e.g., vertical REMs could be correlated with the dream of a bouncing ball. This gave rise to the controversial idea that the dreamer was watching the dream images exactly as he would if awake.

The congenitally blind have complex tactile dreams instead of visual ones; touch being their usual means of experiencing the external world. When blindness occurs after the age of five visual imagery remains for varying periods, gradually becoming rare (children who go blind before they are five do not have visual dreams; M. F. DeMartino [1959], p. 93). This lent some weight to the theory that the REM process was due to memory traces in the brain of things seen before. It was then discovered that all blind people have REMs (if the eye muscles are intact), but of a frequency too low to be detected by a standard EOG. Thus, REMs can exist independently of visual imagery.

It is still unclear how and why the REM process happens, either when the subject is awake or sleeping. Contortional eye movements are also observed in REM sleep, but not when the subject is awake.

Experimental results published by W. C. Dement in 1960 showed that behavioural changes such as apathy or irritability were produced by REM sleep deprivation. This deprivation was compensated by increased amounts of REM sleep on subsequent undisturbed nights.

In 1963 and 1965 G. Moruzzi distinguished between tonic and phasic events in REM sleep. Tonic events are long and sustained, such as the low voltage, mixed frequency EEG. The superimposed phasic events are brief and sporadic, like the REMs. G. Grosser and A. Siegal extended this division to non-REM sleep in 1971. Attempts have been made to separate and compare 'tonic' and 'phasic' dream reports.

NON-REM MENTATION

The issue of non-REM, or sleep onset, mentation is still being argued. The emphasis has changed from whether or not dreams occur in non-REM sleep to how these dreams differ from REM ones. The earlier distinction was that in REM sleep the dreamer saw complex imagery in a progressive sequence, while non-REM dreams were shorter, consisting of abstract thoughts in brief, unrelated scenes. Some scientists remain unconvinced of the existence of non-REM dreams, believing these to be trivial background thoughts which happen more or less continually throughout the day, only being recalled in a relaxed state.

More experiments have revealed that the two types of dreams are in fact very similar in coherency, dramatic content, and length. The main dispute is whether the 'quality' differences are due to the production or to the retrieval mechanisms of the brain. The ability of a dreamer to recall far more REM dreams than non-REM ones upon experimental awakening must also be taken into account.

A. Maury used the term 'hypnagogic' in 1848 to describe 'visions' occurring between wakefulness and deep sleep. It is often used as well for hypnopompic experiences; i.e., when arousing from sleep. Many artists and scientists have recorded flashes of inspiration at these times (e.g., A. Mavromatis [1987], ch. 8), which correspond to intervals of non-REM mentation.

It is argued on page 41 that the Akkadian word *munattu* occasionally referred to hynopompic visions, or to day-dreams. Prognostic dreams seen during the first watch of the night (i.e., covering sleep onset) were accepted cautiously at Mari (page 35).

SIMPLIFIED SLEEP CYCLES

The first sleep cycle covers the beginning of stage 1 non-REM to the end of the first REM period. Subsequent sleep cycles are from the end of one REM period to the end of the next, lasting about ninety minutes.

Most of the studies of non-REM mentation derive from awakenings in stage 2 non-REM.

Stage W(akefulness)	Subject is awake and alert, trying to get to sleep. REMs and eyelid blinks.
Stage 1 non-REM	Subject is drowsy. Slow rolling eye movements or none.
Stage 2 non-REM	5-10 minutes later. Minimal or no eye movements.
Stages 3 and 4 non-REM	After varying times, the subject is in a light sleep. High voltage slow waves show on EEG: when 20-50% of output, stage 3; over 50%, stage 4. Stage 4 often ends with a change in the sleeper's position.
REM	Some time during the second hour of sleep. Subject in deep slumber.
Stages 1 and 2 non-REM	Subject 'emerges' from a deep sleep into a lighter one.
(Stages 3 and 4 non-REM	These become very brief in the second half of the night.)
REM etc.	

REM sleep periods occur regularly, three to five times, throughout the average seven hours slumber of a healthy young adult. They last from a few minutes to over forty, becoming longer as the night progresses, with shorter non-REM intervals in between. REM sleep constitutes 20-25% of the total night's sleep. The first REM period usually contains less 'dreamlike' mentation than the others. Normally several distinct dream episodes happen successively in a single REM period, so one may experience as many as ten or twenty dreams a night.

RECALL

One thing is certain, everyone dreams in REM sleep in some form of sensory image - visual, tactile, auditory, olfactory (very rare), and opinions differ over the existence of gustatory experiences. A possible reluctance 'to have dreams' has led some 'non-dreamers' to claim that they were thinking when laboratory instruments showed them to have been in REM sleep when awakened. There is no way of telling whether or not a person had a dream independently of their report.

On average, a dream is recalled after awaking naturally every two days, usually the last one of the night. Experiments have found this dream to be the longest and most bizarre and exciting.

It is very difficult to remember a dream unless the sleeper wakes during or shortly after it. Significant differences in recall rates have been noticed between abrupt and gradual laboratory awakenings. Even a momentary distraction at arousal may prevent recollection. A recalled dream is soon forgotten unless its subject-matter was very vivid or relevant to the dreamer.

There are two categories of explanations for the general differences in dream recall: the first based on dream content; the second focusing on some property of sleep which impairs the memory process. Modern psychoanalytical theories of emotional repression (page 15) can only account for some cases of forgetting.

The ability to remember dreams also depends upon the individual dreamer, on his attitude towards dreams, and his development of fantasy. Many psychologists have commented upon the increase in their patients' dream recall when undergoing psychoanalysis.

An Akkadian ritual dealing with forgotten dreams is discussed on pages 107-108.

IS MODERN PSYCHOANALYSIS RELEVANT TO MESOPOTAMIAN DREAMS?

The student of any culture's dreams is 'obliged' to apply the tenets of Western orientated psychoanalysis to his dream reports. He is offered a choice of fiercely opposed Schools, a clear and balanced account of which is presented by J. A. Hadfield [1954]. An outline of the basic psychoanalytical views of dreams is given below.

A major contribution of S. Freud was the discovery that dreams are not random and irrational, however their content may appear, but have a function and a form. He distinguished two types of thought processes:

i). Primary process, or the highly condensed, metaphorical form of thinking appearing in dreams. This dream work uses pictures seen in the day (day residues) symbolically to express complex feelings, and to resolve tensions between incompatible desires. The symbolism is necessary to avoid the censor of the conscious self.

ii). Secondary process, or the reality-orientated, linguistic thinking of the day; the rationale separating humans from animals.

S. Freud regarded the primary process as a primitive and undeveloped form of secondary mental activity. The two processes are now envisaged as separate entities. It has been suggested that dreams form a vital part of a nightly procedure whereby waking experiences are consolidated as memories, and incorporated into oneself (B. Tedlock [1987], p. 14). The secondary process concentrates on enabling us to master external reality (W. Kracke [1987], pp. 39-40).

It is generally accepted in scientific circles that dreams attempt to solve problems within the dreamer's personality, or between him and the world. Experiments in sleep laboratories have shown that daytime stress is often followed by emotional dreams. Two theories have arisen as to the purpose of such dreams: firstly, that thereby mastery is gained over the distressing circumstances; secondly, that harsh reality is compensated for by stressful dreams of opposing emphasis. The psychoanalytical Schools differ as to what is the basic emotion being repressed, and hence expressed only symbolically in the dream: e.g., aggression and power seeking (Adler); sex (Freud). (Modern 'symbolic dreams' are completely different from the Mesopotamian 'symbolic-message dreams' discussed on pages 22-23.)

Even today there is a common, popular view that dreams can be messages from or via supernatural sources. Modern research separates prognostic, or paranormal, dreams into the following categories:

i). Dreams which are apparently precognitive, but which sometimes can be explained more simply as subconscious perception by one of the sleeper's senses: e.g., dreaming of an explosion, and awakening to a smell of gas. This process has been confirmed experimentally by producing dreams from external stimuli.

ii). Telepathic dreams are those in which the dreamer apparently receives truthful information of contemporary events: e.g., at the moment of an absent relative's death. Since this information could not have been obtained by normal methods of communication, nor by inference from previous knowledge, such dreams are caused by telepathy, if one accepts its existence.

iii). Clairvoyant dreams (page 24), for which there is no explanation at the moment.

The main bar to scientific acceptance of telepathic dreams is that no fully proven case has been established, as yet. The vital factors are the verification of the dream's priority, and that it was reported immediately to impartial witnesses. Scientists also have difficulty in accepting that the human mind is capable of predicting events without basing its conclusions on previous experience or rational deduction.

J. A. Hadfield [1954, pp. 231-233] presented some complicated theories explaining precognitive dreams as being due to the different concepts of the nature of time held by the conscious and subconscious. A more understandable idea is that we dream about lots of possible events, the majority of which never happen, but when one is fulfilled we remember our 'premonitory' dream.

The differences between psychoanalytical and Mesopotamian (or, for that matter, any ancient, Eastern, or 'primitive' culture) dream theories concern the origin of a dream and its time aspect. A significant dream in Mesopotamia was a message from the gods, predominantly concerning the future of the dreamer. On the other hand, any precognitive aspect to dreams is admitted very reluctantly in psychoanalysis. Modern studies tend to ignore these dreams, and some Schools even deny their existence. Attention is concentrated on dreams envisaged as normal manifestations of the mind, which explain the dreamer's present state by reference to his past. However, the Mesopotamians classified these dreams as irrational (A. L. Oppenheim's [*DB*] 'symptomatic dreams'), having no mantic importance and, therefore, insignificant. In conclusion, the difference between the two systems is such that neither examines in depth the category of dreams most important to the other.

CHAPTER 3: THE CLASSIFICATION OF MESOPOTAMIAN DREAMS

The chapter begins with a brief discussion of the two main categories of Mesopotamian dreams: prognostic dreams (including clairvoyant ones; pages 15-23); and symptomatic dreams (pages 23-24). This is followed by a presentation of the words used by the Mesopotamians to describe a dream's quality (pages 25-31), and of other terms for a dream (usually *šuttu*(MÁŠ.GE_6); pages 31-40). The chapter ends by mentioning some of the links the Mesopotamians made between dreams and reality (pages 40-41).

PROGNOSTIC DREAMS

Three kinds of prognostic dreams can be distinguished in the Akkadian sources, listed below on a descending scale of clarity and direct contact with the divine sender:

i). Message dreams containing a clear statement, requiring no interpretation.

ii). Symbolic-message dreams, which have to be decoded.

iii). Dream omens, which are interpreted from Dream-Books.

MESSAGE DREAMS

Message dreams were regarded in Mesopotamia as a clear and direct communication from the deities, as opposed to the 'coded' omens. DB, p. 190 suggested that incubated dreams formed the pattern for all recorded message dreams. That does not imply that all message dreams were incubated. (The few examples of Mesopotamian incubation are discussed in chapter 19.)

Four characteristics of ancient Near Eastern message dreams (a-d below), as defined in *DB,* pp. 187-197 (presented first and inset), require alteration in the light of the following evidence for Mesopotamia. Most of the Mari dream reports (*AEM* 1/1, pp. 455-482) were unavailable to A. L. Oppenheim, and may reflect different notions from Mesopotamia proper.

a). A deity, or his messenger, clearly gives a message containing advice

> or a warning. Usually, only this figure appears in the dream, and only once is the figure a human being. Nabonidus records the appearance of the deceased king Nebuchadrezzar II (Nabonidus 8, col. VI lines 12-16), but this text is a piece of propaganda, whereby the appearance of the major Neo-Babylonian monarch indicated his 'approval' of the usurper, Nabonidus. An attendant accompanied Nebuchadrezzar, but it is unclear whether he was human or divine.

While it is true that the dream figure frequently is a lone deity, other figures do appear. Marduk and Sin appear together at Nabonidus 1, col. I line 18, but only Marduk speaks. We do not possess any examples of a divine messenger, unless one counts the three dreams of *Ludlul bēl nēmeqi,* Tab. 3, whereby the sufferer is cured. However, these pose problems if taken as message dreams (W. G. Lambert [*BWL*], pp. 23-24 and 27).

The dream reported by the *šabrû*-priest to Ashurbanipal (Cylinder B, col. V lines 49-84; M. Streck [*VAB* 7], pp. 116 and 118; also G. Smith [1871]. pls. 22-23, obv. 25 to rev. 11; M. Streck [*VAB* 7], pp. 190 and 192) records that he saw Ishtar and the king.

A dream of Addu-duri (*AEM* 1/1, No. 227) provides us with an instance of several human beings appearing in a dream, what is more they were people known to her personally, since she names the two ecstatics. (See also a named *šangû*-priest appearing in the second symbolic-message dream on *ARM* 10, No. 50, obv. 14.)

The inscriptions of Ashurbanipal contain two examples of the dream message being given in writing, as noticed by *DB,* pp. 201-202:

i). King Gyges of Lydia sees the writing of Ashurbanipal's name (*Annals,* col. II line 97 (M. Streck [*VAB* 7], p. 20); also 3 *R.* 28-29, rev. 15):

97). *ni-bit* MU-*ia ina* MÁŠ.GE$_6$ *ú-šab-ri-šu-ma* AN.ŠÁR DINGIR *ba-nu-u-a*

Ashur, the god, my creator, caused him to see the writing of my name in a dream.

ii). A Babylonian youth sees on a pedestal a written message describing the fate of rebels (*Annals,* col. III lines 118-121; M. Streck [*VAB* 7], p. 32):

118). *ina u$_4$-me-šu-ma* 1-*en* ^{LÚ}GURUŠ

119). *ina šat mu-ši ú-tul-ma*

120). *i-na-aṭ-ṭa-al* MÁŠ.GE$_6$

121). *um-ma ina* UGU *ki-gal-li ša* ^{d}30 *ša-ṭir-ma*

[118] On that day a certain young man [119] lay down at night, and [120] he started dreaming [121] thus:

Upon the pedestal of Sin('s statue) was written . . . .

Both these 'dreams' are highly dubious since in the first Gyges is then urged by Ashur to pay homage to Ashurbanipal, while at the time of the second Babylonia was in revolt against Assyria.

b). The recipient is a socially important figure (a king or priest), who receives the dream as a privilege. The only example of a female recipient is a Hittite queen.

The recipients of message (and symbolic-message) dreams in the Mari letters are anything but kings (in fact no royal dreams are recorded); nine out of seventeen dreamers were female. It is rare that any indication of rank is given (the dream of *ARM* 10, No. 51 occurred to a *šangû*-priest).

The extant Neo-Assyrian message dreams are seen by men. We have noted examples above of a foreign king, a priest, a young man, to say nothing of the whole Assyrian army (pages 1-2). *ABL* 1021 (= *SAA* 10, No. 361), obv. 13' to rev. 1, contains a dream report from an official[?], who claimed that Bel (i.e., Marduk) promised that he would receive favour in Assyria; yet, so far, this has not been the case. *ABL* 923, obv. 7 stated that Ashur spoke to Sennacherib in a dream (pages 39-40). Esarhaddon mentioned that he saw dreams (page 156), but gave no details. On the other hand, Ashurbanipal only recorded the dreams of other people in his inscriptions.

Nabonidus is the main recipient of Neo-Babylonian dreams, but his mother received one from Sin (Nabonidus 24, col. II lines 5-12).

c). A message dream occurs at times of crisis.

It is not clear from the Mari letters that the message dreams occurred at particularly critical moments, even though the majority refer to public matters. In fact, some of the messages appear mundane: e.g., the king should look after himself (*ARM* 10, No. 51), and a temple (or house, É) is not to be rebuilt in the same location (*AEM* 1/1, No. 234).

The dreams recorded by Ashurbanipal do seem to happen at moments of crisis, but this is probably due to their use as propaganda (see above).

Nabonidus' dreams consist mainly of various deities ordering him to restore their temples. Sin promised Nabonidus' mother that her son would renovate Ehul-hul (Sin's temple at Harran), where she resided.

d). The dreamer accepts the message submissively, and "only rarely does a dialogue (. . . .) ensue".

Dialogue is a common feature of the Mari dream reports (see already P. C. Couprie [1960], p. 185), and occurs also in:

i). The *šabrû*-priest's dream, between the dream figures of Ishtar and Ashurbanipal.

ii). *ABL* 1021 (= *SAA* 10, No. 361), between Bel and the dreamer.

iii). Nabonidus 1, col. I lines 16-33, between Marduk and the dreamer.

iv). Nabonidus 8, col. VI lines 17ff., between Nebuchadrezzar and both the attendant and the dreamer.

The main criterion of a Mesopotamian message dream is that a figure (usually divine) gives an unequivocal message to the dreamer. B. Kilborne [1987, p. 176] missed this point when he stated that message dreams were not interpreted because of the lower social position of the dream interpreter in relation to the dreamer. Throughout his discussion, based on *DB,* B. Kilborne insisted that the types and values of Mesopotamian dreams depended upon the social status of the dreamer, rather than the content. The writer and *DB,* p. 240 have found no proof for this position. B. Kilborne [1987, p. 178] attributed this view to A. L. Oppenheim, for whom it was the sex of the recipient, if anything, which mattered [*DB,* p. 190].

DB, p. 226 described message dreams as examples of the objective-passive approach to spiritual phenomena. The dreamer lies in his bed, receiving a message originating from outside himself; he may speak, even object to the order (e.g., Nabonidus 1), but cannot move. The decision to send such a dream lies entirely at the whim of the deity. Incubation rituals (chapter 19) introduce no element of compulsion, only creating a situation favourable for a visitation, if the god is so inclined. (Objective-active and subjective approaches are discussed on pages 20-23 and 24 respectively.)

SYMBOLIC-MESSAGE DREAMS

The writer prefers the designation 'symbolic-message dreams' to A. L. Oppenheim's 'symbolic', because these dreams are really a sub-category of message dreams. The divine message is now expressed indirectly by symbols. The dreamer sees diverse objects and people performing various actions, most of which are usually taken from his realm of experience. The associations between a symbolic-message dream and its explanation are very rarely obvious, or even intelligible, to us when explained.

This type of dream is mainly recorded in the Mesopotamian epics, where it occurs to heroic recipients, being a motif to propel the action. These literary symbolic-message dreams are always accompanied by their interpretations, which come from other heroic figures or deities.

An example of a symbolic-message dream is when Gilgamesh dreams of the arrival of his boon companion-to-be, Enkidu, and his dreams are interpreted by his divine mother (the *Epic of Gilgamesh,* Tab. 1, col. V line 25 to col. VI line 30). *DB,* p. 207 also offered the passage where Ea/Enki sent a dream to Atrahasis telling him to build an Ark to escape the imminent Flood (the *Epic of Gilgamesh,* Tab. 11, lines 186-187; not lines 195-196 as in *DB*). It should be noted that this episode is described in the different versions either as a dream, or as Ea speaking (ostensibly) to a reed hut (pages 231-232).

DB, p. 190 claimed that women more commonly experienced symbolic(-message) dreams in the ancient Near East than men, yet gave no examples of Mesopotamian female recipients. However, the evidence for Mesopotamia seems to show roughly equal numbers of men and women. There are four possible examples of women seeing symbolic-message dreams: three from Mari - Kakkalidi's dream reported on *ARM* 10, No. 10; and both dreams of Addu-Duri on *ARM* 10, No. 50. The fourth is the extremely fragmentary report of Etana's wife's dream about a plant which would cure her infertility, (the Late Version of the *Legend of Etana,* Tab. 1/B).

These two Mari letters, together with three late reports mentioning astral bodies seen in dreams, appear to disprove the statement of *DB,* p. 207 that symbolic(-message) dreams occur only in Mesopotamian epics (with the Sumerian exception of Gudea's Cylinder A; *DB,* pp. 211-212). In the second dream account of Nabonidus 8, at col. VII, lines 31ff., Nabonidus asks Nebuchadrezzar II to interpret a previous dream about astral bodies. In *YOS* 1, No. 39 (dated to Nabonidus Year 7) an official briefly describes two astronomical dreams he has seen, promising to investigate them. Several instances of astral bodies seen in dreams are listed on BM 77058 (= 83-1-18, 2434; *Recueil de Travaux* 19 [1897], pp. 101-102), which is dated to Years 14-15 of a king ^{m}*Ar-ta-ak*$^{!}$(*ri*)-*ša*$^{!}$(*ta*)-*as-su;* i.e., an Artaxerxes of the Achaemenid era (E. F. Weidner [1921-1923], p. 299). It is possible that these experiences were not regarded as symbolic-message dreams, but as astronomical omens observed in a dream.

DREAM OMENS

Dream omens, like all omens, were sent by the gods, but needed interpretation. This was of a commonplace type, since a Dream-Book (pages 99-101) was used, in which certain actions, things, etc., seen in a dream meant the same regardless of the dreamer's personality. Any differentiations in the apodoses were made on financial or health grounds, not psychological types:

i). The Middle Babylonian tablet of dream omens from Elam (V. Scheil [1913]; *DB,* pp. 257-259) contains forecasts which alter with status: e.g., col. I lines 16'-17', according to whether the dreamer was a poor man *(lapnu)* or an important person *(kabtu);* col. III lines 14-15, whether a poor man or a freedman *(muškēnu).*

ii). Differences are noted for an important person or a freedman in the *Dream-Book;* e.g., Tab. C, rev. col. IV lines 21-22. Tablet C also presents varying predictions for someone in captivity or an invalid at rev. col. IV lines 25-26.

iii). The incubation rituals of *ROP* state that the same dream 'omens' will have one meaning if the ceremony is being performed for an invalid, and another if it is to discover if the supplicant will achieve his desire (lines 69-70).

We do not possess enough information to enable us to decide how frequently such matters entered omen interpretation.

A late tablet in a private collection (*JCS* 29 [1977], p. 72) sheds some light on Mesopotamian views of dream interpretation: line 6:

6). DIŠ MÁŠ.GE$_6$.MEŠ-*šú ana* KA *tup-pi ú-pa-aš-šir* ŠÀ. BI *là* DÙG.GA *ṣal-lu$_4$* ⌜X⌝ [. . . .]

If he/someone interpreted his dreams according to the tablet - His heart will be saddened (lit., not happy); the sleeper . [. . . .]

CLAIRVOYANT DREAMS OR THE OBJECTIVE-ACTIVE APPROACH

In the objective-active approach to spiritual phenomena the dreamer's soul, or a part of it, is believed to leave the sleeping body and, somehow, visit the people and places seen in the resultant dream. Such dreams are called clairvoyant ones, in which the dreamer observes straightforward enactments of events that will repeat themselves exactly in later reality, thus no interpretation is required. This is distinct from "clairvoyance", whereby hidden or distant objects (such as missing people) are 'seen' when awake or in a trance.

a). The Uses Of The Verb *abālu*

DB, pp. 226-227 argued that the use of the verb *abālu,* "to bring, to carry", in dream contexts showed the presence of this concept. We possess six relevant attestations:

i). *TCL* 1, No. 53, lines 27-28:

27). *ša te-te-né-ep-pu-ši*

28). *šu-na-tu-ia it-ta-na-ab-ba-la-nim*

27-28 Whatever you do, my dreams will constantly carry (the news) to me.

ii). *NADR* contains two mentions (in lines 6 and 12) of a dream "which was brought to me (the dreamer)", *ib-bab-lam-ma.*

iii). The phrase *mūšu lib-lam-ma dà-lí-lí-ka lud-lul,* "May Night bring me (a favourable dream), and I will proclaim your glory!" occurs on *NROD,* rev. 8 and 17.

iv). *CT* 39, pl. 42d + K. 7991 + 9194, col. I line 8:

8). [. . . . . .] ⌜X⌝ KI-*šu* MÁŠ.GE$_6$ *ub-la-áš*$^!$(*ma*)-*šú* NA BI *šib-sat* DINGIR

[. . . . . .] . with him; Night brought a dream to him - A god's anger <is directed against> that man.

v). *NROD,* rev. 9 calls the Dream God Anzagar *ba-bi-lu a-me-lu-ti,* "the carrier of mankind".

vi). Gilgamesh asks in his succesive dream incubations in the *Epic of Gilgamesh,* Tab. 4: KUR-*ú bi-i-la šu-ut-ta a-mat* (*damiqti*$^?$) *lu-mur,* "O Mountain, bring me a dream! Let me see (a favourable$^?$) matter!"

However, as A. L. Oppenheim noted, these phrases cover different dream concepts:

i). The objective-passive, in which dreams are brought to the dreamer, as in message dreams (iii and vi above) or symptomatic dreams (iv).

ii). A secondary passive approach (ii) that refers to symptomatic dreams, in which the *N*-stem of *abālu* is used analogously to the *N*-stem of *šakānu,* "to be placed upon (i.e., to occur to)", when describing various ills or omens that have happened to someone.

iii). The objective-active, in which the dreamer's soul is aided by a god (v). This epithet of the Dream God may indicate that he transported men in their sleep, but this would have been an unusually intimate act of gods to ordinary men. Perhaps the meaning of the title is more along the lines of "the bringer (of dreams) to mankind".

In (i) a brother is warning his sister to behave herself in his absence, with the threat of "Big Brother is watching you", so it does not necessarily mean that the dreamer's soul travels freely, as *DB,* p. 226 believed.

b). Dream Travel

The fact that a dream is described as occurring in a certain place does not automatically make it a clairvoyant one. For instance, the first dream on *ARM* 10, No. 50 was set in the temple of Belet-ekallim, but it is a symbolic-message dream. *DB,* p. 227 excluded the travel dreams of the *Dream-Book* (*DB,* pp. 267-269) on the basis of their being omens, and requiring interpretation.

J. V. Kinnier Wilson [1958, pp. 303-304] regarded the Eagle's dream locating the Plant of Fertility in the heavens as a clairvoyant dream (the Late Version of the *Legend of Etana,* Tab. 4/B, lines 1-14). However, the literary reports of dream travel are motifs impelling the action, and so cannot be taken on their own as evidence for the existence of the objective-active approach.

c). Death Dreams

The other literary examples of dream travel involve visits to the Underworld, and are classified here as Death Dreams, together with those in which the dreamer foresees someone's death, often his own. (Note also the unusual dream omen protases of visiting the Underworld or Heaven [*DB,* pp. 259 and 283].)

Enkidu receives two dreams announcing his impending death on Tab. 7 of the *Epic of Gilgamesh,* which *DB,* p. 196, and pp. 213-214 regarded as clairvoyant dreams. The first, in col. I, is only extant on Hittite fragments, thus non-Mesopotamian and possibly atypical. Enkidu is privileged in some way to witness Anu, Ea, Enlil and Shamash debating whether or not Enkidu and Gilgamesh should be killed in retaliation for their murders of the divine Bull of Heaven and Humbaba. Gilgamesh is reprieved, but not Enkidu. *DB,* p. 196 firmly denied any possibility of soul travel, claiming that Enkidu would have recounted his journey to Gilgamesh, yet still believed this dream to be best classified as a clairvoyant one. As yet, we do not possess the complete text of this epic. In addition, the purpose of the episode was to narrate Enkidu's doom, and any 'scientific' detail was probably regarded as irrelevant. In the second dream account Enkidu descends to the Underworld (col. IV lines 15-54).

The *Underworld Vision of an Assyrian Crown Prince* describes how the protagonist made offerings in his desire to see the Underworld (obv. 29-40), which he does in a dream (rev. 1-28). Then Nergal expels him to await his appointed date of death (rev. 28). It is implied that the dreamer consequently changed his wicked ways.

On Tab. 5, lines 2ff., of the Late Version of the *Legend of Etana* the hero's wife has a dream foretelling the death of Etana and, possibly, her own as well.

In conclusion, the varied usages of *abālu*, and the paucity of references, combined with the fact that the only examples of travel in dreams are either literary devices or dream omens, makes one hesitate to accept the existence of the objective-active approach to dreams in Mesopotamia.

SYMPTOMATIC DREAMS

We possess some requests for 'pleasant' dreams: e.g., in a ŠU.ÍL.LÁ-incantation to Nabu, *LM* 54, rev. 22:

22). *i-na šat mu-ši lid-mi-qa* MÁŠ.GE$_6$.MEŠ-*u-a*

May my dreams be pleasant during the night!

Such phrases usually occur in lists of general favours sought from the gods and not in any incubatory context, so we should probably view them as wishes for pleasant symptomatic dreams; i.e., devoid of terrifying images, and with no mantic import.

Any type of bad dream in Mesopotamia was due to the dreamer's previous impiety, resulting in the absence of the protective canopy of his personal deities. (See chapter 7 on the personal deities in the context of dreams.) This enabled various ill-natured powers to attack and produce unpleasant symptomatic dreams and their intensified form, nightmares (chapter 4). For example. *SpTU* 3, No. 80, rev. 30-35 (see S. M. Maul [1994], p. 251):

30). *ina qí-bi-ti-ku-nu* DINGIR *ze-na-a* ^{d}*iš$_8$-tár ze-ni-[ti]*

31). *šá it-ti-ía ze-nu-ma* Á.MEŠ GISKIM.MEŠ HUL.MEŠ *iš-ku-nu-ni*

32). *ù* MÁŠ.GE$_6$.MEŠ *pár-da-a-ta šá at-ta-aṭ-ṭa-lu*

33). *uk-ku-lu* MÁŠ.GE$_6$.MEŠ-*ú-a lum-mu-na i-da-tu-ú-a*

34). *ina* DUG$_4$.GA-*ku-nu* DINGIR.MEŠ GAL.MEŠ DINGIR *ze-na-a* ^{d}*iš$_8$-tár ze-ni-ti*

35). *ina u$_4$-mu an-ni-i li-is-li-mu it-ti-ía*

[30] At your command (,Ea, Shamash, and Marduk,) the wrathful god (and) the wrathful goddess, [31] who are angry with me, and imposed on me ill-boding ominous happenings (and) signs, [32] and the frightening dreams which I constantly see - [33] my dreams are very obscure (and) my omens are very unfavourable - [34] at your command, O great gods, the wrathful god (and) the wrathful goddess [35] will become reconciled with me on this day.

Symptomatic dreams were rarely described in further detail after the appropriate 'adjective' (pages 25-31), apart from nightmares about ghosts (pages 59-61) and about sexual matters (pages 62-65).

DB, p. 227 regarded both pleasant and unpleasant irrational dreams (see page 14) as 'symptomatic', reflecting the purity of the dreamer, and examples of the subjective approach. The *SOED*'s definitions of "subjective" indicate that such dreams originate from within the dreamer, with unpleasant ones possibly being psychosomatic symptoms of his guilt. However, A. L. Oppenheim presented the irrational dreams as:

> "the dreams which are not considered as originating within the individual, but as happening to him, partly as a consequence of his momentary state of health, of mind, etc., and partly on account of malevolent magic activities of outside forces."

He subdivided his subjective approach, separating symptomatic dreams from those described in the Wisdom Literature, which gave:

> "a purely rationalistic and materialistic explanation of the dream-experience".

The writer found no evidence to justify this subdivision. In *DB*'s example of the *Counsels of a Pessimist,* the distinction depends on the implications of the terms *qūlu* and *kūru,* "stupor" and "depression", which are shown on pages 44-45 to be rather more serious than A. L. Oppenheim's "worries and cares" - a view approaching modern psychoanalysis. *Ludlul bēl nēmeqi* is *DB*'s other example of Mesopotamian Wisdom Literature dealing with dreams, in which Marduk's wrath is the cause of all the woes (pages 57-58). In addition, the writer prefers to regard all symptomatic dreams as another example of the objective-passive approach.

B. Kilborne [1987, p. 178] misunderstood the nature of symptomatic dreams. He preferred the designations 'realist' or 'physicalist', believing that the dreams were linked to physical causes, which they clearly are not, from a Mesopotamian view-point. He denied that it was the dream content which led to these dreams not being interpreted, but the dreamer's feelings that they were unimportant. Yet it was their very irrationality which revealed that symptomatic dreams were not a divine message, except indirectly as an indication of one's state of grace. Also, unpleasant symptomatic dreams were certainly not insignificant to the Mesopotamians, as is shown by all the rituals intended to remove their pollution, discussed in chapters 12-17.

It should be noted that the term 'symptomatic dream' can be applied to dreams indicating an illness of which the dreamer is not consciously aware (see G. Devereux [1966]).

DESCRIPTIONS OF A DREAM'S QUALITY

The descriptive terms discussed in this section refer to symptomatic dreams, except for *aqrat, šūqurat,* and *šāšât,* which apply to a Death Dream and to several symbolic-message dreams in the *Epic of Gilgamesh* occurring on Tablets 4 and 7; while *šalimtum* and *la damāqu* could refer to prognostic dreams. The references in the Mari letters describe prognostic dreams.

PLEASANT AND FAVOURABLE DREAMS

The table on page 26 lists the verbs, and their derivatives, which describe pleasant dreams in the Akkadian sources. It reveals (contrary to *DB,* p. 229) that pleasant dreams were described by both singular and plural forms; the singular being used especially in dream rituals, as one might expect. It shows also that there are other 'adjectives' used than *damqāte* (*DB,* p. 229), a form not even attested! (The derivatives of *damāqu* are translated along the lines of 'pleasantness', when referring to symptomatic dreams, and of 'favourableness', when in ominous contexts, or when the evil of a dream is mentioned or implied.) Derivatives of *damāqu* were most commonly used, then of *kânu,* and of *naṭālu* (only in Mari letters). There are two attestations of *banât,* both occurring on *ADRC,* col. II lines 58-60. *banât* is used here in connection with, or as an alternative to, the relevant stative of *damāqu* (these two verbs are almost synonymous in ominous contexts; *CAD* B, p 83b). *šūquru* appears twice, in the *Epic of Gilgamesh,* at Tab. 4, line 29:

29). [*š*]*u-ut-tu*$_4$ *šu-qu-rat* [. . . .]

The dream is very valuable [. . . .]

and Tab. 7, col. II line 20a (page 68).

Finally, there is one attestation of a derivative of:

i). *aqāru:*

the *Epic 0f Gilgamesh,* Tab. 7, col. II line 21a (page 68).

ii). *na'adu:*

AEM 1/1, No. 82, lines 5-9:

5). ^{m}*Ia-si-im-*^{d}*Da-gan*

6). *šu-ut-*[*t*]*a-am iṭ-ṭú-ul*

7). *šu-ut-t*[*um*] *ra-bé-et ù na-a*$_4$*'-da-at*

8). [*t*]*e-er-tam* [*š*]*a šu-ut-ti-šu ú-še-pí-iš-ma*

9). [*šu-ut-t*]*a-šu na-aṭ-la-*[*at*]

[5] Iasim-Dagan [6] saw a dream. [7] The dream is important and deserves attention. [8] I caused an extispicy to be performed concerning his

dream, and [9] (it confirmed that) his [dream] was seen (i.e., meaningful).

Translation	Verb	Stative sing.	Stative pl.	Adj. sing.	Adj. pl.
"valuable, unusual"	*aqāru*	*aqrat* ND	--	--	--
"very valuable"	*šūquru*	*šūqurat* ND	--	--	--
"excellent"	*banû*	*banât* D	--	--	--
"favourable, pleasant"	*damāqu*	*damqat* D ND	*damqā* ND	(*damiqtu*) *dēqtu* ND	--
		SIG₅-*at* ND	--	SIG₅.GA D ND SIG₅+P D ND	--
"very favourable, very pleasant"	*dummuqu*	--	*dummuqā* ND	--	
"unambiguous"	*kânu*	*kīnat*/ GI.NA-*at* D ND	*kīnā* ND	ZI.DA *(kittu)* D	--
"deserves attention"	*na'ādu*	*na'dat* ND	--	--	--
"seen" (i.e., meaningful)	*naṭālu*	*naṭlat* ND	--	--	--
"important"	*rabû*	*rabêt* ND	--	--	--
"beneficial"	*šalāmu*	--	--	*šalimtum* ND	--
"good"	*ṭâbu*	--	--	--	DÙG.GA.MEŠ (*ṭābāti*) ND

D = Technical dream literature   ND = Non-technical dream literature
P = Phonetic complement   All the adjectives and statives are 3rd fem. forms.

iii). *rabû:*

AEM 1/1, No. 82, line 7 (see ii).

iv). *šalāmu:*

PBS 1/2, No. 53, rev. 22-24:

22). *šu-ut-ta*

23). *ki ip-šu-ra ul i-di*

24). *ša-lim-tim ul i-⌈di* X⌉ [X]

[22-24] When he recounted (his) dream I/he did not know (if it was) beneficial. I/he did not know . [.]

v). *ṭâbu:*

STT 135, obv.$^{?}$ 7:

7). MÁŠ.GE_6.MEŠ DÙG.G[A.MEŠ]

good dreams

Generally, 'pleasant' terms were used descriptively to distinguish the dreams so denoted from bad ones. It is rare for direct comparisons to be made in the same portion of text, but see e.g., *NADR,* lines 7-8.

A secondary use involves the magical power of words, whereby describing a dream as pleasant compels it to become so. This concept is present especially in the rituals involving an *egirrû* (pages 156-157).

UNPLEASANT AND UNFAVOURABLE DREAMS

Although unpleasant dreams were far more important to the Mesopotamians than pleasant ones, this distinction is not mirrored by the number of different 'adjectives' (contrary to *DB,* p. 229). However, we do possess more attestations of unpleasant terms.

The table below reveals that (contrary to A. L. Oppenheim [*DB*], p. 231; also see [1966], p. 346) bad dreams were not always:

> "anonymous; their individual manifest content remains hidden behind the (grammatical) plural in which they are consistently referred to in Akkadian".

Again, the majority of the attestations in the singular occur in the dream rituals. The use of the terms is purely descriptive

Derivatives of *lemēnu* and *parādu* were most commonly used. Those from *lemēnu* are always in the form HUL(+), except for *Cap.* 4, line 6 (*lem-né-⌈e-ti⌉*; page 111), and, possibly, *LKA* 139, obv. 26' (duplicated by *LKA* 140, obv. 16'):

26'). [*i*]*na* MÁŠ.GE$_6$ *l*[*e-mut-ti*$^?$] ⌜X⌝ [(. . . .) *ú-š*]*ab-ru-nin-ni-ma*

In a [bad$^?$] dream [(. . . .) they (the angry personal gods)] reveal to me.

Translation	Verb	Stative sing.	Stative pl.	Adj. sing.	Adj. pl.
"confused"	*dalāhu*	--	--	--	*dalhāte* D
"unfavourable, unpleasant"	*la damāqu*	--	*lá damqā* ND	*là damiqtu* (NU SIG$_5$.GA) ND	--
"obscure"	*ekēlu*	--	--	*ikiltu* D	--
"very obscure"	*ukkulu*	--	*ukkulū* * ND	--	--
"incorrect"	*haṭû*	--	--	*haṭi(t)tu* D	*haṭāti* ND
"bad"	*lemēnu*	HUL *(lemnet)* D	HUL.MEŠ *(lemnā)* ND	HUL *(lemuttu)* D ND HUL+P D ND	HUL.MEŠ D ND *lemnēti* ND
"not seen" (i.e., meaningless)	*úl naṭālu*	*úl naṭlat* ND	--	--	--
"frightening"	*parādu*	*pardat* ND	*pardā* ND	*parittu* D ND	*pardāti* D ND
"false"	*sarāru*	--	*sarrā* ND	LUL.LA *(sarratu)* D ND	--
"bewildering"	*šūšû*	*šāšât* ND	--	--	--
"baleful"	*là ṭâbu*	--	--	--	là DÙG. GA.MEŠ *(la ṭābāti)* ND

D = Technical dream literature   ND = Non-technical dream literature

P = Phonetic complement

All the adjectives and statives are 3rd fem. forms, except for *, which is a 3rd masc. form.

Next come derivatives of *haṭû, šūšû* (see on), and of *là ṭâbu.* Then there are two examples of derivatives of *sarāru* (see on) and of *la damāqu:*

i). R. Borger [1969], §5:
máš.ge$_6$ nu sig$_5$.ga
šu-ut-tu là da-mì-iq-tú
An unpleasant dream

ii). *BIN* 6, No. 179, rev. 18-19:
18). *šu-na-t[ù]-ni*
19). *lá dam-qá*
[18] Our dreams [19] are unfavourable.

There is one attestation derived from:

i). *dalāhu:*
ADRC, col. IV line 7.

ii[a]). *ekēlu:*
ADRC, col. III line 37

ii[b]). *ukkulu:*
SpTU 3, No. 80, rev. 33 (page 23).

iii). *úl naṭālu: AEM* 1/1, No. 142, line 23 (page 30)

Four of these descriptive terms are rarely attested, in any grammatical, form with omens:

i). The verb *dalāhu* is normally used in connection with *têrētu,* the ominous organs examined in extispicy. If the omens were "confused", they did not correspond to any known protasis, and could not be interpreted. The charm list *BAM* 377, col. III lines 16-18, contains the more 'normal' adjective *pardāti* when duplicating the charm instructions of *ADRC,* col. IV lines 5-7 (page 283).

ii). *ekēlu* means "to be dark", so a translation along the lines of "obscure" seems appropriate for an ominous context.

iii). *YOS* 10, No. 52 (duplicated by No. 51; correct *YOS* 10, p. 11) is an augural text presenting omens deduced by the haruspex from the physical appearance of sacrificial birds (J. Nougayrol, *RA* 61 [1967], pp. 23-68; as opposed to the lamb of *DB,* p. 207). The comparison of the apodoses of col. IV lines 21 and 22 indicates that *sarāru*(LUL.LA) means "false", in the sense of "misleading":
21). *šu-na-at šar-ri-im ki-na*
- The king's dreams will be unambiguous.
22). *šu-na-tu-šu sà-ar-ra*

- His dreams will be false.

The Akkadian version of *ZI*, line 4 transcribes LUL.LA by *pardu.*

iv). *šāšât* is the *Š* stative of *ešû.* Gilgamesh describes the dreams he received as a result of his incubations on Tab. 4 as *ka-liš šá-šá-át,* "totally bewildering".

The writer has been unable to find an example of *la banû* as mentioned in *DB,* p. 229. *CAD* N_2, *naṭālu* 2g, pp. 124-125, offered *CT* 39, pl. 36, rev. 108 as an instance of *ahû* describing dreams:

108). DIŠ MIN MÁŠ.GE_6 *ahīta*(BAR) *it-ta-*[*ṭal* . . . .]

If ditto (i.e., a man [. . . . . .] to the temple of his personal god) (after) he had seen a strange dream [. .].

(Also see *CAD* $Š_3$, p. 407b, on the unpublished tablet IM 67692, line 265.)

DESCRIPTIVE TERMS FROM MARI

There are indications from Mari that the time of night when a dream occurred was a factor in deciding its value. The haruspex Shamash-in-matim reported to the king: *AEM* 1/1, No. 142, lines 20-23:

20). *aš-šum šu-ut-tim*

21). *ša Sa-am-mé-e-tar e-pu-uš*

22). *šu-ut-tum ši-i ba-ri-ri-tum-ma*

23). [*ú-u*]*l na-aṭ-la-at*

[20-21] I performed (an extispicy) regarding the dream of Sammetar. [22] That dream (occurred in) the first watch (of the night), and [23] it was not seen (i.e., it was of no importance).

The idea that dreams seen at the beginning of sleep were to be treated with caution is perhaps illustrated by *ARM* 10, No. 50, obv. 13. Addu-duri described a frightening symbolic-message dream she saw, qualifying it with:

13). *šu-ut-ti an-ni-tum ša ba-ra-ar-*⌈*tim*⌉

This dream of mine was (one) from the first watch (of the night).

She goes on to recount other experiences which support the dream's dire forecast.

Mesopotamian dream reports rarely mention the time when a dream was seen [*DB,* p. 187], indicating that the time aspect either had never been relevant or was no longer significant. A few references to *munattu* (pages 34-35) suggest that the Mesopotamians occasionally distinguished between nocturnal dreams, those of the early morning (the third watch) and/or day-dreams. Thus, the phrase, as expressed at *NADR,* lines 4-6, may not always have been a formula:

4). MÁŠ.GE$_6$ *an-ni-[tú]*

5). *ša ina ba-ra-ar-ti qab-li-ti šat ur-[ri]*

6). *ib-bab-lam-ma*

[4] This dream, [5-6] which was brought to me during the first watch (of the night), the middle watch, (or) the third watch, ...

AKKADIAN TERMINOLOGY

The usual Akkadian word for "a dream" is *šuttu,* or its logogram MÁŠ.GE$_6$. It has been translated consistently in this study as "dream", although occasionally "vision" may be preferable. At times it is difficult to know whether a reported image derived from a trance, or was seen while awake or in a dream: the recipient possibly being uncertain himself. The possible links between oneirology and (ecstatic) prophecy in Mesopotamia deserve detailed investigation. There are other Akkadian words for "dream", but we can rarely tell what, if any, distinctions the Mesopotamians drew between them.

tabrīt mūši, "NOCTURNAL VISION"

Contrary to *DB,* p. 225, *tabrīt mūši* is only attested syllabically. The writer has found no certain evidence that it was equated with the logogram MÁŠ.GE$_6$, or that this logogram was abbreviated to MÁŠ. The logogram MÁŠ.GE$_6$ is clear in both *ABL* 1021 (= *SAA* 10, No. 361), obv. 14' and 16'. [MÁ]Š does appear on Tab. 2, line 3 of the Middle Assyrian Version of the *Legend of Etana,* which J. V. Kinnier Wilson [1985, p. 70] interpreted as *šutta,* based on the Late Version [ibid., p. 110]. If this rendition is correct, it is the only recorded instance of MÁŠ.GE$_6$ being abbreviated.

We possess only three literary examples of *tabrīt mūši,* all from late Neo-Assyrian texts:

i). Ashurbanipal Cylinder B, col. V, lines 49-52 (M. Streck [*VAB* 7], p. 116):

49). *ina šat mu-ši šú-a-tu šá am-hu-ru-ši*

50). 1-*en* ^{LÚ}*šab-ru-u ú-tu-ul-ma i-na-ṭal* MÁŠ.GE$_6$

51). *i-gi-il-ti-ma tab-rit mu-ši šá* ^{d}XV *ú-šab-ru-u-šu*

52). *ú-ša-an-na-a ia-a-ti um-ma*

[49] During that night (in) which I (Ashurbanipal) prayed to her (Ishtar), [50] a certain *šabrû*-priest lay down, and started dreaming.

[51-52] He awoke, and he repeated to me the nocturnal vision which Ishtar caused him to see, thus:

ii). The same incident is also recorded on G. Smith [1871], pls. 22-23, obv. 25-26 (M. Streck [*VAB* 7], p. 190):

25). *am-šá-la iš-tén šab-ru-ú ša ina šá-at mu-ši* ⸢*ú*$^{?}$⸣-[*tu-lu-ma i-na-ṭa-lu* MÁŠ.GE$_6$]

26). ⸢*i*⸣-*gi-il-ti-ma tab-rit mu-ši šá* ^{d}*Iš-tar šá Ar*[*ba-ìl*^{KI} *ú-šab-ru-u-šu ú-ša-an-na-a ia-a-ti*]

[25] Yesterday a certain *šabrû*-priest, who [lay down at night, started dreaming]. [26] He awoke, and [he repeated to me] the nocturnal vision which Ishtar of Arbela [caused him to see:]

iii). The third examplar comes from the literary text the *Underworld Vision of an Assyrian Crown Prince,* rev. 1:

1). [^{m}*Ku-um*]-*ma-a-a* NÁ-*ma tab-ri-it mu-ši i-na*-[*ṭ*]*a-al ina* MÁŠ. GE$_6$-*šú* (the rest of the line is broken)

Kumma lies down, and he sees a nocturnal vision. In his dream . . . .

The expression *tabrīt mūši* appears to be a synonym for *šuttu,* which occurs in the same passages as well (see also the Biblical phrase (in the King James' Version) "vision of the night": e.g., *Gen.* 46: 2; and *Job* 33: 15). This equivalence is indicated in the lexical text *malku* = *šarru,* Tab. 3, contained on *SpTU* 3, No. 120, col. I lines 53-55:

53).	*tab-rit mu-*⸢*ši*⸣ "nocturnal vision"	*šu-ut-tum* "dream"
54).	*ma-ad-ru-*⸢*ú*⸣ --	MIN "ditto" (i.e., dream)
55).	*mu-na-ma-*⸢*tum*⸣ "waking dream"	*mu-na-at-tum* "waking dream"

(*madrû* is not cited in the modern Akkadian dictionaries; *munattu* is discussed below.)

munattu, "EARLY MORNING" AND "WAKING DREAM"

a). "Early Morning"

The logograms relating to *munattu* in two lexical texts show it was a temporal designation, denoting the very early morning. The logogram of *munattu* given in erim.huš = *anantu,* Tab. 2, line 263, gìr.babbar, is rendered by *šēp ūmi (aliktu)* of *CT* 18, pl. 14b, rev q and r, namely, the "(approaching) foot of day", a poetic expression for "dawn, very early morning". (babbar.ra itself means "the going out of the sun, sunrise", Akk. *ṣīt šamši* [an.ta.gál = *šaqû,* Tab. C, line 40; *MSL* 17, p. 196].)

i). erim.huš = *anantu,* Tab. 2, lines 261-263 [*MSL* 17, p. 41]:

261).	[máš].ge$_6$	*šu-ut-tum*	"dream"
262).	[ù].li	*hi-iš*$^{?}$*/il*$^{?}$*-tum*	?
263).	[gìr].babbar.ra	*mu-na-at-tum*	"early morning"

hištu cannot be translated due to a scarcity of attestations. *CAD* H, *hiltu* B, p. 188b rendered *hištu* as "dream", possibly connected with *hâlu,* "to seep out", so perhaps "pollution (in a dream)". Sexual dreams are mentioned in the Akkadian sources (pages 62-65), but previously people have been too ready to state that problematic words denoted "wet dreams" (see the note on *gilittu;* pages 68-69). *AHw* 1, *hiltu* I, p. 345b offered the 'safe' translation *„etwa „Schlaf"?"* deduced from the context. P. C. Couprie [1960, p. 186] suggested that *hiltu* (originally as *hīštu*) possibly was derived from *hâšu,* "to see", which is only attested lexically [*CAD* H, *hâšu* D, p. 147a].

ii). *CT* 18, pl. 14b, rev. n-r (*malku* = *šarru,* Tab. 6, lines 206-210):

n).	[*h*]*a-aš-tu* "pit"	*šu-ut-tum* "dream"
o).	[*p*]*i-*⌈*rit*⌉*-tu* "fright"	MIN "ditto" (i.e., dream)
p).	[*m*]*u-na-ma-tu* "early morning"	*mu-na-at-tum* "early morning"
q).	[*še*]*-ep u*$_4$*-mì* "foot of the day"	MIN "ditto" (i.e., early morning)
r).	[*še*]*-ep u*$_4$*-mì a-lik-*⌈*tú*⌉ "approaching foot of day"	MIN "ditto" (i.e., early morning)

(*šu-ut-tum* in rev. n appears to be an error for *šu-ut-ta-tú,* since the pair *haštu* and *šuttatu* occur in other texts: e.g., *Šurpu,* p. 50, Commentary B (K. 4320), line 20.

The modern Akkadian dictionaries claim that *munāmātu* (in rev. p) is the plural of *munattu.* It is probably just an alternative, like the rest of the column; see also *SpTU* 3, No. 120, col. I line 55 on page 32.)

The *Epic of Irra,* Tab. 5 lines 42-44, provides us with a literary example of *munattu* as "early morning":

42). *ka-ṣir kam-me-šú* ^{m}*Kab-ti*-DINGIR.MEŠ-^{d}*Marduk* DUMU ^{m}*Da-bi-bi*

43). *ina šat mu-ši ú-šab-ri-šú-ma ki-i šá ina mu-na-at-ti id-bu-bu a-a-am-ma ul ih-ṭi*

44). *e-da šu-ma ul ú-rad-di a-na muh-hi*

42 Kabti-ilani-Marduk, son of Dabibi, (was) the author of this text. 43 He (Irra/Ishum) caused him to see (the text) during the night and, in the early morning, when he recited (the work), neither did he omit anything 44 nor did he add a single line in this respect (i.e., to the composition).

b). "Waking Dream"

munattu is contrasted with *šuttu*(MÁŠ.GE$_6$) in three literary passages:

i). *Ludlul bēl nēmeqi,* Tab. 3, lines 7-8:

7). [*u*]*r-ra u mu-šú iš-te-niš a-na-a*[*s-su-us*]

8). MÁŠ.GE$_6$ *mu-na-at-tú mal-ma-liš šu-um-r*[*u-ṣa-ku*]

7 I wail day and night alike. 8 [I am] equally wretched (in) dream (or) *munattu.*

After Marduk sent the third dream to the sufferer, indicating the abatement of his divine wrath, the beginning of the redemption process is announced in line 46:

46). [*ina*] *mu-na-at-ti iš-pu-ra ši-pi*[*r-ta*]

He (Marduk) sent me a message [in] a/the *munattu.*

(The meaning "early morning" is also possible for this line.)

ii). *Cap.* 1 + 3, obv. 3-4 (see S. M. Maul [1994], pp. 197-203):

3). ⸢EN ^{d}UTU⸣ *šar$_4$* AN-*e u* KI-*tim* :! KA.INIM.MA DIŠ NA *lu ina* MÁŠ.GE$_6$ *lu ina m*[*u-na-at-ti*]

4). *lu mu-du-u lu la mu-du-u* UBUR-*šú ú*-⸢X⸣-[. . . .]

3 Incantation: "O Shamash, the king of heaven and earth."

Incantation rubric: (It is the text) if a man, whether in a dream or in a [*munattu*], 4 whether knowingly or unknowingly, his breast he [. . . .].

(The tablet 81-2-4, 166 is not related to this entry, as R. I. Caplice [1965, p. 111] claimed.)

The same incantation appears, with an appropriate ritual, on *KAR* 228 (see E. Ebeling [1955], pp. 144-148). Here, someone else 'seizes' the man's breast in a *munattu* but *šuttu* is not mentioned: rev. 12-13:

12). KA.<INIM>.MA ŠU.ÍL.LÁ.KÁM *ṣi*!*(šìr)-bit* UBUR

13). *ša mu-na-at-ti*

[12] Incantation rubric: It is (the text of) a ŠU.ÍL.LÁ-incantation (for) seizure of the breast [13] in (lit., of) a *munattu.*

iii). *CT* 23, pls. 15-22 +, col. II lines 18'ff. contain a ritual dealing with the appearance of a ghost. The problem is described in a fragmentary incantation to Shamash: lines 22'-23':

22'). [. . . . *šá* GID]IM DAB-*šu-ma ina* MÁŠ.GE$_6$ *u mu-na-at-ti*

23'). KI-*šú* IGI.I[GI-*ru* . . .]

[22'-23'] [. . . . (a man) whom] a ghost seized or met with (i.e., appeared to him) in dream or *munattu* [. . .]

W. G. Lambert [*BWL,* p. 295] wrote that *munattu* was:

> "the early-morning period of light sleep and waking . . . . but in all the passages where the meaning is plain 'waking time' is clearly correct."

(see also *CAD* M$_2$, p. 200a), thus both deny *munattu* has any ominous significance. Therefore, according to his view, in the passages above being awake is compared to a dream = dreaming (i.e., being asleep); this contrast was more usually expressed by *e-ri u ṣal-li,* "awake or sleeping".

Instead, the writer believes that two ominous incidents are being compared (as in the phrase *šuttu u bīru,* see page 40), one occurring during the night and one in the early morning. Accordingly, *munattu* should be translated in this context as "waking dream", with the intention of covering both the nuances of a dream occurring in the morning, as the dreamer is coming out of deep sleep (see also *DB,* p. 225), and a day-dream.

The possibility of dreams being seen during the day is indicated by the fragmentary line *BMS* 12 (with *LM* 40) + K. 20155, rev. 113 (page 95), and the Old Babylonian letter *TCL* 18, No. 100, obv. 8-9:

8). *a-na-ku mu-ša-am* ⸢*ù ka*⸣*-ṣa-tam*

9). *šu-na-ti-ka-ma a-na-ṭa-al*

[8-9] I myself see dreams (about) you (in the) night and early morning.

***purussâ amāru,* "TO SEE AN ORACULAR DECISION"**

Two logograms are used for *purussû,* "a decision", in Akkadian texts: KA.AŠ.BAR and EŠ.BAR. J. Klein [1970-1971, pp. 121-122] argued that these words originally represented two different concepts in Sumerian: secular judicial activity and divine oracular decisions respectively.

The logograms became interchangeable but the division of meaning continued in the Akkadian sources (see *AHw* 2, p. 882). We are concerned here with the meaning "a decision (granted by an omen from the gods)" or "an oracular decision". A further development occurred in the celestial omens of *Enūma Anu Enlil* where the apodoses are called *purussû*s and the protases *ittu*(GISKIM), "ominous sign, omen" (F. Rochberg-Halton [1982], pp. 367-368).

ROP contains the only examples of the phrase *purussâ amāru* known to the writer. This phrase occurs in several incantation rubrics and desired ritual results, with reference to the observation of shooting stars (lines 88, 91, and 100) and of an ox's movements (line 121). It also represents some type of vision, for which the recipient had to lie down; *purussû* is used in *ROP* both interchangeably with and in apposition to *šuttu,* "dream":

i). Lines 44-51 - the supplicant wishes to speak with his personal deities. The rubric (line 48) refers to a *purussû* (and/or) a dream, while the ritual result (line 51) is "You lie down, and you will see an oracular decision".
 Lines 52-60 have the same purpose but do not mention a visual experience.

ii). Lines 61-70 - the incantation petitions for a dream (line 64); the rubric (line 65) for a *purussû;* while the ritual result (line 68) is "You lie down, and you will see a dream". Dream 'omens' are given in lines 69-70.

iii). Lines 71-84 - the first incantation mentions dream 'omens' in lines 74-75, yet the rubric (line 76) concerns a *purussû,* as does that of the second incantation (line 81). The result of the first ritual (lines 81c-d) is "You lie down, and you will see an oracular decision (and/or) a dream". The second ritual's result refers only to a *purussû* (line 84). (The rubric line 81a has been attached erroneously.)

These complexes, together with lines 1-43, have been treated in this study as examples of dream incubation instead of vision seeking.

The similarity of the subject-matter of *ROP* with the range of topics ascribed to *purussû* on *KAR* 44, rev. 2 (the exorcist's list of manuals) has been pointed out before (e.g., E. Reiner [1960a], pp. 29-30):

2). EŠ.BAR MUL.MEŠ MUŠEN.MEŠ *u* GU_4.MEŠ MÁŠ. ANŠE.MEŠ

Oracular decision(s) from (lit., of) stars, birds, and cattle, (and) wild animals.

Examples of all these categories can be found in *Šumma ālu.*

bīru, "DIVINATION (BY EXTISPICY)" AND "VISION"

The Sumerian word máš appears in the logograms of both *bīru*(MÁŠ), primarily meaning "divination (by extispicy)", and *šuttu*(MÁŠ.GE_6), "divination of the night" (i.e., "a dream"). There are two passages, both in ŠU.ÍL.LÁ-incantations addressed to Gula, which indicate that a prognostic dream and a *bīru* were regarded as comparable sources of omens. It is unclear which nuance of *bīru* is meant.

i). *LM* 7, rev 38-42 (duplicated by *LM* 11, obv. 9'-13'):

38). *ina* MÁŠ.GE_6 *u bi-ri šá* GAR-*n*[*a*]

39). *ina* HUL AN.GE_6 ^{d}30 *šá ina* ITI NENNI U_4 NENNI GAR-[*na*]

40). *ina* HUL Á.MEŠ GISKIM.MEŠ HUL.MEŠ *là* DÙG. G[A.MEŠ]

41). *šá ina* É.GAL.MU *u* KUR.MU GÁL-[*a*]

42). *pal-ha-ku ad-ra-ku u šu-ta-du-ra-*[*ku*]

[38] As a result of dream(s) and *bīru*(s) which occur to [me]; [39] as a result of the ill portent of the lunar eclipse which occurs/occurred in month X, (on) day Y, [40] (and) because of the evil of ill-boding (and) baleful ominous happenings (and) signs, [41] which are (occurring) in my palace and (throughout) my land: [42] I am afraid, I am worried, and [I am] constantly terrified.

(Lines 39-41 constitute the *attalû*-formula, see page 149.)

ii). *STT* 59, rev. 12-13:

12). *ina bi-ri u šu-ut-ti it-ta-na-áš-kan-am-ma*

13). *pal-ha-ku-ma a-ta-*⌜*nam-da*⌝*-ru*

[12] As a result of *bīru*(s) and dream(s which) repeatedly occur to me, [13] I am afraid, and I am constantly (living) in fear̥.

(There are several duplicates of this incantation: e.g., *BMS* 6, obv. 71 to rev. 96; and *LM* 19, obv., which addresses Belet-ili (a name for the Mother Goddess) instead of Gula.)

The linking of *bīru* with *šuttu* has led some modern editors to translate the former as "dream, vision" in certain passages where it occurs on its own. A study of the context usually reveals that this is an erroneous translation (see page 40 for exceptions), and that extispicy is being referred to in phrases well-known elsewhere in the technical corpus.

One such passage is Nabonidus 4*, col. II lines 52-56:

52). *i-na pal-e-a k[i-n]im ina pu-luh-tú šá* ^{d}INANNA *A-ga-dè*^{KI} GAŠAN-*ia*

53). *bi-ri ab-re-e-ma* ^{d}UTU *ù* ^{d}IŠKUR

54). *i-pu-lu-'u-in-ni an-na ki-i-nu*

55). *šá* ⌜*ka*⌝*-šá-du te-me-en-na É-ul-maš šu-a-ti*

56). UZU *dum-qí i-na* UZU SILA$_4$-*ia iš-kun*

[52] In my legitimate reign, in dread of Ishtar of Agade, my lady, [53] I performed an extispicy, and Shamash and Adad [54] answered me with unambiguous assent. [55-56] He (Shamash) placed a favourable omen (lit., flesh of good luck) in the flesh of my (sacrificial) lamb regarding obtaining the foundation document of that Eulmash (Ishtar's temple at Agade).

The context makes it clear that an extispicy was performed. However, S. Langdon [1915-1916, p. 113 and notes 1 and 3-4] translated these lines as if they referred to a dream. SILA$_4$ in line 56 was taken to mean an astronomical omen seen in a dream, with the result that he claimed that *bīru* was used in Neo-Babylonian royal inscriptions in the sense of "dream, dream oracle". The mistranslation possibly arose from the similar sections on the same cylinder in which Nabonidus received divine messages in dreams (*šuttu*(MÁŠ.GE$_6$)) about temple restorations: col. I lines 67-70; and col. III lines 36-37.

J. N. Postgate [*NRGD*] took three fragmentary texts to mean that divine instructions concerning the endowment of certain temples were issued in dreams or visions, *bīru.* However, in these texts, the messages originated from the patrons of the haruspex, Shamash and Adad, while the the phrase *bīra barû* ("to perform a divination (by extispicy)"), indicates that the instructions were revealed on a sheep's entrails, and not by dreams or visions:

i). *ADD* 738, obv. 6' to rev. 8' (= *NRGD,* No. 36 on pl. 22; *SAA* 12, No. 22):

6'). [*bi-r*]*i ab-re-e-ma*

7'). [*ina* UGU$^{?}$ $^{(URU)}$*Šab*]-*bu* URU *ša* AMA LUGAL

8'). [^{d}UT]U <*u*> ^{d}IŠKUR *ina bi-ri ud-du-ni*

[6'] I performed [an extispicy]. [7'-8'] [Shamash] <and> Adad informed me in the extispicy (about) Shabbu, the city of the king's (i.e., my) mother.

ii). *OrNS* 17 [1948], pls. 27-30 (after p. 272), obv. 14-15 (= *SAA* 12, No. 86; and see *NRGD, pp.* 121-122):

14). UGU É *á-ki-it šá* EDI[N *b*]*i-ri ab-re-e-ma*

15). ^{d}UTU *u* ^{d}IŠKUR *iq-bu-ni*

[14] I performed an extispicy concerning the *bīt akiti* (a religious structure) of the open country, and [15] Shamash and Adad addressed me.

iii). *KAV* 39, obv.$^{!}$ 1'-2' (the true obverse was thought to be the reverse in *KAV*; = *SAA* 12, No. 87; and see *NRGD,* pp. 122-123):

1'). [*ina* UGU$^{?}$ ^{d}*Za-ba*$_4$*-b*]*a*$_4^{?}$ *bi-ri ab-re-e-ma* ^{d}*Šá-maš u* ^{d}IŠKUR *áš-'a-al-ma*

2'). *um-ma* ^{d}*Za-ba*$_4$*-ba*$_4$ DUMU AN.ŠÁR *šu-ú* ^{d}*Šá-maš u* ^{d}IŠKUR *ina bi-ri ú-du-ni*

[1'] I performed an extispicy [concerning Zababa], and I asked Shamash and Adad, [2'] "(Was) he Zababa, the son of Ashur?" Shamash, and Adad informed me in the extispicy.

J. N. Postgate [*NRGD,* p. 122] restored [*ina* UGU$^{?}$ É ^{d}*Za-ba*$_4$*-b*]*a*$_4^{?}$, at the beginning of obv.$^{!}$ 1'.

These lines are part of a historical preamble to a royal endowment, similar to (i) and (ii) above. The king's question at obv$^{.!}$ 2' (Had he seen Zababa?) may have arisen from some kind of visionary experience, possibly recounted in the missing first lines of the tablet. If so, then this text is an example of extispicy being used to question the gods after 'a dream'. (The passage is translated differently in *SAA* 12.)

DB, p. 354 regarded obv$^{!}$. 1'-5' as an example of statues of gods (restoring [*ṣalam*(?)] in obv.$^{!}$ 3') being made according to a "vision" (the *bīru* of obv$^{!}$. 1'). This is plausible, but Shamash and Adad (the patrons of extispicy) were unlikely to have replied to the king's questioning by granting another vision (the *bīru* of obv.$^{!}$ 2'), as A. L. Oppenheim claimed.)

In (i) and (iii) above the recipient of the presumed dream was Sennacherib. The fulsome letter *ABL* 923 (= *SAA* 10, No. 174), addressed to his grandson, Ashurbanipal, recounts at obv. 7:

7). AN.ŠÁR *ina* MÁŠ.GE$_6$ *a-na* AD.AD-*šú ša* LUGAL EN-*ia* ABGAL *iq-ṭi-b*[*a-áš-šú*]
Ashur spoke to the grandfather (lit., the father of the father) of the king, my lord, a sage, in a dream.

Since the intention of this passage was to praise Ashurbanipal's wisdom, it may only be hyperbole.

Two further attestations of *bīru* cannot be viewed as alluding to extispicy, and must refer to a type of vision:

i). *SpTU* 2, No. 21, obv. 16:

16). *at-ta man-nu šá ina* MÁŠ.GE$_6$ *u bi-ri* IGI.IGI-*ru* KI-*ia*$_5$
Whoever you are, who are repeatedly seen by me in dream(s) and vision(s),

The ritual is concerned with detaching a recurrent dream apparition (obv. 1).

ii). *Ludlul bēl nēmeqi,* Tab. 3, lines 35-38:

35). *la ta-pal-lah iq-ba-a ú-šá*-X [. . . . .]
36). *mì-mu-u* MÁŠ.GE$_6$ *i-ṭul ù ina mim-ma* [. . . .]
37). *iq-bi-ma a-hu-la-pí ma-gal šum*-[*ru-uṣ-ma*]
38). *a-a-um-ma šá ina šat mu-ši ib-ru-u bi-*[*ra*]

35 "You must not fear", she said to me . . . [. . . . .] 36 something (of) a dream he saw, and through something [. . . .] 37 She spoke, "Deliverance (from your) very exhausted [state], 38 whoever saw a vision during the night".

(These lines occur in the account of the third dream, presumably referring to the previous two.)

It is unclear how, and if, this meaning of *bīru* and that of *munattu* as "a waking dream" are related.

birûtu, "DIVINATION?"

birûtu (like *bīru*) is a derivative of the verbal root *brī,* "to observe, to inspect", and is only attested lexically. The Akkadian dictionaries disagree as to its meaning: *AHw* 1, *birûtu* 1, p. 130a translated it as *„(Traum)-Gesicht",* but there is no evidence to support this rendition; whereas *CAD* B, p. 268a has "divination", the preferable general translation, probably limited to extispicy.

DREAMS AND REALITY

That the Mesopotamians were well aware of the difference between a dream and reality is shown by the use of *na/egeltû* at the end of various literary dream reports (see *CAD* N_1, *nagaltû,* pp. 106-107). Yet, occasionally images or actions seen in dreams were treated as if they had occurred in waking life; as, for example, in the rituals dealing with nightmarish dream content (pages 114-115), especially the act of sorcery mentioned on 81-2-4, 166.

Message dreams were frequently used as a means of reinforcing deeds or speech, by revealing apparent divine support. For example, *ARM* 10, No. 100 is an attempt to seek legal redress from the king by claiming that the god Dagan had told the writer-dreamer that only Zimri-Lim could help her. See also Nabonidus 8 (page 16); *ABL* 1021 (page 17); and the dream reports concerning Gyges and a Babylonian in Ashurbanipal's inscriptions (pages 16-17).

It is possible that 'omens' seen in dreams were taken as 'real'; see the late dream reports about astral bodies mentioned on page 19. The view of *DB,* p. 205 that *JAOS* 38 [1918], pp. 82-85 referred to a series of extispicies observed in a dream can no longer be maintained. Instead, this tablet belongs to a Middle Babylonian haruspical genre studied by F. R. Kraus [1985]. These texts present the extispicy report obtained in response to a specific question, sometimes concerning prognostic dreams. (The issue of extispicy being used 'to confirm' prognostic dreams is not covered in this volume.)

The *tamītu* CBS 12578 (E. Leichty [1990]) asks if a seriously ill person will recover. It is unclear whether an extispicy regarding the health of this (presumably) important person would have been performed as a matter of course, or whether it was carried out because the invalid had seen contradictory prognoses in dream(s), as indicated by the two extremely rare *ezib*-clauses on the reverse:

1). *e-zib šá ina* MÁŠ.GE_6 *i-mu-ut*

2). *e-zib šá ina* MÁŠ.GE_6 TI-*uṭ*

[1] Disregard (the fact) that he died in a dream! [2] Disregard (the fact) that he recovered in a dream!

See page 62 for the statement in the *Sumerian King List* that an incubus was Gilgamesh's father.

CHAPTER 4: SLEEP DISORDERS

E. D. Weitzman [1981, Table 1 on pp. 384-385] listed the many sleeping and awakening disorders known today. Some of these can be found in the Akkadian sources:

i). 'Bad sleep' - disturbed or excessive sleep (pages 43-45).
ii). Nocturnal bruxism or teeth grinding (pages 45-46).
iii). Nocturnal enuresis or bed-wetting (pages 46-47).
iv). Sleep-talking (page 47).
v). Snoring (pages 47-48).
vi). Somnambulism or sleep-walking (page 48).
vii). Nightmares (pages 48-65).

VAT 7525 and the fragmentary 'sleep omens' discussed in F. Köcher and A. L. Oppenheim [1957-1958, pp. 73-75] offer examples of ii-vi above. These particular disorders occur when the muscles are 'uncontrolled', during stages 3-4 non-REM sleep (see chapter 2).

'BAD SLEEP'

There are frequent references to a disturbed night or unpleasant sleep (see *CAD Ṣ, ṣalālu,* pp. 67-69), which could consist of:

i). Oppressive sleep caused by demons.
ii). Sleep interrupted by visitations from demons or ghosts.
iii). Restless sleep or insomnia caused by illness or worrying over problems: e.g., *TCL* 18, No. 152, edge 33-35:

33). *i-na ni-iz-iq-ti-ka*
34). *mu-ši-a-tim*
35). *ú-ul a-ṣa-la-al*

33-35 I cannot fall asleep at night due to worrying about you.

Whatever the reason a "bad night" was evidently something to be dreaded: e.g., *JNES* 33 [1974], p. 290, line 24:

24). dingir.mu ge$_6$ hul.zi.e nam.ba.ni.íb.šid.dè.en
i-li ana mu-[š]i lem-nu la ta-man-[na-an-ni]

O, my personal god, (please) do not deliver [me up] (i.e., abandon me) to a bad night.

STT 275, col. IV line 23 is a charm to ensure repose:

23). [. . . .] ⌜X⌝ *šit-tu u* MÁŠ.GE$_6$.MEŠ HU[L.MEŠ] ⌜SIG$_5$⌝.MEŠ

[. . . .] . (is a stone) to make favourable (both) sleep and bad dreams.

The overwhelming power of sleep is indicated both by the use of the verbs *maqātu,* "to fall upon", and *rehû* (primarily meaning "to beget") in the sense of "to cover with, to pour over", and by the passage in the *Epic of Gilgamesh,* Tab. 11, col. IV line 198 to col. V line 218 where the hero unsuccessfully attempts to fight Sleep, as a preliminary to overcoming Death.

Yet, too deep a sleep, with its numbing effect, was regarded as oppressive and unnatural: *Ludlul bēl nēmeqi,* Tab. 2, lines 71-72:

71). *a-lu-ú zu-um-ri i-te-di-iq ṣu-ba-ti*

72). *ki-ma šu-uš-kal-li ú-kàt-ti-man-ni šit-tú*

[71] The *alû*(-demon) has donned my body (as) a garment. [72] Sleep covers me like a large hunting-net.

Marduk's removal of this affliction is mentioned on Si 55 (*BWL,* pls. 13-14), rev. 11-12:

11). *šit-ti la ṭa-ab-tu re-ha-a ṣa-la-*[*li*]

12). *ki-ma qu-ut-ru im-ma-lu-ú* AN-*e uš-ta-r*[*iq*]

[11] Unpleasant sleep, the pouring out of slumber, [12] he took far [away] like smoke with which the heavens get filled.

qūlu AND *kūru* IN THE *COUNSELS OF A PESSIMIST*

Obverse 17 to reverse 20 of the *Counsels of a Pessimist* (*BWL,* pl. 30) refer to bad sleep and dreams:

17). [*a-a*] *im-qut a-na lìb-bi-ka le-mut-tu$_4$ šit-tu$_4$*

18). [*qu*]-⌜*ú-lu*⌝ *ù ku-*⌜*ú*⌝*-ru i-du-uk-ka šu-us-si*

19). [*qu*]-⌜*ú*⌝*-lu ù ku-ú-ru i-ban-ni šu-ut-ta*

20). [*l*]*u* MÁŠ.GE$_6$ *mu-lam*$^{!}$(*šal*)*-mì-na-at ú ši kur lìb-bu-uk*

[17] [Do not let] bad sleep attack your heart! [18] Drive away stupor and depression from your body (lit., side)! [19] Stupor and depression will produce a (bad) dream. [20] Although the dream worries (lit., makes bad) . . . your heart.

(*AHw* 3, *šuttu(m)* I, p. 1293a emended rev. 20 to *ina*$^{!}$ MÁŠ.GE$_6$ *mu-ši*$^{!}$, but the writer has not come across this expression elsewhere.)

The words *qūlu* and *kūru* often occur together, along with other synonyms for "daze, worry", etc. Passages in *Šurpu* indicate that such moods originated from demonic attacks: e.g., the list of woes at Tab. 7, lines 1-36 due to the *dimītu*-disease, *māmītu* ("curse/oath"), and the *ahhazu*-disease demon:

17). ki šà.dib.ba dingir.re.e.ne.ke$_4$.e.ne.ne.ne sag.sum.mu silig. silig.g[a.a.meš]

18). *a-šar ki-mil-ti* DINGIR *šú-nu i-hi-iš-šu-ma qu-la i-na*[*m-du-u*]

19). lú dingir.bi an.da.ri.a gaba mu.un.re.eš túg.gim dul.la.⸢a. meš⸣

20) *a-me-lu ša* DINGIR-*šú it-ti-šú is-su-ú im-hu-ru-ma* GIM *ṣu-ba-ti ik-tu-mu-šú*

17-18 They (the demons) rush to the place of divine wrath, and they inflict stupor. 19-20 They encountered the man whose personal god has withdrawn from him, and covered him like a garment.

33). lú.u$_{18}$.lu.bi ù.di níg.me.gar gá.gá.da.na ul$_4$.gal tu.tu.lu. d[è]

34). *a-me-lu šu-a-tu$_4$ qu-lu ku-ru iš-šá-kin-šum-ma ma-gal ur-t*[*a-am-mi*]

33-34 Stupor (and) depression have settled upon this man, and he is very exhausted.

This passage (see also *Šurpu,* Tab. 5-6, lines 1-6, and 11-16) suggests that *qūlu* and *kūru* were envisaged as serious conditions, more severe than might appear from the *Counsels of a Pessimist.* The words have been translated diversely, but their general sense is of being utterly weary and devoid of all will power (M. Held [1961], pp. 16-17). (*qūlu* was one of the results when Anzu stole the Tablet of Destinies from Enlil, putting the divine order in abeyance: *Bin Šar Dadmē* (M. Vogelzang [*BŠD*]), Tab. 1, line 84). It is difficult to imagine how anything as vivid as a (bad) dream could be produced by this plight. *DB,* p. 227 regarded these states in a more 'light-hearted' tone, namely, anxiety and cares produce dreams.

NOCTURNAL BRUXISM

Bruxism, or grinding one's teeth, is mentioned on VAT 7525 (*AfO* 18 [1957-1958, pls. 5-9), col. I lines 41-42:

41). [DIŠ LÚ] *i-na ṣa-la-li-šu ši-*[*i*]*n-*[*ni-šu*] ⸢*i*⸣ *ka-ṣa-aṣ*

42). [*i-na*]*-an-zi-iq*

41 [If a man] grinds [his] teeth in his sleep - 42 [He will] have worries.

Bruxism may lead to dental damage if carried to excess. *BAM* 30 (= *LKA* 136) is devoted to rituals to prevent a man from grinding his teeth. One of these rituals treats bruxism in sleep, rev. 47'-53' (see also *BAM* 157, obv. 6'-9'; where the skull is to be in place for three days):

47'). DIŠ NA *ina i-tu-li-šú* ZÚ.MEŠ-*šú*
48'). *i-kaṣ-ṣa-aṣ gul-gul* LÚ.U_{19}.LU
49'). TI-*qé ina* A LUH-*si* ÌxGIŠ ŠÉŠ
50'). 7 U_4.MEŠ *ina* SAG.DU GIŠ.NÁ-*šú* GAR
51'). *ina* IGI *i-tu-li-šú*
52'). 7-*šú i-na-ši-iq*
53'). 7-*šú i-le-ek-ma* TI-*uṭ*

47'-49' If a man grinds his teeth while lying down (asleep): You take a man's skull. You wash (it) in water. You anoint (it) with oil. 50' You place (it) at the head of his bed (for) seven days. 51'-52' He kisses (it) seven times before lying down. 53' He licks (it) seven times. He will recover.

NOCTURNAL ENURESIS

Bed-wetting usually occurs in the first third of the night's sleep (E. D. Weitzman [1981], p. 406). This sleep disorder is mentioned in the 'sleep omens' (KÀŠ-*šú iš-tin: AMT* 65/4, lines 8'-9'; *AMT* 66/2, line 7'; and *CT* 28, pl. 41b, line 11'), as is voiding excrement in one's sleep ($ŠE_{10}$-*šu iz-zi: AMT* 66/2, line 8'; and *CT* 28, pl. 41b, line 10').

Several remedies for enuresis are recorded, including the fragmentary *BAM* 115, obv. 14' and rev. 4'-7'. The ritual cited by the namburbi text catalogue *Cap.* 1 + 3, obv. 1-2 (see S. M. Maul [1994], pp. 197-203):

1). [*ana* HUL KI.N]Á NITA *u* MÍ *lu ina* GE_6 *lu ina kàl* u_4-*mi lu* [. . . .]
2). *lu e-nu-ma ina* KI.NÁ-*šú* KÀŠ-*š*[*ú iš-ti-nu*]

(S. M. Maul [1994, p. 197, n. 344] stated that there was not room at the beginning of obv. 1 for R. I. Caplice's [1965, p. 108] restoration of [NAM.BÚR.BI HUL KI].NA.)

is one of those found on *STT* 239 (and duplicates; S. M. Maul [1994], pp. 379-383), obv. 1-4:

1). [*ana* H]UL KI.NÁ *lu* NITA *u* MÍ *lu ina* GE_6 *lu ina ka*[*l* u_4-*mi*]

2). [*lu i*]*na* AN.BAR$_7$ *ina* KI.NÁ X-*šú-nu e-nu-u lu šu-te-*[*nu-u*]

3). [*e-nu-ma ina*] KI.NÁ-*šú* KÀŠ-*šú iš-ti-nu* HUL KI.NÁ *š*[*ú-a-tú*$^?$]

4). [*ana* NA *ú*]*l* SÁ.SÁ GIŠ.NÁ *šá ina* UGU *ni-lu i-za*[*k*$^?$- . . . .]

[1] [For the] evil of a bed - whether of a man or of a woman, whether during the night or throughout the whole [day], [2] [or] at midday on the bed their X is changed or replaced, [3] [whenever] he urinates [in] his bed - the evil of [that$^?$] bed [4] will not reach [to (i.e., affect) the man], the bed upon which he lies down . . [. . . .]

R. I. Caplice [1965, p. 110] had suggested that *Cap.* 1 (+ 3), obv. 1-2 referred to *Cap.* 13, lines 14'ff., which now forms part of the namburbi ritual catalogue *Cap.* 5 (+)$^?$ S. M. Maul [1994], p. 207 (+) *Cap.* 13 (+) 36 (see S. M. Maul [ibid.], pp. 204-210).

SLEEP-TALKING

The 'sleep omens' list a range of sounds that a man might make during his sleep: weeping *(bakû);* speaking *(dabābu);* groaning *(labû);* roaring *(ramāmu);* shouting *(šasû);* and laughing *(ṣâhu):* e.g., VAT 7525 (*AfO* 18 [1957-1958], pls. 5-9), col I lines 39-40:

39). [DIŠ LÚ] *i-na ṣa-la-li-šu iṣ-ṣí-ih*

40). *ma-di-iš i-ma-ra-aṣ*

[39] [If a man] laughs in his sleep - [40] He will become very ill.

BAM 30, rev. 54' presents the first line of an unidentified tablet containing remedies for noises made in sleep:

54'). DIŠ NA *ina* KI.NÁ-*šú* KA.KA-*si iṣ-ṣe-né-eh*

If a man repeatedly shouts (or) laughs (while asleep) on his bed.

Another medical text, *AMT* 86/1, col. II line 4 (page 54), stated that talking in his sleep was one of the symptoms indicating that a man had been bewitched.

SNORING

There are three 'sleep omens' concerned with snoring: *CT* 37, pl. 49b + K. 14843, obv. 7, and 18-19:

7). DIŠ *i-ih-hu-ur* KUR ÁŠ DINGIR-*šú* KI-*šú sa-*[*lim*]

If (a man) snored (while asleep in his bed) - Achievement of purpose. His personal god will be reconciled with him.

18). DIŠ *i*$^{!}$*-na-ah-hu-ur sa-di-ir* UD.[. . . .]

19). DIŠ *ina* GE$_6$ AN.BAR$_7$ *e-ma* NÁ *i-na-ah-*[*hu-ur* . . . .]

[18] If (a man) snores (while asleep in his bed) - Regular(ly) . [. . . .]

[19] If (a man) snores (while asleep in his bed) during the night (or) day (lit., midday) (or) whenever he sleeps [. . . .]

SOMNAMBULISM

Somnambulists are usually children or adolescents, who may perform complex actions in addition to walking, sometimes endangering themselves. After not more than fifteen minutes they awake, or return to bed, or fall into deep sleep elsewhere (E. D. Weitzman [1981], p. 405).

Sleep-walking is referred to in three fragmentary 'sleep omens': the sleeper rises from his bed (*AMT* 65/4, lines 10'-11'); he gets up and falls down (K. 6530, lines 6, and 7-8; *Rivista degli Studi Orientali* 4 [1913], pl. 7, after p. 1004).

NIGHTMARES AND NIGHT TERRORS

Researchers in sleep laboratories distinguish between nightmares and night terrors. The table on page 49 is based upon C. Fisher, J. Byrne, A. Edwards, and E. Kahn [1970], and chapters one and fourteen in S. J. Ellman and J. S. Antrobus [1991].

S. Freud classified certain regularly occurring nightmares (or anxiety dreams) as 'typical', which meant the same for everyone; e.g., one's teeth falling out or being extracted; appearing naked in public; falling; being chased and attacked by objects or people; death of a loved one; and being lost. However, a modern study found such dreams to be rare (p. 175 in S. J. Ellman and J. S. Antrobus [1991]).

Some instances of these 'typical' nightmares can be found in the Akkadian texts:

i). A. L. Oppenheim [*DB,* p. 289] noted the existence of three fragmentary dream omens concerning teeth, possibly their removal (restoring *it-tab-*[*la*], *DB,* p. 331), on his Tab. C, fragment 1 (*CT* 20, pl. 3b + K. 8339 + 11781), col. II lines 1'-3'.

ii). He also mentioned (*DB,* p. 228) *OrNS* 16 [1947], pp. 200-201 + Kraus No. 54 + K. 5939 + Kraus No. 59, col. II lines 18-19:

18). DIŠ *ina* ŠÀ MÁŠ.GE$_6$-*šú* *e-ri-*⌈*iš*⌉*-ši-šú* GIN.GIN-*m*[*a*?] ⌈x⌉

19). NA BI *a-di-ra-tu-šú là* TE.ME[Š-*šú*]

[18] If he frequently walks about naked within his dream(s) and? . –

[19] The misfortunes of that man will not approach him.

iii). The nightmare of a town attacking the dreamer by falling on him (pages 51-52).

iv). Sexual dreams are discussed on pages 62-65.

Night Terror	Nightmare
Occurs in stages 3-4 non-REM, mainly in first 2-3 hours of sleep, when most stage 4 is present. Two-thirds happen in first non-REM period.	Occurs later in the sleep, in any REM period.
Physiologically intense experience, becoming more intense with longer amounts of stage 4 before the attack. Heart rates almost triple; increased respiratory rates and amplitude. These changes suddenly happen.	Less intense, possibly due to muscle 'control'. Gradual acceleration of heart and respiratory rates.
Writhing or sitting up or sleep-walking; piercing screams or swearing.	Feeling of paralysis in the dream, and inability to call out properly.
	Feeling of oppression on the breast, interferring with respiration.
Feeling of intense dread.	Feeling of intense dread.
Single, brief, vivid incident of sparse mentation associated with physiological signs of anxiety: e.g., being crushed; suddenly struck; enclosed; abandoned; choking. May last longer in children.	Prolonged, elaborate mentation and 'typical' dreams (see above).
Mental confusion on awakening. Difficult to waken dreamer.	No mental confusion. Easy to waken dreamer.
Uncommon to rare experience, usually decreasing with age.	Not uncommon.

CAUSES OF NIGHTMARES

Most psychoanalytical Schools regard nightmares as failed attempts to resolve conflicts within the dreamer's personality (see J. A. Hadfield [1954], ch. 9). The bad dream is the revival of the original experience, or problem, but the dreamer recoils from it in terror, awaking before a solution is reached. So the process has to be repeated, either during the same night or the next. Alternatively, there is the physiological or 'heavy supper' theory, which believes that all dreams are caused either by indigestion, or by bodily or emotional disturbances (J. A. Hadfield [1954], pp. 5-9).

References indicating the Mesopotamian ideas about the probable origins of bad dreams have to be sought in cuneiform texts outside the technical dream literature. Our main source of information is the various lists of woes, in which unpleasant dreams are merely one of a number of disasters afflicting a person.

The role of the personal deities in the context of dreams is dealt with in chapter 7, including effects of their anger.

DEMONS

An incantation directed against an unknown demon appears on several tablets (e.g., the lists on *ZA* 69 [1979], pp. 34-35 and 38; and *SpTU* 3, No. 82, col. IV lines 12-15), accompanied by reliefs known from amulets to avert the demoness Lamashtu. It is unclear how the incantation and the reliefs came to be associated. (*DB,* p. 231 believed that this incantation referred to actions by the dreamer's enemies.) A composite text is presented below:

1). ÉN *šá mal-di* GIŠ.NÁ.MU *e-ti-qu*

2). *ú-pa-lìh-an-ni ú-šag-ri-ra-an-ni*

3). MÁŠ.GE$_{6}$.MEŠ *pár-da-a-ti ú-kal-lim-an-ni*

4). *ana* ^{d}*Bí-duh* Ì.DU$_{8}$.GAL KI-*ti i-pa-qí-du-šú*

5). *ina qí-bit* ^{d}MAŠ IBILA SAG.KAL DUMU *ra-a'-mu*

6). *ina qí-bit* ^{d}*Marduk a-šib É-šag-íla*

7). UMUN KÁ.DINGIR^{KI} ^{GIŠ}IG *u* ^{GIŠ}SAG.KUL *lu ti-da-a*

8). *ki-i a-na ki-din šá* DINGIR.MEŠ EN.MEŠ *an-da-qut* TU$_{6}$ ÉN

[1] Incantation: "(Regarding the demon) who crossed the edge$^{?}$ of my bed; [2] (who) frightened me (and) caused me to panic; [3] (and who) showed frightening dreams to me, [4] they deliver him (the demon) to Biduh, the chief door-keeper of the Underworld. [5] At the command of Ninurta, the foremost heir (and) the beloved son, [6] also at the command of Marduk, who dwells in Esagila, [7] the Lord of Babylon, may you know, (O) door and bolt, [8] that I have entered into the divine protection of the gods, my lords, (so keep this demon out of my house)." Incantation formula.

(*SpTU* 3, No. 82, col. IV line 13, most unusually has *pàr-* instead of *pár-* in composite line 3.

The reading ^{d}*Bí-duh* Ì.DU$_8$.GAL follows K. Deller (pages 14-16 in *Nouvelles Assyriologiques Brèves et Utilitaires,* 1991.)

a). alû

The *alû*-demon could make its victim have sexual dreams (pages 62-63) and other nightmares: *CT* 16, pl. 27, lines 32-33 (revised by unpublished duplicates, courtesy of M. J. Geller):

32). a.lá hul lú.ra ma.mú.da.gim šu bí.in.ra.ra.e.a hé.me.en

33). MIN (i.e., A.LÁ HUL) *šá* LÚ *ki-ma šu-ut-ti ú-šar-*[. . . . *at-ta*]

(Whether) you are the evil *alû*(-demon) who afflicts (lit., hits) a man as in a dream;

(M. J. Geller has withdrawn his restoration of line 33 since *UHF,* p. 137. The Akkadian has an unclear variant.)

b). Lamashtu

CT 17, pl. 25, lines 5-7 equated the personified *di'u*-disease with the Lamashtu-demoness:

5). [^{d}d]im$_8$.me : *la-maš-tu$_4$ pa-šit-tu$_4$* : ka.muš.ì.kú.[e]

6). [ù] nu ku.ku ù nu.du$_{10}$.du$_{10}$.da.[àm]

7). *ul ú-šá-aṣ-lal šit-ta ul uš-ṭa-a-bi*

[5] (The *di'u*-disease) is the Lamashtu(-demoness), the Obliterator. [6-7] It does not let (one) sleep, nor does it make sleep pleasant (lit., good).

c). šēdu

VAT 7525 (*AfO* 18 [1957-1958], pls. 5-9) presents us with two accounts of nightmares, ascribing them to demonic influence; col. III lines 28-35:

28). DIŠ LÚ *i-nu-ma*$^!$*(giš) ṣa-al-lu a-lum*$^!$ *im-ta-na-*⌜*qú*$^!$⌝ *ta-šum*

29). *ù i-ha-az-zu-ma la iš-im-mu-šu*

30). LÚ *šu-ú* ^{d}LAMMA *ù še-e-du i-na zu-*⌜*um-ri*$^!$*-šu*$^!$⌝ *ra-ki-is*

---

31). DIŠ LÚ *i-nu-ma ṣa-al-lu*

32). *a-lum im-ta-na-qú-ta-šum*

33). *ù i-ha-az-zu-ma i-še-mu-šu*

34). *še-ed lu-um-nim i-na zu-um-ri-šu*

35). *ra-ki-is*

[28] If a man, while he lies asleep, (dreams that) a town repeatedly falls upon him, [29] and he sighs, but nobody hears him - [30] A *lamassu* and a *šēdu* are fastened to his body.

[31] If a man, while he lies asleep, (dreams that) [32] a town repeatedly falls upon him, [33] and he sighs, and someone hears him - [34-35] A very evil *šēdu* is fastened to his body.

These two omens reveal some confusion on the part of the compiler because, normally, the pair *lamassu* and *šēdu* occur in texts as two types of benevolent spirits, as designations for the personal deities (H. Vorländer [1975], pp. 25-26). Gods could only walk *(alāku)* or stand *(izuzzu)* at a person's side, whereas demons fastened *(rakāsu)* themselves to their prey, from whence they had to be expelled by exorcism, or bribed away by gifts or substitute victims. Therefore, the use of the verb *rakāsu* in line 30 above makes it very unlikely that this section referred to the benevolent spirits. There was also a *šēdu*-demon, more commonly described as "evil" *(lemnu)*: e.g., *NROD,* obv. 42.

ILL HEALTH

BAM 155 enumerates prescriptions for symptoms caused by *qāt*(ŠU) *eṭemmi* GIDIM), 'the Hand of a Ghost' [*AHw* 3, *šugidimmakku,* p. 1260a]. Column II lines 2'-3' mentions dead men appearing and, presumably, bad dreams:

2'). ÚŠ.MEŠ IGI.MEŠ MÁŠ.GE$_6$.MEŠ *i-na-aṭ*$^{?}$-[*ṭal*$^{?}$ . . . .]

3'). *ù* ŠU GIDIM *kim-te-šú*

[2'] He repeatedly sees dead men, he sees$^{?}$ dreams [(- This is due to) . . . .] [3'] and 'the Hand of a Ghost of his Family'.

AMT 86/1 is discussed under the heading of sorcery (page 54). A close inter-relation between nightmares and the dreamer's health is not necessarily illustrated by this text, as *DB,* p. 230 claimed, because of the association with sorcery.

ND 4368 (pages 80-81) presented the Dream God Zaqiqu as an agent of disease, bringing the *qāt Zaqīqi* ailment, about which nothing is known.

a). Epilepsy

The nature and occurrence of the dreams of epileptics varies with the cycles of their illness (pp. 156-158 in M. D. DeMartino [1959]). The dreams frequently are frightening or of an erotic nature. They become pleasant for a while after a seizure, and sometimes shortly beforehand. One type of epileptic dreams during the seizure, while the other type does not: both types have a dreamless night's sleep afterwards.

'Dream equivalents' of epileptic fits have been identified, which occur during the seizureless intervals. These brief and very vivid dreams (not always unpleasant) are accompanied by sensations such as burning in the throat or coldness in the limbs.

The Mesopotamian medical texts dealing with epilepsy (see M. Stol [1993]) mention dreams or visions in a seizure, especially the section *TDP,* p. 196, Tab. 26 (M. Stol's Tab. 28), lines 58-68 and 71-79. The invalid sees "(something) like" *(kīma)* various animals, dead people, his daughter, and topographical features, all of which are connected with different diagnoses relating to epilepsy. In addition, the sufferer may 'see' the disease demons seizing him: e.g., BM 47753 (M. Stol [1993], pp. 156-157; duplicated by *STT* 91 + 287) obv. 44 (in his 'sleep'); rev. 9; and rev. 14-15 (where he even talks with his attacker).

The letter *PBS* 7, No. 17, rev. 22-25 (= *AbB* 11, No. 17) connects good health and pleasant dreams and, presumably, a similar link existed between ill health and nightmares:

22). *a-[n]a-ku ša-al-ma-ku*
23). *ù a-wi-lum ša-li-im*
24). *ù šu-na-⸢tu⸣-ú-a*
25). *[m]a-⸢di-iš⸣ [d]a-am-qá*

[22] I myself am well, [23] and the man (i.e., my supervisor) is well, [24] and my dreams are very pleasant.

SORCERY

There are several terms denoting witches and wizards in Akkadian, the majority deriving from the verbs *epēšu,* "to do", and *kašāpu,* "to bewitch". References to sorcerers abound in incantations, legal documents, and letters from the Old Babylonian period onwards. A special series, *Maqlû,* was developed to combat sorcery. Yet, despite all the apparent evidence, it is probable that, as in other societies, sorcery was more commonly used as an explanation for calamities than was really practised.

Sorcery could cause bad dreams as well as alienating one's personal deities, who themselves then sent nightmares (see page 60).

a). *AMT* 86/1

The medical text *AMT* 86/1 describes the symptoms indicating that a man has been bewitched, together with the relevant prescriptions: col. II lines 3-7:

3). DIŠ NA SAG.DU-*su iṣ-ṣa-na-bat-su šit-t*[*a* . . . .]

4). MÁŠ.GE$_6$.MEŠ-*šú pár-da ina šit-ti-šú iq-b*[*i*$^!$ . . . .]

5). *bir-*⌜*ka*⌝*-šu ka-si-a ba-ma-as-su šim-m*[*a-tu* (X X)]

6). UZ[U].<MEŠ>-⌜*šú*⌝ *ru-ṭi-ib-*[*ta*] *im-ta-*⌜*na-al-lu-u*⌝

7). LÚ ⌜BI⌝ *ka-ši-ip*

[3] If a man's head constantly afflicts him; (in his) sleep [. . . .]; [4] his dreams are frightening; he spoke in his sleep [. . . .]; [5] his knees are paralyzed; his chest has paralysis; [6] (and) his skin (lit., flesh) is constantly covered with moisture - [7] That man is bewitched.

(*DB*, p. 230 restored "he has po[llutions repeatedly] in his sleep" for line 4.)

b). Assur Photo 4129 (*Archiv Orientální* 17 [1949], pages 190-192)

This tablet contains rituals to perform if a man has enemies, which resemble those directed against witches. Obverse 1-13 lists the favourable effects which will occur after the performance, suggesting that the opposite states are present as a result of the enemies' activities:

13). MÁŠ.GE$_6$.MEŠ-*šú a-na* SIG$_5$

His dreams (will turn to) very pleasant (ones).

c). *LKA* 155

LKA 155 (duplicated by *ŠRT*, pl. 7 + K. 9896) is a ritual against sorcery. Dreams are mentioned in a broken passage on rev. 8-10, as part of a list of calamities afflicting the sufferer as a result of his bewitchment.

d). *Maqlû*

T. Abusch [1989, pp. 45-48] stated that a late stage in the demonization of the Mesopotamian witch, as portrayed in the anti-witchcraft series *Maqlû*, occurred when dreams were connected with witches and witchcraft. He regarded Tab. 7, lines 170-177 as a good example of this association. However, this dream reference forms part of a passage asking for general favours and the averting of the sorcery: line 174:

174). [MÁŠ.GE$_6$] *e-mu-ru ana* SIG$_5$*-ti liš-šak-na*

May [the dream] which I saw become pleasant (lit., be placed as to goodness)!

The only other mention of dreams in *Maqlû* (in G. Meier's edition) is in a catalogue of disasters: Tab. 7, line 123:

123). HUL MÁŠ.GE$_6$.MEŠ Á.MEŠ GISKIM.MEŠ HUL.MEŠ là DÙG.GA.MEŠ

The evil of bad (and) baleful dreams, ominous happenings (and) signs.

It is clear from these lines, and the other examples in this section on sorcery, that witchcraft was regarded as a cause of nightmares but T. Abusch [1989, pp. 46-47] goes much further:

> "As we examine the stages of development of the text [*Maqlû*], we are struck by the degree to which the notion of witchcraft has merged with the idea of the dream, especially in the newly added tablets VI - VIII. To dream an evil dream is to be bewitched. The evil dream experience underlies the imagery and purpose of *Maqlû.* Standard conceptions of bewitchment are overlaid or replaced by images drawn from or associated with the experience of dreaming. The terrifying dream carries with it a double set of metaphors: images associated with dreams generally (clouds, smoke) and images associated with terrifying dreams specifically (evil gods). These images are then equated with witchcraft (. . . .) Perhaps the witch appears in the dream. In any case, she becomes the one who sends the dream or its associated forms and the one to whom they are to be returned . . . .
>
> . . . . The witch's earlier demonic power to send illness-causing demons now links up with her power as a wind (sic) to send dreams. In fact, dreams are themselves demonic powers or beings. Dreaming, moreover, may be perceived as a unitary experience and force in which the witch is both a demonic power who sends the dream and the demonic dream itself. . . . . one of the main purposes of the *Maqlû* ceremony was to purge and protect the patient from the fearful dream experiences of the night and to assure him that these dreams would not recur."

T. Abusch [1990, pp. 55-56] linked this concept of witchcraft as an evil dream with the introduction of Nusku and the expansion of his role within *Maqlû* as the short morning ceremony was transformed into the canonical all night version, which continued into the next morning. Nusku is addressed as a protective light, who has and will protect the petitioner from dreams - witchcraft [ibid., p. 17], as on *NROD,* obv. 39-48.

The writer, working from G. Meier's edition of *Maqlû* (T. Abusch has identified many more tablets), cannot find any evidence to support these theories. T. Abusch [1990, p. 17, n. 34] promised to elaborate upon his views elsewhere. The two specific mentions of dreams on Tab. 7 occur in fairly standard passages, found in other genres. Nusku does appear in two dream rituals: *NADR,* to make a bad dream favourable by fire and sympathetic magic; and *NROD,* to obtain a pleasant dream. Yet, from our evidence (see Table 6 on page 136), he is not the deity predominantly invoked in dream rites.

e). *SpTU* 2, No. 22

SpTU 2, No. 22 is a Seleucid text containing instructions for charms to deal with various misfortunes, some of which mention dreams and witchcraft.

Column I Lines 30'-38'

These lines give instructions for making a charm after *zērūtu*(HUL.GIG) had been performed against a victim on the 4th. of Abu (Abu being July - August). *zērūtu* literally means "hatred", and became a synonym for witchcraft, perhaps even denoting a particular category. One of the anticipated effects of this charm was:

> 35'). MÁŠ.GE$_6$.MEŠ SIG$_5$.MEŠ
> (His) dreams will become favourable.

Column I Lines 39'-46'

Line 39' summarizes and repeats the list of woes of col. I lines 16'-25' (see page 59 for the dream references in lines 19'-21'), going on to state that these ills were the result of sorcery:

> 39'). DIŠ NA *gi-na-a šu-dur* ŠU.BI.AŠ.ÀM NA BI *kiš-pi ep-šu-uš*
> If a man is constantly frightened; ditto - Witchcraft is being practised against that man.

Column I line 44' presents the desired ritual result:

> 44'). MÁŠ.GE$_6$.MEŠ HUL.MEŠ Á.MEŠ GISKIM.MEŠ SIG$_5$.MEŠ
> The bad dreams, the (unfavourable) ominous happenings (and) signs will become favourable.

Column II Lines 8'-16'

This section is another list of woes. Lines 12'-16' mention that the sufferer's nightmares:

12'). MÁŠ.GE_6.MEŠ-*šú pár-da*

13'). ina MÁŠ.GE_6-*šú* ÚŠ.MEŠ *i-dag-gal*

[12'] His dreams are frightening; [13'] he looks at dead people in his dream(s);

were caused by:

15'). LÚ BI ŠU NAM.LÚ.U_{18}.LU DIB-*tì* ^d^*Marduk*

16'). UŠ-*šú*

[15'] 'the Hand of Mankind' (and/or) the divine wrath of Marduk [16'] pursue (i.e., persecute) that man.

(R. Labat [*TDP,* p. 177, n. 30] claimed that 'the Hand of Mankind' ailment was caused by witchcraft, but this equation still has to be proved. E. K. Ritter and J. V. Kinnier Wilson [1980, p. 29] believed that *qāt amēlūti* denoted "delusions of persecution".)

f). *STT* 256

The fragmentary obverse of *STT* 256 contains a list of woes at obv. 1-11, with obv. 5 mentioning that:

5). *i-na* MÁŠ.GE_6 ÚŠ.MEŠ IGI.IGI-*ma*[*r*]

He repeatedly sees dead people in his dreams.

All of these troubles are due to *qāt amēlūti* (obv. 11; see the note under (e) on this ailment).

THE WRATH OF MARDUK

The most detailed description of the effects of Marduk's wrath is in the literary composition *Ludlul bēl nēmeqi,* also known as the *Poem of the Righteous Sufferer.* The narrator is the Kassite 'noble' Shubshi-meshre-shakkan, whose plight is the result of Marduk's inexplicable hostility, although the god is blamed indirectly through fear of blasphemy. Tablet 1 presents the indignities inflicted upon the narrator by humans. Tablet 2 deals with the enigma of the Righteous Sufferer, going on to record the attacks of disease demons, and the inability of the relevant ritual experts to cope with them. Tablet 3 contains three 'dreams' by which the victim is cured, and he begins to recover physically and socially. This theme is continued on various fragments.

The phrases concerning dreams are:

i). Tab. 1, line 54:

54). *at-til-ma ina šat mu-šu šu-ut-ti pár-da-at*

I lay down, and my dream was frightening during the night.

ii). Tab. 3, lines 7-8:

7). *[u]r-ra u mu-šú iš-te-niš a-na-a[s-su-us]*

8). MÁŠ.GE$_6$ *mu-na-at-tú mal-ma-liš šu-um-r[u-ṣa-ku]*

[7] I wail day and night alike. [8] [I am] equally wretched (in) dream (or) waking dream.

(See pages 32-35 on the meanings of munattu.)

Two fragmentary texts bear a close resemblance to parts of the first two tablets of *Ludlul bēl nēmeqi* in their description of the effects of divine wrath. The bilingual text 4 *R*^{2}. 22, No. 2 was included by S. M. Maul [1988, pp. 331-333] in his collection of ÉR.ŠÀ.HUN.GAs. It ascribes the calamities to Marduk in line 3' and, although the name of the deity is missing in K. 2765 (*BWL,* pl. 19), we can probably blame Marduk again.

i). 4 *R*^{2}. 22, No. 2, lines 4'-7':

4'). [ud.da í]b.ta.sùh.sùh ge$_6$.da íb.⸢lù⸣.[l]ù

5'). *ina u$_4$-mi uš-šu-uš ina mu-ši dul$_6$-luh*

6'). ⸢ù⸣ma.mú.da.ta bu.bu.luh.e in.na.mar

7'). *ù ina šu-ut-ti gi-tál-lu-tu$_4$ šá-kin-šú*

[4'-5'] During the day he is confused, (whilst) throughout the night he is perturbed, [6'-7'] and he is very frightened by dream(s).

ii). K. 2765 (*BWL,* pl. 19), obv. 7':

7'). *at-til-ma ina šat mu-ši šu-ut-t[i pardat*$^?$]

I lay down, and during the night [my] dream [was frightening$^?$].

We have already noted Marduk's wrath as one of the causes of the troubles listed on *SpTU* 2, No. 22, col. II lines 8'-16' (page 57).

In the light of the passages above, it is surprising that there is only one example of Marduk being invoked in dream incantations and once with Shamash (Table 6 on page 136). A few passages in incantations outside the technical dream literature describe Marduk's power in relation to dreams, but other deities are similarly credited (see pages 137-138).

SPECIFIC NIGHTMARES

Different types of Mesopotamian nightmares are described on *SpTU* 2, No. 22, col. I lines 19'-21':

19'). MÁŠ.GE$_6$.MEŠ-*šú* HUL.MEŠ *ina* MÁŠ.GE$_6$-*šú* ÚŠ.MEŠ IGI.MEŠ GAZ *lìb-bi* TUK-*šú*

20'). MÁŠ.GE$_6$ IGI *là* DAB-*át ina* MÁŠ.GE$_6$-*šú* GIM *šá* KI MÍ *uš-ta-hu*$^!$(*ri*)

21'). *u* A.RI.A-*šú i-ṣar-ru-ru*

19' His dreams are bad; he repeatedly sees dead people in his dream(s); he panics; 20' (his) dream does not seize the eye; in his dream(s he is) like one who has sex with a woman, 21' and his sperm flows out;

It is not clear what is meant by the dream not seizing the eye; perhaps it refers to forgetting a dream, a particular contribution of the angry personal deities (pages 91-92). Sexual dreams are discussed on pages 62-65.

THE APPEARANCE OF DEAD PEOPLE OR GHOSTS IN DREAMS

The predominant use of *mītu*(ÚŠ) is as an adjective, "dead", describing animals and people. It became a noun, "a dead person", *mītu*(AD$_6$), as distinct from "a living man", ^{LÚ}*balṭu*(TI), as well as a collective term "dead people", *mītūtu* (ÚŠ.MEŠ), describing both corpses and ghosts; in fact, it was used in many texts as a synonym for "ghosts".

An *eṭimmu*(GIDIM) is a ghost, which may return to visit the living when they are awake or asleep. A diagnosis in *TDP* defined an *eṭimmu* as "the likeness of a dead person", *ár-da-na-an mīti*(ÚŠ); e.g., p. 124, Tab. 13, col. III line 26. (*ardanānu*/*dinānu* is used to denote a substitute figurine in exorcistic rituals; see *CAD* D, *dinānu,* pp. 148-150 for examples.)

A ghost arose from the Underworld to torment those alive, in revenge for the cessation of funerary offerings (*kispu,* discussed extensively in A. Tsukimoto [1985]) on which it was dependent. It was an unfair fact of Mesopotamian life that not only was a person responsible for the deceased members of his family (see M. Bayliss [1973]), but that ghosts could return to anyone with whom they had been associated while alive (*CT* 16, pls. 10-11, col. V lines 34-53). Mesopotamian ghosts were demonic, and were not dispelled by daylight: *BMS* 53, obv. 6'-8':

6'). ^{d}UTU GIDIM *mu-pal-li-hi ša iš-tu u$_4$-mì ma-a'-du-ti*

7'). EGIR-*ia rak-su-ma là* ⸢DU$_8$⸣-*ru*

8'). *ina kal* u_4*-mi* UŠ.UŠ-*an-ni ina kal* GE_6 *up-ta-na-*⌈*lah*⌉-*an-ni*

6'-7' O Shamash! The ghost, the one who frightens me, which has been fastened to my back for many days, and will not be loosened, 8' constantly pursues (i.e., persecutes) me all through the day, (and) repeatedly frightens me throughout the night.

At times the *utukku*(UDUG)-demon has the nuance of "ghost" (e.g., the *Epic of Gilgamesh,* Tab. 12, line 84 on page 79), as does the *zaqīqu*-demon (pages 78-79), and it is not clear how these demon-ghosts were differentiated from the ghost par excellence, the *eṭimmu.*

In many other societies the sensation of heavy pressure on the chest experienced during nightmares is attributed to a ghost touching the dreamer while he is asleep. This pressure is possibly referred to on *Cap.* 1 + 3, obv. 3-4, and *KAR* 228, rev. 12-13 (pages 34-35). Generally, though, Mesopotamian ghosts appeared in unpleasant dreams rather than causing them.

A frequent complaint in those lists of woes which mention dreams is that:

ina MÁŠ.GE_6-*šú* ÚŠ.MEŠ IGI.IGI-*mar*/IGI.MEŠ

He repeatedly sees dead people in his dreams.

This phrase occurs on:

i). *BAM* 315, col. III line 5 (with the plural [MAŠ].GE_6.MEŠ).

ii). *BAM* 316, col. II line 8'.

iii). BM 64174 (= 82-9-18, 4143), line 4 (*AfO* 35 [1988], p. 21).

iv). *SpTU* 2, No. 22, col. I line 19'.

v). *SpTU* 2, No. 22, col. II line 13' (with *i-dag-gal,* "he looks at", instead of *amāru).*

vi). *STT* 95 + 295, col. III line 133 (the *mi* on the copy is to be corrected to IGI!.IGI!-[*mar*]).

vii). *STT* 256, obv. 5.

The cause of these calamities was sorcery (v, vii); or the wrath of a (personal) god or goddess (iv, vi, and presumably iii), which in turn was sometimes brought about by sorcery (i, ii); or Marduk's wrath (v).

The *Clod Incantation* (Table 9 on pages 182-183) describes various dreams (not all of which are nightmares), including seeing dead people: e.g., *ADRC,* col. II lines 2-4:

2). *kir-b*[*a-an*] HUL MÁŠ.GE_6 EN.NUN.AN.USAN EN.NUN. $MURUB_4$.[BA] EN.NUN.U_4.ZAL.⌈LA⌉

3). *a-mu-ru a-tam-ma-ru* AD.MU ÚŠ-*ta a-mu-[r]u um-mi mi-*⌈*ta*⌉ *a-mu-ru*

4). DINGIR <IGI> LUGAL IGI IDIM IGI NUN *a-mu-ru* AD_6 IGI ^{LÚ}TI IGI

2-3 O Clod, the evil of the dream which I saw, which I saw repeatedly (during) the first watch (of the night), the middle watch, (or) the third watch - (in) which I saw my dead father; (or in) which I saw my dead mother; 4 (or in) <which I saw> a god; (or in) which I saw the king; (or in) which I saw an important person; (or in) which I saw a prince; (or in) which I saw a dead person; (or in) which I saw a living person;

This passage is repeated in an abbreviated form on *ADRC,* col. III lines 29-30.

Some ghost rituals were to avert the effects of a ghost appearing in dreams:

i). *CT* 23, pls. 15-22 +, col. II lines 22'-23' (page 35), where a ghost was confronting the sufferer in dreams and waking dreams.

ii). The unpublished text K. 2781, line 2:

2). *ina* MÁŠ.GE_6 KI NENNI A NENNI *là* GUR-*ma*

You will not return in a dream to (lit., with) X, the son of Y.

iii). *KAR* 21, rev. 7-20 begins with a fragmentary incantation addressed to Utu, "the king of the ghosts". A ritual follows, whose title (line 11) mentions someone repeatedly seeing dead people. Reverse 19-20 contain an incantation to Shamash:

19). ^{d}UTU *aš-šum* NENNI A NENNI *šá* MÁŠ.GE_6.MEŠ-*šú pár-da*

20). *i-da-tu-šú lem-na dal-ha-ma la šà-ṭir*

19 O Shamash! On account of X, the son of Y, whose dreams are frightening, 20 whose omens are unfavourable, confused, and (the remainder$^?$) is uninscribed (lit., it is not written).

(Dead men have been appearing to someone, but whether in a dream or not is unclear, though line 19 suggests this possibility.)

Two of the rituals concerned with dream content are to make charms to deal with ghosts seen in dreams: *CT* 23, pls. 15-22 +, col. IV lines 13-14; and *SpTU* 4, No. 134, rev.$^?$ 7-8. In addition, the recurrent dream apparition to be repelled by the rites on *SpTU* 2, No. 21, obv. may have been a ghost, since the ritual complex obv. 3-30 resembles ghost rituals involving substitute figurines (page 200).

SEXUAL DREAMS

a). Incubus And Succubus

It seems likely that the Mesopotamians, like many other societies, regarded erotic dreams as unpleasant symptomatic dreams, or even nightmares, caused by a demon sexually assaulting the dreamer, pressing down upon and exhausting the sleeper. The male incubus had sex with female dreamers, the female succubus with men.

The Mesopotamian incubus is, today, usually taken to be the *lilû*-demon, while the succubus is either the *lilītu-* or the *ardat lilî*-demoness (associated with Lilith of Jewish mythology). We know very little about the *lilû*-demon, and only one reference suggests any connection with an incubus, namely, the problematical statement in the *Sumerian King List* (T. Jacobsen [1939]): col. III lines 17-18:

17). ^{d}Giš.bil.ga.meš

18). ab.ba.ni líl.lá

$^{17\text{-}18}$ The father of deified Gilgamesh (was) a líl.

(Gilgamesh's parents are usually taken to be the goddess Ninsun and Lugalbanda, another deified ruler of Uruk.) T. Jacobsen [1989, p. 275, n. 51] wondered if this statement indicated that sexual dreams were "considered as in some sense real". Not much is known about the *lilītu*-demoness either. Hemerologies reveal that the *ardat lilî*-demoness could pick a man as mate *(hâru)*: e.g., *Iraq* 21 [1959], pls. 14-15, obv. 14, rev. 33 and 45.

The *alû*-demon is much more likely as a cause of sexual dreams; it has already been noted as afflicting men in dreams (page 51). A most suggestive passage is *CT* 16, pl. 27, lines 18-23 (supplemented by unpublished duplicates, courtesy of M. J. Geller):

18). [a.lá] hul ⸢ki.ná ge$_6$.a lú⸣ ù.sá.ta ⸢in.úr⸣.ra.u$_8$.a hé.me.en

19). MIN (i.e., A.LÁ HUL) *šá ina ma-a-a-al mu-ši* LÚ *ina šit-ti i-re-e[h-h]u-ú at-ta*

20). a.lá hul ù.sá kar.kar.re lú.a túm.mu.dè in.gub.gub.bu.u$_8$.a hé.me.en

21). MIN *e-kim šit-ti šá* LÚ *ana ta-ba-li iz-za-az-zu at-tú*

22). a.lá hul dingir ge$_6$.a gin.gin šu pil.lá ní nu te.u$_8$.⸢a⸣ hé.me.en

23). MIN DINGIR *mut-tal-lik mu-ši šá qa-ti lu-'a-a-ti la i-šah-hu-tu at-tú*

$^{18\text{-}19}$ You are the evil *alû*(-demon), who has sex with a man during (his) sleep, in (his) bed at night. $^{20\text{-}21}$ You are the evil *alû*(-demon), the one who takes away sleep, (and) who stands (ready) to carry (it)

away from a man. [22-23] You are the evil *alû*(-demon), the (evil) god who roams around at night, who does not shy away from unclean hand(s).

If sexual dreams were considered to be nightmares, it is not surprising that only one such dream is mentioned amongst the omens of the Mesopotamian *Dream-Book,* and then in an apparent royal version (*DB,* p. 293): K. 273 + 1994b + 9064, obv. 12' [*DB,* pl. 13]:

12'). [DIŠ B]ÁRA *ina* MÁŠ.GE$_6$-*šú* KI MÍ *ṣa-lil* [. .]

[If] the king sleeps with a woman in his dream [. .]

On the other hand, there are several dream omens containing the logogram UM, which represents an action done to wild animals, a corpse, men, and women by the dreamer (*DB,* pp. 290-291, and A. L. Oppenheim [1969], pp. 155-157). A. L. Oppenheim [ibid., p. 157] suggested a verb like "to kiss". *ABZ,* p. 95, No. 134 tentatively proposed that UM in these omens was equivalent to *ṭehû,* which means "to approach", sometimes sexually (see *AHw* 3, *ṭehû(m)* I, §3, p. 1384b for examples).

The Middle Babylonian tablet of dream omens from Elam contains a section (col. III lines 8-10) describing a man "going", *alāku*(GIN), to a wild animal, an adolescent girl (*DB,* p. 258 translated "hi[s] daughter"), and his sister (V. Scheil [1913, p. 55] read DAM, i.e., "wife"; *DB,* p. 258 translated "mother-in-law"). The phrase *ana sinništi alāku* means "to have intercourse" (*CAD* A$_1$, p. 321b), so the last two of these references may allude to sexual dreams, while the first perhaps refers to bestiality.

Socially taboo forms of sexual behaviour in Mesopotamia included a man having sex with various female members of his family (e.g., the list given on *CT* 29, pl. 48, line 14, of mother, sister, daughter, and mother-in-law). Sex with one's sister could result in: *TDP,* p. 108, Tab. 12, col. IV line 17:

17). [DIŠ *ina* Ú]R.KUN-*šú* SÌG-*iṣ* ŠU [d]*Šu-lak ana* NIN-*šú* TE-*hi* ŠU [d]30 GÍD-*ma* GAM

[If] he is affected [in] his 'loins' - (It is) 'the Hand of Shulak' ailment (because) he had sex with his sister; (alternatively, it is) 'the Hand of Sin' ailment. He will have (a) protracted (illness), and he will die.

(R. Labat misread the signs at the end of the line in *TDP.*)

and death, if with one's mother: *Hammurabi's Law Code* (R. Borger [*BAL*]. pp. 2-46), §157:

§157). *šum-ma a-wi-lum wa-ar-ki a-bi-šu i-na sú-un um-mi-šu it-ta-ti-il ki-la-li-šu-nu i-qal-lu-ú-šu-nu-ti*

If a man has lain in his mother's 'lap' after <the death> of his father - They shall burn both of them.

Dreams of such behaviour (occurring especially to men, p. 73 in M. F. DeMartino [1959]) are presented in the incantation K. 2315 + 3125 + 83-1-18, 469 (*Analecta Biblica* 12 [1959], pls. 21-22). Lines 56-90 list various unfavourable omens which the petitioner requests the deities to dispel from him, including lines 83-86:

83). MÁŠ.GE$_6$.⸢MEŠ⸣ *pár-⸢da-a-ti⸣ lu-u aṭ-⸢ṭul⸣ lu-u iṭ-ṭù-lu-ú-n*[*i*]

84). GISKIM.ME[Š *lem-n*]*a-a-ti lu-ú a-tam-⸢mar⸣ lu-u i-tam-ma-ru-ú-n*[*i*]

85). MÁŠ.GE$_6$.MEŠ *⸢pár⸣-da-a-⸢tú⸣ lu!-u i-tam-mar-ru-⸢ni ina⸣* MÁŠ.GE$_6$*-ía ana* AMA*-ia$_5$ ba-ni-ti-⸢ia⸣*

86). *ana* {AMA} *⸢e⸣-mi-ti*<*-ia*> *ana a-ha-ti-ia lu-u aṭ-⸢hi⸣*

[83] Whether I or those (of my family) have seen frightening dreams; [84] whether I or they repeatedly see unfavourable omens; [85-86] whether they repeatedly see frightening dreams; whether in my dream(s) I have sex with my mother, my begetter, (or) with <my> mother-in-law, (or) with my sister.

Šumma ālu contains omens dealing with sexual matters, three of which concern wet dreams, and have conflicting apodoses:

i). *CT* 39, pl. 44, line 9:

9). DIŠ NA *ina* ⸢GE$_6$⸣ TE*-ma ina* MÁŠ.GE$_6$*-šú ni-il-šú bul-lul* NA BI ZI.GA TUK

If a man has an erection during the night and, as a result of his dream, he is bespattered by his semen - That man will have a loss.

This is a good example of the symbolic associations in some Mesopotamian omens: semen flows out, so losses will occur; also of the punning element (surrounding ZI.GA here), because the potency rituals were called ŠÀ.ZI.GA = *niš libbi,* "rising of the heart".

ii). *CT* 39, pl. 45, lines 25-26:

25). DIŠ NA TE*-ma* {*u*} *ina* GE$_6$*-šú ig-lut* NA BI ZI.GA DUGUD IGI*-mar*

26). DIŠ NA *ina* MÁŠ.GE$_6$*-šú* MIN (i.e., *ig-lut*)*-ma ni-il-šú bul-lul* NA BI NÍG.SIG$_5$*-ta$_5$* {*ta$_5$*} Á.TUKU TUK*-ši*

[25] If a man has an erection, and during the night has an ejaculation - That man will experience (lit. see) a heavy loss.

> [26] If a man has an ejaculation as a result of his dream, and is bespattered by his semen - That man will have good luck (or) profit.

A fragmentary reference to a sexual dream also occurs on *CT* 39, pl. 36, rev. 109:

> 109). DIŠ MIN *ina* MÁŠ.GE$_6$-*šú* *ana* MÍ TE-*ma* *l*[*a*? . . . .]
>
> If ditto (i.e., a man [. . . .] to the temple of his personal god) (after) he sexually approached a woman in his dream and did [not? . . . .]

The writer has not come across any rituals which either avert sexual dreams, or cancel their effect.

CHAPTER 5: A FRIGHT IN THE NIGHT

DREAD OF DREAMS

Recent studies have found blandness to be the usual emotional tone of dreams but, nevertheless, unpleasant emotions (mainly fear and anxiety) are twice as likely as pleasant ones (p. 175 in S. J. Ellman and J. S. Antrobus [1991]). This emotional grading was deduced from the dream content, and disagreed with the statements of the subjects that most of their dreams were pleasant!

Prognostic dreams and nightmares are mentioned in the Akkadian sources more frequently than pleasant symptomatic dreams because the last type did not require any action from the dreamer. A nightmare indicated that the gods were angry with the dreamer, while an awesome prognostic or Death Dream sent by the gods involved future toil, or contained depressing news. Such dreams, therefore, were often dreaded:

i). *ADRC,* col. III lines 41-42:

41). MÁŠ.⌈GE_6⌉ *šá ina* GE_6 *an-né-e a-mu-ru*

42). *pal-ha-ku-ma ad-ra-ku-ma šu-ta-du-ra-ku*

[41] (Following) the dream which I saw during this night (i.e., last night), [42] I am afraid, and I am worried, and I am constantly terrified.

(This is even though line 43 allowed for the possibility of the dream being favourable.)

ii). After each of his dream incubation episodes, Gilgamesh exclaims: e.g., the *Epic of Gilgamesh,* Tab. 4, line 98:

98). [*u*]*l* DINGIR *e-ti-iq am-mi-ni ha-mu-ú* UZU-*ú-a*

(If) a god did not pass by, why is my flesh numbed?

iii). The *Underworld Vision of an Assyrian Crown Prince,* rev. 29:

29). *a-gal-ti-m*[*a*] *ki-ma eṭ-li ta-pi-ik da-me šá ina šu-ṣe-e i-di-ši-šú it-tan-al-la-ku* EN *bir-ki ik-tùm-mu-šú-ma i-tar-*[*r*]*a*[?]*-ku lìb-bu-u-š*[*ú*]

I woke up, and like a young man who has shed blood (and) wanders alone in a marsh, whom a runner (lit., lord of the knees) has trapped, so that his heart pounds;

Nabonidus is atypical in claiming on Nabonidus 4*, col. III lines 36-37:

36). *ina* MÁŠ.GE_6 *i-na šat mu-ši a-na e-peš É-ul-maš*

37). *tu-šab-ra-an-ni šu-ut-ti ih-di lìb-bi*

[36-37] You (Anunitu) caused me to see (your desire) for the

(re)building of Eulmash (her temple at Sippar) in a dream during the night. My heart rejoiced at (this) dream.

Under these circumstances it is not surprising that *CT* 18, pl. 14b, rev. o equated *pirittu,* "fright", with *šuttu,* "dream" (page 33). The ÉR.ŠÀ.HUN.GA K. 4637 + *OECT* 6, pl. 17 (S. M. Maul [1988], No. 72) associated these two experiences on obv. 22'-23':

22'). máš.ge$_6$ ní.te.na ⌈X⌉ [. . . . .]

23'). *ina šu-ut-ti u pi-r*[*it-ti* . . . .]

22'-23' In dream and fright . [. . . . .]

Gilgamesh overhears Enkidu bemoaning his fate after seeing the gods determine his death in a dream (page 22). Gilgamesh cries out on Tab. 7, col. II lines 20-22 (O. R. Gurney [1954]):

20a). [*šu-ut-tu š*]*u-qu-rat-ma pi-rit-tu$_4$ ma-a'-da-at* [:]

20b [. . . .] *ha-ma-a ki-ma zu-*⌈X⌉-[. . . .]

21a). [*pul-hu*? *ma*]-⌈*a'*⌉-*du šu-ut-tu aq-rat* :

21b). *ana ba*[*l-ṭi*] *i-zi-bu na-sa-sa*

22). [*šu-ut-t*]*u$_4$ ana bal-ṭi ni-is-sa-ta i-zib*

20a [The dream] was very valuable, but the fright is great. 20b [. . . .] are paralyzed, like . . [. . . . 21a The dread? was] great, (but) the dream is valuable. 21b To a healthy [man] they (the gods) left lamentation. 22 [The dream] left grief to a healthy man.

AN *ezib*-CLAUSE IN NEO-ASSYRIAN HARUSPICAL ENQUIRIES

One of the rarer *ezib*-clauses interests us, namely No. 7d in *AGS* = No. 6c in *PRT:*

(e-zib šá) i-na mūši(GE$_6$) *gilittu*(ŠÀ.MUD/LUH-*tú*) *pi-rit-ti*/ ŠÀ.MUD *āmuru*(IGI-*ru*)

(Disregard (the fact) that) I saw terror (or) fright during the (preceding) night!

This phrase could refer either to the nocturnal appearance of ghosts or demons or, more probably, in the light of the connections between *pirittu* and *šuttu,* to bad dreams (as it is taken by the modern Akkadian dictionaries). If so, then it is evidence that the Mesopotamians regarded nightmares as defiling experiences.

E. G. Klauber [*PRT,* p. XX] suggested that this *ezib*-clause alluded to wet dreams. Several writers have attributed the sexual nuance of "pollution (in a dream)" to *gilittu,* and to associated derivatives of *parādu:* e.g., A. Goetze's [1939, p. 16] note on *pardu* in line 5. However, *galātu* (the verb from which *gilittu* derives) has the primary meaning of "to tremble, to become frightened". Also, when *gilittu* occurs with *pirittu* in lists of synonyms, both mean "fear, terror": e.g., *KAR* 234, obv. 20-21:

20). *lu-u gi-lit-tu₄ lu-u* MÁŠKIM *lem-nu lu-u ha-a-a-at-tu₄*

21). *lu-u pi-rit-tu₄ ša ina* GE₆ *ug-da-na-la*$^{!}$*(an)-t*[*an*$^{!}$*-ni*]

[20] Whether (it is) terror, or an evil *rābiṣu*(-demon), or panic, [21] or fright which constantly terrifies [me] during the night,

It is true that *galātu* does have the secondary nuance of "to have an ejaculation", but mainly in the omen series *Šumma ālu* and in obvious sexual contexts (see page 64 for examples). Hence, this usage is a specialized one, and is not to be assumed for its derivatives.

The relevant *ezib*-clause is attested in the following haruspical enquiries (complete restorations have been omitted):

MUSEUM NUMBER	*AGS*	*PRT*	*SAA* 4
BM 98981 rev 3'	--	--	272
Bu. 91-5-9, 168 rev. 2'-3'	--	57	134
K. 1288, rev. 5	150	--	267
K. 2747 + BM 98976 (+) Sm. 1214, rev. 6-7	142 = K. 2747	99 = Sm. 1214	56
K. 11446, rev. 2	153	--	271
K. 11474, rev. 4-5	147	--	276
K. 11477, rev. 3-4	98	--	129
K. 11490, rev. 7-8	60	--	14
K. 11492 + Sm. 412, rev. 2	50 = K. 11492	26 = Sm. 412	108
K. 11494 + 11501 + 12637, rev. 7-8	17 = K. 11494 18 = K. 11501	9 = K. 12637	63
K. 11512, rev. 6	148	--	225
K. 11521, rev. 4'-5'	145	--	185
K. 11579, rev. 5	86	--	136
Sm. 2485 + 83-1-18, 555 rev. 8-9	68	--	84
82-5-22, 484 rev. 4-5	84	--	217
83-1-18, 527 rev. 5	152	--	270
83-1-18, 541 rev. 3-4	104	--	264

CONNECTIONS BETWEEN DREAMS, DEMONS, AND THE UNDERWORLD

DEMONIC DREAMS

As well as believing that various demons could cause nightmares (pages 50-52), there are indications that the Mesopotamians envisaged dreams themselves, and the Dream God (chapter 6), as having a demonic aspect:

i). The instructions for the charm mentioned on *ADRC,* col. IV lines 5-7 also appears in three charm lists. *BAM* 377, col. III lines 16-18, places these instructions in the sixth group, together with charms against the *alû-* and *mimma lemnu*-demons.

ii). The dream vision of *SpTU* 2, No. 21 is addressed on obv. 16-21 in terms reminiscent of those addressed to demons. The queen of the Underworld, Ereshkigal, is asked to separate this apparition from the petitioner (obv. 24). The ritual burying of the substitute figurine (obv. 29) is akin to ceremonies intended to ward off demons and ghosts (page 200).

iii). One name for the Dream God was Zaqiqu/Ziqiqu, and there was a category of demons called *zaqīqu,* who dwelt in the Underworld (pages 78-79).

iv). The medical text ND 4368 (pages 80-81) places Zaqiqu alongside other demons, as an agent commissioned by the great divine triad to cause illness.

v). The incantation addressed to the Dream God as Anzagar on *ADRC,* col. IV lines 8-13, invokes him by terms more suited to a demon, or an Underworld deity.

vi). The lexical text erim.huš = *anantu,* Tab. 1 line 216 (page 83) puts Anzagar in a section dealing with different demons.

vii). Two ghost rituals on *CT* 23, pls. 15-22 + invoke Anzagar (pages 84-85).

THE KING OF THE UNDERWORLD AND DREAMS

The *lipšur*-litany IM 67638 (*Iraq* 31 [1969], pls. 38-40) lists the entourage of various deities, including that of Nergal at lines 36'-39'. Unusually, the Dream God Mamu is placed in the retinue of Nergal, instead of that of Shamash (pages 73-74):

36'). ^{d}U.GUR *lip-šur ina É-mes-lam*

37'). ^{d}*Ma-am-me-t*[*u₄*] *lip-šur šar-rat* GÚ.DU$_8$.A^{KI}

38'). ^{d}*Ma-mú lip-šur* EN MÁŠ.GE$_6$.MEŠ

39'). ^{d}*I-šum lip-šur* SUKKAL ^{d}U.GUR

36' May Nergal, (dwelling) in Emeslam (his temple at Kutha, modern

Tell Ibrahim), absolve! [37'] May Mammetu, the queen of Kutha, absolve! [38'] May Mamu, the lord of dreams, absolve! [39'] May Ishum, the vizier of Nergal, absolve!

A simile involving a dream is used to describe Nergal's powers on 4 *R*^{2}. 24, No. 1 + K. 4925 lines 52'-54':

52'). [^{d}n]è.eri$_{11}$.gal ⸢ur⸣.sag ^{su}u[san].bi

53'). [šà.áš.d]u nam.kala.ga.a.ni rib.ba$^!$ ma.⸢mú⸣.gim za.ra nu mu.[. . . .]

54'). [*gít-m*]*a-lu šá dan-nu-us-su šu-tu-qat ki-ma šu-*⸢*ut*⸣*-ti ina* ⸢*ṣer-ri*⸣ [. . . .]

[52'] O Nergal, the noble hero, [53'-54'] whose power/strength is surpassing. Like a dream he cannot [. . . .] through/at the door-pivot.

It is frustratingly typical of our sources that the verb referring to "dream" is missing in both the Akkadian and Sumerian. J. Böllenrücher [1904, p. 30; his lines 46-48] suggested that perhaps the silence of the dream as it approached the bed was meant *(„Meinte der Dichter vielleicht die Geräuschlosigkeit des Traumes, der mit unhörbarem schritt über die Schwelle ans Lager tritt?").* However, the references in *CAD Ṣ, ṣerru* A, p. 137b, where demons are described as passing through the door-pivot, together with the mention of Nergal's invincibility, indicates that doors were not barriers to demons, diseases, and dreams. *DB,* p. 234 proposed the restoration MU.[UN.GI$_4$], "he cannot [be stopped]" for line 52'.

SLEEP AND DEATH

The Akkadian verbs of lying down, *nâlu*(NÁ) and *ṣalālu,* describe both sleeping and being dead. The *Epic of Gilgamesh,* Tab. 10, col. VI line 33 has occasionally been taken to denote a close correspondence between Sleep and Death - in Greek mythology Hypnos and Thanatos were sons of Nyx/Night. *CAD Ṣ, ṣallu,* p. 74a read:

33). *sal*(or *šal*)*-lu u mītu kî ahāmeš* [*šunu*]

How alike are the sleeper(?) and the dead!

W. G. Lambert [1980, pp. 53-57] proposed the alternative of death being compared to a prison (his lines 25-27):

33). *šal-lu ù mi-tu*$_4$ *ki-i a-ha-meš-*[*ma*]

34). *šá mu-ti ul iṣ-ṣi-ru ṣa-la*[*m-šú*]

35). LÚ.U$_{18}$.⸢LU⸣*-ú* LÚ *e-dil* :

[33] The prisoner and the dead person are alike, [but] [34] Death's likeness cannot be drawn, [35] (yet) *lullû,* (i.e.,) Man, is locked up.

OFFERINGS TO THE DEAD AFTER A DREAM WAS SEEN AT MARI

A possible (but unclear) connection between the dead and dreams is given in a Mari letter (*Die Welt des Orients* [1986], p. 11) which ordered the presentation of a specific *kispu*-offering because someone had seen a dream. Obverse 3 to lower edge 7:

3). *a-na* ⸢*ki*⸣-*is-pí-im*
4). *ša* LUGAL.MEŠ *i-nu-ma*
5). ^{md}*Da-gan-Na-ah-mi*
6). *šu-ut-am*
7). *i-mu-ru*

[3] (N amounts of bread, beer, and flour) for the *kispu*-offering [4] of the kings, because [5] Dagan-Nahmi [6-7] saw a dream.

The dream report A. 15 (*RA* 42 [1948], pp. 128 and 130), rev. 50-52, states that the dreamer was going to offer a *pagrum*-sacrifice to Dagan. *pagrum* means "corpse", and W. L. Moran [*ANET*^{3}, p. 623, n. 8] suggested that this may have been a sacrifice associated with a cult of the dead. (See *ARMT* 21, pp. 160-161, n. 20 on the Mari ritual *pagrâ'um.)*

CHAPTER 6: THE MESOPOTAMIAN DREAM GOD(S)

The Mesopotamians believed that dreams were caused by external powers, who were sometimes benevolent (as when various deities sent message dreams or pleasant symptomatic dreams, sometimes malevolent (see pages 50-58 on the different causes of nightmares). This belief persists today, with several psychoanalysts recording the necessity of convincing patients that their dreams originated within themselves. For some reason the Mesopotamians also developed the concept of a Dream God (in fact, the sources provide us with four main names: Mamu; Sisig; Za/iqiqu; and Anzagar), yet his functions are ill-defined, and he is rarely mentioned in the technical dream literature.

^{d}MA.MÚ

The normal logogram for *šuttu,* "dream", in the Akkadian texts is MÁŠ.GE_6, but occasionally MA.MÚ(.D) is used instead:

i). 4 *R^2*. 22, No. 2, line 6' (page 58).

ii). 4 *R^2*. 24, No. 1 + K. 4925, line 53' (page 71).

iii). *ADRC,* col. III line 3c.

iv). 79-7-8, 77 obv. 26 (manuscript **f**) offers this alternative logogram in the incantation rubric on *ADRC,* col. II line 71, instead of the MÁŠ.GE_6 of the other two duplicates.

MA.MÚ mainly occurs in Sumerian texts (see A. Falkenstein [1966], pp. 57-64 for examples, and also the *Sumerian Flood Story,* line 149. Notice that on Gudea's Cylinder A (*TCL* 8, pls. 1-30) the variant MA.MU occurs (e.g., col. I line 29), and also MÁŠ.GE_6 (col. I line 27).

There are various references to ^{d}MA.MÚ (i.e., to a personified and deified "dream") which place the god within the retinue of Shamash:

i). The *lipšur*-litany K. 2096 (*ABRT* 1, pp. 56-59) has been joined to K. 13246 since *DB,* p. 232 and E. Reiner [1956], pp. 144-145: obv. 13 (duplicated by the unpublished tablet K. 11631, line 4'):

13). ^{d}UTU *^{d}A-a ^{d}Bu-ne-ne ù ^{d}Ma-mú-*[*da*] ⌜X⌝ EN *É-babbar* AŠ

Shamash, (his wife) Aja, (his vizier) Bunene, and Mamuda, . the lord of Ebabbar .

ii). Some Old Babylonian tablets call upon various deities to witness the transactions written upon them. Two examples mention Mamu (both times as ^{d}*Ma-mu*): C. H. Gordon [1952], No. 46, rev. 13: IGI ^{d}UTU ^{d}*A-a* IGI ^{d}*Ma-mu,* "before Shamash (and) Aja, before Mamu"; and VS 7, No. 27, rev. 16-17: ^{16} IGI ^{d}UTU IGI ^{d}*A-a* ^{17} IGI ^{d}*Ma-mu.*

iii). Shamash's entourage is given in col. I lines 29-35 of the God List *KAV* 63:

34). ^{d}*Ma-mú* | ^{d}⌈*Šu*⌉-[*ut-tu*$^{?}$]

Mamu (is the) deified dream$^{?}$

(The restoration follows E. F. Weidner [1924-1925], p. 12.)

iv). The God List *SpTU* 3, No. 108 enumerates Shamash's entourage in col. I lines 29-34, with Mamu appearing in line 34.

v). The God List an = *Anum,* Tab. 3, as presented on *CT* 24, pl. 31, col. IV line 84, unusually describes Mamu as female, a daughter of Shamash, and gives 'her' a brother, Sisig (see page 87 for a possible explanation of this).

84). ^{d}MA.MÚ | DUMU.MUNUS ^{d}UTU.KE$_4$

Mamu (is) a daughter of Shamash

The *lipšur*-litany IM 67638 atypically puts Mamu in Nergal's retinue in lines 36'-39' (pages 70-71).

THE TEMPLE TO MAMU AT BALAWAT

It seems that during the ninth century B.C. Mamu was more important than the scarcity of references would imply. Ashurnasirpal II erected a temple to him at Balawat (ancient Imgur Enlil), which was later embellished by Shalmaneser III. Four inscriptions recording this building by Ashurnasirpal II (BM 90980 (= Rm. 1082), BM 90981 (= Rm. 1083), BM 135121 (No. 73), and an unnumbered and unpublished tablet; L. W. King [*AKA* 1], pp. 167-173, gives a composite copy of the first three, and pl. 63 is a photograph of BM 90980, obv.; and see A. K. Grayson [1991], No. 101.50, on pp. 319-321) do not describe Mamu's functions, but there is no reason to suppose that he was not the Dream God Mamu. No extant non-literary texts mention dream experiences of these two monarchs. No later rulers are associated with building activities or offerings at the site.

Accounts of the earlier excavations at Balawat can be found in D. Oates [1974], S. Lloyd [1980], pp. 150-154, and J. Curtis [1982]; and of the resumed excavations of 1989-1990 in *Iraq* 55 [1993], pp. 30-35. Most of the attention has been focused upon the large wooden gates decorated with bronze plates bearing reliefs and inscriptions: two pairs were installed by Ashurnasirpal II, and another, larger, pair by Shalmaneser III (the latter are exhibited in the British Museum).

To date, Mamu's temple is the only building excavated to any degree of completeness (D. Oates [1974], pp. 176-177). From the point of view of this study, the results have been disappointing, since no temple library, nor any religious or ritual tablet, has been found, only economic and legal documents, dating mainly date from 697-671 B.C. (B. Parker [1963]). Presumably these transactions were those of the temple personnel; one of whom was called ^{d}*Ma-mú-Iq-bi.* B. Parker [ibid., p. 89] mentioned another collection of tablets found at Balawat whose dates reveal that it remained occupied until the Fall of Assyria in 612-610 B.C., when the site was abandoned for a long time.

The only reference to Balawat, apart from the material found there, is a mention of the town as one of twenty-seven which joined Ashur-danin-apli's revolt against his father, Shalmaneser III, at the end of his reign (A. K. Grayson [1996], No. 103.1, col. I line 45, on p. 183).

Aerial photography has shown Balawat to be lying within a triangle formed by three 'hollow way' routes; i.e., sunken tracks produced by traffic throughout the centuries (D. J. Tucker [1994], pp. 109-110). One of these routes was the main Neo-Assyrian road from Nineveh to Arrapha (modern Kirkuk). Balawat was strongly fortified in the ninth century B.C., and covered a sizable area for a provincial town. The ninth century B.C. buildings were built on a mound, probably the remains of earlier occupation. Different reasons have been propounded to explain why Ashurnasirpal II refounded the town, naming it Imgur Enlil (see especially D. Oates [1974], pp. 174-175):

i). Nineveh was the military headquarters in the reign of Ashurnasirpal II, and the campaigns of his first five years were to the north and east; i.e., the army would start off down this main road.

ii). M. E. L. Mallowan [1956, p. 79] suggested that the royal palace at Balawat was a country residence. A bronze plate from one of the gates depicts Ashurnasirpal II receiving the tribute of the governor of Suhi outside Balawat's walls (see J. Curtis [1982], pp. 116-118).

It is assumed that Shalmaneser III resided here, from the erection of 'his' gates. In Years 8 and 9 he fought in Babylonia, and would have used this road.

None of these suggestions explain why Ashurnasirpal II constructed (or rebuilt) a temple to Mamu within the palace precincts: BM 90980 (= Rm. 1082), obv. 21 to rev. 2:

21). URU *šu-ú a-na eš-šu-te* DAB-*bat*

22). ^{URU}*Im-gúr-*^{d}BAD MU-*šu ab-bi*

23). É KUR *ši-i ina li-bit* É.GAL-*ia*

1). *lu-ú ad-di ṣa-lam* ^{d}*Ma-mú* EN-*ia*

2). [*ina lì*]*b-bi lu ú-še-šib*

[21] I reorganized (lit., seized anew) this city. [22] I named it Imgur-Enlil. [23 to 2] I erected this temple within the environs of my palace, (and) I caused a statue of Mamu, my lord, to dwell inside.

J. Curtis [1982, p. 119] proposed that the palace was built because Balawat was already a major religious site, possibly the cult centre of the Dream God. As yet there is no textual evidence to support this idea.

A temple to a Dream God strongly indicates incubation. D. Oates [1974, p. 175] speculated that the Assyrian king slept in this temple on his first night out of Nineveh (28 km. away; ibid., p. 174) in order to receive a dream concerning the future campaign. This is an extremely attractive idea, but this motive does not appear in the few Mesopotamian sources on incubation except, perhaps, in the literary work the *Epic of Gilgamesh,* when the hero solicits dreams before attacking Humbaba (see chapter 19). Following this argument, since many Neo-Assyrian expeditions were to the west, one would expect to find a temple in a corresponding position on the main route in that direction - as yet undiscovered.

At the moment, however unsatisfactory it may be, we do not know why Ashurnasirpal II erected a temple to Mamu, nor why Shalmaneser III continued to endow it, nor why royal patronage apparently ceased. The shrine existed to 694 B.C., at least, because it is mentioned on BT. 115 (*Iraq* 25 [1963], pl. 23), which is dated by that year's eponym, Ilu-itti-ia.

MAMU AND PLEASANT SYMPTOMATIC DREAMS

The only reference to Mamu in a dream rite occurs on *ADRC,* col. IV lines 39-40:

39). ^{d}ma.mú dingir.ma.mú.da.ke$_4$

40). dingir.mu inim še.ga.še.ga ù.tu.ud.da

[39] O Mamu, the god of dreams, [40] (and$^?$) my personal god, create a favourable state (of affairs for me)!

These lines form part of an incantation in a ritual to obtain a pleasant dream. It will be argued on pages 207-208 that these ceremonies sought to ensure pleasant symptomatic dreams by the dreamer's purification and by the appeasement of his angry personal deities. In this passage, either Mamu is described as the personal god of the supplicant (probably only for ritual purposes), or both deities are considered equally responsible for pleasant dreams (see chapter 7 on the role of the personal deities in the context of dreams).

Mamu is also mentioned in a request for a pleasant symptomatic dream in the non-dream incantation 4 R^2. 59, No. 2 + K. 3369 (duplicated by *LKA* 29k). The obverse contains a long catalogue of woes, while the reverse seeks favours from the personal deities and restoration to grace: rev. 25-28:

25). *šub-ra-an-ni-ma* MÁŠ.GE$_6$ SIG$_5$-*ta*$_5$ *luṭ-ṭúl*

26). MÁŠ.GE$_6$ *a-na-ṭa-lu lu-u* SIG$_5$-*at* : MÁŠ.GE$_6$ *a-na-ṭa-lu lu-u* ⌈GI⌉.NA-*at*

27). MÁŠ.GE$_6$ *a-na-ṭa-lu ana* SIG$_5$-*ti tir-*⌈*ra*⌉

28). ^{d}*Ma-*⌈*mú*⌉ DINGIR *šá* MÁŠ.GE$_6$.MEŠ *ina* SAG.MU *lu* GUB-*an*

[25] Let me see a pleasant dream, and may I see (it)! [26] May the dream which I see be pleasant! May the dream which I see be reliable! [27] Turn the dream which I see to good luck! [28] May Mamu, the god of dreams, (be) constantly at my head!

(*LKA* 29k, rev. 22' has the variant *ina i-di-ia lu ka-a-a-an,* "(be) constantly at my side!", for the end of line 28.)

^{d}SIG.SIG

We have noted already (page 74) that the God List an = *Anum* attributed a brother to a feminine Mamu: *CT* 24, pl. 31, col. IV line 85:

85). ^{d}SI.SI.IG | DUMU ^{d}UTU.KE$_4$

Sisig (is) a son of Shamash

The late version, *SpTU* 3, No. 107, presents this line, with a gloss, in col. III line 137:

137). ^{d}SÌG$^{Zi\text{-}qi\text{-}qu}$SÌG | DUMU ^{d}UTU.KE$_4$

The correlation of two names of the Mesopotamian Dream God, the Sumerian Sisig ("the one who constantly blows" or "the winds") and the Akkadian Zaqiqu ("a breeze", see on) is reinforced by *ZI,* line 1, where its Akkadian manuscript has *Zi-qi-qu,* but its two Sumerian texts have SI.SI.IG and SIG.SIG - all without the divine determinative. All these passages invalidate the generally accepted, yet unproven, identification of Anzagar with Zaqiqu [*CAD* Z, *zaqīqu,* p. 60b; *AHw* 3, *zīqīqu,* p. 1530b]. These lines (with CBS 1529, rev. 13, on page 80) are the only references to the god Sisig that the writer has found, and only *ZI* suggests that he was a Dream God. (References cited here under ^{d}*Zaqīqu*/*Ziqīqu* offer more examples of the equation with the logogram SI.SI.IG, etc., also with LÍL.LÁ.)

^{d}*Zaqīqu/Ziqīqu*

The Akkadian name of the Dream God was Zaqiqu, also written Ziqiqu, which is not known in a logographic form. *zaqīqu* is a derivative of the verbal root *zīq* (not *zūq* as in *DB,* p. 233) or, possibly, from *zqq* [*AHw* 3, p. 1499b]. The word has been given many nuances by modern translators, which are briefly mentioned below (also see *DB,* pp. 223-225 and T. Jacobsen [1989]).

NUANCES OF *zaqīqu*

a). Wind And Nothingness

The associated verb, *zâqu,* means "to blow", and *zaqīqu* is equated in lexical texts with words denoting wind, storms, etc. [*CAD* Z, p. 58b]. *zaqīqu* usually refers to a mild breeze, but may imply a storm: e.g., the *Verse Account* (*BHT,* pls. 5-10), col. VI line 20':

20). [. . . . *ep-š*]*e-ti-šú ub-ba-at za-qí-qí*

[All of $^{?}$] his (Nabonidus' deeds are destroyed by the *zaqīqu.*

CAD Z, p. 60b stated that *zaqīqu* only refers to a wind in lexical texts and in a few passages concerning the north wind. It preferred the meaning "ghost" (see b), from the equation with LÍL.LÁ, as in the names of certain demons (see page 87). Accordingly, expressions used in lamentations, literary texts, and royal inscriptions to portray the total destruction of a site such as *ana zaqīqi manû,* "to count as wind", and *ana zaqīqi târu,* "to turn into wind", are rendered as "to count as ghosts" and "to turn into a haunted place", respectively [*CAD* Z, p. 59].

In some passages *zaqīqu* expresses "nothingness": e.g., the *Verse Account,* col. I line 20':

20'). *ib-ta-ni za-qí-qí*

He (Nabonidus) created wind (i.e., none of his achievements lasted or were of any value).

b). A Wind Demon Or A Type Of Ghost

The verb *zâqu* describes the swift movements of various demons whilst attacking mankind [*CAD* Z, pp. 64-65]. The *zaqīqu*-winds developed into a category of Mesopotamian demons, which was characterized by forms of *našarbuṭu,* "to rush forth": e.g., *CT* 16, pl. 15, col. V lines 37-40:

37). ù munus.nu.meš ù nita.nu.meš

38). *ul zi-ka-ru šu-nu ul sin-niš-a-ti šú-nu*

39). e.ne.ne.ne líl.lá bú.bú.meš

40). *šú-nu za-qí-qu mut-taš-rab-bi-ṭu-ti šú-nu*

[37-40] They are neither men nor women, they are the *zaqīqu*s, who constantly rush along.

OrNS 39 [1970], pls. 54-55 (after p. 464), col. I lines 4-10 reveals that *zaqīqu*-demons were envisaged as being similar to ghosts, and dwelling in the Underworld/ grave:

4). líl.lá.⌜e.ne hul⌝.a.meš urugal.la.ta

5). im.⌜ta⌝.è.a.meš

6). *za-qí-qu lem-nu-ti iš-tu qab-rì it-ta-ṣu-ni*

7). ki.sì.ga.a.dé.a.meš!(an) urugal.la.ta

8). im.⌜ta⌝.è.a.meš

9). *a-na ka-sa-⌜ap⌝ ki-is-pi u ⌜na⌝-aq mé-e*

10). *iš-tu qab-rì* MIN (i.e., *it-ta-ṣu-ni*)

[4-6] The evil *zaqīqu*(-demons) come out from the grave. [7-10] They come out from the grave for the presentation(s) of funerary offerings and libation(s) of water.

The idea of the *zaqīqu*-demons residing in the Underworld is reinforced by the *Epic of Gilgamesh.* Enkidu descended to the Underworld to retrieve the *pukku* that Gilgamesh had dropped, but was detained because he disobeyed all the instructions which would have allowed him to return to the world of men. Ea tells Gilgamesh how to talk with Enkidu after this has happened - Tablet 12, lines 83-84, and the Sumerian version, *Gilgamesh, Enkidu, and the Netherworld,* lines 242-243 (see A. Shaffer [1963]):

242). ab.làl.kur.ra gál im.ma.an.tag$_4$

83). *lu-man tak-ka-ap* KI-*tì ip-te-e-ma*

243). si.si.ig.ni.ta šubur.a.ni kur.ta mu.ni.in.e$_{11}$.dè

84). *ú-tuk-ku šá* ^{d}*En-ki-dù ki-i za-qí-qí* ⌜*ul*⌝*-tú* KI-*tì* ⌜*it-ta*$_5$⌝*-ṣa-a*

[242, 83] Scarcely had he (Gilgamesh) opened a hole in the earth/ Underworld, [243, 84] The *utukku* of Enkidu, his servant, came out from the Underworld like a *zaqīqu.*

(*utukku* normally refers to another type of demon, but in this passage it seems to mean “ghost”.)

AHw 3, *zīqīqu* §3, p. 1530a, had another category, *„ein nicht aggressiver Totengeist (//eṭemmu)”,* with a note that the distinctions of “wind” and the two varieties of “wind demon” are not always clear cut.

c). Human Soul

When *zaqīqu* is used with *amīlūtu,* "mankind", or *nišū,* "people", it appears to mean "human soul" (see T. Jacobsen [1989], pp. 274-275 on this nuance of líl; and *DB,* p. 235, for an alternative explanation): e.g.:

i). *KAR* 307, obv. 34:

34). [*ina* SUHUŠ? KAL]A.GA KI-*tì* AN.[T]A *zi-qi-qu* NAM. LÚ.U_{18}.LU *ina* ŠÀ *ú-šar-bi-iṣ*

He (Marduk) caused the *ziqīqu*(s) of mankind to lie down on the strong [foundation?] of the Upper Earth.

ii). The Third House of *bīt rimki* (*JCS* 21 [1967], p. 3), line 13:

13). sìg.sìg.ga nigin nam.lú.u_{18}.lu.ke_4 šu.min ma.ra.ni.íb.gi_4.gi_4

zi-qí-qa šá nap-har ni-ši ú-šá-an-na-ka

The *zaqīqu*(s) of all mankind report to you (, Shamash).

(The 'Forerunner' text CBS 1529 (*Acta Sumerologica* 17 [1995], pp. 125-126) offers this variant at rev. 13:

13). [d]Si-si-ig-e ad nam-lú<-u_{18}>-lu-k[e_4]

Sisig, the father of mankind, ...)

THE DREAM GOD [d]ZA/IQIQU

The only evidence we have that Zaqiqu was a Dream God is that the *Dream-Book* was called ([d])*Za/iqīqu* from the incipit of its first incantation *(ZI).* (Zaqiqu is not always prefixed with the divine determinative, possibly indicating his minor or demonic status; see page 101 for variants of the title in the catalogue references.) C. J. Gadd [1948, p. 74] believed that *ZI* was a brief introductory myth, which described Zaqiqu as the first to interpret dreams and as residing in Agade. However, *ZI* mentions that Zaqiqu had been sent to Agade, whereupon he caused someone to dream (the manuscripts vary as to the category), and that a third person interpreted them. E. I. Gordon [1960, pp. 129-130, n. 57] suggested that an allusion may have been made to Naram-Sin as "the luckless ruler of Agade".

ND 4368 (*Iraq* 18 [1956], pl. 25) provides us with the only reference to the deity Zaqiqu outside the dream literature and lexical texts. J. V. Kinnier Wilson [1957] stated that this fragmentary and difficult tablet formed part of a companion medical series to the diagnostic omen series SA.GIG; both belonging to the lore of the exorcist. The listed diseases are termed 'Hands' of various demons who, in turn, are designated as the *šēdu*-demons and agents of the divine triad: column VI lines 9-13:

9). DIŠ GIG-*ma* IZI ŠUB ⸢X (X) X⸣-*ma ú-ta-ni-ú*
10). ⸢X⸣ *ti* ⸢*là* TUK ŠU⸣ ^{d}*Za-qí-qí* ^{d}ALAD
11). *šá-né-e* ⸢^{d}⸣[BAD] *ana ina* ŠU ^{d}*Za-qí-qí* KAR-*šú*
12). ⸢X X X⸣ *na* KA.A.AB.BA AN.BAR NÍTA *u* MÍ
13). ⸢*ina* GÚ⸣-*šú* GAR *u* ^{GIŠ}GEŠTIN.KA_5.A ŠÉŠ.MEŠ-*su-ma* TI

[9] If he falls ill, and . . . (.) . . . . . . [10] . . . . - (It is due to) 'the Hand of Zaqiqu', the *šēdu*(-demon), [11] the agent of [Enlil].

In order to save him from 'the Hand of Zaqiqu': [12-13] You place around his neck . . . . *imbû tâmti,* (and) 'male' and 'female' iron. You repeatedly anoint him with the 'fox-wine'-plant. He will recover.

See the note on *ADRC,* col. IV line 6 (page 310) on the designation of minerals as 'male' or 'female'.)

(J. V. Kinnier Wilson [1957, p. 42] tentatively translated ^{GIŠ}*karān šēlebi*(GEŠTIN.KA_5.A) as "solanum-(berries)".

That an ailment was named after Zaqiqu is no indication of his importance; see the list of the many 'Hand' diseases in *TDP,* pp. XXII-XXIII.

a). *Zaqīqu* As A Means Of Divine Communication

CAD Z, p. 59, §1 2' (based on *DB,* p. 235) presents passages in which *zaqīqu* "refers to a specific manifestation of the deity", which may or may not reply to human enquiries. *AHw* 3, p. 1530b, §4a placed the same citations under *„Traum-(gott)".* In the passages below, the basic problem is whether *zaqīqu* is a human ritual expert or a spiritual entity. The writer inclines towards the former.

The protagonist of *Ludlul bēl nēmeqi* unsuccessfully sought omens and remission of his suffering on Tab. 2, lines 6-9, including:

8). *za-qí-qu a-bal-ma ul ú-pat-ti uz-ni*

I appealed to a *zaqīqu,* but he did not enlighten me (lit., did not open my ear).

P. C. Couprie [1960, p. 186] stated that here *zaqīqu* had to be a ritual expert, paralleling the other practitioners, and certainly one would expect a reference to a human, rather than to a spiritual being or a "specific avenue of communication with the god" [*DB,* p. 235]. This *zaqīqu* is distinguished from the *šā'ilu* (often translated as "dream interpreter") of line 7.

ZA 61 [1971-1972], pp. 50-61, col. III lines 142-143 records a (similar?) consultation:

> 142). ^d^*Am-na ina bi-ri* [. . . . .]
>
> 143). *za-qí-qu ina šat m*[*u-ši* . . . .]
>
> 142 Amna by an extispicy [. . . . .]. 143 *zaqīqu* during the night [. . . . . . .]

This time it is possible that the Dream God Zaqiqu is meant, to parallel Shamash (^d^*Am-na*).

Nabu addresses Ashurbanipal on *ABRT* 1, pp. 5-6 (= *SAA* 3, No. 13), obv. 1-18, with no indication as to the nature of the experience. The king prays to Nabu (obv. 19-22) but, on obv. 23 the answer does not come directly from Nabu:

> 23). *e-tap-la za-qí-qu* TA IGI ^d^PA EN-*šú*
>
> A *zaqīqu* replied from the presence of (lit., before) Nabu, his lord.

Obverse 24-26 contains the message, Ashurbanipal prays again (rev. 1-5), and Nabu replies (rev. 6-11), by unknown means. Thus, in only one of the three times that the god 'speaks' to Ashurbanipal is a *zaqīqu* mentioned.

The dialogue is not presented as occurring in a dream, and *DB,* p. 235 stated that this *zaqīqu* was not a Dream (God), against F. R. Kraus [1936, p. 88], but was the insubstantial carrier of the divine message. Still, the description of the Dream God Anzagar as "the medium of Nannaru" (i.e., of Sin) on *SDR,* line 32, is brought to mind.

M. Streck [*VAB* 7, p. 347, n. 11] proposed another alternative; this *zaqīqu* was a type of *Wahrsagepriester* or *bārû,* who was especially concerned with incantations against ghosts. It is possible that a ritual expert uttered an inspired speech in a temple while standing in front of a statue of Nabu.

I. L. Finkel [1983, p. 76, n. 5] regarded *AnSt* 33 [1983], p. 79, rev. 6' (pages 235-236) in the light of *ABRT* 1, pp. 5-6. He believed that *zaqīqū*-spirits approached Kurigalzu, who was lying awake trying to incubate a dream, and allayed the king's fears in a way similar to that in which the *zaqīqu:*

> "which comes from Nabû to Assurbanipal before he falls asleep and makes him relax."

We noted above that there is no indication that the episode recorded on *ABRT* 1, pp. 5-6 occurred in a dream, or even at night. On the other hand, Kurigalzu does see a dream but it is unclear how the *zaqīqu*s were involved or if the dream resulted from an incubation.

In conclusion, it seems that *zaqīqu* occasionally denoted a professional, who may have prophesied and/or supervised the incubation process (remembering the *bīt zaqīqi* in the successive dream incubations on the *Epic of Gilgamesh,* Tab. 4, page 225).

^{d}AN.ZA.GÀR/AN.ZAG.GAR.RA

In earlier studies this name was written as ^{d}ZA.GÀR (J. Dyneley Prince [1912-1913], ZAQ.QAR) yet, recently, perhaps since *DB,* the custom has been to write it as AN.ZA.GÀR. T. Jacobsen [1989, p. 274, n. 46] rendered it as *Ìl-za-kàr,* designating it as an early loan from Proto-Akkadian (see *DB,* p. 232). The writer has kept to AN.ZA.GÀR, but is unsure as to why ^{d}ZA.GÀR has become 'incorrect'.

The lexical texts and God Lists 'prove' that Anzagar was a Dream God:

i). an = *Anum,* as on:

^{a} *CT* 24, pl. 32, col. IV line 110:

110). AN.ZA.GÀR | DINGIR.MA.MÚ.DA.KE$_4$

Anzagar (is) the god of dreams

^{b} *SpTU* 3, No. 107, col. III line 170:

170). AN.ZA.$^{\text{ZA.GA.ÁR}}$GÀR | ^{d}UTU MA.MÚ.DA.KE$_4$

Anzagar (is) the Shamash of dreams

^{c} *CT* 24, pl. 39, col. XI line 11:

11). ^{d}AN.ZA.GÀR | MIN | *ša šu*$^{!}$(AN)*-na-ti*

Anzagar (is) ditto (i.e., the Enlil) of dreams.

(Correct *DB,* p. 233, which stated that Bêl replaced the name of Enlil.)

ii). D.T. 46 (*BA* 5 [1906], pp. 655-656), line 7:

7). ⸢AN⸣.ZAG.⸢GAR.RA⸣ | ^{d}*En-*⸢*líl*⸣ *šá* MÁŠ.GE$_6$.[MEŠ]

Anzagar (is) the Enlil of dreams

iii). erim.huš = *anantu,* Tab. 1, line 216 [*MSL* 17, p. 19]:

216). ⸢AN.ZAG$^{?}$⸣.GAR.RA | DINGIR *šá šu-ut-ti*

Anzagar (is) the god of dream(s).

iv). izi = *išātu,* Tab. A, col. II line 15' [*MSL* 13, p. 174]:

15'). AN.ZAG.GAR | DINGIR *ša šu-na-ti*

Anzagar (is) the god of dreams.

ANZAGAR IN RITUALS TO OBTAIN A PLEASANT DREAM

The Dream God is called Anzagar on *SDR,* lines 25-26:

25). *ú-ma-'i-ir-ma* AN.ZA.GÀR DINGIR *šá* MÁŠ.GE_6.MEŠ

26). *ina šat mu-ši-im li-paṭ-ṭi-ra ár-ni-ia*$_5$ *lu-uš-lim*$^!$(*me*) *šèr-ti lu-ta-líl ana-ku*

[25] (If) he (Sin) should send Anzagar, the god of dreams, [26] so that during the night he will absolve me of my sin(s, then) I shall become well (again, and) I shall be cleansed of my transgression.

There are varying opinions as to who sends Anzagar (see page 394), but line 32 seems conclusive:

32). AN.ZA.GÀR *na-áš-pár-ti* ^{d}NANNA-*r*[*i*$^!$]

O Anzagar, the medium of Nannaru (i.e., Sin)

Anzagar is invoked on *NROD,* rev. 9-10:

9). [AN].ZAG.GAR.RA AN.ZAG.GAR.RA *ba-bi-lu a-me-lu-ti*

10). DUMU *šip-ri ša ru-bi-i* ^{d}*Marduk*

[9] O Anzagar, O Anzagar, the bringer (of dreams) to mankind; [10] the messenger of prince Marduk.

(See page 21 on the epithet *bābilu.*)

The minor status of Anzagar is indicated in that the first reference from *SDR* and that of *NROD* come from ŠU.ÍL.LÁ-incantations to the major deities Sin and Nusku respectively. The second passage from *SDR* occurs in the ritual, being uttered while the censer was placed in position. Anzagar is described in *SDR* as the agent of Sin, and of Marduk in *NROD,* even though Marduk is not mentioned elsewhere in the ritual. Perhaps any of the major Mesopotamian deities could order Anzagar to send pleasant symptomatic dreams.

A DEMONIC ANZAGAR

Three texts conflict with the above definition of Anzagar's function, for they connect him with demons, ghosts, and the Underworld:

i). The incantation at *ADRC,* col. IV lines 8-13 describes Anzagar in terms more suited to demons. (The feminine verb in line 12 suggests the existence of an otherwise unknown consort.)

ii). erim.huš = *anantu,* Tab. 1, line 216 (page 83) appears in a section dealing with different kinds of demons.

iii). Anzagar is invoked in difficult Sumerian incantations in two ghost rituals on *CT* 23, pls. 15-22 +: col. I line 25' (duplicated by *OrNS* 24

[1955], p. 243, line 5) mentions him together with Shamash and Asalluhi; and col. I lines 58'-62' alongside Shamash, Ea, and the Underworld deities Ereshkigal and her son, Ninazu. More evidence is required to enable us to decide whether Anzagar occurs in these two rites as an agent of purification or as a god resident in the Underworld.

Although not necessarily related to the god Anzagar, the logogram AN.ZA. GÀR is rendered in Akkadian by *dimtu,* "tower". *DB,* p. 236 speculated that the Dream God lived in a "memorial pillar". T. Jacobsen [1989, p. 274, n. 46] believed that Ilzakar (sic) derived from the verbal root *zkr,* "to remember":

"The God Izakar (sic) is thus the deified dream notion."

The writer is not sure what this definition means, since Mamu was the deified dream.

H. Jacobson [1976] suggested that the concept of Anzagar as a Dream God was related to the use of stone pillows or head-rests known from the Bible (e.g., *Gen.* 28: 11, when Jacob saw a ladder connecting heaven and earth in a dream) and Egyptian tombs. He supported his idea with obv. 59-60 in the *Annals* of Tukulti-Ninurta II, based on the translation of W. Schramm [1970, p. 157]. Tukulti-Ninurta II (890-884 B.C.) apparently spent the night in a place of UŠ.ME.TA-stone, where the gods resided. However, A. K. Grayson [*ARI* 2, §470 on p. 102; now see [1991], No. 100.5] translated this passage differently, following the reading of *CAD* A_2, *asumittu,* p. 348a, whereby ^{NA_4}*ús-me-ta* is an 'ordinary' stone stele erected to the gods, helping to identify the town where the king stayed overnight. Obverse 59-60:

59). *iš-tu* ^{URU}*Da-ia-še-ti at-tu-muš ina pu-ut* ^{URU}*Íd ina* SAG *e-ni šá ku-up-ri*

60). *a-šar* ^{NA_4}*ús-me-ta šá* DINGIR.MEŠ GAL.MEŠ *ina lìb-bi* ⌜*ša*⌝*-zu-ni* GAR-⌜*an be*⌝*-di*

59-60 I moved on from Dajashetu. He (i.e. I) pitched camp, spending the night within . . . before Idu, at the head of the bitumen spring, a place of the stele of the great gods.

SUMMARY

Despite the difficulties surrounding the four main names for the Mesopotamian Dream God, the important point is that such a deity existed. No other type of divination or religious experience was either personified or patronized in this way, although after the Kassite era the deities invoked in extispicy were limited to Shamash and Adad.

We do not know why or when the concept of a Dream God emerged. A. L. Oppenheim [*DB,* p. 232] was convinced that it arose from the view of (unpleasant) symptomatic dreams as demonic powers. While this was probably the reason for the name Zaqiqu; it is the existence of Mamu's temple at Balawat (remembering that 'modern' excavations began in 1956, the year of *DB*'s publication), and the presence of Mamu and Anzagar in rituals to obtain a pleasant (symptomatic) dream that argue against his statement:

> "The Dream-god exists only with respect to this specific [demonic] aspect but remains meaningless and non-existent when dreams are considered as to their mantic implications, or where they are reserved for certain individuals as a means of communication with the deity."

Yet, *DB,* p. 233 had noted the role of Anzagar as a transmitter of divine messages.

If a link with prognostic dreams is proposed as a reason for a Dream God, then the problem is that most message dreams are presented as coming directly from the deity concerned, not via a Dream God. As yet, no Dream God has been associated correctly with dream interpretation (see page 80).

Some reason must lie behind the existence of the four names, but any classification remains doubtful because of the scarcity of attestations outside lexical texts. (A late God list, *SpTU* 3, No. 107, col. III line 171, is the sole source for another name (^{d}MÁŠ.GE$_{6}$) for the deified dream (usually ^{d}MA.MÚ).) The four names may represent designations varying with eras or areas, or different aspects of the dream experience, or a combination of these factors. It is noteworthy that these names were kept distinct, with a correlation only evident between Sisig and Zaqiqu, even though the extant evidence suggests that the Dream God was a minor deity. The writer has classified the names according to the divisions in dream types deduced in chapter 3; i.e., as if they represent different facets of the Dream God or of dreams.

The classification proposed here may not have been adhered to rigidly by the Mesopotamians because two incantations appear to use two names of the Dream God:

i). A Sumerian incantation in a ghost ritual on *CT* 23, pls. 15-22 + invokes an.za.gàr ^{d}ma.mú.da in col. I lines 58' and 61'.

ii). The Akkadian manuscript of *ZI,* line 1 addresses *Zi-qi-qu* ^{d}*Ma-mú* (see pages 323-324).

It is also possible that in both cases the epithet dingir.ma.mú.da.ke$_{4}$, "the god of dreams", was meant, as on *ADRC,* col. IV line 39, where it describes Mamu himself.

Since MA.MÚ is the most common word for dream in Sumerian texts, one would like to be able to assert that Mamu was an early Dream God, being the personification of the dream experience; however, the writer is unaware of any reference to him in Sumerian texts. The only Sumerian Dream God attested is Anzagar (see page 88). The existence of a Neo-Assyrian temple to Mamu at Balawat suggests that, by the ninth century B.C., he was regarded as the patron of incubation and, perhaps, of message dreams.

The dreams predominantly mentioned in Akkadian texts are symptomatic. This was the type of dream which affected the bulk of the population, and numerous rituals were developed to annul their effects. Some of these ceremonies, together with dream omens, were combined in a series called (^{d})*Za/iqīqu;* i.e., the *Dream-Book* (pages 99-101). Therefore, it seems that Zaqiqu represented the unpleasant, demonic side of dreams. Problematically, it is possible that Zaqiqu is connected with incubation, carried out by the putative ritual expert called *zaqīqu* and in the *bīt zaqīqi* of the *Epic of Gilgamesh.* Zaqiqu is not mentioned in the lexical texts, except once as a gloss to Sisig.

The basic division into message dreams and symptomatic dreams may have existed in Sumerian times: Sisig occurs in two tablets of Sumerian proverbs (manuscripts **I** and **II** of *ZI*). The God List an = *Anum* stated that Mamu and Sisig were sister and brother; thereby either denoting the two aspects of dreams, or an attempt to reconcile the different names for the Dream God [*DB,* pp. 232-233]. It must be noted that neither Sisig nor Zaqiqu are definitely attested with a dream-related epithet - the Akkadian of *ZI,* line 1 is restored.

It is interesting that two of the names of the Mesopotamian Dream God were associated with "wind": Sisig = Zaqiqu. T. Jacobsen [1989, p. 274] wrote:

> "The point of similarity is apparently the evanescence of the dream world, on awakening it is gone like the wind."

We have noted the existence of the *zaqīqu*(LÍL.LÁ) wind demon. The same logogram appears in the names of the demons *lilû*(^{LÚ}LÍL.LÁ), *lilītu*(^{MÍ}LÍL.LÁ), and *ardat lilî*(KI.SIKIL.LÍL.LÁ). Page 62 stated that the *lilû* is normally regarded as the Mesopotamian incubus, and the other two as succubi. *ardat lilî* incantations also associate her with the *zaqīqu* wind demon: e.g., she is called a *ziqīqu* (*YOS* 11, No. 92, line 23; see W. Farber's collations at *ZA* 79 [1989], p. 16); and she emerges from the *bīt zaqīqi* (page 226). The *alû*-demon, another candidate for an incubus, was also connected with strong winds (*CAD* A_1, p. 376b). Note the mentions of a "ram of the storm" in two dream incantations, at *ADRC,* col. III lines 33 and 52.

Anzagar complicates matters, being involved in the sending of pleasant symptomatic dreams, while also having a demonic aspect (see already *DB,* p. 233). In rituals to obtain a pleasant dream, he seems to convey such dreams to the sleeper at the command of other deities. It is unclear how he differs from Mamu, who is also invoked in this type of ritual. There is no evidence connecting the demonic Anzagar with Zaqiqu. Anzagar also occurs in both Sumerian and Akkadian sources. In the Sumerian epic *Lugalbanda in Hurrumkurra* (see W. W. Hallo [1983] on lines 256-376) Anzagar gives the hero detailed instructions about a sacrifice: lines 339-340:

339). An.za(.an).gàr.ra dingir.ma.mú.da.ke_4

340). ^{d}Lugal.bàn.da ní.te.ni gu_4.gim ur_5 im.$ša_4$

339 Anza(n)gar, the god of dreams, 340 bellowed like a domesticated ox (at) Lugalbanda himself.

CHAPTER 7: THE PERSONAL DEITIES AND DREAMS

Each individual possessed his own 'guardian angel' in the form of a personal god and/or a personal goddess. These deities could be identified with any major or minor Mesopotamian divinities. In return for reverence (the *Counsels of Wisdom,* lines 135-141), the personal deities guaranteed physical well-being, by deflecting the attacks of demons, disease, and sorcery (yet they could be alienated by sorcery, page 60); and caused one's affairs to prosper. The phrase "to have a god" became synonymous with "to thrive, to be prosperous", etc. If the personal deities believed themselves to be neglected, or if their protégé sinned, they would abandon the individual, and had to be coaxed back. This 'alienation' can be understood if we regard these gods as personifications of a person's 'luck'.

THE PRESENCE OF THE PERSONAL DEITIES

The presence of the personal deities guaranteed pleasant symptomatic dreams: e.g., the charm title on *SpTU* 2, No. 22, col IV line 5:

5). *ana* NA DINGIR-*šú u* XV-*šú ina* SAG-⌈*šu*⌉ GUB-*zi-ma* MÁŠ.GE_6 SIG_5-*tú na-ṭa-lu*

So that a man will cause his personal god and/or his personal goddess to stand at his head (while he sleeps), and (also) in order to see a pleasant dream:

There are two other charms intended to obtain pleasant dreams, *BAM* 315, col. IV lines 27-31 and 32-36 (pages 167-168), with the title: col. IV lines 27-28:

27). *ana* DINGIR *u* $^{d}EŠ_{18}$.TÁR GEŠTUG.MEŠ-*šú* BAD. BAD-*u*

28). MÁŠ.GE_6 SIG_5-*ta na-ṭa-li*

[27] In order that (his) god and/or goddess instruct him (lit., open his ears) [28] (and in order) to see a pleasant dream:

It is stated on pages 207-208 that the ceremonial acts of rituals to obtain a pleasant dream purified the dreamer so he could become reconciled with his wrathful personal deities. Accordingly, these deities play a major part in the ceremonies:

i). Incantations similar to DINGIR.ŠÀ.DIB.BAs were recited in the ritual complexes of *ADRC,* col. IV lines 21-30 and 31-41b.

ii). Censers were set out to the dreamer's personal god at *ADRC,* col. II line 50, and to both the personal deities at col. IV lines 21-22.

iii). Allusions are made in the accompanying incantations to the anger of these deities and to the dreamer's sins: in addition to (i), on *ADRC,* col. II lines 25[?], 47, and 57; and *SDR,* lines 23-26.

We have already mentioned (pages 76-77) the incantation on *ADRC,* col. IV lines 38-40, in which the Dream God Mamu (possibly the personal god of the dreamer, for ritual purposes) and/or the personal deities are regarded as a source of pleasant dreams.

The only other reference to the personal deities in the technical literature occurs on *NADR,* line 18, a ritual using fire to make a bad dream favourable. On manuscript **b** (79-7-8, 77) of *NADR* the personal deities and a lamp (the symbol of Nusku, to whom the appended incantation is addressed) are appealed to at the very end of the ceremony.

THE WRATH OF THE PERSONAL DEITIES

SpTU 2, No. 22, col. III lines 38-43, contains instructions for a stone necklace intended to reconcile irate personal deities to its wearer. The desired ritual result indicates that they could cause bad dreams (and/or that their absence had allowed such dreams to reach the sufferer), line 43:

43). *ki-ṣir* ŠÀ DINGIR-*šú u* ^{d}XV-*šú* DU_8-*šú* MÁŠ.GE_6.MEŠ SIG_5.MEŠ

The anger of his personal god and/or his personal goddess will become separated from him. (His) dreams will become pleasant.

BAM 234, obv. 1-9 lists some of the effects of the wrath of the (personal) deities: obv. 6-8:

6). *i-na* KI.NÁ-*šú* MUD.MUD-*ud ri-mu-tu* TUK-*ši a-du bi-nu-te-šú ana* DINGIR *u* LUG[AL]

7). *lìb-bi-šú ma-li mi-na-tu-šú* DUB.DUB-*ak pi-qa la pi-qa i-pár-ru-ud*

8). *ur-ra u* GE_6 *la* NÁ-*lal* MÁŠ.GE_6.MEŠ *pár-da-a-ti* IGI.DU_8.A.MEŠ

6-8 He is constantly afraid in his bed; he has *rimûtu* throughout his body[?]; his heart is full (of anger) towards god and king; his limbs are constantly 'collapsing'; again and again he is afraid (so that) he cannot sleep day or night; he repeatedly sees frightening dreams;

(Also see *LKA* 139, obv. 26' on pages 27-28, and *CT* 39, pl. 42d, col. I line 8 on page 21.)

Page 60 lists examples of a person seeing dead people in his dreams due to the anger of his personal deities.

FORGETTING DREAMS

An item in a fragmentary list of woes, *BAM* 231, obv. 10, is:

10). [MÁ]Š.GE$_6$.MEŠ-*šú ma-a'-da* MÁŠ.[GE$_6$].MEŠ IGI *la ú-kal*

(He has) many dreams; he cannot recall the dreams which he saw;

It is now known that we have several dreams in a night's sleep, frequently being unable to remember a single one in the morning (chapter 2). In the view of the Mesopotamians, forgetting the details of a dream was a disaster, because one would be unable to perform a ritual to avert its possible evil consequences. For instance, a vital part of the substitution rituals was the recounting, *pašāru*(BÚR), of the dream content to the object which was destroyed in its place (chapter 14).

VAT 7525 (*AfO* 18 [1957-1958], pls. 5-9), reveals that an irate personal god could make his protégé forget his dreams: col. I lines 31-32:

31). DIŠ LÚ *šu-ut-tam ša i-im-ma-ru la ú-ka-al*

32). DINGIR-*šú* ⌜*it*⌝-*ti*-[*š*]*u ze-e-nu*

[31] If a man cannot recall the dream which he sees - [32] (It means that) his personal god is angry with him.

SpTU 2, No. 22, col. I lines 16'-25', lists woes which were caused by divine wrath. Line 20' (page 59) mentioned that "(his) dream does not seize the eye", possibly referring to the sufferer forgetting his dream(s).

We possess one ritual to counteract a forgotten dream: *ADRC,* col. III lines 18-19:

18). DIŠ NA MÁŠ.GE$_6$ *iṭ-ṭul la ú-kal lu* MÁŠ.GE$_6$ *la ina-ṭ*[*al*]

19). 4/7 *uṭ-ṭe-e-ti šá* ^{Ú}*à-ta-wi-ši ana* (IGI) IZI ŠUB-*ma ina* SAG-*šú* GAR-*ma* SIG$_5$

18 If a man saw a dream, (but) he cannot recall (it), or he did not see a dream:

> [19] You throw four/seven grains of the *atā'išu*-plant onto (var., in front of) a fire. You place (the fire$^{?}$) at his head (while he is lying down). It (the dream) will be favourable.

In some way this ceremony purified the bedroom and its occupant. The *atā'išu*-plant (still not definitely identified) was used in other Mesopotamian rituals as a fumigant [*CAD* A_2, p. 481a] so, presumably, the stench drove evil spirits away. On the other hand, this plant was also offered to gods, so perhaps it was fragrant, burnt as a peace-offering to the personal deities.

The title at *ADRC,* col. II line 24 appears to have been attached erroneously to the ritual which follows on the tablet, one to obtain a pleasant dream (chapter 18):

> 24). DIŠ ⌈NA⌉ MÁŠ.GE$_6$.⌈MEŠ *pár-da*⌉*-a-ti ina-*⌈*ṭal*⌉ *u* MÁŠ. ⌈GE$_6$⌉ HUL$^!$(⌈*ù*⌉) *là* ⌈DAB⌉
>
> If a man sees frightening dreams, or he cannot recall a bad dream:

DB, p. 232 believed that *NADR,* lines 4-6 alluded to a forgotten dream, which could still affect the dreamer for weal or woe. (Note that this incantation is addressed to Nusku (line 3), not to the "God of Dreams" as claimed.)

> 4). MÁŠ.GE$_6$ *an-ni-*[*tú*]
>
> 5). *ša ina ba-ra-ar-ti qab-li-ti šat ur-*[*ri*]
>
> 6). *ib-bab-lam-ma šá at-ta* Ì.ZU *ana-ku la i-du-*[*ú*]
>
> [4] This dream, [5-6] which was brought to me during the first watch (of the night), the middle watch, (or) the third watch, and (about) which you yourself understand, (but) I do not -

However, the verb "to recall" is rendered in Akkadian by *kullu*(DAB), not by *idû,* which means "to know, to understand". Also, the phrase:

> (the evil) X which you (the deity invoked) understand, but I do not understand,

is a common one in apotropaic incantations [*CAD* I/J, p. 21b]. This statement emphasized the helplessness of the petitioner and, hopefully, its flattery induced the god to aid him by identifying the source of the problem, thus enabling the subsequent ritual to combat it.

maṣṣar šulme u balāṭi, "A GUARDIAN OF WELL-BEING AND HEALTH"

H. Vorländer [1975, pp. 8-26] argued that various terms described the functions of the personal deities, and came to denote these gods: e.g., *NROD,* obv. 46-48:

> 46). *ma-ṣar šul-me u* TI.LA *šu-kun* UGU-ia_5

47). ^{d}*še-e-du na-ṣi-ru u* DINGIR *mu-šal-li-mu šu-uz-ziz ina* SAG.MU

48). *lit-tar-ru-u'-in-ni kal mu-ši a-di na-ma-ri*

(O Nusku,) [46] establish a guardian of well-being and health for (lit., over) me! [47] Make a protecting *šēdu*(-spirit) and the god who keeps (one) well stand at my head (while I sleep)! [48] May they continually guide me all through the night, until dawn!

We are interested here in the designation *maṣṣar šulme u balāṭi*(TI.LA), "a guardian of well-being and health", along with the analogous expression *rābiṣ* (MÁŠKIM) *šulme*(SILIM), "the overseer of well-being".

TEXTUAL REFERENCES

maṣṣar šulme u balāṭi is used in a phrase expressing wishes for good health, etc., from the sender of a letter to its recipient:

i). In Old Babylonian letters, e.g., *CT* 43, pl. 10, No. 24, obv. 7-8; and *PBS* 7, No. 105, obv. 11-12:

ma-aṣ-ṣa-ar šu-ul-mi-im ù ba-la-ṭi i-na re-ši-ka a-a ip-pa-ar-ku

May a guardian of well-being and health never leave you (lit., your head)!

ii). In Neo-Assyrian letters to the kings Ashurbanipal (e.g., *ABL* 1381 (= *SAA* 10, No. 132), rev. 1-2) and Esarhaddon (e.g., *ABL* 453 (= *SAA* 10, No. 245), obv. 8-9):

^{d}X *ma-aṣ-ṣar šùl-me u* TI.LA TA LUGAL EN-*ia lip-qi-du*

May god X appoint a guardian of well-being and health to the king, my lord!

The continual presence of the personal deities is frequently requested in incantations: e.g. *BMS* 6, rev. 123-124 (restored from *PBS* 1/1, No. 12, rev. 34-35; *SpTU* 2, No. 18, rev. 22'; and *STT* 60 + 233 + unnumbered fragment (O. R. Gurney [1981-1982], p. 93), rev. 31):

123). *lit-tal-lak* DINGIR *mu-šal-lim ina* Á-*ia*$_5$ *lu ka-a-an*

124). *a-a ip-par-ku* MÁŠKIM SILIM *ina* EGIR-*ia*$_5$

(O Shamash,) [123] may the god who keeps (one) well continually walk at my side! [124] May the overseer of well-being never leave from (being) behind me!

The physiognomic omen on *OrNS* 16 [1947], pp. 200-201 + Kraus No. 54 + K. 5939 + Kraus No. 59, col. II line 17 presents a feature of the *rābiṣ šulme*'s role:

17). DIŠ *šu-na-tu-ú-a dam-qa* MÁŠKIM *šul-me* NA [X] ⸢X⸣

If (a man says,) "My dreams are favourable" - The overseer of the man's health [is present$^?$].

A RITUAL OBJECT

Two examples of the creation of a tangible *maṣṣar šulme (u balāṭi)* are mentioned below: a charm necklace (*BMS* 12 (with *LM* 40) + K. 20155); and an inscribed figurine, worn around the neck as an amulet (*KAR* 26). The described tasks of these objects are identical to those of the personal deities, and they were intended to cast a similar protective shade over their wearers. Such objects were more powerful than other examples of their category, which possessed only one or two functions. In effect, a physical personal god was produced, which could even reconcile angry deities to the wearer (*KAR* 26, obv. 49).

a). *BMS* 12 (with *LM* 40) + K. 20155

BMS 12 (with *LM* 40) + K. 20155, obv. 11-13, provides instructions for the manufacture of a charm necklace composed of four replicas of the *anhullu* (AN.HÚL)-plant in alabaster, gold, lapis lazuli, and *mēsu*-wood, interspersed with four beads of the same materials. Each of these materials is shown to have had a particular ritual meaning (obv. 67 to rev. 73). The necklace was intended both to prevent misfortunes and to protect against attacks of types of sorcery (obv. 1).

The incantation to Marduk (obv. 17 to rev. 94) lists the victim's troubles, including at obv. 57:

57). *pár-da* MÁŠ.GE$_6$.MEŠ-*ú-a*

My dreams are frightening.

It states that, at Marduk's command; obv. 64:

64). *a-a* TE-*a* HUL MÁŠ.GE$_6$.MEŠ Á.MEŠ GISKIM.MEŠ *šá* AN-*e* KI-*tim*

the evil of dreams, of ominous happenings (and) the signs of heaven and earth will not approach me.

Reverse 105-114 is an incantation 'switching on' the appropriate magical powers of the necklace before it is placed around the sufferer's neck. It is described on rev. 105 as:

105). *at-ta* AN.HÚL ⸢*ma*⸣-*ṣar šùl-me šá* ^{d}*É-a u* ^{d}*Asal-lú-hi*

O you (sing.) *anhullu*(-replica), the guardian of well-being, (the agent) of Ea and Asalluhi.

The aspect of this *maṣṣar šulme* (*u balāṭi*)'s role most relevant to this study is given on rev. 113, which is unfortunately broken on both *BMS* 12 (with *LM* 40) + K. 20155 and the duplicate *LM* 44, line 10':

> 113). *ina ma-ṣar šul-me* ⌜GE$_6$⌝ *u* ⌜*kàl*$^?$ U$_4$⌝ [M]ÁŠ.GE$_6$ SIG$_5$-*ta lu-mur* : *luṭ-ṭul*
>
> May I experience (or) may I see favourable dream(s during) the night and all$^?$ the day through (the agency of) a guardian of well-being!

b). *KAR* 26

The title *KAR* 26, obv. 1-10 lists possible misfortunes which might be afflicting a person, including at obv. 4-5:

> 4). MÁŠ.GE$_6$.MEŠ *pár-da-te* HUL.MEŠ *là* DUG.GA.MEŠ
>
> 5). IGI.IGI-*mar*
>
> $^{4\text{-}5}$ He repeatedly sees frightening, bad, (and) unpleasant dreams.

All of these woes will be averted by the manufacture of a cedar figurine of a "mad lion" (see F. A. M. Wiggermann [1992], pp. 172-174 on this creature). Its tasks are presented on obv. 46-51 (no dream mention), in an incantation to Marduk and his consort, Ṣarpanitu/Erua, and it is described as:

> 46). ^{GIŠ}ERIN *ma-*⌜*ṣar*⌝ *šul-mé ba-l*[*a*$^!$-*ti*] DINGIR *el*$^!$-*la* [UR].IDIM
>
> A mad [lion] of cedar, a guardian of well-being (and) health, a pure god,

This figurine was probably hung around the neck as an amulet, because it was threaded onto a gold band (rev. 9). Yet, it had to be large enough to bear the inscription of an incantation to Marduk (as Asarri), or just the first line (rev. 11-12), in order to make it efficacious.

The protective figurines of the dream ritual on *ADRC,* col. II lines 19-23, were not interred as in other rituals (see chapter 16), but were placed at the dreamer's head. This recalls *NROD,* obv. 46-48 (pages 92-93), which asks Nusku to ensure that the petitioner's personal deities stand guard at his head during the night. Perhaps these figurines were another version of a visible *maṣṣar šulme u balāṭi.*

CHAPTER 8: DREAM RITUAL SOURCES

The tablets presenting dream rituals predominantly date from the Neo-Assyrian to Seleucid eras, even though Sumerian sources were used to compile the ritual section of the *Dream-Book* (page 100). (Another Sumerian incantation, *YOS* 11, No. 63, mentions a dream at rev. 24, and the rubric of rev. 30 is ge_6.šè.da.kam, "To appease the night".)

In contrast, the earliest known tablet of dream omens was the now lost text Babylon 36383 (*DB,* pp. 313-314; pl. 5), which came from Kassite levels. Its obverse contained an early form of Tab. 9 of the *Dream-Book,* and references to places known to have existed in the Old Babylonian period suggest that there was an even earlier version.

NOTES ON TABLE 2

Table 2 on pages 98-99 lists the sources of dream rituals, omitting the literary examples of incubation (page 221).

i). The various tablets covering parts of the dream ritual collection *KAR* 252 have been edited together under the collective title the *Ashur Dream Ritual Compendium (ADRC)* on pages 249-312. (See page 101 for further details on its structure.)

ii). *AfO* 18 [1957-1958], pl. 10 + *AfO* 19 [1959-1960], p. 119 constitutes the *Substitute King Ritual.* Column B lines 21-29 mention dreams, in connection with guardian figurines (chapter 16).

iii). *BAM* 315 and 316; *BAM* 376, 377, 384, and 400; *CT* 23, pls. 15-22 +; *SpTU* 2, No. 22; *SpTU* 4, No. 134; *STT* 107 (+) 246; and *STT* 275 are charm lists, whose relevant sections are presented in chapter 13.

iv). BM 66559 (= 82-9-18, 6552; pages 178-179) and K. 11406 (pages 337-338) are clod substitution rituals (chapter 14).

v). The *Nusku Apotropaic Dream Ritual (NADR),* pages 314-316 and 317-319, consists of K. 3333 + 8583 + Sm. 1069, col. II lines 1-18, with the duplicate 79-7-8, 77 rev. 3'-17'.

vi). The *Nusku Ritual to Obtain a Pleasant Dream (NROD),* pages 339-348, is based upon *KAR* 58, obv. 39 to rev. 18.

vii). The main manuscript of *Rituals to Obtain a Purussû (ROP),* pages 349-377, is *STT* 73, lines 1-84, and only the tablets covering these lines have been listed in Table 2.

viii). The *Shamash-shum-ukin Dream Ritual (SDR),* pages 379-396, is based on BM 78432. It is so called because line 19a reveals that it was intended for use by this Babylonian ruler.

ix). *SpTU* 2, No. 21, obv. (pages 401-405) deals with a recurrent dream apparition.

x). 81-2-4, 166 (pages 407-410) is concerned with a witchcraft action seen in a dream.

<u>TABLE 2: SOURCES OF DREAM RITUALS</u>

TEXT	**Ashur**	**Kuyunjik**	**Sippar**	**Sultantepe**	**Ur**	**Uruk**	**Various**
ADRC	*BAM* 376* (= *KAR* 213) *BAM* 377* *BAM* 384* *KAR* 53 (N^{5}) *KAR* 252 (N^{87}) *LKA* 132* (N^{426})	K. 3286 (= *ŠRT,* pl. 3) K. 3333 + 8583 + Sm. 1069* K. 3758* K. 4103 + 1330+ 15911 K. 5175 + 6001* K. 8171 + 11041 + 11684 + 14058* 79-7-8, 77* 81-2-4, 233*		*STT* 107 (+) 246* *STT* 245 *STT* 247 *STT* 275*			*SLTN* 149 (S Ni)
		AfO 18, pl. 10 + 19, p. 119					
	BAM 315 *BAM* 316						
	BAM 376 *BAM* 377 *BAM* 384		*BAM* 400				
			BM 66559				
		CT 23, pls. 15-22 +					
		K. 11406					

TABLE 2 (Continued): SOURCES OF DREAM RITUALS

TEXT	Ashur	Kuyunjik	Sippar	Sultantepe	Ur	Uruk	Various
NADR		K. 3333 + 8583 + Sm. 1069 79-7-8, 77					
NROD	*KAR* 58 *LKA* 132	*CT* 51, No. 149 K. 7664 + 9302 + 9494 K. 9000 K. 11706 + 13288				*SpTU* 2, No. 8 *SpTU* 2, Nos. 10 (+) 9	
ROP				*STT* 73	*UET* 7, No. 118		*YOS* 11, No. 75 (Un)
SDR	*LKA* 39 (VAT 13854)	*ABL* 450 BM 78432 *BMS* 1 *LM* 1 + K. 17283 *LM* 2	E. Combe [1908], No. 6 Si 884 Si 904	*STT* 56			
						SpTU 2, No. 21	
						SpTU 2, No. 22	
						SpTU 4, No. 134	
		81-2-4, 166					

* = sections additional to *ADRC*, edited separately

N = Tablets excavated from the private house of a family of exorcists, N4 of O. Pedersén [1986].

S Ni = Sumerian Nippur

Un = Unknown provenance

THE *DREAM-BOOK*

The series Zaqiqu, namely the *Dream-Book* (*DB*, pp. 256-306, with related material; and A. L. Oppenheim [1969]) is an omen compendium with a difference, because it contains both dream omens, and the instructions for ceremonies to avert bad dreams and to obtain pleasant ones. In this way, it unites material concerning two different Mesopotamian views of dreams: the omens, or divine communications requiring interpretation after the compendium's examples; and symptomatic dreams, reflecting the dreamer's cultic purity.

Tablets 1, 10, and 11 (of which only the first line is known, from the colophon of Tab. 10; and corresponding to *ADRC*, col. III line 61) contain the instructions for the ceremonies, while Tablets 2-9 list the omens. As A. L. Oppenheim [*DB,* p. 295] commented, this structure mixes two Mesopotamian literary styles: the one of *Šumma ālu,* in which some omen sections are immediately followed by appropriate apotropaic rites (e.g., *CT* 40, pls. 12-14 (Tab. 9 or 11), dealing with omens concerning parts of a door); the other exemplified by the anti-witchcraft series *Maqlû,* which has a separate "Ritual Tablet". This tablet lists the first lines of the incantations written out in full on the other eight tablets, together with the ritual actions to accompany their recitation.

A. L. Oppenheim [*DB,* pp. 295-296] believed that the *Dream-Book* was compiled from a *Proto-Zaqiqu* (or the omen tablets) and a collection of dream rituals, sometime between 713 B.C. (the colophon of *KAR* 252 (i.e., *ADRC*) dates it to the eponym Ashur-bani, the governor of Nimrud) and the date of the Kuyunjik material from Ashurbanipal's Library. He found allusions to his supposed dream ritual collection at:

i). *KAR* 44, obv. 14:
   14). MÁŠ.⌜GE$_6$⌝ [H]UL$^!$ SIG$_5$.GA
   To make a bad dream favourable

ii). *BAM* 400 (correct *DB,* p. 295 to Si 81), col. III line 1:
   1). 13 ⌜MÁŠ⌝.GE$_6$ [SIG$_5$]
   Thirteen [to make] a dream [favourable]

KAR 44 lists the manuals used by the exorcist, and obv. 14 certainly refers to an apotropaic dream ritual compendium. A. L. Oppenheim regarded *BAM* 400 as an incantation catalogue, believing this reference to be an abbreviation for the thirteen tablet series "Dreams" (he omitted SIG$_5$) of *KAR* 44. However, *BAM* 400 is a guide to charm necklaces, in this case of thirteen beads (pages 166-167). At the moment, we do not know the details of the compilation process of the *Dream-Book.*

The antiquity of the sources of the ritual section of the *Dream-Book* is indicated by the first two incantations on K. 3758 (Tab. 1), which are not divided by a line. E. I. Gordon [1960, p. 129] pointed out that obv. 1-7 *(ZI)* appears on two Sumerian Proverb tablets: *PBS* 12/1, No. 29 and *PBS* 13, No. 38. This was missed by A. L. Oppenheim, but he had noticed [*DB,* p. 296] that obv. 8-11 occurs on another Sumerian Proverb tablet from Nippur, *SLTN* 149 (see *ADRC,* col. III lines 4-15).

A. L. Oppenheim [*DB,* p. 293] also identified a royal *Dream-Book,* K. 273 + 1994b + 9064 [*DB,* pl. 13].

The *Dream-Book* appears in two library/literary catalogues:

i). S. Parpola [1983] edited enumerations of tablets belonging to individual ritual experts. There are four mentions of the *Dream-Book,* all as *iškar* (ÉŠ.GÀR) *Za-qí-qu,* "the series Zaqiqu":

a). *ADD* 944 (+) 943, col. III line 2' (= S. Parpola's No. 1; and *SAA* 7, No. 49) - from an exorcist.

b). *JNES* 42 [1983], p. 17a (K. 4753 + 5711) + *ADD* 980 (+) *JNES* 42, p. 17b (K. 12722) (= S. Parpola's No. 2; and *SAA* 7, No. 50, but not (+) K. 12722): col. I line 15' and col. II line 10' - from two haruspices; and col. III line 10' - from a doctor.

ii). K. 14067 + Rm. 150 (W. G. Lambert [1976]) is a list of texts grouped under personal names, for what reason is unclear. Line 20 reads:

20). [ÉŠ.GÀ]R $^{d⌈}$*Zi*⌉-*qi-qu*.

THE ASHUR DREAM RITUAL COMPENDIUM (ADRC)

ADRC is not systematically arranged either by purpose or by ritual technique. Several dream ritual tablets seem to have been copied indiscriminately on to one large one. This would explain the repetitions of the:

i). ŠU.ÍL.LÁ-incantation to Shamash at col. I lines 73-77, and col. III lines 4-15.

ii). Incantation to the "ram of the storm" at col. III lines 33-36 and lines 52-55 (accompanied by different rites).

iii). Several clod substitution rituals (with minor differences).

The whole of extant Tab. 10 (K. 4103 + 13330 + 15911) of the *Dream-Book* appears at *ADRC,* col. III lines 47-61; and the second incantation of Tab. 1 (K. 3758) occurs at *ADRC,* col. III lines 4-15.

The last section on *ADRC,* col. IV lines 42-47, is a namburbi ritual intended to appease an angry personal goddess, with no mention of dreams. Page 113 offers two possible explanations for its inclusion. Two other passages seem to have been included arbitrarily: col. IV lines 17-18 and 19-20. These were in a fragmentary condition when copied, as is revealed by the scribal comment *hi-pí eš-šu,* "new break".

The existence of dream rituals external to *ADRC* leads one to wonder if these rites were as formally organized as most of the other series listed on *KAR* 44. It is probable that the dream rituals were loosely grouped together, like the namburbi ceremonies (R. I. Caplice [1965], pp. 107-108).

CHAPTER 9: DREAM RITUAL PURPOSES AND CATEGORIES

The primary task of many societies' medical rites is to discover the cause of the complaint either by observing the symptoms, or by investigating the sufferer's background (often by divination) to discover which malefic power is responsible. A technique (e.g., a charm) is chosen to counteract the cause, with the purpose of dispelling demons, propitiating angry deities, etc. However, the blandly laconic titles (when given) of the extant Mesopotamian dream ceremonies do not explain the complex's purpose, often stating merely that the rite is to be used: e.g., *ADRC,* col. I line 13: "If a man saw an ill-portending dream". (The titles of ceremonies concerned with detailed dream content are, by necessity, more informative; see page 114.) The choice of terms describing the dream (pages 25-31) within the ritual complexes does not seem to be relevant in determining either purpose or technique. Accordingly, an analysis has been made of the incantation rubrics and the desired results of the dream rites in order to determine purpose categories. (The results are summarized on pages 109-110.) It must be remembered that a ceremony may have possessed more than one purpose, and that categories deduced from linguistic arguments may not correspond to Mesopotamian practice.

RITUAL PURPOSES DEDUCED FROM INCANTATION RUBRICS

When an incantation was to be recited during a Mesopotamian ceremony, and is written out in full on the tablet describing the ritual (as opposed to the citation of its first line), it can appear:

i). Enclosed in the ritual section, along with the other instructions: e.g., K. 8171 + 11041 + 11684 + 14058, lines 11'-14'.

ii). More usually, in a separate ruled-off section (e.g., *ADRC,* col. III lines 52-55). What is known as 'an incantation rubric' often follows, indicated by KA.INIM.MA at the beginning of the line. It states either the purpose underlying the recitation of the particular incantation, or the category of incantations to which it belongs. The ritual acts to accompany the incantation are given in a third ruled-off section, or in the next line immediately after the rubric.

There are thirty-three incantations occurring in separate sections and attached to a dream ritual (Table 5 on pages 131-134). However, only seventeen rubrics are useful for our analysis (Tables 3 and 4 on pages 115-118). Two additional rubrics (*NROD,* rev. 18; and *SDR,* line 28), which state that the incantations above them belonged to the ŠU.ÍL.LÁ-incantation category, have not been included in this analysis. Another occurrence of KA.INIM.MA has been omitted since the statement of purpose is missing (*ADRC,* col. IV line 41b).

Analysis of these seventeen rubrics reveals the following purposes of dream rituals. (Restorations, etc., in the transliterations have been omitted).

1). To Avert The Evil Of A Bad Dream Which Has Already Been Seen

BÚR = *pašāru,* "To Dissolve"

i). MÁŠ.GE$_6$ HUL BÚR.RU.DA.KÁM, "It is (the text) to dissolve a bad dream" - *ADRC,* col. I line 6; col. II line 71; col. III line 16.

As far as can be deduced from the extant ritual, the first part of col. I line 6 does not refer to an incantation at all. It has been included here because its structure resembles that of the rubrics, rather than that of the desired results (pages 106-109), although it is not introduced by KA. INIM.MA.

Column III line 16 occurs immediately after the end of the relevant incantation, not in a separate section. Unusually, on both manuscripts, the text is prefixed by KA.KÉŠ, which means "spell (lit. knot)", Akkadian *kiṣru.*

ii). MÁŠ.GE$_6$ HUL-*tì* BÚR-*ri,* "To dissolve a bad dream" - *ADRC,* col. III line 45 (see the alternative rubric in line 45a (2/i below)).

iii). HUL MÁŠ.GE$_6$ HUL-*tì* BÚR, "To dissolve the evil of a bad dream" - *ADRC,* col. III line 49.

2). To Make Favourable A Bad Dream Which Has Already Been Seen

SIG$_5$ = *damāqu, D*-Stem, "To Make Favourable"

i). HUL MÁŠ.GE$_6$ SIG$_5$.DA.KE$_4$, "It is (the text) to make the evil of a dream favourable" - *ADRC,* col. III line 45a (see the alternative rubric in line 45 (1/ii above)).

ii). MÁŠ.GE$_6$ HUL SIG$_5$.DA.KE$_4$, "To make a bad dream favourable" - *ADRC,* col. III line 56.

This rubric appeared on *ROP,* line 81a, as an 'incorrect' alternative to line 81 (3/II i below).

(In late texts the grammatically correct ending of .A.KÁM, seen in (1/i) became corrupted to .A.KE$_4$, as above.)

<u>3). To See A Dream</u>

I. *dabābu* And *arkata*(EGIR) *parāsu*, "To Speak" And "To Discover The Future"

i). KI DINGIR-*šú* *u* ^{d}EŠ$_{18}$.TÁR-*šú* *da-ba-bi-im-ma* EGIR NÍ-*šú* *pa-ra-si*, "To speak with his personal god and his personal goddess, and to learn (i.e., to discover) his future" - *ROP*, line 56.

II. IGI.DU$_8$ = *amāru*. "To See"

i). EŠ.BAR IGI.DU$_8$, "To see an oracular decision" - *ROP*, lines 42, 65, and 81 (see page 36 on the relation between *purussû* and *šuttu*, "dream", in this text).

The alternative rubric in line 81a (2/ii above) of making a bad dream favourable is not suited to the overall incubative nature of this tablet.

ii). EŠ.BAR MÁŠ.GE$_6$ IGI.DU$_8$, "To see an oracular decision (and/or) a dream" - *ROP*, line 48.

III. *nâlu*(NÁ) And *šubrû*, "To Lie Down" And "To Cause To See"

i). NÁ-*ma* DINGIR MÁŠ.GE$_6$ SIG$_5$ *šub-re-e*, "To lie down and to cause the god to show (you) a pleasant dream" - *ADRC*, col. IV line 41a.

IV. *tebû* And *amāru*(IGI.DU$_8$), "To Advance" (lit.) And "To See"

i). DIŠ NA *ana* Á.ÁŠ *te-bi* EŠ.BAR IGI.DU$_8$, "If a man (wants) to see an oracular decision upon starting on an enterprise" - *ROP*, line 76.

<u>4). Preventive</u>

la IGI.LÁ = *amāru*, "Not To See"

i). MÁŠ.GE$_6$ *pa-rit-tu$_4$* *là* IGI.LÁ, "(In order) not to see a frightening dream" - *ADRC*, col. II line 21.

<u>5). Miscellaneous</u>

IGI.DU$_8$ = *amāru*, "To See"

i). *ša* MÁŠ.GE$_6$ *i-kil-ta* IGI.DU$_8$, "(For the person) who sees an obscure dream" - *ADRC*, col. III line 37.

Five purpose categories have been deduced from seventeen incantation rubrics. We will now see if there is any support for them from an analysis of the desired ritual results.

RITUAL PURPOSES DEDUCED FROM DESIRED RITUAL RESULTS

A phrase or word occurs at the end of most dream rituals, giving the desired result of the ritual actions upon the dream or upon the dreamer. We possess thirty-four ritual results (Tables 3 and 4 on pages 115-118). Four more results, too broken to be useful, (*ADRC,* col. I line 59; col. II lines 56-57; col. III line 60; and 81-2-4, 166 upper edge 19), and one set of 'omens' (*ROP,* lines 69-70) have not been included in this analysis. (Restorations, etc., in the transliterations have been omitted.)

1). To Avert The Evil Of A Bad Dream Which Has Already Been Seen

It is possible to subdivide these references (the largest group) into two slightly different results:

i). To turn the evil away from the dreamer.

ii). To nullify the evil.

However, it must be remembered that these sections depend upon our translations of the relevant Akkadian verbs, so we may be making more of a distinction than actually existed.

I. To Turn The Evil Away From The Dreamer

a). *etēqu,* "To By-pass"

i). *i-ti-iq-šu,* "(The evil of the dream) will by-pass him" - K. 8171 + 11041 + 11684 + 14058, line 23'.

b). *parāku,* "To Obstruct (i.e., To Affect Adversely)"

i). HUL MÁŠ.GE$_6$ *šu-a-tu$_4$ ana* IGI-*šú ul i-pa-ri-ik,* "The evil of that dream will not obstruct him" - *ADRC,* col. I line 15.

ADRC, col. I line 18 has the result: *ana* LÚ *šu-a-tu$_4$ i-pa-ri-ik,* "It (the ritual) will obstruct (the path$^?$) to that man".

c). TAR = *parāsu,* "To Separate"

i). TAR-*is,* "He (the dream apparition) will be separated (from the dreamer)" - *SpTU* 2, No. 21, obv. 30.

ii). HUL$^?$-*šá* TAR-*is,* "Its evil$^?$ will be separated (from the dreamer)" - *ADRC,* col. I line 27.

d). *úl* TE = *ṭehû,* "Not To Come Near (i.e., Not To Affect Adversely)"

i). HUL MÁŠ.GE$_6$ *a-na* LÚ *úl* TE-*a,* "The evil of the dream will not come near to the man" - *ADRC,* col. II line 18.

ii). HUL.BI *ana* LÚ *úl* TE-*e,* "Its evil will not come near to the man" - *ADRC,* col. I line 6.

iii). MÁŠ.GE_6-*šú úl* TE-*šú,* "His dream will not come near to him" - *ADRC,* col. I line 12.

iv). *ADRC,* col. IV line 30b is an alternative to line 30 (3/II iv below) - *ana* IGI X [(X)] ⌜X⌝ *úl* TE, "Before . [(.)] . it will not come near to . .".

Neither this desired result, nor the ritual of throwing something into the river, agrees with the accompanying incantation, which is intended to reconcile the angry personal deities so that the petitioner will see a pleasant dream. Thus, it would appear that the whole ritual section (*ADRC,* col. IV lines 30a-b) has been incorrectly appended to the incantation by the compiler of *STT* 275.

II. To Nullify The Evil

a). BÚR = *pašāru,* "To Dissolve"

i). BÚR, "It (the evil of the dream) will be dissolved" - *ADRC,* col. I line 72; col. III line 17.

ii). BÚR-*ir,* "It (the evil of the dream) will be dissolved" - *ADRC,* col. I line 78; and 79-7-8, 77 rev. 19', 20', 23', and left edge 26'.

iii). MÁŠ.GE_6 BÚR-*ir,* "The dream will be dissolved" - *ADRC,* col. III line 46.

This has a variant result of NAM.BÚR.BI in line 46a (4/II i below).

iv). HUL MÁŠ.GE_6 BÚR-*at,* "The evil of the dream will be dissolved" - *ADRC,* col. III line 51.

It would appear that lines 51 and 46 (iii above) have been confused, since a third person masculine stative should accompany the masculine noun HUL, not a feminine stative as here. The logogram BÚR-*at* can only be read as a feminine stative *(pašrat)* in Akkadian, suggesting the reading *pašir* (the masculine stative) for BÚR or BÚR-*ir.*

b). DU_8 = *paṭāru,* "To Dispel"

i). HUL-*šú* DU_8, "(The dream's) evil will be dispelled" - *ADRC,* col. III lines 38 and 58.

<u>2). To Make Favourable A Bad Dream Which Has Already Been Seen</u>

I. SIG_5 = *damāqu, G*-stem, "To Be Favourable"

i). SIG_5, "It (the dream) will be favourable" - *ADRC,* col. III lines 3 and 19.

II. SILIM = *šalāmu*, "To Be Beneficial"

i). SILIM.MA, "It (the dream) will be beneficial" - *NADR,* line 18.

<u>3). To See A Dream</u>

I. IGI.DU$_8$ = *amāru*, "To See"

i). EŠ.BAR IGI.DU$_8$, "You will see an oracular decision" - *ROP,* line 43 (see page 36 on *purussû* in this text).

II. *nâlu*(NÁ) And *amāru*, "To Lie Down" And "To See"

i). NÁ-*ma* EŠ.BAR IGI.DU$_8$, "You lie down, and you will see an oracular decision" - *ROP,* lines 51 and 84.

ii). NÁ-*ma* EŠ.BAR MÁŠ.GE$_6$ *ta-am-mar,* "You lie down, and you will see an oracular decision (and/or) a dream" - *ROP,* lines 81c-d are a variant for line 84 (i above).

iii). NÁ-*ma* MÁŠ.GE$_6$ IGI-*mar,* "You lie down, and you will see a dream" - *ROP,* line 68.

iv). NÁ-*ma* MÁŠ.GE$_6$ SIG$_5$-*tu$_4$*/SIG$_5$ IGI-*mar,* "You lie down, and you will see a pleasant dream" - *ADRC,* col. IV lines 30 (SIG$_5$) and 41b (SIG$_5$-*tu$_4$*).

<u>4). Miscellaneous</u>

I. GIŠ.TUK = *šemû*, "To Listen"

i). A.RA.ZU.BI GIŠ.TUK, "His prayer will be heard" - *BAM* 315, col. IV line 31 (page 167).

II. NAM.BÚR.BI, "Apotropaic Ritual"

i). *ADRC,* col. III line 46a, has the alternative 'averting' result for line 46 (1/IIa iii above). (See pages 110-114 for a discussion of the relationship between dream and namburbi rituals).

III. SILIM = *salāmu*, "To Become Reconciled"

i). *ina ze* ⌜X X⌝ SILIM-*mu,* "They (the angry personal deities) will become reconciled by . . ." - *BAM* 315, col. IV line 36 (page 168).

IV. *šakānu*, "To Exist"

i). *ADRC,* col. I line 50 has the broken result: [. . . .] *ša-ki-in-šu,* "[. . . .] exists for him". Presumably something on the lines of good luck or protection is given to the dreamer as the outcome of this extremely fragmentary ritual.

SUMMARY OF RITUAL PURPOSES

The main purpose categories deduced from the incantation rubrics are supported, and augmented, by those deduced from the desired ritual results. Tables 3 and 4 on pages 115-118 present the various dream rites (61 complexes, excluding the alternatives *ADRC,* col. III lines 45a-46a and *ROP,* lines 81a-d, and the literary examples of incubation) with their purpose and ritual technique. The following list gives the number of examples for each purpose category:

i). To avert the evil of a bad dream which has already been seen, either by diverting it from the dreamer or by nullification = 35.

ii). To make favourable a bad dream which has already been seen = 9.

iii). To see a dream = 12; with its subdivisions: rituals to obtain a pleasant dream = 7; and incubation = 5.

iv). Miscellaneous = 4 (see page 110).

v). Preventive = 1.

Since we possess far more desired ritual results, these have been used to classify a ritual's purpose, even if this conflicts with its incantation rubric. Only thirteen complexes have both rubric and result (see below) and, on the whole, the same purpose category is given (8 cases), but direct clashes do occur (5 cases). The latter probably arose from the compilation processes surrounding the dream texts, whereby originally separate incantations and rituals became associated.

Incantation Rubric			**Ritual Result**		
ADRC, col. III lines 16, 45*, 49	BÚR	A	col. III lines 17, 46*, 51	BÚR	A
ADRC, col. III line 37	IGI.DU$_8$	M	col. III line 38	DU$_8$	A
ADRC, col. III line 56	SIG$_5$	F	col. III line 58	DU$_8$	A
ROP, line 42	IGI.DU$_8$	O	line 43	IGI.DU$_8$	O
ROP, lines 48, 76, 81°	IGI.DU$_8$(+)	O	lines 51, 84°	NÁ and *amāru*	O
ROP, line 81a°	SIG$_5$	F	lines 81c-d°	NÁ and *amāru*	O
ADRC, col. III line 45a*	SIG$_5$	F	col. III line 46a*	NAM.BÚR.BI	A
ADRC, col. II line 71	BÚR	A	col. III line 3	SIG$_5$	F
ADRC, col. I line 6	BÚR	A	col. I line 6	*úl* TE	A

* and ° are alternatives on different manuscripts

A = averting F = making favourable M = miscellaneous O = obtaining

The purposes of dream ceremonies which have neither an incantation rubric nor a ritual result have been classified as follows:

i). In general, the instructions for charms are classified according to their titles. The charm on *ADRC,* col. IV lines 8-14, is considered as one to make dreams favourable, from the phraseology of the incantation; and those on *CT* 23, pls. 15-22 +, col. IV lines 13-14, and *SpTU* 4, No. 134, rev.$^{?}$ 7-8, as ones to avert, from the context.

ii). Some rites have been compared with others using the same techniques, thus:

a). *ADRC,* col. I lines 12a-g (an *egirrû* ritual) - to avert.

b). *ADRC,* col. I lines 51-59; BM 66559; and K. 11406 (clod substitution rituals) - to avert.

c). *ADRC,* col. II lines 24-57; *NROD;* and *SDR* - to obtain a pleasant dream.

d). K. 8171 + 11041 + 11684 + 14058, lines 7'-14' (a ritual using fire) - to avert.

iii). The incantation rubric (and content) have been used to assign:

a). *ADRC,* col. II lines 19-23 - preventive.

b). *ROP,* lines 52-60, 61-70, and 71-84 - incubation.

iv). The purposes of the *Substitute King Ritual,* col. B lines 21-24 and lines 25-29, are deduced from the phrases written on the figurines - to obtain a pleasant dream, and to avert, respectively.

v). The rituals with a 'miscellaneous' purpose have been re-allocated:

a). From a dream point of view, the intention of the charms mentioned on *BAM* 315, col. IV lines 27-31 and 32-36 was to obtain a pleasant dream.

b). An averting purpose is indicated by the incantation phraseology of *ADRC,* col. I lines 28-50, and 81-2-4, 166.

DO NAMBURBI RITUALS EXIST FOR BAD DREAMS?

The word *namburbû*(NAM.BÚR.BI), in its Sumerian form, means "(a ritual for) the dissolving of it (the portended evil)", so these are apotropaic ceremonies. Namburbi rituals were intended to avert or dispel the evil portended by a bad omen. This was frequently specified in the title as "the evil of X" (NAM.BÚR.BI HUL X); the evil being identified by its present ominous appearance, not by its future outcome. These rites are responses to the omens of the *Šumma ālu* and *Šumma izbu* series, while references in Neo-Assyrian letters connect them with astronomical phenomena (*ABL* 23 = *SAA* 10, No. 240) and earthquakes (*ABL* 355 = *SAA* 10, No. 56). The wide range of topics covered by the namburbi genre is indicated by *KAR* 44, rev. 6:

6). NÍG.AK.A.MEŠ NAM.BÚR.BI Á.MEŠ AN *u* KI-*tim ma-la ba-šá-a*

magical (averting) actions - apotropaic ritual(s for) all (lit., as many as there are) the signs of heaven and earth;

J. Bottéro [1985a, p. 61] subdivided the namburbi rites into ritual and popular types: the ritual ones being the elaborate ceremonies presented and analysed by R. I. Caplice [*Cap.* Nos.; and (1974), pp. 7-9]; whereas the popular ones were much briefer, and may not have involved a ritual expert. E. Leichty [*ŠI*, p. 11] had already suggested that peasants had 'home remedies' for averting the evil consequences of a malformed birth.

Some texts entitled NAM.BÚR.BI show a development within the genre, namely a positive purpose unrelated to omens: e.g.:

i). Against sorcery - *Cap.* 40 (S. M. Maul [1994], pp. 446-452).

ii). To prevent illness from affecting the royal army - *Cap.* 37.

iii). To bring trade to various professionals - *KAR* 144.

R. I. Caplice denied (on rather arbitrary grounds) that some of the entries in the catalogues of namburbi rituals (*Cap.* 1 + 3 (duplicated by *Cap.* 2 and 4), S. M. Maul [1994], pp. 197-203; *Cap* 5 (+)$^{?}$ S. M. Maul [ibid.], p. 207 (+) *Cap.* 13 (+) 36, [ibid.], pp. 204-210; and *Cap.* III = *SpTU* 1, No. 6) were such rites, while accepting others in this broader sense. He specifically disallowed the existence of namburbi texts directed against bad dreams [1965, pp. 110-111], although the rituals on *ADRC* and the Kuyunjik tablets edited here have been so defined by E. Ebeling [1954, p. 5, 2g] and J. Bottéro [1985a, p. 30]. (The dream ceremonies were not included in S. M. Maul's more recent discussion [1994] of the namburbi rites.) The references to dreams in the namburbi text catalogues are:

i). *Cap.* 1 + 3, obv. 3-4 (page 34).

ii). *Cap.* 4, line 6:

6). ⌜*ana* HUL⌝ MÁŠ.GE$_6$.MEŠ Á.MEŠ GISKIM.MEŠ *ha-ṭa-a-ti lem-né-*⌜*e-ti*⌝ [. . . .]

For the evil of incorrect (and) bad dreams, ominous happenings (and) signs [. . . .]

R. I. Caplice [1974, pp. 8-9] argued that the lack of this type of apotropaic ritual for astronomical portents suggested that such omens were covered by the *Universal*

Namburbi texts, those tablets containing long lists of unfavourable omens: e.g., S. M. Maul [1994], pp. 467-483. Actual astronomical (and meteorological) observations have been found inserted into one copy of this example, *CT* 41, pls. 23-24 + 80-7-19, 123 + S. Langdon [*TI*], pl. 4, col. I lines 25-34. In fact, we do possess individual ceremonies for an eclipse (*Cap.* 65, see page 395) and for a falling star (*Cap.* 35, see page 205).

Bad dreams are also mentioned in the lists of some *Universal Namburbis:* e.g.:

i). *Cap.* 55 (S. M. Maul [1994], pp. 474-475) is extremely fragmentary, but appears to present a list of evils which had occurred within a man's house: rev. 10':

10'). [. . . . *in*]*a* MÁŠ.GE$_6$.MEŠ *pár-da-a-*[*te* . . .]

[. . . .] in frightening dreams [. . . .]

ii). The *Plague Amulets* (E. Reiner [1960]; and S. M. Maul [1994], pp. 185-189, on the group with this introduction): lines A-B:

A). NAM.BÚR.BI HUL MÁŠ.GE$_6$.MEŠ

B). Á.MEŠ GISKIM.MEŠ HUL.MEŠ *là* DÙG.GA.MEŠ

A-B (This is) an apotropaic ritual (for) the evil of bad (and) unpleasant dreams, ominous happenings (and) signs.

iii). *OECT* 6, pl. 22 + *BMS* 62, obv. 10-11 (page 137).

However, there is no obvious reason why bad dreams could not be dispelled by specific namburbi rituals, since their insubstantiality posed no more problem (when sympathetic magic was involved; see on) than a bird flying overhead and away.

The general nature of the dream attestations in the namburbi genre, combined with the use of 'adjectives', suggests that unpleasant symptomatic dreams are the subject-matter. Such dreams contained no prognostic import, but certainly were regarded as evil, indicating the personal deities' absence and, hence, of future troubles: *NADR,* line 8:

8). *šum-ma* HUL HUL-*šá a-a ik-šu-dan-ni*

If (the dream) is bad, may its evil not reach me!

A. L. Oppenheim [*DB,* p. 219] believed that all the dream ceremonies applied to "enigmatic" dreams; i.e., to symbolic-message dreams. The writer has not found any evidence that these dreams were regarded as harmful.

E. Ebeling [1954] presented a fragmentary namburbi tablet, No. 3 (Assur Photo 4148), which may refer to a dream omen: obv. 12'-13' mentions seeing "the evil of the thunder (*rigmu*(GÙ)) of Adad" (some divine symbol?) in dreams.

Namburbi rites were based on the use of sympathetic magic:

i). If the ominous object could not be destroyed directly, for practical reasons, a partial or symbolic destruction was carried out instead: e.g., pouring beer into an ants' nest in the wall (*Cap.* 9 + 23 (and duplicates); S. M. Maul [1994], pp. 211-216 and 350-353).

ii). At other times a simulated enactment of the portended evil was performed, symbolically fulfilling the dire prediction, so that it could not happen (again): e.g., damaging minor parts of a house (*Cap.* 42; S. M. Maul [1994], pp. 484-494).

iii). In the many cases when the ominous object was inaccessible because it was too mobile, distant, or insubstantial, the impending evil was transferred to a suitable substitute, which was subsequently destroyed, eliminating the disaster as well: e.g., birds hovering overhead (*Cap.* 25; S. M. Maul [1994], pp. 234-248).

Even the direct destruction of an ominous object involved sympathetic magic because of the belief that this action annulled the evil portended by the object.

Accordingly, the dream rituals involving substitution by a clod, clay pellets, or a reed (chapter 14), or by figurines (chapter 16), although not designated NAM. BÚR.BI, should be regarded as namburbi rites, until there is unequivocal evidence to the contrary.

NAM.BÚR.BI occurs at the conclusion of two ceremonies on *ADRC,* but there are problems attached to each usage:

i). 81-2-4, 233 obv. 10-11 contains a different incantation rubric and ritual for *ADRC,* col. III lines 45-46 - a clod substitution ritual. The purpose of the alternative section (= *ADRC,* col. III lines 45a-46a) is to make the evil of the dream favourable (HUL MÁŠ.GE_6 SIG_5.GA.KE_4), and the ritual is called a NAM.BÚR.BI (*DB,* p. 343 misread the signs as NAM *ina lìb-bi*). The ritual actions still involve reciting an incantation over a clod, then throwing it in the river (see Table 10 on pages 186-187). Except for the rubric, this would be proof that the Mesopotamians regarded clod substitution rituals as namburbi rites.

ii). The last section on *ADRC* (col. IV lines 42-47) is not concerned with dreams but with a wrathful personal goddess, and it is unclear why it was appended. Its ritual is designated NAM.BÚR.BI by both manuscripts for these lines so, possibly, the reason for linking it with the dream rites is that these were also regarded as namburbi ceremonies. However, the preceding rituals are to obtain a pleasant dream in the coming night, and used incantations resembling DINGIR.ŠÀ.DIB.BAs, so perhaps the connection was the appeasement of the angry personal deities.

Shamash's epithet at 4 R^2. 17 + K. 3206 + 5326 + 16854, rev. 15-16 surely cannot be explained away by the common association of Á.MEŠ and GISKIM.MEŠ with dreams:

15). *mu-hal-liq rag-gi mu-pa-áš-šìr nam-búr-bé-e*
16). Á.MEŠ GISKIM.MEŠ HUL.MEŠ MÁŠ.GE_6.MEŠ *pár-da-a-ti là* DÙG.GA.MEŠ

(O Shamash, you are) [15] the destroyer of the wicked; the releaser of the namburbi(s for) [16] unfavourable ominous happenings (and) signs, (and for) frightening (and) baleful dreams.

(*DB,* p. 219 wrongly attributed this incantation to Anu; also note the different, and lengthy translation.)

RITUALS CONCERNED WITH DREAM CONTENT

Most of the dream rituals were intended to deal with the possible adverse effects of any unpleasant symptomatic dream. There are four rites concerned with specific nightmarish dream content:

i-ii). Two charms were supposed to prevent one from seeing dead people in dreams: *CT* 23, pls. 15-22 +, col. IV lines 13-14; and *SpTU* 4, No. 134, rev.[?] 7-8 (page 165).

iii). *SpTU* 2, No. 21, obv. aimed to separate a recurrent demonic dream apparition from its victim.

iv). 81-2-4, 166 contains a ritual to purify the dreamer after the witchcraft action of earth being thrown over him in a dream, and his subsequent abandonment by the (personal) god. *DB,* p. 307 regarded this as a clairvoyant dream, but it seems to be a nightmare.

These last two examples are the most complex apotropaic dream ceremonies we possess, with detailed titles, the presentation of offerings to a deity (Shamash), and the use of substitute figurines (chapter 16).

Dream content is to be recited to the substitute clay pellets or reed, and in the clod ritual K. 8171 + 11041 + 11684 + 14058 (see chapter 14). Some versions of the *Clod Incantation* (Table 9 on pages 182-183) mention possible dreams and nightmares.

In addition, there are references to undiscovered rituals dealing with dream content:

i). *ADRC,* col. III lines 59-60, states that occasionally the dreamer himself could interpret and neutralize his own dreams:

59). DIŠ MÁŠ.GE$_6$ ina ŠÀ MÁŠ.GE$_6$ IGI-*ma ip-šur* ⌈*am-mar* ŠA$_6$⌉ *u* BÚR-*at*

60). *ana* SIG$_5$ *u* HUL NU ⌈X X⌉

[59] If he saw a dream within a dream, and he interpreted whatever was favourable or able to be interpreted - [60] (The dream) will not [affect him$^?$] for good or evil.

ii). K. 8171 + 11041 + 11684 + 14058, line 24', is just a title:

24'). [DIŠ <LÚ> ina M]ÁŠ.GE$_6$-*šú* MÁŠ.GE$_6$ HU[L-*ta i*]*ṭ-ṭul* *ana*$^!$(*ina*) *là* SÁ.SÁ-*šú*

[If <a man>] saw a bad dream [in] his dream - In order that (its evil) does not reach him:

iii). The fragment *AMT* 79/1 forms the colophon of a large tablet of remedies for the effects of *mišittu* upon various parts of the body. Column IV line 47' shows that an unknown tablet (or part of one) enumerating prescriptions for dream content belonged to the medical corpus:

47'). DIŠ NA *ina* MÁŠ.GE$_6$-*šú* ⌈X⌉ [. . . .] ⌈IGI. IGI-*mar*⌉

If a man repeatedly sees . [. . . .] in his dream(s):

(*DB*, p. 230 suggested the restoration "[dead people]". This is certainly a possibility, but there is the alternative of a recurrent dream figure, as on *SpTU* 2, No. 21, obv. 1.)

TABLE 3: APOTROPAIC AND PROPHYLACTIC DREAM RITUALS

Text	See Chapter	Technique	Pur-pose	INC No.[1]	INC Rubric[2]	Ritual Result[3]
ADRC, col. I lines 1-6	17	misc.	A	--	1/i	1/Id ii
ADRC, col. I lines 7-12	12	*egirrû*	A	--	--	1/Id iii
ADRC, col. I lines 12a-g	12	*egirrû*	A	--	--	--
ADRC, col. I lines 13-15	14	fire - reed	A	--	--	1/Ib
ADRC, col. I lines 16-18	17	misc.	A	--	--	1/Ib
ADRC, col. I lines 19-27	14	fire - oil	A	40	--	1/Ic ii
ADRC, col. I lines 28-50	17	misc.	M[4]	41-42	--	4/IV
ADRC, col. I lines 51-59	14	clod	A	43-44	--	--
ADRC, col. I lines 60-72	14	clod	A	1-2	--	1/IIa i
ADRC, col. I lines 73-78	12	ŠU.ÍL.LÁ	A	3	--	1/IIa ii
ADRC, col. I line 79 to col. II line 18	14	clod	A	4	--	1/Id i
ADRC, col. II lines 19-23	16	G figurine	P	5	4	--

TABLE 3 (Cont.): APOTROPAIC AND PROPHYLACTIC DREAM RITUALS

Text	**See Chapter**	**Technique**	**Pur-pose**	**INC No.**[1]	**INC Rubric**[2]	**Ritual Result**[3]
*AD*RC, col. II line 58 to col. III line 3g	15	alkali - 1 feet - 1 water - 1	F	9	1/i	2/I
ADRC, col. III lines 4-17	12	ŠU.ÍL.LÁ	A	10	1/i	1/IIa i
ADRC, col. III lines 18-19	7	grains on fire	F	--	--	2/I
ADRC, col. III lines 20-38	14	clod	A	11	5	1/IIb
ADRC, col. III lines 39-46 (alt. lines 45a-46a)	14	clod	A	12	1/ii 2/i	1/IIa iii 4/II
ADRC, col. III lines 47-51	17	vinegar	A	13	1/iii	1/IIa iv
ADRC, col. III lines 52-58	15	feet	A	14	2/ii	1/IIb
ADRC, col. III lines 61-68	13	3 charms	A	--	--	--
ADRC, col. IV lines 1-4	13	3 charms	A	--	--	--
ADRC, col. IV lines 5-7	13	charm	F	--	--	--
ADRC, col. IV lines 8-14	13	charm	F	15	--	--
ADRC, col. IV lines 15-16	13	charm	A	--	--	--
BAM 400, col. III line 1 (+)	13	charm	F	--	--	--
BM 66559	14	clod	A	20	--	--
CT 23, pls. 15-22 +, col. IV lines 13-14	13	charm	A	--	--	--
K. 8171 +, lines 7'-14'	14	fire - oil	A	47	--	--
K. 8171 +, lines 15'-23'	14	clod	A	48-50	--	1/Ia
K. 11406	14	clod	A	51-53	--	--
NADR	14	fire - reed	F	54-55	--	2/II
SpTU 2, No. 21, obv. 1-30	16	S figurine	A	34-35	--	1/Ic i
SpTU 4, No. 134, rev.[?] 7-8	13	charm	A	--	--	--
STT 107 (+) 246, rev. 12'-16'	13	charm	A	--	--	--
STT 275, col. IV line 23	13	charm	F	--	--	--
Substitute King Ritual, col. B, lines 25-29	16	G figurine	A	--	--	--
79-7-8, 77 rev. 18'-19'	14	fire - reed	A	--	--	1/IIa ii
79-7-8, 77 rev. 20'	15	oil	A	--	--	1/IIa ii
79-7-8, 77 rev. 21'-23'	14	pellet	A	57	--	1/IIa ii
79-7-8, 77 left edge 24'-26'	14	pellet	A	--	--	1/IIa ii
81-2-4, 166	16	S figurine	M[4]	37	--	--

TABLE 4: RITUALS TO OBTAIN A PLEASANT DREAM AND INCUBATION

Text	See Chapter	Technique	Pur-pose	INC No.[1]	INC Rubric[2]	Ritual Result[3]
ADRC, col. II lines 24-57	18	--	O	6-8	--	--
ADRC, col. IV lines 21-30b	18	--	O	16-17	--	3/II iv 1/Id iv
ADRC, col. IV lines 31-41b	18	--	O	18-19	3/III i	3/II iv
BAM 315, col. IV lines 27-31	13	charm	M[4]	--	--	4/I
BAM 315, col. IV lines 32-36	13	charm	M[4]	46	--	4/III
NROD	18	--	O	22-23	--	--
ROP, lines 1-43	19	incubation	I	24-25	3/II i	3/I
ROP, lines 44-51	19	incubation	I	26	3/II ii	3/II i
ROP, lines 52-60	19	incubation	I	27	3/I i	--
ROP, lines 61-70	19	incubation	I	28	3/II i	3/II iii
ROP, lines 71-84	19	incubation	I	29-30	3/IV I 3/II I	-- 3/II i
(alt. 81a-d)			(F)		2/ii	3/II ii
SDR	18	--	O	31 & 56	--	--
SpTU 2, No. 22, col. IV lines 5-6	13	charm	O	--	--	--
Substitute King Ritual, col B lines 21-24	16	G figurine	O	--	--	--

Notes To Tables 3 And 4

A = averting F = making favourable G = guardian figurine

I = incubation M = miscellaneous O = obtaining pleasant

P = preventive S = substitute figurine

(1) The incantation numbers are those of Table 5 on pages 131-134.

(2) The numbers refer to the discussion of the incantation rubrics on pages 103-105.

(3) The numbers refer to the discussion of the ritual results on pages 106-109.

(4) See point (v) on page 110.

(5) The following alternative rituals have been omitted:

i). *ADRC,* col. IV lines 25a-d (a charm) and 30a-b (clod ritual[?]) - apart from the ritual result of line 30b (page 107) these are not discussed at all.

ii). *SDR,* lines 37-40 - not discussed at all.

iii). Si 884 (manuscript **d** of *SDR*) rev. 1'-3' - not discussed at all.

iv). *SpTU* 2, No. 21, obv. 31-40 (chapter 16).

(6) The following sections have been omitted:

i). *ADRC,* col. III lines 59-60, which does not contain a ritual (pages 114-115).

ii). *ADRC,* col. IV lines 17-20 and 42-47 (page 101), because they do not refer to dreams.

iii). The title K. 8171 +, line 24' (page 115).

iv). The fragmentary rituals of 81-2-4, 233, obv. 1-2 and 12ff.- not discussed at all.

(7) See chapter 19 for the literary examples of incubation.

CHAPTER 10: GENERAL NOTES ON THE DREAM RITUALS

Understanding how the dream rites were performed is beset with problems, due to lack of information. The ritual instructions are very terse, more notes ordering the procedure than detailed manuals. There would have been traditional ways to make a figurine, certain physical attitudes to maintain while reciting an incantation, methods of preparing the ingredients, etc., which our texts assume the ritual expert knew, and would perform automatically, so no details are given. This terseness occurs in all Mesopotamian ceremonies, but the dream rites are a prime example. R. I. Caplice [1974, pp. 9-13] enumerated the main components of namburbi rituals, according to a formalized structure. No such pattern, or even most of his elements, can be identified for dream rites, although other ceremonies comply. (Restorations, etc., in the transliterations have been omitted in this chapter.)

It must be remembered that, although the tablets of dream rituals date from the Neo-Assyrian period onwards, there is no proof that any were performed then (apart from *SDR,* see page 208), so our sources may be scholarly collections of defunct rites.

THE PARTICIPANTS

Most Mesopotamian non-royal rituals involved only the relevant professional and the sufferer-supplicant. The majority of the verbs in the dream rites (as in all Mesopotamian ceremonies) are given by logograms, with no indication as to their subject. These logograms are usually transcribed by the second person singular, and regarded as applying to the practitioner.

This convention arises from the general belief throughout all the world that a society's ritual experts have been divinely appointed to practise, and empowered by a long apprenticeship to a skilled master. Therefore, if an 'unqualified' person managed to acquire both the ingredients and the knowledge of a rite, it would probably be ineffectual since he would be unable to put its forces into motion. Also, it is generally assumed that the Mesopotamian masses were illiterate, thus restricting the use of the craft manuals to the professional elite. It is unclear how large a part oral transmissison played in the training of the practitioners.

Sometimes the logograms could equally apply to the client, who is normally indicated by the third person singular. Occasionally the ancient scribes wrote out the verbs syllabically. Such writings in the dream texts show that the dreamer could perform ritual actions, recite incantations (see page 128), and recount dream content to a substitute. It is probable that he did all this at the professional's command, even if there is no mention of the latter.

Although there may have been popular namburbi rites (page 111) not involving a practitioner, most of the dream ceremonies were too complex to be carried out unsupervised. Knowledge of the appropriate incantations was required, even if some of the ritual actions seem basic: e.g., placing a foot on the ground (pages 193-194).

The evidence predominantly concerns Mesopotamian ritual experts attached to the court or to official circles. There are several, probably unanswerable, questions:

i). Was every type of specialist found in every major town, at least?

ii). Elsewhere, did one person cover a variety of professions in greater or lesser detail, as would be the case of a medicine man or wise woman of a village?

iii). Did varying degrees of competence attract clientele from different social strata, or were the services of a practitioner, in effect, only available to the nobility or the rich?

iv). How many times would a 'normal' individual consult a professional, and for the same troubles (e.g., after every bad dream)?

THE EXORCIST WAS THE NEO-ASSYRIAN DREAM RITUAL EXPERT

It is suggested that, by the Neo-Assyrian period, the exorcist or ***āšipu*** had subsumed oneirology within his professional expertise. (The logogram $^{(LÚ)}$MAŠ. MAŠ indicated the exorcist, and can be transcribed either by *āšipu* or *mašmaššu; ABZ,* No. 74.)

a). Unpleasant Symptomatic Dreams

i). Dreams, in general, were dreaded by the Mesopotamians, and were regarded as having a demonic aspect (chapter 5).

ii). Nightmares were caused by angry deities, demons, and sorcery (pages 50-58).

iii). The methods used to combat unpleasant symptomatic dreams reveal that a bad dream was not insubstantial, but an evil miasma besmirching the dreamer. This was treated as a physical entity which could be: transferred to a substitute, and destroyed (chapter 14 and pages 200-201); or driven away by a pure substance (pages 191-193).

iv). The exorcist diagnosed supernatural agents for the maladies he remedied, proceeding to exorcise both agent and ailment by such techniques as charms, flour circles, and substitute figurines (*KAR* 44, rev. 3, obv. 6 and 10), all of which occur in the dream rituals.

v). An unidentified compendium of rites "to make a bad dream favourable" (MÁŠ.GE_6 HUL SIG_5.GA) is listed amongst the exorcist's craft manuals on *KAR* 44, obv. 14 (page 100).

vi). KAR 44, rev. 6 mentions namburbi rituals, and on pages 110-114 it is argued that some apotropaic dream rites belong to this category.

vii). The only reference to a specific ritual expert on *ADRC* is at col. II line 66, which recalls the 'legitimizing formula' of *ROP,* line 52 (see on):
66). *ša* UR.SAG ^{d}*Marduk* DUMU ^{d}*É-a ana-ku*
I am (the servant) of the hero Marduk, the son of Ea.

b). Rituals To Obtain A Pleasant Dream

i). *ABL* 450 (= *SAA* 10, No. 298) is extremely important because it informs us that *SDR* was performed in the Neo-Assyrian period. The exorcist Nabu-nasir wrote to Esarhaddon giving an abbreviated version of the ritual actions on obv. 9-17 (manuscript $\mathbf{G_1}$).

ii). *NROD* contains two different one line rituals on obv. 51 and 51a. The former identifies the professional involved as the exorcist (^{LÚ}MAŠ. MAŠ).

c). Incubation

i). The only definite mention of a practitioner in the incubation rituals (chapter 19) is the 'legitimizing formula' of *ROP,* line 52:
52). *ra-am-ku šá* ^{d}*É-a* DUMU *šip-ri šá* ^{d}*Asal-lú-hi ana-ku*
I am the (ritually) bathed of Ea, (and) the messenger of Asalluhi.
It is possible that *ramku* was another designation of the exorcist: see *Ludlul bēl nēmeqi,* Tab. 3, lines 23-24; W. Mayer [*UFGB*], pp. 65-66; and *JNES* 15 [1956], p. 138, lines 109-111, with *CAD* $Š_I$, **šangammāhu,* pp. 376-377.

One minor obstacle to regarding the exorcist as the dream ritual expert arises from the catalogues of practitioners' tablets edited by S. Parpola [1983]. He deduced [ibid., pp. 8-9] that these tablets were not needed for professional purposes, but one tablet of the *Dream-Book* was recorded as coming from an exorcist (page 101). However, a tablet of dream omens, VAT 14279 (*DB,* pl. 10), was excavated from N^4 in Neo-Assyrian Ashur, a private house with a large archive and library belonging to a family of exorcists (O. Pedersén [1986], N4: 530).

RITUAL TECHNIQUES

Ethnographical studies have revealed that, although there are many different magical practices attested throughout the world, each society tends to adhere to a limited number. The range of techniques used may be further limited by the knowledge of the individual practitioners. A technique will be applied to a multitude of purposes and, sometimes, comparisons of these purposes enable us to learn more about the underlying theories of the technique. This is especially true of the use of figurines and substitutes in Mesopotamian dream rituals.

Dream ceremonies are non-calendrical rites, being performed at moments of crisis for a particular individual in a private setting. The apotropaic and prophylactic rituals (46 examples; Table 3 on pages 115-116) have been classified according to their techniques:

i). Charms (17) and amulets (chapter 13) = 17 examples.

ii). Substitution rites, involving the transference of the evil to another object, and the latter's destruction (chapter 14). The substitutes are clods (8 examples), or clay pellets (2); rituals using fire are also based on principles of sympathetic magic: burning a reed (3); and soaking something in oil (2) = a total of 15 examples (see (iv) for substitute figurines).

iii). The purification of the dreamer (chapter 15), by alkali solution (1), or oil (1), or water (2), or by feet actions (2) = 5 examples.

iv). Guardian (2) and substitute (2) figurines (chapter 16) = 4 examples.

v). The power of words (chapter 12): creating "an oracular utterance", *egirrû* (2); and reciting a ŠU.ÍL.LÁ-incantation (2 copies of the same ritual) = 4 examples.

vi). Miscellaneous (chapter 17): too broken to determine (3); and a libation of vinegar (1) = 4 examples.

(The above numbers of charms and guardian figurines include those used in ceremonies intended to obtain a pleasant dream.)

LEGAL CONCEPTS IN MESOPOTAMIAN RITUALS

According to the Sumerian myth *Enki and the World Order,* Enki placed the Sun God, Shamash, in charge of justice throughout heaven and earth (lines 373-379; C. A. Benito [1969]); thus, Shamash became the supreme judge of demons, ghosts, gods, and humans. Various incantations express this idea when asking Shamash "to pass judgement on my case" (e.g., *ADRC,* col. III lines 4-5), either by releasing the sufferer from his woes or by punishing witches and other wrong-doers. The Fire Gods Gibil and Nusku (the companions of Shamash) are appealed to similarly: e.g., *NADR,* line 4 (Nusku).

Actual legal practices or derivatives can appear in the ceremonies. The main examples from dream rites are the use of a clod (page 180) or cutting a hem (page 189) to symbolize severance of ties between a bad dream and the dreamer.

The presentation of offerings occurs in two rituals against dream content (each made to Shamash): *SpTU* 2, No. 21, obv. 5; and more detailed on 81-2-4, 166 obv. 5-9. The acceptance of these gifts obliges the deity to help the petitioner in his cause, and to make the ritual efficacious.

Oaths are as binding on supernatural powers as on humans (see the ghost rituals discussed on page 200).

THE SETTING OF THE APOTROPAIC AND PROPHYLACTIC DREAM RITES

TIME OF DAY

Most of the rituals would have been brief; note though, *ADRC,* col. I lines 1-6, which stretched over at least three days. Not surprisingly, they were performed in the early morning, on the day (after) the dream was seen (e.g., *ADRC,* col. III line 50), before the dream's evil took a firm hold of its victim. The matutinal nature is indicated by several phrases, sometimes used in combination:

i). *la-am* GÌR-*šú ana* KI GAR-*nu,* "before he has placed his foot upon the ground" - *ADRC,* col. I line 5; col. III lines 1 (with minor variants), and 50. This expression appears in other, non-dream, rituals (e.g., *CAD* K, *kabāsu,* p. 6b; *CAD* Q, *qaqqaru,* p. 114a), and is unrelated to the method whereby the dreamer is purified by touching the ground with his foot (pages 193-194).

ii). DIŠ LÚ *ina mu-ši-ti-šú* MÁŠ.GE$_6$ HUL-*ta* IGI-*ma uš-ta-dir ina še-ri har-pí ina te-bi-šú* + (i), "If a man saw a bad dream during the night, and became worried: In the early morning, upon his arising," (but) + (i above) - K. 8171 + 11041 + 11684 + 14058, lines 7'-8'.

iii). *be-lu₄ pa-tan,* "without having eaten" - *ADRC,* col. I lines 8-9, and 13, with (i) + (iv). "Without" is usually *balu,* and the modern Akkadian dictionaries offer no examples of this Assyrian? form. The idea of performing a 'ritual' on an empty stomach is common in Mesopotamian medical prescriptions [*CAD* B, *balu,* p. 72].

iv). *ina šēri ha-ar-pí* KÁ *ú-ka-al-lu-šú,* "in the early morning, (while) the door detains him" (i.e., before he leaves the house) - *ADRC,* col. I line 20.

v). *ina še-e-ri,* "in the morning" - 79-7-8, 77 rev. 20'.

vi). *la-am* ᵈUTU.È.A, "before sunrise" - *ADRC,* col. I line 12a.

One wonders about the practicality of some of these time clauses, and if dreamers delayed their daily business until a practitioner arrived.

Dream rituals for protective purposes could be performed at times other than in the morning. *ABL* 22 (page 199) states that no special time was appointed for the burial of the guardian figurines made in the *Substitute King Ritual.* While those of *ADRC,* col. II lines 22-23, presumably, were placed around the bed-head (lit., "your head", line 23) at sometime before the man lay down.

LOCATION

There are indications that, as we would expect, some rituals were enacted in the dreamer's bedroom:

i). Actions were carried out on or over the bed, or while the sufferer was still in bed: e.g., *ADRC,* col. III line 2.

ii). Figurines (*ADRC,* col. II lines 22-23) were placed at a man's head, presumably at the bed-head.

iii). The technique of placing one foot on the ground while the other remained on the bed (pages 193-194).

In the *Substitute King Ritual,* one pair of guardian figurines was buried in the king's bedchamber (col. B line 24), while other pairs were interred throughout the palace, the second relevant pair in the courtyard (col. B line 29).

The substitution rituals offer the probability of two consecutive ritual locations: starting in the bedroom, as the scene of the 'crime', and moving to the place of disposal - a river-bank for the clods, or a cross-roads for the clay pellets. The substitute figurine in *SpTU* 2, No. 21 was buried at the corner of a wall (obv. 29; see page 200).

There is no evidence that these dream rites occurred in an enclosed and purified area, as was the case for many namburbi rituals. The burial site of the substitute figurine on *SpTU* 2, No. 21, obv. 29, was encircled by flour, but this was to confine the dream apparition, paralleling demon and ghost ceremonies (page 200).

A common phrase in Mesopotamian rituals is that an action is to be performed or an incantation recited "before Shamash". According to the context, which is not always helpful, this can mean either merely beneath the sun's rays: e.g., *ADRC,* col. I line 72, where an incantation is to spoken over a clod before it is cast away; or before a representative emblem or statue: e.g., probably, *ADRC,* col. I line 78, where a ŠU.ÍL.LÁ-incantation is recited. (See *NADR,* line 2, where the dreamer holds the hem and reed before the lamp, the symbol of Nusku, who is invoked in the following incantation (lines 3-13).)

CHAPTER 11: INCANTATIONS IN THE DREAM RITUALS

For convenience, the verbal rites, or incantations, found in the dream rituals are studied separately from the physical actions, or technique. It must be remembered, however, that often the two are closely associated, both expressing the desired ritual result by speech and symbolism respectively. Therefore, they ought be studied together, as has been done with the clod substitution rituals and the *Clod Incantation* (pages 180-181). M. Mauss [1972, p. 57] believed that every non-verbal rite had a corresponding phrase - to a certain extent this is true of the dream rituals. He also doubted [ibid., p. 54] whether entirely wordless rites ever existed, stating [ibid., p. 56] that an apparent silence does not mean that the ritual expert is not uttering an incantation inaudibly: a matter impossible to prove. Most of the 'complete' dream rituals contain incantations (see Table 5 on pages 131-134).

The functions of an incantation are: to issue commands to specified supernatural beings; to add to the effectiveness of the non-verbal rites by specifying their intended result; and to connect the ritual to a particular supplicant. The practitioner may either invoke deities to help him, often attracting their attention by the presentation of suitable offerings, or dispel a malevolent force, controlling it through the use of its name. The word 'incantation' has been used here to cover the possibilities of the phrases being 'a spell' (compelling action) or 'a prayer' (entreaty). It is not always easy to tell from a text which type is meant, and both kinds co-exist in most cultures.

The inherent magical power of an incantation only works if the formulae are uttered faultlessly under the correct ritual conditions; according to prescribed methods of recitation, accompanying actions, and stances (e.g., *šukênu,* "to prostrate oneself", on *ADRC,* col. II line 38). If all these conditions are fulfilled, then the incantation will be effective, regardless of the purity of the speaker's intentions. On the other hand, a bungled performance might nullify the incantation, perhaps even turning its energies against the reciter. *PRT ezib* 7e is a clause covering the possibility of a bad rendition of an haruspical inquiry:

> *ina* KA DUMU ^{LÚ}HAL ÌR-*ka ta-mit up-tar-ri-du*
>
> (Disregard (the fact) that) the question was hurried (i.e., garbled) in the mouth of the haruspex, your servant.

The choice of one of the many Mesopotamian verbs loosely meaning "to speak" in a particular incantation has been taken to indicate the way in which that incantation was to be delivered (e.g., E. K. Ritter [1965], p. 309, n. 16; R. I. Caplice [1974], p. 13). It is possible that *manû,* "to recite", involved a formal intoning, because it is normally used when it is the ritual expert who is to utter the phrases. Yet, note the use of *i-ma-nu-ma,* "he (the dreamer) recites", at *ADRC,* col. I line 23 (see page 119 on the significance of the third person singular). *dabābu,* "to speak", and *qabû,* "to say", are generally taken to refer to the sufferer (i.e., to the dreamer).

On *SpTU* 2, No. 21 the dreamer may have been given a chance to present his problem alongside the pre-formulated incantations: obv. 14:

> 14). *ana* ^{d}UTU DU_{11}.DU_{11} ^{d}UTU *i-šem-me* INIM-*su*
> He speaks to Shamash (in his own words$^{?}$, and) Shamash will hear his speech.

The concept of ad libbing might also be meant at *NADR,* line 18 where the dreamer (or the professional, depending on the manuscript) prays *(karābu)* to the lamp and to the personal deities.

At times, only the practitioner recited the incantations, often on behalf of his client; at other times the latter spoke, probably repeating after the expert. *ROP* contains two almost identical incantations in lines 44-47 and 52-55, except that the latter was to be uttered by the ritual expert alone, indicated by the 'legitimizing formula' at the beginning of line 52 (see page 121), which empowered him to act.

The linguistic features of incantations such as alliteration, assonance, and repetition are inevitably hidden in translations.

INCANTATION CATEGORIES IN THE DREAM RITUALS

ABRACADABRA INCANTATIONS

The use of a mysterious language, possibly meaningless in detail, even to the ritual expert, results in so-called 'abracadabra incantations'. These may develop for a variety of reasons:

i). The words were deliberately invented when the incantation was first composed.

ii). The words derive from foreign or archaic languages not generally understood. For example, lines 15-22 of *YOS* 11, No. 5 are in Elamite (see ibid., p. 4), and lines 10-11 of No. 65 state that the appended incantation was in Subarian. The later copies of Sumerian incantations contain grammatical errors, indicating that Sumerian was imperfectly known at the time of copying.

iii). The incantation has become corrupted over the years, due to imperfect oral repetition or incorrect copying.

The abracadabra incantation on *ADRC,* col. II lines 19-20, seems to have been deliberately composed because it contains rhythm and cohesion. It may have been copied into other rituals. *ADRC,* col. II lines 19-20:

19). én hu-ub-ba hu-ub-ba ab-ni a-⸢ra⸣-a ⸢e⸣-ra-a
20). uš-ru-⸢lu$_4$$^{?}$⸣ uš-lu-lu ⸢tu$_6$⸣ én

A similarly patterned incipit occurs on *ADRC,* col. IV lines 42-43, in a ritual to appease a wrathful personal goddess:

42). én hu-ub-ba hu-ub-ba ab-na : a-ra-tu è a-ra-ba-tu è
43). ^{d}EŠ$_{18}$.TÁR.MU *ina uz-zi ha-am-mat* (to be said again once or twice)

The latter part of the above incipit is given on *AMT* 103, col. II line 32', in a medical ritual dealing with ailments of the temple (lines 32'-35'):

32'). én a-ra-tu e a-ra-ba-tu e ti-la [. . . .]
33'). šu dù-dù-meš šu ne-ne a-meš eridu^{ki}-ke$_4^{!}$(ga) mu-un-du [. . . .]

DINGIR.ŠÀ.DIB.BA-INCANTATIONS

W. G. Lambert [1974] edited some DINGIR.ŠÀ.DIB.BA-incantations, and discussed the genre. A few texts have this incantation rubric, which gives the group its name:

KA.INIM.MA DINGIR ŠÀ.DIB.BA GUR.RU.DA.KÁM
Incantation rubric: It is (the text) for appeasing (lit., turning back) an angry deity.

We do not know if these incantations formed a series, as is implied by *KAR* 44, obv. 4; nor if they were a sub-category of ŠU.ÍL.LÁ-incantations (see on). The examples we possess reveal that there was no precise order. In the majority, the deity invoked is the petitioner's unnamed personal god, often also with the personal goddess, but other deities may be addressed as well. The rationale behind these texts is the belief that all misfortunes were because the sufferer had offended the gods in some way.

Incantations analogous to those edited by W. G. Lambert are found in rituals to obtain a pleasant dream, namely, in the ritual complexes of *ADRC,* col. IV lines 21-30 and 31-41b. The *bīt rimki* purification series (on *BBR* 26 + K. 8921 + 10131, col. V lines 78-81) offers another example of such incantations in a ceremonial context.

ŠU.ÍL.LÁ-INCANTATIONS

W. Mayer [UFBG] analysed ŠU.ÍL.LÁ-incantations in depth. (The word is occasionally written ŠU.ÍL.LA (e.g., manuscript **B** of *ADRC,* at col. III line 17) or ŠU.ÍLA (e.g., manuscript **A** of *ADRC,* at col. I line 78).) There is a large number of these incantations (lit., "the raising of the hand (in prayer)"). They are found in different types of ceremonies: e.g., in namburbi rituals; in rites against demons; in rites against witchcraft; in *bīt rimki;* and in *mīs pî.* They were not arranged in a formal series, although certain exemplars tend to appear together. Some texts are identified by the incantation rubric:

KA.INIM.MA ŠU.ÍL.LÁ ^{d}X.KÁM

Incantation rubric: It is (the text of) a ŠU.ÍL.LÁ-incantation to deity X.

Other texts are assigned to this group by similarities in content and structure. W. G. Kunstmann [1932, pp. 54-79] classified the incantations with this rubric as *„allgemein"* ŠU.ÍL.LÁs, and the others as *„spezielle"* (see also W. Mayer [*UFBG*], pp. 8, and 13-16). The latter can be subdivided into two types: by their intended purpose (e.g., apotropaic dream rituals); or by the title given to them by the Mesopotamians (e.g., NAM.BÚR.BI).

W. Mayer [*UFBG,* pp. 11-13] went on to define a ŠU.ÍL.LÁ-incantation as a ritual petitionary prayer of an individual, being a pre-formulated text used in a ritual, entreating a deity to help him against specific evils, or to generally improve his situation. Occasionally the petitioner personalized a ŠU.ÍL.LÁ-incantation by filling in the names in the *annanna*-formula (page 138).

W. G. Lambert [1974-1977, p. 198] stated that W. Mayer's definition of a ŠU. ÍL.LÁ-incantation as a *Bittgebet* (petitionary prayer) "cannot be proved". He suggested, instead, that the rubric ŠU.ÍL.LÁ meant that such incantations did not belong to any specific category, unlike a DINGIR.ŠÀ.DIB.BA, for instance. This would explain the presence of ŠU.ÍL.LÁ-incantations in rituals with different purposes.

A ŠU.ÍL.LÁ-incantation often mentions the ritual acts already performed, or to be carried out by the speaker (e.g., *SDR,* line 20).

Page 151 discusses the recitation of a ŠU.ÍL.LÁ-incantation to Shamash as a dream ritual. Three other ŠU.ÍL.LÁs appear in two elaborate rituals to obtain a pleasant dream: *NROD,* obv. 39-50, and rev, 1-17; and *SDR,* lines 1-27.

TABLE 5: THE INCANTATIONS IN THE DREAM RITUALS

SEPARATE INCANTATIONS

Text Reference	Ritual Technique	No. of INCs.	Sub-INCs	Addressee: Deity	Addressee: 'Tool' and Misc.	Language
1 *ADRC*, col. I lines 60-65	Clod	2	--	UTU	--	S
2 *ADRC*, col. I lines 66-70			--	UTU	--	S
3 *ADRC*, col. I lines 73-77	ŠU.ÍL.LÁ	1	--	UTU	--	S
4 *ADRC*, col. I, 79 - II, 16	Clod	1	a = 79-9	--	Clod	A
			b = 9-14	--	*lipšur*	A
			c = 14-16	Shamash	--	A
5 *ADRC*, col. II lines 19-20	Figurine	1	--	--	Abraca-dabra	?
6 *ADRC*, col. II lines 29-37	O	3	--	UTU	--	S
7 *ADRC*, col. II lines 39-47			--	Various	--	S
8 *ADRC*, col. II lines 51-55			--	--	*ēru*-wood staff	S
9 *ADRC*, col. II lines 58-70	P (2x) + feet (1)	1	a = 58-68	--	?	A
			b = 68-70	Marduk	--	S
10 *ADRC*, col. III lines 4-15	ŠU.ÍL.LÁ	1	--	Shamash/ UTU	--	A+S
11 *ADRC*, col. III lines 20-36	Clod	1	a = 20-24	Shamash	--	A
			b = 25-33	--	Clod	A
			c = 33-36	--	"ram of the storm"	A
12 *ADRC*, col. III lines 39-44	Clod	1	a = 39-42	Ea	--	A
			b = 43-44	--	?	A

TABLE 5 (Continued): THE INCANTATIONS IN THE DREAM RITUALS

SEPARATE INCANTATIONS (Continued)

Text Reference		Ritual Technique	No. of INCs.	Sub-INCs	Addressee: Deity	Addressee: 'Tool' and Misc.	Language
13	*ADRC*, col. III lines 47-48	Vinegar	1	a = 47	--	?	(S)
				b = 48	--	*lipšur*	A
14	*ADRC*, col. III lines 52-55	Feet	1	--	--	"ram of the storm"	A
15	*ADRC*, col. IV lines 8-13	Charm	1	a = 8-12	Anzagar & consort	--	A
				b = 13	Shamash & Marduk	--	A
16	*ADRC*, col. IV lines 23-25	O	2	--	PD	--	S
17	*ADRC*, col. IV lines 28-29			--	PD	--	A + S
18	*ADRC*, col. IV lines 31-37	O	2	--	PD	--	A
19	*ADRC*, col. IV lines 38-40			--	PD	--	S
20	BM 66559, obv.	Clod	$1^?$	?	--	Clod	A
21	K. 5175 + 6001, col. I lines 1'-4'	INC. only	--	--	?	?	S
22	*NROD*, obv. 39-50	O	(2)	--	Nusku	--	A
23	*NROD*, rev. 1-17			a = 1-8	Nusku	--	A
				b = 9-17	Various nocturnal beings	--	A
24	*ROP*, lines 1-20	I	2	--	Gula	--	A
25	*ROP*, lines 21-41			--	Gula	--	A
26	*ROP*, lines 44-47	I	1	--	Various	--	A

TABLE 5 (Continued): THE INCANTATIONS IN THE DREAM RITUALS

SEPARATE INCANTATIONS (Continued)

Text Reference	Ritual Technique	No. of INCs.	Sub-INCs	Addressee: Deity	Addressee: 'Tool' and Misc.	Lang-uage
27 *ROP*, lines 52-55	I	1	--	Various	--	A
28 *ROP*, lines 61-64	I	1	--	--	WC	A
29 *ROP*, lines 71-75	I	2	--	--	WC	A
30 *ROP*, lines 77-80			--	--	WC	A
31 *SDR*, lines 1-27	O	1	--	Sin	--	A
32 Sm. 543, lines 1'-6'	INC. only	--	--	?	?	S
33 Sm. 543, lines 8'-10'	INC. only	--	--	--	Tamarisk	S
34 *SpTU* 2, No. 21, obv. 7-11	Figurine	2	--	Shamash	--	A
35 *SpTU* 2, No. 21, obv. 16-26			--	--	Figurine	A
36 *ZI*	INC. only	--	--	SIG.SIG/ Zaqiqu	--	A + S
37 81-2-4, 166 obv. 12 to rev. 15	Figurine	1	a = obv. 12 -rev. 12, 15	Shamash	--	A
			b = rev. 13-14	--	*lipšur*	A

INCANTATION PHRASES INCLUDED IN THE RITUAL

Text Reference	Ritual Technique	No. of INCs.	Addressee: Deity	Addressee: 'Tool' and Misc.	Lang-uage
38 *ADRC*, col. I lines 9-10	*egirrû*	1	--	*egirrû*	A
39 *ADRC*, col. I lines 12d-g?	*egirrû*	1	--	*egirrû*	A
40 *ADRC*, col. I lines 24ff.	Fire	1	(Gibil)	--	A

TABLE 5 (Continued): THE INCANTATIONS IN THE DREAM RITUALS

INCANTATION PHRASES INCLUDED IN THE RITUAL (Continued)

Text Reference		Ritual Technique	No. of INCs.	Addressee		Lang-uage
				Deity	'Tool' and Misc.	
41	*ADRC*, col. I lines 36-41?	Misc.	2	?	?	A
42	*ADRC*, col. I lines 43ff.			Shamash	--	A
43	*ADRC*, col. I line 52	Clod	2	Shamash	--	A
44	*ADRC*, col. I lines 54ff.			--	Clod	A
45	*ADRC*, col. III line 3d	P	1	?	?	A
46	*BAM* 315, col. IV lines 34-35	Charm	1	Shamash	--	A
47	K. 8171+, lines 11'-14'	Fire	1	Gibil	--	A
48	K. 8171+, lines 17'-18'	Clod	3	--	Clod	A
49	K. 8171+, lines 20'-22'			--	Clod	A
50	K. 8171+, line 22'			--	*lipšur*	A
51	K. 11406, col. I lines 3'-4'	Clod	3?	PD	--	A
52	K. 11406, col. I lines 5'-8'			Shamash	--	A
53	K. 11406, col. I lines 9'-11'			--	Clod?	A
54	*NADR*, lines 3-13	Fire	2	Nusku	--	A
55	*NADR*, line 14			--	Reed	A
56	*SDR*, lines 32-33	O	1	Anzagar	--	A
57	79-7-8,77 rev. 23'	Pellets	1	?	?	A

Notes

A = Akkadian
I = Incubation
O = To obtain a pleasant dream
PD = Personal deities of dreamer
WC = Wain constellation
Con. = Constellation
No. INCs. = Number of incantations per ritual
P = Purification
S = Sumerian

Nos. 38-39 are *egirrû* sentences (pages 156-157). *SDR* is unusual in that it contains a separate incantation (No. 31) as well as an included phrase (No. 56).

The following 'incantations' have been omitted from this analysis because, although they do occur on tablets containing dream rites, it is unclear if they concern dreams. In any case, most are too fragmentary to be useful:

i). *ADRC*, col. IV lines 42-43 (see page 129).
ii). *KAR* 53, rev. 15-21.
iii). *LKA* 132, rev. 7-9.
iv). 81-2-4, 233 obv. 12ff.

STRUCTURE

The thirty-seven examples of 'separate' incantations are reduced to thirty-five because *ADRC,* col. I lines 73-77 and col. III lines 4-15 are basically the same ŠU. ÍL.LÁ-incantation (page 151), and *ROP,* lines 52-55 and 61-64 are the same, although uttered by different people (page 128). Several incantations are internally split into sub-incantations, each addressing a different supernatural being, forming (in effect) distinct incantations (e.g., *ADRC,* col. I line 79 to col. II line 16 = Nos. 4a-c). Four incantations are unattached to ritual actions: BM 66559, obv.; Sm. 543, lines 1'-6', and 8'-10'; and *ZI.*

The discusssion of the structure of dream incantations is based primarily upon the 'separate' incantations, which can be subdivided into:

i). 'Proper' incantations (Table 6 on page 136), mainly invoking a single deity. Sometimes additional gods may be called upon (e.g., *ADRC,* col. IV lines 8-12 (No. 15a) petitions Anzagar (and his consort), while line 13 (No. 15b) appeals to Shamash and Marduk); or supplications are made to numerous deities (e.g., *ROP,* lines 44-47).

ii). DINGIR.ŠÀ.DIB.BA-incantations to the dreamer's personal deities.

iii). 'Tool' incantations, addressed to an object used in the ritual (e.g., the *Clod Incantation;* Table 9 on pages 182-183).

iv). The so-called abracadabra incantations.

'Proper' incantations and the *Clod Incantation* possess the most formal structure (elements of which can be seen in the other types).

In most of the ceremonies to obtain a pleasant dream several incantations were recited in turn: *ADRC,* col. II lines 29-37, 39-47, and 51-55; *ADRC,* col. IV lines 23-25, and 28-29; *ADRC,* col. IV lines 31-37, and 38-40; and *NROD,* obv. 39-50, and rev. 1-17. Two incantations occur in a clod substitution ritual (*ADRC,* col. I lines 60-65, and 66-70), and two in a substitute figurine rite (*SpTU* 2, No. 21, obv. 7-11, and 16-26).

INVOCATION

The deities invoked in the dream incantations are predominantly either gods of fire or light (Gibil, Nusku, Shamash, Sin), or gods of magic (Ea, Marduk): both categories being enemies of demons and wrong-doers. The Dream Gods Anzagar and Zaqiqu are addressed twice. The incubation rituals of *ROP* invoke Gula and various nocturnal beings.

TABLE 6: 'PROPER' INCANTATIONS IN THE DREAM RITUALS

Addressee			Separate INCs:	Included
Deity	'Tool'	Misc.	Nos.	phrases: Nos.
Anzagar (& consort)			15a	56
Ea			12a	
Gibil				(40), 47
Gula			24, 25	
Marduk			9b	
Nusku			22, 23a	54
Shamash/UTU			1, 2, 3, 4c, 6, 10, 11a, 34, 37	42, 43, 46, 52
Shamash & Marduk			15b	
Sin			31	
Zaqiqu/SIG.SIG			36	
Personal deities			16, 17, 18, 19	51?
Various			7, 23b, 26, 27	
	Clod		4a, 11b, (12b), 20	44, 48, 49, 53
	Figurine		35	
	ēru-wood staff		8	
	Reed			55
	Tamarisk		33	
		"ram of the storm"	11c, 14	
		Wain constellation	28, 29, 30	
		Unknown	9a, 13a, 21, 32	41, 45, 57

The INCantation numbers are those of Table 5 on pages 131-134.

'Proper' incantations begin with an invocation of varying length. This summons the deity by the enumeration of some of his epithets and his benevolent actions towards mankind in the past (e.g., *ROP,* lines 13-14 and 19-20). The intention being that the flattered deity will turn his attention towards the supplicant, and help in the ways outlined by the choice of appellation. Occasionally the deity will be addressed by another title later in the incantation.

The dream incantations mainly call upon the deities to provide justice and light. None of these deities (apart from the Dream Gods) are invoked by an epithet relating to dreams, although examples are known outside the technical literature:

a). Ea, Shamash, And Asalluhi

OECT 6, pl. 22 and *BMS* 62 have been joined now [*DB*, p. 219] (and are on permanent loan to the Louvre Museum), forming an incantation to Ea, Shamash, and Asalluhi in a *Universal Namburbi* ritual with several duplicates (see S. M. Maul [1994], pp. 467-483): obv. 10-11:

10). *mu-pa-si-su* Á.MEŠ GISKIM.MEŠ HUL.MEŠ

11). MÁŠ.GE$_6$.MEŠ [*pár*]-*da-a-ti* HUL.MEŠ *là* DÙG.GA. MEŠ

(You are) [10] the obliterators of unfavourable ominous happenings (and) signs, [11] (also of) frightening, bad, (and) unpleasant dreams.

(A namburbi rite for a snake invokes the same deities with this expression but replaces the first word with *mu-pa-áš-ši-ru*, "the dissolvers": e.g., *Iraq* 18 [1956], pl. 14, lines 17-18; see S. M. Maul [1994], pp. 300-303.)

b). Marduk

i). *SpTU* 3, No. 81, obv. 6-9:

6). [én sa.h]ul du$_8$.ù.da [e]n ^{d}marduk.e.da.àm

7). [. . . .] *ina* MÁŠ.GE$_6$.MEŠ HUL.MEŠ *là* DÙG.GA. ME[Š]

8). [(. .) Á.MEŠ G]ISKIM.MEŠ *ha-ṭa-a-ta pár-da-a-t*[*a*]

9). [. . . . S]IG$_5$-*tì tur-ru* EN ^{d}*Marduk it-ti-ka*

[6] [Incantation:] "(The ability of) loosening the evil [sinew] is (yours) lord Marduk. [7] [. . . .] in bad (and) unpleasant dreams, [8] [(. .)] incorrect (and) frightening [ominous happenings] (and) signs, [9] [. . . .] (the ability) to turn to good luck is with you, lord Marduk."

ii). *Šurpu,* Tab. 4, lines 21-22:

21). MÁŠ.GE$_6$ HUL-*tì du-um-mu-qu bu*

22). HUL MÁŠ.GE$_6$.MEŠ Á.MEŠ GISKIM.MEŠ *ana* LÚ *là* TE-*e bu*

[21] to make favourable a bad dream *bu**; [22] not to (allow) the evil of dreams. ominous happenings (and) signs come near to a man (i.e., affect him) *bu**.

(*bu** = line 2: *bul-lu-ṭu šul-lu-mu* ^{d}*Marduk it-ti-ka-ma,* "It is within your power, O Marduk, to heal and preserve".)

c). Shamash

For Shamash, see 4 R^2. 17 + K. 3206 + 5326 + 16854, rev. 15-16 on page 114.

Anu is invoked by a dream epithet in a ŠU.ÍL.LÁ-incantation, but is not addressed in the dream incantations. *BMS* 6, obv. 7-8 (duplicated by *LKA* 50, obv. 5'-7'; and *CT* 51, No. 211, lines 10-12):

7). *pa-šir* MÁŠ.GE_6.MEŠ HUL.[MEŠ]

7a). *ha-ṭa-a-te pár-da-a-*[*te*]

8). Á.MEŠ GISKIM.MEŠ HUL.MEŠ

(O Anu, you are) [7-7a] the dispeller of bad, incorrect, (and) frightening dreams, [8] (also of) unfavourable ominous happenings (and) signs.

INTRODUCTION OF THE PETITIONER AND THE PRESENTATION OF OFFERINGS

It seems that it was thought unnecessary to further cajole the deity after the invocation, so most examples move directly to the request (pages 140-143).

In six cases the speaker introduces himself, using an abbreviated form of the *annanna*-formula (W. Mayer [*UFBG*], pp. 46-52), *ana-ku* NENNI A NENNI: *NROD,* rev. 4; *ROP,* lines 34 and 64; *SDR,* line 15; *SpTU* 2, No. 21, obv. 10; and 81-2-4, 166 rev. 2. The expanded version is thought to read:

ana-ku NENNI A NENNI *šá* DINGIR-*šú* NENNI *u* ^{d}EŠ$_{18}$.TÁR-*šú* NENNI-*tu*$_4$

I myself, X, the son of Y, whose personal god (is) A, and/or whose personal goddess (is) B.

The close relationship between the personal deities and their obedient worshipper, or protégé, was sometimes envisaged as a parental one, as in a variant of the *annanna*-formula (e.g., *SDR,* lines 13a-b):

ana-ku X DUMU DINGIR-*šú šá* DINGIR-*šú* etc.

I myself, X, the son of his personal god, whose personal god is etc.

Offerings are presented to a deity in rituals to obtain a pleasant dream, in incubation rites, and in two ceremonies directed against nightmarish dream content (*SpTU* 2, No. 21, and 81-2-4, 166). These offerings are not always mentioned in the incantation, but are at *SDR,* lines 19a-20.

S. Sperl [1994, p. 223] believed that the purpose of the statements regarding the offerings and the petitioner's actions (e.g., *SDR,* line 21) was to show that the correct procedures were being followed.

COMPLAINT

In the complaint the supplicant briefly describes the terrors he is experiencing, hoping to move the deity to pity his plight: e.g.:

i). *ADRC,* col. III lines 41-42 - the dreamer is frightened after seeing a bad dream.

ii). *SDR* reveals the uneasy transfer of this incantation from rituals against a lunar eclipse into a dream rite (page 149). Lines 12-13 contain the standard *attalû*-formula about the eclipse, while lines 25-26 request a dream indicating the reconciliation of the personal deities as a result of the dreamer's purification.

iii). 81-2-4, 166 rev. 4-10 - earth was thrown over the sufferer in a dream, bewitching him (echoing the ritual title at obv. 1-3).

iv). The complaint is far more elaborate in the *Clod Incantation* (Table 9 on pages 182-183) where many possible dreams and nightmares are recounted to the clod, thereby transferring their evil to it.

ESTABLISHMENT OF A RELATIONSHIP BETWEEN THE DREAM AND A SUBSTITUTE

Not surprisingly, this section only appears in incantations connected with substitution rituals (chapter 14). In the clod rituals the *kirṣu*-formula (page 179) establishes a problematical relationship between the dreamer (sic) and the clod (pages 180-181), while the complaint section associates the clod with the bad dream, and describes the disintegration of them both. In the clay pellet and reed substitution rituals, the evil of the dream is transferred by a straightforward recital of the nightmare.

After the bad dream has been associated with the reed in *NADR,* lines 9 and 13 contain the firm denial:

la ia-ut-tu-un ši-i

May it (the nightmare) not be mine!

DB, p. 298, n. 197 had commented upon the use of this phrase, which is adapted from a formula more usually appearing at the end of an incantation, and intended to endow that incantation with greater authority, hence effectiveness. The formula is:

ÉN *ul ia-ut-tu-un* ÉN ^{d}X

(This) incantation is not mine, (it is) the incantation of god X.

The standard sequence of 'healing' deities is Ea, Asalluhi, Damu, Gula, and Ningirim. E. K. Ritter [1965, pp. 309 and 312] classified incantations invoking the last three deities, along with those containing the above formula, as belonging to *asûtu,* the 'purely' medical lore, as opposed to the magical lore of the exorcist, or *āšipūtu.*

However (see already R. Biggs [*ŠZG*], p. 39), an exorcistic usage is indicated by the adapted use of this formula in *NADR,* and by its appearance (sometimes abbreviated) in incantations directed against various demons: e.g.:

i). Lamashtu - *Lamaštu,* Tab. 1, col. II lines 20-21 (*ZA* 16 [1902], pp. 141-200); and incantations designed to calm a baby (W. Farber [*SKS*], §32, lines 12-14; §34, lines 16-17; also see §25, lines °368-370).

ii). *māmītu,* "curse/oath" (personified as a daughter of Anu) - *BMS* 61, line 20.

iii). *mimma lemnu,* "Anything evil" - *SpTU* 3, No. 82, col. II line 25.

Another occurrence of the formula is in ŠÀ.ZI.GA, No. 19, line 21 (= *LKA* 97, col. II line 21), which is not exorcistic, but nevertheless belongs to *āšipūtu* since ŠÀ.ZI.GA is mentioned in the list of the exorcist's manuals (*KAR* 44, obv. 14).

lipšur-PHRASES

These are exorcistic phrases predominantly found in *lipšur*-litanies (see E. Reiner [1956] on this genre), but also occurring elsewhere. The most extensive list in the dream incantations is found on *ADRC,* col. II lines 9-14 (No. 4b). Other examples of *lipšur*-phrases occur on: *ADRC,* col. I lines 36-41; *ADRC,* col. III line 48 (No. 13b); K. 8171 + 11041 + 11684 + 14058, line 22'; and 81-2-4, 166 rev. 13-14 (No. 37b). These attestations are standard exemplars, apart from two which the writer has not found elsewhere:

i). *ADRC,* col. II line 13:

13). GIŠ⌈ŠÀ.GIŠIMMAR⌉ *li*!(*ku*)-⌈*qad-di*⌉-*šá-an-ni*

May! 'the offshoot' of the date palm purify me!

ii). 81-2-4, 166 rev. 14:

14). [Ú].BABBAR TIN-*an-ni-ma*

May 'the white [plant]' heal me!

REQUEST - DREAM REFERENCES

A number of the 'separate' incantations do not mention dreams at all; even in incubation ceremonies (*ROP,* lines 1-20, 21-41, 44-47, and 52-55), or rituals to obtain a pleasant dream (*ADRC,* col. II lines 29-37, 39-47, and 51-55; *ADRC,* col. IV lines 23-25, and 28-29; *ADRC,* col. IV lines 31-37; and *NROD,* obv. 39-50, and rev. 1-17). This implies a lack of incantations especially designated for these purposes. We have already noted that some DINGIR.ŠÀ.DIB.BA-incantations and ŠU.ÍL.LÁs were adapted for use in rituals to obtain a pleasant dream, with the ŠU. ÍL.LÁ-incantation on *SDR,* lines 1-27, being firmly attested in rites against a lunar eclipse (page 149).

There are three styles of references to dreams in the request section of the incantations:

i). 'May the dream be turned to good luck!'

ii). 'May the evil of the dream be averted!'

iii). Miscellaneous

Usually, only one dream request appears in an incantation, unless it is split into sub-incantations (e.g., *ADRC,* col. I line 79 to col. II line 14 (No. 4a-b) - to avert; with col. II lines 14-16 (No. 4c) - to turn to good luck).

a). Turning The Dream To Good Luck

In four cases deities are asked to turn a bad dream already seen into good luck:

i). *ADRC,* col. I line 75 (a) = *ADRC,* col. III lines 8-9 (b):

a). níg.sig$_5$.ga.aš gub$^?$.ba.ab

Make (the dream) stand for good luck!

b). níg.ša$_6$.ga.aš ku$_4$.ni.íb

ana SIG$_5$-*tì* [*tir-ra*]

Turn (the dream) into good luck!

ii). K. 11406 contains part of the ŠU.ÍL.LÁ-incantation of *ADRC* above, line 7':

[MÁŠ.GE$_6$ *a-mu-ru a-na* S]IG$_5$ *tir-ra*

Turn [the dream into] good luck!

iii). *ADRC,* col. II lines 14-16 (No. 4c):

lu dam-qat = "May (the dream) be favourable!";

lu ki-na-at = "May (the dream) be reliable!";

a-na SIG$_5$-*ti tir-ra* = "Turn (the dream) into good luck!"

iv). *ADRC,* col. IV lines 11-12, asks the Dream God Anzagar and a possible consort:

⌈HUL *te-pu*⌉-*šá ana* ^{MÍ}SIG$_5$ GUR-*ra*

Turn to good luck the evil which you did to me (i.e., sending a bad dream)!

(repeated as ⌈*mim-mu-ú*⌉ *te-pu-šá ana* ⌈^{MÍ}⌉SIG$_5$ *te-e-ri*).

If, by an unlikely chance, the dream should already be favourable, the dreamer naturally wanted to ensure that its good luck would not by-pass him:

i). *ADRC,* col. III line 43 (No. 12b):

dam-qat ma-a du-muq-šá UGU *ia-ši* KUR

If my dream) is favourable, (then say:) 'May its good luck reach me!'

ii). *NADR,* line 7:

šum-ma dam-qat du-muq-šá a-a i-ši-ṭa-a[*n-ni*]

If (this dream) is favourable, may its good luck not pass [me] by!

b). Averting A Bad Dream

A general request occurs in *NADR,* line 8:

šum-ma HUL HUL-*šá a-a ik-šu-dan-ni*

If (this dream) is bad, may its evil not reach me!

In most cases this request is associated with ritual actions ensuring that this aversion will happen: e.g., in the *Clod Incantation* (Table 9 on pages 182-183); *SpTU* 2, No. 21, obv. 16-26; and 81-2-4, 166 obv. 12 to rev. 15. On *ADRC,* col. III line 48 (No. 13b) the wind is requested to carry off the dream's evil.

The incantation mentioning the mysterious "ram of the storm" (*ADRC,* col. III lines 33-36 (No. 11c) and 52-55) uses a simile to describe the desired result of the ritual: *ADRC,* col. III lines 35-36:

35). *ki-i na-*⌈*kap* GÍR⌉^{II} *a-*⌈*na*⌉ *a-si-di la i-qar-ri-bu*

36). HUL MÁŠ.GE$_6$ *šá ina* GE$_6$ IGI.DU$_8$ *la* TE-*a la i-*⌈*qar-ri*⌉*-ba ía-ši*

[35] Just as the tip of the feet cannot approach the heel, [36] (so) the evil of the dream which I saw during the night cannot come near, (and) cannot approach me.

c). Miscellaneous

These references are mainly related to the purpose underlying the ritual to which the incantation belongs:

i). To obtain a pleasant dream:

a). *ADRC,* col. IV lines 39-40:

[39] ^{d}ma.mú dingir.ma.mú.da.ke$_4$ [40] dingir.mu inim še.ga.še.ga ù. tu.ud.da

[39] O Mamu, the god of dreams, [40] (and$^{?}$) my personal god, create a favourable state (of affairs for me)!

b). *NROD,* rev. 7 and 17:

mūšu lib-lam-ma

May Night bring me (a favourable dream)!

ii). On *SDR,* lines 23-26, the petitioner requests a dream indicating his renewed purity and reconciliation with his angry personal deities.

iii). To obtain a dream omen: *ROP,* line 64:
MÁŠ.GE_6 IGI
May he (the petitioner) see a dream!
(and *ROP,* lines 71-75, and 77-80 by analogy).
ROP, lines 1-20, 21-41, and 44-47 are requests for "an oracular decision", *purussû,* which probably means a dream in this text (page 36). *ROP,* lines 61-64 mention speaking with one's personal deities, perhaps in a dream.

iv). *SpTU* 2, No. 21, obv. 10-11, explains that Shamash is being petitioned because of a recurrent dream apparition.

v). The purpose of *ZI* is unclear.

REQUEST - OTHER REFERENCES

In a few incantations the supplicant seems to feel that, while he has the god's attention, he may as well ask for some general benefits concerning his well-being. The topics raised are:

i). Prosperity - *ADRC,* col. II line 63; *ADRC,* col. III lines 10-15; and K. 11406, line 8'.

ii). Reconciliation with one's enemies - *ADRC,* col. II lines 64-65.

NROD, obv. 39-50 is a request for divine protection during the night.

CONCLUSION OF THE INCANTATION

Some of the DINGIR.ŠÀ.DIB.BA-incantations and ŠU.ÍL.LÁs, together with 81-2-4, 166 obv. 12 to rev. 15, conclude with a promise to praise the deity, if the latter, in turn, will fulfil his side of the 'bargain', by granting the petitioner's requests. The closing formulae are:

i). *SDR,* line 27:
ana dà-ra-a-ti lud-lul dà-lí-lí-ka
I will proclaim your glory forever.

ii). *ADRC,* col. IV lines 25 and 29; *NROD,* rev. 8 and 17; and 81-2-4, 166 rev. 15:
dà-lí-lí-ka/ku-nu lud-lul
I will proclaim your glory.

The existence of two identical requests and conclusions on *NROD,* rev. 1-17 (No. 23ab) show it is really two distinct incantations, although there is no dividing line between them.

iii). *NROD,* obv. 49-50:
nar-bi-ka lu-šá-pi IGI ^{d}UTU *ud-da-kám*
I will extol your greatness all day long before Shamash.

INCIPITS

The inclusion of an incantation in *UFBG* shows that W. Mayer regarded it as a ŠU.ÍL.LÁ-incantation. (Restorations, etc., in the transliterations have been ignored. The numbers are those of Table 5 on pages 131-134.)

***ana* DINGIR.MU *mì-na-a* DÙ-*uš* ⁝ *ana* ^{d}XV.MU *mì-na-a ah-ṭi* : DINGIR-*ia*$_5$ *iz-nu-u* KI-*ia*$_5$** = *ADRC,* col. IV line 28 (No. 17)

DINGIR.ŠÀ.DIB.BA-incantation.

áš búr-bi bal-bi ur-šè i-gi-bi = *ADRC,* col. III line 47 (No. 13)

***at-ta man-nu šá ina* MÁŠ.GE$_6$ *u bi-ri* IGI.IGI-*ru* KI-*ia*$_5$** = *SpTU* 2, No. 21, obv. 16 (No. 35)

To the figurine of the recurrent dream apparition.

at$^{!}$-ti* ^{MUL}mar.gíd.da.an.na *šá* AN-*e* KI-*ti ni-ir-ki* ^{d}*Nin-urta ma-šad-da-ki* ^{d}*Marduk = *ROP,* line 71 (No. 29)

To the Wain constellation. (Manuscript **b** (*UET* 7, No. 118) has two options for the unusual KI-*ti* of manuscript **A** (*STT* 73), GAL-*ti* : *at-ti.*

ROP, lines 61-64 (No. 28, page 146) is an incantation closely resembling this one.

***at-tu-nu* MUL.MEŠ *šá mu-ši-ti* ^{d}En.bi.luh ^{d}Nin.bi.luh ^{d}En.bi.luh.ha** = *ROP,* line 44 (No. 26)

UFBG, p. 428, *die Sterne als Gruppe 6.* To various supernatural beings.

Apart from the initial line, which contains a 'legitimizing formula', *ROP,* lines 52-55 (No. 27, page 147) contain the same incantation, but are spoken by the ritual expert instead.

dingir.mu hé$^{!}$.silim.ma.mu ama ^{d}inanna.mu hé.silim.ma.mu níg.dùg.ga. mu ^{d}utu hé.gub = *ADRC,* col. IV line 23 (No. 16)

DINGIR.ŠÀ.DIB.BA-incantation. (Only manuscript **A** (*KAR* 252) has the last phrase from níg.)

dingir.mu ša$_{6}$.ga mu.un.túm.a ⁝ dingir.mu sag.kal pa.è an.ta.gál = *ADRC,* col. IV line 38 (No. 19)

DINGIR.ŠÀ.DIB.BA-incantation. (Manuscript **P** (*KAR* 53) has a different ending to this incipit, repeating dingir<.mu> sag.kal pa.è instead of an.ta.gál.)

***^{d}É-a šàr* ABZU *pa-ti-iq* AN-*e u* KI-*tim ba-nu-u* UN.MEŠ** = *ADRC,* col. III line 39 (No. 12)

UFBG, p. 381, Ea 5. (There are different versions of line 40, see page 277.)

e-piš lum-ni na-ki-su* ZI-*ti mur-te-du-u ek-le-te = *ADRC,* col. IV line 8 (No. 15)

To Anzagar (and his consort).

^{d}Gi-bil* EN HUŠ KALA.GA *tap-pe-e* ^{d}UTU *šàr* X *at-ta = K. 8171 + 11041 + 11684 + 14058, line 11' (No. 47)

UFBG, p. 386, Gira 10. This incantation is included within the ritual instructions, and appears to be unfinished.

An extremely fragmentary incantation to Gibil occurs at *ADRC,* col. I lines 24ff. (No. 40), which seems to be different to No. 47.

hu-ub-ba hu-ub-ba ab-ni a-ra-a e-ra-a = *ADRC,* col. II line 19 (No. 5)

Abracadabra incantation. (This incantation, and possible related ones, are discussed on page 129.)

***il-tu$_{4}$ réme-ni-tu$_{4}$ mu-bal-li-ṭa-at* AD$_{6}$** = *ROP,* lines 1 and 21 (Nos. 24 and 25)

UFBG, p. 387, Gula 6. These incantations are identical except for lines 14-18 and lines 34-39 respectively.

kir-ba-an kir-ba-an ina kir-ṣi-ka ka-ri-iṣ kir-ṣi = *ADRC,* col. I line 79 (No. 4)

The *Clod Incantation.* (Manuscript **E** (*STT* 245) has *ramānu*(NÍ-*ú*)-*ka* for the final *kir-ṣi,* confusing two formulae (see page 179).

K. 8171 + 11041 + 11684 + 14058, lines 17'-18' (No. 48) has this incipit included within the ritual instructions, with more of the incantation appearing in lines 20'-22' (Nos. 49 and 50).

ADRC, col. III line 25 (No. 11b) has a different incipit, but lines 25-33 are basically the same incantation as No. 4 (see Table 9 on pages 182-183):

25). LAG *bi-nu-ut ap-si-i at-ta-ma ina kir-ṣi-ia ga-ri-iṣ*

ADRC, col. I line 52 (No. 43) contains a fragmentary phrase in the instructions, which addresses the Clod, and continues in No. 44, lines 54ff. The ideas expressed are analogous to those of the *Clod Incantation,* but appear in a different form:

52). LAG-*an* X (X) *kul-lat* HUL MÁŠ.GE_6 *is la* [. . . . . .] X X

^{giš}ma.nu ^{giš}tukul kala.ga dingir.re.e.ne.ke$_4$ = *ADRC,* col. II line 51 (No. 8)

To a staff of *ēru*-wood.

^{MUL}MAR.GÍD.DA DUMU.MUNUS ^{d}*A-nim* GAL-*tu$_4$ kal-lat É-kur kul-lul-tu* = *ROP,* line 77 (No. 30)

UFBG, p. 430, ^{MUL}*ereqqu* 4. (Manuscript **b** (*UET* 7, No. 118) has *kut-tùm-tú* for *kul-lul-tu.*)

^{MUL}Mar.gíd.da.an.na ^{MUL}MAR.GÍD.DA *šá-ma-mi šá ni-ir-šá* ^{d}*Nin-urta* = *ROP,* line 61 (No. 28)

To the Wain constellation (see the note on pages 374-375). *UFBG,* p. 430, ^{MUL}*ereqqu* 3.

Lines 61-63 closely resemble *ROP,* lines 71-73 (No. 29, page 144).

nam.tar.zu hé.en.tar.re nam.tar.zu hé.en.tar.re = *ADRC,* col. II line 39 (No. 7)

Various deities are requested to appoint the apotropaic nature of the *kušāru.*

^{d}*Nusku* SUKKAL *ṣi-ru mu-tal-*[. . . .] = *NROD,* rev. 1 (No. 23)

ŠU.ÍL.LÁ-incantation to Nusku. *UFBG,* p. 406, Nusku 5.

^{d}*Nusku šàr mu-ši mu-nam-mir uk-li* = *NROD,* obv. 39 (No. 22)

Probably a ŠU.ÍL.LÁ-incantation to Nusku. *UFBG,* p. 406, Nusku 4. (Manuscript $\mathbf{C_1}$ (*LKA* 132) invokes Nusku by his symbol, the lamp, ^{d}*Nūru* (ZÁLAG$^{!}$).

^{d}Nusku tap-pe-e* ^{d}UTU *at-ta = *NADR,* line 3 (No. 54)

UFBG, p. 407, Nusku 12. Included within the ritual instructions.

***ra-am-ku šá ^{d}É-a* DUMU *šip-ri šá ^{d}Asal-lú-hi ana-ku* DINGIR.MEŠ GE$_6$-*tì ina* [. . . . (. .)]** = *ROP,* line 52 (No. 27)

Addressing various supernatural beings. (It does not contain *attunu,* as stated in *UFBG,* p. 428.)

See *ROP,* lines 44-47 (No. 26, page 144), where the same incantation is spoken by the prospective dreamer, without the initial 'legitimizing formula', the incipit here.

si.si.ig a.ga.dè^{ki}.šè ì.gi$_4$.a = *ZI,* line 1 (No. 36)

To the Dream God Sisig. (Manuscript **II** (*PBS* 12/1, No. 29) has sig.sig a.ga. dè^{ki}.šè ì.gi$_4$.in)

This is the Sumerian incipit of *ZI,* the first incantation of the *Dream-Book,* with the Akkadian incipit on manuscript **A** (K. 3758) being: *Zi-qi-qu Zi-qi-qu ^{d}Ma-mú* DINGIR *šá* [MÁŠ.GE$_6$..MEŠ].

^{giš}šinig giš.dili [. . . .] = Sm. 543, line 8' (No. 33)

To the tamarisk.

šu-ut-ti ba-na-at e-gir-ru-ú-a da-mì-iq = *ADRC,* col. II line 58 (No. 9)

(Manuscript **f** (79-7-8, 77) has the predicate *dam-qa-at* instead.)

This is a most peculiar incantation, compiled from many different formulae, and having no formal structure:

i). Lines 58-60 resemble the *egirrû* sentence on *ADRC,* col. I lines 9-10.

ii). Line 63 expands the ideas of *ADRC,* col. III lines 12-15.

iii). Line 66 is a type of 'legitimizing phrase'.

iv). Lines 68-70 are in Sumerian, while the preceeding lines are in Akkadian. Lines 69-70 contain the ZI.PÀD-formula (W. Mayer [*UFBG*], pp. 351, and 353-354), a common concluding expression.

ta-at-tap-ha* ^{d}UTU *ina* KUR ^{GIŠ}ERIN *ri-šu-nik-ka* DINGIR.MEŠ *ha-da-tak-ka a-me-lu-tú = *ADRC,* col. III line 20 (No. 11a)

UFBG, p. 414, Šamaš 35.

UDU.NÍTA *mé-he-e* GÍR IM *ṭa-ab-hu ik-ka-lu mi-tu-tu* = *ADRC,* col. III line 52 (No. 14)

This incantation mentions the "ram of the storm", who is regarded here as the addressee, although it is dead.

ADRC, col. III lines 33-36 (No. 11c) is the same incantation (with minor variants), with the incipit: UDU.NÍTA *mé-he-e* GÍR IM *ṭu-ub-ha.*

^{d}**utu X X an.ki.bi.da me.en gar kur.kur.ra.ke$_4$** = *ADRC,* col. I line 60 (No. 1)

To Utu.

^{d}**UTU *ana*** ^{d}***Í-gì-gì suh$_4$-hu-ru pa-ni$^{!}$-ka*** = *SpTU* 2, No. 21, obv. 7 (No. 34)

To Utu.

^{d}**utu di.ku$_5$ X an.ki.bi.da.ke$_4$** = *ADRC,* col. I line 66 (No. 2)

To Utu.

^{d}**utu di.ku$_5$ me.en di.mu tar.ru.da.ab**
^{d}**UTU *da-a-na-ta di-ni di-in*** = *ADRC,* col. III lines 4-5 (No. 10)

Bilingual ŠU.ÍL.LÁ-incantation to Shamash. *UFBG,* p. 414, Šamaš 34. (Manuscript **I** (*SLTN* 149) has the alternative verbal form tar.dè.)

ADRC, col. I lines 73-77 (No. 3) is fundamentally the same ŠU.ÍL.LÁ-incantation (page 151), with the incipit: ^{d}utu di.ku$_5$.mah di.ku$_5$.da me.en.

^{d}**UTU DI.KU$_5$ *ṣi-i-ru*** = 81-2-4, 166 obv. 12 (No. 37)

UFBG, p. 414, Šamaš 37.

^{d}**utu sag.kal dingir.re.e.ne.ke$_4$** ^{d}**utu pa.è.da.e.dè** = *ADRC,* col. II line 29 (No. 6)

To Utu.

W. Mayer [*UFBG,* p. 414] numbered two fragmentary incantations invoking Shamash:

i). Šamaš 32 = *ADRC,* col. I lines 28ff. (unnumbered on Table 5 on pages 131-134), which appears within the ritual instructions.

ii). Šamaš 33 = *ADRC,* col. II lines 1-16 (sic), whose beginning is that of the *Clod Incantation* (No. 4a), with *lipšur*-phrases (No. 4b), changing to address Shamash in lines 14-16 (No. 4c).

Zi-qi-qu Zi-qi-qu ^{d}***Ma-mú*** **DINGIR *šá* MÁŠ.GE$_6$.MEŠ** = *ZI,* line 1 (No. 36)

See under si.si.ig a.ga.dè^{ki}.šè ì.gi$_4$.a (page 147).

^{d}30 ^{d}NANNA-*ru šu-pu-u* SAG.KAL DINGIR.MEŠ = *SDR,* line 1 (No. 31)

ŠU.ÍL.LÁ-incantation to Sin. *UFBG,* p. 408, Sîn 1.

Manuscript **A_1** (*BMS* 1), rev. 54, states that it contains several incantations from the *bīt rimki* series. The incipit and accompanying rite occur on the ritual tablet of this series: *BBR* 26 + K. 8921 + 10131, col. III lines 52-53. *LM* 12, line 23' also presents the incipit [ÉN] ⌜^{d}30 ^{d}NANNA⌝-*ru* [. . . . .]; W. Mayer [*UFBG,* p. 490] allocated this tablet to *bīt rimki.*

The *bīt rimki* series was performed, on the occasion of a lunar eclipse, to purify the king. The incantation indicates this function by:

i). Concentrating on the luminous aspect of Sin as the Moon God, encouraging him to return to the skies.

ii). Including the *attalû*-formula (see W. Mayer [*UFBG*], pp. 100-102), albeit rather clumsily placed at lines 12-13, and only on manuscripts **A_1** (*BMS* 1) and **B_1** (*LM* 1 + K. 17283):

12). *ina* HUL AN.GE$_6$ ^{d}30 *šá ina* ITI NENNI U$_4$ NENNI GAR-*na*

13). HUL Á.MEŠ GISKIM.MEŠ HUL.MEŠ *là* DÙG.MEŠ *šá ina* É.GAL.MU *u* KUR.MU GÁL-*a*

[12] As a result of the ill portent of the lunar eclipse which occurs/occurred in month X, (on) day Y, [13] (and because of) the evil of ill-boding (and) unpleasant ominous happenings (and) signs which are (occurring) in my palace and (throughout) my land:

The association of this incantation with a lunar eclipse is shown additionally by its use in a namburbi ritual against that type of bad omen: *Cap.* 65, obv. 13'. The ritual on obv. 9'-14' closely resembles the beginning of that of *SDR* (see page 395).

ŠU.ÍL.LÁ-incantations could contain a variety of requests for favours, including some specific dream mentions. At *SDR,* lines 25-26 four manuscripts (**A**, **b**, **A_1**, **B_1**) mention the Dream God Anzagar, and ask for a sign (in a dream) that the sufferer has been purified and reconciled with his personal deities. What is unusual is that manuscripts **A** (BM 78432) and **b** (E. Combe [1908], No. 6) continue with a ritual designed to obtain a pleasant dream. One wonders if it is significant that these two tablets were especially compiled for Shamash-shum-ukin (*SDR,* line 19a). It is unclear how and why an incantation firmly linked to a ritual for a lunar eclipse should have become adapted to a dream ritual. *SDR* is attested separately in the Neo-Assyrian letter *ABL* 450 (= *SAA* 10, No. 298), obv. 9-17 (manuscript **G_1**).

The tablet K. 10151 (E. G. Perry [1907], pl. 3) illustrates a problem surrounding the citation of incantation incipits. Lines 1-2 are the same as those of *SDR,* but from then on the text is completely different, being *UFBG,* p. 408, Sîn 2. Lines 1-3:

1). ÉN ^{d}30 U_4.SAKAR [. . . . .]
2). ^{d}30 *ed-di-i*[*š-šú-u* . . . . . .]
3). DINGIR *nam-ru kàl k*[*i*$^{?}$ . . . .]

Finally, although the incipits of two fragmentary Dream Incantations are missing, parallels exist for the extant lines:

i). Sm. 543, lines 1'-6' (No. 32) - this appears as the conclusion of other incantations: e.g., in two bilingual exorcistic incantations against demons: *CT* 16, pl. 11, col. VI lines 31-42 (see also *UHF,* lines 354-357 and 506-509); and *Šurpu,* Tab. 7, lines 80-87.

ii). K. 5175 + 6001, col. I lines 3'-4' (No. 21) are common concluding phrases: e.g., *ASKT* 9, rev. 26-29 (an incantation against *māmītu,* "curse/oath").

CHAPTER 12: THE POWER OF WORDS

THE RECITATION OF A ŠU.ÍL.LÁ-INCANTATION

Almost the same ŠU.ÍL.LÁ-incantation to Shamash appears on *ADRC,* col. I lines 73-77 and col. III lines 4-15, with the same accompanying ritual (col. I line 78 and col. III line 17). The first passage is in Sumerian, while the second is bilingual (Sumerian with an interlinear Akkadian translation).

This 'special' ŠU.ÍL.LÁ-incantation is unusual in several ways:

i). A 'special' ŠU.ÍL.LÁ normally forms part of an elaborate ceremony, whereas it is the 'pure' ones that constitute a rite in themselves; i.e., often the recitation of the incantation itself is the rite (W. Mayer [*UFBG*], p. 19). Here, the recitation of a 'special' ŠU.ÍL.LÁ suffices as the ritual.

ii). The text is very short, mentioning neither the troubles afflicting the speaker, nor ritual actions (W. Mayer [*UFBG*], p. 18).

iii). It appears in two separate places on *ADRC.* Column III offers a different incipit (lines 4-5) and an extra concluding line and rubric (lines 14-16). One wonders if we have the complete ŠU.ÍL.LÁ text, or whether, originally, there were two distinct incantations, or only one, which has become corrupted.

THE CREATION OF "AN ORACULAR UTTERANCE", *egirrû*(INIM.GAR)

'ORDINARY' UTTERANCES

The basic meaning of *egirrû/igirrû/girrû* is "a placed word" (INIM.GAR), which is taken to denote "an (overheard) utterance". *egirrû* is usually followed by the adjectives *damqu,* "favourable", or *lemnu,* "unfavourable", hence the nuance of expressing good or bad wishes.

The 'ordinary' sense of an *egirrû* is a comment made about, and often overheard by, a person as he goes about his business: e.g., *Ludlul bēl nēmeqi,* Tab. 1, line 53:

> 53). *ina pi-i su-qí le-mun* INIM.GAR-*ú-a*
> My reputation is bad in the mouth of the street.

The deities were frequently asked to ensure that the petitioner would constantly hear favourable things about himself from all sides: e.g., *CT* 16, pl. 8, lines 280-281:

280). igi.mu.ta inim.gar sig_5.ga hé.en.dug_4.ga :

281). *ana pa-ni-ia e-gir-ri* SIG_5-*tì liq-qa-bi*

280-281 May a favourable utterance be spoken to my face!

Šurpu, Tab. 5-6, lines 154-155, compares an (unfavourable) *egirrû* to "a curse/ oath", *māmītu:*

154). inim.gar sag.ba hul nam.[lú].u_{18}.lu.ke_4

155). *ana e-gir-re-e ma-mit lem-ni* [*šá*] *a-me-lu-ti*

154-155(The goddess Uttu spun a thread) against an utterance, the evil curse of mankind.

ORACULAR UTTERANCES

We do not possess much information about divination by *egirrû*s and, while it was thought to be restricted to human speech, it seemed that this was because the listener could interpret the overheard utterance to suit himself (cledonomancy), hence it was not a scholarly practice. This appears more probable than A. L. Oppenheim's [1954-1956, p. 55] view that cledonomancy was either restricted to priestly circles, or was not widely practised.

It has become obvious since that an *egirrû* may derive from a wider spectrum of auditory experiences, which are deemed to be ominous, possibly by hindsight. So far, we have evidence that the sounds of animals and birds, and the messages of ecstatics at Mari were called "utterances" (see on). Also see pages 156-157, where a phrase given in a dream ritual is called an *egirrû.*

a). Human Speech

At certain times, whose significance eludes us, an overheard utterance was considered by the Mesopotamians to have portentous force. A. L. Oppenheim [1954-1956] discussed this nuance, and concluded that it corresponded to the Greek *kledon.* A person overheard a word or phrase spoken by another, and managed 'to interpret' it so that it related to a problem or an idea, over which he was pondering, unbeknownst to the speaker. Such an utterance was regarded as having been inspired by the gods, thereby revealing their intentions towards the listener's plans.

b). Animal And Bird Cries

CT 39, pls. 41-42 (*Šumma ālu,* Tab. 95) covers *egirrû*s in lines 1-33:

1). DIŠ LÚ *ana* DINGIR *i-kar-rab-ma* INIM.GAR *ar-hiš i-ta-nap-pal-*⌈*šú*⌉ *ar-hiš im-man-gar ìl-šu taṣ-lit-su iš-me*

If a man prays to a god, and an utterance promptly replies to him, (or) promptly is consenting/agreeable - (It means) his personal god heard his prayer.

It appears that a man prays to his personal god, then the first cry he hears afterwards is the response *(egirrû)* to his request. The verb referring to the utterance in this text is always *i-pu-ul-šú,* "answered him". (*apālu* is also used when Shamash and Adad give their verdict by placing signs on a sheep's innards during an extispicy.)

This tablet indicates that certain scholarly rules existed for "utterances" when words were not involved. It does not mention human speech or sounds, only the different creatures whose cries might provide the response: donkeys, oxen, rams, dogs, pigs, goats, and birds (lines 26-33). Therefore, the references to the number of times "yes" *(annu)* or "no" *(ula)* occurred (lines 3-14) are probably to be regarded as general affirmative or negative results according to some unspecified principles, rather than auditions of the actual words. Another factor influencing the outcome was the direction of the utterance in relation to the listener (lines 15-25).

c). Messages From Ecstatics At Mari

ARM 10, No. 4 indicates that an *egirrû* at Mari could be an oracle, which was subsequently expanded and amplified by the same prophet in 'cryptic and magical' language, a fact which does not come over in translation. Queen Shibti wrote to her husband Zimri-Lim telling him about the consultations she had made regarding the future of the expedition he was planning against Ishme-Dagan I of Assyria (1781-1741 B.C.), and their results. Obverse 3-11:

3). *aš-šum te₄-em gi-ir-ri-im*
4). *ša be-lí i-la-ku it-ta-tim*
5). *zi-ka-ra-am ù sí-in-ni-iš-tam*
6). MAH *áš-ta-al-ma i-gi-ir-⌈ru⌉-ú-um*
7). *a-na be-lí-ia ma-di-iš da-mi-iq*
8). *a-na Iš-me-ᵈDa-gan qa-tam-ma*
9). *zi-ka-ra-am ù s[í]-in-ni-iš-tam*
10). *áš-ta-al-ma i-gi-ir-ru-šu*
11). *ú-ul da-mi-iq*

[3] Concerning the plan of campaign [4] which my lord undertakes, [5-6] I have asked for omens from the male and female ecstatic(s), and the oracular utterance [7] for my lord is very favourable. [8-10] Likewise, I have asked the male and female (ecstatics about) Ishme-Dagan, and the oracular utterance concerning him [11] is unfavourable.

The writer has followed A. Finet, who noted [1982, p. 51] that he had collated this tablet in the Aleppo Museum, and that G. Dossin's copy [*ARM* 10, pl. 3] was scrupulously exact. On the other hand, J.-M. Durand [1982, p. 43, and n. 2] also collated this tablet, but read *aš-qí* at the beginning of obv. 6, instead of MAH. Earlier, W. von Soden (*Ugarit Forschungen* 1 [1969], p. 221) suggested that the signs were to be read *ú*$^{!}$*-qí,* and translated as „*die Vorzeichen wartete ich ab*". P. Römer [1971, p. 50] accepted this version, but placed these signs at the end of obv. 4.

The different renditions of A. Finet and J.-M. Durand have given rise to diverging opinions of the divinatory procedure whose results are described in *ARM* 10, No. 4. As will be seen, both solutions are problematic. Regarding the proposal of A. Finet, the sign MAH is rarely attested in the Mari repertoire of cuneiform signs [1982, pp. 51-52]. It seems that, in this letter, the writing of obv. 5-6 represents ^{LÚ} *u* ^{MÍ}*mahhêm*(MAH), an uncommon practice. Elsewhere in the Mari texts, *mahhû* is expressed by ^{LÚ}GUB.BA.

J.-M. Durand [1982, p. 43] translated *ARM* 10, No. 4, obv. 3-6 as:

> *"Relativement à la nouvelle de l'expédition future de mon seigneur, j'ai fait boire les 'signes', mâle et femelle, et j'ai posé mes questions."*

He argued [ibid., p. 44] that 'the signs' denoted people, mediums, who subdued their consciousness by drinking an unknown liquid, becoming mouthpieces for the gods. The professional may have been the *āpilum* [ibid., pp. 45-46], and the liquid, blood, water, or wine - from Biblical (dubious) and Classical examples of such a process [ibid., pp. 48-49]. A similar procedure is supposedly attested on *ARM* 10, No. 6, rev. 1'-2':

> 1'). [*aš-šu-um ṭe*$_4$*-em* K]Á.DIN[GIR.RA^{KI}]
> 2'). [*it-t*]*a-*⌜*tim aš-qí*⌝ *áš-ta-al-m*[*a*]

which he translated [*AEM* 1/1, p. 44] as:

> *"Au subjet de Babylone, après avoir fait boire les signes, j'ai posé mes questions."*

It may be possible that the word "omen, sign" came to be used in the sense of "prophet". J.-M. Durand [1982, p. 44] offered the example of BÁRA, "throne dais", being used for "king" (see *DB,* pp. 293-294, especially n. 184, for such a usage in a possible royal tablet of dream omens, K. 273 + 1944b + 9064 = *DB,* pl. 13). A major problem is that on both *ARM* 10, Nos. 4 and 6 the signs he transliterated as *aš-qí* are emended or broken respectively.

C. Wilcke [1983] took a path between the theories of A. Finet and J.-M. Durand. He adopted the reading *aš-qí* in obv. 6, but did not follow J.-M. Durand's idea of drink induced trances. Instead, the queen plied the populace (male and female) with wine to obtain public opinion about Zimri-Lim's proposed campaign, and recorded what she heard, but the words are convoluted for ordinary speech.

If the theories of either A. Finet or J.-M. Durand are correct, then the letter *ARM* 10, No. 4 raises several interesting points relating to our definition of *egirrû*. The queen consulted some ecstatics, whose message is called, quite rightly, "an utterance". This oracular speech was by no means overheard by chance, being a 'direct' response to a question. Also, it was interpreted by the ecstatics after their trances, in response to further questioning by the queen.

Another Mari letter, *AEM* 1/1, No. 196, suggests that an *egirrû* was an oracle. The sender mentions that he had received the following order: obv. 7-10:

> 7). *i-na a-al* DINGIR-*lim wa-aš-ba-at*
> 8). *i-g[e-e]r-ru-ú-um ša i-na* É DINGIR
> 9). *i-[ba-a]š-š[u]-ú ú te-še-mu-ú*
> 10). *a-[n]a ṣe-r[i-i]a šu-up-ra-am*
>
> [7] You reside in the town of the god. [8-10] Send to me the *egirrû*(s) which occur and you hear in the temple (lit., the house of the god).

By the time of Ashurbanipal (in Mesopotamia proper), *egirrûs* were regarded as something different from prophetic messages: e.g., Cylinder B, col. V lines 93-96 (M. Streck [*VAB* 7], p. 120):

> 93). [*ina tukulti* ^{d}*Aššur u*] ^{d}*Marduk* DINGIR.MEŠ GAL.MEŠ EN.MEŠ-*ia*
> 94). *šá ú-tak-kil-ú-in-ni*
> 95). *ina* GISKIM.MEŠ MÁŠ.GE$_6$ INIM.GAR *ši-pír mah-he-e*
> 96). *qé-reb* ^{URU}*Tul-li-iz* ŠI.ŠI-*šú aš-kun*
>
> [93] [Trusting in Ashur and] Marduk, the great gods, my lords, [94] who encouraged me [95] by omens, by a dream (see lines 49ff.), by an oracular utterance, (and by) the message of an ecstatic, [96] I accomplished his (the Elamite king's) decisive defeat within Tulliz.

(Also see (ii) below.)

ORACULAR UTTERANCES AND DREAMS

Whatever the scope of an *egirrû,* several passages indicate that the Mesopotamians held a nocturnal dream (both prognostic - (i), and (ii) below, and the Ashurbanipal passage above; and symptomatic (iii)) and a day-time auditory experience to be analogous ominous experiences: e.g.:

i). S. Greengus [1979], No. 23, obv. 12'-14':

12'). *a-na La-ma-sà-ni be-⸢el⸣-tim [aš]-pu-ur*

13'). *ù šu-na-a-t[im] ù i-gi-ir-re-e*

14'). *ša a-mu-ru ù e-eš-mu-ú aš-pu-ur-ši*

[12'] [I] wrote to Lamassani, (my) lady, [13'-14'] informing her (about) the dreams and oracular utterances which I (respectively) saw and heard.

ii). Esarhaddon Assur A, col. II lines 18-22 (R. Borger [1956], p. 2, §2):

18). *i-da-at dum-qí*

19). *ina* MÁŠ.GE$_6$ *u ger-re-e*

20). *ša šur-šu-di kar-ri*

21). *šul-bur* BAL-*ia*

22). *it-ta-nab-šá-a* UGU-*ia*

[18] Favourable omens [19] in dream(s) and by oracular utterance(s) [20] concerning the firm establishment of my throne, [21] (and) the prolongation of my reign [22] constantly occurred to me.

iii). *ADRC,* col. II lines 58-60:

58). ÉN *šu-ut-ti ba-na-at e-gir-ru-ú-a da-mì-⸢iq⸣*

59). *ma-har* ^{d}30 *u* ^{d}UTU *dam-q[at]* : *ma-har* ⸢^{d}⸣30 ⸢*u*⸣ ^{d}UTU *dam-[qat]*

60). *ma-har* ^{d}30 *u* ^{d}UTU *dam-[qat]* : *šu-ut-ti ba-na-at e-gir-ru-ú-a* SIG$_5$

[58] Incantation: "My dream is excellent. My oracular utterance is favourable. [59] (The dream) is pleasant before Sin and Shamash. (The dream) [is] pleasant before Sin and Shamash. [60] (The dream) [is] pleasant before Sin and Shamash. My dream is excellent (and) my oracular utterance is favourable."

The divine message received in the dream recorded on the *Weidner Chronicle* is called an *egirrû* at obv. 33 (page 234). (The reference in the *Epic of Tukulti-Ninurta I* (*MAOG* 12/2 [1938], p. 15), col. IV line 45, to *e-g[ir] šu-ut-ti-ia* has been collated by P. Machinist to *e-⸢em⸣*; see *CAD Š$_3$,* p. 407b.)

There is no evidence to support the idea of S. Parpola [*LAS* vol. 2, p. 214] that the *egirrû* mentioned in the incantation of *SDR* (line 22) was a dream-oracle.

a). The Creation Of An Oracular Utterance As A Dream Ritual

An *egirrû* is used in two rituals on *ADRC,* col. I lines 7-12, and 12a-g, to avert the evils of an unpleasant symptomatic dream. In the more complete rite, the dreamer says: lines 9-10:

9). MÁŠ.GE$_6$ *at-tu-lu*

10). [*ma-har*] ^{d}30 *u* ^{d}UTU *dam-qat dam-qat-ma dam-*⌈*qat*$^{?}$⌉ *dam-qa*[*t*]

$^{9-10}$ The dream which I saw is pleasant [before] Sin and Shamash. It is pleasant, and it is pleasant. It is pleasant.

(Note the similar phrasing in an incantation, *ADRC,* col. II lines 58-60, (iii) above.) In this way, "[he] makes a favourable oracular utterance for himself", *i-gir-ri ra-ma-ni-šu* [*ú-da*]*m-mì-iq-ma* (lines 11-12).

There is no indication that the dreamer overheard another person speaking and, since the phrase to be spoken is specified, what was an overheard chance utterance has turned into a ritual formula. B. Landsberger (*MAOG* 4 [1928-1929], p. 316) stated that if unfavourable utterances were heard, one could imagine a good one for oneself *(eg. ramanišu).* Yet, the verb *qabû*(DUG$_4$.GA), "to say", is used in line 9 of the above dream rite.

This is the only certain example of someone creating his own *egirrû* known to the writer. S. Parpola's [*LAS* vol. 2, p. 211 on *LAS* 217] interpretation of *ABL* 1347 (= *SAA* 10, No. 305) is dubious. The *piqittu* who is the subject of this letter is apparently a teething royal baby [*LAS* vol. 2, pp. 109 and 209], so he cannot speak coherently. When the sender wrote on rev. 2:

2). *e-ge-ra-šú as-se-me*

I have heard his oracular utterance.

S. Parpola stated that this meant that the correspondent had heard the baby gurgling in his sleep, thus providing his own *egirrû.* If a dream could be seen concerning the infant (rev. 1; page 237), surely this *egirrû* could have originated from an extraneous source, agreeing with other examples of oracular utterances?

CHAPTER 13: AMULETS AND CHARMS

AMULETS

The Mesopotamian amulets which have survived are usually clay, metal, or stone objects, bearing an inscription and/or reliefs. Small amulets were worn around the neck: e.g., the tablet BM 78613 (= Bu. 88-5-12, 524) discussed by N. Wasserman [1994].

Some larger examples are in "the characteristic amulet shape", a rectangular tablet with a projection at the top, which is pierced through lengthways. The tablet then could either be suspended from a cord or hung on a wooden or metal rod (e.g., J. N. Postgate [1987], p. 57) inside or outside a building. Occasionally other textual genres have this shape: e.g., the *Khorsabad King List* (*JNES* 1 [1942], p. 248) and its duplicate, the *"SDAS" King List* (*JNES* 13 [1954], p. 210). It seems that this shape originated for practical reasons (though it was not widely adopted), and became associated with beneficient content (E. Reiner [1960], p. 155). Such tablets could be hung up for reference purposes (e.g., the King Lists above), or for display: e.g., BM 104410 (= 55-12-5, 460), an inscription of Shalmaneser III in Ninurta's temple at Nimrud. This text can be read like a modern book, instead of turning it over upwards to read the reverse, one turns the 'page' (A. K. Grayson [1991a], p. 19).

Many amulets are limited to one purpose, but see the *Universal Namburbi* incantation written on the *Plague Amulets* (page 112), while pages 50-51 discuss a Lamashtu amulet with an incantation against a demon who has been causing nightmares.

See pages 94-95 on an amulet in the form of a wooden "mad lion" figurine worn around the neck (*KAR* 26), and on a charm necklace (*BMS* 12 (with *LM* 40) + K. 20155), both created as tangible *maṣṣar šulme u balāṭi*s.

CHARMS

Charms consist either of various natural objects placed together inside a leather bag (pages 161-162, and 163) or of stone necklaces (page 163); either being worn around the neck.

The Mesopotamians were keen on listing all possible objects and, in the omen texts, all eventualities. The numerous lists of charms for specific purposes lead one to wonder if all were actually made (also see page 172). If a charm is attested in a rite (e.g., those occurring in the namburbi rituals mentioned on page 166), it probably was made. However, such attestations are rare, and none occur for the dream charms. Archaeology cannot help us since the damp soil of Iraq will have caused the leather bags, their vegetable contents, and the cords to rot long ago. Any stone pebbles/beads remaining will be loose, and not obviously significant to excavators.

Lists of stone necklaces exist, arranged in sections called *ṭurru*(DUR), lit., "a band". The number and/or the order of the stones comprising a particular charm may vary from list to list (e.g., page 167), while the charm itself may occur in different "bands". We do not know if these variations are important; i.e., whether different charms are involved, or if they are only scribal elaborations or errors.

It is not clear, in any society, how charms are envisaged as working for the benefit of the wearer. To their inherent power is added the goodwill of the donor, and the all-important belief of the recipient in their efficacy. Nor is it easy to distinguish between the apotropaic and the beneficent qualities of a charm; frequently both are involved: e.g., a pleasant dream occurs following the repulsion of evil powers. The dream charms have been classified on pages 164-168 according to their titles.

Often amulets and charms are created specifically for a certain person, by a dedicatory inscription, or by phrases spoken during the collection of the ingredients respectively. Such a charm will be efficacious only for that individual, devoid of its powers if lost, or withdrawing them if stolen.

None of the extant dream charms appear to be personalized in this way, but we possess few details about their manufacture, usage, or how long a dream charm was worn. It may have been worn either only at night or for a specific period; there are examples elsewhere of stone necklaces being hung around the sufferer's neck for one day (*Cap.* 20, obv. 5'-6'; S. M. Maul [1994], pp. 278-282), and for seven days (*Cap.* 10, rev. 20; S. M. Maul [ibid.], pp. 336-343, line 51). Alternatively, a dream charm may have been worn until its 'magic' was deemed to be 'discharged', whereupon it may have been returned to the ritual expert to be 'recharged' or a replacement requested. If so, the practitioner probably broke the charm into its separate components from which he could create another charm for somebody else. H. Webster [1948, p. 138] mentioned that in modern Africa a charm which has cured a disease is kept and worn as an ornament, ready to work if the symptoms return. Accordingly, one's personal collection of charms grows throughout one's life.

PHYSICAL CATEGORIES OF MESOPOTAMIAN CHARMS

ina KUŠ

A common type of charm (thirteen examples out of seventeen) was formed of pieces of minerals and plants placed together *ina maški*(KUŠ), "in (a) leather/skin (bag)". Very occasionally the animal whose hide is to be so used is indicated: e.g., on *CT* 23, pls. 15-22 +, col. IV line 14, and *SpTU* 4, No. 134, rev.? 8 a dead cow's? hide is laced up with a dormouse's tendon (see page 165 about this rodent).

In fact, *ina* KUŠ appears to be an abbreviation for two standard phrases found at the end of instructions to make charms:

i). *ina maški*(KUŠ) *ina kišādi*(GÚ)*-šú tašakkan*(GAR*-an*)
You place (the previously mentioned ingredients) in (a) leather (bag) around his (the sufferer's) neck.
(This version has been chosen by the writer, for no special reason.)

ii). *ina maški*(KUŠ) *tašappi*(DÙ.DÙ(*-pí)) ina kišādi*(GÚ)*-šú tašakkan*(GAR*-an*)
(Having placed these ingredients) in (a) leather (bag), you lace (the edges) together. You place (the charm) around his neck.

AHw 1, *epuštu,* p. 231b translated the unit KUŠ DÙ.DÙ.BI as *„Beutel für Ritual".* However, W. Farber [1973], deduced from parallel passages, where *šapû* was written out syllabically, that this verb was represented by DÙ.DÙ*-pí*(= .BI), not *epuštāšu,* "its ritual". (There are no lexical attestations of this equation.) W. Farber [ibid., p. 66] went on to define the meaning of *šapû* from its use in the ritual to make a *lilissu*-kettledrum (*KAR* 60). The skin was placed over the drum's opening, and held in place by cords threaded through prepared holes in the skin and adjacent fastenings, pulling it taut across. Thus, *šapû* means "to lace together".

mēlu

The recitation of an incantation over a *me-eli*(UGU) or *tak-ṣi-ri* (page 163) is prescribed on *ADRC,* col. IV line 14 (see *CAD* M_2, pp. 14-15 for other examples). *mēlu* has been variously translated, with opinions divided between a charm (e.g., E. K. Ritter [1965], p. 310; her 'amulet' equalling a 'charm', as defined in this study), and poultice (e.g., *CAD* M_2, p. 14b; and *AHw* 2, *mêlu,* p. 643b).

mašku and *mēlu* frequently occur together: e.g., in the myth explaining the divine origin of *mēlu*s (*LKA* 146). Ea gives Nabu twenty-one charms all ending with *ina* KUŠ (obv. 24 to rev. 15), which are summarized on rev. 16 as:

16). 21! A-UGU *ša* KA ᵈ*É-a*
Twenty-one! *mēlu*s from the mouth of Ea.

W. Farber [1973, p. 66] regarded both *mašku* and *mēlu* as a leather piece, or a bag, which was filled, and its edges drawn together by a laced cord. (*mēlu* possibly derives from the verb *e'ēlu,* "to bind"; see E. Reiner [1959-1960].) The cord may have been used to hang the leather bag around the neck, or perhaps it was threaded onto another string: e.g., *SpTU* 3, No. 85, col. IV line 24':

> 24'). NA_4.MEŠ *u me*-UGU *ina* GU GADA È *ina* GÚ-*šú* GAR-*an*
>
> You string the stones and/or a *mēlu* onto a flax cord (and) you place (this charm) around his neck.

mašku and *mēlu* are not used as synonyms in other texts (e.g., *STT* 95 + 295, col. I lines 11-12, below), and the writer prefers to understand *mašku* as denoting the leather bag in which the ingredients were placed, while *mēlu* refers to the bag plus contents.

That a *mēlu* had no 'practical' healing value is indicated by its attribution to the lore of the exorcist, on *STT* 95 + 295, col. I lines 11-12:

> 11). 7 Ú.[H]Á! *an-nu-te*
>
> 12). *ina* KUŠ *ina* Ì *ina* KAŠ *me-e-lu lat-k*[*u*] ⌜*ni-ṣir*⌝*-ti* LÚMAŠ.MAŠ
>
> These seven plants (applied) in (a) leather (bag), in oil, (or) in beer (are) a proven charm?, the (craft) knowledge of the exorcist.

The significance of these alternatives is unclear. There are other examples of similar practices in connection with charms: e.g.:

i). *BAM* 315, col. IV lines 27-36 (pages 167-168) contains two charms for the same title. Lines 27-31 concern the manufacture of a leather bag charm. Lines 32-36 have been treated as a charm, but it is unusual that the ingredients are immersed (lit., buried, *temēru*) in honey and ghee for three days.

ii). *Cap.* 20 (S. M. Maul [1994], pp. 278-282) is a namburbi ritual directed against a snake. It presents two rites which mention different stone necklaces. On obv. 4'-6' the necklace is strung, and placed around the sufferer's neck. In the second ceremony various offerings are presented. Then, at obv. 16'-19', the pieces of stone are placed in an oil offering before being placed around the neck (*ana* ŠÀ Ì.GIŠ (stone names) [GAR-*an*]).

takṣīru* AND *mālalu

Following the attribution of *mēlu*s to the exorcist, it is interesting to note that *mēlu*s are not mentioned in the list of his professional manuals, *KAR* 44. However, rev. 3 mentions:

3). *tak-ṣi-ri u ma-la-li*

(tablets of) *takṣīru*s and *mālalu*s;

takṣīru is a derivative of the verb *kaṣāru,* "to tie", and seems to constitute yet another type of charm. F. R. Kraus [1970, pp. 59-60] listed the different renditions, and suggested that it was a stone bead necklace.

Neither of the Akkadian dictionaries is certain what a *mālalu* was, except to suggest the word possibly derives from the verb *alālu,* "to suspend" [*CAD* M_1, pp. 160-161; *AHw* 2, p. 594b]. *mālalu* appears to have two nuances from the citations: the one is a type of liquid container; the other is in the passage above, where it possibly denotes a charm variety. If *takṣīru* is a stone necklace, then possibly *mālalu* denotes the leather bag charms, or *mēlu*s. Then, *KAR* 44, rev. 3 can be interpreted as referring to the numerous charm lists, which otherwise are not mentioned on this tablet. J. Bottéro [1985b, pp. 80-81] had already suggested that this line referred to various types of charms, but did not distinguish between the two words.

DREAM CHARMS

The scope and type of Mesopotamian charms dealing with dreams are shown in Table 7 on page 164.

In addition, there are a few charms mainly concerned with other matters, but which do mention dreams:

i). *BAM* 316, col. II lines 5'-25', contains a list of woes in lines 5'-16', with the purpose in line 15' (amongst several others):

15'). MÁŠ.GE_6.MEŠ-*šú ana* SIG_5-⌈*tì*⌉

(to turn) his dreams to good luck,

A leather bag charm is made, and line 23' presents one desired ritual result:

23'). MÁŠ.GE_6.MEŠ-*šú* SIG_5.MEŠ

his dreams will become favourable;

ii). *BAM* 316, col. VI line 29':

29'). ⌈ana HUL⌉ MÁŠ.GE_6.MEŠ Á.MEŠ GISKIM.MEŠ [HUL. MEŠ/*là* DÙG.(GA.)MEŠ]

For the evil of [bad/baleful] dreams, ominous happenings (and) signs:

iii). *SpTU* 2, No. 22, col. I lines 30'-38' (page 56).

TABLE 7: TYPES OF DREAM CHARMS

Ritual Purpose	Leather Bag	Stone Necklace	*takṣīru* or *mēlu*
To avert (10 examples)	A, III: 61-63 A, III: 64-66 A, III: 67-68 A, IV: 1-2 A, IV: 3 A, IV: 4 A, IV: 15-16 C, IV: 13-14 Q, rev.? 7-8 T, rev. 12'-16'		
To Make Favourable (4 examples)		A, IV: 5-7 S, III: 1 (+) X, IV: 23	A, IV: 8-14
To Obtain A Pleasant Dream (3 examples)	B, IV: 27-31 B, IV: 32-36 P, IV: 5-6		

A = *ADRC* B = *BAM* 315 C = *CT* 23, pls. 15-22 +
P = *SpTU* 2, No. 22 Q = *SpTU* 4, No. 134 S = *BAM* 400
T = *STT* 107 (+) 246 X = *STT* 275

(See the text edition of *ADRC* (pages 249-312) for the text of the charms listed, but not quoted, in the following sections.)

TO AVERT

ADRC, col. III lines 61-68 are contained within one ruled-off section, although three separate charms (a-c below) are listed with the same title. The beginning of col. IV is broken, but the three charms (d-f) enumerated in lines 1-4 (again undivided) probably follow on from the previous column.

a). *ADRC,* Column III Lines 61-63

b). *ADRC,* Column III Lines 64-66

c). *ADRC,* Column III Lines 67-68

d). *ADRC,* Column IV Lines 1-2

e). *ADRC,* Column IV Line 3

f). *ADRC,* Column IV Line 4

g). *ADRC,* Column IV Lines 15-16

h). *CT* 23, Plates 15-22 +, Column IV Lines 13-14

CT 23, pls. 15-22 + is an extensive collection of rituals against ghosts. Column IV lines 13-14 contains a charm against specific dream content:

13). [DIŠ NA *in*]*a* MÁŠ.GE_6-*šú* Ú[Š.MEŠ I]GI.MEŠ ^{Ú}HAR.⌜HAR ^{Ú}⌝[. . . . .]

14). [*ina*] KUŠ ÁB.RI.RI.GA *ina* SA [PÉŠ.GIŠ.ÙR.RA DÙ.DÙ *ina* GÚ-*šú* GAR-*an*]

^{13} [If a man] repeatedly sees dead [people] in his dream(s): Thyme$^{?}$ [. . . . .] ^{14} [you lace together in] a dead cow's$^{?}$ hide with [a dormouse's] tendon. [You place (this charm) around his neck].

(The *arrabu*-rodent is usually taken to be a dormouse, but R. D. Biggs [*ŠZG,* p. 4, n. 25] disputed this identification, stating that there was no evidence that the dormouse ever lived in Mesopotamia. *CAD* A_2, p. 302b offered the alternative of jerboa$^{?}$.)

j). *SpTU* 4, No. 134, Reverse$^{?}$ 7-8

SpTU 4, No. 134 is a fragmentary charm list, the only two extant titles mention repeatedly seeing dead people. Reverse$^{?}$ 7-8 is another ritual against dream content:

7). [DIŠ NA *ina* M]ÁŠ.GE_6-*šú* ÚŠ.MEŠ IGI.MEŠ GAZI^{SAR} KUR.KUR EME UR.GI_7 ^{TÚG}NÍG.DÁRA.ŠU.LÁL

8). [*ina* KUŠ] ÁB.RI.RI.GA *ina* SA <PÉŠ>.ÙR.RA DÙ.DÙ-*pí ina* GÚ-*šú* GAR-*an*

$^{7-8}$ [If a man] repeatedly sees dead people [in] his dream(s): (Pieces of) *kasû, atā'išu*(-plant), the 'dog's tongue'(-plant), (and) a dirty rag you lace together [in] a dead cow's$^{?}$ [hide] with a dormouse's tendon. You place (this charm) around his neck.

(E. von Weiher [*SpTU* 4, p. 44] restored [*ina šer'an*] at the beginning of line 8, but see *CT* 23, pls. 15-22 +, col. IV line 14, above.)

k). *STT* 107 (+) 246, Reverse 12'-16'

12'). DIŠ N[A] ⌜MÁŠ⌝.GE$_6$.<MEŠ> *pár-d*[*a*$^{!}$*-a-ti* . . . .]
13'). BÚR-*ri-šú lu* [. . . . .]

14'). NUMUN ^{Ú}HAB ^{Ú}[. . . . .]
15'). [^{Ú}KUR.K]UR ^{GIŠ}ŠINI[G . . . .]
16'). Trace

The rest of the tablet is broken away.

12'-13' If a man [saw] frightening dream<s>: (In order) to dissolve it (the evil of the dreams) or [. . . . .]

14'-15' Seeds of the *būšānu*-plant, the [. . . .]-plant [. . . . the *atā'išu*-plant], tamarisk [. . . . .]

TO MAKE A BAD DREAM FAVOURABLE

a). *ADRC,* Column IV Lines 5-7

b). *ADRC,* Column IV Lines 8-14

c). *BAM* 400, Column III Line 1

BAM 400 contains titles of stone necklaces, each a charm intended to ward off a specific evil (F. Köcher [1963]). No details of the individual charms are given, only the number of stones comprising them, so one has to look elsewhere (see below for examples). Since it is not a standard charm list, *BAM* 400 has been regarded in various ways:

i). V. Scheil [1925] saw it as an omen catalogue.

ii). J. Nougayrol [1941, p. 76, n. 1] stated that it was a namburbi catalogue. Three of the tabulated charms do appear in such rituals:

  a). Column II line 5' on *Cap.* 20, obv. 4'-6' (S. M. Maul [1994], pp. 278-282).

  b). Column II line 8' on *Cap.* 25a (*OECT* 6, pl. 6) + 24, obv. 17-19 (S. M. Maul [ibid.], pp. 234-248).

  c). Column II line 9' on *Cap.* 10, rev. 17-19 (S. M. Maul [ibid.], p. 341, lines 48-51).

iii). A. L. Oppenheim [*DB*, pp. 295-296] regarded it as a list of incantations (correct his reference from Si 18); see page 100.

BAM 400, col. III line 1:

1). 13 ˹MÁŠ˺.GE6 [SIG_5]

Thirteen (stones) [to make] a dream [favourable]

is probably the charm appearing in three other lists (*BAM* 376, col. I lines 28'-30'; *BAM* 377, col. III lines 20-22; and *BAM* 384, rev. 1-5), albeit these have fourteen stones. Composite lines:

A). ^{NA_4}GUG ^{NA_4}ZA.GÌN *ni-bu* ŠUBA PA NÍR ^{NA_4}BABBAR. DILI

B). ^{NA_4}*hi-li-ba* ZÚ GE_6 KUR-*nu* DAB ^{NA_4}AN.BAR ^{NA_4}ZÁLAG ZÚ SIG_7

C). SIG_7.SIG_7 14 NA_4.MEŠ MÁŠ.GE_6.MEŠ HUL.MEŠ SIG_5

^{A} Carnelian, lapis lazuli, the *(jā)nibu*(-stone), the *šubû*(-stone), the *ajartu*(-shell), the *hulālu*(-stone), the *pappardilû*-stone, ^{B} the *hilibû*-stone, black obsidian, magnetite, iron, the *zalāqu*-stone, green obsidian, ^{C} (and) the *urrīqu*(-stone are) fourteen stones (for a charm) to make bad dreams favourable.

d). *STT* 275, Column IV Line 23

23). [. . . .] ˹X˺ *šit-tu u* MÁŠ.GE_6.MEŠ HU[L.MEŠ] ˹SIG_5˺. MEŠ

[. . . .] . (is a stone) to make favourable sleep and bad dreams.

TO OBTAIN A PLEASANT DREAM

(Other rituals with the same purpose are covered in chapter 18.)

a). *BAM* 315, Column IV Lines 27-36

BAM 315, col. IV lines 27-31 are duplicated by *BAM* 316, col. I lines 20'-24'.

27). *ana* DINGIR *u* ^{d}$EŠ_{18}$.TÁR GEŠTUG.MEŠ-*šú* BAD. BAD-*u*

28). MÁŠ.GE_6 SIG_5-*ta na-ṭa-li pa it hu* ^{NA_4}ZÚ ˹GE_6˺

29). ^{Ú}*nu-ṣa-bu* ^{Ú}*a-ra-ri-a-nu* ^{Ú}EME.UR.GI_7

30). ^{Ú}*a-ra-an-tu* SUHUŠ ^{GIŠ}DÌH *šá* UGU KI.MAH *ina* KUŠ

31). *ina še-rì ana* DINGIR-*šú* KI.ZA.ZA-*ma* A.RA.ZU.BI GIŠ.TUK

32). *ana* KIMIN MUN *eme-sal-lì pul-*[*lu*]*-ur-tú* KÙ. BABBAR *u* KÙ.GI NIR$^{!}$(KID)

33). 3 [*u*$_{4}$]-*me ina* LÀL$^{!}$ Ì.NUN.NA *te-te-*[*mi*]*r ina* U$_{4}$.4. KÁM E$_{11}$-*lam*$^{!}$(*du*)-*ma*

34). *ana* ⌜IGI⌝ <d>20$^{!}$(30) *ki-a-am* DUG$_{4}$.G[A] ⌜X⌝ *sag na ku mu-sal-li-mu*

35). DINGIR *ze-né-e* ^{d}XV z[*e-n*]*é-ti* ^{d}UTU DIB-*ti* SILIM-*mì*

36). DUG$_{4}$.GA *ina ze* ⌜X X⌝ SILIM-*mu*

---

[27] In order that (his) god and/or (his) goddess instruct him (lit., open his ears), [28-30] (and in order) to see a favourable dream: You place (pieces of) . . . black obsidian, the *nuṣābu*-plant, the *arariānu*-plant, the 'dog's tongue'-plant, the *arantu*-grass, (and of) a root of a *baltu* thorn-bush which (grows) over a grave in (a) leather (bag around his neck).

[31] He prostrates himself in the morning before his personal god, and his prayer will be heard.

[32-33] In order ditto (i.e., to "dream"): You immerse (lit., bury) (pieces of) *emesallu*(-salt), *pallurtu*(-plant), silver, and (of) 'proper' gold in honey (and) ghee for three days.

You lift (them) out on the fourth day, and [34] you speak as follows before Shamash!:

"O . . . . the reconciler [35] of the angry god (and) of the angry goddess. O Shamash, propitiate (their) divine wrath!"

[36] You say (this, and) . . . . they will become reconciled.

---

b). *SpTU* 2, No. 22, Column IV Lines 5-6

5). *ana* NA DINGIR-*šú u* ^{d}XV-*šú ina* SAG-⌜*šu*⌝ GUB-*zi-ma* MÁŠ.GE$_{6}$ SIG$_{5}$-*tú na-ṭa-lu*

6). ^{NA_4}ŠUBA ^{NA_4}⌜NÍR⌝ ^{NA_4}AŠ.GÌ.GÌ ina KUŠ

[5] So that a man will cause his personal god and/or his personal goddess to stand at his head (while he sleeps), and (also) in order to see a favourable dream: [6] You place (pieces of) the *šubû*-stone, the *hulālu*-stone, (and of) the *ašgikû*-stone in (a) leather (bag around his neck).

THE CHARM INGREDIENTS

The forty-nine ingredients attested in the dream rituals are listed in Table 8 on pages 169-171. There are:

i). Twenty-eight minerals and shells, out of which thirteen have been identified, two placed as to type, and the remaining thirteen unknown (Nos. 1-28).

ii). Eighteen plants, four of which have been identified, two placed as to type, and twelve are unknown (Nos. 29-46).

iii). Three miscellaneous ingredients - a green frog, an ostrich egg-shell, and a dirty rag (Nos. 47-49).

TABLE 8: THE INGREDIENTS OF MESOPOTAMIAN DREAM CHARMS

	Material	**Identi-fication**	**To avert**	**To Make Favourable**	**To Obtain Pleasant**
1	^{NA4}AN.BAR = *parzillu*	iron	A III: 68 M	S III: 1 D	
2	^{NA4}AŠ.GÌ.GÌ = *ašgikû*	--			P IV: 6 M
3	^{NA4}*(j)ašpû*	jasper		A IV: 5 D	
4	^{NA4}BABBAR.DILI = *pappardilû*	--		S III: 1 D	
5	*aban*(NA$_4$) *gabî*	alum	A IV: 1, 4 M		
6	^{NA4}GUG = *sāmtu*	carnelian		S III: 1 D	
7	^{NA4}*hilibû*	--		S III: 1 D	
8	KA.A.AB.BA = *imbû tâmti*	--	A IV: 15 M		
9a	KA.GI.NA.DAB = *šadânu ṣāb(i)tu*	magnetite	A IV: 1 M		
9b	^{NA4}KUR-*nu* DAB.BA = *šadânu ṣāb(i)tu*	magnetite		S III: 1 D A IV 6 D	
10	KÙ.BABBAR = *kaspu*	silver	A III: 68 M		B IV: 32 H
11	KÙ.GI = *hurāṣu*	gold	A III: 68 M		B IV: 32 H
12	NA$_4$ ^{d}LAMMA = *aban lamassi*	--		A IV: 5 D	
13	*ṭābat*(MUN) *emesalli*	type of salt	A III: 63 M		B IV: 32 H
14	*(jā)nibu*	--		S III: 1 D	
15	^{NA4}NÍG.URUDU.UD	--		A IV: 7 D	
16	NÍR = *hulālu*	--		S III: 1 D	P IV: 6 M
17	PA = *aj(j)artu*	type of shell		S III: 1 D	
18	PIŠ$_{10}$.ITU$_4$ = *kibrītu*	black sulphur	A III: 66 M		

TABLE 8 (Continued): THE INGREDIENTS OF MESOPOTAMIAN DREAM CHARMS

	Material	Identi-fication	To avert		To Make Favourable		To Obtain Pleasant	
19	^{NA4}*sahhû*	--			A IV: 5	D		
20	SIG$_7$.SIG$_7$ = *urrīqu*	--			S III: 1	D		
21	ŠUBA = *šubû*	--			S III: 1	D	P IV: 6	M
22	ÚH.ITU$_4$ = *ru'tītu*	yellow sulphur	A IV: 2	M				
23	NA$_4$ UR = *aban bālti*	--			A IV: 5	D		
24	^{NA4}URUDU NÍTA = *erû zikaru*	'male' copper			A IV: 6	D		
25	^{NA4}ZA.GÌN = *uqnû*	lapis lazuli			S III: 1	D		
26	^{NA4}ZÁLAG = *zalāqu*	--			S III: 1	D		
27	ZÚ GE$_6$ = *ṣurru ṣalmu*	black obsidian			S III: 1	D	B IV: 28	H
28	ZÚ SIG$_7$ = *ṣurru arqu*	green obsidian			S III: 1	D		
29	^{Ú}*arantu*	type of grass					B IV: 30	M
30	^{Ú}*arariānu*	--					B IV: 29	M
31	^{GIŠ}DÌH = *baltu*	type of thorn-bush					B IV: 30	M
32	^{Ú}*elkulla* + ^{Ú}*eli*(UGU)-*kulla*	--	A III: 65 A IV 3	M M				
33	^{Ú}EME UR.GI$_7$ = *lišān kalbi*	--	A IV: 4 Q: 7	M M			B IV: 29	M
34	^{GIŠ}ESI = *ušû*	ebony$^?$	A III: 68	M				
35	GAZI^{SAR} = *kasû*	--	Q: 7	M				
36	^{Ú}HAB = *būšānu*	--	A III: 62 T: 14'	M M				
37	^{Ú}HAR.HAR = *hašû*	thyme$^?$	C IV: 13	M				
38	*(iš)pallurtu*	--					B IV: 32	H
39	^{Ú}KUR.KUR = *atā'išu*	--	A III: 62 Q: 7 T: 15'	M M M				
40	^{Ú}LÚ.U$_{19}$.LU = *amīlānu*	--	A IV: 3	M				

TABLE 8 (Continued): THE INGREDIENTS OF MESOPOTAMIAN DREAM CHARMS

	Material	Identi-fication	To avert		To Make Favourable	To Obtain Pleasant
41	*nikiptu*	--	A IV: 16	M		
42	^{Ú}*nuṣābu*	--				B IV: 29 M
43	^{Ú}SIKIL = *sikillu*	--	A IV: 4	M		
44	^{GIŠ}ŠINIG = *bīnu*	tamarisk	T: 15'	M		
45	^{Ú}*tarmuš*	lupin	A IV: 2, 15	M		
46	Ú.BABBAR = *šammu peṣû*	--	A III: 63	M		
47	LA NUNUZ GA.NU$_{11}$^{MUŠEN} = *haṣab pelî lurmi*	ostrich egg-shell	A III: 67	M		
48	BIL.ZA.ZA SIG$_7$ = *muṣa''irānu arqu*	green frog	A III: 67	M		
49	^{TÚG}NÍG.DÁRA.ŠU.LÁL = *ulāpu lupputu*	dirty rag	Q: 7	M		

A = *ADRC* B = *BAM* 315 C = *CT* 23, pls. 15-22 +

D = *ina* DUR = stone necklace H = in honey and ghee M = *ina* KUŠ = leather pouch

P = *SpTU* 2, No. 22 Q = *SpTU* 4, No. 134, rev.? S = *BAM* 400 and related charm lists

T = *STT* 107 (+) 246

Many of the charm ingredients cannot be positively identified. Sometimes we know that a type of grass or thorn-bush was intended, but often not even that much. No attempt has been made here to study the ingredients in greater detail - a full-scale piece of work in itself, especially since some of the identifications of *DAB* and *DACG* are disputed now.

The Arabian ostrich, which once roamed as far as southern Iraq, became extinct long ago. Ostrich egg-shell cups and fragments are most common from the third and second millennium B.C. strata of Mesopotamian sites (P. R. S. Moorey [1994], p. 128). On the other hand, the ostrich appears as an art motif, and in Assyrian royal inscriptions, of the first millennium B.C. For example, Ashurnasirpal II mentioned large numbers of ostriches in descriptions of royal hunts: e.g., ND 1104 (*Iraq* 14 [1952], pl. 2), col. II lines 88-89 - 200 ostriches were cut down like caged birds; and line 92 - 140 ostriches were captured alive.

CAD L, *lupputu,* pp. 252-253 presents other examples of a dirty rag in charms and medical prescriptions.

We do not know the theory lying behind the composition of the charms; namely, why certain combinations were considered efficacious for dreams, but not, for example, for reconciling angry personal deities. We can be sure that the ingredients would have been significant for the Mesopotamians, probably by sympathetic associations.

IMITATION INGREDIENTS

The ingredients of charms usually depend on local availability. We have seen (page 169) that more minerals were used in the dream charms than plants. This is despite the fact that Iraq does not possess any precious or semi-precious stones or metal ores (e.g., G. Roux [1980], p. 30), having to import them all from distant places. A trade in minerals (and building timber) developed in early times: e.g., obsidian was transported throughout the Near East from c. 7500 B.C. onwards (P. R. S. Moorey [1994], pp. 67-70).

Our evidence about Mesopotamian trade comes from different towns, and from fairly limited time spans, so it is difficult to obtain an overall view of the scale of the activity. The political conditions abroad, and within Mesopotamia, altered the trade's direction and volume; for instance, disruptions changed the materials used for cylinder seals in the Akkadian to Ur III periods (M. Sax, D. Collon, and M. N. Leese [1993], p. 89). P. R. S. Moorey [1994, pp. 74-76] summarized the changes in seal materials, and stated [ibid., p. 77] that a similar pattern broadly applied to beads [ibid., pp. 77-102].

Even in the Neo-Assyrian period (when large areas of the Near East were controlled by the empire, in one way or another), while it would have been profitable to import minerals for royal and official purposes, such as palace and temple decoration and expensive jewellery, one is uncertain about importation for 'magical' uses, especially for the 'ordinary' person. This is even though it is probable that very small stone chips were used for the charms. Therefore, the question as to 'the reality' of the charm lists arises again (see pages 159-160) and, also, if a charm's components varied with supply.

One solution to these problems was the use of imitation ingredients. It is unclear whether their existence arose from a scarcity of the real minerals or from craftsmen reacting to the demands of customers for substitute status symbols. These individuals would still be rich, since imitation stones appear in lists of royal treasures (e.g., the inventory from Kar-Tukulti-Ninurta (modern Telul al-Aqar); see pages 173-174).

GLAZED BEADS

The colour of some stones was changed by their surface having a glaze coating superimposed. The stones most commonly glazed were magnesium silicates (e.g., steatite) or silicates (e.g., quartz) (P. R. S. Moorey [1994], p. 168; details of the glazing processes are presented at ibid., pp. 181-186). Glazed beads appear in Mesopotamia some time in the sixth millennium B.C. [ibid., p. 172]. These were blue or green; by c. 2300 B.C. the glaze was also coloured black, red, and white [ibid., p. 174].

GLASS BEADS

From the middle of the second millennium B.C. economic texts and letters increasingly mention the existence of coloured glasses intended to represent precious stones. The genuineness of a specific stone is emphasized by its designation as KUR.RA = *šadî,* "from a mountain", as opposed to an imitation stone, termed *kūri,* "from a kiln" (A. L. Oppenheim [1970], pp. 10-11; see P. R. S. Moorey [1994], p. 203 on this type of kiln).

We possess *Glass Texts* from the Middle Babylonian period onwards; the Neo-Assyrian series was called *The Door of the Kiln* (all edited in A. L. Oppenheim [1970]). The glass-maker is unattested in the administrative texts [ibid., p. 6]. Two kilns apparently used for glass-making in the early sixth century B.C. were excavated at the south end of Room 47 in the Burnt Palace at Nimrud (M. E. L. Mallowan [1954], p. 77).

Attestations of glass objects in the archaeological record before the Middle Babylonian period are rare and are often accompanied by dating difficulties (P. R. S. Moorey [1994], pp. 190-193). A problem with Mesopotamian sites is that glass exposed to humidity in the soil tends to decompose, and is unrecognizable when excavated (A. von Saldern, p. 204 in A. L. Oppenheim [1970]).

Some of the minerals comprising the dream charms are described in other cuneiform texts as being imitations (for other examples see A. L. Oppenheim [1970], pp. 13-15):

i). *pappardilû* - in the Middle Assyrian inventory of part of the treasure at Kar-Tukulti-Ninurta (VAT 16462; *AfO* 18 [1957-1958], pls. 17-20) thirty-one lumps of glass (*bušlu,* lit., "boiled mass") resembling the *pàppardilû* and *mušgarru* stones are mentioned in col. I lines 27-28. There are also references to ^{NA_4}BABBAR.DILI *ku-ri:* e.g., col. I lines 7-8, 12, and 29.

ii). *sāmtu,* "carnelian" - instructions on how to make various types of this category of glass appear in the *Glass Texts.* See also VAT 16462, col. II line 33; and col. III line 7': ^{NA_4}GUG *ku-ri.*

iii). *ṣurru,* "obsidian" (natural volcanic glass) - see VAT 16462, col. II line 23.

iv). *uqnû,* "lapis lazuli" - the *Glass Texts* contain many examples of making different types of lapis lazuli glass, even coloured red! See also VAT 16462: e.g., col. I lines 32-33; and col. II, lines 3, and 26: ^{NA_4}ZA.GÌN *ku-ri.* Inventories from Qatna (modern Tell Mishrifeh in Syria; *RA* 43 [1949]) describe necklaces with elements composed of boiled *(bašlu)* lapis lazuli: e.g., p. 144, line 74; and p. 178, obv. 3.

('Lapis lazuli' was also used to describe other blue minerals: e.g., a wall peg of the Achaemenid ruler Darius I was actually made from Egyptian Blue (a calcium-copper-tetrasilicate), although inscribed as being of ^{NA_4}ZA.GÌN (E. F. Schmidt [1957], p. 50, fig. 4, with p. 133, and n. 1)).

ADD 1040, rev. 3 is unusual in not mentioning the stone imitated:

3). 1-*en* ⌜*qu-lu*⌝ NA$_4$.MEŠ *ku-u-ri*

One metal loop (with) glass beads.

DYED STONES

A Middle Babylonian chemical text at Berlin, Photo. Bab. K. 713 (*RA* 60 [1966], p. 30), covered the dyeing and subsequent firing of stones to resemble the *pappardilû* or *papparminu* (obv. 1 is broken at the end) and *dušû* stones.

E. Sollberger [1987] studied a bead belonging to Sennacherib (BM 89159):

1). ⌜KUR⌝ ^{md}30-PAP.MEŠ-[SU *šar$_4$* KUR *Aš-šur*^{KI}]

2). ^{NA_4}BABBAR.MIN$_5$ KUR *Aš-*[*šur*^{KI} . . . . . .]

[1] The palace of Sennacherib, [king of Assyria]. [2] A *papparminu*-stone of Assyria [. . . . . .].

X-ray diffraction analysis of this bead revealed that it was chert or chalcedony, which had been dyed black at the ends, and heated [ibid., p. 379]. The bead is striped black, grey, and white, resembling one of the banded agates. P. R. S.

Moorey [1994, p. 100] noted that since there is no recorded source of such agates in Assyria, the reference in line 2 above may indicate that this method was an Assyrian speciality at the time. The Middle Babylonian chemical text mentioned above is called to mind, suggesting that *papparminu* should be read there. E. Sollberger [1987, p. 380] presented an account of a closely corresponding modern method of dyeing stones.

Another example of colouring stones occurs in the Achaemenid period when carbon-coated lime-plaster seals appear, imitating black limestone (P. R. S. Moorey [1994], p. 76).

REPRESENTATIONS

Figurines of frogs or toads have been excavated from the Uruk 3 (= Jemdet Nasr) period onwards, c. 3100 B.C. Similar figurines in clay, frit, and shell, and as stone beads were found at Ur (E. Douglas van Buren [1936-1937], pp. 35-37; C. L. Woolley [UE 2], pl. 142 = U. 1008). A dead or living frog in a leather bag around one's neck (*ADRC,* col. III line 67) would be extremely uncomfortable, due either to the stench (unless it was cured) or to the wriggling, which suggests that a representation was used instead.

Ostriches roamed the open country, the domain of demons and marauding tribesmen. Imitation ostrich egg-shells in gold and silver, serving as a type of cup, were excavated from the Royal Cemetery at Ur (C. L. Woolley [UE 2, p. 283, and pl. 170 = U. 11154). Since the real shell would have to be broken to fit into a leather bag, perhaps any available egg-shell would have sufficed.

P. R. S. Moorey [1994] offered two further instances of the Mesopotamian ingenuity in coping with the demands for rare materials. Gold beads from the Royal Cemetery at Ur had cores of wood, etc., covered with a very thin layer of gold (P. R. S. Moorey [1994], pp. 226-227). A few pieces of ivory were deliberately heated until they turned black, possibly to resemble ebony [ibid., p. 127].

CHAPTER 14: SUBSTITUTION RITUALS

SYMPATHETIC OR SYMBOLIC MAGIC

Sympathetic magic is based upon presumed relationships between animals, humans, objects, and plants, which cause them to affect, or be influenced by, each other. (The topic is discussed by J. G. Frazer [1900], pp. 9-60; M. Mauss [1972], pp. 64-79; and by numerous other writers.)

In addition, some substances and implements were associated with a particular Mesopotamian deity; however, the associations alter with each text. (A. Livingstone [1986, pp. 184-186] believed that the explanation of this was more complicated than variant traditions.) The associations ensured the respective deity's presence at the ceremony, while 'explaining' his role within it and the importance of certain ritual objects. These objects can form a double sympathetic relationship because they represent the god's power and, possibly, enter into the more usual type of sympathetic relationship.

J. G. FRAZER'S LAW OF SIMILARITY AND LAW OF CONTACT

J. G. Frazer [1900, p. 9] propounded the Law of Similarity, namely that like produces like, to explain such relationships. Like may act upon like as well, especially to cure like, by drawing it away to produce the desired opposite: e.g.,, applying water to cure dropsy. The converse is also true, that opposite acts upon opposite - the Law of Opposition. An offshoot of the Law of Similarity is that a figurine can represent the creature or person who is the subject of the ritual, thus any action performed upon the figurine will consequently apply to the real thing. This is a common sorcery technique, and is used in Mesopotamian rituals against ghosts, demons, and dream apparitions (chapter 16).

Although the natural properties are inherent, and the relationships may be firmly rooted in tradition, they still have to be activated by ritual means. A plant could be connected to a stone by a colour, and to another plant by shape; the ritual it is to be used in determines which magical attribute is required, and limits the activation to that particular quality alone.

The process of activating the sympathetic relationship involves J. G. Frazer's [1900, p. 9] second Law, the Law of Contact or Contagion. Objects once in contact, whether actual or assumed, or even occurring accidentally, remain connected, although subsequently physically separated. In this way the essence of an object is seen to be equally present in a piece as in the whole, whether the part be of an individual thing, or of its category. Any action upon a part will affect the whole object from which it has been detached, hence the practice of exuvial magic in sorcery, namely using discarded finger nails, locks of hair, etc.

The two Laws, of Similarity and of Contact, frequently occur in the same ritual, and it becomes extremely difficult to decide which action relates to which Law. The attributes linking like to like form their sympathetic relationships by contact; and, generally, the processes of contact are used only to activate the attributes, enabling their magical powers to work.

The tenets of sympathetic magic can be seen in many Mesopotamian ceremonies, especially in the namburbi rituals (pages 112-113) and purification rites (page 191). The use of substitute figurines in dream rituals is discussed in chapter 16.

Table 10 on pages 186-187 shows the essential coherence of the dream rites involving a clod, clay pellets, or a reed. A ritually prepared substitute is addressed, and the evil of the dream is transferred to it either by reciting an incantation, which mentions the imminent destruction of the clod (hence of the evil), together with various possible dreams (in the *Clod Incantation;* Table 9 on pages 182-183); or by recounting the actual dream content to the substitutes (pellets, reed, and K. 8171 + 11041 + 11684 + 14058 clod rituals). Then the substitute is destroyed in an appropriate manner; the ritual results indicating that the dreamer is now safe from that dream's potential harm.

THE CLOD RITUALS

A substitute clod appears in six rituals:

i). *ADRC,* col. I lines 51-59 (very fragmentary).

ii). *ADRC,* col. I lines 60-72.

iii). *ADRC,* col. I line 79 to col. II line 18.

iv). *ADRC,* col. III lines 20-38.

v). *ADRC,* col. III lines 39-46a.

vi). K. 8171 + 11041 + 11684 + 14058, lines 15'-23'.

In addition, there is K. 11406 (pages 337-338) and BM 66559 (= 82-9-18, 6552; plate 16). The latter is a tablet from Sippar written in the Late Babylonian script. It is extremely difficult to read because the signs in the middle of the lines have become distorted. All the lines on the reverse are too fragmentary to translate. Parts of the obverse can be compared with the *Clod Incantation* (Table 9 on pages 182-183). Obverse 7'-12' describe seeing different people in a dream, as on *ADRC,* col. II line 4. Obverse 13'-15' refer to the disintegration of the clod and the dream's evil in phrases reminiscent of the *Clod Incantation,* but with different verbal forms.

TYPES OF CLOD

The creation of Man from clay is mentioned on *Atra-hasīs,* Tab. 1, lines 189ff., with Text S, col. III lines 5-14 (see also the Sumerian myth *Enki and Ninmah* (C. A. Benito [1969])). As noticed by other writers (e.g., J. Bottéro [1985a], p. 53), this is alluded to in the *kirṣu*-formula of the *Clod Incantation:*

> *ina kir-ṣi-ka ka-ri-iṣ kir-ṣi ina kir-ṣi-ia ka-ri-iṣ kir-ṣi-ka*
> (O Clod,) in the part of you (which) is pinched off, part of me is pinched off, (and) in the part of me (which) is pinched off (is) your pinched-off piece.

ADRC, col. III line 27 goes on to add:

> 27). *ina* NÍ-*ia ba-lil* NÍ-*ka ina* NÍ-*ka ba-lil* NÍ.MU
> In myself is mingled yourself, (and) in yourself is mingled myself.
> (See a similar phrase on page 181 in a ghost ritual involving a figurine.)

The verb *g/karāṣu,* "to pinch off", describes the ritual action performed by the Mother Goddess (as Mami) on *Atra-hasīs,* Tab. 1, line 256. The epithet *binût apsî,* "a product of the Apsu", on *ADRC,* col. III line 25, recalls the statement that Ea (who dwelt in this cosmic region) presented her with the clay (*Atra-hasīs,* Tab. 1, lines 198-203).

It seems clear that *ki/urbānu*(LAG) is a clay clod, but other types of "lump" are attested in the dream ceremonies:

i). LAG IZ.ZI *šá ina* ^{d}UTU.ŠÚ.A GAR, "a lump from a wall which is situated in the west" - *ADRC,* col. I line 71. This could refer to a clod of earth, a piece of brick, or even plaster (see the non-dream rite *ADRC,* col. IV line 45).

ii). LAG is frequently used in parallel to *kirṣu,* "a pinched-off piece". It is unclear if *kirṣu* is related to *kupatinnu,* "clay pellet" (pages 184-185).

iii). LAG MUN *lu* LAG IM, "a lump of salt or a clay clod" - *ADRC,* col. II line 18.

iv). LAG *ša* KÁ *pi-he-e,* "a clod from (the region of) a closed door" - *ADRC,* col. III line 37.

v). *kur-ba-ni ba-li-ti,* "a clod from the waste land" (following *CAD* B, p. 63) - *ADRC,* col. III line 45.

vi). DUG*haṣbu*(ŠIKA), "a potsherd", is mentioned on K. 8171 + 11041 + 11684 + 14058, line 16', but then all the references are to a clod, LAG.

Outside these substitution rites, a LAG is attested on *SDR,* line 36, a ritual to obtain a pleasant dream:

36). *kur-ba-ni* MUN ŠIM*qul-qú-la-ni* ŠIMLI LAG KÁ *ka-mì-i ina* TÚG*ši-ši-ik-ti-šú tara-kás*

You tie lumps of salt, of the *qulqullânu*-plant (and) of juniper, (and) a clod from (the region of) the outer gate into his hem.

THE SYMBOLISM SURROUNDING THE CLOD

As stated on page 179, the clod is identified with the dreamer by the *kirṣu*-formula and by mythology. The dream's evil is transferred to the clod, seemingly to the dreamer's substitute, but read on.

M. Malul [1988, pp. 79-92] presented legal rituals in which the breaking *(hepû)* of clods symbolized the severance of ties between a son and his father. The clod represented the son's personality, so its dissolution wrought a personality change, rendering the son a stranger [ibid., p. 91]. M. Malul [ibid., p. 92] understood the clod in the dream rituals as symbolizing the dreamer, accordingly:

> "its dissolution in the water brought about a symbolic dissolution of the "contaminated personality" of the sufferer, leaving thus a new man."

However, passages in the *Clod Incantation* (Table 9 on pages 182-183) relate the crumbling of the clod to the desired fragmentation and nullification of the dream and its evil: e.g., *ADRC,* col. II lines 6-9:

6). *ki-ma ka-šá-ma ana* A.MEŠ *a-nam-du-ka-ma*

7). *tam-mah-ha-hu tap-pa-⌈as-sa⌉-s[u tap]-⌈pa-ṭa⌉-ru ana* KI-*ka là* GUR-[*ru*]

8). HUL MÁŠ.GE$_6$ *an-ni-ti* [*a-m*]*u-ru ki-ma ka-šá-ma ana* A.MEŠ *li-*[*in-n*]*a-di*

9). *lim-ma-hi-ih lip-pa-⌈sis⌉ lip-pa-ṭir ana* KI-*šú* [*a-a* GUR]

6 Just as I will throw you (O Clod) into (running) water, and 7 you will be soaked, you will disintegrate, [you] will be fragmented, (with the result that) you will not return to your place (i.e., not become a clod again); 8 (so) may the evil of this dream which [I] saw be thrown into water just like you! 9 May it be soaked! May it

disintegrate! May it be fragmented! [May it not return] to its place (i.e., return to me)!

Similar identifications are established in substitute figurine ceremonies (chapter 16), where the destruction of the figurine causes that of the demon, ghost, or witch it is supposed to represent; likewise in namburbi rituals involving a figurine for a dog howling in a house (*Cap.* 12; S. M. Maul [1994], pp. 312-322), or a hissing wild cat in a house (*Cap.* 15).

Since the clod rites state that it is the dream's evil which is dispelled, and their ritual actions are analogous to those of the clay pellet and reed substitution ceremonies (see Table 10 on pages 186-187), it is more logical to understand the clod as representing the (evil of the) dream.

Note that a similar duality of representation arises in the ghost ritual on the obverse of *KAR* 267. Directions are given on obv. 4-5 for making a substitute figurine of the ghost, which is given a human face. It is identified by the inscription on its left shoulder-blade (obv. 6-7) as "the figurine of the ghost, *hajjāṭu*(-demon, or) evil disease which seized X, the son of Y". Yet in the incantation to Shamash (obv. 12-26) the figurine is associated with the sufferer at obv. 17:

17). NÍ-*šú* GIM NÍ-*ia*$_5$ UZU-*šú* GIM *nab-ni-it* UZU-[*ia*$_5$]
He (lit. his self) (is) like myself, (and) his flesh (is) like the appearance of [my] flesh.

A. L. Oppenheim [*DB,* p. 301] stated that, in his ritual Type D (*ADRC,* col. III lines 20-38, and 39-46), the clod was rubbed over the dreamer's body, absorbing the supposed physical miasma of the bad dream, and purifying the dreamer. The verb *kapāru* means "to wipe off", and its *D*-stem has this nuance when used with bread [*CAD* K, p. 179b]. This verb does not appear in the clod rituals, nor is such an action necessary if the substitution rituals are seen as a unit, where verbal transmission suffices.

DB, p. 302 classified the clod ritual K. 8171 + 11041 + 11684 + 14058, lines 15'-23' into a separate category, ritual Type E, because the dream's evil was transferred by recounting the content of the nightmare (line 19') in addition to reciting the *Clod Incantation* (see on). While it is true that the use of both methods of transference in this ritual forms a bridge between the other clod rituals and the rituals involving clay pellets or a reed, this is not enough to distinguish it as a separate category.

TABLE 9: THE *CLOD*

Text Details	Invocation Of The Clod	Establishment Of The Relationship Between The Clod And The Dreamer		Description
		***kiriṣ*-formula**		
ADRC, col. I line 79 - col. II line 9	79 [O Clod,] O Clod,	I, 79 to II, 1 in part of you (which) is pinched-off, part of me is pinched off, (and) in the part of me (which) is pinched off (is) [your] pinched-off piece.		2-3 O Clod, the evil of the dream which I saw, which I repeatedly saw (during) the first watch (of the night), the middle watch, (or) the third watch -
ADRC, col. III lines 25-33 (part of lines 20-36)	25 O Clod, you are the product of Apsu.	25-26 In the part of me	26-27 In myself is mingled yourself, (and) in yourself is mingled myself.	29 (so) the evil [of the dream] which I saw during the night:
K. 8171+ 11041+ 11684+ 14058, lines 17'-22' (in ritual)	17' O Clod,	18' in the part of you		19' He reports to

See also the similar phrases at *ADRC,* col. I lines 51-59 (very fragmentary); and col. III lines 43-44.

INCANTATION

Of The Dream		**Mentions Of The Clod's Imminent Disintegration**	**Parallel Disintegration Of The Dream's Evil**
[3-4] (in) which I saw my dead father; (or in) which I saw my dead mother; (or in) which <I saw> a god; (or in) which I saw the king; (or in) which I saw an important person; (or in) which I saw a prince; (or in) which I saw a dead person; (or in) which I saw a living person;	[5-6] (or in) which I saw knowledge (of something) I did not know; (or in) which I went to an unknown land; (or in) which I repeatedly ate unknown bread; (or in) which I was dressed in an unfamiliar garment -	[6-7] just as I will throw you (O Clod) into (running) water, and you will be soaked, you will disintegrate, [you] will be fragmented (with the result that) you will not return to your place (i.e., not become a clod again);	[8-9] (so) may the evil of this dream which [I] saw be thrown into water just like you! May it be soaked! May it disintegrate! May it be fragmented! [May it not return] to its place (i.e., return to me)!
[30] (in) which I saw a god; (or in) which I saw a king; (or in) which I saw [an important person]; (or in) which I saw a prince; (or in) which I saw a dead person; (or in) which I saw a living person;	[31] (whether) I went to the right, (or) turned to the left (in my dream) -	[28-29] [Just] as you, O Clod, will be thrown into (running) water, and you will be soaked, you will disintegrate, (and) you will be fragmented -	[32-33] may (the evil of the dream) fall into the water just like you (O Clod) and may it be soaked! May it disintegrate, and may it be fragmented!
the clod as many dreams as he saw		[20'-21'] [Just as] I will throw you, O Clod, into the (running) water, and [you] will crumble (and) disintegrate –	[22'] (so) [may] the evil of all the dream(s) which I saw disappear! May it dissolve!

INCANTATIONS

Although the actions of the clod rituals are the same, the accompanying incantations vary for the six main examples (ignoring the variant *ADRC,* col. III line 46a):

i). The *Clod Incantation* (Table9 on pages 182-183) occurs on *ADRC,* col. I line 52[?]; col. I line 79 to col. II line 9; col. III lines 25-33; and as phrases on K. 8171 + 11041 + 11684 + 14058, lines 17'-18' and 20'-22'.

ii). Different incantations to Shamash appear at *ADRC,* col. I lines 54ff., 60-65, and 66-70; col. II lines 14-16; and col. III lines 20-24.

iii). *ADRC,* col. III lines 39-44 is addressed to Ea, containing ideas about the clod and the evil of the dream in lines 43-44, with the variant *lih$_4$-har-miṭ,* "May it crumble!", instead of *lip-pa-ṭir,* "May it be fragmented!"

iv). *ADRC,* col. III lines 33-36 mentions the mysterious "ram of the storm".

All the incantations (apart from the *Clod Incantation*) appear to have been adapted for this ritual technique; three sub-incantations being joined together at *ADRC,* col. I line 79 to col. II line 16, and at *ADRC,* col. III lines 20-36. The incantation mentioning the "ram of the storm" is almost identical to *ADRC,* col. III lines 52-55 (in a rite to make dreams favourable by feet actions; pages 193-194), even though its wording is more suited to apotropaic purposes.

THE CLAY PELLET RITUALS

The clay pellet rituals on 79-7-8, 77 rev. 21'-23' and left edge 24'-26', are basically the same. Seven, or fourteen, clay pellets are formed, the dreamer recounts his dreams over them seven or fourteen times respectively, thereby transferring the dream's evil. Then the pellets are scattered at a cross-roads (accompanied by a phrase, rev. 23').

OTHER RITUAL USES OF PELLETS

As *DB,* p. 304 noted *kupatinnū,* "pellets, pills", are used mainly in Mesopotamian medicine [*CAD* K, *kupatinnu,* pp. 549-550; and *kupputu* A, pp. 552-553], and even then rarely prescribed.

an.ta.gál = *šaqû,* Tab. 3, line 172 [*MSL* 17, p. 156] has the equation ⌜na$_4$⌝kú[š] = *ku-pa-tin-nu,* but in a few texts it seems that the logogram NU.KÁR.KÁR was used instead. These references, along with the magical attestations of *kupputu,* "to form a pellet", provide us with some other examples of ceremonial pellet use:

i). *DB,* p. 304 was only aware of *KAR* 134, a ritual against 'the Hand of a

Ghost'. Obverse 13-16 orders the sufferer's finger nail cuttings to be rolled in clay. The resultant pellet is then to be cast down a well, into the river, or into the box under the door-pivot.

ii). *Cap.* 40, rev. 8-13 (S. M. Maul [1994], p. 449, lines 45-51) is a namburbi ritual to prevent the evil of spittle-magic from affecting a man. Seven clay pellets (NU.KÁR.KÁR) are made, mixed with spittle. They are placed in the mouth, a nostril, and in the hands (the number of pellets does not agree) before being carefully thrown away.

iii). *SpTU* 1, No. 12 is a ritual against a man's enemies. Amongst many other instructions, rev. 6-7 refers to placing seven clay NU.KÁR.KÁR.

It will be seen that there was no standardized magical use of clay pellets in Mesopotamia. In the dream rites, and (i) above, the evil is transferred to the pellets, which are then disposed of. It is not clear why the pellets in the dream rituals were scattered at a cross-roads, rather than thrown into (running) water: *sapāhu,* "to scatter" is rarely attested in rituals [*CAD* S, pp. 151-157]. Cross-roads, and objects found there, possessed magical properties [*CAD* S, *sūq erbetti,* pp. 405-406]. In this context perhaps the evil of the dream was envisaged as being scattered to the four corners of the world. (i) reveals that clay pellets could be thrown into water, although burying them seems more appropriate for returning the ghost and its evil to the Underworld. It is not clear whether any evil is transferred in (ii), or whether the actions are preventive, protecting important parts of the body. We have no idea what happened to the clay pellets in (iii).

RITUALS INVOLVING FIRE

In many Mesopotamian ceremonies fire was both a destructive and a purificatory power. Five dream rituals are centred around "a fire", *išātu*(IZI), or "a lamp", *nūru*(ZÁLAG):

i). 79-7-8, 77 rev. 18'-19'.

ii). *ADRC,* col. I lines 13-15.

iii). *NADR.*

iv). K. 8171 + 11041 + 11684 + 14058, lines 7'-14'.

v). *ADRC,* col. I lines 19-27.

Four of these ceremonies are fragmentary: (ii) and (v) throughout; (iii) has lost its beginning; and (iv) is unfinished. The first three rituals involve burning a substitute reed (pages 188-189 and Table 10 on pages 186-187); the last two concern something soaked in oil (page 190).

TABLE 10: THE DREAM RITUALS

	Text Details	Incantation Addressed To	Purification Of Dreamer	Take Up Substitute Material	Transference Of Recount The Dream
	ADRC, col. I, 51-59 v. frag.	[52] Clod and [54ff.] Shamash			
C	*ADRC*, col. I, 60-72 frag.	[60-65] Shamash --------- [66-70] Shamash		[71] Raise clod from a wall situated in the west	
L	*ADRC*, col. I, 79 to II, 18	[I, 79 to II, 9] Clod, [9-14] *lipšur*-phrases and [14-16] Shamash			
O	*ADRC*, col. III, 20-38	[20-24] Shamash and [25-33] Clod and [34-36] ram of the storm		[37-38] Take a clod from (the region) of a closed door	
D	*ADRC*, col. III, 39-46 --------- alt. 46a	[39-44] Ea ----------		[45-46] Take a clod from the waste land --------- Take [a clod of X]	
	K. 8171 +11041 +11684 +14508, lines 15'-23'	[17'-18'] and [20'-22'] Clod	[15'-16'] Sufferer anoints X with a mixture	[16'] Mentions a potsherd, then [17'] a clod	[19'] He reports to the clod as many dreams as he saw
P E L	79-7-8, 77 rev. 21'-23'			[21'] Roll 7 clay pellets	[21'] He must recount as many dreams as he saw 7x (to pellets)
L E T	79-7-8, 77 left edge, 24'-26'			[24'] Roll 14 clay pellets	[24'-25'] He must recount as many dreams as he saw 14x over (pellets)
R	79-7-8, 77 rev. 18'-19'				[18'] He must recount his dream to a *tārītu* of reed
E	*ADRC*, col. I, 13-15 v. frag.				[14] He recounts to a reed
E D	*NADR* beginning lost, broken in middle	[3-13] Nusku		[1-2] Cuts off (piece of) his right hem. Holds (hem and reed) before lamp.	

USING SUBSTITUTES

The Dream's Evil **Recitation Of INC-antation Mentioning The Dream**	**Destruction Of Substitute**	**More Prayers**	**Result**
[53] Recite the above INC. to clod	(Throw into (running) water; see [54])	[58-59] Prostrate before Shamash. Prayers to unknown	
[72] Recite the above INC. (2x) over clod 3x before Shamash	[72] Throw into river		[72] It (the evil of the dream) will be dissolved
[17] Recite the above INC. over either lump of salt or clay 3x	[18] Throw into river		[18] The evil of the dream will not come near to the man
[38] Recite the above INC. over clod 3x	[38] Throw into (running) water		[38] Its (the dream's) evil will be dispelled
[46] Recite the above INC. over (clod) 7x --------- Recite the above INC. 3x over clod	[46] Throw into (running) water --------- Throw into river		[46] The dream will be dissolved --------- NAM.BÚR.BI
[17'] He says as follows to clod. [23'] Say this to clod.			[23'] (The evil of the dream) will by-pass him
	[22'] Scatter at cross-roads	[22'-23'] Say as follows to Shamash 7x	[23'] It (the evil of the dream) will be dissolved
	[25'] Scatter at cross-roads		[26'] It (the evil of the dream) will be dissolved
	[19'] He must burn(it) in a fire. He blows with his mouth.		[19'] It (the evil of the dream) will be dissolved
	[14] Burns (it) <in> a fire		[15] [The evil of] that [dream] will not obstruct him
[3] He says as follows	[14] He snaps reed into 2/3 pieces. Utters phrase (burn parcel) (More ritual instructions.)	[18] Pray to personal deities and to lamp	[18] It (the dream) will be(come) beneficial

BURNING A REED

a). 79-7-8, 77 Reverse 18'-19'

In this ritual the substitute for the bad dream is a *tārītu* of reed, which *AHw* 3, p. 1330a translated as „*Rohrfasern?*". The evil of the dream is transferred by the dreamer recounting his nightmare to the *tārītu,* which is burnt in a fire. Then the dreamer "blows with his mouth", *ina pi-i-šú i-nap-pah-ma* (rev. 19'): one normally blew through something [*CAD* N_1, *napāhu,* pp. 263-270]. He either blew onto the fire, ensuring that all the evil was transferred, and thoroughly consumed by the flames; or blew the ashes of the *tārītu* far and wide, recalling the scattering of the pellets above.

b). *ADRC,* Column I Lines 13-15

This section of *ADRC* is extremely fragmentary. The rite was to be performed in the morning, before the man had eaten. Line 14 probably refers to actions similar to those of 79-7-8, 77 rev. 18'-19':

14). [. . . .] ⌈X X X⌉ GI ⌈*i*⌉*-pa-šar*!(*šìr*) <*ina*> IZI *i-qal-lu-ma*

[. . . .] . . . he recounts to a reed. He burns (the reed) <in> a fire.

c). *NADR*

Whereas the two previous ceremonies are apotropaic, *NADR* is concerned with making a bad dream pleasant: line 18:

18). *išallim*(SILIM.MA)

It (the dream) will be(come) beneficial.

The option is left open for the dream already being propitious: line 7:

7). *šum-ma dam-qat du-muq-šá a-a i-ši-ṭa-a*[*n-ni*]

If (this dream) is favourable, may its good luck not pass [me] by!

but the rest of the rite indicates that there was an extremely strong probability of its being unfavourable.

The ritual structure is as follows:

i). A piece of the dreamer's hem is cut off, and held before the lamp with a reed joint (GI *kiṣru*) (lines 1-2). The reed has already been plucked out (see lines 9-10).

ii). An incantation is recited to Nusku (lines 3-13), with similarities to the one to Gibil on K. 8171 + 11041 + 11684 + 14058, lines 11'-14'. It describes the theory behind the sympathetic actions, namely, that since the reed and hem cannot return to their original locations, the dream's evil will be unable to return to the dreamer (lines 9-13).

iii), The reed is snapped into two or three pieces, and enveloped by the hem to the accompanying phrase:

14). *⌈ka⌉-ma-ta ka-la-ta ka-sa-ta!(ka)*

(Now) you (the evil of the dream) are captured. You are imprisoned. You are chained up.

Then the speaker mentions burning the parcel before Nusku.

iv). The ground is touched, and the lamp lit (line 15). Lines 16-17 contain a broken section which probably ordered the burning of the parcel in the lamp (possibly after it had been soaked in oil; see the next section).

v). The sufferer prays to the lamp (i.e., to Nusku) (line 18), and also to his personal deities.

There are problems over the persons of the verbs: K. 3333 + 8583 + Sm. 1069 (manuscript **A**) remains in the third person singular, whereas 79-7-8, 77 (manuscript **b**) changes to the second person at the end. The latter manuscript reveals, by the scribal note *hi-pí eš-šú,* "new break", at rev. 13'-15', that its original was partially destroyed by the time it was copied; so some ritual detail around *NADR* line 14 is missing.

Somewhere in the lost beginning the dream must have been recounted to the reed to ensure transference. The snapping of the reed fragments the evil, which is annihilated by the reed's incineration, consequently purifying the dreamer.

As we have seen in (a) and (b) above, the recounting, followed by destruction, were sufficient in themselves. *NADR* reinforces them by the use of a piece of hem, a symbol for the personality and person of its wearer in Mesopotamian law and ritual. M. Malul [1986] argued that ^{TÚG}*sissiktu*(SÍG) was not the hem, but a garment worn close to the loins, from a functional parallelism with different words for lap, etc.

M. Malul [1988, p. 197] gave examples of the wife's hem being cut when she is being divorced; the action symbolically altering her personality so that she was a stranger to her former husband [ibid., p. 209]. The same idea of severance of ties can be seen in this dream ceremony - henceforth the evil of the dream is separated from the dreamer, because he is no longer the man he was [*DB,* p. 299].

It is probable that the instruction to the professional to touch the ground before lighting the lamp (line 15) had a symbolic meaning, at present unknown. J. V. Kinnier Wilson [personal communication, 1992] suggested that the expression implied obeisance before the deity Nusku.

The fragmentary complex *ADRC,* col. I lines 28-50 mentions snapping a reed in line 41, so this may be a reed substitution ritual.

SOAKING SOMETHING IN OIL

The following table summarizes the ritual acts of the very similar rites K. 8171 + 11041 + 11684 + 14058, lines 7'-14' and ADRC, col. I lines 19-27.

Text Reference	Manufacture Of Parcel	Light 'Lamp'	Dream Mention	INCantation To Fire Deity
K. 8171 +, lines 7'-14'	[9'-10'] Take a thorn of a date palm. Wrap it in combed wool and soak it in oil.	[10'] Light a lamp.	(see INC.)	[10'ff.] Say an INC. to Gibil.
ADRC, col. I lines 19-27	[21] Wrap X, and soak it in oil.	[22] Kindle a fire.	[22-23]	[23] Recite an INC. over a thorn.

A. L. Oppenheim [*DB,* p. 303] stated that these passages described:

> "with minute care the preparation of a new wick for the "sacred" fire, i.e., the fire which can be addressed as a divine manifestation of the Fire-god Gibil . . ."

To the writer, the actions recall those of *NADR,* described above. The uncommon ritual object "a thorn of the date palm" appears to be playing a similar role to the reed and, in some way, the combed wool to that of the hem. E. Leichty [1990, p. 303] suggested that the invalid may have been represented in the *tamītu* CBS 12578 by hair from his beard and "wool pillings" (A.GAR.GAR ^{SÍG}HÉ.ME. DA; obv. 9-10), corresponding to the hair and hem mentioned in obv. 3. These examples suggest that other parts of a person's garments, besides the more usual hem, could symbolize an individual in Mesopotamian ceremonies. As in *NADR*, it is uncertain what happened to the oil-soaked parcel of the dream rituals, but it was probably burnt.

CHAPTER 15: THE PURIFICATION OF THE DREAMER

The rituals to cleanse the dreamer, either with purifying substances (pages 191-193) or by his touching the ground with a foot (pages 193-194), support the view that Mesopotamian nightmares were defiling experiences, as suggested by the *ezib*-clause mentioned on pages 68-69.

PURIFYING SUBSTANCES

In purificatory ceremonies the evil is envisaged either personified as a demon bound to its victim, or subjectively as a miasma covering the sufferer. This physical embodiment of the evil enables it to be removed by:

i). Expulsion, according to the Law of Opposition (page 177), whereby a pure substance drives the evil away; in effect consecrating the man (see i and iii below).

ii). The evil is rinsed off into water; in dream rites, while recounting the dream's content to ensure its transference (ii below). Probably this water was disposed of ceremoniously, perhaps into a river: *JNES* 15 [1956], p. 138, lines 100-102:

100). *mim-ma lem-nu mim-ma là* DÙG.GA *šá ina* S[U NENNI] A NENNI GÁL-*ú*

101). KI A.MEŠ *šá zu-um-ri-šú u mu-sa-a-ti šá* ŠU^{II}-*šú*

102). *liš-šá-hi-iṭ-ma* ÍD *a-na šap-lu-šá lit-bal*

[100] Whatever evil (or) unpleasant (thing) is within the body [of X], the son of Y, [101-102] may it be rinsed off with the water from (lit., of) his body and the wash-water of his hands! May the river carry (the evil) off to its depth(s)!

The hands (and feet) were regarded as symbols of power in Mesopotamia (see the different nuances of *qātu,* "hand", in *CAD* Q, pp. 183-198). The legal act of washing one's hands was used to sever the tie between an adopted son and his adoptive father (M. Malul [1988], pp. 97ff.). The same concept lies behind the 'magical' use, whereby the sufferer and his affliction are separated. The evil having been drawn out of the body via the hands, effectively cleansing the whole.

There is one example each of alkali solution, *uhūlu*(NAGA), water, and choice oil, *šamnu*(Ì.GIŠ) *ṭabû*(DÙG.GA), being used to purify the dreamer:

i). *ADRC,* col. II line 58 to col. III line 3g is a ritual complex containing three different rites to make a dream favourable. Column III lines 1-3 order the dreamer to wash his hands in alkali solution, while on his bed, before placing his foot on the ground, and reciting an incantation three times.

ii). After line 3a, which involves feet actions (discussed on pages 193-194), the fragmentary lines 3b-g mention washing hands in a ^{GIŠ}*itqūru*(DÍLI) bowl of water three times while recounting the dream into the water, and/or reciting an incantation three times.

iii). 79-7-8, 77 rev. 20' averts the evil by anointing the dreamer's hands with choice oil in the morning.

A hemerology for 1st. Nisan (March - April) (as on *BAM* 318, col. IV lines 8-12 and *BAM* 316, col. IV lines 22-23) presents a more elaborate oil mixture: composite lines:

A). [1 *in*]*a* ^{ITI}BÁR.ZAG.GAR U_4.1.KÁM

B). ^{NA4}ZA.GÌN.DURU$_5$ [*ina*] Ì+GIŠ *hal-ṣi tara-sà-an* ^{Ú}IN. NU.UŠ HÁD.A SÚD

C). [*ina lì*]*b-bi* Ì+GIŠ ŠUB-*di* EŠ.MEŠ-*su*

D). ^{NA4}ZA.GÌN.DURU$_5$ *ina* SI TÚG-*ka tara-kás e-ma* GIN-*ku ma-gir*

E). GIM DINGIR *ni-iz-mat* ŠÀ-*šú* KUR-*ád* MÁŠ.GE$_6$.MEŠ-*šú* SIG$_5$.MEŠ

[A] The first day in Nisan [1]: [B] You soak (pieces of) *zagindurû*-stone [in] pressed-out oil. You pound (pieces of) dried *maštakal*-plant [C] (and) scatter (them) into the oil. He anoints himself repeatedly (with this mixture). [D] You tie (pieces of) *zagindurû*-stone into the hem of your garment - Wherever you go, it will be favourable. [E] He will obtain his heart's desire like a god; his dreams will become favourable;

Water and oil are common agents of purification in all cultures, and their use in Mesopotamia extended far beyond dream rituals. *Šurpu,* Tab. 9, lines 102-103:

102). ì.dùg.ga ì.zag.ga me.te ^{giš}banšur.ke$_4$

103). [X] X X dadag.ga níg.nam.sikil.la.ke$_4$

[102] Choice oil (and) . . oil are befitting for the (offering) table,

[103] (and, together with) pure [.] . . are the materials for (lit., of) (ritual) cleansing.

Alkali solution (*uhūlu* or *uhūli qarnati*) in the form of soda from plant ash was combined with oils to make soap. Alkali solution also appears in medicinal use, and in the *Glass Texts* (see *AHw* 3, *uhūlu,* pp. 1404-1405; A. L. Oppenheim [1970]; and *DAB,* pp. 312-346 on alkalis generally). The ritual tablet of the series *muššu'u,* "rubbing in" (*AfO* 21 [1966], pp. 16-18), presents other Mesopotamian purifying substances.

FEET ACTIONS

a). *ADRC,* Column III Lines 52-58

This ritual complex is intended to avert the evil of a nightmare, despite the incantation rubric in line 56: "It is (the text) to make a bad dream favourable". The ritual of lines 57-58 is:

57). DÙ.DÙ.BI GÌR-*šú šá* Á *ni-lu ina* KI *um-mad* ÉN 3-*šú* ŠID-*nu-ma*

58). *ana* Á-*šú* 2-*i* BAL-*ma*

[57] Its ritual: He presses (lit., leans) his foot of the side (upon) which he was lying (when he awoke) upon the ground. He recites the (above) incantation three times, and [58] he turns over to his other side.

If the bed was raised, the dreamer would have to be on his back to be able to perform this foot action.

The incantation (lines 52-55) closely resembles that on *ADRC,* col. III lines 33-36, which is appended to a clod substitution ritual (chapter 14).

b). *ADRC,* Column III line 3a

This is a rite to make a dream favourable, and is one of three attached to the complex *ADRC,* col. II line 58 to col. III line 3g. The other two rituals involve straightforward purification of the dreamer (pages 191-192). The accompanying incantation contains a reference to feet actions in col. II line 62:

62). *aš-kun* GÌR *ina* KI *lu da-mì-iq-ti*

I placed (my) foot upon the ground. May there be good luck!

The dreamer recites the incantation while standing with his left foot on the bed and his right foot on the ground.

In some way the dreamer was cleansed by placing (*ummudu* or *šakānu*) a foot upon the ground, while maintaining contact with his bed (the scene of the 'crime'), and uttering an incantation three times. The recitation must be an essential element because, otherwise, a bad dream would automatically be annihilated by the every-day action of leaving one's bed.

Several non-dream texts suggest that the movement was an important feature (the foot, if specified, varies), although the references are to *kabāsu,* "to step on something purposely, to trample" (*CAD* K, p. 6b). In these cases, either something was crushed underfoot literally (an ominous potsherd) or metaphorically (one's sins); or substances were trodden on (e.g., bitumen). That substances were specified indicates the possibility that these purifying materials were more significant than the foot action. The ground played a part in the treatment of a sufferer of the *kīs libbi*-disease. The doctor concludes by touching the patient's buttocks and head fourteen times each, then touching the ground (*BAM* 574, col. I lines 14-16), perhaps directing the illness into it.

A. L. Oppenheim [*DB,* pp. 300-301] believed that (a) and (b) above described an unusual way of arising, so that the demons waiting to pounce (for which there is no evidence) were misled, and abandoned on the other side of the bed. He deduced this from the reference to the dreamer turning over to his other side on *ADRC,* col. III line 58, adding (to get out of bed); and from an erroneous transliteration of *ADRC,* col. III line 3a, namely omitting the GÌR before ZAG-*ka* [*DB,* p. 342], so that the left foot was placed down on the right side of the bed.

CHAPTER 16: FIGURINES

A wide variety of Mesopotamian figurines have been excavated: birds; dogs; lions; mythological creatures; and different anthropomorphic types (see D. Rittig [1977] generally). Individual figurines may be identified further by their insignia or by phrases inscribed upon them, which described their role, thus 'naming' them. In addition, various ritual texts describe the manufacture of figurine types still unattested in the archaeological record.

THE DREAM RITUALS

There are seven dream ceremonies based on the use of figurines, with five different purposes behind them:

- i). *ADRC,* col. II lines 19-23 - to prevent frightening dreams occurring.
- ii). *Substitute King Ritual,* col. B lines 21-24 - to see pleasant dreams in the future; i.e. it has been classified as a ritual to obtain a pleasant dream.
- iii). *Substitute King Ritual,* col. B lines 25-29 - to avert the evil of possible nightmares.
- iv-vi). *SpTU* 2, No. 21, obv. - to separate a recurring dream apparition from the sufferer; one main ritual and two alternatives.
- vii). 81-2-4, 166 - to ward off the effects of a dreamed witchcraft action.

ADRC, COLUMN II LINES 19-23

Lines 19-20 contain a so-called abracadabra incantation, which was discussed on page 129. This has the rubric (line 21), "(In order) not to see a frightening dream". Lines 22-23 order the manufacture of four clay figurines and the recitation of the incantation seven times. Then the figurines are to be placed at the dreamer's head (when he is lying down), not buried as in the other dream rituals. It was suggested on page 95 that these may have been tangible examples of a *maṣṣar šulme u balāṭi.*

SUBSTITUTE KING RITUAL, COLUMN B LINES 21-29

K. 2600 + 3239 + 9512 + 10216 (*AfO* 18 [1957-1958], pl. 10 + *AfO* 19 [1959-1960], p. 119), contains rituals connected with the Substitute King, a role mainly known from the Neo-Assyrian period (see S. Parpola [*LAS* vol. 2], pp. XXII-XXXII). The ceremony was performed when certain types of lunar or solar eclipses, in conjunction with planetary configurations, portended the death of the Assyrian monarch. A living substitute was enthroned, acting as the king in every-day matters, and taking all the bad omens upon himself instead. The Substitute King was probably killed at the end of the dangerous period of the eclipse (usually one hundred days), paralleling the destruction of inanimate substitutes: the expression used is that he goes to his fate.

Column B lines 1-34 present instructions for making pairs of figurines representing various mythological creatures. Each pair was inscribed with a phrase on the lines of:

ṣi-i HUL A *er-ba du-muq* B

Depart evil of A! Enter good luck of B!

Then the figurines were buried in pairs in different places throughout the palace. (See pages 203-204 for a discussion of the two relevant pairs.)

a). Lines 21-24

21). 2 SUHUR.MÁŠ$^{\text{KU6}}$ *ša* ^{GIŠ}ŠINIG *šá* ^{GIŠ}GIDRU *šá* ^{GIŠ}MA.NU *n*[*a*]-*šú-u* [DÙ-*uš*]

22). *ina* MAŠ.SÌLA GÙB-*šú-nu ki-a-am ta-šaṭ-ṭar ṣ*[*i-i* HU]L [X X]

23). *er-ba du-muq* MÁŠ.GE$_6$.[MEŠ *ta-šaṭ-ṭar*]

24). *ina* É *ma-a-a*-[*li te-tem-mer*]

[21] [You make] two tamarisk goat-fish, which hold *e'ru*-wood sticks. [22] You write as follows upon their left shoulder-blade(s):

'[Depart evil of . .!] [23] Enter good luck of dreams!'

[You write (these words, then) [24] you bury] (the figurines) in (the king's) bedchamber.

b). Lines 25-29

25). 2 ALAM.MEŠ *kám-su-ti* [*ša* ^{GIŠ}*bi*]-⌈*ni*⌉ *ša* LÀL Ì.NUN.NA

26). *na-šú-ú* DÙ-*uš ina* MAŠ.SÌLA G[ÙB-*šú-nu*] *ki-a-am* SAR-*ár*

27). *ṣi-i* HUL MÁŠ.GE$_6$.ME[Š HUL].MEŠ *er-ba du-muq* É.GAL

28). SAR-*ár* LÀL Ì.⌈NUN.NA *qa*⌉-*ti-šú*-⌈*nu*⌉ *tu-mal-la*

29). *ina qa-bal* TÙ[R] É.GAL-⌈*lì*⌉ *te-tem-mer*

25-26 You make two [tamarisk] kneeling figurines, which carry honey (and) ghee. You write as follows upon [their] left shoulder-blade(s): 27 'Depart evil of [bad] dreams! Enter good luck of the palace!' 28 You write (these words, then) you fill their hands with honey (and) ghee. 29 You bury (the figurines) inside the palace courtyard.

SpTU 2, No. 21, OBVERSE

This late tablet contains rites dealing with the repeated appearances of a young man in a sufferer's dreams. A summary of the main ceremony, obv. 3-30, follows. A wax figurine representing the dream apparition is made, and its name written upon the left shoulder-blade. Offerings are presented to Shamash, accompanied by an incantation recited three times. Then the dreamer raises the figurine, and addresses Shamash, perhaps in his own words. He recites an incantation three times to the figurine, while washing his hands over it. The text is broken at this point, resuming with the figurine being buried at the corner of a wall, and a magic circle being drawn. The desired result is to separate the apparition from the sufferer; i.e., to stop him from reappearing in the latter's dreams.

Two other rituals, each involving a figurine, are presented on obv. 31-35 and 36-40, but they are very fragmentary. In both cases the figurine is thrown into the river, not interred.

81-2-4, 166

The supplicant has dreamed that someone performed the apparent witchcraft action of throwing earth over him, which resulted in his pollution and neglect by the gods, just as if it had 'really' happened. As *DB,* p. 307 noted, we possess no other references to this type of nefarious deed.

The professional presents various offerings to Shamash. Then the dreamer performs the *mīs pî* ritual, thereby purifying himself, and an incantation to Shamash is recited. A pair of substitute figurines representing the supposed sorcerer or sorceress are made, and the victim washes himself (his hands) over them.

The *mīs pî,* the "washing of the mouth" ceremony, was normally used to consecrate divine statues, bringing them 'to life' (see E. Reiner [1995], pp. 139-143). (The ritual tablet is edited by G. Meier in *AfO* 12 [1937-1939], pp. 40-45, + K. 9278.) There are other examples of the rite being carried out on men, even on a bull, and on a drum [*CAD* M_2, *mīsu* A, p. 112b].

PURPOSES BEHIND THE CREATION AND BURIAL OF FIGURINES

The texts above can be divided according to the purpose of the figurines:

i). Guardians - *ADRC,* and *Substitute King Ritual.*

ii). Substitutes - *SpTU* 2, No. 21, and 81-2-4, 166.

The last two rites are directed against specific dream content (see pages 114-115 for other examples) instead of unspecified nightmares.

GUARDIAN FIGURINES

Certain figurines were buried beneath a building's floor to protect it and its inhabitants from all calamities. Such guardian figurines have been excavated at Neo-Assyrian sites in Assyria from houses (e.g. D. Rittig [1977], pp. 232-237), palaces (e.g., [ibid.], pp. 244-249), and temples (e.g., [ibid.], pp. 240-241). On the other hand, the only examples from Neo-Babylonian sites come from temples or Nabopolassar's (626-605 B.C.) palace at Babylon [ibid., pp. 252-259]: there is no evidence of the practice from private residences.

Many of these figurines were enclosed in brick capsules (D. Rittig [1977], pp. 219-224 and 229-230). The earliest examples come from the Ishtar temple of Tukulti-Ninurta I (1244-1208 B.C.) at Ashur. The basic structure of six burnt bricks sealed with bitumen or clay, completely enclosing the figurines, was used from the temple of Ashur-resh-ishi I (1132-1115 B.C.) at Ashur until the sixth or fifth centuries B.C.

Other varieties of container developed in the first millennium B.C., such as the 'sentry boxes' discovered in the seventh century B.C. Ruined Building at Ur (C. L. Woolley [1926], pp. 691-692). These consisted of three ancient burnt bricks (of a type not made since 2500 B.C.), placed on end to form three sides of a square, with the brick pavement as the roof. The fourth side was left open, facing into the middle of the room. Stone capsules have been found at Nineveh (D. Rittig [1977], 8.3.9-21), and one figurine in a house at Ashur was under an inverted clay vase [ibid., 1.2.1.2].

Guardian figurines were not always enclosed: several have been found loose under the brick pavement (e.g., D. Rittig [1977], 3.1.1-2); and five dog figurines were excavated from a niche in the North Palace at Nineveh [ibid., 16.1.1-5].

It would appear that the Mesopotamian exorcist did not have precise instructions regarding guardian figurines but followed general rules and a standard burial layout. It is noted on pages 203 and 204 that the inscriptions could, and did, vary for the same figurine type. In addition, as far as we can tell from the published excavation details, the figurine burials are not in the locations given in the ritual tablets (although *ABL* 22, obv. 8 explicitly orders adherence to the designated sites; see on), and each excavated site is different. Also, the ritual texts prescribe varying locations for the burials. Even the figurines found at the House of the Exorcist at Ashur differ in insignia, inscriptions, and location from the ritual texts (F. A. M. Wiggermann [1992], pp. 99-100).

The fragmentary letter *ABL* 22 (= *SAA* 10, No. 263) deals with the interment of figurines (unusually called *timru* instead of *ṣalmu*). As S. Parpola [*LAS* vol. 2, p. 17] stated, Esarhaddon seems to have inquired about the burial of figurines in the *Substitute King Ritual* (compare *ABL* 22, rev. 2-9 with col. B lines 21-24). The writer tells the king that the palace practitioners should bury the figurines according to the (ritual) tablet (obv. 8), and also before certain rooms (rev. 5-6), while he will bury figurines likewise where he is staying (rev. 13 to edge 15). It is interesting to see that the king could specify the burial of extra figurines (of an unknown type) as additional safeguards: rev. 7-12:

7). É LUGAL *is-se-niš*
8). *ú-šàh*[!]*-ka-mu-ni*
9). *lit-me-ru ša kal u*$_4$-[*me*]
10). [*š*]*a* GE$_6$ *la pa-*⌈*ris*⌉
11). *im-ma-ti ša lìb-ba-šú-u-ni*
12). *i-*⌈*tam*⌉*-me-er*

7-9 They should bury (the figurines in these places, and) also (lit., together with) (in) the room(s) which the king prescribed. 10-12 It is not determined (whether this interment should be done) during (lit., of all) the day (or) at night, (so) one may bury (them) whenever one pleases.

SUBSTITUTE FIGURINES

The use of substitute figurines is based upon the Law of Similarity (page 177). The method was used in Mesopotamia to:

i). Restrain ghosts and demons (page 200).
ii). Combat sorcery (page 201).
iii). Simulate the destruction of an otherwise inaccessible evil in the namburbi ceremonies (page 201).
iv). Harm individuals in witchcraft (e.g., those mentioned at *Maqlû,* Tab. 4, lines 39-42, see page 202).

a). Ghost And Demon Rituals And *SpTU* 2, Number 21

We have mentioned already (page 70) that the recurrent dream apparition of *SpTU* 2, No. 21 is addressed at obv. 16-21 as if it were a demon, and that the queen of the Underworld is invoked (obv. 24). On the other hand, it may have been a ghost (see pages 59-61 on ghosts appearing in dreams) because the ritual complex obv. 3-30 resembles the ghost ceremonies involving figurines, discussed by J. A. Scurlock [1988, pp. 50-62]. (The fragmentary rites of obv. 31-40 are closer to namburbi practices, page 201.)

The inscription identified the substitute figurine of *SpTU* 2, No. 21 with the dream figure (obv. 4). The dreamer washed his hands over it (obv. 28), thereby releasing himself from the evil association. The figurine was buried at the corner of a wall, and a *šigūšu*(ŠE.MUŠ$_5$)-flour circle is mentioned (obv. 29).

Ghost figurines were usually interred (sometimes accompanied by offerings) under thorn-bushes or in the open country, often in sealed 'coffins', thus returning the ghosts to their rightful abode, the Underworld. The 'grave' was frequently enclosed by a circle of *šigūšu*-flour. An exorcistic ritual offers a reason for the choice of flour: *UHF,* lines 789-790:

789). ^{zì}še.muš$_5$.a [níg.gig gidim.ma.ke$_4$]

790). ki$^!$ giš.ná.da.n[a.ke$_4$ ù.me.ni.hur]

789-790 [Draw] (a flour circle of) šemuš-flour, [(lit.) an unpleasant thing for ghost(s)] (around) the bed's location.

Additional precautions might be taken to prevent the ghost's reappearance: often the figurine was compelled magically to swear an oath not to return; or it could be physically bound or blinded. (The swearing of an oath occurs on *SpTU* 2, No. 21, obv. 15, *i-ta-ma-ma,* "he swears an oath", but it appears that the sufferer performed this, whereas the ghost rituals have the form *tu-tam-ma-šu-ma,* "You make it (the figurine) swear an oath".)

A wall obviously possessed some ritual significance lost to us:

i). A substitute figurine was used against the demoness Lamashtu on *Lamaštu,* Tab. 1, col. II lines 23-27 (repeated at Tab. 3, rev. 34-38; *ZA* 16 [1902], pp. 141-200). The figurine was struck with a dagger, and buried at the corner of a wall. The site was enclosed by a flour circle.

ii). A figurine representing a *māmītu*-demon was made in the Fifth House of the *bīt rimki* ceremony (J. Laessøe [1955], p. 30). Its heart was pierced (obv. 24-25) before it was buried in the *samītu* of a wall (rev. 26) (*CAD* S, p. 117a, "battlemented parapet"; *AHw* 3, p. 1018b, „*Mauersockel*").

b). Anti-Witchcraft Rituals And 81-2-4, 166

The use of substitute figurines on 81-2-4, 166 in connection with sorcery is mirrored in other anti-witchcraft ceremonies. *Maqlû* presents several methods disposing of figurines representing witches and wizards in attempts to combat sorcery:

i). Burning (the translation of *maqlû*): e.g., Tab. 4, lines 132-138.

ii). Placing them in bread and giving them to dogs to eat, which tells us something about the size of these figurines: e.g., Tab. 9, lines 184-187.

iii). Sailing them downstream in a clay boat: e.g., Tab. 9, lines 52-53.

We have seen on pages 191-192 that the dreamer could be purified by washing his hands. In the anti-witchcraft rites, washing over the witch's figurine turned the sorcery back upon her as explained in the Second House of *bīt rimki* (J. Laessøe [1955], pp. 39-40, lines 29-55). In the namburbi ritual *Cap.* 40, the figurines were buried, and the victim washed over the site (probably only his hands) for a month (rev. 4-5; S. M. Maul [1994], p. 448, lines 42-43).

The fate of the figurines of 81-2-4, 166, after the dreamer has washed over them (upper edge 17-18), is unclear.

c). Namburbi Rituals

In a few namburbi rituals, substitute figurines were made of the animal whose actions portended evil, and were thrown into the river: e.g., of a howling dog, *Cap.* 12 (S. M. Maul [1994], pp. 312-322); and of a hissing wild cat, *Cap.* 15. This procedure was possibly followed after seeing a shooting star, *Cap.* 35 (see page 205).

The same actions occur in the alternative rites of *SpTU* 2, No. 21. Obverse 31-40 ordered the casting of the figurine into the river, instead of the burial specified in the main ceremony. It is a shame that these lines are so fragmentary, but they offer additional support to the view that dream namburbi rituals existed (pages 110-114).

APPEARANCE OF THE FIGURINES

Both plaques and, far more commonly, figures in the round have been excavated. The figurines with 'magical' connotations (as distinct from 'religious' images, royal statues, and palace decorations) dating from the thirteenth to sixth centuries B.C. are presented in D. Rittig [1977]. These were intended to stand upright, having either flat bottoms (e.g., [ibid.], 9.1.3] or bases attached (e.g., 1.3.1]. E. Douglas van Buren, who was aware of only a few examples with bases, suggested [1930, p. XLIII] that the figurines either lay flat or were propped up; while others, which tapered, were stuck into the ground. The discovery of a number of clay figurines in a potter's shop at Sippar (E. Douglas van Buren [1930], p. XLII) indicates that certain kinds were manufactured wholesale.

MATERIALS

The cuneiform tablets reveal that figurines could be made from a variety of substances; for example, the list of different figurines made by a witch on *Maqlû,* Tab. 4, lines 39-42:

i). ^{GIŠ}*bīnu*(ŠINIG), "tamarisk".
ii). ^{GIŠ}*erēnu*(ERIN), "cedar".
iii). *iškūru*(DUH.LÀL), "wax".
iv). *ittû*((A.)ÉSIR), "crude bitumen".
v). *kupsu*(DUH.ŠE.GIŠ.Ì), "residue of linseed".
vi). *lipû*(Ì.UDU), "tallow".
vii). *līšu*(NÍG.SILAG.GÁ), "dough".
viii). *ṭiṭṭu*(IM), "clay".

Occasionally materials were mixed together: e.g., *Maqlû,* Tab. 9:

i). line 35 - bitumen and gypsum (*gaṣṣu*(IM.BABBAR)).
ii). line 37 - clay and tallow.

Clay figurines constitute the majority of the excavated examples, sometimes coated with gypsum and painted (D. Rittig [1977], pp. 225-226). The metal ones are primarily of dogs, being bronze (e.g., [ibid.], 16.1.6-11) or copper [ibid., 16.2.1-4]. Most of the figurines modelled from perishable materials have disintegrated long ago. However, a few wooden ones have survived from the temple of Ninurta at Babylon [ibid., 1.2.2.1-4], together with insignia made from copper and onyx. The presence of other metal decorations [ibid., 22-24], found loose or in capsules (page 198), suggests that, originally, they adorned similar wooden figurines, or clay ones, which have been crushed over the centuries [ibid., 1.1.6].

The figurines in the dream rituals were made from clay (*ADRC* and 81-2-4, 166), tamarisk (*Substitute King Ritual;* pages 203-204), or wax (*SpTU* 2, No. 21).

INSCRIPTIONS

The substitute figurine had to be connected with the evil or person it represented in order for it to function: one way was by an inscribed phrase. The ritual texts favour two locations for the inscriptions:

i). The *idu*(Á), "arm, side".

ii). The left *naglabu*(MAŠ.SÌLA), which *CAD* N_1, p. 119a, translated as "shoulder blade", whereas *AHw* 2, p. 711b §2, preferred *„Hüfte"*.

Some excavated figurines have phrases on them, and in a number of places:

i). The back (e.g., D. Rittig [1977], 1.1.5).

ii). The back of the left arm (e.g., [ibid.], 1.1.1); the left and right arms (e.g., [ibid.], 2.1.15).

iii). The right thigh (e.g., [ibid.], 11.1.3).

iv). The left side (e.g., [ibid.], 9.1.2); the left and right sides (e.g., [ibid.], 3.1.1-2).

The phrases do not always correspond with those prescribed in the ceremonies [ibid., pp. 185-205], but the ceremonies do not agree with each other either (e.g., on page 204).

The figurine of *SpTU* 2, No. 21 had its name written on its left shoulder-blade (obv. 4). No details are given, so the 'name' could have been an epithet defining its purpose (see page 204), or more personal: *CT* 23, pls. 15-22 +, col. I line 49':

49'). *šum-ma* ZU-*šú* MU-*šú* SAR-*ár*

You write his name, if you know him (the ghost).

In both cases, it is possible that the ghost or the dream apparition was a (former) acquaintance.

THE FIGURINES OF THE *SUBSTITUTE KING RITUAL*

The figurines in the *Substitute King Ritual* were more elaborate than the roughly anthropomorphic figurines of the other dream rites. The pairs studied here were:

i). Goat-fish, *suhurmāšu*(SUHUR.MÁŠ^{KU_6}), holding *ēru*-wood sticks.

ii). Kneeling figures, carrying honey and ghee.

Similar figurines were discussed by F. A. M. Wiggermann [1992; this ceremony being his Text 6].

Tamarisk was regarded as a major agent of purification and repulsion of evil: e.g., *šēp lemutti ina bīt amēli parāsi* (F. A. M. Wiggermann [1992], Text 1), lines 81-83:

81). GÌR.PAD.DU DINGIR-*ti* ^{GIŠ}ŠINIG *qud-du-ši*

82). GIŠ *el-lu ana bu-un-na-né-e* NU.MEŠ

83). *šá ina* É NENNI A NENNI *ana sa-kap* HUL.MEŠ GUB-*zu*

> [81] The bone of divinity, the holy tamarisk, [82] the pure wood (used) for the features of the figurines, [83] which will stand in the house of X, the son of Y, (ready) to repulse the evil ones.

In this last text, only the figurines of the anthropomorphic deities, "the creatures of heaven", guarding the outer gate were created from tamarisk (F. A. M. Wiggermann [1992], pp. 50 and 60). The monsters, or "the creatures of the Apsu", were of clay; however, the goat-fish [ibid., pp. 184-185] were created from tamarisk. F. A. M. Wiggermann [ibid., p. 79] argued that the kneeling figurines of the *Substitute King Ritual* probably represented minor exorcising deities because they were made of tamarisk.

The nature of the different phrases written upon all the figurines in the *Substitute King Ritual* (page 196) reveals their function as doorkeepers (F. A. M. Wiggermann [1992], pp. 49 and 86), even though they were not always buried in doorways. They were to expel any existing evil from the palace, to prevent new calamities from entering, while allowing good fortune to pass through. F. A. M. Wiggermann [ibid., p. 141] stated that none of the phrases agrees with those given in other ritual texts for the same figurine types.

Although they have no arms, the goat-fish were to hold sticks of *ēru*-wood; the same insignia occurs in the *šēp lemutti ina bīt amēli parāsi* extracts (F. A. M. Wiggermann [1992], Text 2). The possession of a piece of *ēru*-wood endowed its bearer with the divine power to exorcise (pages 213-214).

The writer is unaware of any other instances in the ritual texts where figurines were to "carry" honey and ghee, as distinct from these substances being offered to them. Each of the figurines found in the Ruined Building at Ur (D. Rittig [1977], pp. 250-253) was accompanied by the remains of sacrifices, such as corn grains or the bones of small birds (C. L. Woolley [1926], p. 692); although no mention of these occurs in the extant ritual texts.

CHAPTER 17: MISCELLANEOUS RITUALS

A few sections on *ADRC* pose problems either because they are too fragmentary to be analysed, or because the ritual actions therein do not fit into any of the categories discussed so far, or as covered in the next chapters. The following passages are too broken:

i). Column I lines 1-6 contain a complicated ceremony lasting for at least three days, extremely uncommon for a dream ritual. The application of a dressing in line 3 is more suited to medical cures.

ii). Column I lines 16-18 contain a rite to avert the evil of a bad dream, in which something is bound and enclosed.
See *Cap.* 35 where a fallen star is sealed in clay, and then "the image of well-being[?]" (NU SILIM.MEŠ) is cast into the river (lines 9-11; S. M. Maul [1994], pp. 453-457, lines 15'-17').

iii). The purpose of col. I lines 28-50 is unclear. A reed is snapped at line 41, so perhaps this is a reed substitution ceremony similar to those presented on pages 188-189.

a). *ADRC*, Column III Lines 47-51

This rite, intended to dissolve the evil of a dream, seems to have been cobbled together because:

i). The two lines of the incantation (lines 47-48) do not fit together. The first refers to "a curse", *arratu*(ÁŠ); while the second is a standard *lipšur*-phrase, suitable for any type of evil.

ii). There is no instruction to recite the incantation.

iii). The ritual results of *ADRC,* col. III lines 46 and 51 appear to have become muddled (page 107).

iv). Neither magical averting, nor purificatory, actions are involved, merely a libation of vinegar, *ṭābātu*(A.GEŠTIN.NA), before the dreamer places his foot upon the ground (probably leaving his bed in this case, rather than a feet action ritual; see pages 193-194).

The verb *naqû*(BAL), when occurring in ceremonial contexts, denotes a libation or act of sacrifice [*CAD* N_1, pp. 336-341]. Mesopotamian libations were made to attract the attention of the deities and to secure their goodwill, and it is unusual that no recipient is specified in the passage above. One wonders if vinegar would have been appreciated instead of the more common beer, water, or wine.

One interpretation of this rite is that the vinegar was sprinkled around the room, dispelling the demon who caused the nightmare and/or the evil of the dream by its odour, the basis of ritual fumigations attested in other Mesopotamian ceremonies (see also *ADRC,* col. III lines 18-19 on pages 91-92).

Alternatively, perhaps a libation was made to the demon, along the lines of what was abhorrent to a deity would suit a demon. The Mesopotamians presented *kispu*-offerings to the dead to prevent their returning to the living. Bread, types of flour, and water were offered to ghosts as part of attempts to disperse them (e.g., *CT* 23, pls. 15-22 +, col I lines 31'-32'), and M. J. Geller [*UHF,* p. 136, on his line 844] suggested that a certain 'bag' (^{kuš}a.gá.la) may have contained fragrant plants to appease a demon. The demon's acceptance of the libation would oblige him to leave the sufferer alone, releasing him from hag-ridden sleep. If this supposition is correct, this ritual would be the only example of one designed to deal with the cause of a bad dream, rather than with its dire effects.

CHAPTER 18: RITUALS TO OBTAIN A PLEASANT DREAM

TEXTS

This chapter is predominantly concerned with four elaborate ceremonies, whose structure is given in Table 11 on pages 210-211:

i). *ADRC,* col. II lines 24-57.

ii). *ADRC,* col. IV lines 21-30 (with the omission of the alternatives in lines 25a-d and 30a-b: the former being a charm, and the latter, apparently, a clod substitution).

iii). *ADRC,* col. IV lines 31-41b.

iv). *SDR.*

Additional rituals to obtain a pleasant dream are:

i). *NROD* is regarded in this study as an example of this purpose category because of the requests for a dream on rev. 8 and 17. As may be seen, the alternative one line rites bear little resemblance to those of the group above.

a). Obverse 51 - After reciting the first incantation (obv. 39-50), the exorcist holds the patient's hand while uttering the second ŠU.ÍL. LÁ-incantation (rev. 1-17) three times before Nusku.

b). Obverse 51a - A censer of juniper is set out before a lamp (the symbol of Nusku), and only obv. 39-50 is recited, three times.

ii). Three charms: *BAM* 315, col. IV lines 27-31 and 32-36; and *SpTU* 2, No. 22, col. IV lines 5-6 (chapter 13).

iii). A guardian figurine rite: the *Substitute King Ritual,* col. B lines 21-24 (chapter 16).

PURPOSE

The purpose of *SDR,* as stated in lines 25-26, was to absolve the dreamer of his sins, enabling him to become reconciled with his angry personal deities (so described in lines 23-24):

25). *ú-ma-'i-ir-ma* AN.ZA.GÀR DINGIR *šá* MÁŠ.GE$_6$.MEŠ

26). *ina šat mu-ši-im li-paṭ-ṭi-ra ár-ni-ia$_5$ lu-uš-lim*$^!$*(me) šèr-ti lu-ta-líl ana-ku*

> 25 (If) he (Sin) should send Anzagar, the god of dreams, 26 so that during the night he will absolve me of my sin(s, then) I shall become well (again, and) I shall be cleansed of my transgression.

(Also see the fragmentary ritual result of *ADRC,* col. II lines 56-57.)

The mention of Anzagar suggests that the supplicant's reconciliation would be indicated by a dream. This could be a 'message' dream similar to those of *Ludlul bēl nēmeqi,* Tab. 3, which revealed the abatement of Marduk's wrath, but these dreams were unusual (page 16). Remembering that the Mesopotamians predominantly used 'adjectives', such as "pleasant", to describe symptomatic dreams (page 25), then the ritual results on *ADRC,* col. IV lines 30 and 41b:

> NÁ-*ma* MÁŠ.GE_6 SIG_5(-tu_4) IGI-*mar*
>
> You lie down, and you will see a pleasant dream.

suggest that a pleasant symptomatic dream would occur, due to the renewed protective presence of the personal deities. This could explain the inclusion of these ceremonies on *ADRC,* a compendium mainly consisting of rites to avert unpleasant symptomatic dreams. The rituals to obtain a pleasant dream are not 'proper' incubation ceremonies (see chapter 19), which sought either specific dream omens (*ROP*) or message dreams (the literary examples).

There is no evidence to support E. Behrens' claim [1906, pp. 17-18] that the ritual described on *ABL* 450 (= *SAA* 10, No. 298; manuscript $\mathbf{G}_1$ of *SDR*) was intended to cure the prince Ashur-mukin-palu'a.

RITUAL SETTING

TIME

One might expect that a ritual to obtain a pleasant dream would be performed in the evening, before retiring to bed. However, the only time specification is the "twenty-eighth day" (*ADRC,* col. II line 28). It seems that these rites were performed on an auspicious day, regardless of the hour (see *ADRC,* col. II line 48, where the fumigants were installed "during the day") and, therefore, would appear to have long-term effects.

The Neo-Assyrian letter *ABL* 450 (= *SAA* 10, No. 298), obv. 8, associates the ritual actions of *SDR* with 16th. Ululu. S. Parpola [*LAS* vol. 2, p. 203] connected this ceremony with the rites of Ululu (August - September) mentioned on *KAR* 44, obv. 5, and with other calendrically fixed ceremonies intended to protect the royal family. If he is correct, then it is surprising that this date was chosen because *KAR* 178, col. V line 49 and the Kassite calendar IM 50969 (*Sumer* 8 [1952], after p. 36), col. VI line 16 each state that 16th. Ululu was an unfavourable day.

LOCATION

There is no evidence that the ritual location for these ceremonies was the dreamer's bedroom, unlike the apotropaic and prophylactic rites (pages 124-125). In fact, a location is recorded only in two examples, and then not in detail:

i). *ADRC,* col. II line 27 referred to the open country, but without the usual demarcation of a special area (e.g., *AfO* 18 [1957-1958], p. 296, line 1). Column II line 38, in the same complex, suggests that there were (at least) two locations, even if only different parts of the same area or room, since the practitioner "withdraws", *te-re-qam-ma.*

ii). *ADRC,* col. IV line 21 prescribed "a separate room", *ina bīti*(É) *parsi* (TAR-*si*); a ritual area away from everyday concerns (see *AHw* 2, *parsu(m),* p. 835a, for other instances).

COMMENTS UPON TABLE 11 ON PAGES 210-211

RITUAL I - PRESENTATION OF OFFERINGS

Various offerings are presented to attract the attention of the personal deities, or of Sin, hopefully putting them in a receptive and benevolent mood. *SDR* contains more details than the other examples, and is very similar to a namburbi ritual against a lunar eclipse (*Cap.* 65; page 395), which mentions the same ŠU.ÍL.LÁ-incantation to Sin (see page 149).

INCANTATIONS 1 TO 3

The recitation of several incantations once or thrice formed an important part of these dream ceremonies, more so than for other dream rituals. *SDR* (and *NROD*) include ŠU.ÍL.LÁ-incantations, while the rituals of *ADRC,* col. IV use incantations resembling DINGIR.ŠÀ.DIB.BAs, intended to appease a wrathful deity.

The incantations of *ADRC,* col. II lines 24-57 are not consistent with the ritual acts. Incantation 1 is a Sumerian incantation to Utu, although censers are set out to the supplicant's personal god and before the *kušāru.* One might expect an incantation to the personal god as the *kušāru* is mentioned indirectly in Incantation 2 and, by analogy (see page 212), in Incantation 3. Similarly, in Ritual III another censer is set out before the personal god, but Incantation 3 does not invoke him. In fact, the dreamer's personal god plays a minor role in this complex.

TABLE 11: RITUALS TO OBTAIN A PLEASANT DREAM

	ADRC, Col. II lines 24-57	*ADRC*, Col IV lines 21-30	*ADRC*, Col IV lines 31-41b	*SDR*
TITLE	24-26	21		
RITUAL I	26-28	21-22		29-30
unclear	✓			
set up censer of juniper.	to personal god and before *kušāru*	to personal deities in a separate room		
scatter and present offerings.				set up tamarisk table before Sin. Scatter 24 loaves, flour and dates. Set out confection of honey and ghee.
libate beer		✓		✓
INCANT-ATION 1	[29-37] to UTU	[23-25] DŠDB	[31-37] DŠDB	[1-27] to Sin (ŠIL)
RITUAL II	38			31
referring to incantation	say incantation 3 times			recite incantation 3 times
misc.	prostrate yourself. Withdraw and speak as follows before *kušāru*.			
INCANT-ATION 2	[39-47] to various deities about *kušāru*		[37-40] DŠDB	
RITUAL III	48-50	26-27	41b	31-36
referring to incantation	say incantation	recite incantation 3 times before censer	recite incant-ation 3 times over *ēru*-wood	
place at head or head of bed	place fumigants at your head during the day		place *ēru*-wood at your head	place censer of juniper at head for Anzagar
tie into hem		when censer has burnt out tie ? on left with thread from hem	tie *atā'išu*-plant into hem	tie lumps of salt, *qulqullânu*, juniper, and clod from outer door into hem

TABLE 11 (Continued) RITUALS TO OBTAIN A PLEASANT DREAM

	ADRC, Col. II lines 24-57	*ADRC*, Col IV lines 21-30	*ADRC*, Col IV lines 31-41b	*SDR*
RITUAL III continued	48-50	26-27	41b	31-36
pound	*atā'išu*-plant in juniper oil	sweet reed		
anoint or wash	anoint with mixture	anoint with cypress oil		wash or rinse hands and feet in *aprušu*- and *qulqullânu*-plants
sprinkle	*kasû*-plant mixed in pure water			
place censer of juniper	before personal god			
referring to incantation	say as follows	say as follows		
INCANT-ATION 3	51-55 to *ēru*-wood staff	28-29 DŠDB		32-33 phrase to Anzagar
RITUAL IV	56		30	33
referring to incantation	say incantation		say this 3 times	say this
misc.	prostrate yourself			
RITUAL RESULT	56-57	30	41a	

DŠDB = DINGIR.ŠÀ.DIB.BA (to the personal deities) ŠIL = ŠU.ÍL.LÁ

RITUAL III - PROTECTION AND PURIFICATION OF THE DREAMER

The manual acts of this detailed section are the most important of the whole rite. *SDR* reverses the order of tying objects into the dreamer's hem and his purification.

a). Protection

The sleeper was to be protected during the night by a censer or a piece of *ēru* (^{GIŠ}MA.NU)-wood placed at his head. An *ēru*-wood weapon(^{GIŠ}*kakku* (TUKUL)) was regarded as possessing special qualities enabling it to avert demonic attacks (pages 213-214). Its presence at the bed-head (*ADRC*, col. II (see on) and col. IV line 41b) would prevent the dreamer seeing nightmares caused by demons (pages 50-52) so he would have pleasant dreams.

Censers were prescribed on *ADRC,* col. II line 50, to ensure the presence of the personal deity (see the charm title *SpTU* 2, No. 22, col IV line 5 on page 89), and again on *SDR* to entice Anzagar into coming with the message of reconciliation. (The censer of *ADRC,* col. IV lines 21-30 is made to serve the two purposes of Rituals I and III.)

ADRC, col. II line 48, also mentions the placing of fumigants at the sleeper's head. This could be an additional repellent of demons. It also recalls the ritual dealing with forgotten dreams on *ADRC,* col. III lines 18-19 (pages 91-92), and could refer to the (possibly incorrectly appended) title of col. II lines 24-26, which mentioned inability to remember a bad dream.

Objects were tied into a garment's hem (a symbol of the wearer) in a variety of legal and ritual contexts. (See M. Malul [1988], pp. 179-197; and *ABL* 676 (= *SAA* 10. No. 12), rev. 1'-8', where a list of all the bad omens observed was attached to the Substitute King's hem so that their evil remained, and died with him.) Protection seems to lie behind this practice in the dream rites, as in the hemerology for 1st. Nisan (page 192).

b). Purification

The petitioner was cleansed, either by being anointed with a perfumed oil mixture (*ADRC,* col. II, and col. IV line 27) or by washing with two still unidentified plants, designated as "[the plants] for the appeasement [of an angry god]" (*SDR,* lines 34-35). *ADRC,* col. II line 49 adds the sprinkling of *kasû*-plant mixed with water, thereby purifying the (bed)room as well.

THE CORRESPONDENCE BETWEEN GIŠ*ēru*(MA.NU) AND *kušāru*

ADRC, col. II lines 24-57 connects an *ēru*-wood weapon (pages 213-214), with the ill-defined *kušāru* (pages 214-216) in the following ways:

i). A censer is set out in front of the *kušāru* in Ritual I (lines 27-28), but the subsequent Incantation 1 to Utu alludes to the previously unmentioned *ēru*-wood weapon (lines 32 and 37), asking the gods to appoint its (apotropaic) nature.

ii). Incantation 2 is to be spoken before the *kušāru* (line 38), and this time requests various deities to appoint the (apotropaic) nature of the *kušāru*.

It is unclear why two items, or two names for the same object, were needed. A piece of *ēru*-wood also appears in the complex *ADRC,* col. IV lines 31-41b.

^{GIŠ}*ēru*(MA.NU)

F. A. Wiggermann [1992, pp. 60, 65-69, and 79-85] investigated the significance of *ēru*-wood (Assyrian *e'ru*) in various rituals. He defined ^{GIŠ}*kakku* (TUKUL) specifically as "a mace", whose possession identified the bearer as a deputy of the gods of white magic: Ea or the great gods having assigned its powers, which were guaranteed by Anu. It is also associated with Asalluhi and Marduk.

The identification of *ēru* is disputed; add to F. A. M. Wiggermann's [1992, p. 65] list:

i). Wild pomegranate - J. V. Kinnier Wilson, *Iraq* 50 [1988], p. 81, and n. 24.

ii). Tamarisk$^{?}$ - J. N. Postgate, *The Archive of Urad-Šerūa and his Family* [1988], p. 109 (Roberto Denicola, Rome).

Our sources present three distinct usages of the *ēru*-wood 'weapon':

a). A Hand 'Weapon'

The concept of its being the insignia of the power to exorcise: e.g., *UHF,* lines 162-163:

162). l[ú sili]m.ma sila.a gin.na.mu.d[è]

163). $^{\text{gi[š]}}$[tukul] ^{giš}ma.nu mu$_7$.mu$_7$.a ⸢šu.gá ì⸣-[gál]

162 (When) I, the unharmed man, walk about in the street, 163 the *ēru*-wood [weapon] of the lore of the exorcist is in my hand.

besides possessing this ability in itself, was so firmly rooted in the Mesopotamian ritual tradition that some guardian figurines carried such weapons against evil: e.g., the sticks borne by a pair of goat-fish in the *Substitute King Ritual,* col. B line 21 (page 196).

When Enkidu descended to the Underworld to retrieve the *pukku* dropped by Gilgamesh, one of his instructions was not to carry an *ēru*-wood staff because of the effect it would have: *Gilgamesh, Enkidu, and the Netherworld,* lines 191-192, and the *Epic of Gilgamesh,* Tab. 12, lines 20-21 (the line numbers of the last text are different in A. Shaffer [1963]):

191). ^{giš}ma.nu šu.za nam.ma.e.gá.gá.an

20). *šab-bi-ṭu a-na* ŠU^{II}*-ka la ta-na-áš-ši*

192). gidim ba.e.dè.ur_4.re.eš

21). *e-ṭím-mu i-ar-ru-ru-ka*

[191, 20] Do not carry (**Sum.:** put) an *ēru*-wood (**Akk.** omits) staff (**Sum.** omits) in your hands! [192, 21] The ghosts would panic at you(r appearance).

b). A Drumstick

UHF, lines 727-729, appears to prescribe the beating of a copper drum with a stick. Lines 786-788 inform us that the resultant din caused the demons to abandon their prey. The practice of making loud noises to scare evil spirits away is still current in some parts of the world.

c). A Protective 'Staff' At A Bed-Head

A 'staff' was placed at the bed-head to protect its occupant from the attacks of malevolent beings: e.g., *UHF,* lines 792-794:

792). ^{giš}tukul ^{giš}ma.nu [sag.bi ù.me.ni.gar]

793). udug hul dib.b[a bar.šè hé.em.ta.gub]

794). níg.gig níg.[ak.a nam.ba.te.ge_{26}.e.dè]

[792] [Place] the *ēru*-wood weapon [at his head] [793] (so that) the evil *utukku*(-demon who) passes by [may stand aside, [794] (and so that) disease (and) sorceries [may not approach]!

It is possible that such a 'staff' stood permanently guarding the Mesopotamian monarch's head while he was in bed. The Neo-Assyrian letter *CT* 22, No. 1, from an unnamed ruler (perhaps Ashurbanipal), ordered its recipient to collect various tablets, charms, etc., including, on obv. 14-15:

14). 4 ^{NA_4}GÚ.MEŠ *šá* SAG GIŠ.NÁ LUGAL *u še-pit* LUGAL

15). ^{GIŠ}TUKUL ^{GIŠ}MA.NU *šá* SAG GIŠ.NÁ LUGAL

[14] Four stone charms (lit., stones of the neck) which (are placed) at the head and foot of the king's bed; [15] the *e'ru*-wood weapon which (stands) at the head of the king's bed;

kušāru

Both the meaning and the function of the rarely attested *kušāru* are unclear. The Akkadian dictionaries diverge radically in their translations: *CAD* K, p. 598b, "reed stalk, reed shelter"; *AHw* 1, p. 516b, *„ein breites Band?"*.

Two lexical passages suggest that *kušāru* was connected with marshes and reeds, but they pose problems in themselves. The first, F. Köcher [*KADP*], No. 12, col. I line 79 (uruanna = *maštakal,* Tab. 3, line 87), defines *kušāru* as:

79). [^{Ú}]*gi-rim* ⌜*ša*⌝ *ap-pa-ru* LI.PAD | AŠ *ku-šá-ru*

A *girimmu* of a marsh . . | . *kušāru*

girimmu is a loan-word from Sumerian girim/n, which B. Landsberger [1967, p. 17, n. 52] described as "one of the enigmatic Sumerian root variations of gurun". He also differentiated between girim/n, "flower", and gurun, "fruit, flower", noting that the logograms were used interchangeably in bilingual texts. The Akkadian dictionaries classify *girimmu* as a type of fruit [*CAD* G, p. 88b; *AHw* 1, p. 291a]. In any case, the correspondence in the line above is not helpful in identifying *kušāru* because *girimmus* of various habitats and colours were equated with different plants (see *CAD* G, p. 88b).

The second reference is *CT* 11, pl. 46, col. I line 30 (diri = *watru,* Tab. 4):

30). di.mu.uš | ^{Ú}⌜GISSU⌝ | *ku-šá-*⌜*ru*⌝

The Sumerian words are associated with six other Akkadian ones (lines 31-36): of which two are only attested lexically (*dimmuššatum* and *kumāṣu*); three infrequently (*hīšu, kupû,* and *takkapu*); leaving *ṣillu,* "shade, protection". Moreover, *ṣillu* and *takkapu* do not fit in with the other words, which refer to reed objects, even if the modern Akkadian dictionaries do not agree as to the exact meaning.

The only other mention of *kušāru,* in a ritual context, known to the writer occurs in two incantations directed against the Lamashtu-demoness, *Lamaštu,* Tab. 2 (*ZA* 16 [1902], pp. 141-200):

i). Column I line 47:

47). [*it-t*]*i ku-šá-ri e-di* GÌR^{II}-*ki a-r*[*ak-kas*]

I [am tying] your feet [with] a single *kušāru.*

ii). Column III line 23:

23). *it-ti* ^{GIŠ}ŠINIG *šá*$^!$(*a*) KUR$^!$-*i*$^!$(*bir*) *u ku-šá-ri e-di r*[*u-kus-si*]

[Tie her] with a mountain tamarisk and a single *kušāru!*

These references suggest a type of binding, perhaps magical rather than an actual band. The demoness is certainly not repelled by a protective staff.

Concerning A. L. Oppenheim's note about *kušāru* [*DB,* p. 304, n. 222], this word is also attested on a haruspical or medical commentary text, *CT* 41, pl. 43a, obv. 9:

9). *ku-šá-ri* | *kab-nu*

AHw 1, p. 417b translated *kušāru* in this tablet as *„Reifen",* and *kabnu* as *„Umhüllung";* whereas *CAD* K, p. 22a preferred "(a tree?)" for *kabnu.* *DB*'s lexical reference is from OB Lu A, line 195 (correct from line 194) [*MSL* 12, p. 163], and is now read as:

195). ^{lú}garadin du$_6$.ul.du$_6$.ul · | *mu-pa-hi-ir ku-r*[*u-lim*]

CHAPTER 19: INCUBATION

One of the *SOED*'s definitions of 'incubation' is:

> "The practice of sleeping in a temple or sacred place for oracular purposes."

The archetype is the technique of seeking dreams performed in various Greek and Roman sanctuaries and at the later shrines of Christian saints (e.g., the places described in M. Hamilton [1906]) - Christianity adopted the Classical procedure largely unaltered.

CLASSICAL INCUBATION

The centres of Greek incubation were temples of deceased heroes such as Amphiaraus at Oropus, or Trophonius at Lebadea, and the various temples to Asclepius (the Greek god of medicine), especially at Epidaurus. The majority of the petitioners sought relief from an illness, a disability, or sterility; while some wanted answers to particular problems. Thus, incubation belonged to the field of private divination, relevant only to the individual inquirer.

The incubant was surrounded by an atmosphere of intense expectation; emanating from the other patients' hopes, the preparatory rituals accompanied by explanations from the priests, and the accounts of previous 'miracles' inscribed on tablets around the temple complex. Many of these accounts are extant (e.g., M. M. Austin [1981], No. 126). The early texts describe how the deity or his agent had visited the sleeper, and either performed an 'operation' or gestured, enabling the healed sufferer to walk away the next morning. The later texts record a prescribed course of treatment instead of a direct remedy. Most of the diseases were incurable at the time (e.g., blindness, paralysis) so the cures were ones of faith, resembling those of the modern pilgrims to Lourdes.

Each sanctuary purified the incubant in different ways. He usually sacrificed an animal; at Oropus, he slept upon its hide. Certain restrictions were observed before the incubation, especially fasting or special diets, and sexual abstinence. Sometimes the incubant was shown the god's statue, presenting a form in which the deity could appear (see *DB,* p. 190). Finally, all the incubants went to a special part of the temple called the *abaton,* which may have been an arcade open to the elements on one side, laid down, and slept. The incubant at Lebadea descended alone through a small gap into the bowels of the earth.

It was realised that the incubant might not be healed, either because he did not see a dream, or because his dream was interpreted incorrectly; whereupon he tried again. A 'fee' was demanded after a cure, and texts relate how defaulters were struck down by illness again. Later, the 'fee' was frequently the individual's conversion to Christianity, as well as a financial payment.

Originally, it seems that the priests did not have any medical knowledge. Sanatoria appeared around the temples with the development of the dream prescription, which had to be strictly observed, often for long periods. Many of the ingredients still involved the patient's powers of faith, being items associated with the temple, such as water from the sacred well. So, while the priesthood had acquired a more important role by interpreting the dream, it is unclear if they had obtained, or needed, any medical expertise.

The Romans continued to patronise Greek sanctuaries, besides adding their own, such as the Plutonia. Pluto, the king of the Underworld, was appealed to when approaching death was feared. The therapeutic incubation at these places was different, for the sufferers resided with the priests, who both incubated the dreams and prescribed. These priests may have possessed some rudimentary medical skills.

INCUBATION IN THE ANCIENT NEAR EAST

There are very few accounts of supposed incubation episodes from the whole of the ancient Near East, as distinct from mentions of prognostic dreams. This had been noted already by A. L. Oppenheim [*DB,* pp. 187-188], with examples (correct to *2 Chron.* 1: 7). However, close examination shows that most incidents describe unsolicited dreams, with no formal link in the sources between any ritual mentioned and the dream (also see some of the Mesopotamian examples).

EGYPT

Incubation is not recorded in Egypt until the Ptolemaic era (305-30 B.C.). However, note the statement on the thirteenth century B.C. stela of Qenher-khepeshef that he had slept in the (temple) forecourt; and he also owned a Dream-book (S. Quirke [1992], p. 136).

HITTITE

A. Kammenhuber [1976, pp. 38-41] discussed the Hittite examples. The oldest is the Hittite version of the *Legend of Naram-Sin* (see *ZA* 44 [1938], pp. 54-57, especially lines 9-17), where the king is told by Ishtar to purify himself, and to sleep upon a pure bed in order to receive divine advice.

Murshili II (at the end of the fourteenth century B.C.) referred to incubation in his Plague Prayers (*ANET* ^{3}, pp. 394-396; and R. Lebrun [1980], pp. 192-239). He asked the Hattian Storm God to inform him if more atonement was needed to halt the plague, suggesting (message) dreams (not necessarily incubated) to himself, to priests sleeping upon a pure bed (i.e., incubated), or to anyone.

These two describe (Classical) incubation, in that the intended dreamer purifies himself and sleeps on a pure bed (probably in a sacred area), seeking answers to specific queries. Incubation is also recommended in a ritual against impotency, *KUB* 7, Nos. 5 + 8 + *KUB* 9, No. 27 (*ANET* ^{3}, pp. 349-350, especially *KUB* 7, No. 5, col. IV lines 1-10). Not only may a god send dreams but he may sleep with the sufferer in the dreams.

MARI

There is hardly any evidence about the reception of the several dreams and visions documented in the Mari letters. *ARM* 10, No. 10, obv. 5-6 states that Kakkaldi saw (some kind of vision) in the temple of Itur-Mer, a main god of the city of Mari.

A fiercely debated passage in *ARM* 10, No. 100 could refer to dream incubation in a temple of Dagan. A woman wrote to king Zimri-Lim quoting a message she had received from Dagan, which stated that only the king could restore her kidnapped young girl to her (rev. 22-27). This woman and the deity had conversed together (obv. 9ff.), and we have noted elsewhere (page 18) that dialogues occur in Mari dream reports. The scenario is not described as a dream, but phrases on obv. 7-8 suggest this possibility:

> 7). *ù* $^{[d]}$⌈*Da-gan*⌉ *be-el-ka ú-ṣa-al-*⌈*li-la*⌉*-am-ma*
>
> 8). *ma-am-*⌈*ma*⌉*-an ú-ul il-pu-t*[*a*]*-an-ni*
>
> [7] and Dagan, your lord, made me fall asleep[?], and [8] nobody touched me.

The problem is the verb on obv. 7, because *ṣalālu* is unattested in the *D*-stem (as it seems to be here), the *Š*-stem having the meaning "to make sleep" [*CAD Ṣ*, pp. 67-70]. Some scholars (e.g., W. H. P. Römer [1971], p. 62, n. 4, and p. 63) have preferred to take the verb as *ṣullulu,* "to shelter", connecting it with the statement that nobody touched the 'dreamer', because she was under Dagan's protection.

J.-M. Durand [*AEM* 1/1, p. 472, n. a] took the verb as the *D*-stem of *ṣalālu,* with the technical meaning *"voir pendant son sommeil".* He understood *lapātum* to refer to an opening manual act in an incubation ceremony [ibid., p. 461]. The absence of this gesture indicated that Dagan had commenced the (unsought) dream experience, thus explaining his ignorance of the woman's problem. The irregularity of this process suggested to J.-M. Durand that the recipient was almost certainly a high priestess. His argument is attractive and plausible, but will be strengthened if, and when, more attestations of these technical expressions are discovered.

An even more controversial idea is that of J. M. Sasson [1983, p. 284], who suggested that, at Mari, people could commission others to receive dreams on their behalf, presumably by incubation. This is based upon *ARM* 10, No. 117, obv. 9-11:

9). [*šu-ut-t*]*a a-mu-ra-ak-ki-i*[*m*]

10). [*ù i-na š*]*u-ut-ti-ia* ^{d}*Be*$^{!}$(*nu*)-*el*$^{!}$(*um*)-*te*$_{9}$-[*É-kál-lim*]

11). [*ki-a-am iš-p*]*u-ra-an-*⌈*ni*⌉

[9] I saw [a dream] for you. [10] [In] my dream Belet-[Ekallim] [11] sent me (a message) [thus]:

J. M. Sasson analyzed *a-mu-ra-ak-ki-i*[*m*] as being *amāru* in the first person singular preterite + ventive + second feminine singular Oblique pronominal suffix. (The Oblique case in Akkadian covers the Dative, Genitive, and Ablative of other languages.) He argued that the presence of the ventive indicated a Dative sense, instead of W. L. Moran's [*ANET* ^{3}, p. 632] translation "I had a [dre]am about y[ou]" (using a Genitive nuance; also favoured by J.-M. Durand [*AEM* 1/1, p. 482]). The idea of T. Jacobsen, (presented in J. M. Sasson [1983, pp. 284-285, n. 12], that the sense of obv. 9 was "I have news for you", with the dream reference being 'a password' revealing that the letter actually came from the named sender seems unlikely. There are no other examples of authenticating a letter in this way.

OLD TESTAMENT

In the Old Testament, Solomon sacrifices at Gibeon (*1 Kings* 3: 3-4; *2 Chron.* 1: 3-6), and afterwards God appears in a dream (*1 Kings* 3: 5; *2 Chron.* 1: 7). Similarly, Jacob sacrifices at Beersheba, and sees a vision in the night (*Gen.* 46: 1-4). If the (large number of) offerings were part of an incubatory ceremony, it is strange that no questions were posed, though the dream narrative may suggest their purport. Also, we are not told where the recipients slept.

Incubation is referred to at *Jer.* 29: 8:

i). *King James'* version – "neither hearken to your dreams which ye cause to be dreamed".

ii). *New English version* – "do not listen to the wise women whom ye set to dream dreams".

UGARIT

The Ugaritic text the *Legend of Aqht* (B. Margalit [1989]) is broken at the beginning. Dan'el is encountered performing sacrifices for seven days, before the god El addresses him. Dan'el is promised that, if he returns home and invites the Birth Goddess to his house when he has sex with his wife, a son will be born. There is no indication that El appeared in a dream, nor (as the text stands) that Dan'el or his wife were infertile - he may have had too many daughters. Following J. J. Obermann's study (*How Daniel Was Blessed With A Son, JAOS* Supplement 6 [1946]), it has been widely accepted that this opening scene describes an incubation.

MESOPOTAMIAN INCUBATION CEREMONIES

Only six texts containing accounts of putative Mesopotamian incubation describe any ceremony at all:

i). *ROP* (pages 222-223) - several examples.

ii). The *Epic of Gilgamesh,* Tab. 4 (pages 223-227).

iii). *Atra-hasīs* (pages 227-232).

iv). Nabonidus 8, col. VII lines 1'-15' (pages 233-234).

v). The *Weidner Chronicle* (pages 234-235).

vi). The historical epic fragment BM 47749 (pages 235-236).

Only *ROP* and *Atra-hasīs* explicitly associate the rites with producing a (prognostic) dream.

The desired ritual results of *ADRC,* col. IV lines 30 and 41a, although apparently indicating incubation, belong to rituals to obtain a pleasant (symptomatic) dream (chapter 18).

ROP

There are six incubation rites on *ROP,* remembering that, in this text, the phrase "to see an oracular decision" in the incantation rubrics and in the desired ritual results seems to denote "to see a dream" (page 36). All the ceremonies involve the recitation of an incantation, otherwise they are dissimilar. The lack of a standard incubation procedure is indicated by the comparison below of the most complicated dream rites, lines 65a-68 and 81e-84, with the rituals to obtain omens from shooting stars in lines 88-91 and 100-103. All four complexes sought to discover whether or not the supplicant would achieve his unspecified purpose; the first one also asked about an invalid's recovery.

DREAMS		**SHOOTING STARS**	
Lines 65a-68	**Lines 81e-84**	**Lines 88-91**	**Lines 100-103**
	81e You spend the night.		
	81e GÌR? MAN *ka* TAR-*as*		102 GÌR? MAN! *ka* TAR-*as*
65a You take barley of 1 *harbu.*		88 You take full-grown barley.	100 You take barley of 1 *harbu.*
65a-66 ?			101 ?
66 A youth who has not known a woman grinds (the barley).		88-89 A youth who has not known a woman cleanses himself on an auspicious day. He grinds (the barley).	101 A youth who has not known a woman grinds (the barley).
66-67 You sweep the floor before the Wain constellation. You sprinkle pure water to form a circle.	82-83 You stand alone on the roof at night. You sprinkle pure water 3 times before the Wain constellation and 3 times before Eru'a.	91 You libate pure water.	
67 You set up a censer of juniper and cheap scented flour.	83-84 You scatter cheap scented flour.	88-90 During the night, on the roof, before the Wain constellation, the youth sets fire to a censer of juniper and cheap scented flour. He stands on the outskirts.	102 You place a censer of juniper before the Wain constellation.

DREAMS		SHOOTING STARS	
Lines 65a-68	**Lines 81e-84**	**Lines 88-91**	**Lines 100-103**
68 You recite the incantation (to the Wain constellation) 3 times.	84 You say the incantation (to the Wain constellation).	91 You recite the incantation (to Ninlil) 3 times before the Wain constellation.	103 You recite the incantation (to the stars of the Paths) 3 times before the Wain constellation.

The six incubation rituals on *ROP* are:

i). Lines 42-43 - incantations to Gula. Fragmentary ritual: beer libation; two tablets drawn up; something placed before a star.

ii). Lines 48a-51 - incantation to various deities and astral beings. Fragmentary ritual: censer of juniper set before night stars; incantation recited thrice over tamarisk; personal god drawn in cheap scented flour.

iii). Lines 57-60 - incantation as in (ii), but uttered by the professional (line 52). Fragmentary ritual: cleanse yourself; draw sketches of Ea and Asalluhi. This rite has a different incantation rubric: to speak with one's personal deities (presumably in some type of vision), and to discover the future (line 56).

iv). Lines 65a-68 - incantation to Wain constellation. Ritual: see back. (Dream 'omens' and their meanings are given in lines 69-70.)

v-vi). Lines 81b-c - two alternative incantations to Wain constellation. Ritual: sprinkle water in front of Wain constellation; recite incantation thrice.
Alternative ritual, lines 81e-84, see back.

THE *EPIC OF GILGAMESH,* TABLET 4

It is still unclear how many dream episodes were written on Tablet 4, certainly more than the three of older editions (see *DB,* p. 213), possibly more than the five of more recent ones, following B. Landsberger [1968, p. 102]. The preparations appear to be identical for each example. The best preserved section is at lines 79-100, most of the restorations coming from the other instances. (The transliteration which follows is based on A. R. George's forthcoming edition of the *Epic of Gilgamesh,* which he kindly made available for the writer's thesis.)

79). [*a-na* 20 DANNA *ik-su-pu ku-sa-a-pu*]

80). [*a-na* 30 DANNA *iš-ku-nu nu-bat-tu$_4$*]

81). [50 DANNA *il-li-ku kal u$_4$-mu*]

82). [*ma-lak* ITI *u* U_4.15.KAM *ina šal-šú* u_4*-mu iṭ-hu-ú ana* KUR *Lab-na-nu*]

83). [*a-na* IGI ^{d}UTU *ú-har-ru-ú bu-ú-ru*]

84). [*a*$^?$-(*na*$^?$ . . . . *iš*)-*ku-nu i*-(. . . .)] X X X *pa*

85). [*i-li-ma* ^{d}GIŠ.GÍN.MAŠ *ina muh-hi*] ⌜*šá-di*$^?$*-i*⌝

86). [ZÌ.MAD.GÁ-*su ut-te-qa-a ana* (. . . .)]-⌜*e*⌝-*ni*

87). [KUR]-⌜*ú*⌝ *bi-la šu-u*[*t-ta a-mat* (*damiqti*$^?$)] *lu-mur*

88). [*i-p*]*u-šá-áš-šum-ma* ^{d}[*En-ki-dù a-na* (^{d}GIŠ.GÍN.MAŠ)] ⌜É$^?$⌝ *za-qí-qí*

89). [^{GIŠ}I]G *šar-bi-il-l*[*i*$^?$ *ir-te-ti*] *ina* KÁ-*šú*

90). [*u*]*š-ni-il-šu-ma* [*ina kip-pa-ti* (. . . .)] ⌜*ú*⌝-*ṣur-ti*

91). [*u*$^?$ *š*]*u*$^?$*-ú* GIM ŠE KUR-*e* [(. . . .)-*dam-ma it-t*]*a-til ina* KÁ-*šu*

92). [^{d}GI]Š.GÍN.MAŠ *ina kin-ṣi-š*[*u*] ⌜*ú-tam*⌝-*me-da zu-qat-su*

93). [*šit*]-tu_4 *re-hat* UN.MEŠ UGU-*šu im-qut*

94). [*ina q*]*ab-li-ti šit-ta-šu ú-qat-ti*

95). [*i*]*t-bé-e-ma i-ta-ma-a a-na ib-ri-šu*

96). [*i*]*b-ri ul tal-sa-an-ni am-mi-ni e-re-ku*

97). [*u*]*l tal-pu-tan*^{an}*-ni am-mi-ni šá-šá-ku*

98). [*u*]*l* DINGIR *e-ti-iq am-mi-ni ha-mu-ú* UZU-*ú-a*

99). [*i*]*b-ri a-ta-mar* 3-*ta šu-ut-ta*

100). ⌜*ù*⌝ *šu-ut-ta šá a-mu-ru ka-liš šá-šá-at*

[[79] They broke off a bite to eat at twenty 'miles' (lit., double-hours). [80] They set up an overnight camp (after another) thirty 'miles'. [81] They went fifty 'miles' during (that) day. [82] (It was) a march of one month and fifteen days, (but) they arrived at the Mountain of Lebanon on the third day.

[83] They dug out a pit before Shamash. [84] They placed . (. . . .)] . . . . [to$^?$ (. . . .) [85] Gilgamesh went up to the top] of the mountain$^?$. [86] [He presented his (offering of) cheap scented flour to (. . . .)] . . [87] (He said):

"[O Mountain], bring me a dream! Let me see [a message (of good luck$^?$)!]"

[88] (Meanwhile) [Enkidu] made a 'house$^?$ of Zaqiqu' for him, for [(Gilgamesh)]. [89] [He fastened] a door (against) the storm in its doorway. [90] [He] made him (Gilgamesh) lie down (in it), and (he surrounded the site) [by a circle (. . . .)] diagram. [91] [He] himself$^?$,

like the corn of the mountain [(. . . .) . , and he laid] down at its doorway.

92 Gilgamesh leant his chin on his knees. 93 Sleep, (which) is poured out over mankind, fell upon him. 94 (However), [during] the middle watch (of the night) he woke up (lit., he ended his sleep). 95 [He] arose, speaking to his friend (Enkidu):

96 "My friend, (if) you did not call to me, why am I awake? 97 (If) you did not touch me, why am I bewildered? 98 (If) a god did not pass by, why is my flesh numbed? 99 My friend, I have seen a third dream, 100 and the dream which I saw was totally bewildering."

Gilgamesh offers cheap scented flour on the mountain top to someone unknown (lines 85-86). He asks the Mountain for a dream (line 87), presumably seeking indications as to the outcome of his intended attack on the Guardian of the Cedar Forest, Humbaba, who dwelt upon the Mountain of Lebanon.

a). *bīt*(É) *zaqīqi*

The most interesting part of the episode is Enkidu's construction of a *bīt zaqīqi* (the signs ⌜É?⌝ *za-qí-qí* occur only on K. 10777, col. III line 5; *OrNS* 54 [1985], p. 26, transliteration only). This was a 'proper' building with a strong door (line 89), probably built from wood lying to hand, and surrounded by a protective circle (line 90). The context certainly suggests that "the house of zaqiqu" was a special hut used for incubation, "a temple of the Dream God Zaqiqu".

A problem with this attractive hypothesis is that other attestations of the rare phrase *bīt zaqīqi* connect it either with the meaning of *zaqīqu* as "wind and nothingness" (page 78; (i) below), or as "a wind demon or a type of ghost" (pages 78-79; (ii) and (iii) below).

i). A description of a deserted town appears in the balag-incantation mu.tin nu.nuz dím.ma (*CLAM* 1, pp. 222-242), a + 4 to a + 5:

a+4). [. . . .] X [. . . .] é.líl.lá ba.si.si.ig

X X É *zi-qí-qí šá uš-qa-am-ma-*[*mu*]

a+5). [. . . .] X úru líl.lá ba.gi_4.gi_4

[X] X URU *šá ana za-qí-qí i-tu-ru*

a+4 . . the *bīt ziqīqi* which is completely silent; a+5 . . the town which is turned to the wind.

ii). A *bīt zaqīqi* is attested lexically twice in ea A = *nâqu* [*MSL* 14], on Tab. 4, line 273 [ibid., p. 366] and, in expanded form, on Tab. 4/4 = 25, line 193 [ibid., p. 387], as gá.líl.lá = *bīt*(É) *zi/za-qi-qu* (gá is the *Emesal* equivalent of é). The references are in lists of various types of "houses".

In the expanded version (Tab. 4/4 = 25, lines 193-200) gá.líl.lá is also equated with such places as "the house of the open country", É *ṣe-ri* (line 195), "the house of the earth/Underworld", É *er-ṣe-tú* (line 197); and "the house of [the grave[?]]", É ⌈*qa*⌉-[*ab-rum*[?]] (line 199); the other equations are too fragmentary.

iii). S. Lackenbacher [1971] edited four texts which formed her '*ardat-lilî* tablet' (Group 2). Reverse, col. I lines 2'-5' contain a description of the *ardat lilî*-demoness (which is repeated, with minor variants, on rev., col. III lines 1-4):

2').	én ki.sikil	*ar-da-tu*
3').	edin.na.líl.lá	*ša* É *za-qí-qí*
4').	ki.sikil.líl.lá	*ana ar-da-tu*
5').	ab.ba gur.gur.kam	*ina ap-ti it-ta-nu-ru*

[2'] Incantation: "The young girl [3'] of the *bīt zaqīqi* (**Sum.:** of the open country of the *zaqīqu*), [4'-5'] repeatedly returns through the window to the (human) young girl."

(The scribe confused *ardatu*(KI.SIKIL) with *ardat lilî*(KI.SIKIL. LÍL.LÁ), reversing them in lines 2' and 4'. Note that *bītu,* usually written by É, transcribes EDIN, normally *ṣēru.)*

T. Jacobsen [1970, pp. 339-340, n. 28] stated that edin.líl.lá in line 103 of the Sumerian myth *Inanna and Bilulu* appeared to be a house in the desert, supporting his view by (iii) above. All these citations can be taken as referring to actual buildings, away from the settled areas, with no obvious ritual significance. The Akkadian dictionaries translate *bīt zaqīqi* as "a haunted place" (*CAD* Z, p. 60b; *AHw* 3, p. 1530a, *zīqīqu(m),* 2b).

If we are correct in assuming that, in the dream context of the *Epic of Gilgamesh,* the *bīt zaqīqi* was a ritual hut, then there is a possible connection with the reed hut called *kikkišu* mentioned in the various accounts of how Atrahasis received the message from Ea to build the Ark in order to escape the imminent Flood (see pages 231-232).

There is no evidence to support A. L. Oppenheim's [*DB,* pp. 215-216] statement that a breeze came out of the pit (well), putting Gilgamesh to sleep, and causing his dreams. In fact, it is unclear if and how the pit dug at line 83 is related to the hut and the incubation episode. S. Dalley [1991, p. 127, n. 33] suggested that the digging and the flour offering were connected with a rite to appease the demons of the open country. She pointed out that one piece of advice given to Gilgamesh by the elders of Uruk before he set out against Humbaba was: Old Babylonian (Yale) Version (M. Jastrow and A. T. Clay [1920], pls. 1-7 and frontispiece photograph), Tab. 3, col. VI line 268:

> 268). *i-na nu-ba-ti-ka hi-ri bu-ur-tam*
> Dig a well at your night's resting place!

Gilgamesh is made to lie down (line 90), yet is described as sleeping with his chin leaning on his knees (line 92); i.e., sleeping upright. A. L. Oppenheim [*DB*, p. 216] believed that Gilgamesh slept "in the rather unnatural position of a person squatting on the ground". He explained this as a possible imitation of the 'contracted' burial position, and perhaps necessary to induce prognostic dreams.

S. Parpola [1993, p. 192, n. 120] regarded Gilgamesh as a mystic, from a Kabbalistic view-point, one element being:

> "the special technique (pressing head between knees) he uses for attaining dreams."

He referred to the discussion of 'Elijah's posture' (*1 Kings* 18: 42) by M. Idel [1988, pp. 78-96]. However, many of the examples offered there associated this pose with weeping (which in itself brought visions), or the position was used to 'survey' the angels' dwellings. Such visions are far more religiously orientated than Gilgamesh's symbolic-message dreams. In addition, Gilgamesh's chin was on, not between, his knees.

Another, albeit prosaic, explanation is that Gilgamesh sat with his back against the hut's wall, his head (= chin) on his knees, utterly exhausted after their forced march (see lines 81-82).

ATRA-HASĪS

The uproar from numerous Mankind prevents Enlil from sleeping, so he sends in turn: a plague; drought; famine; and the Flood. He is thwarted in his attempts to annihilate Mankind by Ea/Enki, who advises the hero Atrahasis.

Ea and Atrahasis converse (Tab. 1, lines 366-367), and Ea recommends that Mankind ignores all the deities except Namtar (the Plague God), offering him a baked (loaf) and cheap scented flour (Tab. 1, lines 378-383). Namtar is embarrassed into relenting. The same advice is given to persuade Adad to bring rain (Tab. 2, col. II lines 9-14).

a). Atrahasis And The Famine

There is an unexplained change, and distancing, in the communication between Ea and Atrahasis when dealing with the third calamity: Tab. 2, col. III lines 9-10 (also see lines 7-8):

9). [X X-*a*] ^{d}*En-*⌈*ki*⌉ *ta-mi-ma*

10). [*uz-na i-š*]*a-ak-ka-na i-na šu-na-a-ti*

[9] He (Atrahasis) swears by [. . .] of Enki. [10] [He pays] attention in dreams.

The rest of the Old Babylonian text is extremely fragmentary, as are the Late Babylonian duplicates BE 390999 and BE 36669/24a (W. G. Lambert and A. R. Millard [1969], pls. 4, 9-10; and pl. 5 respectively).

The situation has been improved with the publication of IM 124473 (A. R. George and F. N. H. Al-Rawi [1996]), Tab. 5 of a Standard Babylonian version of *Atra-hasīs* from Sippar. Reverse 59-74 describe an incubation ceremony (based on [ibid.], pp. 175, and 182):

59). *u šu-ú At-ra-ha-sis a-me-lu* :

60). *u*$_4$*-me-šam-ma ib-ta-nak-*(*ki*)

61). *maš-šak-ku i-zab-bi-*⌈*lu gi*⌉*-par* ÍD :

62). *e-nu-ma miṭ-ra-tu*$_4$ *šá-*(*hur-rat*)

63). *mu-šu i-zu-uz-ma ni-qú-ú iq-qí*

64). *ši-it-tu*$_4$ *il-la-*⌈*ku*$^{?}$ X⌉*-am-tu*$_4$:

65). *iz-za-kár ana miṭ-ra-ti*

66). *lil-qé-ma miṭ-rat li-bil* ÍD

67). ⌈*liš-šá*⌉*-kin šu-bul-tu*$_4$ *ma-har* ^{d}*É-a be-lí-ia*

68). *li-mur-ma* ^{d}*É-a li-ih-su-sa-an-ni*

69). *ana-ku ina mu-ši šu-ut-ta lu-mur*

70). *iš-tu iš-pu-ra mi-ṭir-tu*$_4$:

71). *ana pu-ut* ÍD *it-ta-šab i-*(*bak-ki*$^{?}$)

72). *ana pu-ut* (ÍD$^{?}$) X (X) X-*ma*$^{?}$ LÚ :

73). *ana* ABZU *it-ta-rad* ⌈*gim*⌉*-lat-su*

74). *iš-me-e-*⌈*ma*⌉ ^{d}*É-a ri-gim-šu*

[59] And he himself, the man Atrahasis, [60] complains in tears daily. [61] He carries *maššakku* (to) a river meadow. [62] When the *miṭirtu*-canal was still, [63] he divided the night, and he performed a sacrifice. [64] (As) sleep came . . . [65] He addresses the *miṭirtu*-canal,

[66] "May the *miṭirtu*-canal take (it)! May the river carry (it)! [67] May the gift be delivered before Ea, my lord! [68] May Ea see (it), and may he heed me [69] so that I myself may see a dream during the night!"

[70] After he commissioned the *miṭirtu*-canal, [71] he sat down facing the river, (and) he cries[?]. [72] Facing the river, the man . (.) . . [73] (Meanwhile,) his favour descends to the Apsu. [74] Ea heard his call.

(A. R. George and F. N. H. Al-Rawi [1996, p. 183, n. 49] interpreted the very unusual phrase "he divided the night" as meaning he arose at midnight.)

Ea replies by sending Atrahasis two messengers, the *lahmu*s (see F. A. M. Wiggermann [1992], pp. 164-166) and his vizier Ushmu. The former convey an acknowledgement of Atrahasis' gift (rev. 92-94), while the latter utters an unhelpful adage (rev. 102). There is no specific mention of these appearing in a dream, but the context suggests a strong probability. A broken section follows, and it is unclear whether Ea gave any advice or acted himself. (The fragmentary Late Babylonian tablet BE 39099, rev. col. II lines 18-28 (also see lines 29-43) recounts that the bar holding back the fishes was breached in some way.)

The incubation ceremony is not as simple as it might appear. A. R. George and F. N. H. Al-Rawi [1996, pp. 173-174] believed that Atrahasis poured out *maššakku*-powder on to the water's surface, both as an offering and as a means of divination. They supported their argument with Gudea Cylinder A, col. XX lines 5-8, where the king performed an extispicy, cast barley (*še'u*(ŠE)) on to flowing water, and incubated a dream. However, instead of regarding the scattering of the barley as part of an incubation ritual while, at the same time, using the same barley in the very minor divinatory technique of aleuromancy to confirm an extispicy [ibid., p. 174], this passage could refer to three unrelated and undescribed divinatory methods: the first two to discover if the time was auspicious to start rebuilding; and the third to obtain details of the temple (col. XX, lines 9-12).

In the Old Babylonian version of IM 124473, line 61, Atrahasis carries *maššakku* in the morning ([*i-n*]*a še-re-ti;* Tab. 2, col. III line 6), yet the dream ritual is not performed until the dead of night.

The few other texts mentioning *maššakku/muššakku* connect it with the *šā'ilu* ([LÚ]ENSI), usually translated as "dream interpreter", but who had other functions. (The writer intends to discuss this ritual expert, and his feminine counterpart, the *šā'iltu*([MÍ]ENSI), elsewhere.) The commentary tablet K. 3291 (*BWL,* pls. 15-17) on *Ludlul bēl nemēqi,* obv. 27':

27'). *maš-šak-ku sur-qí-nu šá* [LÚ]⌈ENSI⌉

maššakku (is) the (usual) offering of the *šā'ilu.*

The way in which the *šā'ilu* uses *maššakku* is only described once, and there is no mention of dreams. On two occasions various ritual experts are trying to discover the reasons for divine wrath:

i). 4 *R*^{2}. 22, No. 2, lines 10'-11':

10'). ensi.e še.e.ta i.bí.a nu mu.un.na.an.bad.bè

11'). *šá-i-lu ina mu-uš-šá-ak-ka ul i-pe-te-šú*

The *šā'ilu* cannot enlighten him by *muššakku* (**Sum.:** by barley, by the smoke).

ii). *Ludlul bēl nemēqi,* Tab. 2, line 7:

7). *ina ma-áš-šak-ka* ^{LÚ}ENSI *ul ú-šá-pi di-i-ni*

The *šā'ilu* cannot elucidate my situation by *maššakku.*

The Late Version of the *Legend of Etana,* Tab. 2, lines 131-136 records the numerous offerings Etana has made in the hope of begetting a son, and divination is not practised: line 135:

135). *ig-dam-ra maš-šak-ki-ia* ^{MÍ}ENSI.MEŠ

The *šā'iltus* have used up my *maššakku.*

maššakku was a type of scented powder: the lexical text *malku* = *šarru,* Tab. 3, as on *SpTU* 3, No. 120, col. IV line 217:

217). *mu-šak-*⌜*ku*⌝ | *maṣhatu*(ZÌ.MAD.GÁ)

muššakku (equals) cheap scented flour.

Cheap scented flour is used in many non-dream ceremonies (see *CAD* M_1, pp. 330-331). In other incubation rituals it is offered by Gilgamesh (Tab. 4, line 86); used to draw a figure of the intended dreamer's personal deity (*ROP,* line 51); burnt with juniper in a censer (*ROP,* line 60); and scattered *(nasāku)* on a roof top (*ROP,* lines 83-84). The suggestion that *maššakku* was scattered for aleuromancy was mentioned on page 229; alternatively, *DB,* p. 222 suggested that it was burnt and omens deduced from the resultant smoke patterns (libanomancy; see also 4 *R*^{2}. 22, No. 2, lines 10'-11' above). Perhaps the fumes from the censer were intended to induce dreams/visions.

If not *maššakku*, something was definitely thrown on to the *miṭirtu*-canal, and descended to Ea. In contrast to Gudea Cylinder A, col. XX line 6, where barley was cast on to moving water (A. R. George and F. N. H. Al-Rawi [1996], p. 173, n. 39), the movement of the water through this irrigation canal had ceased, and Atrahasis threw his offering on to the still *(šuharruru)* water.

Line 63 does not help us to decide what this substance was. *niqû* means "offering, sacrifice", mainly of animals or birds (*CAD* N_2, pp. 252-259), and the expression *niqâ naqû* means "to perform a sacrifice" (*CAD* N_2, pp. 337-338).

When the verb *naqû* denotes "to pour out (as a libation)", the substance is usually specified, replacing *niqâ*. The namburbi rituals list various substances cast into a river, including beer, dates, types of flour, and plants; nothing from a sacrificed creature. These were offerings, but not necessarily to Ea or to the River; e.g., *Cap.* 6, obv. 25-26 (S. M. Maul [1994], pp. 304-310), to Marduk and Shamash.

Until further evidence is obtained, the writer believes that Atrahasis' incubation ceremony merely consisted of an offering to Ea, perhaps of *maššakku.*

The Assyrian recension of *Atra-hasīs,* on Text S, is different: rev. col. V lines 27-33 (see the fragmentary Old Babylonian version, Tab. 2, col. III lines 6-14):

27). [EN *ta-ši-im-t*]*i* ^{m}*A-tar-hasīs*(GEŠTUG) LÚ
28). [*a-na* EN-*šú* ^{d}*É*]-*a* GEŠTUG^{II}-*šu pi-ta-at*
29). [*i-ta-m*]*u it-ti* DINGIR-*šu*
30). [*ù šu* ^{d}*E*]-*a it-ti-šú i-ta-mu*
31). [*i-še*] KÁ DINGIR-*šu*
32). [*i-n*]*a pu-ut* ÍD *il-ta-kán ma-a-a-al-šu*
33). ⌜*ù*⌝ *me-eṭ-ra-tu šu-hu-rat*

[27] [The Lord of Understanding], the man Atrahasis, [28] listened (lit., opened his ear) [to his lord, Ea]. [29] [He spoke] with his god, [30] [and he, Ea,] spoke with him. [31] [He sought] the gate of his god. [32] He places his bed facing the river. [33] The *miṭirtu*-canal is still.

(Nothing more is recorded.)

b). Atrahasis And The Flood

As W. G. Lambert [1960, p. 119] commented, the tale of Ea's communication with Atrahasis concerning the imminent Flood seems to have been modified throughout the centuries. W. G. Lambert believed that originally Ea whispered through the reed hut's walls to the hero listening on the other side; thereby not breaking his vow to Enlil not to aid the humans, by ostensibly addressing the *kikkišu:*

i). On the Assyrian recension (BM 98977 + 99231; *Journal Of Semitic Studies* 5 [1960], p. 116), Ea has entered Atrahasis' house, the latter hearing the god's footsteps (obv. 1-8). Ea starts addressing the *kikkišu* of his own accord (obv. 13-16), after a fragmentary speech from the hero (W. G. Lambert and A. R. Millard [1969], p. 122).

ii). The version from Ugarit (*Ugaritica* 5 [1968], p. 441, No. 167; W. G. Lambert and A. R. Millard [1969], p. 132) states that Ea repeated the gods' words to the *kikkišu* (obv. 12-13).

iii). There are different translations of the extremely fragmentary Sumerian Flood Story (*PBS* 5, No. 1 and pls. 76-77). They agree that Ziusudra (the Sumerian Atrahasis) is told to stand by a side wall (iz.zi.da) and listen while an unnamed god (probably Enki) speaks to him (lines 152-155). Although line 149 mentions a dream (in a disputed passage), this seems to be a separate incident (W. G. Lambert and A. R. Millard [1969], p. 142).

The statement that Ea's message was via a dream (prognostic, if not incubated) occurs on the *Epic of Gilgamesh,* Tab. 11. Ea talks to various deities (lines 15-19), and repeats their words both to the *kikkišu* and the *igāru,* "wall" (lines 19-20). Later on, when Ea is denying that he warned Atrahasis, he says that he sent the hero a dream (lines 186-187).

Two other texts mention a dream, although in these cases it is only stated that Ea interpreted the dream, so he did not necessarily send it:

i). On *Atra-hasīs,* Tab. 3, the hero asks Ea to teach him the meaning of a dream he has seen (col. I lines 11-14). Ea tells Atrahasis to pay attention to his words (col. I lines 17-18), then proceeds to address the wall and the *kikkišu* (col. I lines 20-21). The dream's interpretation consists of explicit details on constructing an Ark.

ii). Ea says "I will interpret (presumably a dream)", *a-pa-aš-šar,* on CBS 13532, rev. 2 (a Nippur fragment, *Babylonian Expedition of the University of Pennsylvania (Series D),* 5 [1910], p. 8; W. G. Lambert and A. R. Millard [1969], p. 126).

A ceremonial use of a *kikkišu* reed hut is mentioned on *ABL* 4 (= *SAA* 10, No. 210), obv. 7-9 (a letter dealing with a namburbi rite for an earthquake), which describes it as in a secluded area *(qersu),* and entered by the king; also see *ABL* 183 (= *SAA* 10, No. 211), obv. 6-9. (We do not know how the *kikkišu* reed hut differed from the more frequently attested *šutukku* reed hut, also used in rituals; see *CAD* $Š_3$, pp. 411-412.) In the various *Atra-hasīs* episodes, the *kikkišu* could be either a special ritual site, or an ordinary hut which is momentarily given a special function in the communications between god and man. There are no indications in the different versions that Atrahasis incubated this dream, but the previous episode of the famine suggests the possibility. The *kikkišu* may be connected with the *bīt zaqīqi* in the *Epic of Gilgamesh* (pages 225-226) which, outwardly, was a sturdy shelter built by Enkidu, who had not received any religious training. (The 'practical' citations of *kikkišu* [*CAD* K, p. 352b] refer to a reed fence surrounding a field.)

NABONIDUS 8, COLUMN VII LINES 1'-15'

A. L. Oppenheim [*DB,* p, 205] regarded this incident as:

> "one of the few unequivocally described incubation-dreams in cuneiform literature."

After seeing Nebuchadrezzar II in a dream (col. VI; page 16), Nabonidus proceeds to seek another divine message. The break at the beginning of col. VII continued the account of the Nebuchadrezzar dream episode and, perhaps, some ritual detail. Column VII lines 1'-15':

Break

1'). [. . . . ^{d}]*Dil-bat* ^{d}UDU.IDIM SAG.UŠ
2'). [. . . .] ^{MUL}ŠU.PA ^{MULd}ŠÀM
3'). $^{[MUL]}$GAL *a-ši-ib ša-ma-me*
4'). [*sur*]-⸢*qin*⸣-*nu ra-ab-bu-tì*
5'). *áš-tak-kan-šu-nu-ti-ma*
6'). *a-na* TIN U$_4$.MEŠ *ru-qu-ti*
7'). ⸢*kun*⸣-*nu* ^{GIŠ}GU.ZA *la-bar* BAL-*e*
8'). *du-um-mu-qa a-ma-tu-ú-a*
9'). *ina ma-har* ^{d}*Marduk be-lí-ia*
10'). *ú-sa-al-li-šú-nu-ti*
11'). *a-na-al-ma ina šat mu-ši*
12'). ^{d}*Nin-<tin->ug$_5$-ga be-*[*e*]*l-ti*
13'). *mu-bal-li-ṭa-at mi-i-tú*
14'). SUM-*at* ZI-*tì ru-uq-tú*
15'). *ap-pa-li-is-ma*

$^{1'-5'}$ I placed a very large offering (before) Venus, Saturn, [. . . .], Arcturus, the ŠÀM-star, (and) Jupiter, (who) dwell in the heavens. $^{6'-10'}$ I inquired of them in front of Marduk, my lord, regarding (my) long life (lit., life of distant days), established rule, lasting reign, (and) my very favourable matters. $^{11'}$ I lie down, and during the night $^{12'-15'}$ I saw Nintinugga (i.e., Gula), my lady, the one who heals the dying, the giver of long life.

(There are traces of a line before line 1 in *MVAG* 1, also omitted here. The restoration at the beginning of line 4' follows E. Reiner [1960a, p. 24, n. 2]. A. L. Oppenheim [*DB,* p. 205] followed the restoration of S. Langdon [*NBK*] for the same line, having the stars acting "as exalted witnesses", [*mu*]*-kin-nu ra-ab-bu-tim.)*

The ceremony is part of Nabonidus' consultation of various astral beings. We are not told the nature of his later nocturnal experience involving Gula. If it was a dream, then it is unusual (compared to his other dream reports) both in that Nabonidus did not record this fact and in that no precise message was received. Gula's (brief) appearance is regarded as confirming the king's request for a long life and secure reign.

THE *WEIDNER CHRONICLE*

The Neo-Babylonian temple library discovered at Sippar in 1986 (*Iraq* 48 [1987], pp. 248-249) has yielded another copy of the *Weidner Chronicle* (see A. K. Grayson [*ABC*], No. 19; and I. L. Finkel, *JCS* 32 [1980], pp. 72-75). F. N. H. Al-Rawi [1990] used this tablet, IM 124470 [ibid., pp. 11-13], to present a revised edition of the composite text.

The 'chronicle' is actually a literary letter from a king of Isin to the ruler of Babylon (or Larsa, modern Tell Senkereh), most probably from Damiq-ilishu (1816-1794 B.C.) to Apil-Sin (1830-1813 B.C.) (or Rim-Sin I (1822-1763 B.C.) at Larsa) (F. N. H. Al-Rawi [1990], p. 1), with a historical section. The first part of letter recommends that the recipient maintains his rule over Babylon by continuing the offerings in Esagila. The writer goes on to mention a dream he saw, in which he received advice on a specific plan: obv., composite lines (based on F. N. H. Al-Rawi's [1990] rendition):

10). *a-na* ^{d}*Nin-kar-ra-ak-a* GAŠAN-*ia b*[*é-le*]-*et É-*⸢*gal-mah*⸣ *ni-qa-a* ⸢*aq*⸣-*qí-*⸢*šim*⸣-*ma*

11). *ut-nen-ši su-pe-e-šá aṣ-bat-ma* [*a*]-⸢*ma*⸣-*a-ti* <*šá*$^{?}$> *ina lìb-bi* [*eš*]-*te-né-ú šá-a-šú a*[*q-bi*]-⸢*šim*⸣ <*um-ma*> *lu-ú a-na-ku-ma*

[10] I performed a sacrifice to Ninkarrak (i.e., Gula), my lady, the mistress of Egalmah (the temple of Ninisina (again Gula) in Isin). [11] I prayed to her. I besought her with supplications, and I [told] her the matters <which$^{?}$> my heart constantly strives after. Indeed, I myself (spoke) <thus>: (lines 12-13).

14). KÙ-tu_4 ^{d}*Gu-la be-el-t*[*i ṣ*]*ir-tú i-na šat* ⸢*mu*⸣-*ši iz-zi-za-n*[*im-m*]*a* ⸢INIM.MEŠ⸣-*ia* [*iš-me*]-⸢*ma*⸣ *ki-niš i-ta-*⸢*ma*$^{!}$ *it-ti*⸣-*ia*

Holy Gula, the exalted lady, stood by me during the night. [She heard] my words, and spoke with me truthfully (lines 15-32).

33). *e-zib šá ina* MÁŠ.GE$_6$-*ia* EŠ.BAR *iq-qa-ba-a*

Apart from the oracular decision which was pronounced in my dream . . . .

The reason for regarding this dream incident as an incubation is similar to that for Nabonidus' above. Namely, the goddess is petitioned, and later appears at night in a dream (obv. 33). (F. N. H. Al-Rawi [1990, p. 1] described the episode as a "nocturnal vision".) However, the sacrifice and the prayers are a standard way of approaching the gods so need not have an incubatory function.

A more serious obstacle to accepting this incident as an incubation is that, while the petitioner (a king of Isin) asked for dominance in Mesopotamia (obv. 12-13), Gula replied that Marduk has determined the elevation of Babylon (where the letter's recipient resided), and mentioned long life (obv. 34ff.). Thus, the incident appears to be a glorification of Babylon and of Marduk (as is the remainder of the *Weidner Chronicle*), and suspect evidence for the practice of incubation.

ANATOLIAN STUDIES 33 [1983], PAGE 79

Reverse 5'-8' of the fragmentary tablet BM 47749 (= 81-11-3, 454):

5') ^{m}*Ku-ri-gal-zu* {DIŠ} *a-na É-sag-íla* ⌜*i-te*⌝*-ru-u*[*b* X X (X)]

6'). *za-qí-qí iṭ-hu-šu-ma pu-uh-pu-hu-ú su*$^?$ *bu* ⌜X⌝ [X (X)]

7'). *ṣa-lil ina m*[*a*]-⌜*a-a*-IL-*ti*⌝*-šú* ^{m}*Ku-ri-gal-zu* MÁŠ.GE$_6$ *i-na-*[*ṭal*]

8'). *ina še-*⌜*rim*⌝ *ina ṣi-*⌜*it* ^{d}UTU-*ši* MÁŠ⌝.GE$_6$ *ana* ^{LÚ}GAL. MEŠ *i-puš*$_4$ [*tè-ma*$^?$]

$^{5'}$ Kurigalzu entered Esagila [. . (.)] $^{6'}$ The *zaqīqu*s approached him, and anxiety . . . [. (.)] $^{7'}$ he lies asleep. Kurigalzu saw a dream (while) in his bed. $^{8'}$ In the morning, at dawn, he made [a report$^?$ (on his)] dream to his nobles (which follows on the rest of the reverse).

(The translation of *pu-uh-pu-hu-ú* and the restoration at the end of rev. 8' come from I. L. Finkel [1983].)

There is no doubt that Kurigalzu saw a dream. However, a lacuna in the text leaves us uncertain as to the role of the *zaqīqu*s and if he slept in Esagila, instead of in his palace. Pages 81-83 discussed the idea that sometimes *zaqīqu*(s) denoted a ritual expert (possibly a prophet or a supervisor of the incubation process), instead of the spiritual beings which I. L. Finkel [1983] preferred.

The obverse records the distress of a woman called Qatantu. I. L. Finkel [1983, p. 76] suggested that the reason for Kurigalzu's incubation was connected with her plight, perhaps barrenness (or failure to produce a son), and to discover whether or not it was a permanent condition. If Qatantu was his wife, this would have been a serious matter because Kurigalzu was probably one of the Kassite rulers of that name (I. L. Finkel [1983], p. 75, n. 4). *AnSt* 33 [1983], p. 79 is not an example of medical incubation because the queen should have been the dreamer.

I. L. Finkel [1983, p. 76, n. 5] believed that the nobles interpreted Kurigalzu's dream. Instead, the king may have recounted the results of his 'incubation' to allay their fears about the succession and the turmoil into which the realm might be thrown.

SUMMARY

No overall pattern can be deduced from the few examples of Mesopotamian incubation, though the practice varies from the Classical pattern.

One major difference is that while the bulk of the evidence shows that Classical incubation was available to, and practised by, 'ordinary' people, only the late source *ROP* indicates this possibility in Mesopotamia. The cuneiform literary sources, due to their nature, involve either heroes or kings, who were identified with the state.

a). Location

In opposition to the definition quoted at the beginning of this chapter, there is no statement that Mesopotamian incubation was practised in temples (perhaps this was understood). The presence of the putative *zaqīqu* professionals on *AnSt* 33 [1983], p. 79 strongly suggests that this incident (if it was incubation) occurred in Esagila. The "temple of the Dream God Zaqiqu" in the *Epic of Gilgamesh,* Tab. 4 is quite different. This was surrounded by a circle (line 90), thus in a sacred area.

Since the ceremonies of *ROP* were performed for a non-royal individual, they may have taken place at a private residence, even on the roof (lines 62 and 82). Only in lines 66-67 is a sacred area demarcated, by a circle of pure water.

b). Participants

The exorcist *(āšipu)* carried out the ceremonies of *ROP* (see page 121), aided in one complex by "a youth who has not known a woman" (line 66). The purification of the participants is only recorded in line 57, and applies to the practitioner (perhaps this was done automatically). The sole mention of the intended dreamer is in line 60, but the statements, for example, at line 84, "You lie down, and you will see an oracular decision", must refer to him to make sense.

See pages 81-83 on the possible *zaqīqu* professionals. Atrahasis, Enkidu, and Gilgamesh were not ritually qualified, though probably this was irrelevant in literary compositions.

c). Time

As one would expect, the rites were performed at night. Gilgamesh's and Enkidu's preparations were made after an overnight camp had been pitched. On *ROP,* lines 43, 48, 66-67, and 82-83, offerings were placed before certain constellations. It is possible that their emblems were meant [*DB,* p. 205] but *ROP,* lines 81e and 82, describes a ceremony at the dead of night. This is surprisingly late, perhaps due to its association with shooting star rituals (see pages 222-223). Atrahasis also performed a ritual late at night (IM 124473, rev. 62-63).

d). The Deities Invoked

Although there were Dream Gods (chapter 6), they played an insignificant part in all types of Mesopotamian dream rites, and are not even mentioned in the incubation examples. We will probably never know if incubation was practised in Mamu's temple at Balawat (pages 74-76).

Various astral and nocturnal beings are addressed on *ROP,* as well as Gula. The personal deities are not invoked, even when the ritual's purpose was for the suppli-cant to speak with them (complexes lines 44-51 and 52-60). Atrahasis addressed Ea.

e). Motives

ROP, lines 70, and 74-76, queries whether or not an undefined purpose would be achieved. One ceremony could be used for two different aims: line 64, with the 'omens' in lines 69-70.

Regarding incubation for medical purposes *(ROP),* no cure or divine prescrip-tion was sought, only the revelation of the gods' decision about the patient's recovery. The *tamītu* CBS 12578 mentions dreams concerning an invalid's chances (page 41), but it is unclear how these dreams occurred. (See pages 235-236 on *AnSt* 33 [1983], p. 79).

It is possible that *ABL* 1347 (= *SAA* 10, No. 305) attests to a doctor having seen a dream regarding his young patient: rev. 1-3:

1). *šu*[!]*-tu-šú de-eq-*⌜*tú*[!]⌝ *am-rat*

2). *e-ge-ra-šú as-se-me*

3). *ú-m*[*a-a*] *šùl-mu a-dan-niš*

[1] His (the baby's) favourable dream has been seen (on his behalf[?],

and) [2] I have heard his oracular utterance. [3] Now, he is extremely healthy.

See page 225 for the motive behind Gilgamesh's incubations. Atrahasis sought solutions for the famine and the Flood sent by Enlil.

OTHER POSSIBLE REFERENCES TO INCUBATION IN MESOPOTAMIA

DB, p. 233 believed that obv. 9' of the fragmentary Middle Assyrian letter BM 104727 (= 1912-5-13, 2; *Journal of the Royal Asiatic Society* 1904, p. 415 + Sm. 2116, implied that the haruspex *(bārû)* could incubate dreams:

9'). [^{d}*Nin-urta-tuku*]*l-*^{d}*Aš-šur ba-*⌈*ru-tam ip*⌉*-pu-šú šu-na-a-ti i-ta-nam-ma-r*[*u* . . . .]

They perform extispicies (lit., the craft of the haruspex), (and) they repeatedly see dreams [(for) Ninurta-tukulti-Ashur . . . .]

"They" are anonymous and, although dreams are apparently incubated, there is no reason to suppose that the same people were doing both actions. Instead, it seems that various divination experts were working simultaneously with different techniques over a political wrangle between Assyria and Babylonia at c. 1133 B.C. (see J. A. Brinkman [*PHPKB*], pp. 101-104 for the historical background). (A. R. George (*JNES* 52 [1993], p. 297) has identified and joined two unpublished duplicates, BM 55498 (= 82-7-4, 72) and BM 55499 (= 82-7-4, 73), and plans a new edition.)

A chronicle fragment about the First Dynasty of Isin (2017-1794 B.C) (*CT* 13, pl. 45b; A. K. Grayson [*ABC*], pp. 190-191) describes someone seeing a dream after taking tribute to Ekur: obv., col. I line 8':

8'). [. . . . -*i*]*l-ma* MÁŠ.GE$_6$ *i-na-aṭ-ṭal*

[He lay] down, and he started dreaming (lit., he sees a dream).

The incompleteness of the lines makes it difficult to establish the context. A. K. Grayson [*ABC,* p. 190] suggested that obv., col. I lines 6'-10' contained an attempt either to secure confirmation of earlier approval from Enlil or to inquire about another scheme.

The practice of incubation may be recalled in an incantation to Marduk (*AfO* 19 [1959-1960], p. 57, lines 111-112):

111). *e-nu-ma at-ta-i-lu-uš i-du-uš-šú*

112). *at-mu-šu nu-us-su-uq-ma sè-kàr-šú šu-šur*

[111] When I lie down at his (Marduk's) side, [112] his message is well-

chosen, and his discourse correct (i.e., appropriate).

The recipient of the divine communication had lain down beside a statue of Marduk, probably in a temple, and had seen a dream/vision.

TEXT EDITIONS

MANUSCRIPTS

Notes To The Following Tables

T = Text exists in transliteration only

X_1 = Tablet does not belong to the technical dream literature

Lower case = Tablets in Babylonian script

Upper case = Tablets in Assyrian script

Roman numerals = Sumerian texts

Page numbers refer to (additional) sections of tablets not included in the composite texts.

PUBLICATION DETAILS

Publication Details	Symbol(s)
plates 1-2	*SDR* – **A**
plates 3-4	*ADRC* – **B**; *NADR* – **A**; pages 313-319
plate 5	*ADRC* – **G**; *ZI* – **A**; pages 321-324
plate 6a	*ADRC* – **H**
plate 6b	pages 399-400
plate 7	*ADRC* – **M**
plate 8	*ADRC* – **D**; pages 325-326
plate 9	*ADRC* – **C**; pages 327-329
plates 10-12	*ADRC* – **f**; *NADR* – **b**; pages 331-333
plate 13	pages 407-410
plate 14	*ADRC* – **j**; pages 335-336
plate 15a	*SDR* – $\mathbf{d_1}$
plate 15b	*SDR* – **c**
plate 16	(see pages 178-179)
plate 17	*NROD* – **B**
plate 18	*NROD* – **C**
plate 19	pages 337-338
plate 20	*NROD* – **E**
ABL 450	*SDR* – $\mathbf{G_1}$
BAM 376	*ADRC* – $\mathbf{B_1}$
BAM 377	*ADRC* – $\mathbf{A_1}$
BAM 384	*ADRC* – $\mathbf{C_1}$

Publication Details	**Symbol(s)**
BMS 1	*SDR* - $\mathbf{A_1}$
E. Combe [1908], No. 6 - T	*SDR* - **b**
CT 51, No. 103	*ROP* - **D**
CT 51, No. 149	*NROD* - **G**
KAR 53	*ADRC* - **P**
KAR 58	*NROD* - **A**
KAR 213	*ADRC* - $\mathbf{B_1}$
KAR 252	*ADRC* - **A**
LKA 39	*SDR* - $\mathbf{F_1}$
LKA 132	*ADRC* - **N**; *NROD* - **F**
LKA 138	*ROP* - $\mathbf{A_1}$
LM 1 (+ K. 17283)	*SDR* - $\mathbf{B_1}$
LM 2	*SDR* - $\mathbf{E_1}$
PBS 12/1, No. 29	*ZI* - **II**
PBS 13, No. 38	*ZI* - **I**
PSBA 40 [1918], pl. 7	*SDR* - **A**
SLTN 149	*ADRC* - **I**
SpTU 2, No. 8	*NROD* - **d**
SpTU 2, Nos. 10 (+) 9	*NROD* - $\mathbf{a_1}$
SpTU 2, No. 21	pages 401-405
STT 56	*SDR* - $\mathbf{C_1}$
STT 73	*ROP* - **A**
STT 107 (+) 246	*ADRC* - **K**
STT 245	*ADRC* - **E**
STT 247	*ADRC* - $\mathbf{E_1}$
STT 275	*ADRC* - $\mathbf{D_1}$
ŠRT, pl. 3	*ADRC* - **H**
UET 7, No. 118	*ROP* - **b**
YOS 11, No. 75	*ROP* - **c**

MUSEUM NUMBERS

Museum Number	See Number	Publication Details	Symbol
BM 35182		*CT* 51, No. 103	*ROP* - **D**
BM 66559		plate 16	(pages 178-9)
BM 78432		PSBA 40 [1918], pl. 7 and plates 1-2 here	*SDR* - **A**
BM 134542		*CT* 51, No. 149	*NROD* - **G**
Bu. 88-5-12, 335	BM 78432		
CBS 4567		*PBS* 12/1, No, 29	*ZI* - **II**
CBS 14188		*PBS* 13, No. 38	*ZI* - **I**
K. 155		*BMS* 1	*SDR* - $\mathbf{A}_1$
K. 898		*ABL* 450	*SDR* - $\mathbf{G}_1$
K. 2823 + 3332 + 11347 + 11722 + 15427 + * K. 17283		*LM* 1 and * extra	*SDR* - $\mathbf{B}_1$
K. 3286		*ŠRT*, pl. 3 and plate 6a here	*ADRC* - **H**
K. 3332	K. 2823 +		
K. 3333 + 8583 + Sm. 1069		plates 3-4	*ADRC* - **B** *NADR* - **A** pages 313-319
K. 3758		plate 5	*ADRC* - **G** *ZI* - **A** pages 321-324
K. 4103 + 13330 + 15911		plate 7	*ADRC* - **M**
K. 5175 + 6001		plate 8	*ADRC* - **D** pages 325-326
K. 6001	K. 5175 +		
K. 7664 + 9302 + 9494		plate 17	*NROD* - **B**
K. 8171 + 11041 + 11684 + 14058		plate 9	*ADRC* - **C** pages 327-329
K. 8583	K. 3333 +		
K. 9000		plate 18	*NROD* - **C**
K. 9302	K. 7664 +		
K. 9494	K. 7664 +		

Museum Number	See Number	Publication Details	Symbol
K. 11041	K. 8171 +		
K. 11347	K. 2823 +		
K. 11406		plate 19	pages 337-382
K. 11684	K. 8171 +		
K. 11706 + 13288		plate 20	*NROD* - **E**
K. 11722	K. 2823 +		
K. 13288	K. 11706 +		
K. 13330	K. 4103 +		
K. 14058	K. 8171 +		
K. 15427	K. 2823 +		
K. 15911	K. 4103 +		
K. 17283	K. 2823 +		
Ni. 2757		*SLTN* 149	*ADRC* - **I**
Si 18		E. Combe [1908], No. 6 - T	*SDR* - **b**
Si 884		plate 15a	*SDR* - $\mathbf{d}_1$
Si 904		plate 15b	*SDR* - **c**
Sm. 543		plate 6b	pages 399-400
Sm. 1069	K. 3333 +		
Sm. 1382		*LM* 2	*SDR* - $\mathbf{E}_1$
S.U. 51/1 + 25		*STT* 73	*ROP* - **A**
S.U. 51/25	S.U. 51/1 +		
S.U. 51/56		*STT* 245	*ADRC* - **E**
S.U. 51/99		*STT* 247	*ADRC* - $\mathbf{E}_1$
S.U. 51/107		*STT* 56	*SDR* - $\mathbf{C}_1$
S.U. 51/212 (+) 52/10		*STT* 107 (+) 246	*ADRC* - **K**
S.U. 52/10	S.U. 51/212 (+)	*STT* 246	
S.U. 52/74 + 382		*STT* 275	*ADRC* - $\mathbf{D}_1$
S.U. 52/382	S.U. 52/74 +		
VAT 8260		*BAM* 376 and *KAR* 213	*ADRC* - $\mathbf{B}_1$
VAT 8913		*KAR* 53	*ADRC* - **P**
VAT 9026		*KAR* 252	*ADRC* - **A**
VAT 9030		*KAR* 58	*NROD* - **A**
VAT 13615		*LKA* 138	*ROP* - $\mathbf{A}_1$

Museum Number	**See Number**	**Publication Details**	**Symbol**
VAT 13620		*LKA* 132	*ADRC* - **N**
			NROD - **F**
VAT 13823 + 14044		*BAM* 377	*ADRC* – $\mathbf{A_1}$
VAT 14044	VAT 13823 +		
VAT 14060		*LKA* 39	*SDR* - $\mathbf{F_1}$
VAT 17141		*BAM* 384	*ADRC* - $\mathbf{C_1}$
W 22729/5 (+) 22729/18		*SpTU* 2, Nos. 10 (+) 9	*NROD* – $\mathbf{a_1}$
W 22729/18	W 22729/5 (+)	*SpTU* 2, No. 9	
W 22730/3		*SpTU* 2, No. 21	pages 401-405
W 22762/2		*SpTU* 2, No. 8	*NROD* - **d**
YBC 9884		*YOS* 11, No. 75	*ROP* – **c**
79-7-8, 77		plates 10-12	*ADRC* - **f**
			NADR - **b**
			pages 331-333
81-2-4, 166		plate 13	pages 407-410
81-2-4, 233		plate 14	*ADRC* - **j**
			pages 335-336
1932-12-12, 537	BM 134542		
None given		*UET* 7, No. 118	*ROP* – **b**

ASHUR DREAM RITUAL COMPENDIUM (ADRC)

TEXTS

DB, pl. 1 (photograph of **M**, only K. 4103 and K. 13330 separately)

C. D. Gray [*ŠRT*] pl. 3 (**H**)

KAR 53 and 252 (**P** and **A**)

LKA 132 (**N**)

STT 107 (+) 246, and 245 (**K** and **E**)

For details of the British Museum tablets (except for **H** and **M**), see under their respective editions.

STUDIES

J. J. A. van Dijk [*SSA*], p. 9 (on **I**)

A. L. Oppenheim [*DB*], pp. 295-306, and 338 (transliteration of **M**)

R. Borger [1957-1958] (review of *DB,* with collations of the British Museum tablets)

E. I. Gordon [1960], p. 127 and n. 46 (on **I**)

A. Falkenstein [1966], p. 57 (on **I**)

B. Landsberger [1967], p. 14, n. 37 (col. III line 13)

E. Reiner [1967], p. 190 (on **E**, **K**, and $\mathbf{E}_1$)

H. Hunger [*BAK*], No. 236 on p. 80 (colophon of **A**)

J. Klein [1970-1971], p. 119 and notes 11-12 (on **I**)

M.-J. Seux [1976], pp. 368-372 (translation of col. III lines 4-16, 20-36, and 39-44)

J. Bottéro [1985a], pp. 30, 43 (col. I lines 7-12) and 60 (on **I**)

W. Heimpel [1986], p. 144 (col. III line 20)

W. Farber [*TUAT* 2/2], pp. 269-217 (translation of col. III lines 39-58)

B. R. Foster [*BM* 2], p. 674 (translation of col. III lines 20-36; correct to rev. i)

A. R. George and F. N. H. Al-Rawi [1996], p. 174 (col. III lines 21-23)

MANUSCRIPTS

Symbol	Museum Number	Publication Number	Relevant Lines	Lines On *ADRC*
Column I				
A	VAT 9026	*KAR* 252	col. I lines 1-78	1-12, 13-78
B	K. 3333 + 8583 + Sm. 1069	plates 3-4	col. I lines 19'-22' col. II lines 19-23 col. II lines 24-30	2, 4-6 7-11 12a-g
C	K. 8171 + 11041 + 11684 + 14058	plate 9	lines 1'-4' lines 5'-6'	66-70 71-72
D	K. 5175 + 6001	plate 8	col. I lines 6'-10'	73-78
Column I Line 79 To Column II Line 71				
A	VAT 9026	*KAR* 252	col. I line 79 to col. II line 71	I, 79 - II, 71
D	K. 5175 + 6001	plate 8	col. II lines 3'- 16'	I, 79 - II, 12
E	S.U. 51/56	*STT* 245	obv. 1-18 rev. 1'-11'	I, 79 - II, 9 II, 13-19
f	79-7-8, 77	plates 10-12	obv. 1-13, 17-26	II, 58-71
Column III				
A	VAT 9026	*KAR* 252	col. III lines 1-68	1-3, 4-46, 47-68
B	K. 3333 + 8583 + Sm. 1069	plates 3-4	col. III lines 1'-16'	15-28
f	79-7-8, 77	plates 10-12	obv. 14-15 obv. 16 obv. 27-32 obv. 33-34	1-3 3a 3b-g 52-53
G	K. 3758	plate 5	obv. 8-11	5, 7, 9, 11
H	K. 3286	*ŠRT*, pl. 3 and plate 6a	lines 1-10	20-26
j	81-2-4, 233	plate 14	obv. 3-9 obv. 10-11	39-41, 43-44 45a, 46a
K	S.U. 51/212 (+) 52/10	*STT* 107 (+) 246	obv. 4' to rev. 11'	39-46

Symbol	**Museum Number**	**Publication Number**	**Relevant Lines**	**Lines On *ADRC***
Column III (continued)				
M	K. 4103 + 13330 + 15911	plate 7	lines 1'-16'	47-61

I	Ni. 2757	*SLTN* 149	rev. col. II lines 8'-13'	4, 6, 8, 10
Column IV				
A	VAT 9026	*KAR* 252	col. IV lines 1-47	1-25, 26-30, 31-40, 41b
N	VAT 13620	*LKA* 132	obv. 1'-11' obv. 12'-18' rev. 1-3 rev. 4-6	25, 26-30 38-40, 41b 42-43 45-47
P	VAT 8913	*KAR* 53	obv. 1 to rev. 14	38-47

A_1	VAT 13823 + 14044	*BAM* 377	col. III, lines 16-18	5-7
B_1	VAT 8260	*BAM* 376 (*KAR* 213)	col. I line 31'	5-6
C_1	VAT 17141	*BAM* 384	rev. 6-7	5-6
D_1	S.U. 52/74 + 382	*STT* 275	col IV lines 1-6 col IV lines 7-10 col IV lines 11-12 col IV lines 13-15 col IV lines 16-17	23-25 25a-d 21-22 28-29 30a-b
E_1	S.U. 51/99	*STT* 247	rev. 1-8 rev. 9-16	23-25 28-30

Regarding the texts which are not primarily concerned with dreams:

i). **I** is a Sumerian Proverb Collection.

ii). **A_1-D_1** are charm lists.

iii). The obverse of **E_1** contains a ritual enabling a man to regain royal favour and remove his misfortunes, lost through divine wrath.

A was collated by the writer from photographs, and by M. J. Geller in summer 1990. The photographs suggest that the surface of the tablet has deteriorated since E. Ebeling copied it, especially column I.

* * * * *

OBVERSE

<u>Column I</u>

Line 1

A). [*šumma*(DIŠ) *amēlu*(NA)] *šuttu*([MÁ]Š.⸢GE$_{6}$⸣) *ba*$^{?}$ *nu pa-áš-šú*$^{?!}$(*pa*)-*hi* IGI [X X X] *u* ⸢*ha*$^{?}$⸣

Line 2

[. . . . *k*]*ul-lil* U$_{4}$.<1.KÁM> *šutabrû-ma* U$_{4}$.2.KÁM *gi* [. . . .]-⸢*an*⸣ *mūši*

A). [. . . . *k*]*ul-lil* U$_{4}$.<1.KÁM> ZAL.ZAL-*ma* U$_{4}$.2.KÁM *gi* [. . . .]-⸢*an*⸣ GE$_{6}$

B). [. . . . .] ⸢X⸣ GE$_{6}$

Line 3

A). [. . . .] *tasallah*([S]UD) *ina pūti*(SAG.[K]I)-*šú* (erasure) *tašakkan* (GAR-*an*)

Line 4

[U$_{4}$.3$^{?}$].KÁM ^{GIŠ}*šaššuga tubbal tasâk*

A). [U$_{4}$.3$^{?}$].KÁM ^{GIŠ}(erased ^{Ú})MEZ.GÀM È SÚD

B). [ ] SÚD

Line 5

[*ina*] *šikāri u šamni ana pān*$^{!}$ ⸢^{d}⸣*Šamaš tamahhaṣ la-am šēp-šú ana qaqqari iškunu*

A). [*ina*] KAŠ *u* Ì *ana* IGI$^{!}$(KI) ⸢^{d}⸣UTU SÌG-*aṣ la-am* GÌR-*šú ana* KI GAR-*nu*

B). [. . . . . G]AR-*nu*

Line 6

⌜X⌝*-šú-ma* MÁŠ.GE$_6$ HUL BÚR.⌜RU⌝.DA.KÁM *lumun-ša ana amēli úl iṭehhe*

A). ⌜X⌝*-šú-ma* MÁŠ.GE$_6$ HUL BÚR.⌜RU⌝.DA.KÁM HUL.BI *ana* LÚ *úl* TE-*e*

B). [. . . . . T]E-*e*

Line 7

šumma amēlu šutta ha-ṭi-ta e-ta-mar

A). [N]A MÁŠ.GE$_6$ *ha-ṭi-ta e-ta-mar*

B). DIŠ NA MÁŠ.GE$_6$ *ha-ṭ[i-* . . . .]

Line 8

[. . . .] ⌜X-*šú*⌝*-nu pūti-šú la-am šēp-šú ana qaqqari iškunu*

A). [. . . .] ⌜X-*šú*⌝*-nu* SAG.KI$^{!}$-*šú la-am* GÌR-*šú ana* KI GAR-*nu*

B). *la-am* GÌR-*šú ana* KI GAR-*n*[*u* . . . .]

Line 9

[*be-lu$_4$ pa-t*]*an ra-ma-ni-šú* ⌜*ki*⌝*-a-am iqabbi šunat aṭ-ṭu-lu*

A). [*be-lu$_4$ pa-t*]*an ra-ma-ni-šú* ⌜*ki*⌝*-a-am* DUG$_4$.GA ⌜MÁŠ.GE$_6$⌝ *aṭ-ṭu-lu*

B). MÁŠ.GE$_6$ *aṭ-ṭú-l*[*u* . . . .]

Line 10

[*ma-har*] ^{d}*Sîn u* ^{d}*Šamaš dam-qat dam-qat-ma dam-*⌜*qat*$^{?}$⌝ *dam-qa*[*t*]

A). [*ma-har*] ^{d}30 *u* ^{d}UTU *dam-qat* ⌜*dam*⌝*-qat-*⌜*ma dam-qat*$^{?}$⌝ *dam-qa*[*t*]

B). *dam-qat-ma dam-*[. . . . . .]

Line 11

[*ki-a-am*] *iqabbi-ma i-gir-ri ra-ma-ni-šu*

A). [*ki-a-am*] DUG$_4$.GA-*ma i-g*[*ir*]*-*⌜*ri*⌝ *ra-ma-ni-šu*

B). *i-gir-ri ra-ma-ni-š*[*ú* . . . . . .]

Line 12

A). [*ú-da*]*m-mì-iq-ma šutta*(⌜MÁŠ⌝.GE$_6$)*-šú úl iṭehhe*(TE)*-šú*

Line 12a

B[24]). *šumma*(DIŠ) KIMIN *la-am ṣīt šamši*(^{d}UTU.[È.A) . . . . . .]

Line 12b

B). *amēlu*(LÚ) *ina majāli*(KI.NÁ)-*šú* GE_6 [. . . . .]

Line 12c

B). *nignaqqa*(NÍG.NA) *liš-kun maṣhata*(ZÌ.[MAD.GÁ) . . . . . .]

Line 12d

B). *lip-šur ki-a-am liq-*[*bi* . . . .]

Line 12e

B). *dam-qat kīma*(GIM) *aṭ-ṭ*[*ú-lu* . . . .]

Line 12f

B). *i-na* SAR *là* KÚR ⌜X⌝ [. . . . .]

Line 12g

B). *ù šuttu*(MÁŠ.GE_6) *a-n*[*a* . . . .]

Line 13

A). [*šumma*(DIŠ) *amēlu*(NA) *šutta*(MÁŠ].⌜GE_6⌝) ⌜*ha-ṭi*⌝-*it-tu₄ i-mur be-lu₄ pa-tan*

Line 14

A). [. . . .] ⌜X X X⌝ *qanâ*(⌜GI⌝) ⌜*i*⌝-*pa-šar*!(*šìr*) <*ina*> *išāti*(IZI) *i-qal-lu-ma*

Line 15

A). [*lumun*(HUL) *šutti*(MÁŠ.GE_6)] ⌜*šu-a*⌝-*t*[*u₄*] *ana pāni*(IGI)-*šú ul i-pa-ri-ik*

Line 16

A). [. . . . . .] ⌜X X X⌝ *ana ili*(DINGIR)-[*šú*] *ú-te-er-ma ip-šur*

Line 17

A). [. . . . . .] *ip-*⌜*pa-*X X X X X⌝ *ú-*⌜*'i-il-ma*⌝ *ipehhi*(BAD)-*ma*

Line 18

A). [. . . . . .] ⸢*ra*? *ad* DINGIR X X *niš*? *ù*?⸣ *ana amēli*(LÚ) *šu-a-*tu_4 *i-pa-ri-ik*

Line 19

A). [. . . . . .] ⸢X⸣ [X] ⸢X X⸣ [(X)] ⸢X *ša*⸣ *uš-ta-di-*⸢*ir*⸣ *u* <*amēlu*(NA)> *šū*(BI) *ilsi*(DÉ!.A)

Line 20

A). [. . . . . . *ina šēri*] ⸢*ha-ar*⸣*-pí bābu*(KÁ) *ú-ka-al-lu-šú*

Line 21

A). [. . . . . .] ⸢X X⸣ *i-la-wi-ma šamni*(Ì+GIŠ) *i-ṣa-bu*

Line 22

A). [. . . . . .] ⸢X X⸣ *i-šá-tu i-šá-ka-an šuttu*(MÁŠ.GE_6)

Line 23

A). [. . . . . .] ⸢X X *a*⸣ *ana muhhi*(UGU) ^{GIŠ}*ṣillî*(DÁLLA) *i-ma-nu-ma*

Line 24

A). [ÉN . . . .] ⸢X X⸣*-ma ga-aš-ru dan-nu*

Line 25

A). [. . . . .]*-bé-e kul-la-at it-ti lemutti*(HUL-*tì*)

Line 26

A). [. . . . .] *ana ú-*⸢X X⸣*-ma li-ma-a*(-)*ah-ka*

Line 27

A). [. . . . .] ⸢X⸣ [X] ⸢*ša*? *ga ad bi* X⸣ *lumun*(⸢HUL?⸣)*-*⸢*šá*⸣ *paris* (TAR-*is*)

Line 28

A). [. . . . .] ⸢X *uš*⸣-[*ta*]*-di-i*[*r*]*-*⸢*šú-ma pa/ú ru*?*-ti*⸣

Line 29

A). [. . . . .] SÍG ⸢X *an* X⸣ *imitti*(⸢ZAG⸣)*-*⸢*šú*⸣

Line 30

A). [. . . . .] ⌜X X *i*$^{?}$ *šu* X X hé$^{?}$.me.X X⌝

Line 31

A). [. . . . .] ⌜X *um*⌝-*m*[*a* X (X)] ⌜X X⌝ [X] ⌜X X⌝ *imitti*(⌜ZAG$^{?}$⌝)-⌜*šú*⌝

Line 32

A). [. . . . .] ⌜X *lul ib*$^{?}$-*ba* X X X⌝ [X X] ⌜X X X⌝

Line 33

A). [. . . . .] ⌜X X X X⌝ *te l*[*i*](-)*te*-⌜*eb-ba*$^{?}$⌝-*an-ni*

Line 34

A). [. . . . .] *bu* ⌜X⌝ [*b*]*i ti šikitta-šu*(KI.⌜GAR⌝.BI) *nukkiru*(KÚR-⌜*ru*⌝) ⌜*hul-li*⌝<-*iq*> *zēra*(⌜NUMUN⌝)-⌜*šú*⌝

Line 35

A). [. . . . .] ⌜X *ù* X⌝ [(X)] ⌜X⌝ *lum-ni* ⌜*i*$^{?}$-*šu*⌝

Line 36

A). [. . . . .] *šamê*([A]N$^{?}$-*e*) *erṣetim*(KI-*ti*[*m*]) ⌜*it*$^{?}$⌝ *ta*$^{?}$ ⌜*ki*$^{?}$⌝ *šutti* (⌜MÁŠ.GE$_6$⌝) *lemuttu*(⌜HUL-*tu*$_4$⌝)

Line 37

A). [. . . . . .] ⌜*šá*$^{?}$ *ina*⌝ *barārīti*(⌜EN.NUN$^{!}$.AN.USÁN⌝) *qablīti*(⌜EN.NUN.MURUB$_4$.BA$^{!}$(*tu*)⌝) *šāt urri*([E]N.⌜NUN$^{?}$⌝.U$_4$.ZAL.⌜LE⌝)

Line 38

A). [. . . . . .] *šuttu*([MÁ]Š.⌜GE$_6$⌝) *an-ni-tu ina zu-mur amēli*(⌜LÚ⌝) *an-ni-i*$^{!}$(*zag*)

Line 39

A). [. . . . . .] ⌜*li*$^{?}$-*tu*$^{?}$⌝-*r*[*a*] ⌜X X X X⌝ *ina zu-mur a*-⌜*li-ti*$^{?}$-*ka*⌝-*ma*

Line 40

A). [. . . . . .] ⌜X⌝ *u lumun*(HUL) *šutti*(MÁŠ.G[E$_6$]) ⌜X⌝ *ka* ⌜X⌝ *ina zumri*(SU)-*ia*

Line 41

A). [*šar*$_5$ *bēr*(DANNA) *li-is-s*]*i a-a i-tu-*⌈*ra*⌉ *qanâ*(⌈GI⌉) *šu-*⌈*a*⌉*-ti ana* 2 *ta-ha-mi*$^{!}$*-*⌈*iš*⌉

Line 42

A). [. . . . . . *l*]*u-mu-un šutti*(MÁŠ.GE$_6$) *ana pān*(IGI) ^{d}*Šamaš*(UTU) *ana lib-bi tu-*⌈*kal*⌉

Line 43

A). ⌈X⌉ [. . . . . .] ⌈X X⌉ *ši*$^{!}$(*pi*)*-ma* ⌈^{d}⌉*Šamaš*(⌈UTU⌉) *šutta*([MÁ]Š.⌈GE$_6$⌉) ⌈*an*⌉*-ni-ta ana mah-ri-*⌈*ka*⌉

Line 44

A). *ki-n*[*u* . . . . . .] ⌈X X⌉ URU *la* ⌈X *ak*⌉ *sa*$^{?}$ *la lumun*(HUL)*-šá*

Line 45

A). *úl iṭehhe*(T[E-*e*) . . . . *k*]*a*$^{?}$ ⌈*ta*$^{?}$⌉ *di* ⌈*in*⌉ *ši pa-nu-*⌈*ša*⌉

Line 46

A). *ú-*⌈X⌉-[. . . . .] ⌈X X *im*$^{?}$⌉ *mi ku*

Line 47

A). ⌈*a*-X⌉ [. . . . .] *lumun*(HU]L$^{?}$)*-šá* [*p*]*a-ṭe-*⌈*er*⌉

Line 48

A). *kīma*(⌈GIM⌉) DING[IR X] ⌈X X X *ib* X⌉ [. . . . . .] ⌈X X⌉ *ap* ⌈*pa*$^{?}$*-šìr*$^{?}$*-ma*$^{?}$⌉

Line 49

A). *ma-*⌈*har* X X X X X⌉ *tar ku* ⌈X⌉ [. . . .] ⌈X X *tar*$^{?}$ X⌉

Line 50

A). ⌈*ta*⌉*-ka*[*r*]*-*⌈*rab*⌉*-m*[*a*] ⌈X⌉ [. . . .] *šá-ki-*⌈*in-šu*⌉

Line 51

A). *šumma*(DIŠ) *šutta*(MÁŠ.G[E$_6$ X]-⌈X*-ma*⌉ *lumun*(⌈HUL⌉)*-šá* ⌈*uš*⌉-[*t*]*a-*⌈*di*⌉*-ir* [. . . .] ⌈X⌉.TA.AB

Line 52

A). *kirbān*(LAG-*a*[*n*) X (X)] *kul-lat lumun*(⸢HUL⸣) *šutti*(MÁ[Š.GE$_{6}$]) *is l*[*a* . . . . . .] ⸢X X⸣

Line 53

A). ⸢*ana*⸣ *muhhi*(UG[U)-*šú ta-m*]*a-an-nu-*[*m*]*a* [*ana*] *pān*([IG]I) ^{d}*Šamaš*(⸢UTU⸣) [. . . . .]

Line 54

A). *ta*$^{?}$-⸢*ma*⸣-[. . . .] ⸢*ki*⸣-*ma kir-*⸢*ba*⸣-[*ni*] *ina mê*(A.MEŠ) *t*[*a*$^{?}$]-⸢X⸣ [. . . . .]

Line 55

A). *ih*/*ah-h*[*u*$^{?}$ . . . .] ⸢^{d}⸣*Šamaš*(UTU) ⸢*di*$^{?}$-*in*$^{?}$⸣ [X (X) *e*]-⸢*la*⸣-*a-ti* [*u šap-la-a-ti*]

Line 56

A). *ma-la* [X] ⸢X *bi* X X⸣ [X (X)] ⸢X X *qu kir*/*un* (X)⸣ [. . . . .]

Line 57

A). *ana me*/*šip ki*[*r*$^{?}$] ⸢X *di qaq*⸣ [X X] ⸢X X *la*⸣ ^{d}*Nusku* [. . . . . .]

Line 58

A). *me*/*šip* ⸢X *si* X X⸣ [(X) ^{d}]*Šamaš*(UTU) *tuš-*[*ke*]*n ana* ^{d}⸢*É*⸣-[*a*] ⸢*u* ^{d}⸣[. . . . .]

Line 59

A). ⸢*u*⸣ *pān*(IGI) ⸢X *ru-ka*⸣ *ta-kar-*⸢*rab-ma*$^{?}$⸣ [(X)] ⸢(X) SIG$_{5}$$^{?}$⸣

Line 60

A). ^{d}utu ⸢X X⸣ a[n.k]i.⸢bi⸣.da me.⸢en gar⸣ kur.ku[r.ra].ke$_{4}$

Line 61

A). ⸢si ^{d}utu X X X en⸣ inim.ma ⸢giš.tuk X⸣ [X X] ⸢X⸣

Line 62

A). di.ku$_{5}$ me.⸢en di⸣.ku$_{5}$.da m[e.en]

Line 63

A). ka.aš.bar ⸢bar⸣.<re> [m]e.⸢e$^{?}$⸣.en ⸢ka⸣.aš.bar.[mu] bar.ra [me.en]

Line 64

A). ⸢máš⸣.ge$_{6}$ ⸢hul níg⸣.ga.mu níg nu.dùg.g[a.mu]

Line 65

A). ⸢lag⸣ a.a$^{?}$ ⸢X X.da.gim⸣ {bi} ⸢X⸣.bi ⸢ha⸣.ba.gul.e

Line 66

én ^{d}utu di.⸢ku$_{5}$⸣ [mah] an.ki.bi.⸢da⸣.ke$_{4}$

A). én ^{d}ut[u di].⸢ku$_{5}$⸣ [mah] an.ki.bi.⸢da⸣.ke$_{4}$

C). [ ] ⸢$^{d?}$⸣utu d[i.]

Line 67

[min (i.e., ^{d}utu di.ku$_{5}$ mah) ku]r.kur.ra.[ke$_{4}$] ⸢di.ku$_{5}$$^{?}$⸣ <me.en> inim.inim.mu

A). [min ku]r.kur.ra.[ke$_{4}$] ⸢di.ku$_{5}$$^{?}$⸣ <me.en> inim.⸢inim⸣.mu

C). [ ].inim.mu

Line 68

[X X] ⸢X X⸣ [X] ma ⸢tu⸣ n[íg$^{?}$ nu].⸢dùg.ga⸣.mu da.a.ni.⸢iš⸣

A). [X X] ⸢X X⸣ [X] ma ⸢tu⸣ n[íg$^{?}$ nu].⸢dùg.ga⸣.mu ⸢da⸣.a.ni.⸢iš⸣

C). ⸢X⸣ [ ] / [d]a.a.ni

Line 69

[. . . .] mu.mu máš.[g]e$_{6}$ ⸢hul⸣.a.mu [s]u nu.⸢dùg.ga⸣.mu

A). [. . . .].mu máš.[g]e$_{6}$ ⸢hul⸣.a.mu [s]u nu.⸢dùg.ga⸣.mu

C). mu.mu m[áš.]

Line 70

[l]ag.gim nu ki uzu$^{?}$.⸢ke$_{4}$⸣ ki.bi.šè <ba>.⸢an⸣.gi$_{4}$.⸢gi$_{4}$⸣.e.dè ⸢tu$_{6}$⸣ én

A). [ ].⸢ke$_{4}$ ki⸣.bi.šè <ba>.⸢an⸣.gi$_{4}$.⸢gi$_{4}$⸣.e.dè ⸢tu$_{6}$⸣ én

C). [l]ag.gim nu ki uzu$^{?}$.ke$_{4}$$^{!}$(nun) ⸢ki⸣.b[i.]

Line 71

DÙ.DÙ.BI *kirbān igāri šá ina ereb šamši šaknat šumēl-*⸢*ka*$^{!}$⸣ *tanaššâ*

A). [ ] LAG [ ].ZI *šá* ^{d}⸢UTU⸣.ŠÚ.A GAR GÙB-⸢*ka*$^{!}$⸣ ÍL-*a*

C). DÙ.DÙ.BI LAG IZ.ZI *šá ina* ^{d}UTU.ŠÚ.A ⸢GAR⸣ G[ÙB-]

Line 72

ana pān ^{d}*Šamaš šipta šalāšīšu ana muh-hi tamannu ana nāri tanaddi-ma pašir*

A). [ ] ⸢ÉN⸣ 3-*šú ana* ⸢UGU⸣ Š[ID$^{?}$]-*nu* Í[D] ⸢ŠUB⸣-*ma* ⸢BÚR⸣

C). *ana* IGI ^{d}UTU ÉN 3-*šú ana muh-hi* ŠID-*nu ana* Í[D] ŠUB-*m*[*a*]

Line 73

[én ^{d}utu] di.ku$_5$.mah ⸢di⸣.ku$_5$.da me.en

A). [én ^{d}utu] di.ku$_5$.mah ⸢di⸣.ku$_5$.da me.en

D). [ ].ku$_5^{!}$([r]u).da me.en

Line 74

[ka.aš.ba]r bar.re me.en ka.aš.bar.mu bar.re me.en

A). [ka.aš.ba]r bar.re me.en ka.aš.bar.mu bar.re me.en

D). [.ba]r.mu bar.re < >.en

Line 75

[máš.ge$_6$] igi bí.⸢in⸣.du$_8$.du$_8$.na níg.sig$_5$.ga.aš gub$^{?}$.ba.ab

A). [máš.ge$_6$] igi bí.⸢in⸣.du$_8$.du$_8$.na níg.sig$_5$.ga.aš gub$^{?}$.ba.ab

D). [ ].ga.aš ku$_4$<.ni>.íb

Line 76

A). [si.sá].bi ga.an.du tab.ba.[m]u sá ga.an.du$_{11}$

Line 77

[níg.u$_4$].da.mu ša$_6$.ga hé.a

A). [níg.u$_4$.d]a.⸢mu⸣ ša$_6$.ga hé.a

D). [. . . . .].da.mu ša$_6$.ga < >.a

Line 78

[X *k*]a X IGI? ⌜d*Šamaš šu-íla*⌝-*ku tanašši-ma pašir*

A). [X *k*]a X IGI? ⌜d*Šamaš šu-íla*⌝-*ku* ÍL-*ma* BÚR

D). [Í]L-*ma* BÚR-*ir*

Column I Line 79 To Column II Line 71

Column I Line 79

ÉN [*kir-ba-an*] *kir-ba-an ina kir-ṣi-ka ka-ri-iṣ* ⌜*kir*⌝-*ṣi* (**E**: *ramāni*)

A). [*ki*]*r-ba-an ina kir-ṣi-ka ka-ri-iṣ* ⌜*kir*⌝-*ṣi*

D). ÉN [*ki*]*r-ba-an ina kir-ṣi-ka ka-ri-i*[*ṣ*]

E). [*kir-b*]*a*!(*is*)-*an*!(*bar*) *kir-ba-an* / [*ki*]*r-ṣi-ka ga-ri-iṣ ramāni*(NÍ{*ú*}.MU)

Column II Line 1

ina k[*ir-ṣ*]*i-ia ka-ri-iṣ ki-ri-i*[*ṣ-ka*] (**E**: *ramān-ka*)

A). [. . . . .] ⌜X⌝-*ṣi ki*-⌜X⌝ [X X]

D). *ina k*[*ir- -i*]*a ka-ri-iṣ ki-ri-i*[*ṣ-ka*]

E). [-*ṣ*]*i-ia ga-ri-iṣ ramān*(NÍ{*ú*})-*ka*

Line 2

kir-b[*a-an*] *lu-mun šutti barārīti qablī*[*ti*] *šāt urri*

A). [. . . .]⌜X⌝ M[ÁŠ.G]E$_6$ [E]N.NUN.AN.⌜USÁN⌝ EN.N[UN].⌜X⌝ [X]

D). *kir-b*[*a-an*] HUL EN.NUN.AN.USÁN EN.NUN.MUR[UB$_4$.BA] / EN.NUN.⌜U$_4$⌝.ZA[L.]

E). [LAG] *lu-mun* MÁŠ.GE$_6$ / [ ].⌜NUN⌝.A[N.US]ÁN EN.NUN.MURUB$_4$.[ ] / [ ].NUN.U$_4$.ZAL.⌜LA⌝

Line 3

a-mu-ru a-tam-ma-ru abī mīta a-mu-[*r*]*u um-mi mi*-⌜*ta*⌝ *a-mu-ru*

A). [ ] ⌜X.MU ÚŠ⌝-*ta* IGI ⌜X X⌝ [ ]

D). *a-mu-ru a-tam-ma-ru* AD.MU ÚŠ *a-mu-*[ ] / AMA.⌜MU⌝ *mi*-⌜*ta*⌝ *a-mu-ru*

E). [*a*]*m-mar a-tam-m*[*a-*] / [*me*]-*ti a-m*[*u-r*]*u um-mi me-e-ti a*-⌜*mu*⌝-[ ]

Line 4

ila <āmuru> šarra āmuru kabta āmuru rubâ a-mu-ru mīta āmuru ^{LÚ}*balṭa āmuru*

A). DINGIR [IGI] ⸢LUGAL IGI IDIM⸣ [ ] ⸢AD$_6$⸣ IGI ⸢^{LÚ}TI⸣ [ ]

D). ^{d}*Šamaš*(UTU) < > LUGAL IGI IDIM IGI NUN [IGI] / AD$_6$ IGI ^{LÚ}TI IGI

E). [. . . .] ⸢X⸣ [. . . .] NUN *a-mu-ru*

Line 5

ihza là mūdâ āmuru ana māti là mūdâ ⸢*al*⸣*-li-ku akla là mūdâ a-*⸢*tak*⸣*-*[*ka*]*-lu*

A). ⸢NÍG.ZU⸣ [X] ⸢*là* ZU X X X X ZU GIN$^?$ X⸣ NINDA *là* ZU *a-t*[*ak-ka-lu*]

D). NÍG.ZU *là* ZU IGI *ana* KUR *là* ZU GI[N-*ku*] / NINDA-*la* *là* ZU *a-*⸢*tak*⸣*-*[ ]*-lu*

E). [.Z]U *là* ⸢ZU⸣*-ú a-mu-ru* / [ ]-⸢*ú* *al*⸣*-li-ku* / [. . . . . -*k*]*a*$^!$-*lu*$^!$(*ku*)

Line 6

ṣubāta là mūdâ al-lab-šú ki-ma ka-šá-ma ana mê a-nam-du-ka-ma

A). ⸢TÚG⸣ *là* Z[U] ⸢*al-lab-šú ki-ma*⸣ *ka-šá-ma ana* A.⸢MEŠ⸣ *a-nam-*[ ]

D). TÚG *là* ZU *al-lab-*[ ] / *ki-ma ka-šá-ma* ⸢*ana*⸣ [ ] ⸢*a-nam*⸣*-du-ka-ma*

E). [ZU-*ú a*]*l-*⸢*lab*$^!$*-šú*⸣ / [ ] *ana* A.MEŠ *a-n*[*am*]*-*⸢*du*⸣

Line 7

tam-mah-ha-hu tap-pa-⸢*as-sa*⸣*-s*[*u tap*]*-*⸢*pa-ṭa*⸣*-ru ana ašri-ka là tatur*[*ru*]

A). *tam-mah-ha-hu* ⸢*tap*⸣*<-pa>-*⸢*as-sa*⸣*-s*[*u*] DU$_8$*-ru* *ana* KI-*ka là* G[UR-*ru*]

D). *tam-mah-ha-*[ ] / *tap-pa-sa-as-su* [-*r*]*u ana* KI-*ka là* GUR-[ ]

E). [*tap*]*-*⸢*pa-ṭa*⸣*-ru* / [*tutār*(GUR]-*ár*)

Line 8

lumun šutti an-ni-ti [a-m]u-ru ki-ma ka-šá-ma ana mê li-[in-n]a-di

A). HUL MÁŠ.⸢GE$_6$⸣ *an-ni-⸢ti* *ki-ma*⸣ *ka-šá-ma* ⸢*a-na*$^!$ A.MEŠ⸣ *l[i-*]

D). HUL MÁŠ.GE$_6$ *an-n[i-ti* *-š]á-ma* *ana* A.MEŠ *l[i-*]

E). [*a-m]u-ru* / [*-in-n]a-di*

Line 9

lim-ma-hi-ih lip-pa-⸢sis⸣ lip-pa-ṭir ana ašri-šú [a-a itūr]

A). *lim-ma-hi-ih lip-pa-⸢sis⸣ lip-pa-ṭir*$^!$(⸢*nir*⸣) *ana* KI-*šú* [*a-a* GUR]

D). *lim-ma-hi-ih lip-*[. . . . . .] ⸢X X⸣ [X (X)]

E). [*li*]*p*$^!$-⸢*pa*⸣-*ṭir*

Line 10

li-bir nāra libbalkit šadâ lip-⸢ṭur ina⸣ zumrīja li-[. . . . . .]

A). *li-⸢bir⸣* ÍD BAL-*it* KUR-*a lip-⸢ṭur ina* SU⸣.MU *li-*[. . . . . .]

D). *li-bir* Í[D . . . .]

Line 11

kīma qut-ri ⸢li⸣-tel-⸢li⸣ šamê [kīma ^{GIŠ}*bī]ni nas[hi]* ⸢*ana*⸣ *ašri-⸢šú a⸣-a i[tūr]*

A). GIM *qut-ri* ⸢*li*⸣-*tel*-⸢*li*⸣ AN-⸢*e*⸣ [GIM ^{GIŠ}ŠI]NIG ⸢ZI⸣-[*hi*] ⸢*ana* KI-*šú a*⸣-*a* G[UR]

D). GIM$^!$(*be si*) ⸢X⸣ [. . . . .]

Line 12

^{GIŠ}*bīnu lillil-an-ni* ^{Ú}[*ma*]*štakal lipšur-an-⸢ni⸣*

A). ^{GIŠ}⸢ŠINIG⸣ KÙ-*an-ni* ^{Ú}[IN].⸢NU.UŠ⸣ BÚR-*an-⸢ni⸣*

D). ⸢GIŠ⸣[. . . . .]

Line 13

^{GIŠ}*libbi gišimmari li*$^!$-⸢*qad-di*⸣-*šá-an-ni nāru lim-hur-an-ni*

A). ^{GIŠ}⸢ŠÀ.GIŠIMMAR⸣ *li*$^!$(*ku*)-⸢*qad-di*⸣-*šá-an-ni* ⸢ÍD⸣ *lim-hur-an-ni*

E). [. . . . . .]-⸢*an*⸣-[*ni*] / [. . . . .]-*n*[*i*]

Line 14

lid-di-na melamma-šá-ma [lemutta] lit-bal ^{d}*Šamaš*$^{!}$ *šunat a-mu-ru*

A). *lid-di-na* ME.LÁM-*šá-ma* ^{MÍ}[HUL] ⸢*lit-bal*⸣ ^{d}UTU$^{!}$ MÁŠ.GE$_6$ *a-mu-ru*

E). [ ] *lit-ba*[*l*] / [-*r*]*u*

Line 15

lu dam-qat ^{d}*Šamaš šunat a-m*[*u*]-⸢*ru*⸣ *lu ki-na-at*

A). *lu dam-qat* ^{d}UTU ⸢MÁŠ.GE$_6$⸣ *a-m*[*u*]-⸢*ru*⸣ *lu* GI$^{!}$.NA-*at*

E). *lu* SIG$_5$-*at* / [IG]I *lu ki-na-at*

Line 16

^{d}*Šamaš šunat a-mu-*⸢*ru*⸣ *a-na damiqti tir-ra*

A). ^{d}UTU MÁŠ.GE$_6$ *a-mu-*⸢*ru*⸣ *a-na* ⸢SIG$_5$-*te te-e*⸣-*er*

E). [ ] ⸢SIG$_5$⸣-*ti tir-ra*

Line 17

DÙ.DÙ.BI *lu kirbān ṭābti lu kirbān ṭiṭṭi šipta šalāšīšu ana muhhi tamannu*

A). DÙ.DÙ.BI *lu* LAG ⸢MUN *lu*⸣ LAG IM ÉN 3-*šú ana* ⸢UGU ŠID⸣-*nu*

E). [*lu ana*] ⸢LAG MUN⸣ *lu ana* LAG IM / [ ] 3-*šú* ŠID-*nu*

Line 18

ana nāri (**E**: [*m*]*ê*) *tanaddi-ma lumun šutti ana amēli úl iṭehhâ*

A). *ana* ⸢ÍD⸣ ŠUB-*di-ma* HUL ⸢MÁŠ⸣.G[E$_6$$^{!}$] *a-*⸢*na*⸣ LÚ *úl* TE$^{!}$

E). [*ana mê*(A].MEŠ) ŠUB-*di* / [.G]E$_6$ *ana* LÚ *úl* TE-*a*

Line 19

én hu-ub-ba hu-ub-ba ab-ni a-⸢ra⸣-a ⸢e⸣-ra-a

A). én hu-ub-ba hu-ub-ba ab-ni a-⸢ra⸣-a ⸢e⸣-ra-a

E). [ ] ⸢X⸣-ni

Line 20

A). uš-ru-⸢lu$_4$$^{?}$⸣ uš-lu-lu ⸢tu$_6$⸣ én

Line 21

A). KA.INIM.MA *šuttu*(MÁŠ.GE$_6$) *pa-*⌈*rit-tu$_4$*⌉ *là amāri*(⌈IGI.LÁ⌉)

Line 22

A). DÙ.DÙ.⌈BI⌉ 4 *ṣalmāni*(NU$^!$(NA)) *zikar*(⌈NITA⌉) *u sinniš*(MÍ) *šá ṭiṭṭi*(IM) *teppuš*(⌈DÙ⌉*-uš*) *šipta*(ÉN) *sebîšu*(7-⌈*šú*⌉)

Line 23

A). *ana muhhi*(⌈UGU⌉) *tamannu*(ŠID-*nu*)*-ma ina rēši*(⌈SAG⌉)*-ka tašakkan*(⌈GAR-*an*⌉)

Line 24

A). *šumma*(DIŠ) *amēlu*(⌈NA⌉) *šunāti*(MÁŠ.GE$_6$.⌈MEŠ⌉) ⌈*pár-da*⌉*-a-ti ina-*⌈*ṭal*⌉ *u šutta*(MÁŠ.⌈GE$_6$⌉) *lemutta*(HUL$^!$(⌈*ù*⌉)) *là ukâl*(⌈DAB⌉)

Line 25

A). ⌈AMA$^?$⌉-^{d}*ištari*(EŠ$_{18}$.⌈TÁR⌉)*-šú* ⌈X X X (X)⌉*-ma* ŠU *su ku šú ana libbi*(ŠÀ) *ili*(DINGIR)*-šú*

Line 26

A). ⌈X X X X *su hi* X X X⌉ *damiqta*(⌈SIG$_5$$^?$-*a*⌉) IGI.⌈DU$_8$⌉ U$_4$.28. ⌈KÁM⌉

Line 27

A). ⌈X⌉ [X X] ⌈X⌉ *u$_4$-me ana ṣēri*(⌈EDIN⌉) *tuṣṣi*(⌈È⌉)-⌈*ma*⌉ *nignaq*(NÍG. NA) $^{⌈GIŠ⌉}$*burāši*(⌈LI⌉) *ana pān*(IGI) *ili*(DINGIR)-⌈*šú*⌉ *tašakkan* (GAR-*an*)

Line 28

A). *nignaqqa*(⌈NÍG⌉.[NA]) $^{⌈LÚ⌉}$*marṣu*(⌈GIG⌉) *ana pān*(IGI) *ku-šá-r*[*i išakkan*(GAR-*a*]*n*)*-ma* ⌈*ki*⌉*-a-a*[*m*] *taqabbi*(DUG$_4$.GA)

Line 29

A). én ^{d}utu(over erasure) sag.⌈kal dingir.ṛe.e⌉.[ne.ke$_4$] ^{d}utu ⌈pa.è⌉.da. [e].dè

Line 30

A). ^{d}ut[u lu]gal an.⌈ki.a⌉ lu[gal] ^{d}a.nun.⌈na⌉.[k]e$_4$.⌈ne⌉

Line 31

A). ⌈^{d}utu⌉ ur.sag kala.ga ⌈lugal⌉ ^{d}i.gi$_4$.⌈gi$_4$⌉.n[e]

Line 32

A). ⌈^{d}⌉utu ^{giš}ma.nu ⌈^{giš}⌉tukul ⌈kala.ga⌉ dingir.re.e.⌈ne⌉.ke$_4$

Line 33

A). igi.zu.šè [hé.dad]ag.ga.àm

Line 34

A). di[ngir.m]u ⌈á⌉.zi.da.mu hé.⌈en.gub.bé⌉

Line 35

A). ⌈^{d}⌉inanna.mu ⌈á⌉.gùb.bu.mu$^{!}$(zu) ⌈hé⌉.en.⌈gub.bé⌉

Line 36

A). an.ki.a igi.zu.⌈šè hé⌉.en.⌈gub.bé⌉

Line 37

A). dingir ⌈nam⌉.tar ⌈^{giš}⌉ma.nu ⌈hé.en⌉.tar.re.e.⌈dè⌉ tu$_6^{!}$(ka) én

---

Line 38

A). *šalāšīšu*(3-*šú*) *taqabbi*(DUG$_4$.GA)-*ma tuš-kèn te-re-qam-ma ana pān*(⌈IGI⌉) *ku-šá-ri* ⌈*ki*⌉-*a-am taqabbi*(DUG$_4$.GA)

Line 39

A). én [n]am.tar.zu hé.en.⌈tar⌉.re ⌈nam⌉.tar.zu hé.en.tar.re

Line 40

A). ⌈^{d}⌉en.⌈líl⌉ [n]am.tar.⌈zu hé⌉.en.tar.r[e] ^{d}nin.⌈líl nam.tar⌉. [zu] ⌈hé.en. tar⌉.re

Line 41

A). ^{d}nin.⌈urta dumu⌉.sag é.kur.ra.ke$_4$ nam.tar.zu hé.⌈en.tar.re⌉

Line 42

A). ^{d}⌈nusku⌉ sukkal.mah ^{d}en.líl.⌈lá.ke$_4$ nam⌉.tar.zu ⌈hé.en.tar⌉.re

Line 43

A). ^{d}⌈nanna⌉ lugal urím$^{!}$(šeš.⌈ká⌉)⌈^{ki}⌉.ke$_4$ n[am.ta]r.⌈zu hé.en.tar⌉.re

Line 44

A). ⌈^{d}utu lugal kalam⌉.ma.ke$_4$ ⌈nam.tar⌉.[z]u ⌈hé.en⌉.tar.re

Line 45

A). ⸢^{d}iškur lugal⸣ an.ki.a nam.tar.zu hé.en.t[ar.r]e

Line 46

A). ⸢^{d}asal.lú.hi dumu.sag abzu⸣.ke$_4$ ⸢nam⸣.tar.⸢zu hé⸣.en.tar.[re]

Line 47

A). dingir.⸢mu⸣ ama.⸢^{d}inanna.mu silim.ma⸣.a[b]

Line 48

A). [*šalāšīšu*(3]-⸢*šú*⸣) *taqabbi*([D]UG$_4$.⸢GA⸣)-*ma ina libbi*(ŠÀ) *u$_4$-me qut-āra*(PA) *ina rēši*(SAG)-*ka tašakkan*(GAR-⸢*an*⸣) ⸢${}^{\text{Ú}}$⸣*atā'iša* (KUR.KUR)

Line 49

A). [*i-na šaman*(Ì+GIŠ)] ${}^{\text{[ŠI]M}}$*burāši*(⸢LI⸣) *tasâk*(SÚD) *tapaššassu* ([ŠÉ]Š-*su*) *kasê*(⸢GÀZI⸣${}^{\text{SAR}}$) *mê*(A) *ellūti*(⸢KÙ⸣) *tasallah*(⸢SUD⸣)

Line 50

A). *nignaq*(⸢NÍG.NA⸣) [${}^{\text{ŠIM}}$*burāši*(LI) *ana*] *pān*(⸢IGI⸣) *ili*(DINGIR)-*šú tašakkan*(GAR)-*ma* [*k*]*i*-⸢*a-am*⸣ *taqabbi*(⸢DUG$_4$⸣.GA)

Line 51

A). én ${}^{\text{giš}}$ma.⸢nu ${}^{\text{giš}}$⸣t[ukul kala.g]a dingir.re.e.⸢ne.ke$_4$⸣

Line 52

A). ⸢gissu⸣ {ga} dùg.ga [ig]i.⸢zu⸣.šè gá.gá

Line 53

A). dingir.⸢mu á⸣.zi.da <gin.na>.mu.dè

Line 54

A). ⸢ama.${}^{d?}$⸣inanna.mu á.gùb.b[u] <gin.na>.mu.⸢dè⸣

Line 55

A). ⸢di.da⸣ hé.en.silim.mu ⸢eš.bar⸣ [hé.en.ba]r.re ⸢én⸣

Line 56

A). [*šalāšīšu*(3]-⸢*šú*⸣) *taqabbi*(⸢DUG$_4$⸣.GA)-*ma* ⸢*tuš*⸣-*kèn tanâl*(NÁ)-*ma šutta*(MÁŠ.⸢GE$_6$⸣) [X] *u mim-ma*

Line 57

A). ⌜*ú-gal*⌝-*li*-⌜*lu* X⌝ [. . . . . .]

Line 58

ÉN *šu-ut-ti ba-na-at e-gir-ru-ú-a da-mì*-⌜*iq*⌝

A). [ ] ⌜*šu*⌝-*ut*-⌜*ti*⌝ *ba-na-at* ⌜INIM⌝.GAR-*ú*-⌜*a*⌝ [ ]

f^{1}). ÉN *šu-ut-ti* *dam-qa-at* ⌜*e*⌝-[*gi*]*r*-⌜*ru*⌝-*ú-a* *da-mì*-⌜*iq*⌝

f^{17}). ÉN *šu-ut-ti* *ba-na-at* *e-gir-ru-ú-a* ⌜*da*⌝-[ ]

Line 59

ma-har ^{d}*Sîn u* ^{d}*Šamaš dam-q*[*at*] : *ma-har* ⌜^{d}⌝*Sîn* ⌜*u*⌝ ^{d}*Šamaš dam*-[*qat*]

A). [ ] ⌜^{d}30⌝ *u* ^{d}UTU *dam-q*[*at*] *ma*-⌜*har* ^{d}⌝30 [*dam-qat*]

f^{2}). *ma-har* ^{d}30 *u* ^{d}UTU *dam-qa* : *ma*-⌜*har*⌝ [3]0 ⌜*u*⌝ ^{d}UTU *dam*$^{!}$-*qa*

Line 60

ma-har ^{d}*Sîn u* ^{d}*Šamaš dam*-[*qat*] : *šu-ut-ti ba-na-at e-gir-ru-ú-a damiq ina qí-bi-ti*-⌜*ki šar*⌝-[*rat*] ^{d}*Nin-líl*

A). *ma-ha*[*r* 3]0 ⌜*u*⌝ ^{d}⌜UTU⌝ *da*[*m-qat*
in]*a* ⌜*qí-bi-ti* *šar*⌝-*r*[*a*-]

f^{3}). *ma-har* ^{d}30 *u* ^{d}UTU *dam-qa* :
ina ⌜*qí-bit* *šar*⌝-*ra-tú* ^{d}*Nin-líl*

f^{18}). *ma-har* ^{d}30 *u* ^{d}UTU *dam-qa* : *šu-ut-ti ba-na-at e-gir-ru-ú-a* SIG$_5$ *ina* *qí-bi-ti*-⌜*ki*⌝ [*šar-rat*] ⌜^{d}*Nin*⌝-*líl*

Line 61

šá ina ba-lu-uš-šá pu[*russê la i*]*p*-⌜*pa-ra*⌝-*su aš-kun du-un-qu*

A). *šá* *ina* ⌜*ba*⌝-*lu-uš-šá* E[Š.BAR *la* *i*]*p*-⌜*pa-ra*⌝-*su* *aš*-⌜*kun*⌝ [ ]

f^{4}). ⌜*ša*⌝ *ina* *ba-lu-uš-ša* *ši-mat ma-a-ti* *la* *iš*$^{!}$-*šim-mu* / *aš-kun* *du-un-qu*

f^{19}). *ša* < > *ba*-[ ]-⌜*uš*⌝-*ša* *ši-mat šamê*(AN-*e*) *u erṣetim*(KI-*tim*) *la* *iš-šim-m*[*u*] / *aš-ku*[*n* SI]G$_5$

Line 62

lu da-mi-iq-tu$_4$: *aš-kun šēpa ina qaqqari lu da-mi-iq-ti*

A). [*l*]*u* ⌈*da*⌉*-mi-iq-tu*$_4$ *aš-k*[*un*] *šēpē*(⌈GÌR$^{II?}$⌉) *ina* KI *lu da-mi-i*[*q-*]

f^{5}). *lu da-mì-iq-tu*$_4$: *aš-kun* GÌR$^{!}$ *ina* KI *lu da-mì-iq-ti*

f^{20}). *lu da-mì-iq-tu*$_4$: *aš-kun* GÌR *ina* KI *lu da-mì-*⌈*iq*⌉-[ ]

Line 63

šá u$_4$*-me lu da-am-qá-nim* : *ša arhi lu da-am-qa-nim ša šatti lu da-am-*⌈*qa-nim*⌉

A). *šá u*$_4$*-me lu da-am-qá-n*[*im*] *ša* ⌈ITI *lu*⌉ *dam-qá-*⌈*nim šá* MU⌉ *lu da*[*m-qá-nim*]

f^{6}). *ša u*$_4$*-me lu da-am-qa-nim* : *ša* ITI *lu da-am-qa-nim* / *ša* MU.AN.NA *lu da-am-*⌈*qa-nim*⌉

f^{21}). *ša* [*-m*]*a da-am-qa-nim* :

Line 64

ša it-me-a-am li-ip-šu-ra ša i-ze-ni$^{!}$*-am* ⌈*li*⌉*-ip-š*[*u-r*]*a na-šu-ú lid-di-na*

A). ⌈*šá it*⌉*-ma-a lip-šu-ru šá i*[*z-nu-u li*]*p-šu-ra na-šu-ú lid-*[ ]

f^{7}). *ša it-me-a-am li-ip-šu-ra* / *ša i-ze-ni*$^{!}$(*er*)*-a* ⌈*li*⌉*-ip-p*[*aṭ-r*]*a na-šu-ú lid-di-na*

f^{21}). *ša it-me-a-am li-ip-šu-*⌈*ra*⌉ *ša* ⌈*i-ze*⌉-[ ] / [ ]*-di-na*

Line 65

la mu-du-ú ana qātē-ia$_5$ *liš-kun*

A). ⌈*la*⌉ *mu-du-ú* ⌈*ana*⌉ [*-i*]*a* ⌈*liš*⌉*-ku*[*n*]

f^{8}). *la mu-du-ú ana* ŠU^{II}*-ia*$_5$ *liš-*⌈*kun*⌉

f^{22}). *la mu-du-ú ana* ⌈ŠU⌉[ ]

Line 66

ša qarrādi ^{d}*Marduk mār* ^{d}*É-a ana-ku a-a ip-rik*

A). ⌈*šá*⌉ ⌈UR⌉.SAG ^{d}*Marduk* DU[MU] ^{d}*É-a* ⌈*ana*⌉-[ ]

f^{9}). *ša qar-ra-du* ^{d}*Marduk* DUMU ^{d}*É-a ana-ku*

f^{23}). [^{d}*Marduk* DUM]U ^{d}*É-a ana-ku a-a ip-rik*

Line 67

lum-⌜nu⌝ li-mu-ra-an-ni-ma pu-uz-ra li-mid

A). ⌜*lum-nu*⌝ *li-mu-ra-an-ni-ma* [*p*]*u-uz-ra li-m*[*id*]

f[10]). *lum-ni li-mu-ra-an-ni-ma pu-uz-ra li-mi-id*

f[23]). ⌜*lum-ni*⌝ [(. . . .)] / [(X X) *l*]*i-mu-ra-an-ni-ma p*[*u*]-⌜*uz*⌝-*ra li-mid*

Line 68

ina lìb-bi lum-ni ana lemutti a-a ab-bal-kit ᵈmarduk dumu.sag abzu.ke$_4$

A). ⌜*ina*⌝ *libbi*(ŠÀ) [ ]-*ni ana* HUL-*tì a-a ab-*< >-⌜*kit*⌝ ᵈm[ar]duk dumu.sag ⌜abzu⌝.k[e$_4$]

f[11]). *ina lìb-bi lum-ni ana* HUL-*tì a-a ab-bal-kit* / ᵈmarduk dumu.sag abzu.ke$_4$

f[24]). *ina lìb-bi lum-ni ana* HU[L-] / [.s]ag abzu.ke$_4$

Line 69

ša$_6$.ga zíl.zíl.bi za.a.kám

A). š[a$_6$.g]a zíl.zíl.[b]i za.a.k[ám]

f[12]). ša$_6$.ga zíl.zíl.bi za.a.kám

f[25]). ⌜ša$_6$⌝.ga zíl.zíl.bi za.a.kám

Line 70

zi.an.na hé.pàd zi.ki.a hé.pàd

A). zi.an.[n]a hé.pàd zi.ki.[h]é.pà[d]

f[12]). zi.an.na hé.pàd zi.ki.a hé.pàd

f[25]). zi.an.na h[é.]

Line 71

KA.INIM.MA MÁŠ.GE$_6$ HUL BÚR.RU.DA.KÁM

A). KA.⌜INIM⌝.M[A] MÁŠ.GE$_6$ HUL ⌜BÚR⌝.[.D]A.K[E$_4$]

f[13]). KA.INIM.MA MÁŠ.GE$_6$ HUL BÚR.RU.⌜DA⌝.KÁM

f[26]). [.M]A ⌜MA⌝.MÚ HUL BÚR.RU.D[A.]

REVERSE

Column III

Line 1

DÙ.DÙ.BI *e-nu-ma amēlu šutta īmuru-ma la-ma šēp-šú ina qaqqari iš-ku-nu*

A). DÙ.DÙ.BI *e-nu-*⸢*ma* LÚ MÁŠ⸣.GE$_6$ IGI.DU$_8$ *la-*⸢*ma*?
GÌR?⸣-[GAR-*n*]*u*

f[14]). KÌD.KÌD.BI *e-nu-ma* LÚ MÁŠ.GE$_6$ IGI.DU$_8$!(ZI)-*ma la-ma*
GÌR-*šú ina* KI *iš-ku-nu*

Line 2

ina muhhi erši-šú ina uhūli qātē-šú imessi!*-ma*

A). *ina* ⸢UGU⸣ GIŠ.NÁ-*šú ina* NAGA ŠU^{II}-*šú* LUH!-⸢*si*⸣-*ma*

f). *ina* UGU GIŠ.NÁ-*šu ina* NAGA! ŠU^{II}-*šú* LUH!(Ú)-*ma*

Line 3

šipta šalāšīšu imannu-ma idammiq

A). ÉN 3-*šú* ŠID-*nu-ma* SIG$_5$

f). ÉN 3!(Ú)-*šú* ŠID-*ma* SIG$_5$

Line 3a

f[16]). KÌD.KÌD.BI *šanû*(2-*ú*) *šēp*(GÌR) *šumēli*(GÙB)-*ka ina muhhi* (UGU) *erši*(GIŠ.NÁ) *šēp*(GÌR) *imitti*(ZAG)-*ka ina qaqqari*(KI) *tašakkan*(GAR)-*ma šipta*(ÉN) *šalāšīšu*(3-*šú*) *tamannu*(ŠID-*nu*)

Line 3b

f[27]). [. . . .] ⸢X *na*⸣ *šá-ni-a qātē*(ŠU^{II})-*ka* ^{GIŠ}*itqūri*(DÍLI) *šalāšīšu*(3-*šú*) *te-me-es*!(*e*)-[*si* . . . .]

Line 3c

f). [*e-nu-ma t*]*e-me-es-su-ú šutta*(MA.MÚ) *šu-a-ti šalāšīšu*(3-*šú*) *ana libbi*(SÀ) *mê*(A) *tapaššar*(BÚR) [. . . .]

Line 3d

f). [. . . .]-*ú-ti li-il-qú-nim*!*-ma šalāšīšu*(3-*šú*) *qātē*(ŠU^{II})-*ka te-me-es-s*[*i* . . . .]

Line 3e

f). [*e-nu-ma*] *qātē*([Š]U^{II})-*ka te-me-es-su-ú šipta*(ÉN) *an-ni-tú šalāšīšu*(3-*šú*) *tamannu*([Š]ID)-⸢*ma*? *šu*⸣ [. . . .]

Line 3f

f). [. . . . .] ⌜X⌝ *bi* X *a* NU HUL [. . . . . .]

Line 3g

f). [. . . . .] ⌜X⌝-*ma ana bīti*(É)-*ka* [. . . . . .]

Line 4

én ^{d}utu di.ku$_5$ me.en di.mu tar.ru.da.ab

A). én ⌜^{d}⌝utu ⌜di⌝.ku$_5$$^{!}$(ru) me.en di.mu tar.ru.da.ab

I). ^{d}utu di.ku$_5$ me.en di.mu tar.dè

Line 5

^{d}*Šamaš da-a-a-na-ta di-ni di-in*

A). ^{d}[UT]U *da-a-a-na-ta di-ni di-in*

G). ^{d}UTU *da-a-*[ ]

Line 6

ka.aš.bar bar.ra me.en ka.aš.bar.ra.mu bar.ra ⌜me.en⌝

A). ka.⌜aš⌝.bar bar.ra me.en ka.aš.bar.ra.mu bar.r[a] ⌜me.en⌝

I). ka.aš.bar bar.re me.en ka.aš.mu bar.ra < >

Line 7

pa-⌜*ri*⌝*-is purussê at-ta purussû-a-a puru*[*s*]

A). *pa-*⌜*ri*⌝*-is* EŠ.BAR *at-ta* EŠ.BAR-*a-a* TAR-*u*[*s*]

G). TAR-*is* E[Š].BAR [ ]

Line 8

máš.ge$_6$ igi bí.in.du$_8$.a níg.ša$_6$.ga ku$_4$.ni.íb

A). ⌜máš⌝.[g]e$_6$ igi bí.in.du$_8$.a níg.⌜ša$_6$⌝.ga ka ⌜X⌝ [X g]ub.b[a$^{?}$]

I). máš.ge$_6$ igi ba.ni.in.du$_8$.a / ša$_6$.ga.aš ku$_4$.ni.íb

Line 9

šu-⌜*ut*⌝*-ti a-mu-ru a-na damiqti* [*tir-ra*]

A). *šu-*⌜*ut*⌝*-ti a-mu-ru a-na* SIG$_5$-*tì* [*tir-ra*]

G). *šunātē*(MÁŠ.GE$_6$.MEŠ) [ ]

Line 10

si.sá.bi ga.an.du tab.ba.mu sá ga.àm.du$_{11}$

A). ⌜si.sá⌝.bi ga.an.du tab.ba.mu sá g[a.an.]

I). si.sá.bi ga.du / tab.ba$^{!}$.mu sá ga.àm.du$_{11}$

Line 11

i-šá-riš lul-lik-ma tap-pe-e l[u-uk-šu-ud]

A). ⌜*i*⌝-*šá-riš lul-lik-ma tap-pe-e l[u-uk-šu-ud]*

G). i-*šá*-⌜*riš*⌝ [ ]

Line 12

A). ^{d}utu níg.u$_{4}$.da.mu níg.⌜ša$_{6}$⌝.[ga hé.a]

Line 13

A). ^{d}*Šamaš*(UTU) *šá u$_{4}$-me*-⌜*ia*⌝ *l[u$^{!}$(šá)-u damiqti*(SIG$_{5}$-*ti*)]

Line 14

A). ^{d}utu níg.iti.da.⌜mu⌝ ní[g.ša$_{6}$.ga hé.a]

Line 15

^{d}*Šamaš šá arhi-ia lu dam*-⌜*qá-at*$^{?}$⌝

A). ^{d}UTU *šá* ITI-*ia l[u*]

B). [ ] *lu dam*-⌜*qá-at*$^{?}$⌝

Line 16

KA.KÉŠ MÁŠ.GE$_{6}$ HUL BÚR.RU.DA.KÁ[M]

A). KA.KÉŠ MÁŠ.GE$_{6}$ [ ]

B). ⌜KA⌝.KÉŠ MÁŠ.GE$_{6}$ HUL BÚR.RU.DA.KÁ[M]

Line 17

ana pān ^{d}*Šamaš* ŠU.ÍL.LA *tamannu-ma paš[ir]*

A). *ana* IGI ^{d}U[TU .L]A ŠID-[ ]

B). *ana* IGI ^{d}UTU ŠU.ÍL.LA ŠID-*nu-ma pašir*(BÚ[R])

Line 18

šumma amēlu šutta iṭ-ṭul la ú-kal lu šutta ina-ṭ[al]

A). DIŠ < > MÁŠ.⌜GE$_{6}$⌝ *i[ṭ-*] ⌜*lu*⌝ MÁŠ.GE$_{6}$ ⌜*ina*⌝-[ ]

B). DIŠ NA MÁŠ.GE$_{6}$ *iṭ-ṭul la ú-kal lu* MÁŠ.GE$_{6}$ *ina-ṭ[al]*

Line 19

7 (**B**: 4) *uṭ-ṭe-e-ti šá* ^{Ú}*à-ta-wi-ši ana* (**B** adds: *pān*) *išāti tanaddi-ma ina rēši-šú tašakkan-ma idammiq*

A). 7 *uṭ-ṭ*[*e-*]*-ši ana* IZI ŠUB-*ma ina* S[AG-]

B). 4 *uṭ-ṭe-e-ti šá* ^{Ú}*à-ta-wi-ši ana* IGI IZI ŠUB-⌈*ma*⌉ / *ina* SAG-*šú* GAR-*ma* SIG_5

Line 20

ÉN *ta-at-tap-ha* ^{d}*Šamaš ina šadî* ^{GIŠ}*erēni ri-šu-nik-ka ilānu ha-da-tak-ka a-me-lu-tú*

A). ÉN [KU]R ^{GIŠ}ERIN *ri-šu-*⌈*ni*⌉*-ka* DI[NGIR.]

B). ÉN *ta*!(⌈*it*⌉)*-tap-ha* ^{d}UTU *ina* KUR ^{GIŠ}⌈ERIN⌉ / *ri-šu-nik-ka* DINGIR.MEŠ *ha-da-tak-ka a-me-*[ ]-⌈*te*⌉

H). ÉN *ta-at-tap-ha* ^{d}UTU *ina* KUR ^{GIŠ}[ERIN] / ⌈*ri*⌉*-šu-nik-ka* DINGIR.MEŠ *ha-da-*⌈*tak*⌉*-k*[*a*] *a-me-lu-tú*

Line 21

na-šak-ka mār ^{LÚ}*bārî* ^{GIŠ}*erēna*

A). *n*[*a-*] ^{LÚ}HAL [ ]E[RIN]

B). *na-šak-ka* DUMU ^{LÚ}HAL ^{GIŠ}ERIN

H). *na-šak-ka* DUMU ^{LÚ}HAL ^{GIŠ}*eri_4-nu*

Line 22

^{MÍ}*al-mat-tu_4 ku-uk-ku-šú maṣhata la-pu-un-tu_4 šamna šá-ru-u*

A). $^{M[Í]}$[*-t*]*u_4* ZÌ.MAD.GÁ ⌈*lu-up*⌉*-p*[*u-u*]*n-tú* [ ]-⌈*ú*?⌉

B). ^{MÍ}*al-mat-tú* ⌈ZÌ⌉.MAD.⌈GÁ⌉ / *la-pu-un-tú* Ì+GIŠ *šá-ru-u*

H). *al-mat-tu_4 ku-uk-ku-šú* ZÌ.MAD.GÁ / *la*!*-pu-un-tu_4* Ì+GIŠ / ⌈*šá*⌉*-ri*!(⌈*ti*⌉)

Line 23

ina šá-ru-ti-šú na-ši puhāda

A). [ ]*-ti-šú* [*n*]*a-ši* ^{UDU}⌈$SILA_4$⌉

B). *ina šá-ru-ti-šú na-ši* ⌈^{UDU}$SILA_4$⌉

H). *ina šá-ru-ti-šú na-ši pu-ha-du*

Line 24

ana-ku na-šá-ka-ak-ka kirbāna bi-nu-ut ⸢*ap*⸣*-s*[*i*]*-i*

A). [

-*a*]*k-k*[*a*] LAG *bi-nu-ut* ⸢*ap*⸣*-s*[*i*]*-i*

B). *ana-ku*

na-šá-ka-ak-ku LAG *bi-nu-ut* ABZU

H). [X X] ⸢X⸣-*iddina*(AŠ$^{?}$) *mār*(DUMU) *ili*(DINGIR)-*šú*

na-šá-⸢*ka-ak-ka*⸣ / [*kir-ba-n*]*u bi-nu-ut* ⸢ABZU⸣

Line 25

kirbān bi-nu-ut [*ap*]*-si-i at-ta-ma ina kir-ṣi-ia ga-ri-iṣ*

A). [*ap*]*-si-i at-ta-ma i*[*na -ṣ*]*i-*⸢*ia*⸣ *ga-*⸢*ri*⸣*-iṣ*

B). LAG *bi-nu-ut* ABZU *at-ta-ma* / *ina kir-ṣi-ia ga-ri-iṣ*

H). [*kir-ba-nu* AB]ZU *at-*⸢*ta*⸣*-m*[*a*]

Line 26

kir-ṣi$^{!}$*-ka ina kir-ṣi-ka ga-ri-iṣ kir-ṣi*

A). [-*k*]*a ina kir-*⸢*ṣi*$^{?}$⸣*-k*[*a -r*]*i-iṣ kir-ṣi*

B). *kir-ṣi*$^{!}$(*iṣ*)*-ka* / *ina kir-ṣi-ka ga-ri-iṣ kir-ṣi*

H). [ ]-⸢*iṣ*$^{?}$⸣ *kir-*⸢*ṣi*$^{?}$⸣

Line 27

ina ramāni-ia ba-lil ramān-ka ina ramāni-ka ba-líl ramāni

A). [ ] ⸢*ba*⸣*-lil* NÍ-*k*[*a* -*k*]*a ba-líl* NÍ.MU

B). *ina* NÍ-*ia ba-líl* NÍ{*ú*}*-ka ina* NÍ-*ka ba-líl* NÍ

Line 28

[*k*]*i-ma at-ta kirbāna ana mê tannaddû-ma* ⸢*tam-mah*⸣*-ha-hu tap-pa-*⸢*sa-su*⸣

A). [*a*]*t-*⸢*ta*⸣ ⸢LAG⸣ *ana* A.M[EŠ] ⸢*tam-mah*⸣*-ha-hu*

tap-pa-⸢*sa-su*⸣

B). [*k*]*i-ma at-ta* LAG *ana* A.MEŠ ŠUB-*ma*

Line 29

A). ⸢*tap*⸣*-pa-ṭa-ru lumun*(HU[L) *šutti*(MÁŠ.GE$_6$)] *šá ina mūši*(GE$_6$)

āmuru(IGI.DU$_8$)

Line 30

A). *ila*(DINGIR) *āmuru*(IGI.DU$_8$) *šarra*(LUGAL) *āmuru*(IGI.D[U$_8$) *kabta*(IDIM)] *āmuru*(IGI) *rubâ*(NUN) *āmuru*(IGI) *mīta*(⌈ÚŠ⌉) *āmuru*(IGI) *balṭa*(TI) *āmuru*(IGI)

Line 31

A). *imna*(ZAG) *attalka*(GIN-⌈*ka*⌉) *šumēla*(GÙB) *a-sah-ru*

Line 32

A). *ki-ma ka-a-šá-ma ana mê*(A.MEŠ) *limqut*(ŠUB-*ut*)-*ma lim-ma-hi-ih lip-*⌈*pa-sis*⌉

Line 33

A). *u lip-pa-ṭir*$^{!}$ *immer*(UDU.NÍTA) *mé-he-e patar*(GÍR) *šāri*(IM) *ṭu-ub-ha*

Line 34

A). *ikkalū*(GU$_7$.MEŠ) *mītūtu*(BA$^{!}$(NÍTA).ÚŠ.MEŠ) *išattû*(NAG-*ú*) *šārumma*(IM-*um-ma*)

Line 35

A). *ki-i na-*⌈*kap*⌉ *šēpē*(⌈GÌR^{II}⌉) *a-*⌈*na*⌉ *a-si-di la i-qar-ri-bu*

Line 36

A). *lumun*(HUL) *šutti*(MÁŠ.GE$_6$) *šá ina mūši*(GE$_6$) *āmuru*(IGI.DU$_8$) *la iṭehhâ*(TE-*a*) *la i-*⌈*qar-ri*⌉*-ba ía-ši*

Line 37

A). KA.INIM.MA *ša šutta*(MÁŠ.GE$_6$) *i-kil-ta amāri*(IGI.DU$_8$) DÙ.DÙ.BI *kirbāna*(LAG) *ša bābi*(KÁ) *pi-he-e*

Line 38

A). *teleqqi*(TI-⌈*qí*⌉) *šipta*(⌈ÉN⌉) *ana muhhi*(⌈UGU⌉) *šalāšīšu*(3-*šú*) *tamannu*(ŠID-*nu*) *ana mê*(A.MEŠ) *tanaddi*(ŠUB-*di*) *lumun*(HUL)-*šú ippaṭṭar*(DU$_8$)

Line 39

ÉN ^{d}*É-a šàr apsî pa-ti-iq šamê u erṣetim ba-nu-u nišē*

A). ÉN ^{d}*É-a šàr* ABZU *pa-ti-qu* AN-*e u* KI-*tim ba-nu-u* UN.MEŠ

j). [ ]⌈*É*⌉*-a šàr*! ABZU *pa-ti-iq* AN-*e u* KI-*tim* / [U]N.MEŠ

K). ÉN ⌈d⌉[ ] ⌈X AN⌉ *u* ⌈KI-*tim*⌉ *b*[*a*!-]

Line 40

mu-uṣ-ṣi-ru uṣurāti na-din nindabê šá ilāni rabûti [. . . .] ⌈*ú*⌉ *kit-ti pa-ri-is purussê šá ilāni ahhē-šú* [. . . .] X-*ma di-ni di*!*-in purussû-a-a purus*

A). *mu-*⌈*uṣ-ṣi-ru*⌉ GIŠ.HUR.MEŠ *e-piš ú-sa-*⌈*te*⌉ *pa-ri-is* EŠ.BAR *šá ili*(DINGIR) *u amēli*(LÚ)

j). *mu-uṣ-ṣi-ru* GIŠ.HUR.MEŠ *na-din* NIDBA *šá* DINGIR.MEŠ GAL.MEŠ / [. . . .] ⌈X⌉ *kit-ti pa-ri-is* EŠ.BAR *šá* DINGIR.MEŠ ŠEŠ.MEŠ-*šú* / [. . . .] X-*ma di-ni di*!(*ki*)*-in* EŠ. BAR-*a-a* TAR-*us*

K). *mu-u*[*ṣ-* . . . .] ⌈*ú*⌉ *k*[*it-t*]*i* ⌈*pa-ri*⌉-[*i*]*s*! ⌈EŠ!.BAR!⌉-*a šá* ⌈DINGIR⌉.[ ]

Line 41

šutta šá ina mūši an-né-e a-mu-ru :

A). [M]ÁŠ.⌈GE_6⌉ *šá ina* GE_6 *an-né-e a-mu-ru*

j). [*in*]*a* GE_6 *an-ni-i a-mu-ru* :

K). MÁŠ.[*-m*]*u-*⌈*ru*⌉

Line 42

pal-ha-ku-ma ad-ra-ku-ma šu-ta-du-ra-ku

A). *pal-ha-ku-ma ad-ra-ku šu-ta-du-ra-ku*

K). *pal-ha*!(⌈*ía*⌉)*-k*[*u a*]*d-ra-ku-ma šu-ta-*⌈*du-ra*⌉-[ ]

Line 43

dam-qat ma-a du-muq-šá eli ia-ši likšud ma-a ki-ma kur-ba-an-ni šá ina pāni-ka

A). *dam-qat ma-a du-muq-šá* UGU *ia-ši*
KUR *ma-a ki-ma* LAG *šá ina* IGI-*ka*

j). *dam-qat ma-a* SIG$_5$-*šá ana muhhi*(⌈UGU⌉)-*ia* /
[. . . .] *ma*!(*is*)-*a* GIM LAG *šá ina* IGI-*ka*

K). ⌈*dam*!⌉-[ ]-*šá*!(*a*) *i*[*na*!] *muh-hi-ia*
⌈X-*id*⌉ *ma kur-ba-an-ni* / *ina* IGI-⌈*ka*⌉

Line 44

ana mê ad-du-u ina mê [*li*]*m-ma-hi-ih lip-pa-sis u lih$_4$-ih-har-miṭ* ⌈TU$_6$⌉ ÉN

A). *ana* A.MEŠ *ad-du-u ina* A.MEŠ *lip-pa-sis*
lih$_4$-har-miṭ ⌈TU6⌉ ÉN

j). *ana* A.MEŠ ŠUB-*ú* / [*li*]*m-ma-hi-ih lip-pa-si-is u*
li-ih-har-miṭ TU$_6$! ÉN

K). [-*d*]*u-u ina* A.MEŠ *lip*-⌈*pa-sis u*⌉
lih$_4$-har-< > ⌈TU$_6$⌉ ÉN!(⌈EN⌉)

Line 45

KA.INIM.MA *šutti lemutti pašāri* DÙ.DÙ.BI! *kur-ba-ni ba-li*-⌈*ti*⌉

A). KA.INIM.MA MÁŠ.GE$_6$ HUL-*tì* BÚR DÙ.DÙ.BI!(TA)
kur-ba-ni ba-li-⌈*ti*⌉

K). KA.INIM.[ ]-*tì* BÚR-*ri* KÌD.⌈KÌD⌉.[B]I
kur-ba-an-ni / *ba*-⌈*li*⌉-[ ]

Line 46

teleqqi šipta sebâ ana muhhi tamannu-ma ana mê tanaddi-ma šuttu pašir

A). TI-*qí* ÉN 7.TA.ÀM *ana* UGU ŠID-*nu-ma ana*
A.MEŠ ŠUB-*ma* MÁŠ.GE$_6$ BÚR-*ir*

K). TI!(⌈AN⌉)-⌈*qí*⌉ [.T]A.À[M] ⌈*ana*⌉ UGU ŠID-*nu ina*
A.MEŠ ŠUB-*di* / *šunāte*(MÁŠ.G[E$_6$.M]EŠ) *p*[*a*?]-⌈*šá*?⌉-*a-ri*

Line 45a

j[10]). [KA.INIM].MA HUL MÁŠ.GE$_6$ SIG$_5$.GA.KE$_4$

Line 46a

j). [DÙ.DÙ.BI *kirbān*(LAG) (X)] *teleqqi*(TI-*qí*) *šipta*(ÉN) *šalāšīšu* (3-*šú*) *ana muhhi*(UGU) *tamannu*(ŠID-*nu*) *ana nāri*(ÍD) *tanaddi* (ŠUB)-*ma* NAM.BÚR!.BI(over erasure)

Line 47

én áš búr-bi bal-bi ur-šè i-gi-bi

A). én áš búr-bi bal-bi ur-šè i-gi-bi

M). [ba]l-b[i]

Line 48

šunat aṭ-ṭú-lu lumna šāru lit-bal

A). MÁŠ.GE_6 *aṭ-ṭú-lu* HUL IM *lit-bal*

M). [ ] HUL I[M]

Line 49

KA.INIM.MA *lumun šutti lemutti pašāri*

A). KA.INIM.MA HUL MÁŠ.GE_6 HUL-*tì* BÚR

M). [ ] MÁŠ.GE_6 [ ]

Line 50

DÙ.DÙ.BI *u_4-um šutta e-mu-ru la-am šēp-šú ana qaqqari iškunu*

A). DÙ.DÙ.BI *u_4-um* MÁŠ.GE_6 *e-mu-ru la-am* GÌR-*šú ana* KI GAR-[*n*]*u*

M). [-*u*]*m* MÁŠ.GE_6 *e-mu-ru l*[*a-*]

Line 51

ṭābāta inaqqi šēp-šú ana qaqqari išakkan lumun šutti pašrat

A). A.GEŠTIN.NA BAL-*qí* GÌR-*šú ana* KI GAR-*an* HUL MÁŠ.GE_6 BÚR-[*a*]*t*

M). [ ] BAL-*qí* GÌR-*šú ana* KI GAR-*a*[*n*]

Line 52

ÉN *immer mé-he-e patar šāri ṭa-ab-hu ik-ka-lu mi-tu-tu*

A). ÉN UDU.NÍTA *mé-he-e* GÍR IM *ṭa-ab-hu ik-ka-lu mi-tu-tu*

f). [-*a*]*b-hu ik-k*[*a-*]

M). [( ) .NÍ]TA *mé-he-e* GÍR IM [ ] / [ ]-*ka-l*[*u* -*t*]*u-ti*

Line 53

u šu-nu ik-ka-lu šārumma šutta šá ina mūši an-né-e a-mu-ru

A). [ ] *šu-nu ik-ka-lu* IM-*um-ma* MÁŠ.GE$_6$ *šá ina* GE$_6$ *an-né-e a-mu-ru*

f). [MÁ]Š.GE$_6$ *šá* ⸢*i*⸣-[*na*]

M). *u šú-nu ik-k*[*a-*] / [ ] GE$_6$ *an-ni-i* [ ]

Line 54

ki-ma na-kap šēpi-ia ana a-si-di-ia la i-qar-ri-bu šutta

A). *ki-ma na-kap* GÌR-*ia ana a-si-di-ia la i-qar-ri-bu* MÁŠ.GE$_6$

M). [ ]-*ma na-kap* [ ]-⸢*si-di-ia*⸣ *l*[*a*] / [ ].GE$_6$

Line 55

šá a-mu-ru la iṭehham-ma la i-qar-ri-ba TU$_6$ ÉN

A). *šá a-mu-ru la* TE-*am-ma la i-qar-ri-ba* TU$_6$ ÉN

M). *šá a-*⸢*mu*⸣*-r*[*u*]

Line 56

KA.INIM.MA MÁŠ.GE$_6$ HUL SIG$_5$.DA.KE$_4$

A). KA.INIM.MA MÁŠ.GE$_6$ HUL SIG$_5$.DA.KE$_4$

M). ⸢KA⸣.INIM.MA M[ÁŠ.]

Line 57

DÙ.DÙ.BI *šēp-šú šá idi ni-lu ina qaqqari um-mad šipta šalāšīšu imannu-ma*

A). DÙ.DÙ.BI GÌR-*šú šá* Á *ni-lu ina* KI *um-mad* ÉN 3-*šú* ŠID-*nu-ma*

M). DÙ.DÙ.BI[!] GÌR[!](*áš*)-*šú šá* ⸢Á X⸣ [ ]

Line 58

ana idi-šú šanî ibbalakkat-ma lumun-šú ippaṭṭar

A). *ana* Á-*šú* 2-*i* BAL-*ma* [H]UL-*šú* DU$_8$

M). *ana* Á-*šú* 2-*i* BAL-*ma* [ ]

Line 59

šumma šutta ina libbi šutti īmur-ma ip-šur ⸢*am-mar*⸣ *damqat u pašrat*

A). DIŠ MÁŠ.GE$_6$ *ina* ŠÀ MÁŠ.GE$_6$ IGI-*ma ip-šur* ⸢*am-mar* ŠA$_6$ X X X⸣

M). DIŠ MÁŠ.GE$_6$ *ina* ŠÀ MÁŠ.GE$_6$ IGI-*ma i*[*p*-] / *u* BÚR-*at*

Line 60

ana damiqti u lemutti NU ⸢X X⸣

A). *ana* SIG$_5$ *u* HUL NU ⸢X X⸣

M). *ana* SIG$_5$ *u* H[UL]

Line 61

šumma amēlu šunāti pár-da-a-te iṭ-ṭul šunātu-šú ana lemutti šaknā-⸢*šú*⸣

A). DIŠ NA MÁŠ.GE$_6$.MEŠ *pár-da-a-te iṭ-ṭul* MÁŠ.GE$_6$.MEŠ-*šú ana* HUL GAR-⸢*šú*⸣

M). DIŠ NA MÁŠ.GE$_6$.MEŠ *pár-da-a-ti i*[*ṭ*-]

Line 62

A). *lumun*(⸢HUL⸣)-*ši-na* <*ana*> *pašāri*(BÚR) *ù ana amēli*(NA) *là ṭehê* (TE-*e*) *zēr*(NUMUN) ^{Ú}*būšāni*(HAB) ^{Ú}*atā'iša*(KUR.[KUR])

Line 63

A). *šamma peṣâ*(⸢Ú.BABBAR⸣) *ṭābat*(MUN) *eme-sal-lì ina* K[UŠ]

Line 64

A). *šumma*(⸢DIŠ⸣) *amēlu*(N[A]) *šunāti*(⸢MÁŠ.GE$_6$⸣.MEŠ) *pár-da-te i*[*ṭ-ṭul*]

Line 65

A). ⸢X⸣ [X].⸢MEŠ?⸣ $^{[Ú]}$⸢*el-kul*⸣-*la* $^{⸢Ú⸣}$*eli*(⸢UGU⸣)-*k*[*ul-la* . . . .]

Line 66

A). *kibrīta*(P[IŠ$_{10}$].⸢ITU$_4$⸣) *i*[*na* KUŠ]

Line 67

A). *šumma*(⸢DIŠ⸣) ⸢KIMIN⸣ *hasab*(LA) [*pelî*(NUNUZ)] *lurmi*(⸢GÁ.NU$_{11}$⸣)^{MUŠEN} *muṣa''irāna*(⸢BIL.ZA⸣.ZA) *arqa*(⸢SIG$_7$⸣)

Line 68

A). *parzilla*(AN.BAR) *kaspa*(KÙ.BABBAR) *hurāṣa*(KÙ.GI) *sīkāt* (KU.KU) ^{GIŠ}*ušî*(⌈ESI⌉) *ina* [KUŠ]

Column IV

Line 1

A). [. . . .] ⌈*a*⌉ *šá* ^{GIŠ}MÁ $^{\text{NA}_4}$*šadâna*(⌈KA⌉.GI.⌈NA⌉) *ṣābita*(DAB) *aban* (NA$_4$) *ga-bi-*⌈*i*⌉

Line 2

A). [^{Ú}*tar-m*]*uš ru'tīta*(ÚH.⌈ITU$_4$⌉) *ina* ⌈KUŠ⌉

Line 3

A). $^{\text{[Ú]}}$*amīlāna*([L]Ú.U$_{19}$.LU) ^{Ú}*el-kul-la* ^{Ú}*eli*(UGU)*-kul-la ina* KUŠ$^{!}$

Line 4

A). *aban*([N]A$_4$) *ga-bi-i* ^{Ú}*sikilla*(SIKIL) ^{Ú}*lišān kalbi*(EME.UR.GI$_7$) *ina* KUŠ

Line 5

$^{\text{NA}_4}$*aš-pu-u* $^{\text{NA}_4}$*sah-hu-ú aban bālti aban lamassi*

A).	$^{\text{[N]A}_4}$*aš-pu-u*	$^{\text{NA}_4}$*sah-hu-ú*	NA$_4$ UR NA$_4$	^{d}LAMMA
A$_1$).	$^{\text{NA}_4}$*aš-pu-u*	⌈*sah-hu*⌉*-u*	UR	^{d}LAMMA
B$_1$).	*aš-pu-u*	*sah-hu-u*	UR	^{d}LAMMA
C$_1$).	$^{\text{NA}_4}$*aš-*⌈*pu-ú*⌉	$^{\text{NA}_4}$*sah-hu-*⌈*ú*⌉ [		]

Line 6

$^{\text{NA}_4}$*šadâ-nu ṣābita* $^{\text{NA}_4}$*erî zikari ina rikis kitî tašakkak*

A).	[ ]-⌈*nu*⌉	DAB.BA	$^{\text{NA}_4}$URUDU NÍTA *ina* DUR ⌈GADA⌉ È-*ak*
A$_1$).	$^{\text{NA}_4}$KUR-*nu*	DAB	
B$_1$).	KUR-*nu*	[DA]B	
C$_1$).	$^{\text{⌈NA}_4\text{⌉}}$[	]	

Line 7

$^{\text{[N]A}_4}$NÍG.⌈URUDU⌉.UD *abnē šunāti* ⌈*dal*⌉*-ha-a-ti dummuqi*

A). $^{\text{[N]A}_4}$NÍG.⌈URUDU⌉.UD NA$_4$.MEŠ MÁŠ.GE$_6$.MEŠ ⌈*dal*⌉*-ha-a-ti* SIG$_5$

A$_1$). 5 NA$_4$ MÁŠ.GE$_6$.MEŠ *pár-da-te*

C$_1$). [ ].MEŠ [ ]

Line 8

A). [ÉN *e-piš l*]*um-ni na-ki-su napišti*(ZI-*ti*) *mur-te-du-u ek-le-te*

Line 9

A). [X (X)]-⌈*ša-ti*⌉ *ka-ti-mu nu-ul-la-a-te*

Line 10

A). [*mur*]*-te-ed-d*[*u*]*-*⌈*ú*⌉ *lumun*(HUL) *ka-tim-ti mu-ši ur-ri*

Line 11

A). [A]N$^?$.⌈ZAG.GAR.RA⌉ *lemutti*(HUL) *te-*⌈*pu*⌉*-šá ana damiqti* (^{MÍ}SIG$_5$) *tīrra*(GUR-*ra*)

Line 12

A). [X (X)] ⌈ X *mim-mu-ú*⌉ *te-pu-šá ana damiqti*(⌈^{MÍ}⌉SIG$_5$) *te-e-ri*

Line 13

A). [UGU$^?$]-⌈*ni* ^{d}⌉*Šamaš*(UTU) ⌈*li-da*⌉*-mi-*⌈*iq* UGU$^?$⌉*-ni* ^{d}*Marduk lidammiq*(HÉ.⌈ŠA$_6$⌉)

Line 14

A). [X-*šú*$^?$ *šipta*(É]N) *an-ni-tú ana muhhi*(UGU) *me-eli*(UGU) *tak-ṣi-ri tamannu*(ŠID)*-ma ina kišādi*(⌈GÚ⌉)*-šú tašakkan*(GAR-*an*)

Line 15

A). [. . . .] ⌈X⌉ *šunāti*(MÁŠ.GE$_6$.MEŠ) *šu-te-qí* ^{Ú}*tar-*⌈*muš*⌉ *imbû tâmti*(KA.A.AB.BA)

Line 16

A). [. . . *ni-ki*]*p-tú zikar*(NÍTA) *u sinniš*(MÍ) *ina* KUŠ

Line 17

A). [*lumun*(HUL) *idāti*(Á].MEŠ) *ittāti*(GISKIM.MEŠ) *ana*$^!$ *amēli* (⌈NA⌉) ⌈*là*⌉ *ṭehê*(⌈TE.E.DÈ⌉) *qān šalāli*(GI.ŠUL.HI)

Line 18

A). $^{[hi\text{-}pi]\ ⌈eš\text{-}šú⌉}$ *áš* GE$_6$ ^{NA_4}*ajarta*(⌈PA⌉) ^{Ú}*imhur*(IGI)-*lim imbû tâmti* (KA.A.AB.⌈BA⌉) *ina* KUŠ

Line 19

A). $^{⌈hi⌉\text{-}pi\ eš\text{-}šú}$ *ha bu* ^{Ú}*harmuna*(HAR.HUM.BA.⌈ŠIR⌉) ^{Ú}*ēda*(DILI) *zēr* (NUMUN) ^{Ú}*ēdi*(DILI) *ina* KUŠ

Line 20

A). $^{hi\text{-}pi\ eš\text{-}šú}$ ⌈^{Ú}⌉*ēda*(DILI) ^{Ú}*el-kul-la* ^{Ú}*ašla*(NINNI$_5$) *imbû tâmti*(KA.⌈A⌉.AB.BA) *ina* ⌈KUŠ⌉

Line 21

ilu-⌈*šu pa-ṭi*-X GIM$^{?}$⌉ *ina muhhi*$^{?}$*-šú* ⌈*ana*⌉ *ṭehê* : DÙ.DÙ.BI *nignaq* ^{ŠIM}*burāši ina bīti parsi*

A). ⌈DINGIR-*šu pa-ṭi*-X GIM$^{?}$⌉ *ina* ⌈UGU$^{?}$⌉-*šú* ⌈*ana* TE-*e*⌉ :
NÍG.NA ⌈^{ŠIM}⌉LI *ina* É TAR-*si*

N$^{3'}$). DÙ.DÙ.BI
NÍG.NA ^{GIŠ}LI *ina* É TAR-*si*

D$_1$^{11}). [N]ÍG.NA ^{ŠIM}⌈LI X⌉ *u* [(X)] TAR$^{!}$(⌈*bi*⌉)-*si*$^{!}$(*ad*)

Line 22

ana (**D$_1$**: *mahar*) *ili-šú u* ^{d}*ištari-šú tašakkan-ma šikāra* (*rēštâ*) *tanaqqi kam taqabbi*

A). *ana* ⌈DINGIR⌉-⌈*šú*⌉ < > ⌈^{d}EŠ$_{18}$.TÁR$^{?}$-*šú*⌉ GAR-⌈*an*$^{?}$⌉
⌈X⌉ ⌈UR$_5$.GIM⌉ DUG$_4$.GA

N). *ana* DINGIR-*šu* / *u* ^{d}XV-*šú* GAR-*ma*
kam DUG$_4$.GA

D$_1$). IGI DINGIR-*šú* GAR-*an* /
[K]AŠ.SAG ⌈BAL UR$_5$⌉.GIM DUG$_4$.GA

Line 23

én dingir.mu hé$^{!}$.silim.ma.mu ama.^{d}inanna.mu hé.silim.ma.mu [níg.dùg].ga.⌈mu ^{d}utu⌉ hé.⌈gub⌉

A). ⌈én dingir.mu hé$^{?}$.silim.ma⌉.mu ⌈ama⌉.^{d}inanna.⌈mu
hé.silim.ma.mu⌉ [níg.dùg].ga.⌈mu ^{d}utu⌉ hé.⌈gub⌉

D$_1$^{1}). ⌈én⌉ [di]ngir.m[u] ⌈hé$^{!}$.silim$^{!}$⌉.[m]a.mu / am[a.^{d}inann]a.mu
[ ].⌈silim$^{!}$.ma⌉.mu

E$_1$). [di]ngir.mu ⌈hé$^{!}$⌉.silim.m[u] / [am]a.^{d}inanna.mu
⌈hé⌉.silim.ma.mu / ⌈á⌉.zi.da dingir.mu [h]é.silim.ma.mu

Line 24

igi.mu ama.^{d}inanna.mu hé.gub : igi ^{d}nin.urta lugal ^{giš}⸢tukul⸣.ke$_4$ hé.gub

A). ⸢X X X X .^{d}inanna⸣.mu ⸢hé.gub⸣ : igi ⸢^{d}nin.urta⸣ [tuku]l.ke$_4$ ⸢hé⸣.gub

D$_1$). igi ⸢ama.$^{d!}$⸣.[ ] ⸢hé⸣.gub / [ig]i ⸢^{d}⸣[ ] $^{[gi]š}$[tuku]l.[k]e$_4$ ⸢hé⸣.gub

E$_1$). igi.mu ama.^{d}inanna.⸢mu⸣ hé.gub / igi$^{!}$(bar) ^{d}nin.urta lugal ^{giš}⸢tukul⸣.ke$_4$ hé.gub

Line 25

inim.inim nu.dùg.ga.mu inim nu.silim.ma ⁝ *a-*[*n*]*a ia-a-ši re-ṣa-*⸢*nim*⸣*-ma dà-lí-lí-ku-nu lud-lul* ⸢TU$_6$⸣ ÉN

A). ⸢inim.inim nu⸣.dùg.ga.mu inim ⸢nu.silim⸣.ma ⁝ ⸢*ana*⸣ *ía-ši* ⸢*ru*⸣*-ṣ*[*a-*]*-*⸢*lí-lí-ku*⸣*-nu* ⸢*lud*⸣*-lul*

N$^{1'}$). [ ].⸢dùg.ga.mu$^{!}$ inim⸣ nu.[ ] / ⸢*ana ia*$^{!}$*-ši re-ṣa*⸣*-nim*$^{!}$(*du*)*-ma* ⸢*dà*⸣*-lí-lí-*⸢*ku*⸣< > ⸢*lud*⸣*-*[ ]

D$_1$). [i]nim nu.si.sá / [*-l*]*í*$^{!}$*-lí-ku-nu lud-lul*

E$_1$). inim.inim nu.dùg.ga.mu ⸢inim⸣ nu.silim.ma / *a-*[*n*]*a ia-a-ši* ⸢*re*⸣*-ṣa-*⸢*nim*⸣*-ma* / ⸢*dà*⸣*-lí-lí-ku-nu* ⸢*lud*⸣*-lul* ⸢TU$_6$⸣ ÉN

Line 25a

D$_1^{7}$). [X] ⸢X⸣ [. . . . .] ⸢X⸣ nam.ba.te.gá.dè

Line 25b

D$_1$). [X] ⸢X⸣ [. . . . . *t*]*i* ⸢X⸣

Line 25c

D$_1$). [X] ⸢X X X⸣ [X] ⸢X *ta*$^{?}$⸣ *ma* ⸢X X⸣

Line 25d

D$_1$). [*šipta*(É]N) *tamannu*(⸢ŠID⸣*-nu*) *i*[*na*] *kišādi-šu*(GÚ.BA) *tašakkan* ([GA]R)

Line 26

šalāšīšu ana pān nignaqqi tamannu-ma kīma nignaqqu kurummat-su uqtattû ina šumēli-ka ina qê ina ^{TÚG}*sissikti-ka*

A). ⸢3$^{?}$-*šú*$^{?}$⸣ [ ] ⸢IGI$^{?}$⸣ NÍG.⸢NA ŠID⸣-*nu-ma* ⸢GIM⸣ NÍG.NA ŠUKU-*su* TIL-*ú* *i*[*na*]-⸢X *ina* GU$^{?}$⸣ [ ] ⸢^{TÚG}⸣SÍG$^{!}$(⸢SÍG-*šú*⸣)-*ka*$^{!}$(KEŠDA)

N$^{4'}$). 3-*šú* *ana* IGI NÍG.NA / ŠID-*ma* GIM NÍG.NA ŠUKU-*su* TIL-*u* *ina* GÙB-*ka* / *ina* GU *ina* ^{TÚG}⸢SÍG⸣-*ka*

Line 27

tara-kas qanâ ṭāba tasâk ina šaman ^{GIŠ}*šurmēni tapaššassu-ma : ki-a-am taqabbi*

A). ⸢X X⸣ [G]I ⸢DÙG.GA⸣ < > ⸢*ina* Ì+GIŠ ^{GIŠ}ŠUR.MÌN⸣ ŠÉŠ$^{!}$(⸢SÍG⸣)-*su* : *ki-a-am* [D]UG$_4$.G[A]

N). *tara-kas* GI DÙG.GA SÚD / *ina* Ì ^{GIŠ}ŠUR.MÌN EŠ.MEŠ-*su-ma* *kam* DUG$_4$.GA

Line 28

ÉN *ana ilī mì-na-a e-pu-uš* ⋮ *ana* ^{d}*ištarī mì-na-a ah-ṭi* : *ilu-ia*$_5$ *iz-nu-u itti-ia*$_5$

A). [DIN]GIR.⸢MU*mi*⸣-*n*[*a*]-⸢*a*⸣ *e*-⸢*pu*⸣-*uš* ⋮ ⸢^{d}⸣EŠ$_{18}$.TÁ[R.M]U *mi-na-a ah-ṭi* : DINGIR-*ia*$_5$ *iz-n*[*u*-] K[I]-*i*[*a*$_5$]

N). ÉN *ana* DINGIR.MU *mì-na-a* DÙ-*uš* *ana* ^{d}XV.MU *mì-na-a ah-ṭi* / DINGIR-*ia*$_5$ *iz-nu-u* KI-*ia*$_5$

D$_1$[13]). ÉN *ana* DINGIR.MU *mi-na-a* DÙ-*uš* / *ana* *ilī*(DINGIR.MU) *mi*-⸢*na*⸣-*a ah-ṭi*

E$_1$). ⸢ÉN⸣ *a-na* DINGIR.MU *m*[*i*]-*na-a* *e-pu-*[*u*]*š* / *ana* ^{d}È[Š].TAR.⸢MU⸣ *mi*-⸢*na*⸣-*a ah-*[ ] DINGIR-*ia*$_5$ *iz-nu*-⸢*ú*⸣ KI-*ia*

Line 29

^{d}*iš-tar-ia*$_5$ *is-bu-su eli-ía muruṣ lìb-bi-ia lim-ṭa-ma dà-lí-lí-ku-nu lud-lul* TU$_6$ ÉN

A). ⌈^{d}EŠ$_{18}$.TÁR-*ia*⌉ < >-⌈*bu*⌉-*su* UGU-*i*[*a*$_5$ GI]G ŠÀ-*ia*$_5$
⌈*lim-ṭa*⌉-*ma* *dà-lí-lí*-⌈*ku*⌉-*nu* *lud*-⌈*lul*⌉

N). ^{d}XV-*ia*$_5$ *is-bu-su* UGU-*ía* / GIG ŠÀ-*ia*
lim-⌈*ṭa*⌉-*ma* *dà-lí-lí-ku-nu* *lud-lul*

D$_1$). [GI]G *lìb-bi-ia*
lim-ṭa-ma *dà-lí-lí-ku*-⌈*nu* *lud*⌉-*lul*

E$_1$). ^{d}*iš-tar-ia*$_5$ ⌈*is*⌉-*bu-su* UGU-*ia* / GIG *lìb-bi*-⌈*ia*⌉
lim-ṭa-ma / *dà-lí-lí-ku-n*[*u* *l*]*ud-lul* TU$_6$ ÉN

Line 30

an-nam šalāšīšu taqabbi-ma tanâl-ma šutta damiqta tammar

A). 3-[DU]G$_4$.⌈GA⌉-*ma* N[Á-] ⌈MÁŠ.GE$_6$⌉ S[IG$_5$
]-*mar*

N). 3-*šú* DUG$_4$.GA-*ma* NÁ-*ma* MÁŠ.GE$_6$ SIG$_5$
IGI-*mar*

E$_1$). *an-nam* ⌈3⌉-*šú* DUG$_4$.GA-*ma* / NÁ-*ma* MÁŠ.GE$_6$ SIG$_5$
IGI-*mar*

Line 30a

D$_1$[16]). [*a*]*n-nam šalāšīšu*(3-*šú*) *tamannu*(⌈ŠID⌉) ⌈(X) X X⌉ [X X]-*ma*

Line 30b

D$_1$). ⌈X⌉ *ana nāri*(ÍD) *tanaddi*(ŠUB-*di*)-*ma ana pān*(IGI) ⌈X⌉ [(X)] ⌈X⌉
úl iṭehhe(TE)

Line 31

A). ⌈X⌉ [X] ⌈X SILIM *e*⌉ [. . . . . DU]G$_4$$^?$.⌈GA$^?$⌉

Line 32

A). DIN[GIR X] ⌈X X X⌉ [. . . . .] ⌈X⌉

Line 33

A). ⌈X⌉ [X X] ⌈X⌉ [. . . . .] *taqabbi*(DUG$_4$.GA)-⌈*ma*⌉

Line 34

A). [. . . . . *tir-ra ki-šad-k*]*i* ⌈*šá taš*⌉-*bu-si eli*(⌈UGU⌉)-⌈*ia*$_5$⌉

Line 35

A). [. . . . . *m*]*u* ⸢*ul a-mur*⸣-*ma e-ti-it-eq*

Line 36

A). [. . . *ilī*(DINGIR.MU) *šá itti*(KI)-*i*]*a*$_5$ ⸢*sab*⸣-*s*[*u*$^?$ *šu-u*]*h*-⸢*hi*⸣-*ra pa-ni-ka*

Line 37

A). [^{d}*ištarī*(EŠ$_{18}$.TÁR.MU) *šá e*]-*zi*-⸢*zi*⸣ *l*[*i*]-⸢*nu-uh*⸣ *kab-ta-at*$^!$(*ab*)

Line 38

én dingir.mu ša$_6$.ga mu.⸢un⸣.túm.a ⁝ dingir.mu sag.kal pa.è an.ta.gál

A). [m]u.⸢un⸣.túm.[ ] ⁝ dingir.mu sag.kal pa.è an.ta.gál

N). én dingir.mu ša$_6$.ga mu.túm.a dingir.mu sag.kal pa.è / an.ta.gál

P). én dingir.mu ša$_6$.ga mu.⸢un⸣.[ ] / dingir.mu sag.kal pa.è dingir<.mu> sag.kal pa.è

Line 39

dingir.mu še.ga.še.ga *ía-a-ši* : ^{d}ma.mú dingir.ma.mú.da.ke$_4$

A). [ ].⸢ga *ia*⸣-[*a-š*]*i* : ^{d}ma.mú dingir.⸢ma⸣.mú.ke$_4$

N). dingir.mu še.ga.še.ga *ía-a-ši* ^{d}⸢ma⸣.mú / dingir.ma.mú.da.ke$_4$

P). dingir.mu še.ga.še.ga *ía-ši* / ^{d}ma.mú < >.ma.mú.da.e.ne

Line 40

dingir.mu inim še.ga.še.ga ù.tu.ud.da én

A). [š]e.g[a].š[e.] ù.tu$^!$(ma).ud.da

N). dingir.mu inim še.ga / še.ga ù.tu.ud.da én

P). dingir.mu inim še.ga.še.ga tu.ud.da én

Line 41a

P). KA.INIM.MA *itūli*(NÁ)-*ma ila*(DINGIR) *šutta*(MÁŠ.GE$_6$) *damiqta*(SIG$_5$) *šub-re-e*

Line 41b

DÙ.DÙ.BI *ina muhhi* ^{GIŠ}*ēri šipta šalāšīšu tamannu-ma i-na rēši-ka* (**A**: *rēš erši-ka*) *tašakkan* ^{Ú}*atā'iša ina* ^{TÚG}*sissikti-ka tarakkas tanâl-ma šutta damiqtu tammar*

A). [ ] ŠID-*nu-ma i*[*na*
S]AG GIŠ.NÁ-*ka* GAR-*an* ^{Ú}KUR.KUR *ina* ^{TÚG}SÍG-*ka*
KEŠDA

N). KA.INIM.MA *ina* UGU ^{GIŠ}MA.NU ŠID-*ma ina*
SAG-*ka* GAR-*an* / ⸢X ^{Ú}⸣KUR.KUR *ina* ^{TÚG}SÍG-*ka*
KEŠDA

P). DÙ.DÙ.BI *ina* UGU ^{GIŠ}MA.NU ÉN 3-*šú* ŠID-*nu-ma* / *i-na*
SAG-*ka* GAR-*an* ^{Ú}KUR.KUR *ina* ^{TÚG}SÍG-*ka*
KEŠDA / NÁ-*ma* MÁŠ.GE$_{6}$ SIG$_{5}$-*tu*$_{4}$ IGI-*mar*

Line 42

én hu-ub-ba hu-ub-ba ab-na : a-ra-tu è a-ra-ba-tu è

A). [ ]-⸢ba hu⸣-u[b]-ba ab-na : a-ra-tu è a-ra-ba-tu è

N$^{\text{r1}}$). én hu-ub-ba hu-ub-ba ab-na / a-ra-tu è a-ra< >-tu è

P). én hu-ub-ba hu-ub-ba ab-na a-ra-ba-te e a-ra-ba-te e

Line 43

^{d}*ištarī ina uz-zi ha-am-mat* : ^{d}*ištarī* MIN : ^{d}*ištarī* ⁝ MIN

A). [ ] *ha-am-mat* : ^{d}EŠ$_{18}$.⸢TÁR.MU⸣
MIN : ^{d}EŠ$_{18}$.TÁR.⸢MU⸣ ⁝ MIN

N). ^{d}XV *ina uz-zi*$^{\text{!}}$(*mu*) *ha-mat* KIMIN
KIMIN

P). ^{d}EŠ$_{18}$.TÁR.MU *ina uz-zi ha-*⸢*am*$^{\text{!}}$*-mat*$^{\text{!}}$⸣ MIN
MIN

Line 44

KA.INIM.MA *šib-sat* ^{d}*ištari ana amēli nu-uh-hi*

A). [ ].MA ⸢*šib*⸣-[ ] ⸢^{d}EŠ$_{18}$⸣.TÁR *ana* LÚ *nu-uh-hi*

P). KA.INIM.MA *šib-sat* ^{d}EŠ$_{18}$.TÁR *ana* NA *là ṭehê*(TE-*e*)

Line 45

DÙ.DÙ.BI *si-i-ra igāri šá ṣīt šamši*

A). [ ].⸢BI⸣ *si-i-ra* IZ.ZI *šá* ^{d}UTU.È

N). DÙ.DÙ.BI *še-ra* É.GAR$_{8}$ < > *ereb šamši*(^{d}UTU.ŠÚ.A)

P). DÙ.DÙ.BI *si-i-ri* É.GAR$_{8}$ *šá* ^{d}UTU.⸢ŠÚ.A⸣

Line 46

teleqqi kirbān ṭābti ana muh-hi ta-sár-raq šipta sebî[šu] tamannu

A). [ ] ⌜MUN⌝ *ana muh-hi ta-sár-raq* ÉN ŠID-*nu*

N). TI-*qí* LAG MUN *ina* UGU DUB

P). [ ] / ⌜X⌝ [UG]U ⌜*ta*⌝-*sa*$^{!}$-*raq* ÉN 7-[*šú*]

Line 47

ina še-pit erši-ka tašakkan-ma NAM.BÚR.BI

A). [GÌ]R GIŠ.⌜NÁ⌝-*ka* GAR-*ma* ⌜NAM⌝.BÚR-*ma*

N). *ina še-pit* GIŠ.NÁ-*ka* GAR-*ma* NAM.BÚR.BI

<u>Colophon Of Manuscript A, Column IV Lines 48-57</u>

48). [*ṭuppu*(DUB)] $^{[m]⌜d⌝}$*Nabû*(AG)-*šal-lim* ^{LÚ}*šamallî*(ŠAGANA$_{X}$.LÁ) *ṣehri*(TUR)

49). [X] ⌜X X *te* TÙM⌝ ^{d}*Nabû*(AG) *ṭupšar*(DUB.SAR) *É-sag-íla*

50). [X] ⌜X DA⌝.MEŠ *li-šim ši-mat-su*

51). [*na*]-⌜*an*⌝-*nab-šu ina pî*(KA) *nišē*(UN.MEŠ) *lu-še-li*

52). [^{d}*Ṣarpani-t*]u_4 *na-ram*-⌜*ti*⌝ ^{d}*Marduk*(ŠÀ.ZU$^{!}$(*ṣi*))

53). [*la na-par*]-⌜*ka*⌝-*a lemutta*(^{MÍ}⌜HUL⌝)-*šú li-tas-qar*

54). [^{d}*Gu-l*]*a* ⌜*a-zu*⌝-*gal*-⌜*la*⌝-tu_4 *É-kur*

55). [. . . .] ⌜X X⌝ *ina zumri*(⌜SU⌝)-⌜*šú li*⌝-*ir*-⌜*ku-us*⌝-*ma*

56). [*li-i*]*r-tap-pu-da* ⌜*ka-ma*$^{!}$-*a-tú*⌝

57). ⌜*ša lim-mu* ^{m}⌝*Aš-šur*-⌜*ba*⌝-*ni*$^{!}$(*qaq*) $^{⌜LÚ⌝}$*šá*-⌜*kìn* ^{URU}⌝*Kal*-⌜*ha*⌝

<u>Colophon Of Manuscript M, Lines 16'-18'</u>

16'). *šumma*(DIŠ) *amēlu*(NA) *šunāti*(MÁŠ.GE$_6$.MEŠ) *pár-da-a-ti i*[*ṭ-ṭul*]

17'). DUB.10.KÁM *iškar*(É[Š.G]ÀR) ⌜^{d}*Zi*⌝-[*qi-qu*]

18'). *ekal*(KUR) ^{m}*Aššur*(AN.ŠÁR)-*bān*(DÙ)-*apli*(A) *šar*$_4$ *kiššāti*(ŠÚ) *šar*$_4$ *māt*(KUR) *Aššur*(AŠ)$^{K[I]}$

* * * * *

OBVERSE

Column I

1). [If a man] - dream . . . . [. . .] . .

2). [. . . .] . . should stay like that for a <whole> day, and on the second day . [. . . .] . at night$^{?}$

3). You moisten [a dressing in . . $^{?}$], (and) you place (it) on his forehead.

4). [On the third$^{?}$ day] you dry (and) pound *šaššugu*-wood.

5). You stir (the wood) [into] beer and oil before Shamash. Before he has placed his foot upon the ground,

6). . it/him, and it is the dissolving of the bad dream. Its evil will not come near to (i.e., affect) the man.

---

7). If a man has seen an incorrect dream

8). [. . . .] their . his forehead, before he has placed his foot upon the ground,

9). [without having] eaten, he himself says as follows: "The dream which I saw

10). is pleasant [before] Sin and Shamash. It is pleasant, and it is pleasant. It is pleasant."

11-12). [Thus] he says, and (in this way) [he] makes a favourable oracular utterance for himself. His dream will not come near to him.

12a). If ditto (i.e., lines 7-8): Before sunrise [. . . . . .]

12b). the man upon his bed at night$^{?}$ [. . . . .]

12c). he must set out a censer. [Cheap scented] flour [. . . to . .]

12d). he must recount. He must [speak] as follows: "[. . . . . . .]

12e). it is favourable like (the dream) [which] I saw [. . . . . . .]

12f). in . . . . [. . . . .]

12g). and the dream to [. . . . .]

---

13). [If a man] saw an incorrect dream: Without having eaten

14). [. . . .] . . . he recounts to a reed. He burns (the reed) <in> a fire.

15). [The evil of] that [dream] will not obstruct him.

---

16). [. . . . . .] . . . to [his] personal deity he turned, and he recounted

17). [. . . . . .] . . . . he binds, and he encloses, and

18). [. . . . . .] . . . . it will obstruct (the path$^{?}$) to that man.

---

19). [. . . . . .] . [.] . . [(.)] . . he became worried, and that <man> called out

20). [. . . . . . in] the early [morning], (while) the door detains him (i.e., before he leaves the house),

21). [. . . . . .] . . he wraps, and he soaks (it in) oil.

22). [. . . . . .] . . he kindles a fire. The dream

23). [. . . . . .] . . . he recites over a thorn thus:

24). [Incantation: “. . . . .] . . . the strong (and) the powerful (one$^{?}$)

25). [. . . . . .] . . . . all of the ill-boding omen(s)

26). [. . . . .] . . . .

27). [. . . . .] . [.] . . . . . its evil$^{?}$ will be separated (from the dreamer).

---

28). [. . . . .] . he became worried about it, and . . .

29). [. . . . .] . . . . his right

30). [. . . . .] . . . . . . may . . .

31). [. . . . .] . . . [. (.)] . . [.] . . his right$^{?}$

32). [. . . . .] . . . . [. .] . . .

33). [. . . . .] . . . .

34). [. . . . .] . . . . change its appearance! Destroy its descendant(s)!

35). [. . . . .] . . . [(.)] . he has$^{?}$ misfortune.

36). [. . . . .] heaven (and) earth . . . a bad dream

37). [. . . . . .] which during the first watch (of the night), the middle watch, (or) the third watch

38). [. . . . . .] this dream from the body of this man

39). [. . . . . . .] may$^{?}$ it return . . . . to the body (i.e., womb) of your progenitress$^{?}$ and

40). [. . . . . .] . . the evil of the dream . . . from my body

41). [may it (the evil) be 3,600 ‘miles’ (lit., double hours) distant!] May it not return to me!” You snap that reed into two.

42). [. . . . . .] the evil of the dream you recall before Shamash.

43). . [. . . . . .] . . . . O Shamash, this dream before you

44). . . [. . . . . .] . . . . its (the dream’s) evil

45). will not come [near . . . .] . . . .

46). . . [. . . . .] . . . . .

47). . . [. . . . .] its [evil$^{?}$] is loosened

48). like . [.] . . . . . [. . . . . .] . . . is dissolved$^{?}$, and$^{?}$

49). before . . . . [. . . .] . . . .

50). you pray, and . [. . . .] exists for him.

---

51). If [he saw] a dream, and became worried at its ill portent [. . . .] . . .

52). “O Clod! [. .] all of the evil of the dream . . [. . . . . .] . .

53). [you] recite over [it (the clod)], and [before] Shamash [. . . . .]

54). you$^{?}$ will [. . . .] like/just as the clod in water you$^{?}$ will . [. . . . .]

55). . . [. . . .] O Shamash, the decision(s)$^{?}$ [. (.) of (the regions)] above [and below]

56). as many as [.] . . . . [. (.)] . . . . (.) [. . . . .]

57). to . . . . . [. .] . . . Nusku [. . . . . .]

58). . . . . . [(.)] you prostrate yourself (before) Shamash. To Ea and the god [. . . . .]

59). and before . . . you pray . . and[?] [(.)] (.) .

---

60). "O Utu, you are the . . of heaven and earth, the governor[?] of the lands.

61). . Utu . . . . the hearer of the word . [. .] .

62). You are the judge. You [are] (my) judge.

63). You are the maker of the oracular decision(s). [You are] the maker of the oracular decision(s) [concerning me].

64). The bad dream is my property, [my] unpleasant thing.

65). May its . be destroyed like (this) clod (which) will be . . into water!"

---

66). Incantation: "O Utu, you are the [exalted] judge of heaven and earth.

67). [(You are) ditto (i.e., the [exalted] judge) of] the lands. <You are> the judge. My words

68). [. .] . . [.] . . my unpleasant thing . . . .

69). my [. . .], my bad dream, my ill-health

70). like the clod . . . they <will> return to their places (i.e., leave me alone)!" Incantation formula.

---

71). Its ritual: You lift up (in) your left hand a lump from a wall which is situated in the west.

72). You recite the (above) incantation three times over (the lump) before Shamash. You throw (the lump) into the river. It (the evil of the dream) will be dissolved.

---

73). [Incantation: "O Utu], you are the foremost judge to pass judgement.

74). You are the maker of [the oracular decision(s)]. You are the maker of the oracular decision(s) concerning me.

75). Make [the dream] which I saw stand for good luck!

76). May I prosper! May I obtain a friend!

77). May [the event(s)] of my [day(s)] be favourable!"

---

78). [.] . . you recite (lit., raise) (this) ŠU.ÍL.LÁ-incantation before[?] Shamash. It (the evil of the dream) will be dissolved.

<u>Column I, Line 79 And Column II</u>

79). Incantation: "[O Clod], O Clod, in the part of you (which) is pinched off, part of me (**E**: myself) is pinched off,

1). (and) in the part of me (which) is pinched off (is) [your] pinched-off piece (**E**: yourself).

2-3). O Clod, the evil of the dream which I saw, which I repeatedly saw (during) the first watch (of the night), the middle watch, (or) the third watch - (in) which I saw my dead father; (or in) which I saw my dead mother;

4). (or in) <which I saw> a god; (or in) which I saw the king; (or in) which I saw an important person; (or in) which I saw a prince; (or in) which I saw a dead person; (or in) which I saw a living person;

5). (or in) which I saw/experienced knowledge (of something) I did not know/understand; (or in) which I went to an unknown land; (or in) which I repeatedly ate unknown bread;

6). (or in) which I was dressed in an unfamiliar garment - just as I will throw you (O Clod) into (running) water, and

7). you will be soaked, you will disintegrate, [you] will be fragmented, (with the result that) you will not return to your place (i.e., not become a clod again);

8). (so) may the evil of this dream which [I] saw be thrown into water just like you!

9). May it be soaked! May it disintegrate! May it be fragmented! [May it not return] to its place (i.e., return to me)!

10). May it cross the river! May it cross over the mountain! May it (be) detach(ed) from my body! May it [. . . . . .]!

11). May it ascend to heaven like smoke! May it be as unable to return (lit., not return) to its place [as] an uprooted tamarisk!

12). May the tamarisk purify me! May the *maštakal*-plant absolve me!

13). May! the 'off-shoot' of the date palm purify me! May the river receive (the evil of the dream) from me!

14). May (the river) give its aura to me, and may it carry off [the evil]! O Shamash, (regarding) the dream which I saw,

15). may it be pleasant! O Shamash, may the dream which I saw be reliable!

16). O Shamash, turn the dream which I saw into good luck!"

---

17). Its ritual: You recite the (above) incantation three times over either a lump of salt or over a lump of clay.

18). You throw (the lump) into the river (**E**: (running) water). The evil of the dream will not come near to the man.

19-20). Unintelligible abracadabra incantation.

---

21). Incantation rubric: (It is the text in order) not to see a frightening dream.

22-23). Its ritual: You make four clay figurines[!], male and female. You recite the (above) incantation over (them) seven times. (Then) you place (them) at your head (before lying down).

---

24). If a man sees frightening dreams, or he cannot recall a bad dream:

25). his personal goddess . . . (.) and his hand . . to the heart of his personal god

26). . . . . On the twenty-eighth day

27). . [. .] . day you go out to the open country. You set out a censer of juniper before his personal god.

28). The sufferer sets out a censer before the *kušāru,* and you speak as follows:

---

29). Incantation: "O Utu, the foremost of the gods; O Utu, the manifest;

30). O Utu, the king of heaven and earth, the king of the Anunnaki;

31). O Utu, the mighty hero, the king of the Igigi;

32-33). O Utu, [may] the *ēru*-wood, the mighty weapon of the gods, cleanse (me) before you!

34). May my personal god stand at my right!

35). May my personal goddess stand at my[!] left!

36). May he (the personal god) be present (lit., stand) before you in heaven and (on) earth!

37). May the (personal) god appoint (the apotropaic) nature of the *ēru*-wood!" Incantation formula.

---

38). You say (this incantation) three times, and you prostrate yourself. (Then) you withdraw, and you speak as follows before the *kušāru:*

---

39). Incantation: "May he (Enlil) appoint your (apotropaic) nature! May he appoint your nature!

40). May Enlil appoint your nature! May Ninlil appoint [your] nature!

41). May Ninurta, the eldest son of Ekur, appoint your nature!

42). May Nusku, the grand vizier of Enlil, appoint your nature!

43). May Nanna (i.e., Sin), the king of Ur[!], appoint your nature!

44). May Utu, the king of the Land (i.e., Sumer), appoint your nature!

45). May Ishkur (i.e., Adad), the king of heaven and earth, appoint your nature!

46). May Asalluhi, the eldest son of the Apsu (i.e., of Ea), appoint your nature!

47). Become reconciled with me, O my personal god (and) my personal goddess!"

48-49). You say (this incantation) [three] times. During the day you place fumigants at your head. You pound *atā'išu*-plant [in] juniper [oil]. You anoint him (with this mixture). You sprinkle *kasû*(-plant mixed in) pure water.

50). You set out a censer [of juniper] before his personal god, and you say as follows:

---

51). Incantation: "O *ēru*-wood, [the mighty weapon] of the gods.

52). You lay out pleasant shade [in] front of you.

53). In order for my personal god <to go> at (my) right,

54). (and) my personal goddess <to go> at (my) left,

55). may (the *ēru*-wood) make the verdict (concerning me) well-disposed! [May it make] the oracular decision!" Incantation.

---

56). You say (this incantation) [three] times, and you prostrate yourself. You lie down, and a dream [.] and whatever

57). sin(s) which he committed (against his personal deities) . [. . . . . .]

---

58). Incantation: "My dream is excellent. My oracular utterance is favourable.

59). (The dream) is pleasant before Sin and Shamash. (The dream) [is] pleasant before Sin and Shamash.

60). (The dream) [is] pleasant before Sin and Shamash. My dream is excellent, (and) my oracular utterance is favourable. At your command, queen Ninlil,

61). without whom (**A**:) the oracular [decision(s) cannot be] decided, I established good luck.

62). May there be good luck! I placed (my) foot upon the ground. May there be good luck!

63). May (the events) of the day be favourable for me! May (the events) of the month be favourable for me! May (the events) of the year be favourable for me!

64). May he (my enemy) dissolve whatever he swore against me! May he who is angry[!] with me set aside (his wrath)! May he give (back) to me (that which) was taken away!

65). May one restore to me (whatever I lost) unknowingly!

66). I am (the servant) of the hero Marduk, the son of Ea. May (the evil of the dream) not obstruct me!

67). Should misfortune see me, (then) may it hide itself away!

68). May I not cross over from misfortune to calamity! O Marduk, the eldest son of the Apsu (i.e., Ea),

69). it is within your power to treat (me) kindly, and to make (things) favourable.

70). May you be adjured by the oath of heaven! May you be adjured by the oath of earth!"

---

71). Incantation rubric: It is (the text) to dissolve a bad dream.

REVERSE

Column III

1). Its ritual: When a man has seen a dream, before he has placed his foot upon the ground,

2). he washes his hands in alkali solution upon his bed.

3). He recites the (above) incantation three times. It (the dream) will be favourable.

3a). Its alternative ritual: You place your left foot upon the bed (and) your right foot upon the ground, and you recite the (above) incantation three times.

3b). [. . . .] . . second you wash your hands (in) a bowl three times [. . . .]

3c). [While] you are washing, you recount that dream into the water three times [. . . .]

3d). [. . . .] . . may it take (the dream's evil) from me!" You wash your hands three times [. . . .]

3e). [While] you are washing your hands, you recite this incantation three times, and? . [. . . .]

3f). [. . . . .] . . . . not evil [. . . . . .]

3g). [. . . . .] . and to your house [. . . . . .]

4-5). Incantation: "O Shamash, you are the judge. Judge my case!

6-7). You are the maker of the oracular decision(s). You are the maker of the oracular decision(s) concerning me. (**Akk.**: Make the oracular decision regarding me!)

8-9). Turn the dream which I saw into good luck!

10-11). May I prosper! May I obtain a friend!

12-13). O Shamash, may the event(s) of my day(s) be favourable!

14-15). O Shamash, may the event(s) of my month(s) be favourable!"

16). [It] is the spell (lit., knot) for dissolving a bad dream.

---

17). You recite (this) ŠU.ÍL.LÁ-incantation before Shamash. It (the evil of the dream) will be dissolved.

---

18). If a man saw a dream, (but) he cannot recall (it), or he did not see a dream:

19). You throw seven (**B**: four) grains of the *atā'išu*-plant onto (**B**: in front of) a fire. You place (the fire$^{?}$) at his head (while he is lying down). It (the dream) will be favourable.

---

20). Incantation: "O Shamash, you arose in the Cedar Mountain. The gods rejoice because of you, (and) mankind is pleased by you.

21). The haruspex brings you cedar (as an offering);

22). the widow cheap flour (or) cheap scented flour; the poor woman oil; (while) the rich man

23). brings a lamb from (amongst) his wealth.

24). (However,) I myself bring you a clod, a product of the Apsu.

25). O Clod, you are the product of the Apsu. In the part of me (which) is pinched off,

26). part of you is pinched off, (and) in the part of you (which) is pinched off (is) my pinched-off piece.

27). In myself is mingled yourself, (and) in yourself is mingled myself.

28). [Just] as you, O Clod, will be thrown into (running) water, and you will be soaked, you will disintegrate, (and)

29). you will be fragmented - (so) the evil [of the dream] which I saw during the night:

30). (in) which I saw a god; (or in) which I saw a king; (or in) which I saw [an important person]; (or in) which I saw a prince; (or in) which I saw a dead person; (or in) which I saw a living person;

31). (whether) I went to the right, (or) turned to the left (in my dream) -

32). may (the evil of the dream) fall into the water just like you (,O Clod), and may it be soaked! May it disintegrate,

33). and may it be fragmented! O ram of the storm, slaughter (the evil of the dream) with a sword of wind!

34). The dead eat (and) drink, (but) it is in the wind.

35). Just as the tip of the feet cannot approach the heel,

36). (so) the evil of the dream which I saw during the night cannot come near, (and) cannot approach me."

37-38). Incantation rubric: (It is the text for the person) who sees an obscure dream. Its ritual: You take a clod from (the region of) a closed door. You recite the (above) incantation three times over (the clod). You throw (the clod) into (running) water. Its (the dream's) evil will be dispelled.

---

39). Incantation: "O Ea, the king of the Apsu; the one who fashioned heaven and earth; the creator of mankind;

40). the drawer of the cosmic plans; the giver of the food offering(s) of the great gods; [. . . .] and truth; the maker of the oracular decision(s) concerning the gods, his brothers [. . . .] . and judge my case! Make the oracular decision concerning me!

41). (Following) the dream which I saw during this night (i.e., last night),

42). I am afraid, and I am worried, and I am constantly terrified.

43-44). (If my dream) is favourable, (then say:) 'May its good luck reach me!' (Otherwise, say:) 'May (the evil of the dream) be soaked in the water like the clod which I throw into (running) water before you (Ea)! May it disintegrate, and may it crumble!'" Incantation formula.

45-46). Incantation rubric: (It is the text) to dissolve a bad dream. Its ritual: You take a clod from the waste land. You recite the (above) incantation over (the clod) seven times, and you throw (it) into (running) water. The dream will be dissolved.

45a). [Incantation] rubric: It is (the text) to make a bad dream favourable.

46a). [Its ritual:] You take [a clod (of X)]. You recite the (above) incantation over (it) three times, and you throw (it) into the river. (This is) an apotropaic ritual.

---

47). Incantation: "To dissolve the curse . . . .

48). (Regarding) the dream which I saw, may the wind carry off (its) evil!"

---

49). Incantation rubric: (It is the text) to dissolve the evil of a bad dream.

---

50). Its ritual: (On) the day which he saw the dream, before he has placed his foot upon the ground,

51). he libates vinegar. (Then) he places his foot upon the ground. The evil of the dream will be dissolved.

---

52). Incantation: "O ram of the storm, slaughtered by a sword of wind. The dead eat,

53). and they eat, (but) it is in the wind. The dream which I saw during this night (i.e., last night) -

54). just as the tip of my foot cannot approach my heel (so the evil of) the dream

55). which I saw cannot come near to me, nor approach me." Incantation formula.

---

56). Incantation rubric: It is (the text) to make a bad dream favourable.

---

57). Its ritual: He presses (lit., leans) his foot of the side (upon) which he was lying (when he awoke) upon the ground. He recites the (above) incantation three times, and

58). he turns over to his other side. Its (the dream's) evil will be dispelled.

---

59). If he saw a dream within a dream, and he interpreted whatever was favourable or able to be interpreted -

60). (The dream) will not [affect him$^{?}$] for good or evil.

---

61). If a man saw frightening dreams, (and) his dreams inflict misfortune upon him:

62-63). <In order> to dissolve their evil, (so that) it will not come near to the man: You place seeds of the *būšānu*-plant, (pieces of) the *atā'išu*-plant, the 'white plant', (and grains) of *emesallu*-salt in (a) leather (bag around his neck).

64). If a man [saw] frightening dreams:

65-66). [You place] (pieces of) . [.] . the *elkulla*-[plant], the *elikulla*-plant, (and) black sulphur in (a) [leather] (bag around his neck).

67-68). If ditto (i.e., line 64): [You place] an ostrich [egg]-shell, a green frog, (pieces of) iron, silver, (and) gold, (together with) ebony$^{?}$ powder in (a) [leather] (bag around his neck).

<u>Column IV</u>

1). [. . . .] . . . magnetite, alum,

2). [lupin], (and) yellow sulphur you place in (a) leather (bag around his neck).

3). You place (pieces of) the 'man-like'-[plant], the *elkulla*-plant, (and of) the *elikulla*-plant in (a) leather (bag around his neck).

4). You place (pieces of) alum, the *sikillu*-plant, (and) of the 'dog's tongue'-plant in (a) leather (bag around his neck).

5-6). You thread (beads of) jasper, the *sahhû*-stone, the *bāltu*-stone, the *lamassu*-stone, magnetite, (and) of 'male' copper onto a flax thread,

7). (also) of the NÍG.URUDU.UD-stone: (these are all) stones to make confused dreams favourable.

---

8). [Incantation: "O the] evil-[doer], the one who cuts the throat. The ruler of (lit., the one who constantly follows) darkness.

9). [. (.)] . . the one concealed in vileness;

10). the ruler of the hidden evil of night (and) day;

11).	O Anzagar, turn to good luck the evil which you did to me (i.e., sending a bad dream)!
12).	[O . (.) (fem.)], turn whatever you did to me into good luck!
13).	[.] . may Shamash make favourable! . . may Marduk make favourable!"
14).	You recite this incantation [(n times?)] over a leather bag charm? (or) a stone necklace?, and you place (it) around his neck.
15-16).	(In order) to avert [. . . .] . dreams: You place (pieces of) lupin, *imbû tâmti,* [. . .] 'male' and 'female' *nikiptu*(-plant) in (a) leather (bag around his neck).
17-18).	(In order that) [the evil of ominous happenings] (and) signs do not come near to a man: You place (pieces of) the *qān šalāli*-reed, New [break] . . *ajartu*-shell, the *imhur-līm*-plant, (and of) *imbû tâmti* in (a) leather (bag around his neck).
19).	New break . . You place (pieces of) the *harmunu*-plant, the *ēdu*-plant, (and) seeds of the *ēdu*-plant in (a) leather (bag around his neck).
20).	New break You place (pieces of) the *ēdu*-plant, the *elkulla*-plant, the *ašlu*-rush, (and of) *imbû tâmti* in (a) leather (bag around his neck).
21-22).	His god . . . . to come near upon? him. Its ritual: You set out a censer of juniper to (**D**$_1$: before) his personal god and to his personal goddess in a separate room. You libate (first class) beer. You speak thus:
23).	Incantation: "May my personal god become reconciled with me! May my personal goddess become reconciled with me! May Utu make my [pleasant thing] be present!
24).	May my personal goddess stand before me! May (my personal god) stand before Ninurta, the king of the weapon!
25).	Words unpleasant for me (and) word(s) of non-reconciliation Come to my aid, and I will proclaim your (pl., the personal deities') glory!" Incantation formula.
25a).	[.] . [. . . . .] . do not allow to approach!
25b).	[.] . [. . . . .] . .
25c).	[.] . . . [.] . . . . .
25d).	You recite the (above) incantation. You place (this charm) around the neck of that (man).
26-27).	You recite (the above incantation) three times before the censer. As soon as the censer has used up its offering, you bind (unknown *materia*

	medica) to your left hem with a thread. You pound a sweet reed. You anoint him with cypress oil. You speak as follows:
28).	Incantation: "What did I do to my personal god? What sin did I commit towards my personal goddess? My personal god was angry with me.
29).	My personal goddess was angry with me. May my anxiety decrease, and I will proclaim your (personal deities') glory!" Incantation formula.
30).	You say this (incantation) three times. You lie down, and you will see a pleasant dream.
30a).	You recite this (incantation) three times (.) . . [. .] and
30b).	you throw . into the river. Before . [(.)] . it will not come near.
31).	. [.] . . . [. . . . .] . .
32).	. [.] . . . [. . . . .] .
33).	. [. .] . [. . . . .] you say thus:
34).	"[. . . . . turn back] your [countenance (lit., neck) (towards me)], you (the personal goddess) who are angry with me!
35).	[. . . . .] . I did not see, and I repeatedly transgressed.
36).	[. . . my personal god] is angry [with] me, turn your countenance back towards me!
37).	(As for) [my personal goddess who] is furious, may her emotions calm down!"
38).	Incantation: "O my personal god (who) brings good luck. O my personal god (who is) manifest (and) exalted on high.
39).	My personal god be gracious towards me! O Mamu, the god of dreams,
40).	(and$^?$) my personal god, create a favourable state (of affairs for me)!" Incantation.
41a).	Incantation rubric: To lie down, and to cause the god to show (you) a pleasant dream.
41b).	Its ritual: You recite the (above) incantation three times over (a piece of) *ēru*-wood. You place (the wood) at your head (when lying down) (**A**: at the head of your bed). You tie (a piece of) *atā'išu*-plant into your hem. You lie down, and you will see a pleasant dream.
42).	An unintelligible abracadabra line.
43).	"My personal goddess is masterful in (her) rage. My personal goddess ditto (i.e., is masterful in her rage). My personal goddess ditto."
44).	Incantation rubric: (It is the text) to appease the wrath of the goddess against a man.

45-46). Its ritual: You take plaster of the east wall. You sprinkle a lump of salt upon (the plaster). You recite the (above) incantation seven times.

47). You place (the mixture) at the foot of your bed. (This is) an apotropaic ritual.

Colophon Of Manuscript **A**, Column IV Lines 48-57

48). [(This is) the tablet of] Nabu-shallim, the young apprentice (scribe),

49). [.] . . . . Nabu, the scribe of Esagila

50). [.] . . . may he determine his fate!

51). May (Nabu) remove (the name of) his progeny from the mouths of mankind!

52-53). May [Ṣarpanitu], the beloved of Marduk, [incessantly] proclaim his misfortune!

54-55). May [Gula] the chief female doctor of Ekur, fasten [. . . .] . . in his body!

56). [May he] constantly roam about outside!

57). (The year) of the eponym Ashur-bani, the governor of Nimrud (i.e., 713 B.C.).

Colophon Of Manuscript **M**, Lines 16'-18'

16'). If a man [saw] frightening dreams:

17'). Tablet ten of the series ^{d}*Zi*[*qiqu*].

18'). The palace of Ashurbanipal, king of the world, king of Assyria.

* * * * *

NOTES

Column I

4). Comparison with **A** reveals the correct reading of the sign on **B**, col. I line 20', contrary to *DB*, p. 339 and R. Borger [1957-1958], p. 418.

5). The last sign on **A** is *-nu,* not *-an* as in *KAR.*

6). The last sign on **A** is *-e,* not *-a* as in *KAR.*

7). *e-ta-mar* is one of the rare Assyrian grammatical forms occurring in **A**; see also col. I line 9$^{?}$, and col. III line 50.

9-12). A similar passage to lines 9-10 occurs in col. II lines 59-60.

The restoration of <*lumun*> before MÁŠ.GE$_6$ made in *DB,* p. 300, n. 199 is unnecessary.

9). The restoration [*be-lu*$_4$] comes from line 13. It seems to be an Assyrian form of *balu,* but is not found in the Akkadian dictionaries [*CAD* B, pp. 70-72; *AHw* 1, pp. 100-101].

17). There is no clear *-li-* in the middle of the line as in *KAR.*

The *D*-stem of *e'ēlu* is uncommon [*CAD* E, p. 40a; *AHw* 1, p. 189a].

19-27). See the similar ritual involving a lamp on K. 8171 + 11041 + 11684 + 14058, lines 7'-14'.

The dividing line after line 27 was omitted in *KAR,* as already noted in *DB,* p. 298, n. 196.

21). The use of *-wi-* in a text from Ashur is rare, being used only for an archaising effect (W. von Soden [1967], No. 223); also see col. III line 19.

25). *kullatu* is infrequently followed by a genitive singular noun [*CAD* K, *kullatu* A, pp. 505-506; *AHw* 1, *kullatu(m)* I, pp. 501-502]: see also K. 8171 + 11041 + 11684 + 14058, line 13'.

32). The traces of the last two signs do not resemble *nin-ma* as in *KAR.*

34). The modern Akkadian dictionaries do not offer examples of *šikittu* with *nakāru* [*AHw* 3, p. 1233b]; the more usual verb is *târu.*

39). The sign after -[*r*]*a* may not be *la* as in *KAR;* the third to last sign is possibly *-ti,* not *-tin;* and the penultimate sign perhaps *-ka,* not *ti.*

40). The signs after MÁŠ.GE$_6$ are not *an-ni-tu*$^{?}$ *u* as in *KAR.*

42). The phrase *ana libbi* is rare (perhaps it is an Assyrianism?) [*CAD* L, pp. 164-175; *AHw* 1, pp. 549-551].

49). The third and second signs from the end are not clearly *KAR*'s *im tar.*

51). A verb of seeing is required after MÁŠ.GE$_6$, but the surface of the tablet has been destroyed.

54). *KAR* read the first sign as *um.*

55). Read ⌜*di*$^{?}$-*in*$^{?}$⌝ for *KAR*'s DI KU$_5$.

59). The third sign is not ⌜*nu*⌝-.

61). The fourth sign is not a clear di as in *KAR.*

65). The trace of the sign before the second bi does not resemble hul.

66). *DB,* p. 339 read *uš* for ^{d}utu on **C**, line 1'.

68). *DB,* p. 339 read the trace on **C**, line 2' as *z*/*g*[*i*].

69). *DB,* p. 339 read m[áš] as T[I] on **C**, line 3'.

72). The signs in the middle of **C**, line 6' are not *ana* IGI NÁ as *DB,* p. 339 read, but *ana muh-hi.* The first IGI is clearly there, contrary to R. Borger [1957-1958], p. 418.

73-78). See col. III lines 4-17 where the same ŠU.ÍL.LÁ-incantation (in a bilingual format) and ritual occur.

75). **D**, col. I line 6, has the variant ku$_4$<.ni>.íb, "Turn . . . . into (good luck)".

<u>Column I Line 79 To Column II Line 71</u>

79). *kirṣu* usually corresponds to IM.KÍD rather than IM.Ú as on **E**, obv. 2-3. It would appear that **E** confused two phrases: the *kirṣu*-formula, and that seen in col. III line 27 (page 179).

2-6). Similar lines appear in col. III lines 29-31. None of these actions appears as such in the omen tablets of the *Dream-Book,* which are more specific. There were rituals directed against dream apparitions (*SpTU* 2, No. 21), and against dead men appearing in dreams (*CT* 23, pls. 15-22 +, col. IV lines 13-14; and *SpTU* 4, No. 134, rev.$^{?}$ 7-8 on page 165). It is possible that these lines refer to omen sections of the *Dream-Book:*

- i). The dreamer could descend to the Underworld - Tab. C, obv. col. I lines 71-85 [*DB,* pp. 327-328].
- ii). Gods could be seen - Enlil, in the colophon of Tab. 7 [*DB,* p. 311]; and Tab. C, frag. 1, col. II lines 4'-25' [*DB,* pp. 331-332].
- iii). Tab. 9 [*DB,* pp. 311-314] deals with omens of dream travelling.
- iv). Tab. A [*DB,* pp. 314-318] is concerned with eating. There are references to eating unknown meat (col. II line 12') and an unknown plant (col. IV line 14'), suggesting that NINDA could be rendered as "bread" instead of "food".
- v). Colophons present verbs whose sections do not appear in the extant *Dream-Book:* IGI on Tab. 7; and *labāšu* on Tab. 3 [*DB,* p. 309].

2). There is no need for the additional signs of *DB,* p. 341 after *kir-b*[*a-an*] on **D**, col. II line 5'. In the same line the sign is USÁN, not USAN; read MUR[UB$_4$] for MURU[B], as already noted by R. Borger [1957-1958], p. 418; and the final .[AN] is superfluous.

3). **E**, obv. 6 has the variant [*a*]*m-mar,* "[I] see".

4-5). **E**, obv. 8-12 appears to vary, but the lines are too fragmentary for one to be sure.

4). **D**, col. II line 7' replaced "god" by ^{d}*Šamaš*(UTU).

6). The sign on **D**, col. II line 9' is *al-*, not the *ti*(?) of *DB*, p. 341.

7). Correct *tap-pa-as-sa-su* on **D**, col. II line 11' (*DB*, p. 341) to *tap-pa-as-as-su;* see already R. Borger [1957-1958], p. 418.

8). The signs on **D**, col. II line 12' are *-š*]*á-ma ana,* not *-ṭ*]*u a-na* as *DB*, p. 341 read.

9). The last sign *šu-* of *DB*, p. 341 on **D**, col. II line 13' should be read *lip-*.

12). Read ⌜GIŠ⌝ for the MÁ[Š] of *DB*, p. 341 on **D**, col. II line 16'.

13). The *lipšur*-phrase associated with ^{GIŠ}ŠÀ.GIŠIMMAR is an unusual one, and the writer has been unable to find another attestation. B. Landsberger [1967, p. 14, n. 37] suggested the form *li*$^{!}$(*ku*)*-qad*$^{!}$(*šu*)*-di-šá-an-ni,* used here. W. Mayer [*UFBG*], p. 271 read *lu*$^{!}$*-qad*$^{?}$*-di-šá-an-ni.*

14-16). See 4 R^2. 59, No. 2 + K. 3369, rev. 25-28 (page 77).

17). **E**, obv. 4 has the variant [*lu ana*] ⌜LAG⌝ . . . . *lu ana* . . . ., "[either to] a lump . . . . or to . . . .".

19-20). See col. IV line 42 and page 129.

25). Read ŠU *su* for *KAR*'s *la su.*

26). Read $SIG_5^{?}$*-a* instead of *KAR*'s SIG_5*-tú.*

28). In some way the *kušāru* was regarded as being parallel to the ^{GIŠ}MA.NU of the subsequent lines (page 212).

37). The expression nam.tar tar literally means "to determine the fate of". Lines 37 and 39-46 are requesting various deities to empower the *ēru*-wood/*kušāru,* and the translation is a development of the nuance "to confer an object's characteristic qualities" (see F. Rochberg-Halton [1982], p. 365).

52). J. Krecher [1978, pp. 66-67] argued that gissu was to be read gissu(-n), in which case it cannot be followed by .ga.

58). **f**, obv. 1 has the variant *dam-qa-at,* "pleasant".

Throughout **f** *DB*, p. 342 transliterated *-mi-* for *-mì-;* see already R. Borger [1957-1958], p. 418.

59-60). See a similar passage at col. I, lines 9-10.

59). *dam-qa* of **f** is a third feminine plural stative, compared with the singular verbal form on **A**. The subject in **f** is either "dreams", which appeared in the singular in line 58, or *egirrû* and *šuttu* together, with the feminine unusually predominating over the masculine noun *egirrû.* The different genders of these nouns were carefully distinguished in line 58.

60). *DB*, p. 342 omitted [*šar-rat*] on **f**, obv. 18.

The sign on **A**, col. II line 60 is ⌜*šar*⌝-, not *šìr-* as in *KAR.*

61). The obverse of **f** has the following variants in the middle of the line:

f[4]). ⌜*ša*⌝ *ina ba-lu-uš-ša ši-mat ma-a-ti* (f[19]: AN-*e u* KI-*tim*) *la iš-šim-mu*

Without whom the fate of the land (**f**[19]: of heaven and earth) cannot be determined.

DB, p. 342 transliterated *-sim-* for *-šim-* on **f**, obv. 19.

62). *DB*, p. 342 omitted : on **f**, obv. 20.

63). *da-am-qá-nim* is a third feminine plural stative with the ventive ending, with an understood *amātu* in the plural as its subject: see the use of níg in the similar phrases in col. I line 77 and col. III lines 12 and 14.

69). The sign is ga on **f**, obv. 12, not GÁ as *DB*, p. 342 read.

71). *DB*, p. 342 read [INIM.INI]M.MA on **f**, obv. 26.

<u>Column III</u>

1). On **f**, obv. 14 the signs are actually IGI ZI-*ma*, not the IGI.DU_8-*ma* of *DB*, p. 342; and the preposition is *ina* not *ana*. ZI has been emended to DU_8 instead of being read *itebbi*, "he gets up", but see K. 8171 + 11041 + 11684 + 14058, lines 7'-8', which have *ina te-bi-šú*, "upon his arising".

2). *DB*, p. 342 transliterated **f**, obv. 15 as ina SAG GIŠ.NÁ TU_5 $ŠU^2$-*šú* ÉN. R. Borger [1957-1958, p. 418] had already altered this reading, but NAGA and LUH are not as clear as he implied.

NAGA was rarely used in rituals, the more usual ingredient being *uhūli qarnāti*(NAGA.SI) [*AHw* 3, pp. 1404-1405].

3a). *DB*, p. 342 omitted GÌR before ZAG-*ka*.

3b). R. Borger [1957-1958, p. 418] suggested *te-me-si*? as the reading of the verb.

3c). *DB*, p. 342 restored [*la-ma*] at the beginning.

3f). *DB*, p. 342 read X as *sa*.

4-17). See col. I lines 73-78 where the same ŠU.ÍL.LÁ-incantation (in Sumerian only) and ritual occur.

Lines 5, 7, 9, and 11 appear on K. 11406, col. I lines 5'-8'.

4). **G** contains an incantation to Ziqiqu *(ZI)* at obv. 1-7, before this one to Shamash. *ZI* appears in two Sumerian proverb collections, and comprises the first incantation of the *Dream-Book*. Although there is no dividing line on **G**, the two incantations have been treated separately.

8). **A**, col. I, line 75 had concluded with níg.sig_5.ga.aš $gub^?$.ba-ab, but here it has an unclear variant.

9). **A**, col. III line 9 should begin with *šunat* instead of *šutti*.

The restorations at the ends of lines 11 and 13 come from *BMS* 6, rev. 115-118 and its duplicates (especially *PBS* 1/1, No. 12, obv. 25 to rev. 2; *SpTU* 2, No. 18, rev. 18'-20'; and *STT* 60 + 233 + unnumbered fragment (O. R. Gurney [1981-1982], p. 93), rev. 21-24):

115). *lid-mì/mi-qa* MÁŠ.GE$_6$.MEŠ-*ú-a*

116). MÁŠ.GE$_6$ *aṭ-ṭu-la ana* SIG$_5$-*ti šuk-na*

117). *i-šá-riš lul-lik tap-pe-e lu-uk-šu-ud*

118). *šá u$_4$-me-ia lu-u* SIG$_5$-*tì*

STT 60 + 233 + unnumbered fragment, rev. 22 has this variant for line 116 above:

22). MÁŠ.GE$_6$ *a-na da-*⌈X⌉-[X]-*tú* ^{MÍ}SIG$_5$ *tir-ri*

10). **I**, rev. col. II lines 12'-13' occur in a separate ruled-off section.

16). On **B**, col. III line 2' the second sign is KÉŠ, not the SAR of *DB,* p. 340.

18). It seems as if the Mesopotamians expected to be able to recall a dream next morning and, therefore, equated not having seen a dream with not remembering one.

DB, p. 340 read the end of **B**, col. III line 4' as *la* B[ÚR(?)].

19). See *ABZ,* p. 156, No. 383 on the plant name; and the note on col. I line 21.

On **B**, col. III line 5' the third PI of *DB,* p. 340 should be *-ši.*

20). The Cedar Mountain is normally located either at Mount Hermon on the borders of Lebanon and Syria (M. B. Rowton [1967], pp. 266-267) or at Mount Amanus in Turkey [ibid., pp. 268, and 270]. This would mean that the sun is described here as rising in the west! W. Heimpel [1986, p. 144] suggested that the Cedar Mountain in this passage should be understood as a general term for high tree-covered mountains, rather than a specific geographical location. On the other hand, there is Sumerian evidence for another Cedar Mountain, in the east: e.g., *Enmerkar and Ensuhkeshdanna* (A. Berlin [1979]), line 160:

160). igi.nim.šè kur.šim.^{giš}erin.na.šè

to the east, to the mountain of the fragrant cedars.

The second sign of **B**, col. III line 7' is ⌈*it*⌉-, not *ta-* as *DB,* p. 340 read, and as is grammatically correct; see already R. Borger [1957-1958], p. 418. The final signs on **B**, col. III line 8' are *a-me-*[*lu*]-⌈*te*⌉, instead of *DB*'s *a-me-*[*l*]*ut-tú;* the last sign could possibly be *-tú.* Note that *DB,* p. 301, n. 205 read *a-me-lu-tú,* but there is no LÚ.DIDLI(sic) in the other texts.

22). The *D*-stem of *lapānu* is rarely attested [*CAD* L, p. 82b; *AHw* 1, p. 534b]: **A** uses the *D*-stem verbal adjective, "very poor", as opposed to that of the *G*-stem on the duplicates.

24). **H**, line 7 contains a broken personal name and an expanded identification of the supplicant:

7). [X X] ⸢X⸣-AŠ? DUMU DINGIR-*šú*

[. .] . -iddina, the son of his personal god,

25). A sub-incantation to the Clod begins here, within the incantation to Shamash.

29-31). See the note on col. II lines 2-6.

33). A sub-incantation to the ram of the storm begins here: see also col. III lines 52-55. It is difficult to see how a dream could be destroyed by wind.

34). Perhaps the argument is that the dreamer saw the dead performing these actions in his dream, but from now on his dream is insubstantial and harmless.

38). **K**, obv. 1' contains a trace which may or may not be parallel to this line.

40). **A** contains an abbreviated version of this line, and the variants *e-piš ú-sa-⸢te⸣*, "the giver of help", and *pa-ri-is* EŠ.BAR *šá* DINGIR *u* LÚ, "the maker of the oracular decision(s) concerning god and man".

j has a dividing line between obv. 6 and 7; i.e., between *ADRC,* col. III lines 40-41.

41). *mūšu annû,* lit. "this night", must mean "last night" in such contexts (see also I. L. Finkel [1983], p. 79, on his line 9').

43). *ma-a* is used to introduce direct speech, but not normally within an incantation as here (*CAD* M_1, *mā,* pp. 1-4).

The sign on **A**, col. III line 43 is *-muq-,* not *-ni-* as in *KAR.*

44). *DB,* p. 343 only restored [*li*]*m-* at the beginning of **j**, obv. 9, but there is room for more, as indicated.

46). The phrases at the ends of lines 46 and 51 appear to have become confounded (page 107).

45a). This alternative rubric does not suit a clod substitution ritual.

46a). There is no ruling between obv. 11-12 on **j** but, since an incantation starts at obv. 12, the following lines have been treated separately.

DB, p. 343 read NAM *ina lìb-bi* at the end of **j**, obv. 11.

47). *DB,* p. 338 omitted this line on **M**, so line x + 1 is really line 2'.

48). *DB,* p. 338 omitted the dividing line between lines 2' and 3' on **M**; see already R. Borger [1957-1958], p. 418.

50). *e-mu-ru* is an Assyrian form: see also col. I line 7.

51). *DB,* p. 338 omitted the dividing line between lines 5' and 6' on **M**; see already R. Borger [1957-1958], p. 418.
See the note on line 46.

52-55). Basically the same incantation occurs in col. III lines 33-36, with a different rubric, and involving a clod substitution ritual instead. The incantation has become muddled here: line 52 has *ṭa-ab-hu* (a *G*-stem third plural stative verbal form) instead of the *G*-stem imperative in the ventive, *ṭu-ub-ha*; and *ik-ka-lu* of line 53 should be NAG-*ú.*

53). See the note on col. III line 41.

54). Instead of the *na-qab* of *DB,* p. 338, read *na-kap* (*qáb*) on **M**, line 9'; see already R. Borger [1957-1958], p. 418.

57). The BI of **M**, line 12' is not as clear as *DB,* p. 338 makes out; see already R. Borger [1957-1958], p. 418.

59-60). The *u* BÚR-*ab* of *DB,* p. 338 at the beginning of line x + 12 on **M** in fact belongs to line 15'; see already R. Borger [1957-1958], p. 418. The latter is to be read *u* BÚR-*at ana* SIG_5 *u* H[UL . . . .].

61). The sign at **M**, line 16' is *pár-,* not the *par-* of *DB,* p. 338; see already R. Borger [1957-1958], p. 418.

63). The *Practical Vocabulary of Ashur* (*AfO* 18 [1957-1958], pp. 328-341), line 109 equates ú.babbar, the "white plant", with *hi-*[*l*]*i ṣar-bat-te,* the "sap of the Euphrates poplar" (also see *CAD Ṣ, ṣarbatu,* p. 109). Yet, it seems unlikely that a liquid (however viscous) would have been placed in a leather bag charm.
See page 161 on the abbreviation *ina* KUŠ.

<u>Column IV</u>

1-4). These charms probably refer back to the title of col. III line 64: "If a man saw frightening dreams".

3). This KUŠ has an extra *šá* at the end, not shown in *KAR.*

6). P. R. S. Moorey [1994, p. 212] suggested that the references to 'male' and 'female' (see *CAD* S, *sinnišu,* p. 293b) minerals may have been used to distinguish between darker and lighter colours or shades of the same stone, as in later Classical texts.

7). On $\mathbf{A_1}$ a dividing line comes either side of col. III line 18, i.e., *ADRC,* col. IV line 7. Lines 20-22 on $\mathbf{A_1}$ contain another dream charm (page 167). This second charm can be found also on $\mathbf{B_1}$, col. I lines 28'-30' (thus before *ADRC,* lines 5-7), and on $\mathbf{C_1}$, rev. 1-5 (again beforehand).

Dreams were rarely described as *dalhāti,* "confused" (page 29). The charm list **A_1**, col. III line 18 has the variant 5 NA_4 MÁŠ.GE_6.MEŠ *pár-da-te,* "five stones (for a charm against) frightening dreams".

BAM vol. 4, p. XXV stated that one should compare **A_1**, col. III lines 16-18 with *BAM* 316, col. II lines 2'-3'. However, the latter is a completely different charm, and unconnected with dreams.

8). The *i* in *KAR* is part of *[l]um.*

9). The translation of *nullâtu* follows that of *AHw* 2, *nulliātu,* p. 803a *„Niedertract, Gemeinheit"* rather than that of *CAD* N_2, *nullâtu,* pp. 333-334 "foolish talk, foolishness".

The sign is *-ti* instead of DINGIR *šú* in *KAR.*

12). There is a change of subject in this line, since *te-e-ri* is a feminine singular imperative, perhaps referring to the otherwise unknown consort of Anzagar.

14). See pages 161-163 for the reasoning behind the translations of *mēlu* and *takṣīru.*

16). In later Classical texts, 'masculine' plants were regarded as more effective than 'feminine' ones.

21). The order of **A** has been followed from here on, although differences occur on **N**, **D_1**, and **E_1**, as will be seen from the table below:

ADRC	lines 21-22	23-25	25a-d	26-27	28-29	30	30a-b
N	obv. 3'-7'	1'-2'	--	4'-7'	8'-10'	11'	--
D_1	col. IV, 11-12	1-6	7-10	--	13-15	--	16-17
E_1	--	rev. 1-8	--	--	9-14	15-16	--

22). Read *ana* DINGIR at the beginning of **A**, col. IV line 22 instead of *KAR*'s ÉN.

23). **E_1**, rev. 3 has the variant ⌜á⌝.zi.da dingir.mu [h]é.silim.ma.mu, "May my personal god become reconciled with me on the right!". The scribe wrote one hé.silim.ma.mu too many, since personal deities stood (gub) at a person's side: e.g., *ADRC,* col. II line 34.

24). Read ⌜gub⌝: on **A**, col. IV line 24 instead of *KAR*'s bal.

25). **D_1**, col. IV line 5 has the variant inim nu.si.sá, "dishonest word(s)".

The imperative on **A** is that of *râṣu,* "to come to someone's help", while **N** and **E_1** have the imperative of *rêṣu,* "to help".

25a). The phrase *ina* GÚ.BA GAR is used in several places on **D_1** for the more normal *ina* GÚ-*šú* GAR-*an.*

30a-b). The different ritual on $\mathbf{D}_1$ probably involved a clod. Both the ritual and the desired ritual result do not suit the preceding incantation.

34). The restoration comes from *JNES* 33 [1974], p. 276, line 47, with a change of gender.

35). The correct *Gtn* third masculine singular preterite form of *etēqu* in the Neo-Assyrian period was *e-te-te-eq.*

39). It is very unusual to have one Akkadian word *(iâši)* amongst a line of Sumerian as all the texts have.

41b). **N**, obv. 17 introduces this line with the variant KA.INIM.MA, "incantation rubric".

42). See col. II lines 19-20 and page 129.
N, obv. 19-21 goes on to *NROD,* obv. 39 and then obv. 51a, before rejoining **A**.

44). **P**, edge 12 has the variant *là* TE-*e,* "does not come near".

45). *še-ra* of **N** must be the same word as *sīru,* "plaster" of the other texts. This is apparently the first attestation with initial *š* [*CAD* S, *sīru* A, pp. 319-320; *AHw* 2, *sīru(m),* p. 1050b].
N and **P** have the variant ^{d}UTU.ŠÚ.A, "west".

N and **P** continue with different incantations; on **P** with no dividing line. **N**, rev. 7-9 is an abracadabra incantation. **P**, rev. 15-21 is very fragmentary: line 16 may address Sin, and line 17 possibly refers to a dream. The incantations on both texts may have been intended to appease an angry personal deity, following on from the last section on *ADRC.*

<u>Colophon of **A**</u>

49). H. Hunger [*BAK*], No. 236 on p. 80 read [*ša*]$^{?}$ *itabbalu*(TÙM) at the beginning of the line.

50). H. Hunger read [*kīma*] SAHAR [X] X MEŠ at the beginning of the line.

55). H. Hunger suggested [*murṣa*] X$^{?}$ at the beginning of the line.

57). H. Hunger omitted the first sign.

K. 3333 + 8583 + Sm. 1069 AND NUSKU APOTROPAIC DREAM RITUAL (NADR)

TEXTS

DB, pls. 1-2 (photographs)

STUDIES

R. Borger [1957-1958] (review of *DB,* with collations)

A. L. Oppenheim [*DB*], pp. 298; 300, notes 199-200; 301, n. 205; and 339-341 (The three tablets have been joined since: K. 3333 = his Fragment 4; K. 8583 = Fragment 3; and Sm. 1069 = Fragment 2)

M.-J. Seux [1976], p. 373 (translation of col. II, lines 1-13)

B. R. Foster [*BM* 2], p. 638 (translation of col. II lines 3-13; correct to 79-7-8, 77)

K. 3333 + 8583 + Sm. 1069 forms manuscript **B** of *ADRC.* Only column II lines 1-18 (with the relevant part of 79-7-8, 77), which constitute the *Nusku Apotropaic Dream Ritual (NADR),* are dealt with here. The cuneiform text appears on plates 3-4.

* * * * *

OBVERSE

Column I

1'). One trace at the end of the line

2'). One trace at the end of the line

3'). One trace at the end of the line

Gap of about fifteen lines

19'-22' = *ADRC,* col. I lines 2 and 4-6

23'). [. . . . .]⸢X⸣-*šú*

24'). [. . . . .] UD

25'). [. . . . .] GAR

26'). [. . . . .]⸢X⸣

27'). [. . . . .]⸢X⸣

The rest of the column is broken away

Column II

Lines 1-18 = *NADR*

A = K. 3333 + 8583 + Sm. 1069

b = 79-7-8, 77 rev. 3'-17' (lines 4-15 and 18)

Line 1

A). ⌈*ana*⌉ *pān*(⌈IGI⌉) ⌈*nu-ri*⌉ *qan*(GI) *ki-iṣ-ri i-*⌈*na gi*$^{?}$ *ku zi*⌉ [^{TÚG}*sissikti* (SÍG)]

Line 2

A). *imitti*(ZAG)-*šú i-bat-taq-ma ana pān*(IGI) *nu-ri ú-kal*$^{!}$(*e*) *ki-a-am iqabbi*(DU[G$_4$.GA])

Line 3

A). *um-ma šu-ma* ^{d}*Nusku tap-pe-e* ^{d}*Šamaš*(UTU) *at-*[*ta*]

Line 4

da-a-a-na-ta di-ni di-in šuttu an-ni-[*tú*]

A). *da-a-a-na-ta* *di-ni di-in* MÁŠ.GE$_6$ *an-ni-*[*tú*]

b). [(. .) *da-a*]-⌈*a*⌉-*na*$^{!}$(*la*)-*ta* ⌈*di*⌉-[ ]

Line 5

ša ina ba-ra-ar-ti qab-li-ti šat ur-[*ri*]

A). *ša ina ba-ra-ar-ti* *qab-li-ti* *šat ur-*[*ri*]

b). [ ] EN.NUN.AN.US[AN EN.NUN.M]URUB$_4$.B[A EN.NUN.U$_4$.ZAL.LE]

Line 6

ib-bab-lam-ma šá at-ta tīdû ana-ku la i-du-[*ú*]

A). *ib-bab-lam-ma* *šá at-ta* Ì.ZU *ana-ku* *la* *i-d*[*u-ú*]

b). [*-b*]*a-ab-l*[*am-*] / *šá* ⌈*at*⌉*-t*[*a* *ti-du-ú*] ⌈*a*⌉*-na-*[ ] ⌈*i*⌉*-d*[*u-*]

Line 7

šum-ma dam-qat du-muq-šá a-a i-ši-ṭa-a[*n-ni*]

A). *šum-ma dam-qat* *du-muq-šá a-a* *i-ši-ṭa-a*[*n-ni*]

b). *šum-ma damiqti*(SI[G$_5$-*ti*]) *du-muq-šá* [*ia*]-⌈*ú i*⌉*-še-*[ ]

Line 8

šum-ma lemnet lumun-šá a-a ik-šu-dan-ni

A). *šum-ma* HUL HUL-*šá a-a ik-šu-dan-*[ ]

b). *šum-ma* [*lemutti*(HUL-*ti*) HU]L-*šá ia-ú i*[*k-š*]*ú-dan-ni*

Line 9

la ia-ut-tu-un ši-i ki-ma qanû an-nu-u na-aṭ-pu-ma

A). *la ia-ut-tu-un ši-i ki-ma* GI *an-nu-u na-aṭ-pu-*[ ]

b). *la ia-u*[*t-*] / GIM < > ⸢*an-nu-ú*⸣ *na-aṭ-pu-ma*

Line 10

ana ašri-šú là iturru ù kīma ^{TÚG}*si-is-sik*<*-tu*> *an-ni-tú ina ṣubāti-ia bat-*[*qat*]*-ma*

A). *ana* KI-*šú là* GUR *ù* ^{TÚG}SÍG
an-ni-tú ina TÚG-*ia bat-*[*qat-ma*]

b). [*n*]*i-iṭ-pi-šu la i-t*[*u-ru*] / GIM ^{TÚG}*si-is-sik*<*-tu*>
an-ni-ti bat-qa-tu-ma

Line 11

ana ṣubāti-ia kīma ib-bat-⸢*qu-ma*⸣ *là iturru lumun šutti an-ni-ti*$^!$

A). *ana* TÚG $^{hi\text{-}pi}$ GIM *ib-tu-qu-ma là* GUR HUL MÁŠ.GE$_6$
⸢*an-ni*⸣-[ ]

b). *ana* TÚG-*ia* GIM *ib-bat-*⸢*qu-ma*⸣ [ ] / MÁŠ.GE$_6$
an-ni-ti$^!$

Line 12

šá ina ba-ra-ar-ti ina qab-li-ti ina šat u[*r-ri*] *ib-*[*bab-lam-ma*]

A). *šá ina ba-ra-ar-ti qab-li-ti*
šat u[*r-ri ib-bab-lam-ma*]

b). *šá*$^!$(*ana*) *ina* EN.NUN.AN.USAN *ina* ⸢EN⸣.NUN.MURUB$_4$.BA
ina EN$^!$.NUN.U$_4$.ZAL.⸢LE⸣ *ib-*[*ba-ab-*]

Line 13

a-a ik-šú-dan-ni la ia-tu-un ši-i $^{hi\text{-}pi\ eš\text{-}šú}$ IGI ⸢X⸣ TÚG *bar nu šá ul ma*$^?$ GIŠ

A). *la ia-tu-un ši-i* IGI ⸢X⸣ [. . . . . .]

b). *a-a ik-šú-dan-ni la ia-ut-*[*t*]*u-un ši-i*$^!$ / $^{hi\text{-}pi\ eš\text{-}šú}$ TÚG *bar nu šá*
ul ma$^?$ GIŠ

Line 14

qanâ ana 2-*šú* (**b**: 3-*šú*) *i-ha-*⸢*am*⸣*-meš-ma* $^{\textit{hi-pi eš-šú}}$ [^{TÚG}*si-is*]*-sik-ta ilammi* ⸢*ka*⸣*-ma-ta ka-la-ta ka-sa-ta*$^{!}$(*ka*) $^{\textit{hi-pi eš-šú}}$ [*ana pān*] *ilūti-ka rabīti a-qal-liš*

A). GI *a-na* 2-*šú i-ha-*⸢*mi*⸣-[*iš* . . . .]

b). GI *ana* 3-*šú i-ha-*⸢*am*⸣*-meš-ma* / $^{\textit{hi-pi eš-šú}}$ [^{TÚG}*si-is*]*-sik-ta* NIGIN-*mi* ⸢*ka*⸣*-ma-ta ka-la-ta ka-sa-ta*$^{!}$(*ka*) / $^{\textit{hi-pi eš-šú}}$ [*ana* IGI] DINGIR-*ti-ka* GAL-*ti a-qal-liš*

Line 15

[*k*]*i-a-am iqabbi-ma qaqqara* [*t*]*a-lap-pat-ma ana nūri ta-q*[*ad*$^{!}$]

A). [*k*]*i-a-am* ⸢DUG$_4$.GA⸣ [ ]

b). DUG$_4$.GA-*ma* ⸢KI⸣ [*t*]*a-lap-pat-ma ana* ZÁLAG *ta-q*[*ad*$^{!}$]

Line 16

A). ⸢X X⸣ [. . . . .]

Line 17

A). [*in*]*a pān*(IGI) *nu-*⸢*ri*⸣ [. . . . .]

Line 18

ana ili-ka ^{d}*ištari-*⸢*ka*⸣ *u nu-ri ta-kar-rab*$^{!}$*-ma išallim*

A). *ana* *nu-ri i-k*[*ar-*]

b). *ana* DINGIR-*ka* ^{d}EŠ$_{18}$.TÁR-⸢*ka*⸣ *u nu-ri ta-kar-rab*$^{!}$(⸢*zag*⸣)*-ma* SILIM.MA

19-23	= *ADRC,* col. I lines 7-12
24-30	= *ADRC,* col. I lines 12a-g
	The rest of the column is broken away

REVERSE

Column III

	Break
1'-2'	= *ADRC,* col. III lines 15-16
3'	= *ADRC,* col. III line 17

4'-6'	= *ADRC,* col. III lines 18-19
7'-16'	= *ADRC,* col. III lines 20-28

Column IV

Uninscribed

* * * * *

OBVERSE

Column I

The lines not discussed under *ADRC* or *NADR* (i.e., col. I lines 1'-3' and 23'-27') are too fragmentary to translate. *DB,* p. 339 omitted lines 25'-27'.

Column II

Lines 1-18 = *NADR*

1-2). before the lamp a reed joint . . . . . He cuts off (a piece of) his right [hem], and he holds (the hem and reed) before the lamp. He says as follows,

3). (he speaks) thus: "O Nusku, you [are] the companion of Shamash.

4). You are the judge. Judge my case! This dream,

5-6). which was brought to me during the first watch (of the night), the middle watch, (or) the third watch, and (about) which you yourself understand, (but) I do not -

7). if (this dream) is favourable, may its good luck not pass [me] by!

8). If it is bad, may its evil not reach me,

9). (also may) it (the bad dream) not be mine! Just as this reed was torn out, and

10). cannot return to its place, and just as this hem was cut off from my garment, and

11). cannot return to my garment, because it was cut off - (so may) the evil of this dream

12). which [was brought to me] during the first watch (of the night), during the middle watch, (or) during the third watch,

13). may (its evil) not reach me! (May) it (the bad dream) not be mine! [New break] . . . .

14). He snaps the reed into two (**b:** three) pieces, and [New break]. He wraps the hem around (the reed. He says: "Now) you (the evil of the dream) are captured. You are imprisoned. You are chained up. [New break] I will burn it (the parcel) [before] your (Nusku's) great divinity."

15). He speaks thus. You touch the ground, and you light the lamp.

16). . . [. . . . .]

17). before the lamp [. . . . .]

18). You pray to your personal god, your personal goddess, and to the lamp. It (the dream) will be(come) beneficial.

* * * * *

NOTES

Column II

1). It would appear from the abrupt beginning that the ritual began at the bottom of col. I on **A**, which is missing.

The sign on **A**, col. II line 1 is *ku* instead of *lu,* as in *DB,* p. 340.

5). The first sign on **A**, col. II line 5 is *ša,* not *šá* as *DB,* p. 340 read.

6). Contrary to *DB,* p. 343, the first *ú* on **b**, rev. 6' is not extant.

7-8). **b** uses the first masculine possessive pronoun *jā'û* rather clumsily, instead of the vetitive *(a-a)* of **A**.

7). *DB,* p. 343 read [S]IG$_5$ for SI[G-*ti*] on **b**, rev. 7', and *ia-* is not extant.

8). The sign is -[*š*]*ú-* on **b**, rev. 8', not -[*š*]*u-* as in *DB,* p. 343.

9-11). *DB,* p. 343 read GÍM for GIM on **b**, rev. 9'-10'; see already R. Borger [1957-1958], p. 418.

10). **b**, rev. 9' has the variant [*n*]*i-iṭ-pi-šú,* "[to] whence it was plucked". Also, the penultimate sign is -*t*[*u*]-, instead of -*tu*[*r*], as in *DB,* p. 343.

The sign is *ù* on **A**, col. II line 10, not *u* as in *DB,* p. 340; see already R. Borger [1957-1958], p. 418.

11). It appears that the break on **A**, col. II line 11 only covered the -*ia* of **b**.

12). Read **b**, rev. 11' as BA *ina* EN[!], instead of BA.AN *ina* EN as in *DB,* p. 343.

13). *DB,* p. 343 read -*šu-* for -*šú-* on **b**, rev. 12'; see already R. Borger [1957-1958], p. 418.

14). **b**, rev. 13'-15' contains an expanded ritual. A part of the first "new break" is [^{TÚG}*si-is*], and [*ana* IGI] occurred in the second "new break".

Read *a-na* on **A**, col. II line 14, instead of *ana* as in *DB,* p. 340; see already R. Borger [1957-1958], p. 418.

The last sign on **b**, rev. 14' is -*ka,* not -*ta* as in *DB,* p. 343, and as would be grammatically correct.

15). *DB,* p. 343 omitted *-ma* on **b**, rev. 16'; see already R. Borger [1957-1958], p. 418.

Previously the verbs on **b** had been written out syllabically in the third person singular, from now on the ritual expert is addressed via second person singular forms.

18). *DB,* p. 343 read *u* $EŠ_4$ on **b**, rev. 17', instead of $^{d}EŠ_{18}$.

A, col. II line 18 has the variant *ana nu-ri i-k*[*ar-rab-ma*], "He prays to the lamp".

K. 3758 AND *ZAQIQU INCANTATION (ZI)*

TEXTS

DB, pl. 1 (photograph of **A**)
PBS 13, No. 38 (**I**; correct to CBS 14188)
PBS 12/1, No. 29 (**II**)

STUDIES

C. J. Gadd [1948], p. 74
A. L. Oppenheim [*DB*], pp. 296-297, and 338
R. Borger [1957-1958] (review of *DB,* with collations)
E. I. Gordon [1960], pp. 129-130, n. 57 (Proverb Collections 11 and 18)

K. 3758 forms manuscript **G** of *ADRC.* Obverse 1-7 is an incantation to Ziqiqu *(ZI),* with duplicates on two collections of Sumerian proverbs (**I** and **II**). Its colophon states that it was the first tablet of the series ^{d}*Ziqiqu* (i.e., the *Dream-Book*) as found in Ashurbanipal's Library at Kuyunjik. The cuneiform text appears on plate 5.

* * * * *

OBVERSE

Lines **1-7** = *ZI*
A = K. 3758, obv. 1-7
I = *PBS* 13, No. 38, lines 5-10
II = *PBS* 12/1, No. 29, col. III lines 6'-10'

Lines 1-2

A).	[ÉN *Zi-q*]*i-qu Zi-*⌈*qi*⌉*-qu* ^{d}*Ma-mú ilu*(DINGIR) *šá* [*šunāti*(MÁŠ.GE$_6$.MEŠ)] / [*ana A*]-⌈*ga*⌉*-dè*^{KI} *áš-p*[*ur-ka*]		
I).	si.si.ig	a.ga.dè^{ki}.šè	ì.gi$_4$.⌈a⌉
II).	sig.sig	a.ga.dè^{ki}.šè	ì.gi$_4$.in(?)

Line 3

A).	[*ina A*]-⸢*ga-dè*⸣^{KI}	*mi-na-a*	*te-*[*pu-uš*]
I).	a.ga.dè^{ki}.a	a.na.àm	mu.e.ni.ak
II).	a.ga.dè^{ki}.a /	a.na.àm	ì.ak

Line 4

A).	[*šunāti*(MÁ]Š.GE$_6$.MEŠ)	*pár-da-a-ti*	*áš-*[*ta-kan*$^?$]
I).	máš.ge$_6$	lul.la	im.ma.an.na.gar
II).	máš.ge$_6$	zi.da	

Line 5

A).	⸢^{LÚ}⸣*pa-šìr-ši-na*	[(. . . .)]
I).	^{lú}búr.ru.bi	bí.in.tuku$^!$

Line 6

A).	*ana* : ^{URU}*A-*⸢*ga*⸣-dè⸢^{KI}	*ki-i*⸣ [. . . . .]
I).	⸢a⸣.ga.dè^{ki}.a	a.⸢bi/ga X⸣ [X X] a.gim

Line 7

A).	*ina ra-mì-*⸢*ni*⸣*-šú-m*[*a*]	⸢*tu*⸣-[. . . . .]
I).	[X] ⸢X X⸣ [. . . . .]	⸢tuku⸣

8-11 = *ADRC,* col. III lines 5, 7, 9, and 11

The rest of the tablet is broken away

REVERSE

Break

1'). [. . . .M]ÁŠ.[GE$_6$ . . . .]

2'). [X] ⸢X (X)⸣.MEŠ *ana libbi*(ŠÀ) ⸢X⸣ [. . . . .]

3'). *šumma*(DIŠ) *amēlu*(NA) *ina šutti*(MÁŠ.GE$_6$)-*šú* ⸢X⸣ [. . . . .]

4'). DUB.1.KÁM *iškar*(ÉŠ.G[ÀR) ^{d}*Zi-qi-qu*]

5'). *ekal*(KUR) ^{m}*Aššur*(AN.ŠÁR)-*bān*(DÙ)-*apli*(A) *ša*[*r*$_4$ *kiššati*(ŠÚ) *šar*$_4$ *māt*(KUR) *Aššur*(AN.ŠÁR)^{KI}]

* * * * *

OBVERSE

Lines **1-7** = *ZI*

1-2). O Sigsig, whom I sent to Agade. (**Akk.**: [Incantation:] O Ziqiqu, O Ziqiqu, Mamu, the god of [dreams], I have sent [you] to Agade.)

3). What have you done in Agade?

4). I inflicted a false (**II:** reliable) dream (**Akk.:** frightening dreams) upon him (the sufferer).

5). (However,) he/Agade had an interpreter for them, [(. . . .)]).

6). When to Agade [. . . . .]

7). by itself/himself . [. . . . .]

8-11 = *ADRC,* col. III lines 5, 7, 9, and 11.
The rest of the tablet is broken away.

REVERSE

Break

1'-2' are too fragmentary to translate

3'). If a man in his dream . [. . . . .]

4'). Tablet one of the series [^{d}*Ziqiqu*]

5'). The palace of Ashurbanipal, king [of the world, king of Assyria]

* * * * *

NOTES

Obverse

1-7). E. I. Gordon [1960, pp. 129-130, n. 57] suggested that the original Sumerian proverb may have contained an allusion to Naram-Sin as "the luckless ruler" of Agade.

1). E. I. Gordon [1960, pp. 129-130, n. 57] restored [d(!)] at the beginning of **A**, obv. 1, following the colophons of the *Dream-Book.* However, when Ziqiqu is repeated in this line, there is no divine determinative. The library catalogues discussed on pages 100-101 list the series both with and without the divine determinative. The restoration of *DB,* p. 338 has been followed here.

J. V. Kinnier Wilson [1992, personal communication] suggested restoring [MÁŠ.GE$_6$.MEŠ *ana-ku*] at the end of **A**, obv. 1, translating the line as "O Ziqiqu, Ziqiqu, [I am] Mamu, the god of [dreams]." Thus, *ZI* would be a dialogue between Mamu and Zaqiqu. (Also see page 86.)

2). *DB,* p. 338 restored [URU] at the beginning of **A**, obv. 2, instead of [*ana*], which corresponds to the Sumerian .šè.

E. I. Gordon [1960, pp. 129-130, n. 57] restored *áš-t*[*a*(?!)-*par-ka*] at the end of **A**, obv. 2, while *DB,* p. 338 suggested *áš-b*[*a-ta*].

3). *DB,* p. 338 restored [URU] at the beginning of **A**, obv. 3, instead of [*ina*], corresponding to .a in the Sumerian; and read *te*-[*zi-ib*], at the end of the line instead of a form of *epēšu,* corresponding to Sumerian .ak.

4). E. I. Gordon [1960, pp. 129-130, n. 57] restored [*ta*(?)-*áš-kun-šum*(?)-*ma*] at the end of **A**, obv. 4. A *Gt* form of *šakānu*(GAR) is required, following the Sumerian verbal prefix .im.ma.

The sign is pár- on **A**, obv. 4 not *par-* as in *DB,* p. 338; see already R. Borger [1957-1958], p. 418.

5). *DB,* p. 338 read [*ú*]- at the beginning of **A**, obv. 5, stating on p. 219 that Ziqiqu was asked to dispel the dreams.

DB, p. 338 read -*šar*- for -*šìr*- on **A**, obv. 5.

6). On **A**, obv 6 read *ana* : URU for the URU <<*m*>> of *DB,* p. 338.

7). One would like to be able to read ní.te at the beginning of **I**, line 10, corresponding to Akkadian *ramānu,* but the traces do not agree.

<u>Reverse</u>

1'). A. L. Oppenheim [*DB,* p. 338] omitted this line in his transliteration, so line x + 1 is really line 2'.

2'). *DB,* p. 338 read the first sign as *ana.*

3'). This line presents the incipit of Tab. 2, the start of the omen section of the *Dream-Book.*

4'-5'). These lines have been restored from other extant colophons of the *Dream-Book.*

K. 5175 + 6001

TEXTS

DB, pl. 2 (photograph)

STUDIES

A. L. Oppenheim [*DB*], pp. 301, n. 205; and 341 (= Fragment 5)

R. Borger [1957-1958] (review of *DB*, with collations)

K. 5175 + 6001 forms manuscript **D** of *ADRC*. The cuneiform text appears on plate 8.

* * * * *

Column I

Break

1'). [. . . . .] ⸢X⸣ hé.a.ni

2'). [. . . . . . . hé.e]m.ta.è

3'). [an.gim hé.en.kù.ga k]i.gim hé.en.sikil

4'). [eme hul.gál ba]r.šè hé.em.ta.gub

5'). [ka.inim.ma máš.ge$_6$ hul búr].ru.da.kám

6'-9' = *ADRC*, col. I lines 73-77

10' = *ADRC*, col. I line 78

11'). [. . . . .] ⸢X⸣ sá.sá.e.ne

12'). [. . . . .] ⸢X X dùg.ga⸣.mu$^!$(du$_8$)

13'). One trace at the end of the line

The rest of the column is broken away.

Column II

Break

1'). [. . . . *ili*(DIN]GIR)-*šú u* ^{d}*ištari*(⸢EŠ$_{18}$⸣.T[ÁR)-*šú* . . . . . .]

2'). ⸢*ana*$^?$⸣ [. . . .] ⸢*šá*⸣-*ni-ti* [. . . .]

3'-16' = *ADRC*, col. I line 79 to col. II line 13

The rest of the column is broken away

* * * * *

Column I

Break

1'). [. . . . .] . . . .

2'). [. . . . . . . may] it depart!

3'). [May he become as pure as heaven!] May he become as clean as the earth!

4'). May [the evil tongue] stand [aside]!"

5'). [Incantation rubric:] It is (the text) [to dissolve a bad dream].

6'-9' = *ADRC,* col. I lines 73-77

10' = *ADRC,* col. I line 78

11'-13' are too fragmentary to translate.

The rest of the column is broken away.

Column II

Break

1'). [. . . .] his personal god and [his personal] goddess [. . . . . .]

2'). In order to$^?$ [. . . .] second [. . . .]

3'-16' = *ADRC,* col. I line 79 to col. II line 13

The rest of the column is broken away.

* * * * *

NOTES

Column I

3'-4'). See page 150 on these common concluding phrases.

4'). *DB,* p. 341 omitted [ba]r.šè.

11'). ⌈X⌉ does not resemble the [N]U of *DB,* p. 341.

Column II

2'). *DB,* p. 341 omitted the dividing line between lines 2' and 3'; see already R. Borger [1957-1958], p. 418.

K. 8171 + 11041 + 11684 + 14058

TEXTS

DB, pl. 1 (photograph)

STUDIES

A. L. Oppenheim [*DB*], pp. 302-303, and 339 (= Fragment 1)

R. Borger [1957-1958] (review of *DB*, with collations)

J. Bottéro [1985a], pp. 53-54 (lines 15'-23'; correct from line 24')

J. N. Lawson [1994], pp. 96-97 (lines 15'-24')

K. 8171 + 11041 + 11684 + 14058 forms manuscript **C** of *ADRC*. The cuneiform text appears on plate 9.

* * * * *

	Break
1'-4'	= *ADRC*, col. I lines 66-70
5'-6'	= *ADRC*, col. I lines 71-72
7').	*šumma*(DIŠ) *amēlu*(LÚ) *ina mu-ši-ti-šú šutta*(MÁŠ.GE_6) *lemutta* (HUL-*ta*) *iṭṭul*(IGI)-*ma uš-t*[*a-di-ir*]
8').	*ina še-ri har-pí ina te-bi-šú la-am šēp*(GÌR)-*šú ana qaqqari*(K[I) *iškunu*(GAR-*nu*)]
9').	1 ^{GIŠ}*ṣillî*(DÁLLA) ^{GIŠ}*gišimmari*(GIŠIMMAR) *šá ištāni*(IM.SI.SÁ) *teleqqi*(TI-*qí*) ^{SÍG}*pušikka*(GA.[ZUM.AK(.A)])
10').	*talammi*(NIGIN-*mi*) *šamna*(Ì+GIŠ) *ta-ṣab-bu nu-ra ta-qad ana nu-ri ki-a-a*[*m taqabbi*(DUG_4.GA)]
11').	^{d}*Gi-bil bēlu*(EN) *ruššû*(HUŠ) *dannu*(KALA.GA) *tap-pe-e* ^{d}*Šamaš* (UTU) LUGAL [. . . .]
12').	*šur-*[*b*]*a-ta ba-ìl-la-ta ina ilāni*(DINGIR.MEŠ) *ahhē*(ŠE[Š.MEŠ)-*ka*]
13').	[*k*]*úl-lat šuttīja*(MÁŠ.GE_6.MU) *ša ana-ku* ⸢*i*⸣-[*du-u a-mu-ru*]
14').	*at-ta ti-du-u a-mu-ru ana-ku* [. . . .]

15'). *šumma*(DIŠ) *amēlu*(LÚ) *ina mušīti*(GE$_6$) *šutta*(MÁŠ.GE$_6$) *lemutta* (HUL-*ta*) ⸢*iṭ-ṭul* X⸣ [. . . .]

16'). *ištēniš*(1-*niš*)-*ma i-pa-šá-aš ana ṣīt šamši*(^{d}UTU.È.[A]) *eli*(UGU) ^{DUG}*haṣbi*(ŠIKA) URUDU ⸢X X⸣

17'). *ana*$^!$ *kir-ba-nu ki-a-am iqabbi*(DUG$_4$.GA) *kir-ba-nu ina kir-ṣi-ka*

18'). ⸢*kir*⸣-*ṣi ka-ri-iṣ ina kir-ṣi-ia kir-iṣ-ka ka-ri-iṣ*

19'). *šutta*([MÁŠ].GE$_6$) *ma-la iṭ-ṭú-lu a-na kir-ba-ni i-pa-áš-šar*

20'). [*kīma*(GIM)] *kir-ba-nu ka-a-šá ana mê*(A.MEŠ) *a-nam-du-ka-ma*

21'). [*ta*]*h-ha-ra-ma-ṭu tap-pa-sa*-⸢*as*⸣-*su lumun*(HUL) *šutti*(MÁŠ.GE$_6$) *ma-la aṭṭulu*(IGI.GÁL)

22'). [*lu*] *hal-qat lu na-har-mu-ṭa-at 1 šu bēru*(DANNA) *ina zumrīja* (SU.MU) *lu na-sa-at*

23'). [*ana*] *kirbāni*([LA]G) *iqabbi*(DUG$_4$.GA)-*ma ana mê*(A.MEŠ) *inaddi*(ŠUB)-*ma i-ti-iq-šu*

24'). [*šumma*(DIŠ) <*amēlu*(LÚ> *ina*] *šutti*([M]ÁŠ.GE$_6$)-*šú šutta*(MÁŠ. GE$_6$) *lemutta*(HU[L-*ta*) *i*]*ṭ-ṭul ana*$^!$(*ina*) *là kašādi*(SÁ.SÁ)-*šú*

* * * * *

1'-4' = *ADRC,* col. I lines 66-70

5'-6' = *ADRC,* col. I lines 71-72

7'). If a man saw a bad dream during his night's rest), and became [worried]:

8'). In the early morning, upon his arising, (but) before [he has placed] his foot upon the ground,

9'-10'). you take a thorn of the date palm of the north side. You wrap (this thorn in) combed [wool], (then) you soak (it) in oil. You light a lamp. [You say] as follows to the lamp:

11'). "O Gibil, the red/glowing (and) powerful lord; [you are] the companion of Shamash, king [. . . .].

12'). You are very grand. You are very powerful amongst the gods, [your] brothers.

13'). All of my dream(s) which I myself [know that I have seen]

14'). (and which) you yourself know that I have seen, I myself [. . . .]

15'). If a man saw a bad dream during the night . [. . . .]

16'). together, and he anoints (X with this mixture). To the east, over a potsherd . . .

17'). He says as follows to the clod: "O Clod, in the part of you

18'). (which) is pinched off, part of me is pinched off, (and) in the part of me (which) is pinched off (is) your pinched-off piece."

19'). He reports to the clod as many dreams as he saw. (Then he says:)

20'). "[Just as] I will throw you, O Clod, into (running) water, and

21'-22'). [you] will crumble (and) disintegrate - (so) [may] the evil of all the dream(s) which I saw disappear! May it dissolve! May it withdraw sixty 'miles' (lit., double-hours) from my body!"

23'). He says (this) [to] the clod, and he throws (it) into (running) water. (The evil of the dream) will by-pass him.

24'). [If <a man>] saw a bad dream [in] his dream - In order that (its evil) does not reach him:

* * * * *

NOTES

7'-14'). See *ADRC,* col. I lines 19-27 for a similar ritual involving a lamp.

10'). The first sign is NIGIN not NIGIN$_2$ as *DB,* p. 339 read; see already R. Borger [1957-1958], p. 418.

12'). The sign is *-ìl-,* not *-il-* as *DB,* p. 339 read; see already R. Borger [1957-1958], p. 418.

13'). See the note on *ADRC,* col. I line 25 (page 304) about the rare following of *kullatu* by a genitive singular noun.

Read [*k*]*úl-* for the *kul-* of *DB,* p. 339, and *ša ana-ku* ⌜*i*⌝- instead of *šá ana-ku* X; see already R. Borger [1957-1958], p. 418.

The restoration at the end of the line follows the suggestion of J. V. Kinnier Wilson [1992, personal communication].

14'). This ritual is incomplete, needing the conclusion of the incantation and, probably, a desired ritual result.

15'). The ritual began at the end of this line with some ingredient(s) being either mixed (*bullulu*) or pounded (*sâku*).

16'). The .A is not extant, and *DB,* p. 339 read URUDU as D[U].

17'). The potsherd (^{DUG}ŠIKA) of the ritual is addressed as if it was the clod *(kirbānu)* from which Man was created (pages 179-180).

19'). Read *a-na* for the *ana* of *DB,* p. 339; see already R. Borger [1957-1958], p. 418.

22'). The last signs are definitely *na-sa-at,* not *ne-* as *DB,* p. 339 read. See *AHw* 2, *nesû* II, pp. 781-782 for occasional writings with *na-*.

24'). See S. Parpola [*LAS* vol. 2, pp. 47-48] on the interchanges between *ana* and *ina* in the Neo-Assyrian period.

79-7-8, 77

TEXTS

DB, pl. 2 (photograph)

STUDIES

A. L. Oppenheim [*DB*], pp. 300, n. 202; 303-304; and 342-343 (= Excerpt 1)

R. Borger [1957-1958] (review of *DB,* with collations)

79-7-8, 77 forms manuscript **f** of *ADRC.* Reverse 3'-17' constitute manuscript **b** of *NADR.* Only rev. 18' to left edge 26' are dealt with here. The cuneiform text appears on plates 10-12.

* * * * *

OBVERSE

1-12	= *ADRC,* col. II lines 58-70
13	= *ADRC,* col. II line 71
14-15	= *ADRC,* col. III lines 1-3
16	= *ADRC,* col. III line 3a
17-25	= *ADRC,* col. II lines 58 and 60-70
26	= *ADRC,* col. II line 71
27-32	= *ADRC,* col. III lines 3b-g
33-34	= *ADRC,* col. III lines 52-53
	The rest of the tablet is broken away

REVERSE

	Break
1').	[. . . . . .] ⸢X *ra*⸣ [. . . . .]
2').	[. . . . . .] ⸢X⸣ *še* ⸢X⸣ [. . . . .]
3'-17'	= *NADR,* lines 4-16 and 18

18'). *šumma*(DIŠ) *amēlu*(LÚ) *šutta*(MÁŠ.GE$_6$) *lemutti*(HUL-*tì*) *īmur* (IGI)-*ma ul-ta-di*$^{!}$-*ir*$^{!}$(*ni*) *ana ta-*⸢*ri*⸣-*ti qanî*(GI) *šutta*(MÁŠ. GE$_6$)-*šú* ⸢*lip*⸣-[*šur*]

19'). *ina išāti*(IZI) *li-iq-li ina pi-i-šú i-nap-pah-ma pašir*(BÚR-*i*[*r*])

20'). KIMIN (i.e., DIŠ LÚ MÁŠ.GE$_6$ HUL-*tì* IGI-*ma ul-ta-di-ir*) *ina še-e-ri šamna*(Ì.GIŠ) *ṭāba*(DÙG.GA) *qa-ti-šú tapaššaš*(ŠÉŠ)-*ma pašir*(BÚR-*ir*)

21'). KIMIN 7 *ku-pa-tin-nu ša*$^{!}$(*id*) *ṭiṭṭi*(IM) *tu-*⸢*kap*$^{!}$⸣-*pat šutta*(MÁŠ. GE$_6$) *ma-la iṭ-ṭú-lu sebîšu*(7-*šú*) *ana lìb-bi lip-šur*

22'). *a-na sūq erbetti*(E.SÍR.KA.LÍM.MA) *ta-sà-pah mahar*(IGI) ^{d}*Šamaš*(UTU) ⸢*ki*⸣-*a-am iqabbi*(DUG$_4$.GA$^{!}$(*ni*))

23'). *šunat*(MÁŠ.GE$_6$) *aṭ-ṭú-lu a-šar*$^{?}$ *su am li-il-lik sebîšu*(7-*šú*) *iqabbi* (DUG$_4$.GA)-*ma pašir*(BÚR-*ir*)

LEFT EDGE

24'). KIMIN 14 *k*[*u*]-*pa-tin-nu* ⸢*ša*⸣ *ṭiṭṭi*(⸢IM⸣) [*tu-kap*]-*pat šutta*(MÁŠ. [GE$_6$) *ma-la iṭ-ṭú-lu* 14-*šú*]

25'). *ana muhhi*(UGU) *lip-šur ana*$^{!}$(*ina*) *sūq erbetti*(E.SÍR.K[A.LÍ]M. ⸢MA⸣) *ta-*⸢*sà*⸣-[*pah-ma*]

26'). *pašir*([BÚ]R-*ir*)

* * * * *

REVERSE

Break

1'-2' are too fragmentary to translate

3'-17' = *NADR,* lines 4-16 and 18

18'). If a man saw a bad dream, and became worried: He should [recount] his dream to a *tarītu* of reed (reed fibre$^{?}$).

19'). (Then) he should burn (the *tarītu*) in a fire. He blows with his mouth. It (the evil of the dream) will be dissolved.

20'). Ditto (i.e., If a man saw a bad dream, and became worried): You anoint his hands with choice oil in the morning. It (the evil of the dream) will be dissolved.

21'). Ditto: You roll seven clay pellets. He should recount as many dreams as he saw to (the pellets) seven times.

22'). You scatter (these pellets) at a cross-roads. He says as follows before Shamash:

23'). "May the dream which I saw go to a place . .!" He says (this) seven times. It (the evil of the dream) will be dissolved.

LEFT EDGE

24'-25'). Ditto: [You] roll fourteen clay pellets. He should recount [as many] dreams [as he saw] over (the pellets) [fourteen times]. You scatter (these pellets) at a cross-roads.

26'). It (the evil of the dream) will be dissolved.

* * * * *

NOTES

Reverse

2'). *DB*, p. 343 read the first ⌜X⌝ as *ri.*

18'). *DB*, p. 343 omitted IGI-*ma;* see already R. Borger [1957-1958], p. 418. The final sign is not extant.

20'). The sign is ŠÉŠ not ŠEŠ as in *DB*, p. 343; see already R. Borger [1957-1958], p. 418.

22'). The sign is SÍR not SIR as in *DB*, p. 343; see already R. Borger [1957-1958], p. 418.

23'). Read the eighth sign as *su,* not *šu* as in *DB*, p. 343.

Left Edge

23'). The sign is SÍR not SIR as in *DB*, p. 343; see already R. Borger [1957-1958], p. 418.

81-2-4, 233

TEXTS

DB, pl. 3 (photograph)

STUDIES

A. L. Oppenheim [*DB*], pp. 302, n. 208; and 343-344 (= Excerpt 2)

R. Borger [1957-1968] (review of *DB*, with collations)

81-2-4, 233 forms manuscript **j** of *ADRC*. The cuneiform text appears on plate 14.

* * * * *

OBVERSE

1). [. . . . . . D]ÙG.GA$^{!}$ ⸢X *ši*⸣ *ina še$^{!}$-rim ba-lu pa-tan*

2). [. . . .] ⸢X⸣ *u* ^{d}[X] *šipta*(ÉN) *šalāšīšu*(3-*šú*) *tamannu*(ŠID-*nu*) *ana nāri*(ÍD) *tanaddi*(ŠUB)-*ma$^{!}$ lumnu*(HUL$^{!}$) *pašir*(BÚR)

3-9 = *ADRC*, col. III lines 39-41 and 43-44 (where there is no dividing line as here, between lines 6 and 7).

10-11 = *ADRC*, col. III lines 45a and 46a. (There is no dividing line after line 11.)

12). [én . . . .] hul da en gal ^{d}en.ki.k[e$_{4}$ m]u.un.ši.in.gin.na

13). [. . . . . .] ⸢X⸣.a.ni du$_{8}$.àm

14). [. . . . . .] ⸢X X⸣ [(X)] ⸢X dug$_{4}$⸣.ga ^{d}asal.⸢lú.hi.ke$_{4}$⸣

15). [. . . . .] ⸢X ^{d}⸣[. . . .]

The rest of the tablet is broken away

REVERSE

Break

1'). [*k*]*i*-⸢*i*⸣ *pî*(KA$^{!}$) ^{GIŠ}*lē'i*(LI.U$_{5}$.UM$^{!}$) ⸢*la-bi-ri*$^{!}$⸣-[*šú šaṭir bari*]

* * * * *

OBVERSE

1). [. . . . . .] . . . . in the morning, without having eaten

2). [. . . .] . and . . you recite (this) incantation three times. You throw (it) into the river. The evil (of the dream) will be dispelled.

3-9 = *ADRC,* col. III lines 39-41 and 43-44

10-11 = *ADRC,* col. III lines 45a and 46a

12). [Incantation: ". . . .] evil . great lord Enki, it/he will go to

13). [. . . . . .] . . . . .

14). [. . . . . .] . . [(.)] . . . Asalluhi

15 is too fragmentary to translate.

The rest of the tablet is broken away

REVERSE

Break

1'). [Written (and) collated] according to the text (lit., mouth) of [its] ancient wooden writing-board.

* * * * *

NOTES

Obverse

1-2). The ritual, as it stands today, is incomplete, since we do not possess the incantation to be recited, nor is it clear what is to be thrown into the river (probably a clod).

1). *DB,* p. 343 omitted this line; see already R. Borger [1957-1958], p. 418.

2). *DB,* p. 343 began transliterating the line from ÉN.

Reverse

1'). *DB,* p. 343 read [UG]U GIŠ *li-*u_5*-um* SA[R].

Fragments of at least sixteen writing-boards made of walnut wood covered with beeswax were excavated from the North West Palace of Ashurnasirpal II at Nimrud. Both these and another sixteen ivory writing boards are examined in M. Howard [1955] and D. J. Wiseman [1955].

K. 11406

The cuneiform text appears on plate 19.

* * * * *

<u>Column I</u>

Break

1'). One trace at the end of the line

2'). [. . . . .] ⌈*šab*⌉ *ši*

3'). [. . . . . . *libba-ka l*]*i-nu-uh*

4'). [. . . . .] ⌈X⌉ *iš-du-ud*

5'). [^{d}*Šamaš*(UTU) *da-a-a-na-ta di-n*]*i di-in*

6'). [*pa-ri-is purussê*(EŠ.BAR) *at-ta purussû*(EŠ.BAR)]-⌈*a*⌉-*a purus* (TAR-*us*)

7'). [*šunat*(MÁŠ.GE$_{6}$) *a-mu-ru a-na*] *damiqti*([S]IG$_{5}$) *tir-ra*

8'). [*i-šá-riš lul-lik-ma tap-p*]*e-e lu-uk-šu$_{x}$*(⌈*šud*⌉)-⌈*ud*⌉

9'). [. . . . . . *k*]*i*$^{?}$-*i mah*-⌈*ha*⌉ *mê*(A)-*šú* MÁŠ.G[E$_{6}$ (X)]

10'). [. . . .] ⌈X⌉ *ma a a la da* ⌈X⌉ [X X (X)]

11'). [. . . .] *kīma*(GIM) *kur-ba-ni ina mê*(A.MEŠ) [. . . . (*nadû*)]

12'). [. . . .] *luh* [. . . .]

13'). [. . . .] ⌈X⌉ *ana šapti*(NUNDUN) [. . . .]

14'). [. . . .].⌈MEŠ⌉ *lu* ⌈X⌉ [. . . .]

15'). [. . . . .] ⌈*šá* X⌉ [. . . .]

The rest of the tablet is broken away

* * * * *

<u>Column I</u>

Break

1'-2' are too fragmentary to translate

3'). [. . . .] may [your emotions] calm down!

4'). [. . . . .] . . .

5'). [O Shamash, you are the judge.] Judge my [case]!

6'). [You are the maker of the oracular decision(s).] Make [the oracular decision] regarding me!

7'). Turn [the dream which I saw into good] luck!

8'). [May I prosper!] May I obtain [a friend]!

9'). [. . . . . . just] as$^{?}$ it is soaked in its water (so may) the dream [(X)]

10'). [. . . .] . . . . [. . (.)]

11'). [. . . .] like the clod in (running) water [. . . . (to throw)]

12'-15' are too fragmentary to translate

The rest of the tablet is broken away

* * * * *

NOTES

A clod is mentioned in col. I, line 11', but the preceeding incantation phrases raise problems. Column I line 3' addresses an angry deity, while lines 5'-8' appear in a ŠU.ÍL.LÁ-incantation to Shamash (see *ADRC,* col. III lines 5, 7, 9, and 11) Lines 12'-15' have no obvious parallels in the dream texts. So, although K. 11406 is probably a clod substitution ritual, it does not correspond with the other examples, which form a group (pages 178-179).

Only one trace remains of column II.

NUSKU RITUAL TO OBTAIN A PLEASANT DREAM (NROD)

Only *KAR* 58, obverse 39 to reverse 18 has been studied, together with the tablets duplicating these lines.

TEXTS

CT 51, No. 149 (**G**)
KAR 58 (**A**)
LKA 132 (**F**)
SpTU 2, Nos. 8, and 10 (+) 9 (**d** and $\mathbf{a_1}$ respectively)

STUDIES

E. Ebeling [1918] (edition of **A**)
A. Falkenstein and W. von Soden [*SAHG*], Nos. 77-78 (translation of rev. 1-17 and obv. 39-50 of **A** respectively)
E. Ebeling [*AGH*], pp. 36-43 (edition of **A**)
A. L. Oppenheim [*DB*], p. 298 (obv. 19' of **F**)
H. Donner [1957-1958], p. 392 (**A**, obv. 39 and 44)
R. Borger [1974], p. 191 (*bīt mēseri* connections)
W. Mayer [*UFBG*], pp. 485-486, Nusku 4 (transliteration of *NROD,* obv. 39-50)
M.-J. Seux [1976], pp. 254-255 and 320-321 (translation of **A**, obv. 39-50, and rev. 1-17 respectively)
E. von Weiher [*SpTU* 2], pp. 48-59 (editions of **d** and $\mathbf{a_1}$)
B. R. Foster [*BM* 2], pp. 636, and 637 (translation of *NROD,* obv. 39-50, and **A**, rev. 1-17 respectively)

MANUSCRIPTS FOR THE OBVERSE

Symbol	Museum Number	Publication Number	Relevant Lines	Lines on *NROD*
A	VAT 9030	*KAR* 58	obv. 39-51	39-51
B	K. 7664 + 9302 + 9494	plate 17	col. I lines 40'-48'	39-46
C	K. 9000	plate 18	lines 14'-16'	39-41
d	W 22762/2	*SpTU* 2, No. 8	col. III lines 3'-11'	39-50
E	K. 11706 + 13288	plate 20	obv. 1'-13'	39-50
F	VAT 13620	*LKA* 132	obv. 19'-21'	39, 51a
G	BM 134542 (= 1932-12-12, 537)	*CT* 51, No. 149	rev. 1'-5'	48-50, 51a
-------				
a$_1$	W 22729/5 (+) W 22729/18	*SpTU* 2, Nos. 10 (+) 9	obv. 8'-17'	39-49

The reverse of *NROD* occurs only on **A**, rev. 1-18.

C (R. Borger's [1974, p. 191], exemplar v) indicates by its colophon that it belongs to the *bīt mēseri* series, as does **d** (R. Borger's exemplar Uruk a), both forming part of Piece 5 of Tablets 3 and 4 (see ibid. on **E** and **F**, under his exemplar x).

K. 7664 and K. 9302 have been joined (**B**) since the edition of W. Mayer [*UFBG*].

It is suggested that *SpTU* 2, Nos. 9 and 10 form the same tablet because they supply each other's lacunae. This was brought to the writer's attention by J. V. Kinnier Wilson [1992, personal communication]. Correct E. von Weiher [*SpTU* 2], p. 54 to either No. 10, lines 7'-16' or No. 9, obv. 8'-17'.

KAR 58, obv. 39-51 does not mention dreams, but has been studied because:

i). The ritual on **A** indicates a continuation on to the incantation of rev. 1 17, which mentions Anzagar and dreams.

ii). Its incipit occurs on **F**, which contains rituals to obtain a pleasant dream (*ADRC*), and one to appease an angry personal goddess.

The whole complex *NROD* has been treated as a ritual to obtain a pleasant dream, although it differs from the pattern of those on *ADRC* and *SDR* (Table 11 on page 210), since a dream is requested. A. L. Oppenheim [*DB,* p. 298] regarded **F** as containing a ritual against bad dreams, but there is no mention of nightmares.

* * * * *

OBVERSE

Line 39

ÉN ^{d}*Nusku šàr mu-ši mu-nam-mir uk-li*

A).	ÉN	^{d}*Nusku*	*šàr*	*mu-ši*	*mu-na-mir*	*uk-li*
B).	[	*Nu*]*sku*	*šàr*	GE$_6$	*mu-na-mir*	*uk-*⌈*li*⌉
C).	⌈ÉN⌉	^{d}*Nusku*	*šàr*	GE$_6$	*mu-na-mir*	*uk-*[ ]
d).	ÉN	^{d}*Nusku*	*š*[*àr* . . . .]			
E).	ÉN	^{d}*Nu*[*sku*				]
F).	ÉN	^{d}*Nūru*(ZÁLAG$^{!}$(UTU))	*šàr*	*mu-ši*	*mu-nam-mir*	⌈*uk*⌉*-li*
a$_1$).	[ ]	⌈d⌉*Nusku*	*šàr*	*mu-ši*	*mu-nam-mir*	*ú-mu* :

Line 40

ta-az-za-az ina mu-ši-ma ni-ši ta-bar-ri

A).	*ta-za-az*	*ina*	*mu-ši-ma*	UN.MEŠ	*ta-bar-ri*
B).	[GUB-*az*	]	⌈*mu-ši*	UN$^{!}$⌉.MEŠ	⌈*ta*⌉*-bar-ri*
C).	*tazzaz*([G]UB-⌈*az*⌉)	*ina*	*mu-ši*	UN.MEŠ	*ta-bar-*[ ]
E).	GUB-*az*	[			]
a$_1$).	*ta-az-za-az*	*ina*	*mu-ši*	*ni-ši*	*t*[*a-*]

Line 41

ina ba-li-ka ul šakin nap-tan ina É-kur

A).	*ina*	*ba-li-ki*	*ul* GAR-*in nap-tan ina É-kur*			
B).	[			]	⌈*ul*⌉	*nadin*(SUM-*in*)
C).	[*in*]*a*	*ba-*⌈*li*⌉*-ka*	*šip-ṭu*$^{!}$	*purussû*(EŠ.BAR)	*ul*	⌈X⌉-[ ]
d).	*ina*	*ba-li-ka*	[			]
E).	*ina*	*ba-li-*⌈*ki*⌉	*šip-*⌈*ṭu*⌉	[		]
a$_1$).	[	*b*]*a-li-ki*	*šip-ṭu u*	*pu-ru-us-su-ú*	*u*[*l*	]

Line 42

ᵈše-e-du ha-a-a-ṭu al-lu-hap-pu hab-bi-lu gal-lu-u rābiṣu ilu lem-nu

A). ᵈALAD *ha-a-a-ṭu* *al-lu-hap-pu hab-bi-lu gal-lu-u*
MÁŠKIM DINGIR *lem-nu*

B). [
MÁŠ]KIM DINGIR *lem-nu*

d). *še-e-du* *al-lu-ha*[*p-* . . . . . .] ⌈X⌉ [X X] ⌈X X⌉ [. . . . . .]

E). *še-e-du* *a*[*l*]*-lu-ha-pu* *ha-a-*⌈*a*⌉*-*[
]

a₁). [ ]-⌈*e*⌉*-du* *al-lu-hap-pá* *ha-*⌈*a*⌉*-a-ṭu* :
ra-bi-iṣ *ilū*(DINGIR.MEŠ) [ ]

Line 43

ú-tuk-ku ᴸᵁ́*lilû* ᴹᴵ́*lilītu im-me-du pu-zur šá-ha-ti*

A). *ú-tuk-ku* ᴸᵁ́LÍL.LÁ ᴹᴵ́LÍL.LÁ *im-me-du* *pu-zur*
šá-ha-ti

B). [*-r*]*a* *u*
šá-ha-tú

d). *im-mé-du* *pu-zur* *u*
šá-⌈*hat*⌉

E). *ú-tuk-*[LÍ]L.LÁ ⌈ᴹᴵ́⌉LÍL.LÁ *i*[*m-*
]

a₁). [*ga*]*l₅-lu-ú li-li-tú* *ár-da*[*t*] *li-li-i* : *im-mid* *pu-uz-ru* ⌈*ù*⌉
š[*á-*]

Line 44

ina pān ᵈ*Nūri-ka šu-ṣi sag-hul-ha-zu ṭu-ru-ud ú-tuk-ku kušud lem-nu*

A). *ina* IGI ᵈZÁLAG-*ka* *šu-ṣi* *sag-*⌈*hul-ha*ᴵ*-za*ᴵ⌉ *ṭu-ru-ud*
ú-tuk-ku KUR-*ud* *lem-nu*

B). [. . . . .] *ú-tuk-ka lem-nu*

d). *ina* ⌈IGI⌉ *nūri*(IZI.GAR)*-ka* *šu-ṣi* *sa*[*g-*] /
⌈*ú*⌉*-tuk-ku* *lem-nu*

E). [ ]-*ṣi* *sag-hul-ha-*[. . . .]

a₁). *šu-ṣu* *sag-hul-ha-zu* *ṭu-ru-du*
[ ]

Line 45

^{d}*Šu-lak* (**E** adds: [*il*]*u*) *mut-tal-lik mu-ši ša li-pit-su mu-tú a-mur-ka-ma a-sa-hur ilūt-ka* :

A). ^{d}*Šu-lak* *mut-tal-lik mu-ši ša* TAG-*su* *mu-tú*
a-mur-ka-ma *a-sa-hur* DINGIR-*ut-ka*

B). [ ] ⸢*šá*⸣ TAG-*su* ÚŠ /
[DI]NGIR-*ut-ka*

d). ^{d}⸢*Šu*⸣-*lak* *mut-tal-lik* GE$_6$ *šá li-pi-*[*it*] /
a-mur-ka-ma *as-hur* ⸢X⸣ DINGIR-*ut-ka*

E). [DING]IR *mut-al-lik m*[*u-*] /
[ ]-*ma as-*[ ]

a$_1$). ^{d}*Šu-lak* *mut-tal-lik mu-ši šá li-pit-s*[*u*] /
a-mur-ka-a-ma as-sa-hur DINGIR-*ú-u*[*t*]-*ka* :

Line 46

ma-ṣar šul-me u balāṭi šu-kun eli-ia$_5$

A). *ma-ṣar šul-me u* TI.LA *šu-kun* UGU-*ia*$_5$

B). [ ]-⸢*kun* UGU$^{?}$-*ia*$_5$⸣

d). EN.NUN *šu-lum u* TIN *šu-ku*[*n*]

E). [-*ṣa*]*r šul-me* ⸢*u*⸣ [ ]

a$_1$). EN.NUN *šu-*[*ul-mi*]

Line 47

^{d}*še-e-du na-ṣi-ru u ilu mu-šal-li-mu šu-uz-ziz ina rēšīja*

A). ^{d}⸢ALAD⸣ *na-ṣi-ru* DINGIR *mu-šal-li-mu šu-zi-iz*
ina SAG.MU

d). *še-e-du na-ṣi-ru u* DINGIR *mu-šal-li-mu šu-uz-ziz*
ina [ ]

E). [*n*]*a-ṣi-ra* DINGIR [
]

a$_1$). ^{d}ALAD *na-ṣir u ilū*(DINGIR.MEŠ) *mu-ša*[*l*]-*lim šu-uz-*[
]

Line 48

lit-tar-ru-u'-in-ni kal mu-ši a-di na-ma-ri

A). *[li-it-tar]-ru-ni* *kal mu-ši a-di* *na-ma-ri*

d). *lit-tar-ru-u'-in-ni* *kal* GE$_6$ *a-di-i* *šat ur-ra*

E). [ ]-⸢X⸣-*ni* *kal* [ ]

G). [. . . .] ⸢X X⸣ [. . . .]

a$_1$). *li-it-tar-ru-u'-in-nu* *kal mu-ši a-d*[*i*]

Line 49

^{d}*Nusku gít-ma-lu be-el ta-šim-ti nar-bi-ka lu-šá-pi*

A). [ ] *gít-ma-lu* EN *ta-šim-ti* *nar-bi-ka lu-šá-pi*

d). ^{d}*Nusku* *gít-ma-lu* ⸢EN⸣ [ ] / *nar-bi-ka lu-šá-pi*

E). [. . . . .] ⸢X *pu*⸣ [. . . .]

G). [*be*]-*el* *t*[*a-*]

a$_1$). ^{d}*Nusku* *gít-ma-lu* *be-lu* *ta-šim-tú* : *nar-bi-k*[*a* . . . . .]

Line 50

mahar ^{d}*Šamaš ud-da-kám te* [ÉN]

A). [ ] ^{d}UTU *ud-da-kám*

d). IGI ^{d}UTU *ud-da-kám te* [ÉN]

E). traces of two or three signs

G). [(. . . .) *i*]*na pān*(IGI) ⸢^{d}⸣[. . . .]

Line 51

A). [*kīma annītam iqbû* ^{LÚ}]*āšipu*(MAŠ.MAŠ) *qāt*(ŠU) ^{LÚ}*marṣi*(GIG) *iṣabbat*(DAB)-*ma ana pān*(IGI) ^{d}*Nusku šalāšīšu*(3-*šú*) *iqabbi* (DUG$_4$.GA)

Line 51a

F). *ina pān*(IGI) *nu-ri nignaq*(NÍG.NA) ^{GIŠ}*burāši*(LI) / *tašakkan* (GAR-*an*) *šipta*(ÉN) *šalāšīšu*(3-*šú*) *tamannu*(ŠID-*nu*)

G). [. . . .] ⸢X⸣ *ina pān*(IGI) ^{d}*Nūri*(ZÁ[LAG) . . . .] / [. . . .] ⸢X *ú*⸣ [. . . .]

REVERSE

1). [EN ^{d}]*Nusku sukkallu*(SUKKAL) *ṣi-ru mu-tal-*[*lik mu-ši*]

2). [X X X] ⸢X⸣ *ilāni*(DINGIR.MEŠ) *ša kib-ra-a-ti bēl*(EN) *emūqān* (USU) *ṣīrātu*(MAH.MEŠ-*t*[*u$_4$*])

3). *ša i-na ru-qé*$^{!}$*-ti te-ni-še-e-ti ri-gim-šu i-še-mu-ú*

4). *ana-ku annanna*(NENNI) *mār*(A) *annanna*(NENNI) *ut*$^{!}$(*te*)*-nin-k*[*a*] ⸢X⸣ *di-ni-ia uznā*(GEŠTUG^{II})*-ia pu-te-i*

5). [*aš*]*-šum di-ni-*[*ia re-e-m*]*u*$^{!}$(⸢*i*⸣) *šur-ši-i*

6). [*aš-šum*] *di-nim ša-nim-ma* [X X]*-ma-ta a-meš*

7). *maṣṣarat*([E]N.NUN) *ba-ra-ri-tú maṣṣarat*(EN.NUN) *qab-li-tú maṣṣarat*(EN.NUN) *šat ur-ri*

8). [*mu-š*]*u lib-lam-ma dà-lí-lí-ka lud-lul*

9). [AN].ZAG.GAR.RA AN.ZAG.GAR.RA *ba-bi-lu a-me-lu-ti*

10). *mār*(DUMU) *šip-ri ša ru-bi-i* ^{d}*Marduk*

11). *mu-ši-tu pu-luh-tu ša li-la-a-ti*

12). 3 *maṣṣarāti*(EN.NUN.MEŠ) *ša mušīti*(GE$_6$*-ti*) *e-ra-a-ti na-aṣ-ra-a-te dal-pa-a-te la ṣa-lil-a-ti*

13). *ki-ma at-ti-na e-ra-te-na na-aṣ-ra-a-ti-*[*n*]*a*

14). *dal-pá-ti-na la ṣa-li-la-ti-*⸢*na*⸣

15). *a-na e-ri ṣal-li purussâ*(EŠ.BAR*-a*) *ta-nam-din-na*

16). *te-ep-pu-šá ṣi-bu-ut-ku*<*-nu*> *ta-bar-ra-a kal mu-ši a-di maṣṣarat* (EN.NUN) *šat* ⸢*ur*⸣*-ri*

17). *mušu*(GE$_6$) *lib-lam-ma dà-lí-lí-ka lud-lul*

18). KA.INIM.MA ŠU.ÍL.LÁ ^{d}NUSKU.KÁM

* * * * *

OBVERSE

39). Incantation: "O Nusku, the king of the night; the illuminator of darkness;

40). you are present (lit., stand) during the night, and you watch over mankind.

41). A meal cannot be prepared in Ekur without you.

42). The *šēdu*(-demon), the *hajjāṭu*(-demon), the *alluhappu*(-demon), the *habbilu*(-demon), the *gallû(*-demon), the *rābiṣu*(-demon), 'the evil god',

43). the *utukku*(-demon), the *lilû*(-demon), (and) the *lilītu*(-demoness all) cower away (lit., take refuge) in secret nooks

44). before your divine light. Send away the *saghulhazû*(-demon)! Drive away the *utukku*(-demon)! Defeat the evil one!

45). O Shulak, (**E** adds: the god), the one who roams around at night, (and) whose touch (is) death. I looked at you, and I appeal to your divinity.

46). Establish a guardian of well-being and health for (lit., over) me!

47). Make a protecting *šēdu*(-spirit) and the god who keeps (one) well stand at my head (while I sleep)!

48). May they continually guide me all through the night, until dawn!

49). O noble/perfect Nusku, the lord of understanding, (do this, and) I will extol your greatness

50). all day long before Shamash!" [Incantation] formula.

---

51). [When he has said this] the exorcist takes the hand of the invalid, and he says (the following incantation) three times before Nusku:

51a). You set out a censer of juniper before the lamp. You recite the (above) incantation three times.

REVERSE

1). [Incantation:] "O Nusku, the august vizier; the one who roams [around at night];

2). [. . .] . of the gods of the four quarters (of the world). The lord of overpowering strength . [.]

3). whose voice mankind hears from afar.

4). I myself, X, the son of Y, beseech you (to) grant me knowledge . of my situation!

5). Cause (Shamash/the gods) to have [mercy] regarding the verdict [(on) me]!

6). [As for] the case of another [. .] . . . .

7-8). May the first watch (of the night), the middle watch, the third watch, (and/or) Night bring me (a favourable dream), and I will proclaim your glory!

9). O Anzagar, O Anzagar, the bringer (of dreams) to mankind;

10). the messenger of prince Marduk.

11). O Night, the terror of the evening.

12). O (you) three Watches of the Night, awake, watchful, remaining awake, (and) not lying asleep.

13). While you (fem. pl.) are awake, watchful,

14). remaining awake, (and) not lying asleep,

15). you give oracular decision(s) to those awake or sleeping.

16). You carry out your purpose. You watch all night until (the end of) the third watch.

17). May Night bring me (a favourable dream), and I will proclaim your (masc. sing.) glory!"

18).	Incantation rubric: It is (the text of) a ŠU.ÍL.LÁ-incantation to Nusku.

* * * * *

NOTES

Obverse

39). **F**, obv. 19' has the variant [d]ZALAG[!], but is still addressing Nusku, since his symbol was a lamp.

a$_1$ has the variant *mu-nam-mir ú-mu,* "the illuminator of the day[?]" (*ūmu* is usually written with U$_4$, see *AHw* 3, pp. 1418-1420). E. von Weiher [*SpTU* 2, p. 58] offered a possible reading of the beginning of *SpTU* 2, No. 10, noting that a word for darkness would be more appropriate.

d, col. III lines 1'-2' possibly refer to this incantation, since there is no dividing line:

1'). *ana* ⌈X⌉ [. . . . .]

2'). *kīma*(GIM) *an-n*[*am* . . . .]

41). All the other manuscripts have the variant *ina ba-li-ka šip-ṭu u pu-ru-us-su-ú ul* SUM-*in,* "Divine judgement and oracular decision(s) cannot be given without you.".

42-43). The manuscripts list the demons differently.

43). E. von Weiher [*SpTU* 2, p. 59] suggested that the last sign on **a**$_1$ (No. 10), line 10' was I[GI].

45). It is unclear why the demon Shulak, the overseer of the lavatory (*TDP,* p. 188, Tab. 26, line 13), appears in connection with Nusku.

d, col. III line 8' has the variant *as-hur,* "I appealed".

48). **d**, col. III line 10' has the variant *šat ur-ri,* "(the end of) the third watch (of the night)".

G has a dividing line between rev. 1' and 2'; i.e., between *NROD,* lines 48-49.

49). The translation of M.-J. Seux [1976, p. 255] restored [*Seigneur*] (i.e., EN) after Nusku, which is unsupported by the *SpTU* texts.

50). E. Ebeling [*AGH,* p. 40] restored [*a-di ṣît*] at the beginning of **A**, obv. 50; a restoration again unconfirmed by the *SpTU* texts.

51). The restoration on **A**, obv. 51 comes from E. Ebeling [*AGH*], p. 40.

Reverse

1). The second epithet was applied usually to demons or unpleasant deities.

2). E. Ebeling [*AGH,* p. 40] restored [*nûr*] at the beginning of this line, which does not fit with the traces, and restored ⌜*ap*⌝-[*kal-lu*] at the end, but there does not appear to be room. Instead, J. V. Kinnier Wilson [1992, personal communication] proposed -*t*[*u*$_4$].

4). In the middle of the line E. Ebeling [*AGH,* p. 40] restored [*aš-š*]*um,* but the trace does not resemble -*šum.*

5). The restoration comes from *AHw* 2, *rašû* I, §*Š* 10, p. 962b. E. Ebeling [*AGH,* p. 40] read [*di-ni*]-*i* instead, translating [ibid., p. 41] the whole line as *„was [meinen] Prozeß angeht, laß (mich) mein [Recht] bekommen!"*

6). E. Ebeling [*AGH,* p. 40] read [*zu-kur a*]-*ma-ta a-miš,* translating [ibid., p. 41] *„[sprich(?) das W]ort: Ich habe (ihn) mißachtet!".* M.-J. Seux [1976, p. 320, n. 9] read [*ana*] *di-nim ša-nim-ma [l]a ta-a-lak, "Ne va pas [à] un autre judgement";* stating that he had followed the translation of A. Falkenstein and W. von Soden [*SAHG,* p. 352]: *„zu einem anderen Prozeß mögest du nicht hingehen".*

8). J. V. Kinnier Wilson [1992, personal communication] suggested the reading at the beginning of the line. E. Ebeling [*AGH,* p. 40] read [*mu-ši-t*]*u.* M.-J. Seux [1976, p. 320, n. 10] suggested [*šut-t*]*u,* however, *šuttu* appears more usually written out as *šu-ut-tu* [*CAD Š*$_3$*,* pp. 405-407].

9). A sub-incantation appears to begin in this line, addressed to Anzagar, and personified Night and the three Watches of the Night (the last four being feminine).

12). The verbs should be second feminine plural statives, as on rev. 13-14, instead of singular.

16). The pronominal suffix -*ku*<-*nu*> should read -*kina* (second feminine plural).

RITUALS TO OBTAIN A PURUSSÛ (ROP)

TEXTS

CT 51, No. 103 (**D**)
LKA 138 (**A$_1$**)
STT 73 (**A**)
UET 7, No. 118 (**b**)
YOS 11, No. 75 (**c**)

STUDIES

E. Reiner [1960a] (edition of **A**, mentioning **A$_1$**; correct p. 28 to obv. 2-5)
R. Borger [1961], p. 153 (**A**, line 16)
E. Reiner [1965], p. 248 (line 82)
H. Hunger [*BAK*], No. 380 on p. 116 (colophon of **A**)
H. Hirsch [1968-1969], p. 50, n. 135 (**A**, lines 33, 35, and 73)
M.-J. Seux [1976], pp. 483-485 (translation of **A**, lines 1-20 and 21-41)
O. R. Gurney [1981-1982], p. 93 (corrections to **A**)
W. Horowitz [1989] (lines 61-63 and 71-73)
E. Reiner [1995], pp. 57-71 (lines 61-64 and 71-75; interchange notes 291 and 292 on p. 71), and 72-73

MANUSCRIPTS

Symbol	Museum Number	Publication Details	Relevant Lines	Lines on *ROP*
A	S.U. 51/1 + 25	*STT* 73	1-138	1-138
b	--	*UET* 7, No. 118	obv. 1'-2'	46-47
			3'	48
			4'-7'	48a-51
			8'-10'	61-64
			11'	65
			12'-16'	65a-70
			17'-20'	71-75
			21'	76
			22'-23'	77-80
			24'	81
			25'-27'	81a-84
c	YBC 9884	*YOS* 11, No. 75	1-3	77-78
			4	81a
			5-7	81b-d
D	BM 35182	*CT* 51, No. 103	1'-2'	86-87
			3'-6'	88-91

A_1	VAT 13615	*LKA* 138	obv. 2-5	88-91
			6-8	85-87

A is the only source for lines 1-41 and 92-138. **c** is the only source for lines 81b-d.

The reverse of the Neo-Babylonian tablet **b** is very fragmentary, and we cannot tell if it is related to *ROP* or not. Correct *UET* 7, p. 2 to lines 46-84.

Obverse 1 of $\mathbf{A_1}$ possibly contained a title for the whole tablet. The reverse contains more rituals, apparently seeking omens. The language of these lines is difficult to understand. Reverse 3-6 describes the achievement of a purpose according to the flight of certain birds. The section also appears on *CT* 39, pl. 24, rev. 28-29 (correct *LKA*, p. XIII).

* * * * *

OBVERSE

Column I

1^{A}). [ÉN *ìl-tu*$_4$] *réme-ni-tu*$_4$ *mu-bal-li-ṭa-at mīti*(AD$_6$)

2). [*šá nap*]-⸢*lu*⸣-[*us-sa*] *ba-la-ṭu u na-ás-hur-šá šá-la-*⸢*mu*⸣

3). [*ap-kal-lat*] *ilāni*(DINGIR.MEŠ) *ga-me-rat ab-ra-a-*[*ti*]

4). [*ṣa-bi-t*]*a-át mar-ka*[*s k*]*ip-pat šamê*(AN-*e*) *u erṣetim*(KI-⸢*tim*⸣)

5). [*mu-ki*]*l*-[*l*]*at mar-ka-*⸢*si*⸣ *rabî*(GAL-*i*) *ša É-šár-ra*

6). *ina šamê*(AN-*e*) *šu-tur manzāz*(KI.GUB)-*ki ina* ⸢^{d}⸣*ištarāti*(EŠ$_{18}$.TÁR.MEŠ) *šá-qa-a re-šá-a-ki*

7). ^{d}*A-nu* ^{d}*Enlil*(BAD) *u* ^{d}*É-*⸢*a*⸣ *ilāni*(DINGIR.MEŠ) *abbē* (AD$^{!}$(GAL).MEŠ)-*ki*

8). [*ina ba-l*]*i-*⸢*ki*⸣ *ul i-šá-ka-nu ur-*⸢*ta*⸣

9). [*ba-ni-tú ṣir-tú*] *šá e-la šá-šá la ibbannâ*(DÙ-*a*) *ab-ra-a-ti*

10). [*ù purussê*(EŠ.BAR)] *šamê*(AN-*e*) *u erṣeti*(KI-*ti*) *là ipparrasu* (TAR-*su*)

11). [*ana-ku al-s*]*i-ki du-uš-mu-ú pa-lih-k*[*i*]

12). [*ana marušti*(NÍG.GIG) *i*]*m-hur-an-*⸢*ni*⸣*-ma* ⸢*ina*⸣ *šap-li-ki ak-mi-su*

13). [*ṭè-em ilūti*(DINGIR]-*ti*)-*ki rabīti*(GAL-⸢*ti*⸣) *áš-šu lib-luṭu*

14). [*ta-re-mìn*]-⸢*ni*⸣*-ma ta-ṭè-mìn-ni*

15). [*ki-i annanna*(NENN]I) *mār*(A) *annanna*(NENNI) *marṣa*(GIG) *a*[*n*]*-na-a šá mar-ṣu*

16). [*ina marṣi*(GIG) *an-n*]*i*$^{!}$*-i tu*$^{!}$(⸢*šu*⸣)*-šat-bi-i ana ilāni*(DINGIR.MEŠ) *abbē*(AD$^{!}$(GAL).MEŠ)-*ki a-bu-su ta-ṣab-ba-ti-ma*

17). [*ana qí-bi-ti-k*]*i ṣir-ti ilāni*(DINGIR.MEŠ) *abbē*(AD$^{!}$(GAL).MEŠ)-*ki i-qul-lu-ma*

18). [. . . .] ⸢X⸣ *i-gam-me-lu-šu u sūq*(SILA) *āli*(URU)*-šú ina šùl-me ú-šak-ba-s*[*u*]

19). [*ki-i šá*] *ta-re-mìn-ni-ma ṭè-em ilūti*(DINGIR-*ti*)*-ki rabīti*(GAL-*ti*) *ta-ṭè-m*[*ìn-ni*]

20). [*ṭ*]*e-*⸢*em*⸣ *ilūti*(DINGIR-*ti*)*-*⸢*ki*⸣ *rabīti*(GAL-*ti*) *šup-rim-ma pî* (KA)*-ia*$_5$ *lu-še-ṣi*

---

21). ÉN *ìl-tu*$_4$ *réme-ni-tu*$_4$ *mu-bal-li-*⸢*ṭa*⸣*-at mīti*(AD$_6$)

22). *šá nap-lu-us-sa ba-la-ṭu u na-ás-hur-šá šá-la-mu*

23). *ap-kal-lat ilāni*(DINGIR.MEŠ) *ga-me-rat ab-ra-*⸢*a-ti*⸣

24). *ṣa-bi-ta-át mar-kas* ⸢*kip-pat*⸣ *šamê*(<AN>-⸢*e*⸣) *u erṣetim*(K[I]-*tim*$^{!}$)

25). *mu-kil-lat mar-ka-si rabî*([GAL]-*i*) *ša É-*⸢*šár*⸣*-ra*

26). *ina šamê*(AN-*e*) *šu-tur manzāz*(KI.⸢GUB$^{!}$⸣)-⸢*ki*⸣ *ina* ⸢^{d}⸣*ištarāti* (EŠ$_{18}$.TÁR.MEŠ) *šá-qa-a re-šá-a-ki*

27). ^{d}*A-nu* ⸢^{d}⸣[*Enlil*(BAD) *u*] ^{d}*É-a ilāni*(DINGIR.MEŠ) *abbē*(AD. MEŠ)-*ki*

28). *ina ba-*[*li-ki*] *ul i-šá-ka-nu* ⸢*ur*⸣-*t*[*a*]

29). [*ba*]-⸢*ni-tú*⸣ *ṣi*[*r-tú šá*] ⸢*e*⸣-*la šá-šá la ibbannâ*(DÙ-*a*) *ab-ra-a-t*[*i*]

30). *ù purussê*(EŠ.BAR) *šamê*(AN-*e*) <*u*> *erṣeti*(KI-*ti*) *là ipparrasu* (TAR-[*s*]*u*)

31). *ana-ku al-si-ki du-uš-mu-ú pa-lih-ki*

32). *ana marušti*(NÍG.GIG) *im-hur-an-ni-ma ina šap-li-ki ak-mi*$^{!}$(*mu*)-*su*

33). *ṭè-em ilūti*(DINGIR-*ti*)-*ki rabīti*(GAL-*ti*) *áš-šu mi-*⸢*it*⸣-*ti*

34). *ta-re-mìn-ni-ma ta-ṭè-mìn-ni* [:] *ki-i annanna*(NENNI) *mār*(A) *annanna*(NENNI) *murṣa*(GIG) *šá mar-ṣu murṣa*(GIG) *an-*⸢*nam*$^{?}$ *nin*⸣ *ú*

35). *ú-ru-uh-šú ana* KUR.NU.GI$_{4}$.A *šu-uh-mu-ṭa-at*

36). ^{d}*Anunnakū*(DIŠ.U) *šu-ut ku-dúr-ra šá* LÍL *annanna*(NENNI) *ik-di-ru ú*$^{!}$*-ru-uh* KUR.NU.GI$_{4}$.A *na-šu-šu*

37). *il*(DINGIR)-*šú u* ^{d}*ištar*(XV)-*šu u$_{4}$-um-šu ù šim-ta-šu*

38). *ú-maš-ši-*⸢*ru*⸣-*šu-ma ur-ha šu-te-šu-ra* : ⸢*ù*⸣ *har-ra-an la ta-ri te-bu-ú*

39). *sūq*(SILA) *āli*(URU)-*šú* ⸢*zu*⸣-*mu-ma a-na du-ur da-ri la i-kab-ba-su*

40). *ki-i šá ta-re-mìn-ni-ma ṭè-em ilūti*(DINGIR-*ti*)-*ki rabīti*(GAL-*ti*) *ta-ṭè-mìn-ni*

41). *ṭè-em ilūti*(DINGIR-*ti*)-*ki rabīti*(GAL-*ti*) *šup*$^{!}$*-rim-ma pî*(KA)-*ia lu-še-ṣi*

<u>Column II</u>

42^{A}). KA.INIM.MA E[Š.BAR IGI.DU$_{8}$ DÙ.DÙ.B]I ⸢*a-na*⸣ *pān*(IGI) [. . . . . . *tašakkan*(GAR]-*an*) *šikāra*(KAŠ) *tanaqqi*(BAL-*qí*) 2 *ú-ìl-ti te-'i-i*[*l*$^{!}$]

43). *ina pān*(IGI) ^{MUL}[X X] ⸢X⸣ *mu kil ana* Á ⸢X⸣ *an* ⸢X⸣ [. . . . *t*]*a*$^{!}$*-šak-*⸢*kan*⸣-*ma purussâ*(EŠ.BAR) *tammar*(IGI.DU$_{8}$)

Line 44

A). ⸢ÉN⸣ *at-*[*tu*]*-*⸢*nu*⸣ *kakkabānu*(MUL.MEŠ) *šá mu-ši-t*[*i*] ⸢^{d}⸣En.bi.luh ^{d}Ni[n.bi.luh ^{d}]En.bi.luh.ha

Line 45

A). [*u*] *mu-ši-tu₄ kal-la-tu₄ kut*$^{!}$(*nu*)*-t*[*um*$^{!}$*-t*]*u₄* : ^{d}*É-a* [*šar₄*] *apsî* (A[BZU]) *tuk-lat Eri₄-du₁₀*

Line 46

ilī Sibitti ^{d}VII *a-šib šá-ma-*[*mi ilā*]*nu ellūtu ia-*[*a*]*-t*[*i*] *arad-ku-nu*

A). ⸢DINGIR⸣ IMIN.⸢BI⸣ ^{d}VII *a-šib šá-ma-*[*mi* DINGIR].MEŠ KÙ. MEŠ *ia-*[*a*]*-t*[*i*] ⸢ÌR⸣*-ku-nu*

b). [ ]*-*⸢*ku*⸣*-nu*

Line 47

itti ili-ia₅ u ^{d}*ištari-ia₅ šu-ud-*⸢*bi*⸣*-*[*ba*]*-*⸢*nin*⸣*-ni-ma* : *lu-ú en-še*$^{!}$(*kur*)*-ku di-ni li-di-nu lu-ú dan-na ana-ku purussû-a-a lip*$^{!}$*-ru*$^{!}$*-su*

A). [K]I DINGIR-*ia₅* ^{d}XV-*ia₅* *šu-ud-*[*-ba*]*-*⸢*nin*⸣*-ni-ma* : *lu-ú en-še*$^{!}$(*kur*)*-ku* *di-ni* *l*[*i-*] ⸢*lu*⸣*-ú* ⸢*dan*⸣*-na ana-ku* EŠ.BAR*-a-a lip*$^{!}$*-ru*$^{!}$*-su*

b). KI DINGIR-*ia₅* *u* ^{d}INANNA-*ia₅* [*-u*]*d-*⸢*bi*⸣*-*[ ] / [*-k*]*u* *di-i-ni li-di-nu lu-ú* *dan-na* [ ]

Line 48

[K]A.⸢INIM⸣.MA EŠ.BAR MÁŠ.GE₆ [IGI.DU₈]

A). [K]A.⸢INIM⸣.MA EŠ.BAR M[ÁŠ.GE₆ IGI.DU₈]

b). [ ] EŠ.BAR MÁŠ.GE₆ [ ]

Line 48a

DÙ.DÙ.BI ⸢*ina*⸣ *mušīti ana pān kakkabāni mušīti*

A). DÙ.DÙ.BI ⸢*ina*⸣ GE₆ *ana* IGI MUL.MEŠ GE₆*-tì*

b). [ ] *ana* IGI MUL.MEŠ GE₆*-ti*

Line 49

nignaq ⌜^{ŠIM}⌝*bur*[*āši tašakkan šip*]*tu*$^{!}$ *an-ni-tu*$_{4}$ *šalāšīšu ana muhhi* ^{GIŠ}*bi-ni tamannu-ma*

A). [ ].⌜NA⌝ $^{\text{Š[IM]}}$[GAR-*an* É]N$^{!}$ *an-ni-tu*$_{4}$ 3-*šú ana* UGU ^{GIŠ}*bi-ni* ŠID-*nu-ma*

b). NÍG.NA ⌜^{ŠIM}⌝L[I] / [ ] 3-*šú ana* UGU ^{GIŠ}*bi-ni* ŠID-*ma*

Line 50

[. . . . . .] *tašakkan ina rēš erši-ka*

A). [. . . . . .] GAR-*an* *ina* SAG GIŠ.NÁ-*ka*

b). *ina* SAG GIŠ.[ ]

Line 51

[. . . . *k*]*a ili ram-ma-ni šá maṣhata te-ṣir tanâl-ma purussâ tammar*

A). [. . . . . .] *šá* ZÌ.MAD.GÁ *te-ṣir* NÁ-*ma* EŠ.BAR IGI.DU$_{8}$

b). [. . . . *k*]*a* DINGIR *ram-ma-ni* *šá* ZÌ.MAD.GÁ *te-ṣ*[*ir*] / [-*m*]*a* EŠ.BAR IGI.[ ]

52^{A}). [ÉN *ra-am*]-*ku šá* ^{d}*É-a mār*(DUMU) *šip-ri šá* ^{d}*Asal-lú-hi ana-ku ilānu*(DINGIR.MEŠ) *mušīti*(GE$_{6}$-*tì*) *ina* [. . . . (. .)]

53). [^{d}En.bi.luh] ⌜^{d}Nin⌝.bi.luh *ilānu*(DINGIR.MEŠ) *bēl*(EN.MEŠ) *mušīti*(GE$_{6}$-*tì*) *mu-ši-tu*$_{4}$ *kal*$^{!}$(*e*)-*la-tu*$_{4}$ *k*[*ut-tum-tu*$_{4}$]

54). ⌜^{d}⌝[*É-a*] *šar*$_{4}$ *apsî*(ABZU) *tuk-lat Eri*$_{4}$-*du*$_{10}$ *ilānu Sibitti*(DINGIR.IMIN.BI) ^{d}VII *a-šib šá-ma-mi ilānu*(DINGIR.MEŠ) [*ellūtu*(KÙ.MEŠ)]

55). *ia-*[*a-ti*] *arad*([Ì]R)-*ku-nu itti*(KI) *ili*(DINGIR)-*ia*$_{5}$ ^{d}*ištari*(XV)-*ia*$_{5}$ *šu-ud-bi-ba-nin-ni-ma lu-u en-še*$^{!}$(*kur*)-*ku di-ni li-di-nu purussû* (EŠ.BAR)-⌜*a*⌝-[*a lip-ru-su*]

---

56). KA.INIM.MA *itti*(KI) *ili*(DINGIR)-*šú u* ^{d}*ištari*(EŠ$_{18}$.TÁR)-*šú da-ba-bi-im-ma arkat*(EGIR) *ramāni*(NÍ)-*šú pa-ra-si*

---

57). DÙ.DÙ.⌜BI⌝ *ramān*([N]Í)-⌜*ka*⌝ *tubbib*(DAGAD) *ina*$^{!}$ *rēš*(SAG) *eb-bi u eb-bi-ti uṣurāti*(GIŠ.HUR.MEŠ)

58). *šá* ^{d}*É-a u* ^{d}*Asal-lú-hi te-ṣir-ma itti*(KI) *ili*(DINGIR)-*ka u* ^{d}*ištari* (XV)-*ka*

59). *ta*-⌜X (X) X X (X)⌝ *arkat*(⌜EGIR⌝) *ramāni*(NÍ)-*ka i-par-ra-su-ka*

60). *uṣurta*(GIŠ.⌜HUR⌝) [*an-ni-t*]*ú šá e*-⌜*ṣi*⌝-*ru*$^{!}$-[*k*]*a te-ṣir*

Line 61

ÉN ^{MUL}Mar.gíd.da.an.na ^{MUL}*ereqqi šá-ma-mi šá ni-ir-šá* ^{d}*Nin-urta*

A). ÉN ^{MUL}Mar.gíd.da.⌈an$^{?}$⌉.n[a]$^{?}$ [MA]R.GÍD.D[A]-*mi šá ni-ir*$^{!}$(*ni*)-*šá* ^{d}*Nin-urta*

b). [^{MUL}Mar.gí]d.da.an.na ^{MUL}MAR.GÍD.DA *šá-ma-mi šá ni-ir-šá* ^{d}*Nin-urta*

Line 62

ma-šad-da-šá ^{d}*Mar[duk bu-b]a*$^{!}$*-tu*$^{!}$*-šá mārāt* ^{d}*A-nim šá šamê ellūti*

A). *ma-šad-da-šá* ^{d}*Mar[duk bu-b]a*$^{!}$*-tu*$^{!}$*-šá* *mārat*(D[UMU.MUNUS]) ⌈^{d}⌉*A-nim šá* AN-*e* KÙ.MEŠ

b). *ma-šad-da-šá* ⌈^{d}⌉[ ] / [DUM]U.MUNUS.MEŠ ^{d}*A-nu-*⌈*um*⌉ *šá* AN-*e* KÙ.MEŠ

Line 63

ana pān ^{d}*Aš-šur*^{KI} *nap-ha-tu*$_{4}$ *ana pān Bābili*^{KI} *pānū-šá šak-nu*

A). *ana* IGI ^{d}*Aš-šur*^{KI} ⌈*nap-ha*⌉-[ ] *ana* IGI K[Á. .R]A^{KI} IGI-*šá šak-nu*

b). *ana* IGI AN.ŠÁR *nap-ha-tu*$_{4}$ *ana* IGI KÁ.DINGIR.RA IGI-*šá* [ ]

Line 64

ki-i annanna mār annanna i-bal-lu-ṭu i-šal-li-mu mu-šu lib-lam-ma šutta lūmur

A). *ki-i* NENNI A ⌈NENNI$^{!}$⌉ *i-ba[l-l]u-[ṭ]u i-š[al- m]u-šu lib-lam*$^{!}$(*kid*)-*ma* MÁŠ.GE$_{6}$ IGI

b). [NENN]I *i-bal-lu-ṭu i-šal-li-mu mu-šu lib-lam-ma* MÁŠ.GE$_{6}$ [ ]

Line 65

KA.INIM.MA EŠ.BAR IGI$^{!}$.[DU$_{8}$]

A). KA.INIM.MA EŠ.⌈BAR⌉ IGI$^{!}$(DÙ).[DU$_{8}$]

b). [ ] EŠ.BAR [ ]

Line 65a

DÙ.DÙ.BI *š[e-e]m ša* 1 *har-bi teleqqi ištēnā te-bi-ir*

A). DÙ.DÙ.BI *š[e-e]m ša* 1 ⌈*har*⌉-*bi* TI-*qí* 1.TA.ÀM *te-bi-ir*

b). [ ] *har-bi* TI-*qí* 1.TA.ÀM *te-bi-ir*

Line 66

še bi mi tu na kar rib $^{L[Ú]}$*ṣehru šá sinništa là īdû iṭên ana pān* ^{MUL}*ereqqi*

A). *še bi mi tu na* ⌜X⌝ $^{L[Ú]}$[TU]R *šá* MÍ *là* ZU-*u* ÀRA-*en* *ana* IGI ^{MUL}MAR.GÍD.DA

b). *še* *mi tu na kar rib* TUR ÀRA-*e*[*n*] / [.D]A

Line 67

ūra tašabbit mê ell[*ūti*] *tasallah su-ur-ta tu-sa-ar nignaq* ^{ŠIM}*burāši u maṣhati tašakkan*

A). ÙR SAR ⌜A.MEŠ⌝ KÙ.M[EŠ] SUD *su-ur-ta tu-sa-ar* NÍG.NA ^{ŠIM}LI *u* ZÌ.MAD.GÁ GAR-*an*

b). ÙR SAR A KÙ SUD *su-ur-ta tu-sa-ár* NÍG.NA ^{ŠIM}LI *u* ZÌ.MAD.[ ]

Line 68

šipta šalāšīšu tamannu itti ^{LÚ}*mamman là tadabbub tanâl-ma šutta tammar*

A). ÉN 3-*šú* ⌜ŠID⌝-*nu* KI ^{LÚ}N[A].ME *là* DU_{11}.DU_{11}-*ub* NÁ-*ma* MÁŠ.GE_6 IGI

b). [K]I NA.ME *là* DU_{11}.DU_{11}-*ub* NÁ-*ma* MÁŠ.GE_6 IGI-*mar*

Line 69

šum-ma mim-ma nadin-šú marṣu iballuṭ šum-ma mim-ma là nadin-šú marṣu imât

A). *šum-ma mim-ma* SUM-*šú* GI[G T]I *šum-ma mim-ma là* SUM-*šú* GIG ÚŠ

b). *šum*$_4$*-ma mim-ma* SUM-*šú* GIG TI / [-*š*]*ú* GIG BA.ÚŠ

Line 70

šum-ma ana epēš ṣibûti teppuš šum$_4$-ma mim-ma nadin-šú ṣibût-su ikaššad šum$_4$-ma mim-ma là nadin-šú là ikaššad

A). *šum-ma ana* DÙ-*eš* Á.ÁŠ DÙ-*u*[*š mi*]*m-ma* SUM-*šú* ÁŠ-*su* KUR-*ád* *là* SUM-*šú là* KUR-*ád*

b). *šum$_4$-ma ana* DÙ-*eš* Á.ÁŠ DÙ-*uš* / [-*š*]*ú* *kašād*(KUR-*ád*) *ṣibûti*(ÁŠ) *šum$_4$-ma mim-ma* *là* SUM-*šú là* KUR-*ád* AŠ

Line 71

ÉN *at*$^!$-*ti* ^{MUL}mar.gíd.da.an.na *šá šamê* KI-*ti ni-ir-ki* ^{d}*Nin-urta ma-šad-da-ki* ^{d}*Marduk*

A). ÉN *at*$^!$(*mar*)-*ti* ^{MUL}Mar.gíd.d[a.an.n]a *šá* AN-*e* KI-*ti* *ni-ir-ki* ^{d}*Nin-urta ma-šad-da-ki* ^{d}*Marduk*

b). [.gí]d.da.an.na *šá* AN-*e* GAL-ti $^{: at-ti}$ *ni-ir-ki* ^{d}*Nin-urta ma-šad-da-ka* ^{d}*Marduk*

Line 72

[*bu*]-*ba-tu-ki mārāt* ^{d}*A-n*[*im*] *šá šamê ellūti ina māt Aš-šur*^{KI} *nap-ha-ti*

A). [*bu*]-*ba-tu-ki mārat*(DUMU.MUNUS) ^{d}*A-n*[*im*] *šá* AN-*e* KÙ.MEŠ *ina* KUR *Aš-šur*^{KI} *nap-ha-ti*

b). [DUMU.MUNU]S.MEŠ ^{d}*A-nu* *šá* AN-*e* KÙ.MEŠ *ina* KUR *Aš-šur*^{KI} *nap-ha-a-tú*

Line 73

ina Bābili^{KI} *pānū-ki šaknū ina* [*b*]*a-li-ki mītu là imât ù* ^{LÚ}*balṭu har-ra-an là iṣabbat*

A). *ina* KÁ.DINGIR.RA^{KI} IGI-*ki* GAR-*nu* *ina* [*b*]*a-li-ki* AD_6 *là* ÚŠ *ù* TI *har-ra-an là* DAB-*bat*

b). *ina* KÁ.DINGIR.MEŠ IGI-*ka tašakkan*(GAR-*an*) / [A]D_6 *là* BA.ÚŠ *ù* ^{LÚ}TI.LA KASKAL *là* DAB-*bat*

Line 74

š[*um-m*]*a harrān te-ba-ku* ⌜*ṣi*⌝-[*bu-t*]*i akaššad mim-ma li-di-nu-ni*

A). *š*[*um-m*]*a* KASKAL *te-ba-ku* ⌜*ṣi*⌝-[*bu-t*]*i* KUR-*ád mim-ma* *li-di-nu-ni*

b). [ÁŠ] KUR-*ád mim-ma* *lid-di-nu-ni*

Line 75

šum$_4$-ma harrān te-ba-ku ṣi-[bu-ti] là akaššad mim-ma lim-hu-ru-nin-ni

A). *š[um-m]a [ ] te-[b]a-ku ṣi-[bu-ti] là* KUR-*ád mim-ma lim-hu-ru-nin-ni*

b). *šum$_4$-ma* KASKAL *te-ba-ku* ÁŠ *là* KUR-*ád mim-ma lim-hur-ú-in-ni*

Line 76

[KA.IN]IM.MA *šumma amēlu ana ṣibûti te-bi purussâ amāri*

A). [KA.IN]IM.MA *ana* ⸢Á⸣.[ ] ⸢*te*⸣-*bi* EŠ.BAR IGI.DU$_8$

b). [ ] DIŠ NA *ana* Á.ÁŠ *te-bi* EŠ.BAR IGI.DU$_8$

Line 77

ÉN ^{MUL}*ereqqu mārat* ^{d}*A-[n]im rabītu kal-lat É-kur kul-lul-tu*

A). ⸢ÉN⸣ ^{MUL}MAR.⸢GÍD.DA⸣ DUMU.M[UNUS -*n*]*im* GAL-*tu$_4$* *kal-lat É-kur* ⸢*kul*⸣-[*lu*]*l-tu*

b). [ ]⸢*A*⸣-*nu* GAL-*tú* *kal-lat É-kur kut-*⸢*tùm*⸣-*tú*

c). ÉN ^{MUL}MAR.GÍD.DA DUMU.MUNUS ^{d}*A*-[ ] / *É-kur kal-lat kul-lul-tu$_4$*

Line 78

mu-šim-tu šá šīmāti u mu-za-a'-iz-tu šá kurummāti at-ti

A). *mu-šim-*⸢*tu$_4$*⸣ *šá* NAM.[ ]-*iz*$^!$([*i*]*t*)-*tu šá* {ŠE}.PAD.MEŠ *at-ti*

b). *mu-šim-tú šá* NAM.MEŠ *mu-za-a'-iz-tu šá* PAD.MEŠ *at-ti*

c). *mu-š[im-*] / *u mu-za-a'-iz-tu$_4$ šá* PAD.HÁ *a*[*t*$^!$-]

Line 79

šum-ma mim-ma ki-⸢*a*⸣-[*am šá*] *damqāti zitta lid-di-nu-ni*

A). *šum-ma mim-ma ki-*⸢*a*⸣-[*am šá*] SIG$_5$.MEŠ HA.LA *lid-di-nu-ni*

b). [H]A.LA *lid-di-nu-ú-ni*

Line 80

šum-ma mim-ma ki-a-am šá ahīti ṣi-i-tu$_4$ li-ṣi

A). *šum-ma mim-ma ki-a-a*[*m*] BAR-*tì ṣi-i-ti li-ṣi*

b). *šum$_4$-ma mim-ma ki-a-am šá* BAR-*tì ṣi-i-tu$_4$ li-*{*še*}*-ṣi*

Line 81

KA.INIM.MA EŠ.BAR IGI.DU$_8$

A). KA.INIM.MA EŠ.BAR IGI.DU$_8$

b). [ ] EŠ.BAR IGI.DU8

Line 81a

c). KA.INIM.MA MÁŠ.GE$_6$ HUL SIG$_5$.GA.KE$_4$

Line 81b

c). DÙ.DÙ.BI *mê*(A.MEŠ) *ana pān*(IGI) ^{MUL}*ereqqi*(MAR.GÍD.DA)

Line 81c

c). *tanaddi*(ŠUB-*di*) *šipta*(ÉN) *šalāšīšu*(3-*šú*) *tamannu*(ŠID)-*ma tanâl* (NÁ)-*ma*

Line 81d

c). *purussâ*(EŠ.BAR) *šutta*(MÁŠ.GE$_6$) *ta-am-mar*

Line 81e

[DÙ.DÙ].BI *mušīta tu-šam-ša*$^{!}$ GÌR$^{?}$ MAN *ka taparras*

A). [DÙ.DÙ].BI GE$_6$ *tu-šam-ša*$^{!}$(*ni-ši*) GÌR$^{?}$ MAN *ka* TAR-*a*[*s*]

b). [-*a*]*s*

REVERSE

<u>Column III</u>

Line 82

e-nu-ma nišū ṣal-lu-ma qu-lu šaknu e-diš-ši-ka ina ūri tazzaz-ma

A). *e-nu-ma* UN.MEŠ *ṣal-lu-ma* ⌈*qu-lu*⌉ GAR-*nu e-diš-ši-ka ina* ÙR GUB-*az-ma*

b). *e-nu-ma* UN.MEŠ *ṣal-lu-ma qu-lu* ⌈GAR$^{!}$⌉-[ ]

Line 83

mê ellūti ana pān ^{MUL}*ereqqi šalāšīšu ana pān* ^{d}*E-ru-*⌈*ú*⌉*-a šalāšīšu*$^{!}$ *til-lih maṣhata*

A). A.MEŠ KÙ.MEŠ *ana* IGI ^{MUL}MAR.GÍ[D.D]A 3-*šú ana* IGI ^{d}*E-ru-*⌈*ú*⌉*-a* ⌈3$^{!}$⌉-*šú til-lih* ZÌ.MAD.GÁ

b). [ ] ^{MUL}MAR.GÍD.DA 3-*šú ana* IGI ^{d}*E*-[ ]

Line 84

tanassuk e-nu-ma tassukū an-nam taqabbi tanâl-⌜*ma*⌝ *purussâ tammar*

A). ŠUB-*uk* *e-nu-ma* ŠUB-*ku* *a*[*n*$^{!}$]-*nam* DUG$_4$.GA NÁ-⌜*ma*⌝ EŠ.BAR IGI.DU$_8$

b). [-*u*]*k* *e-nu-ma* ŠUB-*ku* *an-*⌜*nam*⌝ DUG$_4$.G[A]

Line 85

ÉN ^{d}*Nin-líl be-let šamê u erṣetim um-mi ilāni rabûti*

A). ^{d}*Nin-líl be-let* AN-⌜*e ù*⌝ KI-*tim* AMA DINGIR.MEŠ GAL.MEŠ

A$_1$[6]). ÉN ^{d}*Nin-líl be-let* AN *u* KI-*tim* *um-mi* DINGIR.[ ]

Line 86

šá ina ba-li-šá ^{d}*En-líl be-e*[*l*] *šīmāti la* NAM.MEŠ *ki-i annanna mār annanna*

A). *šá ina ba-li-šá* ^{d}*En-líl be-e*[*l* N]AM.MEŠ *la* NAM.MEŠ *ki-i* NENNI A NENNI

D). [. . . . .]-*lu$_4$* N[AM$^{?}$.]

A$_1$). *šá ina ba-li-ša* ^{d}*En-líl be-el*$^{!}$(*lit*) NAM.MEŠ [ ] / *ki-i* NENNI A NENNI

Line 87

ṣibût-su i-kaš-šá-du kakkaba ištu imitti-ia$_5$ lil-su-ma-am-ma ana šumēli-ia lītiq

A). ÁŠ-*su* *i-kaš-šá-du* MUL [T]A ZAG-*ia$_5$* *lil-su-ma-am-ma* *ana* GÙB-*ia* DIB-*iq*

D). [T]A$^{!}$ XV-*ia* ⌜*lil*⌝-*s*[*u*]-*m*[*a*$^{?}$-]

A$_1$). ÁŠ-*su* *kaš-du* MUL TA ZAG-*ia$_5$* ⌜*lil*⌝-*su*-[ ]

Line 88

KA.INIM.MA KA.AŠ.BAR BAR.RE DÙ.DÙ.BI *še'a rabâ teleqqi* [LÚ]*ṣehru šá sinništa là īdû*

A). KA.INIM.MA KA.AŠ.BAR BAR.RE DÙ.DÙ.BI ŠE GAL TI-*qí* [LÚ]TUR *šá* MÍ *là* ZU

D). [.M]A KA.AŠ.BAR BAR.RE ŠE GAL TI-⌈*qí*⌉ [ ]

A_1[2]). KÌD.⌈KÌD⌉.BI ŠE GA[L -*q*]*í* [LÚ]TUR *ša* MÍ *là* ZU

Line 89

ina ūmi šemî ú-ta-lal i-ṭe₄-en-ma ina mušīti ina ú-ri ana pān [MUL]*ereqqi*

A). *ina* U_4 ŠE.GA ⌈*ú*⌉*-ta-lal* ⌈*i*⌉*-ṭe₄-en-ma ina* GE_6 *ina* ÙR *ana* IGI [MUL]MAR.GÍD.DA

D). [.G]A *ú-tal-lal i-ṭe₄-en ina* GE_6 *ina* Ù[R]

A_1). *ina* U_4 ŠE.GA [ ] / *i-ṭe₄-en-ma i-na* GE_6 *i-na ú-ri ana* IGI [MUL]MAR.GÍD.D[A]

Line 90

nignaq [ŠIM]*burāši u maṣhati an-ni-tú* [LÚ]*ṣehru ú-nam-mar-ma ahâti izzaz*

A). NÍG.NA [ŠIM]< > *u* ZÌ.MAD.GÁ *an-*[*n*]*i-tú* [LÚ]TUR *ú-nam-mar-ma* BAR.BAR GUB.BA

D). [ ]LI *u* ZÌ.MAD.GÁ [LÚ]TUR *ú-na*[*m-*]

A_1). [ ] / *ù* ZÌ.MAD.GÁ *an-ni-tú* [LÚ]TUR *ú-nam-mar-ma* BAR.[ ]

Line 91

šipta an-ni-tú šalāšīšu ana pān [MUL]*ereqqi tamannu mê ellūti tanaqqi-ma purussâ tammar*

A). ÉN *an-ni-tú* 3-*šú ana* ⌈IGI⌉ [MUL]MAR.GÍD.DA ŠID-*nu* A.MEŠ KÙ.MEŠ BAL-*qí-ma* EŠ.BAR IGI.DU_8

D). [-*t*]*ú* ⌈3⌉-*šú ana* IGI [MUL]MAR.GÍD.DA ŠI[D-]

A_1). ÉN *an-ni-tú* ⌈3⌉-*šú ana* IGI [MUL]MAR.GÍD.DA ŠID-*nu* A.MEŠ KÙ.MEŠ BAL-[ ]

92^{A}). ÉN *ilānu*(DINGIR.[ME]Š$^{!}$) *rabûtu*(GAL.MEŠ) *šu-ut* ^{d}*A-*[*n*]*im* *ilānu*(DINGIR.MEŠ) *rabûtu*(GAL.MEŠ) *šu-ut* ^{d}*En-líl*(50) *ilānu* (DINGIR.MEŠ) *rabûtu*(GAL.MEŠ) *šu-ut* ^{d}*É-a*

93). *šu-ut* ^{d}*A-nim al-si-ku-n*[*u-š*]*i šu-ut* ^{d}*Enlil*(50) *na-as-hu-ra-ni*

94). *šu-ut* ^{d}*É-a kīma*(⸢GIM⸣) ⸢*dun-qi*⸣*-ku-nu qu-la-ni*

95). *ana-ku annanna*(NENNI) *šá a* [*n*]*a a* [*na*$^{?}$] *lu-ma-ši-ku-nu šit-ku-nu pa-nu-ú-a*

96). *an-na kīna*(G[I.N]A) *ap*$^{!}$(*si*)*-la-*⸢*a*⸣*-nin-ni-ma ina libbi*(ŠÀ) *kakkab* (MUL.MEŠ) *šamê*(AN-*e*) *là manûti*(ŠID.MEŠ)

97). *kab-bu-ti* [. . . *ṣar-h*]*u*$^{!}$*-ti ṣar-ru-ti mi-ih-rat irāti*(GAB MEŠ)*-ku-nu*

98). *kakkabu*(MUL) *ištu*(T[A$^{!}$) *imittīja*(ZAG.MU) *li*]*-su-ma-am-ma a-na šumēlīja*(150.MU) *lītiq*(DIB-*iq*)

99). ⸢*šum*⸣*-m*[*a ana ṣibûti*(Á.ÁŠ) *ištu*(TA)] *arkatīja*([EG]IR.MU) *a-na pānīja*(IGI.MU) *lītiq*(DIB-*iq*)

---

100). K[A.INIM.MA KA.AŠ.BAR BAR.R]E {DIŠ} DÙ.DÙ.BI *še-am ša* 1 *har-bi teleqqi*(TI-*qí*)

101). ⸢X⸣ [. . . . . .] ⸢X⸣ *ir pap*$^{?}$ *ir* ^{LÚ}*ṣehru*(TUR) *šá sinništa*(MÍ) *là īdû* (ZU) *iṭên*(ÀRA-*en*)

102). *ana pān*(IG[I) ^{MUL}*ereqqi*(MAR.GÍD.DA) *nignaq*(NÍG.N]A) ^{ŠIM}*burāši*(LI) *tašakkan*(GAR-*an*) GÌR$^{?}$ MAN$^{!}$ *ka taparras*(TAR-*as*)

103). ⸢X⸣ [. . . . . .] *šipta*(⸢ÉN⸣) *šalāšīšu*(3-*šú*) *ana pān*(IGI) ^{MUL}*ereqqi* (MAR.GÍD.DA) *tamannu*(ŠID)*-ma*

104). *šu*[*m-ma kakkabu*(MUL) *ištu*(TA) *imitti*(ZAG)*-k*]*a a-na šumēli* (150)*-ka ītiq*(DIB-*iq*) *damiq*(SIG$_{15}$)

105). *šu*[*m-ma kakkabu*(MUL) *ištu*(TA) *šumēli*(150)*-k*]*a a-na imitti* (ZAG)*-ka ītiq*(DIB-*iq*) *là damiq*(SIG$_{15}$)

106). *šum-m*[*a kakkabu*(MUL) *ištu*(TA) *pāni*(IGI)*-k*]*a a-na arkati* (EGIR)*-ka ītiq*(DIB-*iq*) *là damiq*(SIG$_{15}$)

107). *šum-m*[*a kakkabu*(MUL) *ištu*(TA) *arkati*(EGIR)*-k*]*a a-na pāni* (IGI)*-ka ītiq*(DIB-*iq*) *damiq*(SIG$_{15}$)

108). *šum-*[*ma* . . .] ⸢X⸣ ^{MUL}*ereqqi*(MAR.GÍD.DA) *ītiq*(DIB-*iq*) *damiq* (SIG$_{15}$)

109). *šum-*[*ma* X X] *šakin*(⸢GAR⸣)*-ma ana libbi*(ŠÀ) ^{MUL}*ereqqi*(MAR. GÍD.DA) *īrub*(TU) *damiq*(SIG$_{15}$)

---

110). ÉN [*a*]*l-si-ku-nu-ši ilānu*(DINGIR.MEŠ) *dajānu*(DI.KU$_5$.MEŠ) *ina šamê*(AN-*e*) *rabûti*(GAL.MEŠ)

111). *ina s*[*u*$^?$*-p*]*e*$^?$*-e šu*$^!$*-ke-ni ak-ta-nar-rab-ku-nu-ši*

112). [*di-p*]*a*$^!$*-ru* ⌜*na*⌝*-mir-tu šá qé-reb šá-ma-me* : *ana* ⌜*nu*⌝*-ri-ku-nu ṣu-mu-rat mit-har-tú*

113). [*ana d*]*a*$^!$*-a-nu-ti-ku-nu nišū*(UN.M[EŠ) *i*]*-qu-lu* : *ana purussê*(EŠ. ⌜BAR⌝)*-ku-nu i-kan-nu-uš en-šu*

114). *ilānu*(DINGIR.MEŠ) *da-a-a-nu šá* [*l*]*a innennû*(BAL-*ú*) *qí-bit-su-un*$^!$

115). *ina šat mu-ši an-né-e mê*(A.MEŠ) *nagbi*(IDIM) *ellūti*(KÙ.MEŠ) *uš-te-še-ra ana pu-ut alpi*(⌜GU$_4$$^{!}$⌝)

116). *dīn*(DI)*-ku-nu ki-na u purussâ*(EŠ.BAR) *ilūti*(DINGIR-*ti*)*-ku-nu rabīti*(GAL-*ti*) *lu-mur-ma qa-ba-a lu-*⌜*uš*⌝*-kun*

117). *šum-ma annanna*(NENNI) *mār*(A) *annanna*(NENNI) *ṣibût*(ÁŠ)*-su i-kaš-šá-du alpu*(GU$_4$) *purussâ*(EŠ.BAR) *lid-di-na* TU$_6$ ÉN

---

118). DÙ.DÙ.BI *ina ūmi*(U$_4$) *šemî*(ŠE.GA) *tal-ta-ad-da-ad* ^{DUG}*lahanna* (LA.HA.AN) *ši* ⌜*šu* (X)⌝ *mu teleqqi*(TI-*qí*)

119). ^{LÚ}*ṣehru*(TUR) *šá sinništa*(MÍ) *là īdû*(ZU-*u*) *ina nāri*(ÍD) *mê*(A. MEŠ) *i-sab-ba nignaq*(NÍG.NA) ^{ŠIM}*burāši*(LI) *u maṣhati*(ZÌ. MAD.GA)

Column IV

120). *ana pān*(IGI) *ilāni*(DINGIR.MEŠ) *mušīti*(GE$_6$-*tì*) *tasarraq* (DUB$^!$(UM)*-aq*) *šikāra (rēštâ)*(KAŠ.SAG) *tanaqqi*(BAL-*qí*) *mê* (A.MEŠ) *šu-nu-te tanašši*(ÍL)*-ma*

121). *šipta*(ÉN) *šalāšīšu*(3-*šú*) *tamannu*(ŠID-*nu*) *ana pu-ut alpi*(GU$_4$) *rab-ṣi šalāšīšu*(3-*šú*) *tanaqqi*(BAL-*qí*)*-ma purussâ*(EŠ.BAR) *tammar*(IGI.DU$_8$)

---

122). *šum$_4$-ma alpu*(GU$_4$) *is-su-us-ma it-bi kašād*(KUR-*ad*) *ṣibûti*(ÁŠ)

123). *šum$_4$-ma alpu*(GU$_4$) *is-su-us-ma là it-bi là kašād*(KUR-*ad*) *ṣibûti* (ÁŠ)

124). *šum$_4$-ma alpu*(GU$_4$) *itbi*(ZI)*-ma lēt*(TE)*-su ana imitti*(15)*-šú iddi* (ŠUB) *là kašād*(KUR-*ad*) *ṣibûti*(ÁŠ)

125). *šum$_4$-ma alpu*(GU$_4$) *itbi*(ZI)*-ma lēt*(TE)*-su ana šumēli*(150)*-šú iddi*(ŠUB) *kašād*(KUR-*ad*) *ṣibûti*(ÁŠ)

126). *šum$_4$-ma alpu*(GU$_4$) *šinnē*(ZÚ.MEŠ)*-šú im-ruq-ma it-bi kašād* (KUR-*ad*) *ṣibûti*(ÁŠ)

127).	*šum$_4$-ma alpu*(GU$_4$) *šinnē*(ZÚ.MEŠ)-*šú im-ruq-ma là it-bi là kašād*(KUR-*ad*) *ṣibûti*(ÁŠ)
128).	*šum$_4$-ma alpu*(GU$_4$) *itbi*(ZI)-*ma ana pāni*(IGI)-*šú illik*(GIN) *kašād* (KUR-*ad*) *ṣibûti*(ÁŠ)
129).	*šum$_4$-ma alpu*(GU$_4$) *itbi*(ZI)-*ma ana arkati*(EGIR)-*šú illik*(GIN) *là kašād*(KUR-*ad*) *ṣibûti*(ÁŠ)
130).	*šum$_4$-ma alpu*(GU$_4$) *itbi*(ZI)-*ma ana imitti*(ZAG)-*šú illik*(GIN) *là kašād*(KUR-*ad*) *ṣibûti*(ÁŠ)
131).	*šum$_4$-ma alpu*(GU$_4$) *itbi*(ZI)-*ma ana šumēli*(150)-*šú illik*(GIN) *kašād*(KUR-*ad*) *ṣibûti*(ÁŠ)
132).	[*šu*]*m$_4$*-⸢*ma*⸣ *alpu*(⸢GU$_4$⸣) *itbi*(⸢ZI⸣)-*ma is-si kašād*(KUR-*ad*) *ṣibûti* (ÁŠ)
133).	[*šum$_4$-ma alpu*(GU$_4$) *itbi*(ZI)-*m*]*a hu-ru-up-pa-šú ušaqqi*(LAL-*qí*) *kašād*(KUR-*ad*) *ṣibûti*(ÁŠ)
134).	[*šum$_4$-ma alpu*(GU$_4$) *it-bi*(ZI)-*m*]*a hu-ru-up-pa-šú uš-ta-píl šu-uz-zu*-⸢*qu*⸣ [*là*] *kašād*(KUR-*ad*) *ṣibûti*(ÁŠ)
135).	[*šum$_4$-ma alpu*(GU$_4$) *itbi*(ZI)-*m*]*a eperē*(SAHAR.HÁ) *ana muhhi* (UGU)-*šú is-lu là kašād*(KUR-*ad*) *ṣibûti*(ÁŠ)
136).	[*šum$_4$-ma*] *alpu*(⸢GU$_4$⸣) *itbi*([Z]I)-[*m*]*a ina qaran*(SI) *imitti*(ZAG)-*šú eperē*(SAHAR.HÁ) *is-lu kašād*(KUR-*ad*) *ṣibûti*(ÁŠ)
137).	*šum$_4$-ma alpu*(GU$_4$) *itbi*(ZI)-*ma ina qaran*(SI) *šumēli*(150)-*šú eperē*(SAHAR.HÁ) *is-lu là kašād*(KUR-*ad*) *ṣibûti*(ÁŠ)
138).	*šum$_4$-ma alpu*(GU$_4$) *itbi*(ZI)-*ma ina šēpē*(GÌR^{II})-*šú mah*-⸢*ra*⸣-*a-ti eperē*(SAHAR.HÁ) *ana arkati*(EGIR)-*šú is-lu là kašād*(KUR-*ad*) *ṣibûti*(ÁŠ)
139).	*gabarî*(GABA.RI) *É-sa-bad šà-ṭír* ⸢$^{m!d!}$⸣*Nabû*(PA$^!$(ÁŠ))-*šab-ši* ^{LÚ}*šamallû*(ŠAMAN.LÁ) *ṣehru*(TUR)
140).	*mār*(DUMU) ^{md}*Nabû*(PA)-*ēriba*(SU) ^{LÚ}*ṭupšarru*(A.BA)

* * * * *

OBVERSE

Column I

1).	[Incantation: "O] merciful [goddess], the one who heals the dying;
2).	[whose favourable glance] (is) life, and whose favourable attention (brings) well-being.
3).	[The wise woman] of the gods, (and) the controller of mankind.
4).	[The holder] of the cable of the circumference of heaven and earth;

5). [the holder] of the great cable of Esharra (Enlil's cosmic abode).

6). Your position is pre-eminent in heaven. Amongst the goddesses your head is high(est).

7). Anu, Enlil, and Ea, the gods, your fathers,

8). cannot establish the command [without] you.

9). [The exalted creator], in whose absence mankind cannot be created,

10). [and the oracular decision(s)] of heaven and earth cannot be decided.

11). [I myself], the slave, the one who fears you, [called out to] you.

12). I knelt before you in supplication [on account of the difficulty] confronting me.

13-16). [(Previously) you took pity upon (lit., had pity for)] me, and you looked after me [(regarding) the decision of] your great [divinity] as to whether he will recover. [(Namely,) whether] you[!] will allow (lit. to cause) [X], the son of Y, this patient who is ailing, to recover (lit., to rise) [from] this [disease]. You can intercede (for him) to the gods, your fathers[!], and

17). the gods, your fathers[!], will pay attention [to] your august [speech].

18). [. . . .] . they will spare him, and they will allow (lit., cause) (him) to walk about the street(s) of his city in good health.

19). [Just as] (previously) you took pity upon me, and looked after [me] (regarding) the decision of your great divinity,

20). (so, this time) send me the (favourable) decision of your great divinity, and I will pronounce (it) (lit., cause it to leave my mouth)!"

---

21). Incantation: "O merciful goddess, the one who heals the dying;

22). whose favourable glance (is) life, and whose favourable attention (brings) well-being.

23). The wise woman of the gods, (and) the controller of mankind.

24). The holder of the cable of the circumference of <heaven> and earth;

25). the holder of the [great] cable of Esharra.

26). Your position is pre-eminent in heaven. Amongst the goddesses your head is high(est).

27). Anu, [Enlil, and] Ea, the gods, your fathers,

28). cannot establish the command without [you].

29). The exalted creator, in whose absence mankind cannot be created,

30). and the oracular decision(s) of heaven <and> earth cannot be decided.

31). I myself, the slave, the one who fears you, called out to you.

32). I knelt before you in supplication on account of the difficulty confronting me.

33-34). (Previously) you took pity upon me, and you looked after me (regarding) the decision of your great divinity about a dying man. (Namely,) whether X, the son of Y, who is ailing (from) . . . disease, and

35). whose path to the Underworld is being hastened;

36). for whom the Anunnaki, who establish the boundary of . ., raise (i.e, produce) the path of the Land of No Return (i.e., the Underworld);

37-38). whose personal god and personal goddess release (prematurely) for him the day of his fate (lit., his day and his destiny); who is proceeding down (this) path, and going away on a journey of no return (i.e., is dying);

39). he will be deprived of the street(s) of his city, and he will never tread (them again).

40). Just as (previously) you took pity upon me, and looked after me (regarding) the decision of your great divinity,

41). (so, this time) send me the (favourable) decision of your great divinity, and I will pronounce (it)!"

<u>Column II</u>

42). Incantation rubric: (It is the text) [to see] an oracular [decision. Its ritual:] Before [. . . . you place]. You libate beer. You draw up two tablets (lit., you tie up two 'bindings').

43). Before the [. .] star . . . . [. . . .] you place. You will see an oracular decision.

---

44). Incantation: "O you stars of the night; Enbiluh; Ninbiluh; Enbiluhha;

45). [and] Night, the veiled bride; Ea, [the king of the Apsu], the support of Eridu;

46). the Sibitti, the divine Seven, who dwell in the heavens, the pure [gods]. (Regarding) myself, your (pl.) servant,

47). allow (lit., cause) me to speak with my personal god (and) my personal goddess and, either may they pass judgement (as to whether or not) I will be weak (i.e., remain ill), or may they make the oracular decision concerning me, (namely, whether or not) I will be strong (i.e., recover)!"

---

48). Incantation rubric: (It is the text) [to see] an oracular decision (and/or) a dream.

48a-49). Its ritual: [You set out] a censer of juniper during the night, before the stars of the night. You recite this incantation three times over (a piece of) tamarisk.

50). You place [. . . . . .]. At the head of your bed

51). [. . . .] You draw (your) own personal god (out) of cheap scented flour. You lie down, and you will see an oracular decision.

---

52) [Incantation:] "I am [the (ritually) bathed] of Ea (and) the messenger of. Asalluhi. O gods of the night . [. . . . (. .)];

53). [Enbiluh]; Ninbiluh; the gods, the lords of the night; Night, the [veiled] bride;

54). [Ea], the king of the Apsu, the support of Eridu; the Sibitti, the divine Seven, who dwell in the heavens, [the pure] gods.

55). (Regarding) myself, your servant, allow me to speak with my personal god (and) my personal goddess and, either may they pass judgement (as to whether or not) I will be weak (i.e., remain ill), (or) [may they make] the oracular decision concerning me!"

---

56). Incantation rubric: (It is the text) to speak with his personal god and his personal goddess, and to learn (i.e., discover) his future.

57-59). Its ritual: You cleanse yourself according to the rules$^{?}$ for a pure man and a pure woman. You draw sketches of Ea and Asalluhi. You . (.) . . (.) with your personal god and your personal goddess. They will decide your own future for you.

60). You draw [this] sketch which I drew for you (accompanying diagram on the tablet).

---

61). Incantation: "The Wain constellation, the waggon of the heavens: whose yoke (is) Ninurta;

62). whose pole (is) Marduk; (and) whose axles (are) the daughters of Anu of the pure heavens;

63). who rises before Ashur, (and) sets its face (lit., faces) before Babylon.

64). May Night bring me (the oracular decision as to) whether (or not) X, the son of Y, will live (and) be well. May I see a dream!"

---

65). Incantation rubric: (It is the text) to see an oracular decision.

65a). Its ritual: You take barley of one *harbu.* Once you . .

66). . . . . A youth who has not known a woman grinds (the corn). Before the Wain constellation

67). you sweep the roof. You sprinkle pure water (to) make a circle. You set out a censer of juniper and cheap scented flour.

68). You recite the (above) incantation three times. (After performing this ritual) you (must) speak with no one. You lie down, and you will see a dream.

69). If (in the resultant dream) something is given to him - The invalid will recover. If something is not given to him - The invalid will die.

70). If you are performing (this ritual) for achieving a desire, (then) if they give him something - He will achieve his purpose. If they do not give him anything - He will not achieve (his purpose).

---

71). Incantation: "O you[!] Wain constellation of the . . heavens: your yoke (is) Ninurta; your pole (is) Marduk;

72). (and) your axles (are) the daughters of Anu of the pure heavens. You rise in Assyria, (and)

73). set your face in Babylon. Without you the dying cannot die and the living cannot go on a journey.

74). If I will achieve my purpose on the journey I am preparing to start, may they (the dream visions) give me something!

75). If I will not achieve my purpose on the journey I am preparing to start, may they receive something from me!"

---

76). [Incantation] rubric: (It is the text) if a man (wants) to see an oracular decision upon starting out on an enterprise.

---

77). Incantation: "O Wain constellation, the eldest daughter of Anu; the veiled bride of Ekur;

78). you are the one who determines the fates, and the distributor of (Man's) food portions.

79). If (there is to be) anything thus [of] good fortune, (then) let them give me a share!

80). If (there is to be) anything thus of misfortune, (then) may expenditure go out!"

---

81). Incantation rubric: (It is the text) to see an oracular decision.

81a). Incantation rubric: It is (the text) to make a bad dream favourable.

81b-c). Its ritual: You sprinkle water in front of the Wain constellation. You recite the (above) incantation three times. You lie down, and

81d). you will see an oracular decision (and/or) a dream.

81e). Its ritual: You spend the night. You cut your . .

REVERSE

Column III

82). When people are sleeping, and there is silence, you stand all alone on the roof.

83-84). You sprinkle pure water three times before the Wain constellation (and) three times before the goddess Eru'a. You scatter cheap scented flour. When you have scattered (this flour), you say this (above incantation). You lie down, and you will see an oracular decision.

---

85). Incantation: "O Ninlil, the lady of heaven and earth; the mother of the great gods;

86). without whom Enlil, the lord of destinies, cannot . . If X, the son of Y,

87). will achieve his purpose, may a star shoot from my right, and may it pass by to my left!"

---

88). Incantation rubric: (It is the text) to make an oracular decision. Its ritual: You take full-grown (lit., large) barley. A youth who has not known a woman

89). cleanses himself on an auspicious day. He grinds (the barley). During the night, on the roof, before the Wain constellation,

90). the youth sets fire to a censer of juniper and this cheap scented flour. (Then) he stands on the outskirts (of the ritual area).

91). You recite this (above) incantation three times before the Wain constellation. You libate pure water. You will see an oracular decision.

---

92). Incantation: "O great gods, those (of the path) of Anu; O great gods, those (of the path) of Enlil; O great gods, those (of the path) of Ea.

93). I call out to you (of the path) of Anu. Those (of the path) of Enlil turn with favour to me!

94). Those (of the path) of Ea, please$^{?}$ (lit., according to your divine grace) pay attention to me!

95). (As for) myself, X, whose face is set (i.e., turned) towards . . your *lumāšu*-(stars),

96). reply to me (with) an unambiguous assent! (Thus,) from amongst the stars of heaven, (which are) innumerable,

97). glowing, [. . . shining], and twinkling (lit., flashing), (which are) in front of you (lit., confront your chests)

98). [may] a star shoot [from my right], and may it pass by to my left!

99). If [(this ritual is being performed) regarding an aim], may it (the star) pass [from] behind me to in front of me!"

---

100). [Incantation rubric: (It is the text) to make an oracular decision.] Its ritual: You take barley of one *harbu*.

101). . [. . . . . .] . . . . A youth who has not known a woman grinds (this corn).

102). You set out [a censer] of juniper before [the Wain constellation] . . . . .

103). . [. . . . . .] you recite the (above) incantation three times before the Wain constellation.

104). If [a star] passed by [from] your [right] towards your left - Favourable.

105). If [a star] passed by [from] your [left] towards your right – Unfavourable.

106). If [a star] passed by [from in front of] you to behind you - Unfavourable.

107). If [a star] passed by [from behind] you to in front of you - Favourable.

108). If [. . . .] . it passed the Wain constellation - Favourable.

109). If [. .] there was, and it entered into the Wain constellation - Favourable.

---

110). Incantation: "[I] called out to you, O gods, the judges (dwelling) in the great heavens.

111). I constantly pray to you in supplication? (and) prostration.

112). O bright torch (i.e., Shamash), which is within the heavens. (The world) strives for your(pl.) light.

113). Mankind pays attention [to] your judicial role. The weak man bows down to your(pl.) oracular decision.

114). O gods, the judges whose command cannot be altered,

115). during this night I will cause pure spring water to flow (down) onto the forehead of an ox.

116). Let me see your unambiguous verdict and the oracular decision of your great divinity, (so that) I may establish the prognosis!

117). If X, the son of Y, will achieve his purpose, let the ox (by its movements) give (him) the oracular decision!" Incantation formula.

---

118). Its ritual: You withdraw (lit., drag yourself) (to a suitable ritual site) on an auspicious day. You take a bottle . . . .

119). A youth who has not known a woman draws up water from a river. A censer of juniper and cheap scented flour

Column IV

120). you swing around (lit., scatter) before the gods of the night. You libate (first-class) beer. You lift up that (river) water, and

121). you recite the (above) incantation three times. You pour out (the water) three times onto the forehead of a recumbent ox. You will see an oracular decision.

---

122). If the ox grunted, and got up - Achievement of purpose.

123). If the ox grunted, and did not get up - Non-achievement of purpose.

124). If the ox got up, and lowered its cheek to its right - Non-achievement of purpose.

125). If the ox got up, and lowered its cheek to its left - Achievement of purpose.

126). If the ox ground its teeth, and got up - Achievement of purpose.

127). If the ox ground its teeth, and did not get up - Non-achievement of purpose.

128). If the ox got up, and went forwards (lit., to its front) - Achievement of purpose.

129). If the ox got up, and went backwards (lit., to its back) - Non-achievement of purpose.

130). If the ox got up, and went to its right - Non-achievement of purpose.

131). If the ox got up, and went to its left - Achievement of purpose.

132). If the ox got up, and lowed - Achievement of purpose.

133). [If the ox got up], and raised its hip - Achievement of purpose.

134). [If the ox got up], and lowered its hip - Great vexation. [Non]-achievement of purpose.

135). [If the ox got up], and stirred up dust in front of itself - Non-achievement of purpose.

136). [If] the ox got up, and stirred up dust with its right horn - Achievement of purpose.

137). If the ox got up, and stirred up dust with its left horn - Non-achievement of purpose.

138). If the ox got up, and stirred up dust behind itself with its front feet - Non-achievement of purpose.

---

139). Written (according to) the exemplar of Esabad (by) Nabu-shabshi, the young apprentice (scribe),

141). the son of Nabu-eriba, the scribe.

* * * * *

NOTES

Lines 1-12 and 19-20 duplicate lines 21-32 and 40-41, and have been used to amend and restore each other.

1). The two incantations are addressed to a "merciful goddess", *ìl-tu$_4$ réme-ni-tu$_4$*. This is almost certainly Gula, in whose temple the original tablet was found (see the note on line 139). Gula describes herself in line 187 of the hymn edited by W. G. Lambert (*OrNS* 36 [1967], pp. 105-132) as *[ìl-tu₄ r]éme-ni-tu₄ ᵈNin-líl a-na-ku-ma,* "I am the merciful [goddess] Ninlil"; and as *re-me-na-ku,* "I am merciful" in line 88. Both lines occur in passages recounting her healing abilities (lines 178-187 and lines 79-91 respectively). In addition, *mu-bal-li-ṭa-at mīti*(AD_6) is the Akkadian rendition of ᵈnin.tin.ug₅.ga, a name for Gula. *STT* vol. 1, p. 6 misinterpreted this epithet, describing the first two incantations of *ROP* as addressing the goddess Antum.

7). The emendation of GAL to AD[!] comes from line 27. The scribe was consistent in his 'confusion' throughout the first incantation: see lines 16-17 also.

11). *dušmû* replaces the more usual *ardu*(ÌR) in this phrase.

16). The restoration at the beginning of the line follows E. Reiner [1960a, p. 31].

She read [ibid., p. 31] *ina mahar*, with a note (n. 12) that something like this was required for the sign AD. R. Borger [1961, p. 153] mentioned that AD was in fact *-i ana.*

See the note on line 7.

17). See the note on line 7.

18). E. Reiner [1960a, p. 32] restored [DINGIR.MEŠ-*š*]*u* at the beginning of this line.

25). O. R. Gurney [1981-1982, p. 93] noted that the sign GAL[!], seen on the tablet's photograph, was now lost.

31). See the note on line 11.

33). E. Reiner [1960a, p. 32] read *mi-i-ti,* with n. 14 stating that that the sign was like *tu.* H. Hirsch [1968-1969, p. 50, n. 135] favoured the reading *mī*[*t*]*ūti.* However, a late orthographical practice was to write a long open syllable as a short closed one, by adding an extra consonant at the end, thus *mi-it-ti* for *mīti.* This practice is especially noticeable in tablets from Sultantepe (W. G. Lambert [1959], p. 125).

34). E. Reiner [1960a, p. 32 and n. 15] emended the end of the line to GIG *an-nam <mar>-ṣu-ú.*

36). E. Reiner [1960a, p. 32 and n. 16] read LÍL, stating that this had been collated, but perhaps was to be omitted.

The Anunnaki and the Mother Goddess as Mammitum are described as determining life and death in the *Epic of Gilgamesh,* Tab. 10, col. VI lines 35-38:

35). *ul-tu ik-ru-bu* [X (X)]

36). ^{d}*A-nun-na-ki* DINGIR.MEŠ GAL.MEŠ *pa*[*h-ru*]

37). ^{d}*Ma-am-me-tum ba-na-at šim-ti it-ti-šú-nu si-ma-tú i-ši*[*m-mi*]

38). *iš-tak-nu mu-ta u ba-la-*⌈*ṭa*⌉

[35] After they blessed (me) [. (.)], [36] the Anunnaki, the great gods, assembled, (and) [37] Mammetum, the creator of destiny, determines fates with them. [38] They have established death and life.

LÍL corresponds to *salā'u,* "to become ill, to enter into a critical stage of illness" [*CAD* S, *salā'u* A, pp. 96-97]. Only the stative of the *G*-stem is attested. Perhaps one could read *šá salih*(LÍL) *annanna*(NENNI), and translate as "the Anunnaki, who establish the boundary (of life) for (lit., of) the critically ill X". Another option is *sili'tu,* "illness", which often occurs in parallel with *murṣu* (*CAD* S, p. 264a).

Column II

43). E. Reiner [1960a, p. 32] read *ina* IGI MUL [X *ina*] *še-rim ana* ⌈Á X X⌉ AN at the beginning of the line. However, the sign is *mu,* not *še-*.

See page 36 on the relationship between *šuttu* and *purussû* in this text.

44). It is unclear who the triad Enbiluh, Ninbiluh, and Enbiluhha were. They surely have some astral significance, considering the context. E. Reiner [1960a, p. 32, n. 17] suggested that these may have been cryptic names for, perhaps, Sin (as the moon), Ishtar (as the planet Venus), and Shamash (as the sun).

46). The Sibitti, the "Seven", appear here as the Pleiades constellation. They were a group of benevolent gods.

47). J. V. Kinnier Wilson [1992, personal communication] suggested the reading *en-še*[!]*-ku* because *adi*(EN) *kašdāku*(KUR-*ku*), "concerning (whether or not) I will obtain", has no specified object. (Note the omens of lines 69-70, showing that the same ritual could be used to obtain an answer about one's health or sucess).

E. Reiner [1960a, p. 32] read *lu-ú te*(?)*-ba*(?)*-a*(?)*-ku* (while commenting [n. 18] that the text was *lu-ú kal na/ba* DIŠ *ku*), translating [ibid., p. 26] "so that, until I carry out my plan, they may give me a favourable decision, or (until) I get up (in the morning[?]), they may give me a favourable sign".

48-48a). These form one line on **A**.

48b-51). Both **A** and **b** contain the diagrams to be drawn, see the plates in *STT* and *UET* 7 for details.

52-53). These lines form basically the same incantation as lines 44-47. The difference being that the latter were spoken by the petitioner, and the former by the ritual expert. This is shown by the use of the 'legitimizing formula' at the beginning of line 52 (see page 121).

55). E. Reiner [1960a, p. 33] restored *ia*-[*ti*] at the beginning of this line, but see line 46.

See the note on line 47 regarding the emendation.

56). The phrase *arkata parāsu* literally means "to decide the past", often in the sense of investigating the circumstances surrounding a lawsuit or an individual's suffering, as on *Ludlul bēl nēmeqi,* Tab. 2, line 6:

6). LÚHAL *ina bi-ir ár-kàt ul ip-ru-us*

The haruspex cannot investigate (successfully my) circumstances by extispicy.

It developed the nuance of "to learn the future (by divination)" when used in connection with omens, as here (A. Goetze, *JCS* 11 [1957], p. 96, n. 4).

E. Reiner [1960a, p. 27] believed that these were direct nocturnal apparitions of the personal deities instead of dreams.

57). See O. R. Gurney [1981-1982, p. 93] for the reading *ina*!.

The translation was proposed by J. V. Kinnier Wilson [1992, personal communication].

59). E. Reiner [1960a, p. 33] read *ta-n*[*am-m*]*ar-ma,* "you will see . . . face to face" [1960a, p. 27], at the beginning of the line, but the traces do not agree.

60). O. R. Gurney [1981-1982, p. 93] read *šá e-ṣi*!*-ru lu*! *te-ṣir* at the end of the line.

The sketch is given to the right of the section lines 57-60, see the plate in *STT* for details.

61). E. Reiner [1960a, p. 33] read the beginning of the line on **A** as ÉN MUL. MAR.GÍD.DA [GIŠ.MA]R.GÍD.DA. The traces could also be read as ⌈MUL?⌉[MA]R.

MULMAR.GÍD.DA is the Great Bear, Plough, or Charles' Wain *(Ursa Major)* constellation, the "waggon" in Akkadian; and MULMAR.GÍD. DA.AN.NA usually is the Little Bear *(Ursa Minor)* constellation. W. Horowitz [1989, pp. 243-244] believed that the Sumerian word for the Little Bear constellation was adopted into Akkadian as a loan-word. In some texts, the loan-word was followed by its Akkadian translation, [(MUL)]*ereqqi šamāmi.*

Following E. Reiner [1995, p. 57, n. 237], it seems that [MUL]MAR.GÍD.DA.AN.NA has been used erronously in *ROP* for the Wain constellation. The ritual attached to lines 61-64 is performed before the Wain constellation (line 66), and the alternative incantation to lines 71-75, namely lines 77-80, addresses this constellation.

62). Anu had many daughters, and it is not clear which ones are meant here.

64). See the similar passages on *NROD,* rev. 8 and 17.

65-65a). These form one line on **A**.

69-70). These lines contain dream 'omens', presenting the relevant meanings in advance, thus dispensing with the need for an interpreter (E. Reiner [1960a], p. 31). See also lines 74-75 (in an incantation), 98-99 (in an incantation), 104-109, and 122-138. Tablet B of the *Dream-Book* contains the 'kenning' *iddinu*(SUM)-*šú,* "(If) they gave X to him" [*DB,* pp. 322-326].

70). **b**, obv. 16' has the variants (*là*) KUR-*ád* ÁŠ, "(Non-)achievement of purpose".

71-73). These lines form basically the same incantation as in lines 61-63 (see the note on line 61), except that here the constellation is addressed in the second person. **b** incorrectly uses the second masculine pronominal suffix *-ka.*

There is no ritual appended to this incantation, and E. Reiner [1960a, p. 27] believed that the one of lines 65a-68 sufficed. Instead, it has been placed with the following incantation (lines 77-80) and the two rituals on lines 81a-d and 81e-84.

71). E. Reiner [1960a, p. 33] emended the KI-*ti* of **A**, line 71 to KÙ-*ti.*

b, obv. 17 presents two variants, *rabûti*(GAL-*ti*) : *at-ti.* There are a few references elsewhere to the "great heavens": e.g., *ROP,* line 110, and the Gula hymn (*OrNS* 36 [1967], p. 120), line 70 (and the note on ibid., p. 131):

> 70). *né-bu-ú* GABA *šá* AN-*e* GAL.MEŠ *uš-ta-nam-da-nu-uš* [d]I-*gì-gì*
>
> The Igigi take counsel with him (Ninurta), the shining . of the great heavens.

The phrase also occurs on *KAR* 109, obv. 8, and on *Iraq* 48 [1986], p. 135, obv. 8'.

73). **b**, obv. 18' has the variant GAR-*an,* "you set".

75). The 'kenning' *imhur,* "he received X", occurs on Tablet B of the *Dream-Book* [*DB,* p. 326].

77). See the note on line 61.

80). The dividing line after line 80 does not occur on the plate of **A**, but E. Reiner [1960a, p. 27] put one there after collation.

81&81e). These lines form one line on **A**.

81c). *YOS* 11, p. 47 incorrectly stated that the end of line 6 offered two alternative readings: *tamannū-ma*/**tazakkar*[*qar*]*-ma.*

81e). The dividing line after **A**, line 81 is unnecessary since the ritual continues over onto line col. III line 82.

E. Reiner [1960a, p. 34] emended the end of the line to *ar*(!)-*kat*(!)-*ka* TAR-*as* (see n. 22), "you will find out your future" [ibid., p. 27]. The same phrase occurs at line 102.

Column III

83). E. Reiner [1960a], p. 27, n. 9] suggested that the Eru'a constellation was intended (*Coma Berenices* and *Canes Venatici*).

84). Disregard *CAD* S, *sarāqu* A, p. 172a and p. 173b, which state that this verb is written ŠUB in **A**, since the verb in *ROP* is *nasāku* instead. The second person present of the *G*-stem of *sarāqu* should be *tasarraq,* not *-uq* in any case.

85-91). The order of these lines is reversed on $\mathbf{A_1}$, obv. 2-8.

86). E. Reiner [1960a, p. 34] read the middle of **A** as *be-e*[*l* NAM.MEŠ] NAM.MEŠ *la* NAM.MEŠ. However, there is no room for this restoration, which is also unsupported by $\mathbf{A_1}$, obv. 7. We want a translation along the lines "without her Enlil cannot determine the fates", but NAM is not the usual logogram for *šâmu.*

88). The incantation rubric is slightly odd, because we expect EŠ.BAR IGI. DU_8, "to see an oracular decision", as before.

91). The next section on $\mathbf{A_1}$, obv. 9-12 again reverses the order of an incantation and its ritual (see *ROP,* lines 85-91). The incantation addresses the Wain constellation, but it is not clear whether or not these lines should be inserted into *ROP.*

D, lines 7'-9' are very fragmentary, with a mention of the Wain constellation.

92). All the stars known to the Mesopotamians were arranged into three bands or 'Paths'. The 'Path of Anu' was in the middle, spanning the

Equator; to the north was the 'Path of Enlil'; and to the south, that of Ea [*RLA* 3, p. 76].

94). E. Reiner [1960a, p. 34] restored the middle of the line *as* ⌜*gi-mi-ir*⌝*-ku-nu,* but the traces do not agree.

95). E. Reiner [1960a, p. 34] read *ana-ku* NENNI *šá a* UD *a-*[*na*(?)] *lu-*.

The meanings of the term *lumāšu* vary with the date of the text [*RLA* 3, p. 80].

96). E. Reiner [1960a, p. 34] read *an-na ki*(!)*-na*(!) *ap*(!)*-li-nin-,* with n. 23 stating that the text had *an-na di ud la i,* which is not obvious from the copy.

97). E. Reiner [1960a, p. 34] read *nam-ru*(!)*-*[*ti*] at the beginning of the line.

The restoration comes from *AHw* 3, *ṣarhu* III, p. 1085b.

O. R. Gurney [1981-1982], p. 97 read EN *mu*!*-ba*[*l-*] for this line, but this does not correspond with the tablet.

100). See the note on line 88 about this incantation rubric.

102). See the note on line 81e about E. Reiner's [1960b, p. 34] emendation.

104-107). The section stating the omens in advance begins at line 104, correct E. Reiner [1960a], p. 28.

110-114). Line 112 quotes the *Shamash Hymn,* line 52 (with *-ku-nu* instead of *-ka*).

E. Reiner [1995, p. 73] now believes that the divine judges are the gods of the night (from line 120), and not Shamash and Adad.

110). E. Reiner [1960a, p. 35] emended GAL.MEŠ to KÙ.MEŠ, but see the note on line 71.

118). E. Reiner [1960a, p. 35] read *ši šu* [*k*]*ud mu.*

Column IV

139). Esabad was a temple of Gula's, probably the one at Ashur [*RLA* 2, p. 474].

See H. Hunger [*BAK*], No. 380 for the reading of the personal name.

SHAMASH-SHUM-UKIN DREAM RITUAL (SDR)

TEXTS

ABL 450 ($\mathbf{G}_1$)

BMS 1 ($\mathbf{A}_1$)

LKA 39 ($\mathbf{F}_1$)

LM 1 and 2 ($\mathbf{B}_1$ + K. 17283; and $\mathbf{E}_1$ respectively)

STT 56 ($\mathbf{C}_1$)

R. F. Harper [1898-1899], p. 130 ($\mathbf{G}_1$)

S. Langdon [1918], pl. 7 (**A**)

J. N. Strassmaier [*AV*], Nos. 6700 (lines 1-7), 7845 (lines $23^{!}$-25), 8063 (lines $2^{!}$-10), and 8297 (lines 1-4), (all for $\mathbf{A}_1$)

STUDIES

J. A. Craig [1894-1895] (edition of $\mathbf{A}_1$)

L. W. King [*BMS*], No. 1 (edition of $\mathbf{A}_1$, using the part of $\mathbf{B}_1$ known to him (K. 3332) and $\mathbf{E}_1$)

M. V. Scheil [*SFS*], No. 18 on p. 104 (description of **b**)

M. Jastrow [1905], pp. 299-300 (translation of $\mathbf{A}_1$, obv. 1-7, 9-11, and 20-21)

E. Behrens [1906], pp. 8 ($\mathbf{G}_1$, rev. 5-9), and 17-18 ($\mathbf{G}_1$, obv. 8-18)

E. G. Perry [1907], No. 2 (edition of $\mathbf{A}_1$, obv. 1-28)

E. Combe [1908], Nos. 2 and 6 (editions of $\mathbf{A}_1$ and **b** respectively, noting $\mathbf{E}_1$ and $\mathbf{G}_1$)

H. Zimmern [1911-1912], pp. 4-5 (translation of $\mathbf{A}_1$, obv. 1-27)

S. Langdon [1918] (edition of **A**, noting the existence of **b**, $\mathbf{A}_1$, and $\mathbf{G}_1$)

A. T. Olmstead [1923], p. 407 (translation of $\mathbf{G}_1$, obv. 8 to rev. 9)

B. Meissner [*BuA* 2], p. 322 (translation of $\mathbf{G}_1$, obv. 8-18)

L. Waterman [*RCAE*], No. 450 (edition of $\mathbf{G}_1$)

W. G. Kunstmann [1932], pp. 69-70 (ritual), and 103

R. H. Pfeiffer [*SLA*], No. 292 (edition of $\mathbf{G}_1$)

A. L. Oppenheim [1941], p. 253 (translation of $\mathbf{G}_1$, obv. 8 to rev. 9)

A. Falkenstein and W. von Soden [*SAGH*], No. 52 (translation of $\mathbf{A}_1$, obv. 1-27, using an unpublished duplicate)

E. Ebeling [*AGH*]. pp. 6-9 (edition of $\mathbf{A}_1$, obv. 1-29, using **A** and **b**; correct W. Mayer [*UFBG*], p. 494)

A. L. Oppenheim [*DB*], p. 233 (ritual)
H. Hunger [*BAK*], No. 407 on p. 120 (colophon of **C_1**)
F. J. Stephens [*ANET* [3]], p. 386 (translation of **A_1**, obv. 1-27)
R. Labat [1970], pp. 284-285 (translation of **A_1**, obv. 1-27, with unspecified duplicates)
S. Parpola [*LAS*], No. 219 (edition of **G_1**)
W. Mayer [*UFBG*], Sin 1 on pp. 490-495 (transliteration of lines 1-28, using **A-c** and **A_1-F_1**; correct his manuscript K (**c** here) to lines 26 onwards)
M.-J. Seux [1976], pp. 278-280 (translation of **A_1**, obv. 1-27, using **A, b, C_1**, and **F_1**)
W. Mayer [1980], p. 422 (corrections to **B_1**).
B. R. Foster [*BM* 2], pp. 682-683 (translation, mainly of **A_1**, obv. 1-27)
S. Parpola [*SAA* 10], No. 298 (edition of **G_1**)
S. Sperl [1994], pp. 221-225 (notes on **A_1**, lines 1-27)

MANUSCRIPTS

Symbol	Museum Number	Publication Number	Relevant Lines	Lines on *SDR*
A	BM 78432 (= Bu. 88-5-12, 335)	S. Langdon [1918], and plates 1-2	obv. 1' to rev. 16	7-8, 19-20b, 21-40
b	Si 18	E. Combe [1908], No. 6	obv. 1 to rev. 10	8, 19-20b, 21-32
c	Si 904	plate 15b	lines 1'-7'	26-31

A_1	K. 155	*BMS* 1	obv. 1-28	1-13, 14-15, 16-18, 19, 20, 21-28
B_1	K. 2823 + 3332 + 11347 + 11722 + 15427 + * K. 17283	*LM* 1 (and * extra)	obv. 1 to rev. 8	1-13, 14-15, 16-18, 19, 20, 21-28
C_1	S.U. 51/107	*STT* 56	obv. 19 to rev. 37	1-11, 14, 15a, 17-19, 20b-c
d_1	Si 884	plate 15a	obv. 1-7	1-7
E_1	Sm. 1382	*LM* 2	lines 1'-5'	4-8
F_1	VAT 14060	*LKA* 39	obv. 1'-7'	10-11, 13a-15, 16
G_1	K. 898	*ABL* 450	obv. 9-17	29, 31, 34, 36

The writer has been unable to consult the unpublished tablet VAT 13854, mentioned as a duplicate to *BMS* 1, obv. 1-28 by R. Borger [*HKL* 2, p. 123].

Only manuscripts **A, b,** and **c** connect the incantation and ritual, both of which mention the Dream God Anzagar (*SDR,* lines 25 and 32 respectively). **A** and **b** were intended for the use of Shamash-shum-ukin (*SDR,* line 19a), hence the name of this ritual to obtain a favourable dream.

S. Langdon [1918, p. 105, and n. 6] stated that only the obverse of **A** was preserved; however, see his edition and his plate 7. Reverse 13ff. appears to offer a very broken second or alternative ritual.

b has only been published in transliteration. Occasionally the rendition of E. Combe [1908], No. 6 has been emended according to the other duplicates, and following the edition of W. Mayer [*UFBG*], pp. 490-494, since W. von Soden collated the text (W. Mayer's text H) after Photo K. 389f. E. Combe's transliteration has been left unaltered for *SDR,* lines 29-32 (i.e., the ritual).

A$_1$, rev. 54 tells us that this tablet formed part of the *bīt rimki* series as collected in Ashurbanipal's Library. The incantation line numbering of *SDR* follows that of **A**$_1$. **B**$_1$ and **E**$_1$ only contain the incantation, but probably also belong to this series. K. 17283 has been joined to **B**$_1$ since the copy of *LM* 1.

C$_1$ is a collection of incantations, with obv. 1-18 addressing Ea, and rev. 38 citing the incipit of one to Adad.

d$_1$, rev. 1'-3' presents a broken ritual, which seems to differ from that of *SDR.*

F$_1$ only covers the incantation. Obverse 3'-4' mentions Ashurbanipal, which may cause confusion in the context of *SDR* (see lines 13a-b and 19a), since Assyrian and Babylonian versions of the same incantation have been merged.

G$_1$ is a Neo-Assyrian letter written by the exorcist Nabu-naser to Esarhaddon, concerning the prince Ashur-mukin-palu'a (separate edition on pages 396-398).

* * * * *

Line 1

ÉN ^{d}*Sîn* ^{d}*Nannaru šu-pu-u ašarid ilāni*

A_1).	ÉN	^{d}30 ^{d}NANNA-*ru*	⸢*šu-pu-ú*⸣	[	]
B_1).	⸢ÉN⸣	^{d}30 ^{d}NANNA-*ru*	[		]
C_1).	⸢ÉN$^{!}$⸣	^{d}30 NAN[NA]-*r*[*u*]	⸢*šu-pu-ú*⸣	[. . . .]	⸢X⸣.MEŠ
d_1).	[		*š*]*u-pu-u*	SAG.KAL	DINGIR.MEŠ

Line 2

^{d}Sîn ed-deš-šu-ú mu-nam-mir uk-li

A_1). ^{d}30 *ed-deš-šu-ú mu-nam-m*[*ir*]
B_1). ⌜^{d}⌝30 *ed-deš-šu-ú* ⌜*mu*⌝-[ ]
C_1). [ ] ⌜*ed-deš-šú*⌝-*u mu-na-*⌜*mir*⌝ *uk-*⌜*lu*⌝
d_1). [ ] *mu-nam-mi uk-li*

Line 3

ša-ki-in na-mir-ti a-na nišē a-pa-a-ti

A_1). *ša-ki-in na-mir-ti a-na* UN.MEŠ [ ]
B_1). *ša-ki-in na-mir-t*[*i*]
C_1). [*n*]*a-*⌜*mir*⌝*-te ana* ⌜UN⌝.MEŠ *a-pa-*[ ]
d_1). [ ] UN.MEŠ *a-pa-a-ti*

Line 4

ana nišē ṣal-mat qaqqadi uš-šu-ru šá-ru-ru-k[*a*]

A_1). *ana* UN.MEŠ *ṣal-mat* SAG.DU *uš-šu-ru šá-*[ ]
B_1). *ana* UN.⌜MEŠ⌝ *ṣal-mat* SAG.DU [ ]
C_1[23]). [.ME]Š *ṣal-mat* SAG.DU *uš-šu-ru šá-r*[*u*$^{!}$]
d_1). [ ] *uš-šu-rù šá-ru-ru-k*[*a*]
E_1). [ ] ⌜*uš-šu-ru*⌝ [ ]

Line 5

nam-rat ṣēt-ka ina šamê e[*l*$^{!}$*-lu-ti*]

A_1). *nam-rat* UD.DA-*ka ina* AN-*e* ⌜X⌝ [ ]
B_1). *nam-rat* UD.DA-*ka* [ ]
C_1[22]). [-*r*]*at* UD.DA-⌜*ka ina*⌝ [A]N$^{!}$-*e e*[*l*$^{!}$*-lu-ti*]
d_1). [*i*]*na* AN-*e* ⌜X⌝-[ ]
E_1). [ ] *ina* AN-*e* [ ]

Line 6

šar-hat di-pa-ra-ka kīma ^{d}Girri ⌜X⌝ [. . . .]

A_1). *šar-hat di-pa-ra-ka* GIM ^{d}GIBIL$_6$ ⌜X⌝ [. . . .]
B_1). *šar-hat di-pa-ra-ka* [ ]
C_1[24]). [-*ha*]*t ṣēt*(UD.DA)-*ka* GIM ^{d}GIBIL$_6$ ⌜X⌝ [ ]
d_1). [G]IM ^{d}GIBIL$_6$ ⌜X⌝ [ ]
E_1). [-*k*]*a* GIM ^{d}[GI]BIL$_6$ [ ]

Line 7

ma-lu-ú nam-ri-ru-ka erṣeta rapāš[*ta*]

A).	[	K]I-⌜*ta* X⌝	[	]-⌜*ti*?⌝
A_1).	*ma-lu-ú nam-ri-ru-ka*	KI-*ta*	DAG[AL-*ta*]	
B_1).	*ma-lu-ú nam-ri-ru-ka*	KI-⌜*ta*⌝	[ ]	
C_1[25]).	[ ]-*u nam-ri-ru-ka*	⌜KI⌝-*tim*	DA[GAL-]	
d_1).	[-*k*]*a*	KI-*tim*	D[AGAL-]	
E_1).	[-*r*]*u-ka*	[ ]		

Line 8

šar-ha nišū ug-da-šá-ra ana a-ma-ri ka-a-⌜*ta̧*⌝

A).	[ ]	*ana a-*⌜*ma*⌝*-ri*	⌜*ka*⌝*-a-*⌜*ta*⌝
b).	[-*r*]*a*	*ana a-ma-ri*	[ ]
A_1).	*šar-ha* UN.MEŠ *ug-da-šá-ra*	*ana a-ma-ri*	*ka-*[ ]
B_1).	[		*k*]*a-a-šá*
E_1).	Trace		

Line 8a

C_1). [X X] ⌜*ana*⌝ *ilūti*(DINGIR-*ti*!(*ut*))-*ka ú-paq-*⌜*qu*⌝ *ka-*⌜*a*?⌝-[*a-na*]

Line 9

^{d}*A-num šamê šá la i-lam-ma-du mì-lik-šú ma-a*[*m-man*]

A_1).	^{d}*A-num* AN-*e šá la i-lam-ma-du*	*mì-lik-šú ma-a*[*m-man*]	
B_1).	^{d}*A-num* AN-*e šá la* ⌜*i*⌝-[		]
C_1).	[ ]-*lam-ma-du*	*mi-lik-šú kab-*[X X X]	

Line 10

šu-tu-rat ṣēt-ka kīma ^{d}*Šamaš bu-uk-ri-*[*ka*]

A_1).	*šu-tu-rat*	UD.DA-*ka*	GIM	^{d}UTU	*bu-uk-ri-*[*ka*]
B_1).	[-*t*]*u-*⌜*rat*⌝	UD.DA-*ka*	⌜X⌝	[	]
C_1).	[	].⌜DA?⌝-*ka*	GIM	^{d}[UT]U [	]
F_1).	[	-*k*]*a*	GIM	⌜d⌝[	]

Line 11

⌜*kám*⌝-*su* [*ma-h*]*ar-ka ilānu rabûtu purussû mātāti* ⌜*šá-kin*⌝ *ina pāni-*[*ka*]

A_1). ⌜*kám*⌝-*su* ⌜IGI-*ka* DINGIR.MEŠ GAL.MEŠ⌝ EŠ.BAR KUR.KUR GAR-*in* *ina* IGI-[*ka*]

B_1). [ ] ⌜IGI$^{?}$⌝-[ ] / [.B]AR KUR.[ ]

C_1). [*ma-h*]*ar-ka* DINGIR.MEŠ G[AL.] / [ ] ⌜*šá-kin*⌝ *ina* IGI-[ ]

F_1). [.BA]R KUR.KUR GAR-*in* [ ]

Line 12

ina lumun attalî ^{d}*Sîn šá ina arhi annanna ūmi annanna iššakn*[*a*]

A_1). *ina* HUL AN.GE$_6$ ^{d}30 *šá ina* ITI NENNI U$_4$ NENNI GAR-*n*[*a*]

B_1). [HU]L AN.G[E$_6$]

Line 13

lumun idāti ittāti lemnēti là ṭābāti šá ina ekallīja u mātīja ibšâ

A_1). HUL Á.MEŠ GISKIM.MEŠ HUL.MEŠ *là* DÙG.MEŠ *šá ina* É.GAL.MU *u* KUR.MU GÁL-⌜*a*⌝

B_1). [HU]L Á.[ ] / [*i*]*na* É.⌜GAL⌝.[ ]

Line 13a

$F_1^{3'}$). [*ana-ku* ^{md}*Aššur*]-*bān*([D]Ù)-*apli*(A) *mār*(DU[MU$^{!}$) *ili* (DINGIR)-*šú*]

Line 13b

F_1). [*šá il*(DINGIR)-*šú* ^{d}*Aš-šur*] ⌜^{d}⌝*ištar*(EŠ$_{18}$.TÁR)-*šú* ^{d}*Aš-šur-*⌜*i*$^{!}$⌝-[*tu*$_4$ (. .)]

Line 13c

F_1). [. . . . *pal-ha-ku* (*u*) *a*]*d-ra-ku u šu-ta-d*[*u-ra-ku*]

Line 14

ilānu rabûtu i-šal-lu-ka-ma ta-nam-[din] mil-ka

A_1). DINGIR.MEŠ GAL.MEŠ i-šal-lu-ka-ma SUM-in mil-ka
B_1). [ ].ME[Š]
C_1). [.ME]Š i-⌈šal-lu-ka⌉ ta-nam-[din]
F_1). [ ]-lu-ka-ma SUM-in [ ]

Line 15

⌈uš⌉-bu pu-hur-šú-nu uš-ta-mu-ú ina šapli-ka

A_1). uš$^{!}$(GUB)-bu pu-hur-šú-nu uš-ta-mu-ú ina KI.TA-⌈ka⌉
B_1). ⌈uš⌉-[ ]-⌈ka⌉
F_1). [-n]u uš-ta-mu-u ina K[I.]

Line 15a

C_1[32]). [. . . .] u ^{d}Í-gì-gì ú-šat-lim-⌈ka⌉ [X X]

Line 16

^{d}Sîn šu-pu-ú šá É-kur i-šal-⌈lu⌉-ka-ma ta-mit ilāni tanaddin

A_1). ^{d}30 šu-pu-ú šá É-kur i-šal-⌈lu-ka-ma⌉ ta-mit DINGIR.MEŠ SUM-[ ]
B_1). ⌈^{d}⌉[ ]-⌈ka⌉-ma / t[a-SU]M-in
F_1). Trace

Line 17

(ūmu) bubbulu u_4-um ta-mit-ti-ka pi-riš-ti ilāni rabûti

A_1). UD.NÁ.ÀM u_4-um ta-mit-ti-ka pi-riš-ti DINGIR.MEŠ G[AL.]
B_1). U[D.]-ti-ka / p[i-] GAL.MEŠ
C_1[33]). [ ] ⌈u_4⌉-um purussê(EŠ.BAR) šá DINGIR.MEŠ [ ]

Line 18

U_4.30.⌈KÁM⌉ *i-sin-na-ka ⌈u_4⌉-um ta-šil-ti ilūti-ka*

A_1). U_4.30.⌈KÁM⌉ i-sin-na-ka ⌈u_4⌉-um ta-šil-ti DINGIR-t[i-]
B_1). [-n]a-ka / [ ]-ka

Line 18a

C_1[34]). [. . . .] *te-diš-ti i-qul-lu-ka*

Line 18b

C_1). [. . . .]⌈X X X X X X⌉[(X)]

Line 19

^{d}*Namraṣīt e-muq la šá-na-an šá la i-lam-ma-du mi-lik-šú ma-am-man*

A). [ ]-*muq la šá-na-an* / [ ]-⌈*du mi*⌉-*lik*-⌈*šú*⌉ *mam-ma*

b). ^{d}*N*[*amraṣīt e*]-*muq la ša-na-an ša la i-l*[*am-*] *mi-lik-šú* [ ]

A_1). ^{d}AŠ.⌈IM_5⌉.BABBAR *e-muq la šá-na-an šá* [*l*]*a i-lam-ma-du mi-lik-šú ma-a*[*m-*]

B_1). [ ]-⌈*na*⌉-*an* / *š*[*á m*]*a-am-man*

Line 19a

ana-ku ^{d}*Šamaš-šum-ukîn arad-ka*

A). [-M]U-GI.NA ⌈ÌR⌉-*ka*

b). *ana-ku* ^{d}GIŠ.NU_{11}-MU-GI.NA Ì[R-]

Line 20

as-ruq-ka ši-riq mu-ši el-la aq-qí-ka re-eš-ta-a ši-kar da-áš-pa

A). [ ] ⌈*ši*⌉-*riq mu-ši el-la* / [ ]-*eš-ta-a ši-kar da-áš-pa*

b). *as-ruq-ka ši-riq mu-ši e*[*l-lu*] / *aq-qi-ka re-eš-ta-a ši-kar* [ ]

A_1). *as-ruq-ka ší-ri*[*q*] GE_6 *el-l*[*u*] *aq-qí-ka re-eš-ta-a ši-kar* [ ]

B_1). *a*[*s-*] ⌈*el-lu*⌉ / *a*[*q-q*]*í re*-⌈*eš*⌉-[ ]

Line 20a

ina ^{GIŠ}GÁN.LAGAB$^{?}$ *qud-du-ši šum-ka az-kur*

A). [ ]-*ši* MU-*ka az-kur*

b). *ina* ^{GIŠ}GÁN.LAGAB$^{?}$ *qud-du-ši* MU-*ka az-*[ ]

Line 20b

al-si-ka be-lí ina qé-reb šamê ellūti

A).	[	*-l*]*í*	*ina*	*qé-reb* AN-*e* KÙ.MEŠ	
b).	*al-si-ka*	*be-lí*	*ina*	*qé-reb* AN-*e* K[Ù.	]
C$_1$).	[ ]-⸢*si*⸣-*ka*	EN	*ina*	*q*[*é*	]

Line 20c

C$_1$[37]). [(X)] ⸢X⸣ *ana ilāni*(DINGIR.MEŠ) *an na* ⸢*ana šu-te-* X⸣ [(X X)]

Line 21

kám-[*s*]*a-ku az-za-az a-še-'e ka-a-šá*

A).	[	*-a*]*z*	*a-še-'e*	*ka-a-šá*	
b).	[ ]*-ku*	*a-za-az*	*a-še-'e*	*ka-*[	]
A$_1$).	*kám-sa-ku*	*az-za-az*	*a-*⸢*še*⸣*-'e* {*ka*}	*ka-*[	]
B$_1$).	*kám-*[*-k*]*u*	*az-za-az*	⸢*a*⸣*-*[		]

Line 22

egirrê dum-qí u mì-šá-ri šu-kun eli-ía

A).	[ ]		*u mi-šá-ri*	*šu-kun*	UGU-*ía*
b).	[ ]	*dum-qí*	*u mi-šá-ri*	*šu-kun*	UGU-[ ]
A$_1$).	INIM.GAR	⸢*dum*⸣*-qí*	*u mì-šá-ri*	GAR-*un*	UGU-[ ]
B$_1$).	INIM.[	*du*]*m-qí*	*u mì*[!](*a*)*-šá-ri*	[	]

Line 23

ilī u ^{d}*ištarī ša iš-tu ūmē ma-a'-du-tú is-bu-su eli-*⸢*ía*⸣

A). [*i*]*š-tu* U$_4$.MEŠ
ma-a'-du-tú *is-bu-su* ⸢UGU-*ía*⸣

b). [ ] *u* ^{d}[ ] *iš-tu* *u$_4$-mu*
ma-a'-du ⸢X⸣ *is-bu-su* [ ]

A$_1$). DINGIR.MU *u* ^{d}EŠ$_{18}$.TÁR<.MU> *ša* ⸢*iš*⸣*-tu* *u$_4$-um*
ma-du-ti *is-bu-su* [ ]

B$_1$). DINGIR.M[U] ⸢^{d}EŠ$_{18}$[?].TÁR[?] *šá* *iš*⸣*-t*[*u*
] / *is-bu-su* UGU-[ ]

Line 24

ina kit-ti u [*mi*]-⸢*šá*⸣-*ri lis-li-mu itti-ia*$_5$: *ur-hi lid-mì-iq pa-da-ni li-šir*

A). [ ]-⸢*šá*⸣-*ri li-is-li-mu* KI-*ía* / [ ]
pa-da-nu li-šir

b). [ ]-*ti u m*[*i-*]-*is-li-mu* [ ]

A$_1$). *ina kit-ti u* NÍG.SI.SÁ *lis-li-mu* KI-*ia*$_5$: *ur-hi lid-mì-iq*
pa-da$^!$(*iš*)-*ni l*[*i-*]

B$_1$). *ina kit-ti* < > NÍG.SI.SÁ *lis*-⸢*li*⸣-*mu* KI-*i*[*a*$_5$] / *ur-hi lid-mì-iq*
pa-d[*a*]-*ni li-š*[*ir*]

Line 25

ú-ma-'i-ir-ma AN.ZA.GÀR *ila šá šunāti*

A). [-*m*]*a* AN.ZA.GÀR *ilāni*(DINGIR.MEŠ) *šá*
MÁŠ.GE$_6$.MEŠ

b). [ ]-*ir-ma* AN.ZA.GÀR [
]

A$_1$). *ú-ma-'i-ir-ma* AN.ZA.GÀR DINGIR *šá*
MÁŠ.GE$_6$.[ ]

B$_1$). *ú-ma-'i-ir-ma* AN.ZA.⸢GÀR⸣ DINGIR *šá*
MÁŠ.G[E$_6$.]

Line 26

ina šat mu-ši-im li-paṭ-ṭi-ra ár-ni-ia$_5$ *lu-uš-lim*$^!$(*me*) *šèr-ti lu-ta-líl ana-ku*

A). [-*r*]*a* ⸢*ár-ni-ia*⸣ / [
-*t*]*a*-⸢*líl*⸣ *ana-ku*

b). [ ]-*ši-im li-paṭ-ṭi-ra* [-*li*]*m*$^!$(*me*) *šèr-ti*
lu-ta-líl [ ]

c). *ina šat mu-ši-i*[*m*] / *lu-uš-lim*$^!$(*me*) *šèr-*[
]

A$_1$). *ina šat* GE$_6$ DU$_8$.MEŠ *ár-ni-ia*$_5$ *lu-uš-lim*$^!$(*me*) *šèr-ti*
lu-ta-l[*íl*]

B$_1$). *ina šat* GE$_6$ DU$_8$.MEŠ *ár-*[ ] / [ ]-*uš-lim*$^!$(*me*) *šèr-ti*
l[*u-t*]*a-líl* [ ]

Line 27

ana dà-ra-ti lud-lul dà-lí-lí-ka

A). [*-l*]*u-*⸢*la*⸣ *dà-lí-lí-ka*

b). [ ]*-ra-a-ti lud-lu-la da-li-li-ka*

c). *ana da-ra-a-ti lud-l*[*ul-*]

A_1). *ana dà-ra-ti lud-lul dà-lí-lí-*[ ]

B_1). ⸢*ana dà-ra*⸣*-ti* [ ]*-lul d*[*a*$^!$*-*]

Line 28

KA.INIM.MA ŠU.ÍL.LÁ ^{d}ZUEN.NA.KÁM

A). [ ].⸢ÍL⸣.LÁ ^{d}ZUEN.NA.KÁM

b). [ ].INIM.MA ŠU.ÍL.LÁ ^{d}ZUEN.NA.[ ]

c). KA.INIM.MA ŠU.ÍL.L[Á]

A_1). KA.INIM.MA ŠU.⸢ÍL⸣.LÁ ^{d}ZUEN.[KÁM]

B_1). KA.INIM.MA [ ]ZU[EN].NA.KE_4

Line 29

DÙ.DÙ.BI ^{GIŠ}*paššūr* ^{GIŠ}*bi-ni ana pān* ^{d}*Sîn tara-kás* 12 *akal ha-še-e* 12 *akal šamaššamī*

A). [ŠINI]G *tašakkan*(GAR-*an*)
12 NINDA *ha-še-e* 12 ⸢NINDA⸣ ŠE.GIŠ.Ì

b). *kikiṭṭu* ^{iṣu}*bînu tašakka-an*
12 AZAG(?)-ŠE / 12 GAR ŠAR

c). DÙ.DÙ.BI ^{GIŠ}BANŠUR ŠINIG$^!$ [
]

G_1) ^{GIŠ}BANŠUR *bi-ni ana* IGI ^{d}30 *tara-kás*

Line 30

suluppa sasqâ tasarraq miris dišpi himēti tašakkan

A). [ ]-⸢*aq*⸣ NINDA.⸢Ì⸣.DÉ LÀL
Ì.NUN GAR-*an*

b). *suluppu* KU-A-TER *tasarraq* / *miris bîni*
himêti

c). ⸢ZÚ⸣.LUM.MA ^{Zì}⸢EŠA⸣ DUB-*aq*$^!$ [
]

Line 31

šikāra tanaqqi [šipta šalāšīš]u tamannu nignaq ^{ŠIM}*burāši a-na* AN.ZA.GÀR *ina rēš erši-šú tašakkan*

A). [KAŠ BAL-*qí* ÉN 3-*š*]*ú* ŠID-⌈*nu*⌉ *ina* SAG GIŠ.NÁ-*šú ana* AN.ZA.GÀR / [NÍG.NA ^{ŠIM}LI GAR-*an*]

b). *šikari tanaqqi* *pân* ^{ilu}[ZA.KAR] / *ina rêš* ^{giš}*ir*[*ši*(?)] *niknakka*(?) *burâši* [*tašakkan*]

c). [BA]L-⌈*qí*⌉ [ŠI]D$^{?}$-[ ]

G$_1$). NÍG.NA ^{ŠIM}LI *a-na* AN.ZA. GÀR / *ina* SAG GIŠ.NÁ *tašakkan* (GAR-*an*)

Line 32

AN.ZA.GÀR *na-áš-pár-ti* ^{d}*Nannari*

A). [A]N.ZA.GÀR *na-áš-pár-ti* ^{d}NANNA-*r*[*i*$^{!}$]

b). ^{ilu}ZA.KAR *na-aš-par-ti* ^{ilu}*Nannaru*

Line 33

A). [. . . . . .] ⌈X X X⌉-*ma uznā*(GEŠTUG^{II}.MEŠ) *liptettâ*(BAD.MEŠ) *taqabbi*(⌈DUG$_4$.GA⌉)-⌈*ma*⌉

Line 34

ina ^{Ú}*áp-ru-šá qul-qú-la-ni qātē-šú u šēpē-šú tamessi*

A). [. . . . . . D]A ŠU^{II}-⌈*šú*⌉ [G]ÌR^{II}-*šú ú-šah-hat-ma*

G1). *ina* ^{Ú}*áp-ru-šá qul-qú-la-ni* / ŠU^{II}-*šú u* GÌR^{II}-*šú* LUH-*si*

Line 35

A). [Ú.MEŠ DINGIR.ŠÀ.DIB.BA] GUR.RU.DA.KÁM

Line 36

kur-ba-ni ṭābti ^{ŠIM}*qul-qú-la-ni* ^{ŠIM}*burāši kurbān bābi ka-mì-i ina* ^{TÚG}*ši-ši-ik-ti-šú tara-kás*

A). [. . . . . .] ⌈X (X)⌉ LAG KÁ.AN.AŠ.A.AN *ina* ^{TÚG}SÍG-*šú* ⌈KEŠDA$^{!}$⌉

G1). *kur-ba-ni* MUN / ^{ŠIM}*qul-qú-la-ni* ^{ŠIM} LI / LAG KÁ *ka-mì-i* / *ina* ^{TÚG}*ši-ši-ik-ti-šú tara-kás*

Line 37

A[13]). [. . . . .] ⸢X⸣ *lu ina* ITI$^{?}$ *ba n*[*é*] ⸢*e*⸣

Line 38

A). [. . . . .] ⸢X X⸣ ^{GIŠ}BANŠUR *tašakkan*(GAR-*an*)

Line 39

A). [. . . . .] ⸢X⸣ *ku da*

Line 40

A). [. . . . .] ⸢X⸣ *su*

The rest of the tablet (**A**) is broken away

* * * * *

TRANSLATION

1). Incantation: "O Sin, the brilliant luminary, the foremost of the gods;

2). O Sin, (the one who is) constantly renewed; the illuminator of darkness;

3). the provider of light to numerous mankind;

4). your rays are released towards the black-headed people.

5). Your shining appearance is bright in the [pure] heavens.

6). Your torch is magnificent, like Girra . [. . . .].

7). Your splendour fills the wide earth.

8). The proudest of the people$^{?}$ vie with one another for the sight of you.

8a). [. .] they constantly pay attention to your divinity.

9). O Anu of the heavens, whose instruction(s) nobody can understand,

10). your shining appearance is pre-eminent like (that of) Shamash, [your] son.

11). The great gods kneel before you. The oracular decision(s) of the lands is placed before [you] (for approval).

12). As a result of the ill portent of a lunar eclipse which occurred in month X, on day Y,

13). (and because of) the evil of unfavourable (and) unpleasant ominous happenings (and) signs which are (occurring) in my palace and (throughout) my land,

13a). [I myself Ashurbani]pal, the son$^{!}$ [of his personal god],

13b). [whose personal god (is) Ashur], (and) whose personal goddess is Ashuritum [(. .)],

13c). [. . . . I am afraid, (and)] I am worried, and [I am] constantly terrified.

14). The great gods ask you, and you give advice.

15). They sat (in) their assembly, (and) debated under [you(r leadership)].

15a). [The Anunnaki] and the Igigi granted you [X X].

16). O Sin, the brilliant one of Ekur, they ask you, and you give the oracle of the gods.

17). The day of the new moon (is) the day of your oracle, the secret of the great gods.

18). The thirtieth day (is) your festival, the day of delight for your divinity.

18a). [. . . .] they pay attention to your renewal,

18b). [. . . .] . . . . . . [(X)].

19). O Namrasit (i.e., Sin), unrivalled (in) strength, whose instruction(s) nobody can understand;

19a). I myself, Shamash-shum-ukin, your servant,

20). scattered a pure offering of the night for you. I libated sweet first-class beer for you.

20a). I invoked you by holy . . .

20b). I called out to you, my lord within the pure heavens.

20c). [(X)] . to the gods . . . . . . [(X X)]

21). I am kneeling, I am standing, (and) I am seeking you.

22). Establish an oracular utterance of good luck and justice for me!

23-24). May my personal god and <my> personal goddess, who have been angry with me for many days, become reconciled with me through my truth and justice! May my way be favourable! May my path be straight!

25). (If) he (Sin) should send Anzagar, the god of dreams,

26). so that during the night he will absolve me of my sin(s, then) I shall become well (again, and) I shall be cleansed of my transgression.

27). (Then) I will proclaim your (Sin's) glory for ever!"

28). Incantation rubric: It is (the text of) a ŠU.ÍL.LÁ-incantation to Sin.

29-30). Its ritual: You install a tamarisk table before Sin. You scatter twelve thyme$^{?}$ loaves, twelve sesame loaves, dates, and *sasqû*-flour. You set out a confection (made of) honey (and) ghee.

31-32). You libate beer. You recite [the (above) incantation three] times. You set out a censer of juniper at the head of his bed for Anzagar. "O Anzagar, the medium of Nannaru (i.e., Sin),

33). [. . . .] . . . and let me hear!", you say.

34). You wash his hands and his feet in the plants *aprušu* (and) *qulqullânu*.

35). They are [the plants] for the appeasement (lit., the turning back) [of an angry god].

36). You tie lumps of salt, of the *qulqullânu*-plant, (and) of juniper, (and) a clod from (the region of) the outer gate into his hem.

---

37). [. . . . .] Ishtar or in the month$^{?}$ . . .

38). [. . . . .] . . you place (on) a table.

39-40 are too fragmentary to translate.

The rest of the tablet (**A**) is broken away

* * * * *

NOTES

1). This incipit occurs elsewhere (pages 149-150). It is possible that the end of **c**, obv. 19 is different.

See *ABZ,* p. 259 regarding W. Mayer's [*UFBG,* p. 491] note on the different versions of NANNA.

4-5). $\mathbf{C}_1$, obv. 22-23 reverses the order of these lines.

5). W. Mayer [*UFBG,* p. 419] suggested the reading D[AGAL.MEŠ] at the end of the line

6). $\mathbf{C}_1$, obv. 24 has the variant UD.DA-*ka,* "your shining appearance".

The trace at the end of $\mathbf{A}_1$ has given rise to different restorations:

i). E. Ebeling [*AGH,* p. 6]: *hi*[*-mi-iṭ-ka*], "your fire" (*himṭu* literally means "scorching, fever").

ii). S. Langdon [1918, p. 107]: *ru*[*š-ši*], "blazing".

iii). W. Mayer [*UFBG,* p. 491]: *hi*[*-miṭ-ka*]$^{?}$.

iv). E. G. Perry [1907, p. 6]: *šár-*[*ru-ri-ka*(?)], "your rays"; H. Zimmern suggested (in [ibid.], p. 15) *r*[*uš-ši-e*].

v). M.-J. Seux [1976, p. 278, n. 11]: *bi*[*r-bir-ru-ka*], "your rays". The writer agrees with W. Mayer [*UFBG,* p. 491] that there is hardly room on $\mathbf{A}_1$ for all this.

The final traces on $\mathbf{C}_1$, obv. 24 and on $\mathbf{d}_1$, obv. 6 are not the same as each other, or as $\mathbf{A}_1$.

8). The correct second singular accusative and genitive personal pronoun was *kâti* or *kâta* (**A**), but in late texts the dative *kâši* or *kâša* ($\mathbf{B}_1$) was also used for the accusative [*CAD* K, p. 288a].

9). W. Mayer [*UFBG,* p. 492] suggested restoring the end of $\mathbf{C}_1$, obv. 27 as *kab*[*-tú mamma*(*n*)]$^{?}$.

11-19). The order of lines 11-13, 14-17, and 18-19 appears to have become muddled, at least going by their sense, although all the manuscripts containing these lines follow the same pattern. Two emended arrangements have been suggested: the more preferable one of M.-J. Seux [1976, p. 279, n. 18] (lines 11, 14-19, and 12-13); and that of F. J. Stephens [*ANET*^{3}, p. 386] (lines 11, 14-15, 12-13, and 16).

12-13). $\mathbf{A}_1$ and $\mathbf{B}_1$ insert the *attalû*-formula (page 149) about a lunar eclipse because they were intended for use in the *bīt rimki* ritual.

13a-c). See page 381.

15). The first sign on $\mathbf{A}_1$, obv. 15 is definitely GUB, despite W. Mayer [*UFBG,* p. 493], which is to be corrected to *uš-,* following $\mathbf{B}_1$, obv. 16.

17). The moon disappeared from the sky around the twenty-eighth of the month (a lunar month is 29½ days), and visited the Underworld (S. N. Kramer [1960], p. 54, line 90), judging the newly arrived dead. The day of the new moon was called UD.NÁ.ÀM, and was associated both with the rebirth of Sin (K. 2164 + 2195 + 3510 (Babylonaica 6 [1912], pls. 1-2), rev. 25-31), and with death and funerary offerings.

$\mathbf{C}_1$, rev. 33 has the variant ⌜*u₄*⌝-*um* EŠ.BAR šá DINGIR.MEŠ G[AL.MEŠ], "the day of the oracular decision of the great gods".

19a). See page 381.

20a). The reading of **b**, obv. 6 follows that of W. Mayer [*UFBG,* p. 493, n. 1 on his *Einschab* DH], after collation by W. von Soden.

The last sign on **A**, obv. 8' is *-kur,* not *-niš* as S. Langdon [1918] copied.

23). The expected form is ^{d}EŠ$_{18}$.TÁR.MU, parallel to DINGIR.MU. J. A. Craig [1894-1895, p. 102] read *-ya,* and S. Parpola [*LAS* vol. 2, p. 213] -MU, but this sign is not extant on $\mathbf{A}_1$, obv. 23.

The ⌜X⌝ of **b**, obv. 10 is probably *-tú,* see **A**, obv. 12'.

25). Various subjects have been proposed for *ú-ma-'i-ir-ma,* namely, who sends Anzagar to the petitioner:

- i). An unspecified he - E. Combe, and E. G. Perry.
- ii). The personal god - F. J. Stephens.
- iii). Sin - S. Langdon, H. Zimmern.
- iv). I (the petitioner) - E. Ebeling, A. Falkenstein and W. von Soden, R. Labat, S. Parpola, and M.-J. Seux. The argument seems to be that the practitioner is commissioning Anzagar by this ritual, on behalf of the petitioner.

26). The emendation in the middle of the line follows the suggestion of J. V. Kinnier Wilson [1992, personal communication].

The transliteration of **b**, rev. 2 follows that of W. Mayer [*UFBG,* p. 494], after collation by W. von Soden.

b has been collated as *lu-ta-líl,* see W. Mayer [*UFBG,* pp. 494-495].

28). W. Mayer [*UFBG,* p. 494] restored the end of **b**, rev. 5 as [.KE$_4$], but **A** and **b** are very close in their sign usage.

29-31). The namburbi against a lunar eclipse, *Cap.* 65, which also cited the incipit of *SDR,* contains a ritual closely resembling that of *SDR.* *Cap.* 65, obv. 9'-14':

9'). ⸢GIM⸣ *an-nam i-te-ep-šú ina* U$_4$.4.KÁM 2 GI.DU$_8$

10'). *ana* ^{d}⸢ZUEN⸣ GAR-*an* 5 ŠUKU.MEŠ 12.⸢TA.ÀM⸣ NINDA ^{Zì}KUM (var. ÁŠ.AN.NA) GAR-⸢*an*⸣

11'). ZÚ.⸢LUM⸣.MA $^{⸢Zì⸣}$EŠA DUB-*aq* NINDA.Ì.DÉ.A LÀL Ì.⸢NUN.NA GAR⸣-*a*[*n*]

12'). ^{DUG}A.DA.GUR$_5$ DU-*an* NÍG.NA ^{ŠIM}LI GAR-*an* KAŠ. S[AG BA]L-⸢*qí*⸣

13'). *ana* IGI ^{d}30 ^{d}ZUEN ^{d}NANNA-⸢*ru*⸣ *šu-pu-*⸢*ú*⸣

14'). 3-*šú tu-šam-na-*⸢*šu*⸣

$^{9'-10'}$ When he has done this, on the fourth day you place two reed altars before Sin. You set out five food portions and twelve loaves of *isqūqu*-flour (var., of emmer). $^{11'}$ You scatter dates and *sasqû*-flour. You set out a confection (made of) honey (and) ghee. $^{12'}$ You correctly install an *adagurru*-vessel. You set out a censer of juniper. You libate (first-class) beer. $^{13'-14'}$ You make him (the petitioner) recite (the incantation) "O Sin, the brilliant luminary" three times before Sin.

Both rituals have been elaborated from the very simple one of *bīt rimki* (which is the same for all the incantations in this section), which also cites this incipit: *BBR* 26 + K. 8921 + 10131, col. III lines 52-53:

52). *ana* IGI ^{d}30 NÍG.NA ^{ŠIM}LI GAR-*an* KAŠ.SAG BAL-[*qí*]

53). ÉN ^{d}30 U$_4$.SAKAR *šu-pu-ú* 3-*šú* ŠID-*nu*

^{52} You set out a censer of juniper before Sin. You libate (first-class) beer. ^{53} You recite the incantation "O Sin, the brilliant luminary" three times.

The letter *ABL* 450 (= *SAA* 10, No. 298; **G**$_1$) shows us that the ritual of *SDR* was actually performed in Neo-Assyrian times. Obverse 8 assigns the ceremony to 16th. Ululu (see page 208). (The line numbers used here are those of *SAA* 10.)

31-32). All three manuscripts vary for these lines. **A** has been followed for the beginning of line 31, then $\mathbf{G_1}$, returning to **A** for line 32.

34). **A**, rev. 10 has the variant *ú-šah-hat-ma,* "you rinse".

36). R. H. Pfeiffer [*SLA,* p. 203] and S. Parpola [*LAS* vol. 1, p. 164] noted an erasure between *-ni* and MUN on $\mathbf{G_1}$, obv. 14. Although there is a gap here, there is no evidence that the surface has been touched.

APPENDIX: *ABL* 450 (= *SAA* 10, No. 298)

OBVERSE

1). [*a-na šarri*(LUGAL) *be-lí-ia*]

2). [*urad*(ÌR)*-ka* ^{md}*Nabû*(AG)*-nāṣer*(PAP*-er*)]

3). [^{d}*Nabû*(AG) *u* ^{d}*Marduk*]

4). [*a-na šarri*(LUGAL) *bēli*(EN)*-ia a-dan-niš*]

5). ⸢*lik-ru*$^{!}$*-bu*$^{!}$⸣ *š*[*ul-mu a-da*]*n-*[*niš*]

6). *a-na* ^{m}*Aš-šur-mukīn*(⸢*mu-kin*⸣$^{[in]}$)*-palū'a*([BA]L*-u-a*)

7). *lìb-bi ša šarri*(LUGAL) *bēli*(⸢EN⸣)*-ia lu* ⸢*ṭa*⸣*-ab-šú*

8). *né-pi-ši ša* ^{ITI}*Ulūlu*(KIN) U_4.16.KÁM

9). ^{GIŠ}*paššūr*(BANŠUR) *bi-ni ana pān*(IGI) ^{d}*Sîn*(30) *tara-kás*

10). *nignaq*(NÍG.NÁ) ^{ŠIM}*burāši*(LI) *a-na* AN.ZA.GÀR

11). *ina rēš*(SAG) *erši*(GIŠ.NÁ) *tašakkan*(GAR*-an*)

12). *ina* ^{Ú}*áp-ru-šá qul-qú-la-ni*

13). *qātē*(ŠU^{II})*-šú u šēpē*(GÌR^{II})*-šú tamessi*(LUH*-si*)

14). *kur-ba-ni ṭābti*(MUN)

15). ^{ŠIM}*qul-qú-la-ni* ^{ŠIM}*burāši*(LI)

16). *kurbān*(LAG) *bābi*(KÁ) *ka-mì-i*

17). *ina* ^{TÚG}*ši-ši-ik-ti-šú tara-kás*

18). *re-e-ši ni-it-ti-ši*

REVERSE

1). *né-ep-pa-áš*

2). *ilānu*(DINGIR.MEŠ) *ša šarri*(LUGAL) *bēli*(EN)*-ia*

3). *šum-ma issi*(TA) ^{m}*Aš-šur-mukīn*(*mu-kin*^{in})*-palū'a*(BAL*-u-a*)

4). *la-ku-ú šu-tu-u-ni*

5). *a-du Aš-šur Bēl*(EN) *u* ^{d}*Nabû*(AG)

6). *ilāni*(DINGIR.MEŠ*-ni*)*-ka issi*(TA) *nišē*(UN.MEŠ)

7). *im-nu-šu-ú-ni*

8). *u*$_4$*-mu u urhu*(ITI) *la ni-ib-ṭi-li*

9). *ša la dul-lu u né-pe-ši*

* * * * *

OBVERSE

1). [To the king, my lord,]

2). [(from) your servant Nabu-nasir:]

3-5). May [Nabu and Marduk greatly] bless [the king, my lord! (There is) great health]

6). to Ashur-mukin-palu'a (i.e., he is very well),

7). (so) the heart of the king, my lord, may be happy!

8). The ritual(s) of Ululu: On the sixteenth day . . . .

9-17 = *SDR,* lines 29, 31, 34, and 36.

18). We have prepared (for the ritual).

REVERSE

1). We are going to do it.

2). (I swear by) the gods of the king, my lord,

3). if, since Ashur-mukin-palu'a

4). was an infant (lit., weak)

5). until Ashur, Bel, and Nabu,

6-7). your gods, counted him amongst the (adult) people,

8). we did not cease day or month

9). (from) any (lit., no) rite or ritual.

* * * * *

NOTES

Obverse

1-4). These lines have been restored after *SAA* 10.

Reverse

3-9). These lines contain an oath which has been rendered in various ways. S. Parpola [*LAS* vol. 2, p. 214, and still in *SAA* 10, No. 298] regarded the *lakû* as a different person to Ashur-mukin-palu'a, and who had to be protected from potential infection from the latter. This "baby" had recently aged enough to be able to speak for himself, and so was counted amongst the people. This view is opposed to that of *CAD* L, *lakû,* §2a, p. 46b which stated that Ashur-mukin-palu'a was an infant, who had become an adult. The writer does not understand why *lakû* cannot refer to the named prince.

E. Behrens, A. L. Oppenheim [1941], R. H. Pfeiffer, and A. T. Olmstead took this passage to refer to a weak (i.e., ailing) Ashur-mukin-palu'a, who is (only just) being counted amongst living men. Only *CAD* B, *baṭālu,* §5', p. 175b could be taken as suggesting that this prince had died recently, not the first three as S. Parpola [*LAS* vol. 2, p. 214] implied.

Sm. 543

TEXTS

DB, pl. 1 (photograph)

STUDIES

A. L. Oppenheim [*DB*], pp. 341-342 (= Fragment 6)

The cuneiform text of Sm. 543 appears on plate 6b.

* * * * *

Break

1'). [lú.u$_{18}$.lu dumu dingir.r]a.⸢na⸣ [hé.en.kù.ga hé.en.sikil hé.en. dagad]

2'). [^{dug}bur.šaka]n.gim [ù.me.ni.luh.luh]

3'). [^{dug}bur.ì.nun].na.gim [ù.me.ni.su.ub.su.ub]

4'). [^{d}utu sag.ka]l dingir.re.e.⸢ne⸣.[ke$_{4}$ šu.na ù.me.ni.sum]

5'). [^{d}utu sag.ka]l dingir.re.e.ne.[ke$_{4}$ silim.ma.na šu sa$_{6}$.ga]

6'). [dingir.r]a [n]a.šè hé.en.ši.[in.gi$_{4}$.gi$_{4}$]

7'). [ka.in]im.ma máš.ge$_{6}$ hu[l búr.ru.da.kám]

8'). [én ^{gi}]^{š}šinig giš.dili [. . . .]

9'). [X (X)] ⸢X⸣ tukul(?) $^{gi[š]}$⸢erin$^{?}$⸣.na [. . . . . .]

10'). One trace at the end of the line

The rest of the tablet is broken away

* * * * *

Break

1'). "[May the man, the son of] his [god, become pure! May he become clean! May he be cleansed!]

2'). [May he be washed] like [a *pūru*-vessel for oil]!

3'). [May he be scrubbed] like [a *pūru*-vessel for ghee]!

4'). [Entrust the man (i.e., the petitioner) to Utu, the foremost] amongst the gods!

5'-6'). (Then) may [Utu, the foremost] amongst the gods, [return] (this) man to [the favourable hand(s)] of his [personal god for his well-being]!"

7'). [Incantation] rubric: [It is (the text) for dissolving] a bad dream.

8'). [Incantation:] "A solitary tamarisk [. . . .]

9'). [. (.)] . a weapon? of cedar? [. . . . . .]

10' is too fragmentary to translate.

The rest of the tablet is broken away.

* * * * *

NOTES

Apart from [INIM.IN]IM.MA in line 7', none of the restorations were noted in *DB*, pp. 341-342]

2'-6'). These lines appear at the conclusion of other incantations (page 150).

6'). *DB*, p. 342 read this line as [*a*]-*na-ku* HÉ.EN.SI[G_5].

SpTU 2, No. 21, OBVERSE

TEXT

SpTU 2, No. 21

STUDIES

E. von Weiher [*SpTU* 2], pp. 104-108

The obverse of this late tablet contains a detailed ritual (with two alternatives in lines 31-35 and 36-40) to deal with the repeated appearances of a young man in a person's dreams. The fragmentary reverse does not appear to be connected with dreams but with the appearance of ghosts. Reverse 26' states that this tablet was left unfinished.

* * * * *

OBVERSE

1). [*šumma*(DIŠ) . . . .] *amēli*(LÚ) *ina šutti*(MÁŠ.GE$_{6}$)-*šú* *ītanammar*(IGI.IGI-*mar*)

2). [. . . . .] ⸢X⸣ ÍL-*šú*

---

3). [DÙ.DÙ.BI *ṣalam*(N]U$^{?}$) ^{LÚ}*ṣehri*(TUR) *šá iškūri*(DUH.LÀL) *teppuš*(DÙ-*uš*)

4). [*šum*(MU)-*šú ina*] *naglabi*([MAŠ].SÌLA) *šumēli*(GÙB)-*šú tašaṭṭar* (SAR-*ár*) *ana pān*(IGI) ^{d}*Šamaš*(UTU) *riksa*(KEŠDA) *tarakkas* (KEŠDA)

5). [*nignaq*(NÍG.NA)] $^{[ŠI]M}$*burāši*(LI) *tašakkan*(GAR-*an*) *šikāra*(KAŠ) *u karāna*(GEŠTIN) *tanaqqi*(BAL-*qí*)

6). [*ana pān*(IGI)] ⸢^{d}⸣*Šamaš*(UTU) *ki-a-am taqabbi*(DUG$_{4}$.GA)

---

7). ÉN ^{d}*Šamaš*(UTU) *ana* ^{d}*Í-gì-gì suh$_{4}$-hu-ru pa-ni$^{!}$-ka*

8). *ana* ^{d}*A-a kal-lat pa-nu-ka šak-na*

9). *ra-áš-bu kun-nu-ú i-lit-ti* ^{d}*A-nu-um*

10). *ana-ku annanna*(NENNI) *mār*(A) *annanna*(NENNI) *šá* ^{LÚ}*ṣehri* (TUR) *ina šutti*(MÁŠ.GE$_{6}$)-*ia$_{5}$ itti*(KI)-*ia$_{5}$ rak-su-ma úl ippaṭṭaru* (DU$_{8}$-*ru*)

11). ^{d}*Šamaš*(UTU) *bēlu*(EN) *rabû*(GAL-*ú*) *áš-šú parāsi*(TAR-*si*) *am-hur-ka*

---

12). *an-nam ana pān*(IGI) ^{d}*Šamaš*(UTU) *šalāšīšu*(3-*šú*) *taqabbi*(DUG$_4$.GA)-*ma ṣalma*(NU) *šu-a-tú*

13). ^{LÚ}*marṣu*(TU.RA) *ina qāti*(ŠU)-*šú šá šumēli*(150)-*šú inašši*(ÍL)-*ma ina imitti*(15)-*šú*

14). *ana* ^{d}*Šamaš*(UTU) *idabbub*(DU$_{11}$.DU$_{11}$) ^{d}*Šamaš*(UTU) *i-šem-me amat*(INIM)-*su*

15). *i-ta-ma-ma a-na mehri*(GABA.RI) *ana salmi*(NU) *ki-a-am iqabbi* (DUG$_4$.GA)

---

16). ÉN *at-ta man-nu šá ina šutti*(MÁŠ.GE$_6$) *u bi-ri ittanammaru*(IGI.IGI-*ru*) *itti*(KI)-*ia$_5$*

17). *ina-an-na ina pān*(IGI) ^{d}*Šamaš*(UTU) *tab-la-ta ek<-me>-ta u kuš-šu-da-ta*

18). *ú-lid-ka ṣēru*(EDIN) *kīma*(GIM) *a-bi-ka*

19). *ú-kan-ni-ka qer-bet kīma*(GIM) *um-mi-ka*

20). *mut-tal-lik qer-bé-e-tú muš-te-'e-ú ur-he-e-tú*

21). *mu-šap-ri-su a-lak-ta at-ta-ma*

22). *is-suh-ka-ma ina zumri*(SU)-*ia$_5$* ^{d}*Šamaš*(UTU) *dajān*(DI.KU$_5$) *ili* (DINGIR) *u amēli*(LÚ)

23). *niš ilī*(DINGIR.MEŠ) *na-as-ha-ta-ma a-lak-ta-ka liprus*(TAR-*us*)

24). [*šar-rat*] ⸢^{d}*Ereš*⸣-*ki*$^{!}$-*gal ina qí-bi-ti-šá a-lak-ta liprus*(TAR-*us*)

25). [^{d}*Asa*]*l-lú-hi maš-maš ilī*(DINGIR.MEŠ) *rabûti*(GAL.MEŠ)

26). [X X]-*e šá* ^{d}*Ea*(IDIM) *a-lak-ta-ka liprus*(TAR-*us*) *te* ÉN

---

27). [*an-nam*] *šalāšīšu*(3$^{!}$-*šú*) *ana ṣalmi*(NU) *iqabbi*(DUG$_4$.GA)-*ma*

28). [*qātē*(ŠU^{II})-*šú*] ⸢*ana*⸣ *muhhi*(UGU)-*šú ana elênu*(UGU-*nu*) *imessi* (LUH-*si*)

---

29). [. . . .] ⸢X⸣-*ma ana tubqāt*(UB) *dūri*(BÀD) *te-qeb-ber-šú zisurrâ* (ZÌ.SUR.RA-*a*) *šá qēm*(ZÌ) *šigūši*(ŠE.MUŠ$_5$)

30). [. . . .] *ina u$_4$-me-šu-ma paris*(TAR-*is*)

---

31). [. . . . . . *k*]*a gu la ana*(over erasure) *muhhi*(UGU) *teṣṣir*(HUR-*ir*)

---

32). [. . . *ṣalam*(NU) ^{LÚ}*ṣehri*(TUR) *šá*] *itti*(KI)-*šú ittanammaru*(IGI.IGI) *ina muhhi*(UGU) *tu-šar-kab*

33). [. . . . . . *ana pān*(IG]I) ^{d}*Šamaš*(UTU) *tamannu*(ŠID-*nu*) *e-ma tamtanû*(ŠID-*nu-u*)

34). [. . . . .] ⸢X⸣-*šu a-di u$_4$-um balāṭi*(TI.LA)

35). [. . . . . . . IGI.IG]I-*mar ṣalmu*(NU) *ana nāri*(ÍD) *tanaddi*(ŠUB-*di*)

---

36). [. . . . .] *ta-nam-bi nu li*[!] *'i* DU_8[!]

37). [. . . . . ŠU]B *šalāšīšu*(3-*šú*) *taqabbi*(DUG_4.GA)-*ma*

38). [. . . . .] *lá ma ina muh-hi-šú tuš-ta-haz*

39). [. . . . .] *ad ne ina libbi*(ŠÀ) *tallak*(GIN-*ak*)

40). [. . . . . . *ṣalma*(NU) *ana*] *nāri*(ÍD) *tanaddi*(ŠUB-*di*)

The rest of the tablet is broken away.

* * * * *

OBVERSE

1). [If . . . .] he repeatedly encounters a man in his dream(s)

2). [. . . . .] . . .

---

3). [Its ritual:] You make a wax figurine of a young man.

4). You write [his name upon] its left hip/shoulder. You install a cultic arrangement before Shamash.

5). You set out [a censer] of juniper. You libate beer and wine.

6). You say as follows [before] Shamash:

---

7). Incantation: "O Shamash, your countenance is turned towards the Igigi.

8). Your countenance is directed towards Aja, (your) bride.

9). (You are) the awesome (and) honoured offspring of Anu.

10-11). I myself, X, the son of Y, pray to you regarding separation, O Shamash, the great lord, because a young man is bound with me in my dream(s), and will not be detached."

12-13). You say this (incantation) three times before Shamash. The sufferer raises that figurine in his left hand and (then) in his right.

14). He speaks to Shamash (in his own words[?], and) Shamash will hear his speech.

15). He swears an oath, and he says as follows to the replica, (namely,) to the figurine:

---

16). Incantation: "Whoever you are, who are repeatedly seen by me in dream(s) and vision(s),

17). now, before Shamash, you are removed (from me). You are forcibly taken away, and you are driven away.

18). The open country begot you like your father.

19). The pasture land treated you kindly like your mother.

20-21). You are the roamer (of) the fields, the seeker (of) the paths, (and) the one who blocks the roads.

22). Shamash, the judge of god and man, expelled you from my body.

23). You are expelled (from my body by) the (oath) of the life of the gods. May (Shamash) divert/block your course (to me)!

24). May [queen] Ereshkigal divert your course by her command!

25-26). May Asalluhi, the exorcist of the great gods (and) the [. .] . of Ea, divert your course!" Incantation formula.

---

27). He says [this (incantation)] three times to the figurine, and

28). he washes [his hands] over it, (namely,) above (the figurine).

---

29). [. . . .] . and you bury it (the figurine) at a corner of the wall. A magic flour circle of *šigūšu*-flour

30). [. . . .] on that day. He (the dream apparition) will be separated (from the sufferer).

---

31). [. . . . . .] . . . you draw upon (it).

32). [. . . the figurine of the young man who] is repeatedly seen by him you cause to ride upon (it).

33). [. . . . . .] you recite [before] Shamash. When? you have recited

34). [. . . . .] . . until the day of (his) recovery

35). [. . . . .] . You throw the figurine into the river.

---

36). [. . . . .] you invoke/name . . . .

37). [. . . . .] . you say three times, and

38). [. . . . .] . . over/upon it you . .

39). [. . . . .] . . you go inside

40). [. . . . . .] you throw [the figurine into] the river.

The rest of the tablet is broken away.

* * * * *

NOTES

4). See page 203 on the different translations of *naglabu.*

7). As E. von Weiher [*SpTU* 2, p. 107] noted, the form should be *pa-nu-ka,* as on obv. 8.

15). *mehru* does not usually occur in rituals, normally referring to written copies or to people of equal rank [*CAD* M_2, *mihru* A, pp. 54-60].

16). See pages 37 and 40 for a discussion of the phrase *ina šutti*(MÁŠ.GE_6) *u bīri.*

26). Asalluhi is frequently described as the son of Ea.

30). The verb at the beginning of the line is either eṣēru, "to draw", or *lamû,* "to surround", probably the latter.

31-35). This appears to be an alternative ritual. It involves the use of a figurine, and an unknown piece of apparatus (a mat?) upon which the figurine rides, i.e., is carried on.

33). *ēma* means "whenever, wherever", and the Akkadian dictionaries cite no examples with verbs of speaking [*CAD* E, p. 136b; *AHw* 1, p. 210b], but see *BAM* 542, col. III line 2 (⌈*e*⌉-*ma* ŠID-*ú*).

38). The *Š*-stem of *ahāzu* is rarely attested in cultic contexts [*CAD* A_1, pp. 180-183]. E. von Weiher [*SpTU* 2, p. 106] translated this line as „ . . *und darüber zündest*(?) *du an"*. However, the noun *išātu* usually precedes *ahāzu* when the meaning of "to kindle a fire" is required.

81-2-4, 166

TEXTS

DB, pl. 3 (photograph)

STUDIES

A. L. Oppenheim [*DB*], pp. 306-307, and 344

R. Borger [1957-1958] (review of *DB*, with collations)

R. I. Caplice [1965], p. 111 (see page 34)

M.-J. Seux [1976], pp. 371-372 (translation of obv. 12 to rev. 15)

The cuneiform text of 81-2-4, 166 appears on plate 13.

* * * * *

OBVERSE

1). [*šumma*(DIŠ) *amēlu*(LÚ) *lu*] *ina šutti*(MÁŠ.⸢GE$_6$⸣) *lu* [. . . . . .]

2). [. . . .] ⸢X⸣ *lu mu-du-*⸢*u*⸣ [*lu là mu-du-u* (. . . .)]

3). [*epere*(SAHAR) *ana mu*]*h-hi-šú iddi*(ŠUB-*di*) [. . . .]

4). [. . . .] *mu qātē*(ŠU^{II})-*šú* DINGIR [. . . .]

---

5). [DÙ.DÙ.BI *an*]*a pān*(IGI) ^{d}*Šamaš*(UTU) *ištēn*(1-*en*) *paṭīra*(GI.[DU$_8$) *tukân*(DU-*an*)]

6). *nīqa*([SÍS]KUR) *tanaqqi*(BAL-*qí*) *imitta*(ZAG) [^{UZU}*himṣa*(ME.HÉ)]

7). *šumê*([UZ]U.ZÚ.ŠEG$_6$) *tu-ṭah-hi* [. . . .]

8). $^{\text{[Z]Ì}}$*šasqâ*(EŠA) *miris*(NINDA.Ì.DÉ.A) *dišpi*(LÀL) [*himēti*(Ì.NUN(.NA)) *tašakkan*(GAR-*an*)]

9). *nignaq*(NÍG.NA) ^{ŠIM}*burāši*(LI) *tašakkan*(GAR-*an*) *šikāra (rēštâ)* (KAŠ.[SAG) *tanaqqi*(BAL-*qí*)]

10). *amēlu*(LÚ) *šuātu*(BI) *mīs pî*(KA.LUH.Ù.DA) *ippuš*(DÙ-[*uš*)(-*ma*)]

11). *ina pān*(IGI) ^{d}*Šamaš*(UTU) *izzaz*(GUB)-*ma kam iqabbi*(DU[G$_4$.GA])

---

12). ÉN ^{d}*Šamaš*(UTU) *dajān*(DI.KU$_5$) *ṣi-*[*i-ru*]

13). *bēl*(EN) *šamê*(AN-*e*) *erṣetim*(KI-*t*[*im*])

14). *bēl*(EN) *elâti*(AN.TA.MEŠ) *u šaplāti*(K[I.TA.MEŠ])

15). *nu-úr* ^{d}*Í-gì-*[*gì u* ^{d}*A-nun-na-ki*]

REVERSE

1). *pa-ri-is purussê*(EŠ.BAR) *ilī*(DINGIR.M[EŠ) *rabûti*(GAL.MEŠ)]
2). *at-ta-ma ana-ku* [*annanna*(NENNI) *mār*(A) *annanna*(NENNI)]
3). *ardu*(ÌR) *pa-lih ilūti*(DINGIR-*ti*)-*k*[*a rabīti*(GAL-*ti*)]
4). *am-hur-ka* ^{d}*Šamaš*(UTU) *re-*[*me-nu-ú*]
5). *epere*(SAHAR) *šá ina šutti*(MÁŠ.GE$_{6}$) *lu ina* [. . . .]
6). *ana muhhi*(UGU)-*ía na-du-u lu i*[*b-ru*]
7). *lu tap-pu-u lu ru-u-a l*[*u* . . . .]
8). *lu mudû*(ZU-*u*) *lu là mudû*(ZU-*u*) *lu* ⌈X⌉ [. . . .]
9). *šá epere*(SAHAR) *ana muhhi*(UGU)-*ía iddû*(ŠUB-*u*) *lu* Š[U . . . .]
10). ⌈*iš*⌉-*šá-a lu ina pî*(KA)-*šû qa* [. . . .]
11). *ut*$^{!}$([*u*]*n*)-*nin ina pān*(IGI) *ilūti*(DINGIR-*ti*)-*ka rabīti*(GA[L-*ti*) (. . . .)]
12). [*ina*] *muhhi*([U]GU) *ṣalme*(NU)-*šú mê*(A.MEŠ) *a-ram-*[*mu-uk*]
13). $^{[GIŠ]}$*bīnu*([ŠI]NIG) *lillil*(KÙ)-*an-ni* ^{Ú}*maštakal*(AŠ.BAD) *l*[*ip-šur-an-ni*]
14). *šammu peṣû*([Ú].BABBAR) *liballiṭ*(TIN)-*an-ni-ma ši-me k*[*u* . . . .]
15). [X] ⌈X⌉ *din ka dà-lí-lí-k*[*a lud-lul*]

16). [*kam*] *iqabbi*([DU]G$_{4}$.GA)-*ma uš-ken ina pān*(I[GI) ^{d}*Šamaš* (UTU)]

UPPER EDGE

17). [*ṣalam*(NU) *zikari*(NÍTA)] ⌈*u*$^{!}$⌉ *ṣalam*(NU) *sinništi*(MÍ) *šá ṭiṭṭi*(IM) *ippuš*(DÙ-[*uš*])
18). [*ana*] *muhhi*(⌈UGU⌉) *irammuk*(TU$_{5}$)-*m*[*a* . . . .]
19). [X (X)] *qātē*([Š]U^{II})-*šú* DINGIR ⌈*i*⌉-[. . . .]

* * * * *

OBVERSE

1). [If a man, either] in a dream or [. . . . . .]
2). [. . . .] . either an acquaintance, [or someone unknown (. . . .)]
3). threw [dust/earth] upon him [. . . .]

4). [. . . .] . the god [. . . .] his hands.

---

5). [Its ritual: You put] one reed [altar in place] before Shamash.

6-7). You perform a sacrifice. You offer the shoulder, [the fatty tissue around the intestines], (and) roasted meat. [. . . .]

8). [You set out] *sasqû*-flour (and) a confection (made) of honey [(and) ghee].

9). You set up a censer of juniper. [You libate (first-class)] beer.

10). (Then) that man (i.e., the dreamer) performs the mouth-washing (ritual).

11). He stands in front of Shamash, and he says as follows:

---

12). Incantation: "O Shamash, you are (from rev. 2) [the exalted] judge;

13). the lord of heaven (and) earth;

14). the lord of (the regions) above and [below];

15). the light of the Igigi [and of the Anunnaki];

REVERSE

1). the decider of the oracular decision(s) concerning [the great] gods.

2). I myself, [X, the son of Y],

3). the servant who fears your [great] divinity,

4). I pray to you, [O merciful] Shamash,

5). (because of) the earth which in a dream or in [. . . .]

6). was thrown upon me. Whether (it was) [a colleague],

7). or a companion, or a friend, or [. . . .],

8). or an acquaintance, or someone unknown, or . [. . . .]

9). who threw (this) earth upon me, or . [. . . .]

10). raised, or with his mouth . [. . . .]

11). I pray before your great divinity [(. . . .)].

12). I bathe in water over his (the thrower's) figurine.

13). May the tamarisk purify me! [May] the *maštakal*-plant [absolve me]!

14). May the 'white [plant]' heal me! Hear . [. . . .]

15). [.] . . [I will proclaim] your glory!"

---

16). He speaks [thus], and he prostrates himself before [Shamash].

UPPER EDGE

17). He makes [a figurine of a man] and a figurine of a woman (out) of clay.

18). He bathes over (them), and [. . . .]

19). [. (.)] his hands the god . [. . . .]

* * * * *

NOTES

Obverse

1). *DB,* p. 344 restored [*ina bi-ri*] at the end of the line. The experiences *šuttu* and *bīru* are discussed on pages 37-40.

2). *DB,* p. 306 restored "[somebody]" at the beginning of this line.

3). *DB,* p. 344 restored [*ina muh*]-*hi,* but see rev. 9, where *ana* occurs.
DB, p. 306 restored "[and he has become depressed(?)]" at the end of the line.

4). *DB,* p. 344 read the first sign as *niš,* but it is a clear *mu.*

7). See E. K. Ritter and J. V. Kinnier Wilson [1980], p. 30 on their line 20 for the rendition of this logogram.

8). *DB,* p. 306 wanted the verb "to scatter", but, in this context the verb is usually *šakānu,* "to place" [*CAD* M_2, p. 109].

9). *DB,* p. 344 restored [GEŠTIN] at the end of the line.

14). Contrary to *DB,* p. 344 the last .TA.MEŠ is not extant on the tablet; see already R. Borger [1957-1958], p. 418.

15). The second *-gì* is not extant, contrary to *DB,* p. 344.

Reverse

5). *DB,* p. 344 restored [*bi-ri*] at the end of the line.

9). *DB,* p. 344 restored Š[U^2] at the end of this line.

10). *DB,* p. 344 restored Š[UB-*u*] at the end of the line, but the sign is definitely not ŠUB.

14). See the note on Ú.BABBAR at *ADRC,* col. III line 63 (page 310).
DB, p. 344 read *lim-me-ru,* but the sign is not *-ru.*

15). Akkadian incantations concluded with various phrases (discussed by W. Mayer [*UFGB*], pp. 307-361), but the traces do not agree with any of the common expressions. The sentence normally preceding *dà-lí-lí-ka lud-lul* was *nar-bi-ka lu-šá-pi.* Phrases involving *balāṭu*(TIN) were usually written out syllabically: *a-di* u_4*-um bal-ṭa-ku or lu-úb-luṭ.*

19). *DB,* p. 344 restored *i*-[*mah-har*] at the end of the line.

GLOSSARY

abracadabra incantation: See pages 128-129.

Adad: Sumerian Ishkur. Storm god, and god of beneficial rain. Patron of extispicy with Shamash.

Agade: An unlocated town in Babylonia.

amulet: An object bearing an inscription and/or reliefs, possessing magical powers to protect a house or a person against evil powers.

Anu: Sky god, head of the gods, dwelling in the topmost heaven. One of the supreme divine triad, with Ea and Enlil. Anu became a remote figure, with his functions being taken over by Enlil.

Anunnaki: General term for an old group of gods dwelling in the Underworld, who originally had some connection with the heavens and Anu. They are often paired with the Igigi.

Anzagar: A Dream God (see pages 83-85).

apodosis: The second part of an omen, the prediction.

apotropaic: Turning away evil.

Apsu: Cosmic home of Ea, a freshwater ocean lying beneath the earth.

Asalluhi: Originally a local god of Kuara, becoming a god of healing and magic. A son of Ea. Associated with Marduk.

Ashur: Assyrian national god, and patron deity of the city of Ashur. One of his consorts was Ninlil, called Mullissu in Assyria.

Ashur: Capital of Assyria until 883 B.C., on the Tigris. Modern Qalat Shergat.

Ashurbanipal's Library: The Neo-Assyrian king Ashurbanipal collected thousands of cuneiform tablets at Kuyunjik, which are registered under various tablet signatures in the British Museum. Nearly all known Mesopotamian literary genres are represented. The 'Library' actually consists of three collections, that excavated by:

i). H. Layard in 1849 in Rooms 40-41 of Sennacherib's palace.
ii). H. Rassam in 1853 in Ashurbanipal's palace.
iii). R. Campbell Thompson in 1927 in the temple of Nabu.

Ashur-mukin-palu'a: A son of Esarhaddon (see S. Parpola [*LAS* 2], p. 25 on obv. 9 of *LAS* 17).

Babylon: Cult centre of Marduk and capital of Babylonia, on the Euphrates.

Bel: Means "Lord"; see Marduk.

bīt rimki: A purification ritual series, performed on the occasion of a lunar eclipse to purify the (Neo-Assyrian) king.

charm: A stone necklace, or leather bag containing various natural objects, worn around the neck, and possessing magical powers for a specific purpose.

clairvoyant dream: See page 20.

colophon: A section at the end of the last column on the reverse of a tablet. Its content varies, but often provides us with information about the tablet's position with a literary, medical, or ritual series, together with the incipit of the next tablet; as well as data on the ancestry of the scribe, and on scribal practices.

Dagan: Originally a corn god, becoming a weather god and connected with the Underworld. He had two cult centres in the Mari sphere of influence, at Terqa (as a lord of funerary offerings) and at Tuttul.

Death Dream: The dreamer visits the Underworld, or foresees his or someone else's death.

DINGIR.ŠÀ.DIB.BA-incantations: Incantations to appease an angry deity, see pages 129-130.

Dream-Book: A collection of dreams with their interpretations.

Ea: Sumerian Enki. God of crafts, creation, magic, water, and of wisdom. A member of the supreme divine triad, with Anu and Enlil. Sometimes a son of Anu. Consort Damkina. Main temple was Eabzu at Eridu. Helps Mankind to survive the Flood. Ea dwelt in the cosmic region Apsu.

Ebabbar: The name of two main temples of Shamash, at Sippar and at Larsa.

egirrû: An "oracular utterance", see pages 151-155.

Ekur: Enlil's temple in Nippur.

Enkidu: Boon companion of Gilgamesh.

Enlil: His functions are uncertain; one of the supreme divine triad, with Anu and Ea. He came to be as powerful as Anu in ordering the universe. Consort Ninlil. Cosmic abode Esharra, between heaven and earth. Main temple Ekur at Nippur.

eponym: In Assyria the years were distinguished by the personal name of a high official, according to a certain order.

Ereshkigal: Queen of the Underworld. Sister of Ishtar. Nergal was her consort in one tradition. She had a son, Ninazu, by Gugalanna.

Eridu: Cult centre of Ea, on the old coast of the Persian Gulf. Modern Abu Shahrain.

ÉR.ŠÀ.HUN.GA: A lament intended to appease a specific angry deity.

Esagila: Marduk's temple at Babylon.

Etana: Sumerian king of the First Dynasty of Kish after the Flood, and legendary hero.

exorcist: Mesopotamian *āšipu* or *mašmaššu.* (It is to be remembered that Mesopotamian demons did not possess their prey, but wrapped themselves around the victim like a garment.)

extispicy, haruspicy: Omens deduced from the entrails of sacrificed animals (usually rams) by the haruspex.

***ezib*-clause:** Various clauses asked Shamash and Adad to "disregard" certain errors which might have been committed during the extispicy ritual preparations, and to grant an omen even if something might not be correct.

Gibil/Girra: A fire god, and a son of Anu.

Gilgamesh: Legendary hero and god, and probably a historical Sumerian king of Uruk at the beginning of the Early Dynastic period. His parents are usually Lugalbanda and Ninsun. His boon companion is Enkidu.

guardian figurine: A figurine buried beneath a building's floor to protect it and its inhabitants from all calamities.

Gula: Main goddess of medicine. Many other goddess became associated with her, hence her other names such as Ninisina. She was sometimes the consort of Ninurta.

haruspex: Mesopotamian *bārû,* who performed extispicy/haruspicy.

hemerology: A calendar listing the favourable or unfavourable days of a month for carrying out certain activities.

Humbaba: Monster guardian of the Cedar Forest, appointed by Enlil. He was killed by Gilgamesh and Enkidu. He had a human body, lion's claws for hands, long hair and a long beard, and a face resembling coiled intestines.

Igigi: Collective term for the gods of heaven. Often paired with the Anunnaki.

incantation rubric: A section following the incantation, usually ruled-off separately, presenting either the purpose of the incantation or its category. It begins with KA.INIM.MA.

incipit: The first line of an incantation or of a tablet.

incubation: A ritual to induce a prognostic dream in response to a particular problem.

Ishtar: Sumerian Inanna. Goddess of battle, fertility, love, and sex, and the planet Venus; the most important Mesopotamian goddess. Her sister was Ereshkigal. She had various local forms, such as Ishtar of Arbela and Ishtar of Agade.

Isin: Modern Ishan Bahriyat.

kispu: Ritual meal regularly offered to the dead, and on special occasions when ghosts were troublesome.

Kuyunjik: The palace mound at Nineveh is known by its Turkish name.

Lamashtu: A demoness mainly attacking unborn and newly born babies; she also brings disease. A daughter of Anu. She had a lion's head, donkey's ears and teeth, a hairy body, long fingers and nails, and bird's talons for feet. The plaques depicted her holding snakes in her hands, while animals suckled at her naked breasts.

***lipšur*-phrases and -litanies:** These phrases are exorcistic, beginning with *lipšur,* "may X absolve", or similar grammatical forms. The litanies are collections of such phrases within incantations.

Lugalbanda: A deified Sumerian king of the First Dynasty of Uruk. His consort was the goddess Ninsun, and they are usually the parents of Gilgamesh.

Mamu: A Dream God (see pages 73-77).

Mari: Modern Tell Hariri, on the Euphrates, in Syria.

Marduk: Main deity of the Babyonian pantheon, and patron of Babylon. By absorbing the functions of several other gods, he acted many areas, especially magic. He became associated with Asalluhi. A son of Ea. His usual consort was Sarpanitu, and Nabu became their son. Main shrine was Esagila at Babylon.

message dream: A prognostic dream, containing a clear statement from the gods, thus not requiring interpretation.

Nabu: God of writing and wisdom. Became Marduk's son. Consort usually was Tashmetu. Main shrine was Ezida at Borsippa (modern Birs Nimrud).

namburbi ritual: "(A ritual for) the dissolving of it (the portended evil)", i.e., a ritual to dispel the evil portended by a bad omen, by the means of sympathetic magic.

Nergal: King of the Underworld. Associated with Erra, a warrior and plague god. A son of Enlil. Main shrine was Emeslam at Kutha (modern Tell Ibrahim). Consort was Ereshkigal, or Mammetu, or others.

Nimrud: Akkadian Kalhu, on the Tigris. Founded by Ashurnasirpal II in 883 B.C. as the Assyrian capital.

Nineveh: This town consists of the mounds of modern Kuyunjik and Nebi Yunus, and the surrounding area, opposite the modern town of Mosul. It was once on the Tigris. Capital of Assyria in the late eighth and early seventh centuries B.C.

Ninlil: Her role is unclear, apart from being the consort of Enlil. She was called Mullissu in Assyria, where she was Ashur's consort.

Ninurta: An agricultural and rain god, who become a war god, associated with Zababa. A son of Enlil. His consort sometimes was Gula.

Nusku: A god of fire and light, whose symbol was a lamp. Vizier and often a son of Enlil.

personal deity: Each person had his own protective deity, who would look after him, if revered correctly, guarding him against evil powers and misfortunes.

prognostic dream: A dream which can be taken to refer to the future, either directly or by interpretation. There are three categories: a message dream; a symbolic-message dream; and a dream omen.

prophylactic: Guarding against disease, and evil.

protasis: The first part of an omen, the description of the observed event or sign.

purussû: "An oracular decision", given by an omen from the gods.

Shamash: Sumerian Utu. Sun god, and god of justice, destroying evil. Consort Aja. Patron of extispicy with Adad. His two main temples, both called Ebabbar, were in Larsa and in Sippar.

Shulak: A demon, the overseer of the lavatory.

Sin: Sumerian Nanna(r) or Zuen. Moon god. Various logograms seem to indicate the different stages of the moon (T. Jacobsen [1976], p. 121):

i). ^{d}*Namraṣīt*(AŠ.IM_5.BABBAR), the new moon (the beginning of the lunar cycle).

ii). ^{d}ZUEN, of which the Akkadian ^{d}Sîn is an abbreviation, denotes the crescent moon.

iii). ^{d}NANNA, the full moon (days 14/15 of the lunar cycle).

A son of Enlil. Consort Nikkal, Sumerian Ningal. Two important shrines were Ehulhul at Harran in Syria, and Ekishnugal at Ur.

Sippar: A town on the Euphrates, one of the cult centres of Shamash. Modern Tell Abu Habba.

Sisig: A Dream God (see pages 77-78).

substitute figurine: Actions are performed over a figurine (or another item) as the substitute for the person or object to be affected by the ritual, for good or bad. Involves sympathetic magic.

Substitute King Ritual: When certain solar or lunar eclipses portended the death of the Assyrian ruler, a substitute was enthroned for about a hundred days, acting as the king and taking all the bad omens upon himself. He was probably killed at the end of the eclipse period.

Sultantepe: Tablets were excavated from this Syrian site in 1951-1952, whose colophons date from 718-612 B.C.

symbolic-message dream: A prognostic dream, whose message has to be decoded by an interpreter, and not by a Dream-Book.

sympathetic magic: Various relationships are seen to exist between objects and creatures, so action on one will affect the other (see pages 177-178).

symptomatic dream: A dream with no mantic import, only pleasant or unpleasant (then a nightmare).

ŠU.ÍL.LÁ-incantation: See page 130.

tamītu: A Babylonian question to Shamash and Adad about a specific problem or plan, or if the inquirer would be protected from all evil in the year to come. The gods replied via extispicy.

Ur: A town on the Euphrates, and a cult centre of Sin. Modern Tell Muqayyar.

Uruk: Modern Warka. Its kings included Gilgamesh and Lugalbanda.

Utu: See Shamash.

Zababa: Originally a local god of Kish, a god of war. Associated with Ninurta.

Zaqiqu/Ziqiqu: A Dream God, a type of demon, and a means of divine communication (see pages 78-83).

TIME CHART

All the dates are B.C. Only periods and kings mentioned several times in this study are noted here.

Early Dynastic	c. 2900 - c. 2340
Agade or Old Akkadian	c. 2340 - c. 2159
Naram-Sin 2254-2218	
Ur III	c. 2113 - c. 2004
Isin-Larsa	c. 2017 - c. 1763
Mari	c. 1820 - c. 1760
Zimri-Lim c. 1775-1757	
Old Babylonian	c. 1894 - 1595
Kassites in Babylonia	c. 1595 - c. 1155
Middle Babylonian	c. 1155 – 732
Neo-Babylonian	626 – 539
Nebuchadrezzar II 604-562	
Nabonidus 559-539	
Old Assyrian	c. 2010 – c. 1700
Middle Assyrian	c. 1500 – 935
Neo-Assyrian	934 - c. 609
Ashurnasirpal II 883-859	
Shalmaneser III 858-824	
Sennacherib 704-681	
Esarhaddon 680-669	
Ashurbanipal 668-627?	Shamash-shum-ukin 667-648 (in Babylonia)
Achaemenids in Babylonia	538 – 331
Seleucids	305 – 64

INDEXES

INDEX OF AKKADIAN WORDS DISCUSSED

INDEX OF TEXTS MENTIONED

1). The references are to cuneiform copies unless followed by P = photograph or T = transliteration.
2). The dream ritual texts are listed under their museum numbers or composite titles

ADDITIONAL ABBREVIATIONS

Cagni, L. [1970]: *Das Erra-Epos.* Studia Pohl 5. Pontificium Institutum Biblicum.
(E): Edition here.
JRAS: Journal of the Royal Asiatic Society.
Küchler, F. [1904]: *Beiträge zur Kenntnis der assyrisch-babylonischen Medizin.* Assyriologische Bibliothek 18. J. C. Hinrichs.
Lambert, W. G., and S. B. Parker [1966]: *Enūma Eliš: The Babylonian Epic of Creation: The Cuneiform Text.* The Clarendon Press.
Lau, R. J. and J. Dyneley Prince [1905]: *The Abu Habba Cylinder of Nabuna'id.* Semitic Study Series. E. J. Brill.
Meier, G. [1937]: *Die assyrische Beschwörungssammlung Maqlû. AfO* Beiheft 2.
Meier, G. [1966]: Studien zur Beschwörungssammlung Maqlû. *AfO* 21, pp. 70-81.
PSBA: *Proceedings of the Society of Biblical Archaeology*
Reiner, E. [1958]: *Šurpu: A Collection of Sumerian and Akkadian Incantations. AfO* Beiheft 11.

PUBLISHED TEXTS

AbB 5, No. 10 – T: 7

ABL 4, obv. 7-9: 232
ABL 22: 124, 199
ABL 23: 110-111
ABL 183, obv. 6-9: 232
ABL 355: 110-111
ABL 450: 396-398 (E)
obv. 8: 208, 395
obv. 9-17 = manuscript $\mathbf{G_1}$ of *SDR*: 99, 121, 149, 208, 243, 245, 379, 380, 381
ABL 453, obv. 8-9: 93
ABL 676, rev. 1'-8': 212
ABL 923, obv. 7: 17, 39-40
ABL 1021, obv. 13' to rev. 1: 6, 17, 18, 31, 41
ABL 1336: 6
ABL 1347, rev. 1-3: 6, 157, 237-238
ABL 1381, rev. 1-2: 93
ABRT 1, pp. 5-6: 82, 87

UNPUBLISHED TEXTS

NON-MESOPOTAMIAN REFERENCES

INDEX

1). The majority of the dream references are indexed as "message dreams", "omens, dream", etc.
2). Only ingredients used in dream rituals and one nocturnal bruxism ritual are recorded.
3). The three letters *S* are listed in the order *S, Ṣ, Š.*
4). The index entries for the Text Editions are limited to the ingredients and to some points in the accompanying notes.

PLATES

Plate 1: BM 78432 (= Bu. 88-5-12, 335)

Obv.

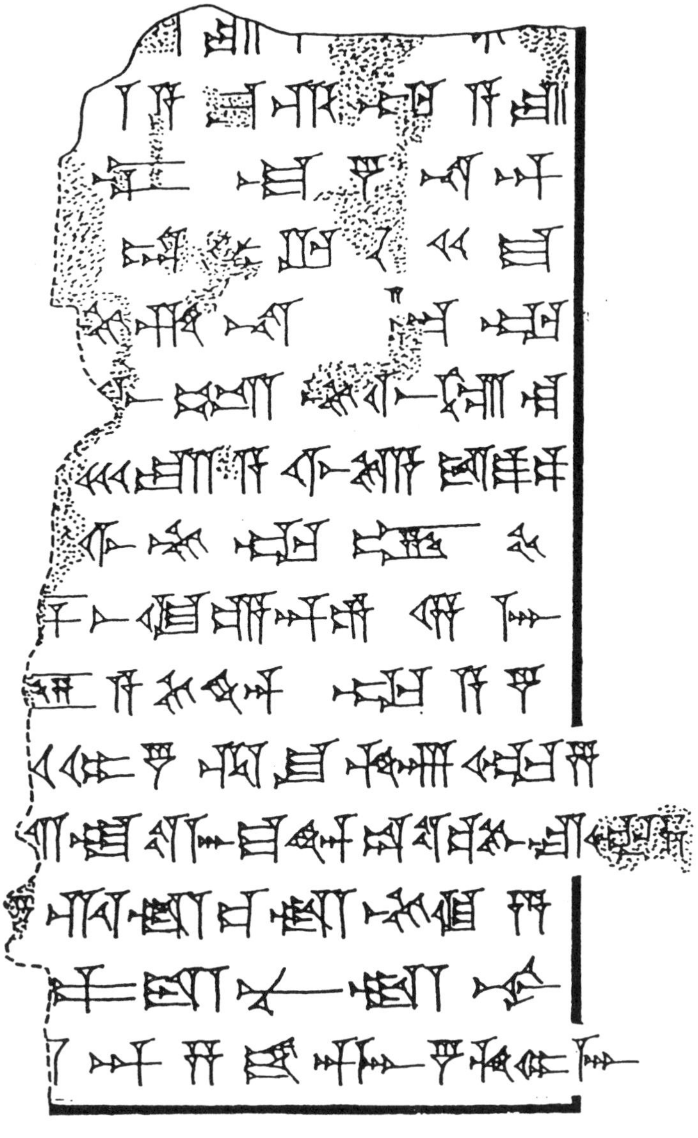

Plate 2: BM 78432 (= Bu. 88-5-12, 335)

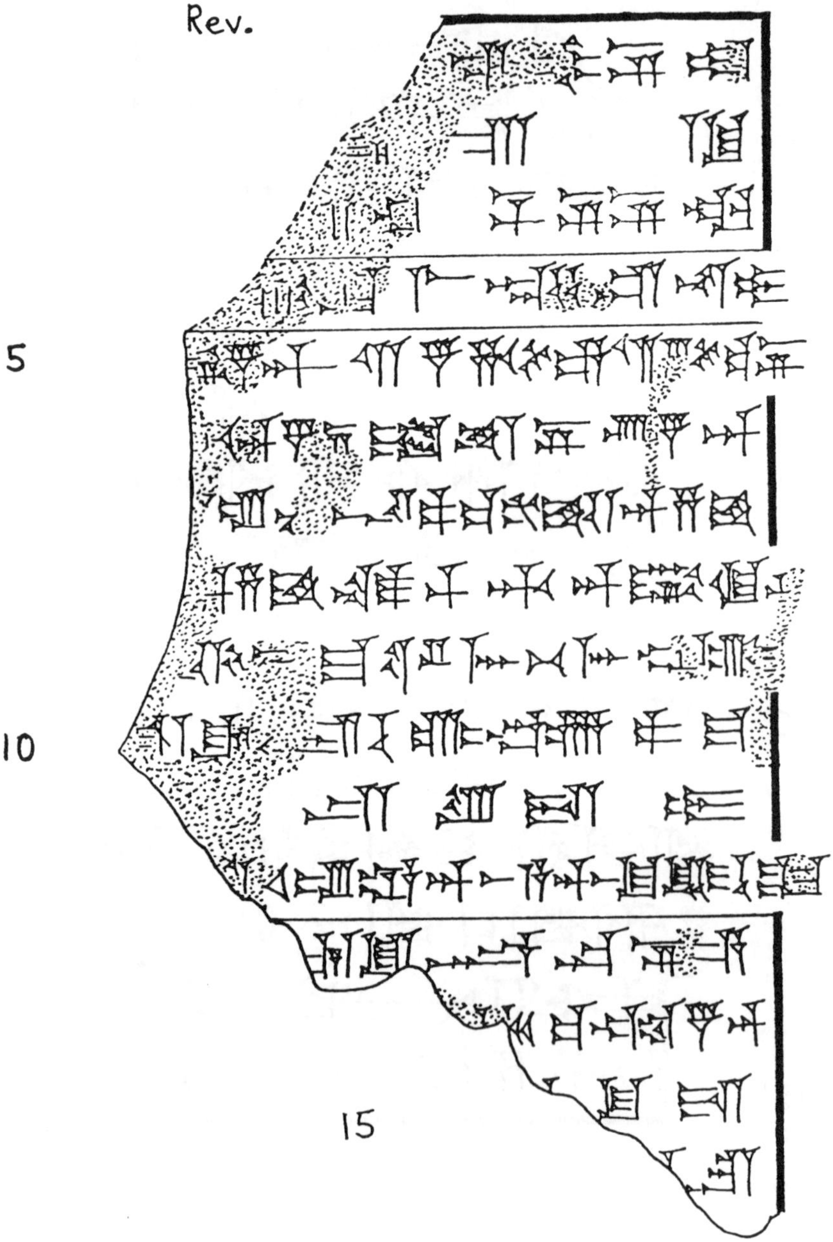

Plate 3: K. 3333 + 8583 + Sm. 1069

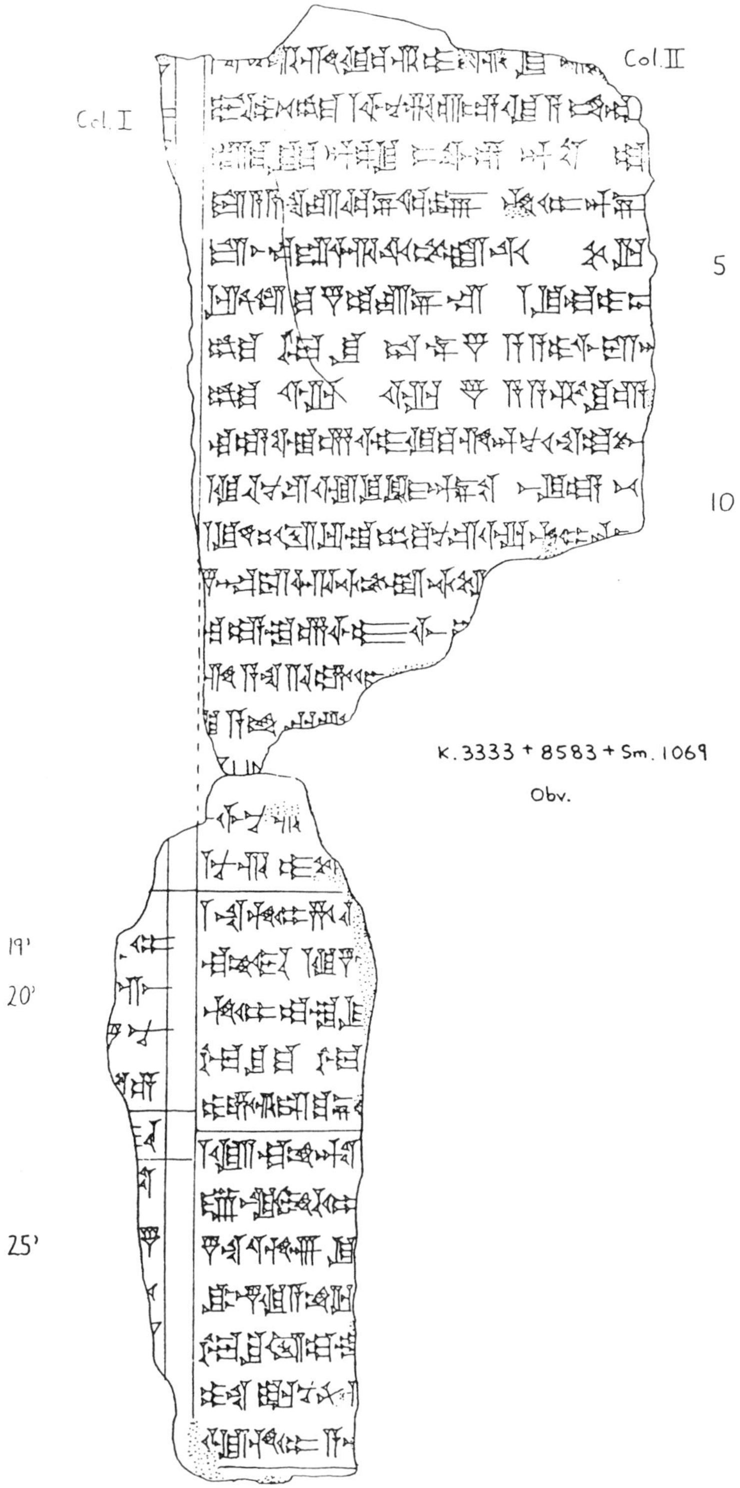

Plate 4: K. 3333 + 8583 + Sm. 1069

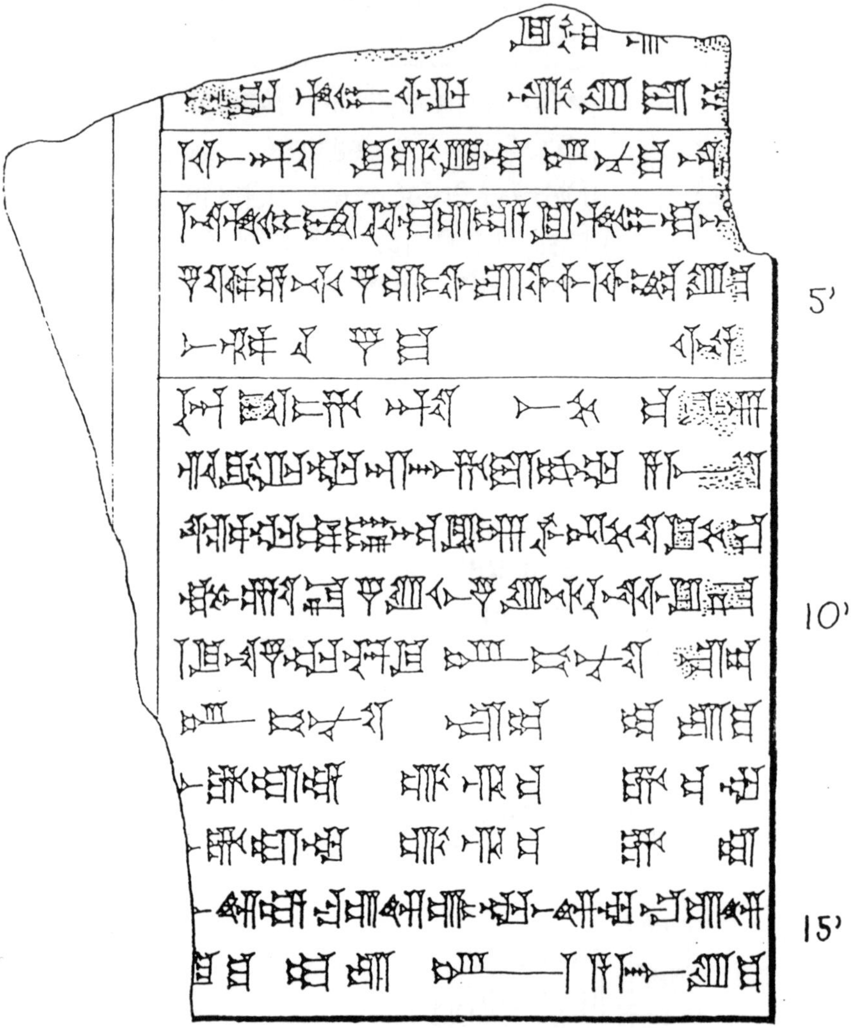

Plate 5: K. 3758

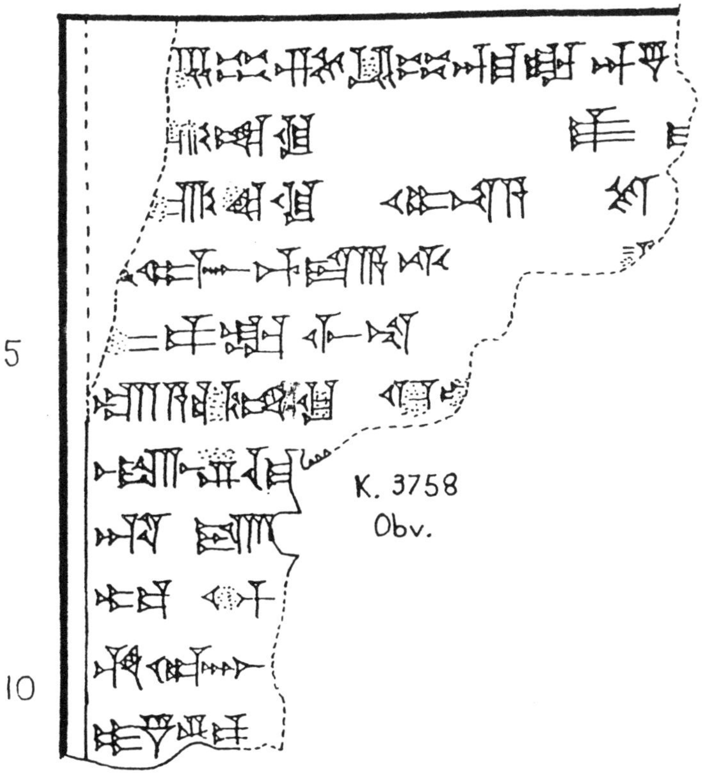

K. 3758
Obv.

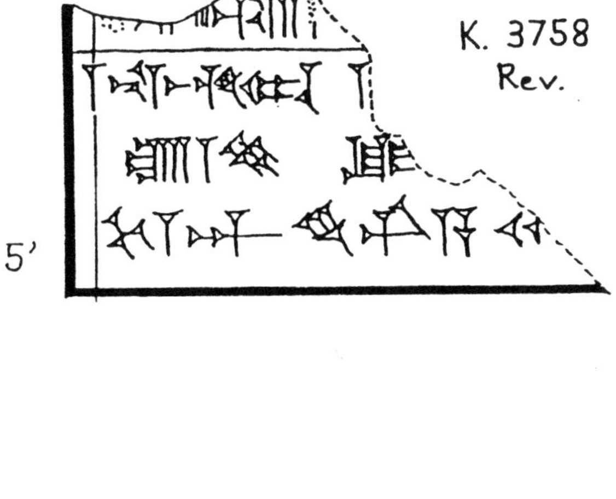

K. 3758
Rev.

Plate 6: K. 3286 and Sm. 543

K. 3286

Sm. 543

Plate 7: K. 4103 + 13330 + 15911

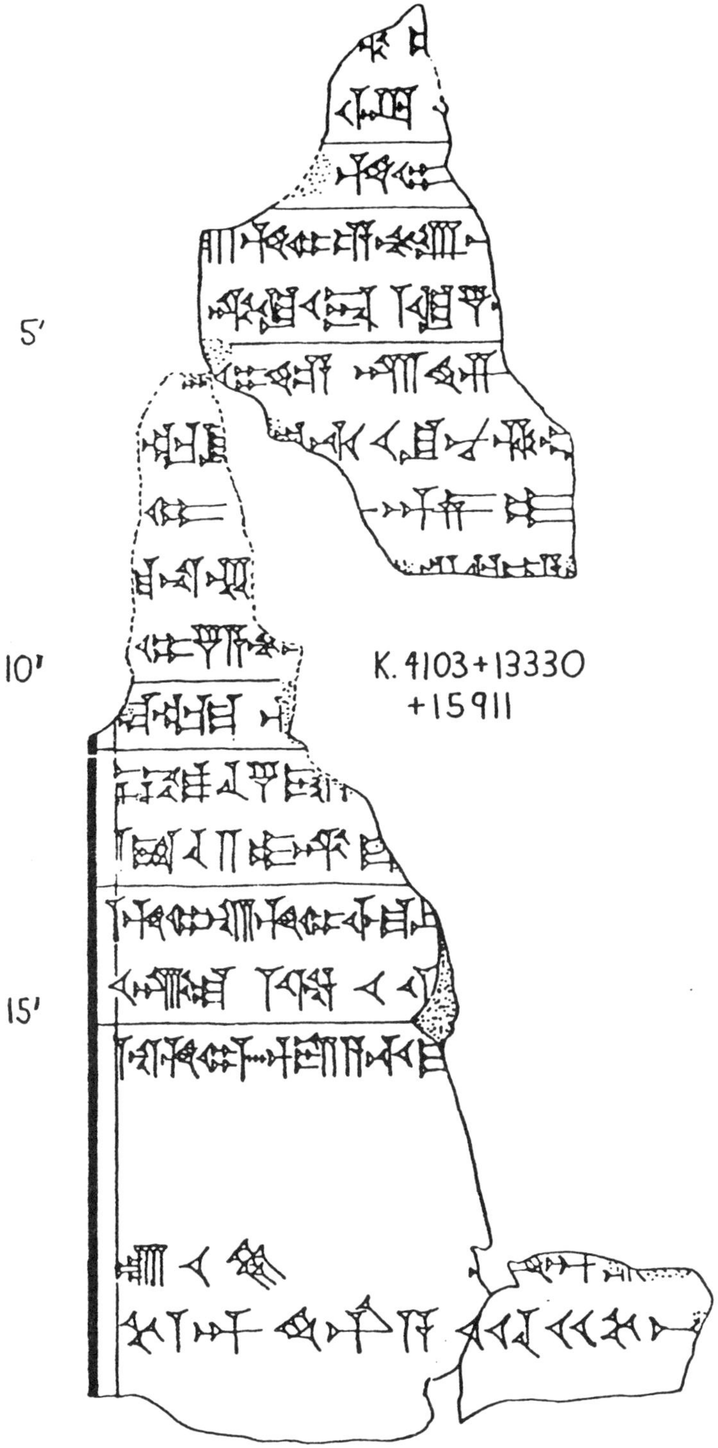

Plate 8: K. 5175 + 6001

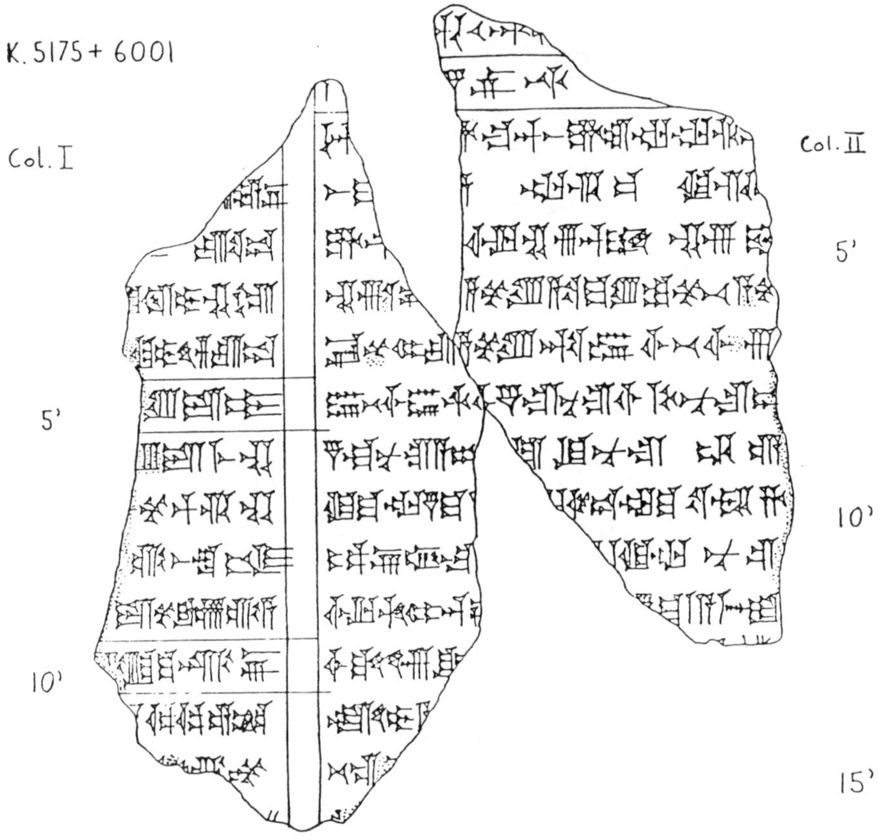

Plate 9: K. 8171 + 11041 + 11684 + 14058

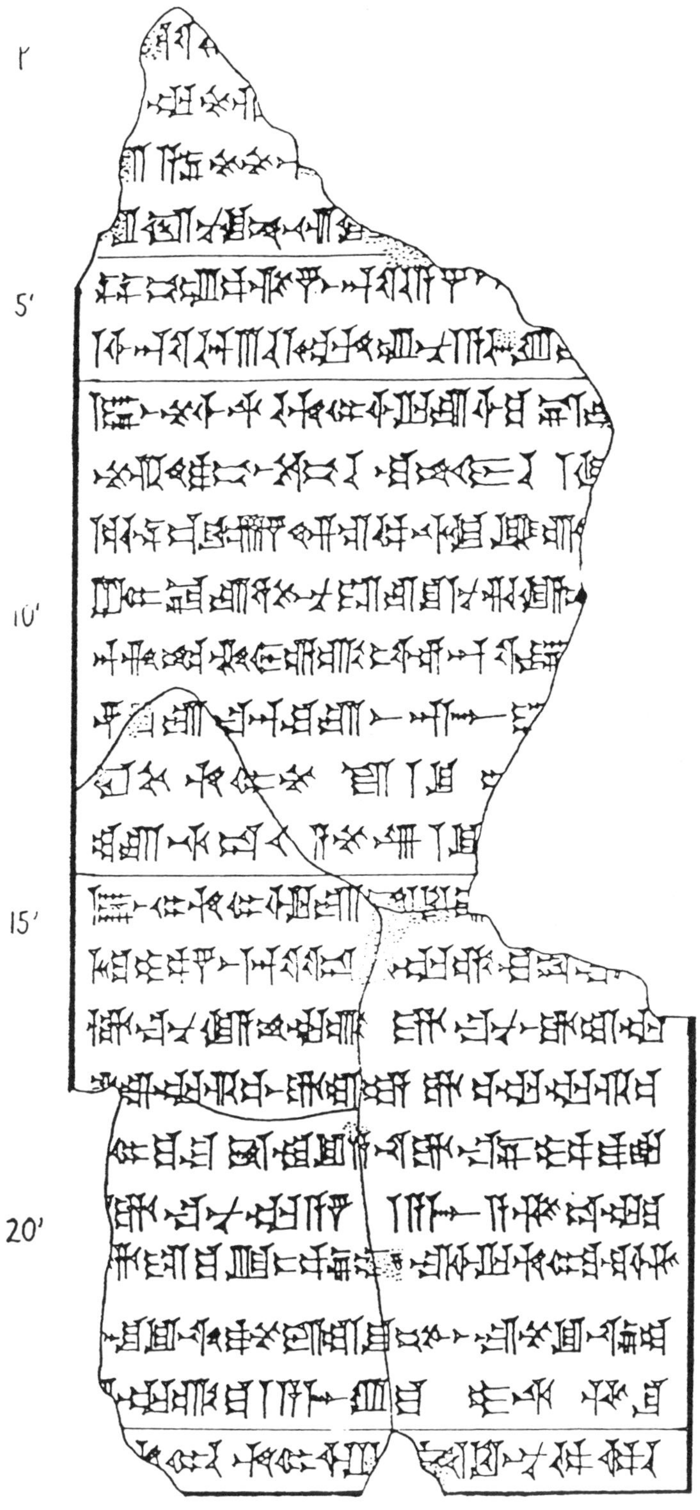

Plate 10: 79-7-8, 77

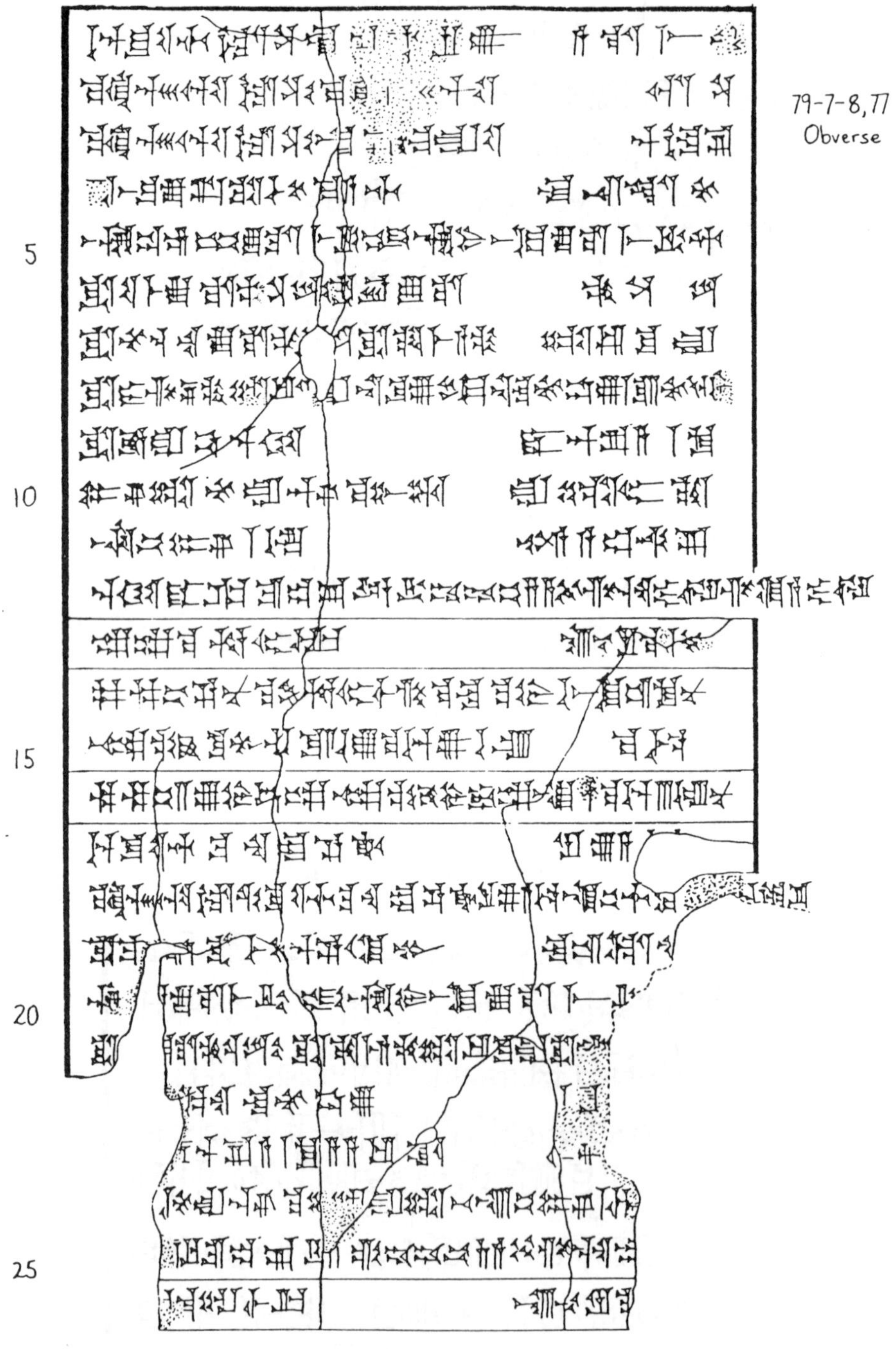

Plate 11: 79-7-8, 77

79-7-8, 77 Obverse (cont.)

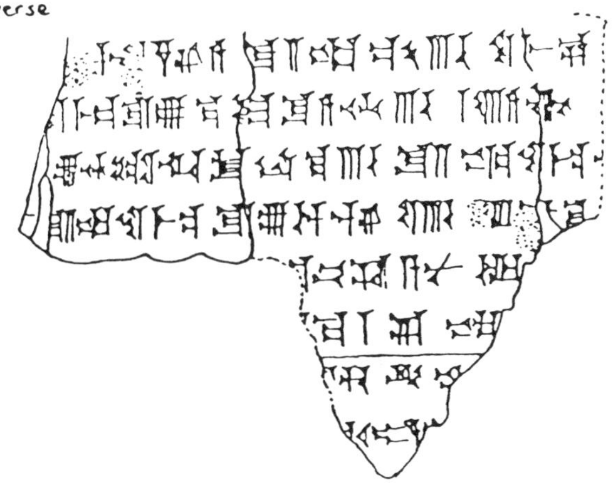

Reverse

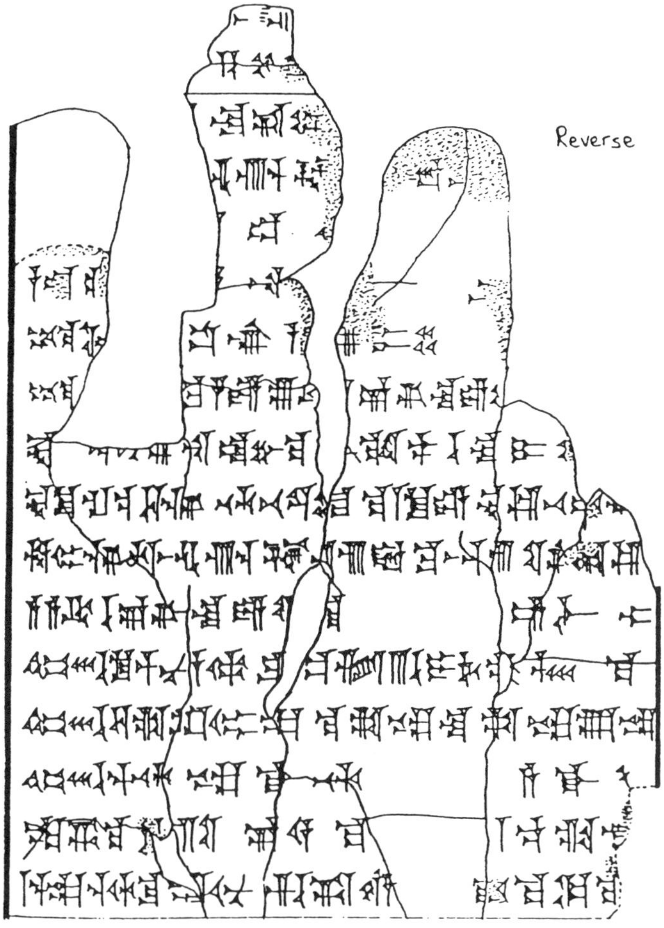

Plate 12: 79-7-8, 77

79-7-8, 77 Reverse (cont.)

20'

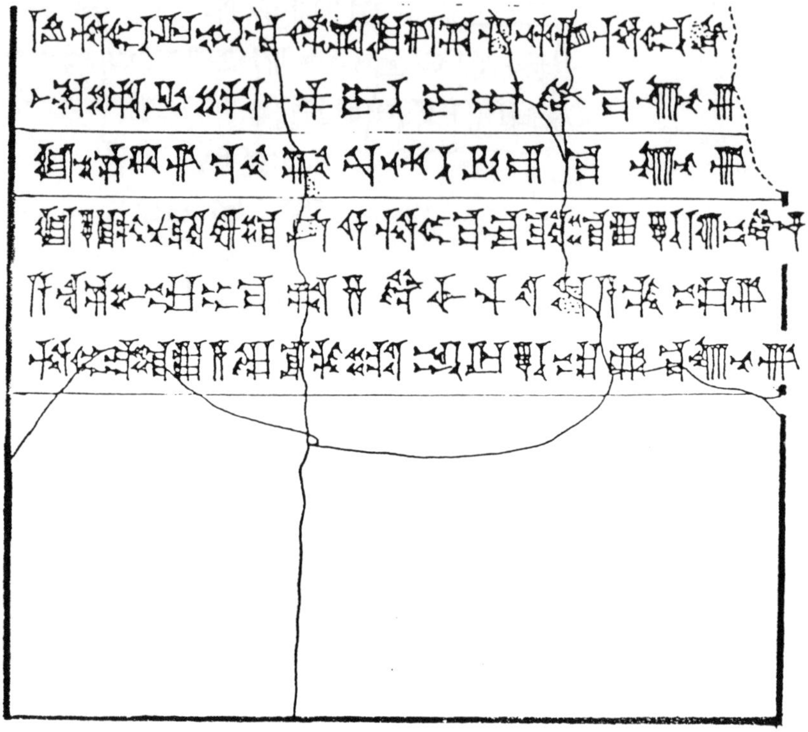

24'

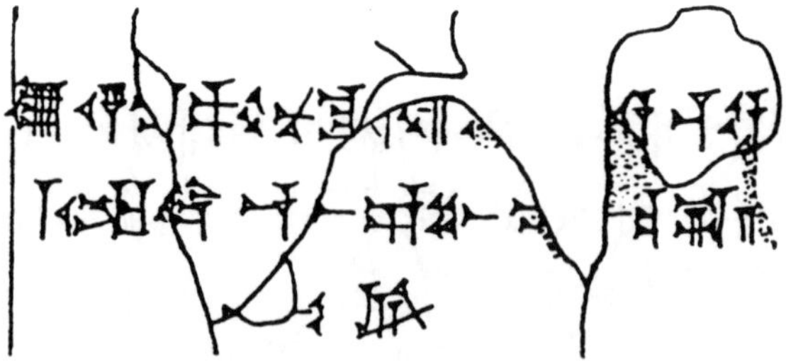

Left Edge

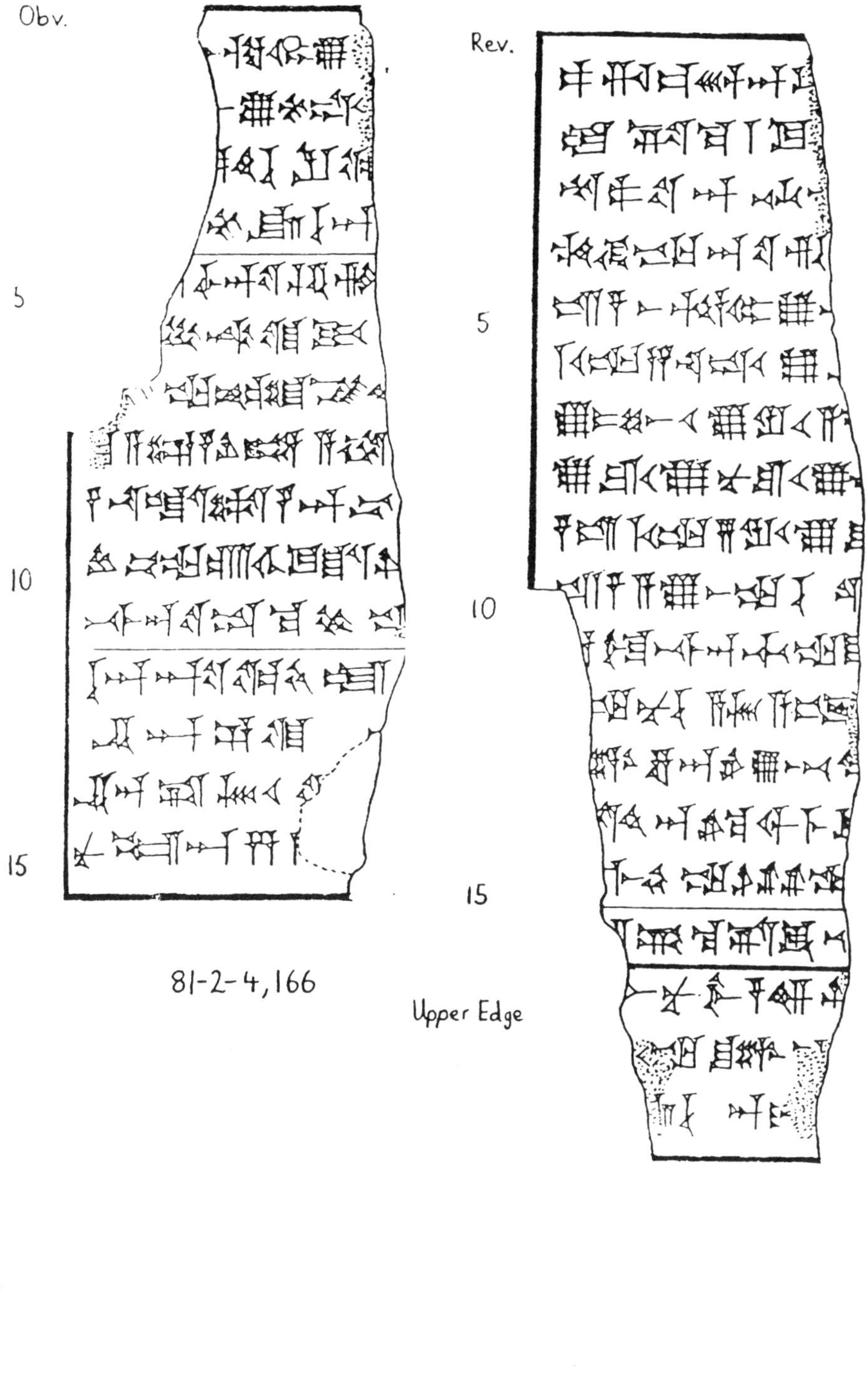

81-2-4,166

Plate 14: 81-2-4, 233

Obv.

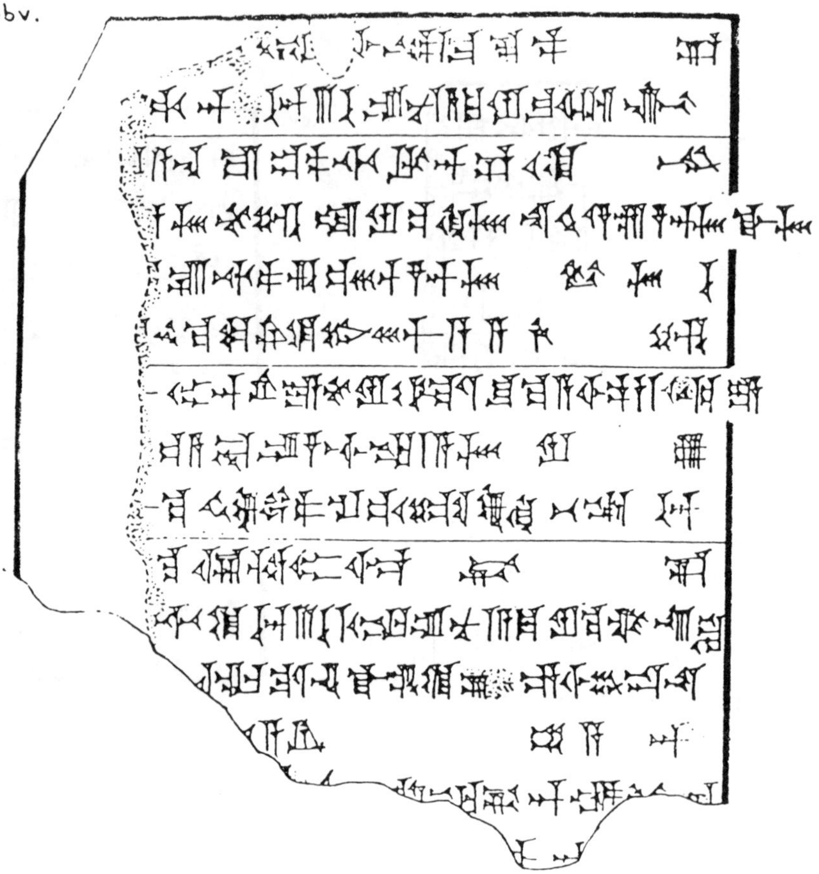

81-2-4, 233

Rev.

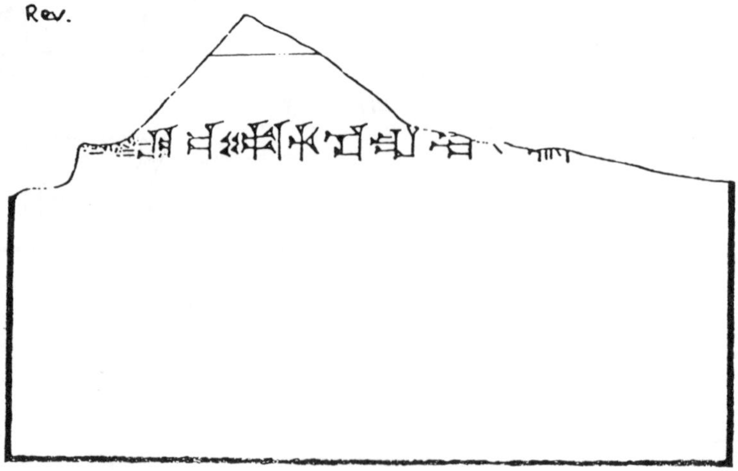

Plate 15: Si 884 and Si 904

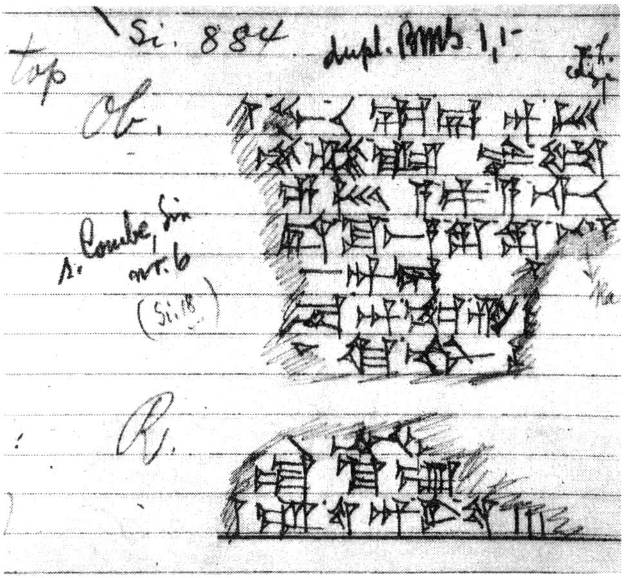

Plate 16: BM 66559

Plate 17: K. 7664 + 9302 + 9494

Plate 18: K. 9000

Plate 19: K. 11406

Plate 20: K. 11706 + 13288